THE MAKING
OF MODERN
TIBET

Revised Edition

A. Tom Grunfeld

An East Gate Book

M.E. Sharpe
Armonk, New York
London, England

An East Gate Book

Copyright © 1996 by M. E. Sharpe, Inc.

Photographs by A. Tom Grunfeld unless otherwise noted.

Library of Congress Cataloging-in-Publication Data

Grunfeld, A. Tom.
The making of modern Tibet / A. Tom Grunfeld. — Rev. ed.
p.   cm.
"An East gate book."
Includes bibliographical references and index.
ISBN 1-56324-713-5 (hardcover : alk. paper). —
ISBN 1-56324-714-3 (pbk. : alk. paper)
1. Tibet (China)—History—1951–   I. Title.
DS786.G76   1996
951'.505—dc20   96-11504
CIP
Printed in the United States of America

The paper used in this publication meets the minimum requirements of
American National Standard for Information Sciences—
Permanence of Paper for Printed Library Materials,
ANSI Z 39.48-1984.

BM (c)   10   9   8   7   6   5   4   3   2   1
BM (p)   10   9   8   7   6   5   4

THE MAKING
OF MODERN
TIBET

To:

My Mother

My Father

In Memoriam, Shandor Amir

Contents

Preface to Second Edition

I completed the research and writing for this book sometime late in 1985, and it was published early in 1987. Much has changed since then, and much, unfortunately, has not.

Tibet has changed considerably. All ethnic minorities now make up nearly 9 percent of China's population. Like the rest of China, Tibet has experienced a return of a market economy, and, coupled with the continuing financial investment by the government in Beijing, economic development is in evidence almost everywhere. Along with a higher material standard of living, especially in the cities, has come a huge influx of ethnic Chinese, particularly in Lhasa, resulting in greater ethnic tensions. Greater openness has also meant the appearance of tens of thousands of foreign visitors each year. Less restrictions have also allowed for more public demonstrations of Tibetan nationalism followed, inevitably, by harsh responses from the authorities. There is now a very different look and feel to Tibet from a decade ago.

A small number of scholars are now permitted to conduct research in Tibet, albeit with considerable constraints. Compared to a decade ago, there are substantially more published sources in Tibetan, Chinese, and English, although there are few actual government documents and these are limited to texts that demonstrate some historic Sino-Tibetan relationship.[1]

Also, in recent years the subject of Tibet has become a worldwide phenomenon, thanks to a concerted campaign on the part of the Dalai Lama's administration to garner support for its cause. This campaign has resulted in an outpouring of published materials in a host of languages and has awakened the international media to the issue of Tibet and its relations with China. While this campaign has generated considerable heat and an army of supporters for the Dalai Lama, it has generated very little light on the subject of Tibet's history because its intent is to create and maintain a political campaign based on emotional moralism rather than on historical realities.

Some things remain problematic for historians. The government of the United States still refuses to release documents concerning Tibet, even those that are almost fifty years old. It is still not possible to get access to historical archives in China or Tibet. The optimism I expressed in my first introduction for a community of Tibetan university-trained historians was premature, and there remain very few who fit this category although there has been a veritable explosion of European and American scholars of Tibet, many of whom have produced work that is both thoughtful and groundbreaking. In China there are also many more Tibetan and Chinese scholars of Tibet, but, unfortunately, they continue to work under considerable political constraints. While this new scholarship is better nuanced and less blatantly polemical, far too much continues to be strongly prejudiced by the ongoing political crusade to which many authors have committed themselves.[2]

The Dalai Lama's publicly stated views have changed slightly, as have the political circumstances in which he finds himself, and these are explored in the new chapter I have added to bring the history of Tibet up-to-date. The Chinese government's posture remains stubbornly the same publicly, although privately (and that's an important contrast from a decade ago in China and Tibet—the ability to hold private discussions with Chinese and Tibetan scholars of Tibet) some experts in China express a far greater range of opinions and historical judgments.

The general outlines of the history of Tibet that I originally laid out in these pages have not changed substantially in spite of the availability of additional sources. I have accounted for whatever changes I felt were relevant to a better understanding of this history.

New York City
December 1995

Notes

1. Heather Stoddard, "Tibetan Publications and National Identity," in *Resistance and Reform in Tibet*, ed. by Robert Barnett and Shirin Akiner (Bloomington: Indiana University Press, 1994), pp. 121–156.

2. Tsering Shakya, "The Development of Modern Tibetan Studies," in Ibid., pp. 1-14.

Acknowledgments

At different times while I was working on this study several people and institutions were kind enough to assist me in a variety of ways which I would like to acknowledge.

When it came to archival research almost every organization I approached proved helpful. They included the Department of Manpower and Immigration of the Canadian government, the Federal Police of Switzerland, the United States Department of the Army, the United Nations High Commissioner for Refugees, and the staffs of the National Archives (Washington, DC), the Public Record Office (London), the India Office Library (London) and the library of the Central Intelligence Agency.

I am also appreciative of the kindness shown to me by the administration of the State University of New York, Empire State College. Their patience, encouragement and material assistance contributed greatly to my finishing this study without excessive delay.

Likewise, many individuals have contributed to this work. They have helped further my understanding of Tibetan history by providing documents, corresponding with me, and allowing me to interview them. Among them are the Dalai Lama, L. Fletcher Prouty, the late Lowell Thomas, Hugh Richardson, George Patterson, Robert Trumbull and several Chinese intellectuals and officials who must remain unnamed. Dr. B.A. Garside was kind enough to supply me with papers from the American Emergency Committee for Tibetan Refugees while Dr. Girija Saklani shared her doctoral dissertation with me and Mr. Niall McDermott helped me with information from the International Committee of Jurists. I wish to point out that the willingness of these individuals to assist me does not necessarily mean that they agree with my conclusions, which are mine alone and for which I solely am responsible.

I also want to make special mention of a travel grant provided for me by the National Endowment for the Humanities; this allowed me to carry out archival research in British government repositories.

Others have helped in a different, but no less important, fashion. From the very beginning, Neville Maxwell and Felix Greene never lost faith in my ability to complete this history. They consistently urged me to persevere. At times their faith in me was the only thing that kept me going. I am extremely grateful.

Even after the manuscript was completed, it was not ready for publication. It needed some solid editing to shape and mold the unwieldy tome into a tightly written, smooth flowing text suitable for publication. It took the skills of Susan Rhodes, without which the manuscript might still be sitting on some dusty shelf.

Additional encouragement and editing came from Larry Jagan and Robert Molteno of Zed Books. Their enthusiasm about the manuscript and willingness to publish the book, despite many obstacles, has also earned my undying gratitude. I am also grateful to Hilary Scannell for her patient and thorough copyediting of the final manuscript.

My most heartfelt thanks goes to those who gave up the most so that I could have the time to research and write this book. Alice, Daniel and Ian unselfishly gave me weeks and months in which they released me from my obligations to them. That is time which can never be made up. I can best show my appreciation and gratitude by being as strongly supportive of their future endeavors as they have been of mine.

Frequently Cited Periodicals

AA	*American Anthropologist* (Washington, DC)
AATA	*Asia and The Americas* (New York)
AAFF	*ASIAN AFFAIRS* (London)
AJ	*Asian Journal* (New York)
AR	*Asian Recorder* (New Delhi)
BR	*Beijing Review* (Beijing)
BIS–USSR	*Bulletin, Institute for the Study of the USSR* (Munich)
BCAS	*Bulletin of Concerned Asian Scholars* (Boulder, CO)
CAJ	*Central Asiatic Journal* (Weisbaden, W. Germany)
CAR	*Central Asian Review* (London)
CNA	*China News Analysis* (Hong Kong)
CT	*CHINA'S TIBET* (Beijing)
CP	*China Pictorial* (Beijing)
CQ	*The China Quarterly* (London)
CR	*China Reconstructs* (Beijing)
CSM	*Christian Science Monitor* (Boston)
CB	*Current Background* (Hong Kong)
CS	*Current Scene* (Hong Kong)
EH	*Eastern Horizon* (Hong Kong)
EW	*Eastern World* (London)
ECMM	*Extracts from the Chinese Mainland Magazines* (Hong Kong)
FES	*Far Eastern Survey* (New York)
FA	*Foreign Affairs* (New York)
FBIS	*Foreign Broadcast Information Service* (Hong Kong)
FCA	*Free China and Asia* (Taibei)
FCR	*Free China Review* (Taibei)

GMRB	*Guangming Ribao* (Enlightenment Daily, Beijing)
HR	*History of Religions* (Chicago)
see Xinhua	*Hsinhua* (New China News Agency, Beijing)
see XRB	*Hsi-tsang Jih-pao* (Tibet Daily, Lhasa)
IOLR	*India Office Library and Records* (London)
IS	*International Studies* (New Delhi)
see RMRB	*Jen-min Jih-pao* (People's Daily, Beijing)
JPRS	*Joint Publications Research Service* (Springfield, VA)
JAH	*Journal of Asian History* (Weisbaden, W. Germany)
JAS	*Journal of Asian Studies* (Ann Arbor, MI)
JAOS	*Journal of The American Oriental Society* (New Haven, CT)
JHKBRAS	*Journal of the Hong Kong Branch of the Royal Asiatic Society* (London)
JRAS	*Journal of the Royal Asiatic Society* (London)
JRCAS	*Journal of the Royal Central Asian Society* (London)
see GMRB	*Kuang-ming Jih-pao* (Enlightenment Daily, Beijing)
MTTC	*Min-tsu Tuan-chieh* (Nationalities Unity, Beijing)
MTYC	*Min-tsu Yen-chiu* (Nationalities Study, Beijing)
NGM	*National Geographic Magazine* (Washington, DC)
see Xinhua	*New China News Agency* (Beijing)
NT	*New Times* (Moscow)
NYT	*The New York Times* (New York)
NY	*The New Yorker* (New York)
N–T	*News-Tibet* (New York)
PA	*Pacific Affairs* (Vancouver, B.C.)
PR	*Peking Review* (Beijing)
PC	*People's China* (Beijing)
PRO	*Public Records Office* (Kew, UK)
RMRB	*Renmin Ribao* (People's Daily)
SPT	*Soviet Press Translations* (Seattle)
SWB	*Summary of World Broadcasts* (Part 3, the Far East, BBC, London)
SCMP	*Summary of The China Mainland Press* (Hong Kong)
TB	*Tibetan Bulletin* (Dharamsala, India)
TJ	*The Tibet Journal* (Dharamsala, India)
TR	*Tibetan Review* (New Delhi)
TSB	*The Tibet Society Bulletin* (Bloomington, IN)
USNWR	*US News and World Report* (New York)
WSJ	*The Wall Street Journal* (New York)
Xinhua	*Xinhua* (New China News Agency, Beijing)
XRB	*Xizang Ribao* (Tibet Daily, Lhasa)

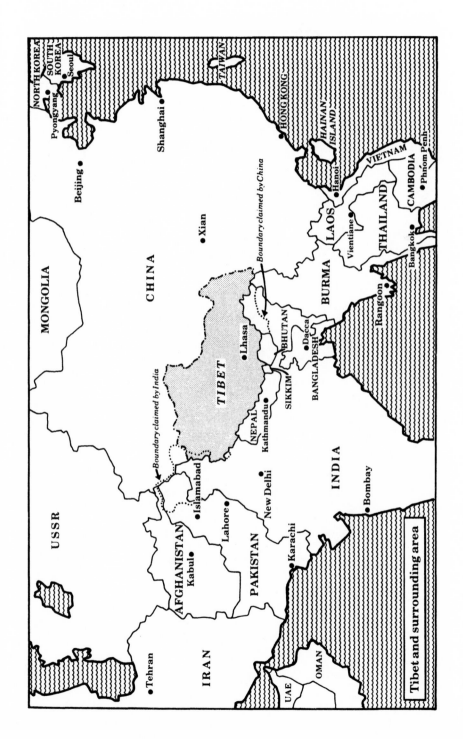

Tibet and surrounding area

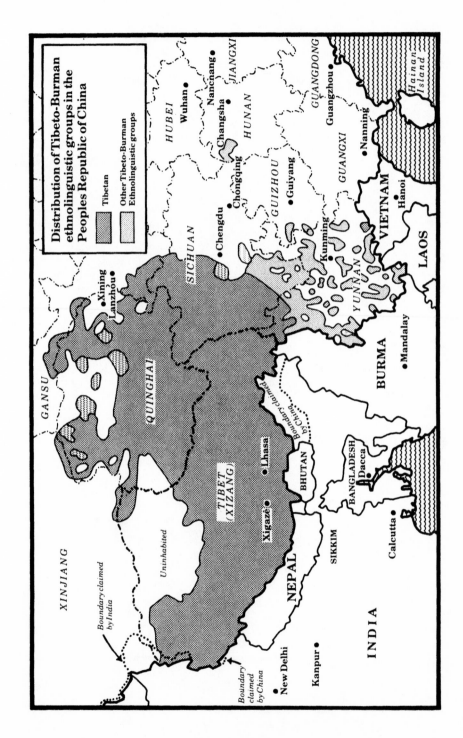

Distribution of Tibeto-Burman ethnolinguistic groups in the Peoples Republic of China

Tibetan

Other Tibeto-Burman Ethnolinguistic groups

THE MAKING
OF MODERN
TIBET

Introduction

"TIBET"—the name alone conjures up visions of mystery and fantasy, visions of spirituality, exotica and mysticism. It is a land so wrapped in obscurity that almost any fantastic tales about it, or allegedly from it, are received with awe and believed, unquestioningly, by countless individuals the world over. A land whose society and history have been so romantically homogenized that many call themselves "experts" after reading a mere handful of texts, assuming that the uniformity of these accounts indicates their accuracy.

On the face of it this cloud of mystery is not surprising. Because of its geographical isolation and total lack of roads and modern communication networks, Tibet escaped, for the most part, the great advances of Western imperialism during the eighteenth, nineteenth, and twentieth centuries. When European travelers, missionaries, merchants, and military forces were combing the world, Tibet remained impenetrable: aloof, separate, and unmolested (with the most minor exceptions).

The popularity of the religions and art of Asia during the latter part of the nineteenth and early twentieth centuries deepened the shroud of mystery. Some people, like Madame Blavatsky (a self-proclaimed spiritual leader) and her Theosophical Society perverted and misrepresented Buddhist and Hindu philosophy to suit their own idealized versions. Another source of misconception was the publication, in 1933, of James Hilton's *Lost Horizon,* a story of a mysterious valley high in the Himalayan wilderness where—in an atmosphere of eternal bliss and South Pacific weather—no one grew old or ill. *Lost Horizon* was published in the middle of a worldwide depression, and its story of a utopian society expressed people's inner desires that such a "perfect" place should actually exist.

But in spite of Tibet's relative isolation and lack of visitors, considerable information about it was available to the serious scholar. The writings of the

3

British colonial official Charles Bell (later Sir) and the numerous articles and books that were an outcrop of the British Younghusband Expedition to Tibet in 1904 are only the most obvious examples. But the people most responsible for perpetuating the false images of Tibet were those least likely to avail themselves of these sources.

This situation was to last, more or less, until 1950. The victory of communism in China in 1949 and the subsequent creation of a strong central government in Beijing (Peking) for the first time in over half a century was to have its repercussions in Tibet—and around the rest of the world. In universities throughout the West, and especially in the United States, scholars were prevented from putting forward views that could be construed as pro-communist. Scholarship on Tibet degenerated into the taking of sides: black and white, wrong and right, good and bad.

Of course, the definitions of "friend" and "foe" depended on which side the speaker was on. Supporters of the Dalai Lama's government in Lhasa appeared to believe that pre-1950 Tibet was an undeniably independent state where the inhabitants were universally happy and smiling through all adversity, a society in which not one soul could find complaint, for all needs were addressed and all were benevolently ruled in a classless paradise. It was this "Shangri-la," so the story continues, that the inhuman, Buddhist-hating Chinese soldiers defiled by enslaving the people for their own ends. Supporters of Beijing, on the other hand, saw Tibet as a society that had been based on the gravest inhumanities, where a handful of aristocracy—both lay and clerical—had enslaved the people in a European-style medieval feudalism that visited the most barbaric punishments and cruelties upon the populace until the People's Liberation Army marched into Tibet to liberate it.[1]

While these scenarios may appear ludicrously simplistic, those who are familiar with the literature on Tibet will find them only slightly exaggerated. Accounts of the past became almost wholly didactic and all critical judgment was suspended. The uprising in Tibet in 1959, which will be discussed in detail below, only exacerbated this dichotomy and made it even more impossible to escape the shackles of polemic.

Although this situation still obtains, we are, at the same time, on the threshold of a new era in Tibetan historiography. Among the refugees a new group is emerging: young (many were born outside Tibet), Western-educated, less orthodox in their religious practices, and with experience of other cultures. This group, exemplified by individuals such as the journalist and scholar Dawa Norbu and by journals such as the *Tibetan Review*,[2] is beginning to question and research. They are more inclined to be critical of their elders and of the "Shangri-la" image that historic Tibet enjoys.

Remarkably enough, this new, more conciliatory attitude is also apparent on the Beijing side. The period following the ousting of the so-called "Gang of Four" in October 1976 and the re-emergence to power of Deng Xiaoping (Teng Hsiao-p'ing) marked a major liberalization of Chinese society. One of the consequences of this new attitude was a call for less dogmatism.[3]

Not only has the call been made generally to Communist Party members and the public at large but, more importantly, to more specialized members of society such as historians. In July 1979 *Lishi Yanjiu* (Historical Studies) published a major article which was soon after reprinted in China's most important newspaper, *Renmin Ribao* (People's Daily), calling on historians to adopt a new attitude to their work.

> It is wrong to evade the fact that bad persons, bad things, shortcomings and errors did occur within our Party. It is even worse to ascribe all achievements and merits to persons who are positively evaluated and all shortcomings and errors to those who are negatively evaluated. This is typical of the metaphysical approach which denies that things develop and are mutable, and considers that what is good is all good and what is bad is all bad.[4]

Absolute objectivity, however admirable, is unattainable; the reader will undoubtedly be able to identify my ideological biases. But the impossibility of being objective does not necessarily invalidate the search for a middle ground. By that I do not mean a sterile, noncommittal middle ground, but a point of view that allows the author to be aware of his or her prejudices and compensate for them. I have made every effort to use materials from most, if not all, contending points of view. I therefore choose to call this book "disinterested and dispassionate history," and I present it as an attempt at historical interpretation without political, religious, economic, or emotional commitments to either side, but rather with a commitment to furthering historical understanding and even "truth"—knowing full well how fleeting and changeable that "truth" can be.

History can never be definitive; scholars continually unearth new sources that challenge accepted interpretations. This study was hampered by a lack of cooperation from certain sources over the seven years it has taken to complete this work. In spite of my continued efforts, the American Department of State and the Central Intelligence Agency have consistently refused to furnish the relevant documents under the Freedom of Information Act. Although the Act was specifically designed to help uncover new historical evidence, and despite the fact that many of the materials I asked for were over thirty years old, the results of my efforts were, with a handful of exceptions, insignificant. Efforts to interview prominent Tibetan exiles have likewise failed—as have efforts to visit Tibet itself. I am also acutely aware that the study does not draw on a host of sources available only in the original Tibetan, Russian, German, or Chinese. But as Hugh Trevor-Roper has so aptly pointed out, all researchers reach a point of diminishing returns where to continue without publishing only postpones the inevitable.

A Note on the Usage of Terms

In the highly emotional state of Tibetan studies, even the choice of certain terms is taken as a political statement.

Ethnically, China is 93 percent Han. The remaining 7 percent of the population is composed of over fifty other ethnic groups. No one disagrees that Tibetans are ethnically different from the Han. However, those who consider Tibet to be an independent state prefer to differentiate between "Tibetans" and "Chinese," implying a political separation. Those who consider Tibet to be a part of China differentiate between "Tibetans" and "Han" because this implies that Tibetans are politically Chinese. In this study I will use the terms "Han" and "Chinese" interchangeably for purely stylistic reasons and not as advocacy for one side or the other. My conclusions on these issues are developed in the body of the study.

A politically-motivated choice of names is also available for two geographical areas with populations that are predominantly Tibetan: Kham and Amdo. Since these names are Tibetan, they are not used in China today. Kham is part of Sichuan (Szechwan) Province, while Amdo is part of Qinghai (Chinghai) Province. Although proponents of a politically autonomous "Greater Tibet" use them specifically to indicate their political views, I use these terms simply to identify areas of ethnic Tibetan inhabitation.

In most writings on Tibet the terms lama and monk are used interchangeably. This is incorrect. Every member of the clergy was a monk; however, not all monks were lamas. This latter term was reserved for monks who had achieved a high status either through being recognized as a reincarnation of a previous lama or, far more uncommonly, by having risen up through the ranks because of hard work and intelligence. I therefore use these terms accordingly.

A Note on the Spelling of Tibetan Words

There are two acceptable orthographies in use for the transliteration of Tibetan words. One is more linguistically accurate, the other is simpler. For example, the two central provinces of Tibet are correctly transliterated as *Dbus* and *Gtsang,* although they are more readily pronounceable as *U* and *Tsang.* In the knowledge that either form is comprehensible to experts, I have elected, for the most part, to use the latter.

The situation is somewhat further confused by the recent adoption in the People's Republic of China of a system of transliteration called *pinyin.* Although it is used universally in China, its use for the Tibetan names would probably make those names incomprehensible to almost all readers. For example, the very name "Tibet" in *pinyin* is "Xizang." This form will therefore only be used for Chinese names, with the more familiar spellings following in parenthesis.

New York City
Spring 1986

1

Tibet as It Used to Be

By all accounts, Tibet is a stunning place. Predominantly a plateau averaging 3,600 m. (12,000 ft.) above sea-level, its landscape includes not only snow-covered mountains but also glaciers and green forest, grasslands and salt lakes. It is surrounded by mountains: the Kunlun range in the north, the Hengduan in the east, the Himalayas in the south and the source of many of Asia's major rivers: the Tsangpo, which meanders first east and then south to become the Brahmaputra ("son of Brahma"); the Mekong, which flows into Burma and Laos; the Salween which also flows into Burma; the Yangzi (Yangtze) and Yellow Rivers, which flow into China proper; the Sutlej into Pakistan; and the Indus flowing west into Ladakh.

Tibetans have learned to live with the rarefied air and the strong winds that are so common in this cold, dry climate. But the Tibetan climate is not uniform like the Arctic; Tibetans live between 1,200 m. (4,000 ft.) and 5,100 m. (17,000 ft.) above sea-level. Tibet's numerous valleys create wide-ranging climatic conditions with little precipitation. The capital city of Lhasa, for example, lies at the same latitude as Cairo and New Orleans, although at an altitude of about 3,600 m. (12,000 ft.). But because it is situated in a valley it gets little snow and its yearly temperature ranges from 10 to 24° C (14–74° F)—fairly temperate conditions.

The remoteness of Tibet and the late introduction of a written script in the seventh century have created almost insurmountable obstacles to piecing together accurate accounts about the origins of Tibet and, for that matter, the Tibetans themselves. Not surprisingly, legends abound. Even the origin of the very name "Tibet" is unknown; the name used by the native inhabitants is "Bod" (or "P'oyul")—"the land of snows."

There are also difficulties in determining the precise geographical boundaries of Tibet. Tibetans live in an area of about 3.8 million sq. km. (1.5 million sq. miles) or about fifteen times the size of the United Kingdom and half the size of the United States. The political boundaries, however (the Tibet Autonomous Region [TAR]), cover an area of only 1.2 million sq. km. (470,000 sq. miles). The population has been estimated from a low of 1,500,000 to a high of 10,000,000 (see Appendix A). Using the figures accepted by Beijing, the TAR therefore covers 12.5 percent of the area of the People's Republic of China (PRC) but is home to under 0.002 percent of the PRC's population.

For the purposes of the general reader Tibet can be divided into several regions. In the central area, with the capital of Lhasa, is the province of U. To the southwest is the province of Tsang, centering on Tibet's second largest town, Shigatse. To the east is the area known as Kham, today politically divided between the province of Sichuan and the TAR. North of Kham is an area known to Tibetans as Amdo, and to the Chinese as Qinghai, while to the far west is Ngari. The area just north of U and Tsang is called the Chang Dang (Chang Tang), the northern plateau with its desolate deserts and seemingly endless grasslands.

The Social Structure

If there is one point of agreement among scholars it is that Tibet's original social order has been irreversibly altered by the influence of Chinese communism and the upheavals of 1959. The attempt to rapidly socialize and modernize the Tibetan way of life after 1959 doomed to failure any hope of preserving the unique lifestyle of these people. But that is where agreement ends, for there are two sharply differing views: one holds that the change was beneficial, the other that it was disastrous.

The changes in Tibetan society since 1959 have certainly made it impossible for anthropologists fully to reconstruct what life was previously like. There were some scholars, such as the American anthropologist/missionary Robert Ekvall and the American-trained Chinese scholar Li Anzhe (Li An-che), who lived among the Tibetans before 1950; but for the most part scholars have been forced to study necessarily inexact replications of that society in the communities of exiles in Nepal and India. In the past decade two American anthropologists have been allowed to conduct fieldwork in Tibet while other Tibetan-speaking Western scholars have traveled freely throughout Tibet.[1]

The best single description of pre-1950 Tibetan society is "feudal." The word is in quotes here only because it has been a catchword in the seemingly neverending political battles over what Tibetan life used to be like. The Chinese tend to use the term in their popular media in a pejorative sense (although many Chinese academic journals have used it more descriptively),[2] and naturally the knee-jerk reaction of China's opponents has been to deny that feudalism ever existed in Tibet or even to go so far as to argue that it was beneficial.[3] The term is used here simply because it is the adjective which comes closest to describing Tibetan society; the parallels between Tibet and medieval Europe are striking.

The Elites

Tibetans were ruled by an unusual form of feudal theocracy that was both _cen-_ _tralized_—in a government in Lhasa headed by a man known, outside of Tibet, as the Dalai Lama—and also _decentralized,_ giving local control to the countless monastic and aristocratic estates. The central government maintained a military force, issued currency and postage stamps, negotiated with other governments and acted as a final court of appeal. The heads of the feudal estates maintained a monopoly of power over all local matters; the central government normally intervened only when the flow of taxes was disrupted. All the officials in Tibet, both lay and ecclesiastic, in Lhasa and on the estates, came from the same small pool of noble families.

At the very top of the social structure was the Dalai Lama, who was both the secular and ecclesiastical ruler of Tibet. Then came the _ger-ba,_ or aristocratic lords, numbering anywhere from 150 to 300 families. These families could be arranged in four distinct groupings. The most exclusive were the _de-bon,_ or families descended from the ancient kings of Tibet. They were followed closely by the _yab-shi,_ or families descended from previous Dalai Lamas. When a new Dalai Lama is found, or chosen (in a manner described below), his family is immediately ennobled, a custom that

> served to anchor the Dalai Lama to the existing system and must be viewed as a strong restraint against his altering the structural status quo since any changes would negatively affect his parents and siblings also.[4]

The third group of aristocracy were called _mi-dra;_ they were families who had been rewarded with ennoblement as a result of some meritorious service by one of their members. These three were the elites of the elite and made up only twenty-five to thirty families. They were extremely wealthy and almost all government officials were drawn from their ranks.

The final group of aristocracy were known as _gyu-ma,_ or "common." These hereditary families were the majority of the nobility, although they were only moderately well-off; some were even poor enough to be forced to carry on trade to supplement their incomes. Despite claims to the contrary, heredity and ennoblement were the only avenues for joining the nobility. The rest of the population were serfs and, in much smaller numbers, slaves and outcasts.

As in all agricultural societies, the source of power and wealth was not titles but land. Land was divided among the three ruling groups: the monasteries, the lay nobility, and the Lhasa government (whose village members were known as "the ones who serve the government"). Although there is some dispute over how much of the arable land each group held, it is generally agreed that the monasteries and the lay nobility controlled well over 50 percent—and the best land at that.[5]

For the lay nobility there were two types of estates. One was the traditional family seat, which was owned outright and could not be sold. It could be confiscated for acts of treason, although this was rare. The other, and more important form, was estates given to the families by the government in exchange for certain obligations such as government service, the orderly collection of taxes, and the supplying of serfs to the Tibetan army. It was this type of estate that promoted the cohesion of the political structure ruling Tibet.

Appointment to government office necessitated the allocation of an estate to cover expenses. There were however very few movable estates. "Family seats" and monastic estates were rarely confiscated. New arable land was hardly ever reclaimed because of the lack of both technical expertise and entrepreneurial motivation. Many of the nobility had only one estate, and single estates were rarely confiscated; the number of estates that were rotated were, therefore, few.

These estates were extremely lucrative. One former aristocrat noted that a "small" estate would typically consist of a few thousand sheep, a thousand yaks, an undetermined number of nomads and two hundred agricultural serfs. The yearly output would consist of over 36,000 kg. (80,000 lb.) of grain over 1,800 kg. (4,000 lb.) of wool and almost 500 kg. (1,200 lb.) of butter.[6] To the estate's proceeds must be added the various perquisites that came with holding office in Tibet.

The nobles' main functions as government officials were quite straightforward: to collect taxes, settle disputes, punish criminals, and act as a liaison between the central government and the area of Tibet they were administering. For this they received little or no formal salary.[7] But this was not a deterrent; on the contrary, there was stiff competition for governmental posts—gifts were even given to obtain one. This was a direct result of the perquisites that accompanied the job. A government official had "unlimited powers of extortion" and could make a fortune from his powers to extract bribes not to imprison and punish people.[8] In some cases the nobles themselves would not even bother going to their posts but would send one of their stewards who, by all accounts, tended to be harsher than the masters. There was also the matter of extracting monies from the peasantry beyond the necessary taxes. Their abuse of privileges, their lack of concern for the bulk of the population, and even their practice of taking "temporary wives" while stationed away from Lhasa, meant that "very few nobles [had] a reputation for integrity."[9]

One of the most unusual aspects of the Tibetan polity was the dual system whereby every lay official had a clerical counterpart. Usually there was a total of 340 officials, evenly divided, although for a brief period in the 1930s and 1940s there were 200 lay officials and 230 clerical. The monk officials were all from the predominant Gelugpa sect and usually from one of the three major Gelugpa monasteries, all situated in the environs of Lhasa: Drepung, Ganden, and Sera. These monk officials were considered more reliable than their lay counterparts for they had fewer vested interests. They did not individually own estates that they had to worry about losing, nor did they have to worry about offending powerful interests since their clerical status gave them protection. This aspect of the system was sometimes abused when a noble family sent their son to a monastery to acquire monkhood (one night in a monastery was sufficient) solely to make him eligible for one of the official clerical positions.

At the top of the pyramid was one man—the Dalai Lama. Tibetans believe that he is an incarnation of the patron deity of Tibet, Chenrezig (known in Indian Buddhism as Avaloketi'svara). Buddhists believe that individuals go through repeated incarnations until they have performed enough meritorious deeds to free themselves from this cycle and propel them into a state of heavenly bliss called *nirvana*. Buddhists further believe that there are *bodhisattvas* who, having reached the very gates of *nirvana*, have unselfishly denied themselves that release and instead have elected to return to earth in a human form in order to help others achieve that state. The Dalai Lama is believed to be an incarnation of Chenrezig, just such a *bodhisattva*.

Confusion begins with the very name itself. The Dalai Lama is referred to in non-Tibetan literature as the "Living Buddha" or the "God King." Neither of these descriptions is apt. A Buddha is one who enters *nirvana;* therefore a living Buddha is a contradiction. Moreover, the Dalai Lama is neither a "God," nor a representative of a supreme deity, but rather the deity's manifestation on earth. The very term *Dalai Lama* is not Tibetan but Mongolian. Since *Dalai* translates as "oceans of wisdom," the entire term could translate as "a lama with oceans of wisdom." In Tibet, however, this term is unknown; there he is referred to as *Gyalwa Rinpoche* (Victorious One) or *Kyabngon Rinpoche* (Precious Protector).

Buddhists hold that all people are reincarnated many times until, if ever, they reach *nirvana*. In Tibet, reincarnation had a unique use—to determine heirs to leadership positions. This form of succession appears to have been institutionalized around the fifteenth century when the Gelugpa sect of Tibetan Buddhism began its rise to undisputed power although it predates this period. This practice proved useful for the clerical elite; it kept control of the transition of power out of the hands of the lay nobility, for religious incarnations could only be identified by the clergy. By occasionally selecting "incarnations" from among non-aristocratic families, the clerical elite were able to prevent any one, or small group of, families from monopolizing power. So successful was the system that it resulted in dozens, if not hundreds, of incarnations at all levels of the ecclesiastic order.

The Dalai Lama was the highest position determined by incarnation. In reality it did not much matter which boy was chosen as the incarnation (only one female was ever chosen) as long as he was bright and alert, for he would spend his life—from the age of anywhere from three to five years old—being socialized to whatever position was planned for him, cut off from all outside influences.

Since an incarnation was chosen young, there was a lengthy period until he reached his maturity when others had to rule. Given the low life expectancy in Tibet it was not uncommon for incarnations to die before, or soon after, their ascendancy to power. This resulted in long periods of rule by advisers, or, in the case of the Dalai Lama, regents. As a measure of the power that regents must have wielded it is important to note that only three of the fourteen Dalai Lamas have actually ruled Tibet. From 1751 to 1960 regents ruled for 77 percent of the time (94 percent if we exclude the exceptionally long reign of the thirteenth Dalai Lama).

A description follows of the process by which the current Dalai Lama was discovered in 1938; it is similar to one described for finding earlier Dalai Lamas by European travelers in the seventeenth century and to the way in which the thirteenth Dalai Lama was "discovered" in the nineteenth century.[10]

Before the thirteenth Dalai Lama died in 1933 he gave some clues as to where he might be reborn. These clues were then combined with a host of other "cosmic" signs to lead the authorities to a particular house. By 1937 official search parties traveled along various routes toward the east, investigating unusual births and rumors of strange phenomena. It was one of these parties that came upon a village in Amdo with a three-story monastery with golden roofs, situated just above a peasant house with carved gables. A boy of the right age was discovered living in the house.

First the lamas in the search party switched clothing with their servants so that the lamas could go into the kitchen and speak to the boy privately without arousing suspicion. The boy is said to have immediately identified the lamas as such despite their servants' clothing and to have been able to pick out objects that belonged to the previous Dalai Lama when presented with duplicates of each object, such as rosaries and canes. And finally he had the proper distinguishing marks: large ears and moles on his torso under his arms, indicating the place where his previous arms were supposed to have been. (Chenrezig is depicted as having large ears and four arms—the moles replaced the second pair.) It was also claimed, if further proof was needed, that the thirteenth Dalai Lama had at one time stayed at the monastery in the village and on passing the peasant house in question, paused and commented to his aides how pretty it was.

The People

The vast majority of the people of Tibet were serfs, or as they were known there, *mi ser* (literally "yellow person").[11]

> Peasants in Tibet, particularly those on the estates belonging to the aristocracy and the monasteries, are in a sense serfs. A tenant peasant is bound to furnish the greater part of his agricultural produce for the use of his landlord, keeping

only enough for the bare support of himself and his family. He is also bound to furnish *ulag* and supplies to his landlord and all government officials traveling through his village. A tenant cannot quit his land without the permission of his *sGer pa* lord. If he wants to go away he must first ask for what the Tibetans call *Mi hkrol shu ba* (petition for man separation). Normally such permission is not granted.[12]

Serfs were "tied" to their masters. They received the right to work the land in exchange for taxes and *ulag,* corvée labor. So powerless were they that they required permission to enter a monastery and even to marry. If two serfs of different lords married, male offspring reverted to the father's lord, while female offspring went to the mother's. Permission to leave the estate—even for the briefest period— for such matters as family visits, pilgrimages, or for some sideline trading required the consent of the lord. Such consent was not readily given and usually came only after all the feudal obligations had been successfully completed.

But, just as there were different classes of aristocrats, so also were there different classes of serfs. *Tre-ba* and *du-jung* serfs were indentured to both monastic and lay nobility. The wealthiest serf group, *tre-ba,* were "taxpayer" serfs. These families held title to hereditary land that could be taken away from them only as a result of the most severe evasion of their feudal responsibilities— a heavy burden of taxes and a transport corvée obligation. This latter tax was especially severe since it obliged the family to have ready animals, fodder, housing, provisions, and guides *at all times* in case government officials, or government-authorized individuals, happened to travel through their area. Since Tibet had no roads and no modern means of transportation, travel was by stages ranging from eight to twenty-three miles, depending on the difficulty of the terrain. At each stage a "taxpayer" family was to provide lodging and provisions for all the travelers and assure their transportation to the next stage, at which point the original "taxpayer" returned home and another "taxpayer" family took over. This responsibility was crucial for the government but onerous for the serf; it required a great deal of surplus income to be always ready, even if visitors came months or years apart. As befitted their status, these serfs had an influential say in village matters and at times were elected as headmen.

Another group of serfs was called *du-jung,* literally "small smoke" ("small households"). These serfs had no hereditary land, but held hereditary serf status for which they were compelled to pay taxes, perform corvée and other feudal obligations. This group had little power and usually rented land or worked as hired hands for the taxpayer serfs.

Yet another group of serfs belonged neither to the monasteries nor to the nobility, but directly to the government. They lived in government villages which they could not leave without permission. Their lands were held in nonhereditary family units. One of the major differences between this group and the previous two is that the monasteries and nobility had their own land (*demesne* land), which the serfs were obliged to work as part of their corvée in addition to the land issued them. This situation did not exist in the government-owned villages.[13]

Historically there was very little class mobility in Tibet, and, for the most apart, serfs were forced to accept the position they found themselves in upon birth. Recent statements such as "there is no class system and the mobility from class to class makes any class prejudice impossible"[14] are inaccurate and reflect politics rather than fact. A serf might acquire wealth, but he would always remain a serf. There was, however, one avenue of escape that was possibly unique to Tibet—the practice of "human lease." It was possible for a serf to arrange with his/her lord to allow the serf to take out a "lease" on himself/herself. This agreement allowed the serf to go anywhere and do anything as long as he or she continued to fulfill some mutually agreed yearly obligation.[15] For example, a lord of a female serf could grant such a contract if she were marrying a male owned by another lord and wished to move to her husband's estate. Since the feudal obligation in this case consisted of a yearly sum of money or some open-ended corvée service, for which the serf could possibly hire someone, it was not a particularly onerous situation. It is not surprising that the lords did not favor these deals and did not enter into such arrangements willingly.

Statistics on the percentage of the population in each of these serf groups are difficult to obtain and those that do exist are not necessarily reliable. In 1959 the Chinese government estimated the social breakdown as follows:

nobility	5%	
clergy	15%	
herdsmen (nomads)	20%	
serfs	60%	(of which 45% were taxpayer, 45% were human lease, 10% other)[16]

It is difficult to give figures about the tax structure in Tibet because it varied by region and even by year. We can conclude, however, that serfs paid three general types of taxes: one to the government in Lhasa, one to the monasteries, and one to their feudal lords. Of course, serfs in monastic estates did not pay the taxes required by the lay nobility; serfs in government villages were also freed from this obligation. Examples of taxes paid yearly to the government include:

tsampa (roasted barley) for monks
prayer festival tax
hay tax
poisonous flower tax (flowers were used in the preparation of paper)
utensil tax
meat tax
taxes held over from years gone by
corvée tax (dam repair, building irrigation canals, etc.)
military tax (wages and supplies for soldiers)

Taxes paid directly to the monasteries for the upkeep of religious functions include:

butter tax
meat tax
wool tax
woolen cloth tax
tsampa

Monasteries also had the right to *take* children to be initiated as monks if the voluntary supply was insufficient.

Note should be made of the existence of slavery in Tibet. Although vehemently denied by apologists for the old order, there is evidence that slaves existed—usually as private household servants. Since there were few families that could afford to feed and shelter them, they could not have been very numerous. Today, Chinese authorities cite a figure of 5 percent of the population having been slaves; this, however, may be too high.

Sir Charles Bell, a British colonial official in India and a renowned Tibet scholar, acknowledged the existence of slaves:

> Slaves are sometimes stolen, when small children, from their parents. Or the father or mother being too poor to support their child would sell it to a man, who paid them "sho-ring," "price of mothers' milk," brought up the child and kept it or sold it as a slave. . . .
>
> Two slaves whom I saw . . . had been stolen from their parents when five years old, and sold in Lhasa for about seven pounds each.[17]

In spite of the overwhelming evidence of a highly stratified society with a huge gulf between the classes, writers continue to ignore this or attempt to justify it on the grounds that it was benevolent. But not all residents of Tibet were blind to the slights around them. One Western-educated Tibetan, writing about the differences between the rich and poor, wrote that they "could have been different races."[18] A foreign resident who lived in Tibet for over two decades admitted that "nobles regard the common people as inferior."[19] Others were simply unable, or unwilling, to face the realities, writing that "the difference between the rich and poor in Tibet really was a very small one,"[20] or the "Tibetan peasant's way of life seemed enviable, for he possessed what all men desire—ample time to enjoy his leisure independently."[21]

The best examples of the upper strata view of Tibet—that Tibet's social structure was benevolent to the people—can be found in a book by Mary Taring, who was born into one of the wealthiest families in Tibet and married into another.

> We thought the government kind to let us have estates. The people were so contented although the difference between their livelihood and their master's was so great. In the light of Buddhism all people are equal. In Tibet everything was done alike for rich and poor. No one can imagine how gay life was in Tibet.[22]

In spite of these views, however, and seemingly without seeing any contradiction, she also mentions that there were outcasts whom no one would consider marrying; that while the poor subsisted on tsampa and butter tea, the wealthy also ate rice and an additional four to five dishes at every meal; that her family had fifteen to twenty servants (one of whom would always carry her up and down stairs when she was a child because she was "lazy"); that the rich used Western-trained doctors at the British Mission or traveled to India for medical care; and that the servants were so ill-trusted that every morning they were only given the food required for one day out of a locked storehouse.[23]

The life of the vast majority of the Tibetans was not "enviable" by any stretch of the imagination. They lived "in small, badly lighted, cold hovels"[24] and ate a mixture of tsampa, butter, and tea, and if they were lucky, some meat. Indeed, the low productivity resulting from the bad diet was a problem.[25] One refugee reports that when his family lived in Tibet, at a level that could be considered lower-middle class in Tibetan terms, they could experience, at most, "two food crises a year."[26] The nomad diet was slightly better in that it had a high concentration of protein (meant, cheese, milk, yogurt); but it lacked vegetables and grains.[27]

In spite of the claim made not long ago that "before the Chinese crackdown in March 1959, the normal Tibetan diet included an inexhaustible flow of butter-tea, large amounts of meat and various vegetables,"[28] a survey made in 1940 in eastern Tibet came to a somewhat different conclusion. It found that 38 percent of the households never got any tea but either collected herbs that grew wild or drank "white tea,"—boiled water. It found that 51 percent could not afford to use butter, and that 75 percent of the households were forced at times to resort to eating grass cooked with cow bones and mixed with oat or pea flour.[29]

The wealthy, on the other hand, lived in opulent splendor. This, of course, has to be understood in relative terms; because of Tibet's isolation, even the upper strata suffered somewhat from being cut off from the world. Nevertheless, they lived in large, thick-walled houses—a matter of no small importance in a climate as changeable as Tibet's. There was little work for them to do, since many government functions and even the running of their estates were often handled by stewards. Women, in particular, did little but prepare for parties that lasted entire days and were filled with such pastimes as gambling with dice or playing mah-jong. Among the populace, a common appellation for the rich was "ones whose lips are always moistened by tea." The rich, of course, were quick to deny any interest in earthly wealth.[30]

One of the main reasons for the creation of the Buddhist religion was the Buddha's abhorrence of the caste system in the Hindu religion. Equality of human beings was an important element in Buddhist dogma. Unfortunately, this did not deter Tibetans from developing their own caste system. A number of professions were considered "unclean"; and while the Buddhist caste system was not as rigid as the Hindu, Tibetan lower castes were ostracized. There were professional, hereditary beggars, metal workers, fishermen and women, musicians, smiths, actors, butchers and undertakers. While attitudes toward these groups varied widely, it is safe to say that the populace was disdainful toward them, and there was little, if any, intermarriage. In some cases these individuals were forced to live on the outskirts of the villages.

A particularly intriguing group of outcasts lived in Lhasa and were known as *Ra-gyap-pa.* They lived in a ghetto, in houses built of animal horns and their monopoly over certain jobs made them relatively well off. It was their function to rid the city of corpses, human and otherwise, and dispose of the night soil. Before 1912 they were also in charge of convicts.

By all accounts, the task of keeping Lhasa clean must have been herculean, for the city could have rivaled the worst present-day metropolis for its filthiness. Garbage was strewn everywhere, and it was common practice for people to relieve themselves anywhere they pleased. Dead animals were said to be a familiar sight. So bad was it that the thirteenth Dalai Lama was "almost always" sick from the smell and the dirt. The nobility routinely carried around scented handkerchiefs for their noses as they rode through the capital's streets.[31]

Education

There were only two formal schools in Tibet, one for the clergy (the Peak School) and one for the laity. Both had as their sole purpose the preparation of students to become government officials. Both took boys from fourteen to twenty years of age, either from the nobility or from the families of former monk officials. Each school had only twenty to thirty boys enrolled at any one time; those with any physical disfigurements were not admitted.

The major source of education was the monasteries, where some monks learned basic literacy. Those who were bright enough and willing even had some opportunity for advancement. Most, however, only learned to recite the necessary prayers from memory. The wealthy hired tutors or, during the twentieth century, began to send their children to India and Sikkim for an Anglo-Indian education, usually at Christian missionary schools.

A final form of education was provided by ad hoc schools run by roving teachers. Sometimes a lord would hire one for his children and even at times allow serf children to attend. Tuition varied widely, and there are reports that children performed duties such as sweeping in lieu of tuition. Because of their transience, it is difficult to estimate how many of these schools there were. One former noble suggests there were about fifty such schools in Lhasa, each serving about seventy-five to one hundred children.[32] In any event, it is clear that a very small percentage of the population received any formal schooling. Recent arguments have been put forward to justify this situation:

> Reading and writing are virtually unnecessary for there is no such thing as a secular literature in Tibet and one of the values of having such a large body of

monks is that in every village in every part of the country there are monks readily available to read the scriptures or recite them. . . .

What intellectual development any layman wants he wants in terms of his knowledge and understanding of the scriptures and this is always open to him. Further knowledge, to anyone with so clear a sense of direction, is meaningless.[33]

The author unwittingly demonstrates the attitude of the upper classes toward the majority of the population. Without an education there could be no possibility of advancement to a government position, nor could there be an attempt to learn of alternative forms of society or break through the monopoly on information so closely guarded by the clergy. Tibet had no radio stations or newspapers, or indeed any printed secular literature, although oral folk literature abounded. There was one Tibetan-language newspaper, published in India, to which only the nobility subscribed.

Nomads

A large, and important, component of Tibetan society was the nomads—a group about whom even less is known than the sedentary population. Their chief importance to the economy of Tibet was their cultivation of the yak, an animal uniquely adapted as a beast of burden in the Tibetan terrain, thriving at altitudes of 3,000 to 5,100 m. (10,000 to 17,000 ft.) above sea-level. There was scarcely a part of the yak that did not have an important use. Its hair was used to make tents; the hair of its tail for religious ceremonies; its hide for boots, belts, bags, case covers; its meat was a valuable source of protein; while the butter from yaks' milk was used for lamps, food, religious sculptures and cosmetics. Its dung was, and still is, the major source of fuel in Tibet.[34]

The nomads—or herdsmen as they are also called—living mostly in Kham and Amdo, were divided into rigid social classes in either tribes or principalities led by hereditary chiefs or monastic lords. There are no reliable population figures. As previously mentioned, in 1959 the Chinese government estimated them at 20 percent of the population. A more recent estimate puts the figure at 48 percent,[35] although without an accurate census the figures are meaningless.

The nomads are a hardy breed, well acclimatized to their environment, often walking barefoot in the coldest weather. They are fiercely independent, with a long-established history of rejecting rule from either Beijing or Lhasa. This independence makes them feel superior to the sedentary population, and in return the nomads are held in some awe by other Tibetans.

Their lives, however, were not easy. They lived in constant fear of raids and had to be prepared for them at all times. It was common to have men sleep outside the tents, in all sorts of weather, to be on the alert for the raiders. Lack of food was a constant problem. If food supplies ran low, the only alternatives were raids on fellow nomads, hunting or banditry. The last was something for which they were particularly infamous.[36]

Women and Marriage

As in most traditional societies, women were considered inferior to men. The very name by which they were known (*kiemen* or *kye-mi*) translated literally to mean "inferior birth" or "lower birth." This was in line with Tibetan Buddhist belief that to achieve *nirvana,* it was necessary to be male; thus a common prayer among women was "may I reject a feminine body and be reborn a male one." It is not surprising, therefore, that a nomad chieftain would state that

> in our land it was considered a great misfortune not to have a child, moreover a son, to carry on the family line. A man's wealth was, first and foremost, measured through the number of sons he had.[37]

Poor women, of course, worked exceedingly hard. They were responsible for the household animals, household tasks, an equal share of the corvée labor, and most of the agricultural work (although superstitious taboos prevented them from plowing). Rich women, on the other hand, did little. Some did interest themselves in the running of the estates, even doing some of the accounting for the family; but, for the most part, in the words of a Western observer, they

> know nothing about equal rights and are quite happy as they are. They spend hours making up their faces, stringing their pearl necklaces, choosing new material for dresses and thinking how to take the shine out of Mrs. So-and-so at the next party.[38]

Marriage was not considered a religious ceremony; indeed, it was more closely tied up with astrology and superstition than religion. For the economically better off serfs and the wealthy a relative or friend usually acted as a go-between for an arranged marriage. Matters such as the dowry and gifts from the bridegroom were topics for negotiation. But these matters were not even discussed until it was determined that the prospective couple's astrological signs were compatible; the date of the proposed marriage was also astrologically selected. Women, for the most part, were not supposed to be informed of the arrangements in advance because it was believed that they would be distressed to know that they were about to be leaving home. Since there were no religious sanctions to marriage and a wedding was costly, the poor did not bother to marry, simply living together without benefit of any ceremony.[39]

The lack of religious sanctions to marriage, the celibacy of much of the male population and the informality of connubial arrangements meant that promiscuity was common. This was especially so among the poor who made up the vast majority of the Tibetan people. Tibetans' "morals are so loose as almost to be nonexistent," complained a British doctor curing venereal disease sufferers, "prostitutes are unnecessary, extramarital intercourse is condoned; it is quite common for a husband to bring for treatment his wife infected during his absence." Among the wealthy, however, a double standard prevailed: men felt free to conduct extramarital relations (relations with servant girls were said to be common), while women were expected to be faithful. There was a law in Tibet that if a man happened to catch his wife in an extramarital affair he had the right to cut off the tip of her nose.[40]

Promiscuity, naturally enough, resulted in children being born out of wedlock. In spite of one anthropologist's assertion that mothers killed these "illegitimate" children,[41] the evidence indicates not only acceptance but indeed a demand for unwed mothers and their offspring as a result of the low birthrate and the strong desire for children.[42] Having children, regardless of marital status, was far more desirable in Tibetan society than being childless.

The lack of any modern medical facilities and knowledge made the act of giving birth fraught with danger for mother and/or child. Children were usually born on the first floor, which also happened to be the stable. Unclean as it was, it was the most private place where a woman could go. The only help available to women was that of other women whose knowledge was based on experience. Since bathing is rare among Tibetans (because of the cold, the lack of water, and the fact that washing irritates the skin and robs it of natural oils necessary for protection from the ultra-violet rays at Tibet's altitude), babies were not washed as they emerged from the womb, but sometimes licked by the mother.

Without any records or surveys it is difficult to determine how high the death rate was among the very young. The current Dalai Lama informs us that his mother had sixteen children, of whom nine were lost.[43] While this figure is quite high it seems to tally with accounts given by long-time residents of Tibet, particularly medical missionaries. Estimates of child mortality range from 40– 75 percent.

There were no religious proscriptions against divorce. It was usually by mutual consent. On the condition that the wife was not responsible, the dowry was returned to her and she was given custody of the children and a share of the wealth accumulated during the marriage. The poor—in line with their marriage practices—divorced simply, just parting company, the wife in most cases taking the children.

Widows, especially those without children, suffered a social stigma similar to that in India and China. The suspicion in which they were held was more acute if the woman was widowed at a young age or more than once. These were considered almost sure signs of witchcraft or demonry and the only escape for these unfortunate women was to join a nunnery.

Perhaps nothing about the Tibetan social system has drawn as much curiosity as the marriage practices. In addition to the more common unions based on monogamy (one husband, one wife) and polygamy (one husband, multiple wives), Tibetans also practiced polyandry—the marrying of one woman to multiple husbands. In spite of the attention it has attracted, and the anthropological work being done in this area, there is considerable dispute as to how common a practice it was.

Polyandry usually took the form of a woman marrying two or more brothers or a father and son(s) when a young man with marriageable sons was widowed. In these cases all the offspring called the oldest husband "father" and the others "uncle." Polygamy usually followed this format too, with a man marrying sisters or a mother and daughter(s). The most common explanation for the practice of polyandry is the economic structure of the family. If a family had just enough land for subsistence it would have been disastrous to have several brothers marry different wives and break up the land into smaller units. By bringing in one wife the land size was preserved, only one person was added to the household, and there was a guarantee that there would not be an overabundance of offspring. One scholar argues that land was not the cause of these nuptial arrangements but rather attributes them to the assignment of corvée labor. Since corvée was assigned to each household, the breaking up of that household would put an additional burden on the remaining members, leaving them with an undiminished level of corvée.

An understanding of the social stratification and the practice of land tenure are necessary prerequisites to understanding the marriage practices among different groups of serfs. Among the poorest of the people, monogamy was the rule as it was among the "small households" (du-jung). Since there were no economic interests involved, these marriages were informal and not prearranged—usually entered into for love. At the other end of the economic spectrum, the nobility, monogamy was also the rule, although polygamy was not uncommon. It should be pointed out that there were two forms of polygamy practiced in Tibet. One was the common practice of a wealthy man marrying multiple wives. Another, however, had to do with inheritance. If a situation arose in which a wealthy family had no male heir, regardless of the number of female children involved, a male would be brought in to become the heir. This male would cut all ties with his biological family, assume the name of his adopted family and marry the female(s).[44]

Health Care

Without sanitary conditions and modern medical care, Tibet was not a healthy place. Venereal disease (estimated to affect 90 percent of the population)[45] and smallpox (afflicting about one-third of the population, including the thirteenth Dalai Lama in 1900, and seven thousand in Lhasa alone in 1927)[46] were chronic, as were cataracts, leprosy (especially in Amdo and Kham) and gastro-intestinal diseases.[47]

Modern medicine was available in Tibet only at the offices of the Chinese and British representatives—and that only after the 1930s. Christian medical missionaries plied their trade in the Kham and Amdo areas from the late nineteenth century on. In both areas their facilities were not often used; when they were, it was usually by the elites.

The doctors of Tibet were monks, especially trained in the use of herbal medication and other forms of spiritual healing. Disease was seen in the holistic terms familiar in other Asian traditional medicines. Physical imbalance was believed to be related to spiritual imbalance, a disturbance of the elements almost certainly resulting from a patient's *karma* or legacy from a previous life. One former missionary related that leprosy was quite prevalent among the sedentary population of Kham. The nomads of the area regarded this as just punishment for having disturbed the spirits of the land.[48]

In addition to the use of herbs and natural treatments, some of which were quite effective, Tibetan medicine was also a conglomeration of blood-letting, exorcisms, the laying on of hands, and "holy" spittle and a belief in the mystical powers of anything that had come into contact with a holy person. This last belief resulted in a premium being placed on the urine and excrement (rolled up in pill form and swallowed) of highly incarnated monks and especially of the Dalai Lama. A Chinese refugee who was formerly a cadre involved with religious work recalled a Communist Party circular about the Dalai Lama's visit to Beijing in 1954. According to this report, the lama defecated into a gold-plated receptacle from which the feces were returned to Tibet to be made into medicine.[49]

In Tibet medicine was inextricably bound with superstition. Since monks were considered to be holy it was concluded that they were capable of performing "holy" acts. One treatment involved the writing of a proper prayer on a piece of paper and blessing it; the patient then swallowed it as the medication.[50] Monks touched the patient to cure such things as headaches.[51] Wearing a properly blessed rosary consisting of human skulls, around one's neck, served as a cure for toothache.[52] Without rejecting the entire system out of hand, it must be recognized that there was much that was harmful as well as beneficial. The skills of the practitioners varied and, as it true almost everywhere else, the quality of care depended on a person's socioeconomic status.

Crime and Punishment

This is yet another area in which little research has been done. Some paint a picture of a law-abiding and passive society.

> the Tibetan countryside, except in certain districts along the eastern border, was mostly free from brigandage.
> Mostly . . . Tibet was a land where a fair degree of personal security prevailed.[53]
> There is no police force because there is no need for it, there is no need for it because there is little crime, and virtually none that cannot be quickly and

easily settled by arbitration ... [because of the] simple fact that the Tibetan people find it more agreeable and more convenient to be law-abiding.[54]

There is no evidence to support these images of a utopian Shangri-la. A frequent visitor to western Tibet reported that brigands ran freely, another called robbers "a regular plague," while a former resident reported "thieves as thick in Lhasa as fleas on a dog," and yet another confirmed that account by relating that he never ventured out at night in Lhasa unless accompanied by a servant and unless carrying a sword and/or revolver because he "lived in constant fear of burglars. . . . " Economics was not always at the root of the crime. Some believed that to kill a rich or lucky man was to acquire his good fortune. All Westerners were considered to be very rich and lucky.[55]

But by and large this state of affairs was a result of poverty and lack of effective law enforcement. The Tibetan army and the Lhasa police force (the only one in the country) were as much the problem as an instrument for its solution. It was believed that the police force itself turned to crime in the evening. Its activities and open corruption were evidently quite profitable. Even a law allowing officials to keep stolen merchandise upon the capture of a criminal was not incentive enough for much police work. It was usually left up to the victim to find and apprehend a criminal. Only then did Tibetan officials assume their judicial functions. Tibetans adapted to the situation as they were compelled to do, for those who could afford it, protection was offered by servants, weapons, and huge mastiffs.[56] In the countryside the most notorious villains were the Khampas (residents of Kham), "infamous in Tibet as brigands. In fact all robbers were generally referred to as Khampas."[57] For these nomads, raiding and protecting themselves against raids were of primary economic concern—to protect or replenish their livestock, their main livelihood.

Monks were not above criminal activity either. In order to make ends meet, poor monks have been known to steal and sell religious artifacts in spite of the threat of severe penalties. Pepper forced under the eyelids and spikes forced under the fingernails were among the prescribed punishments, though we do not know how often these drastic measures were employed. One high lama received five years of solitary confinement, loss of rank and had two estates confiscated for his frequent sexual liaisons with women.[58]

There were no sets of codified laws but rather a mixture of laws handed down by practice. These laws were the Buddhist canons, the royal law of the ancient kings of Tibet, and what could best be called traditional customs. Mediation and arbitration, preferably by monks, were the most common methods for solving disputes. The lack of law enforcement, the absence of detention facilities for criminals and the disruptions caused by long-lasting feuds made mediation the preferable form of conflict resolution in Tibet. This practice was used not only between individuals but also by communities in conflict. Crimes such as trespassing on the grazing fields of others, poaching in animal preserves, the dese-cration of local shrines and banditry were resolved by making restitution, offer-ing gifts, and even giving "life-money" (*mistong,* literally "man indemnity") to the relatives of someone who had been killed.[59] According to one of the brothers of the current Dalai Lama, the practice of giving "life-money" was not uncom-mon; the amount to be paid was dependent on the wealth and status of the victim. For instance, the killing of a high monastic official would require a payment of U.S.$8,000–10,000.[60]

Another unusual form of dispute resolution was to allow for "divine interven-tion"—drawing lots or throwing dice to determine the guilt or innocence of the parties involved, believing that the spirit world would always support the party in the right. When punishment was incurred it varied according to the circum-stances of the crime and the status of the criminal. As far as can be ascertained there were only a handful of jails, and in these the poorest prisoners ran the risk of being starved to death since their families were completely responsible for their well being. In Lhasa the jail was a deep underground pit from which the prisoners were only allowed out once or twice a year to beg for alms. Since prisons were few, other forms of punishment had to be created. One consisted of chaining the criminal's feet about twelve inches apart, the other in placing a yoke around his or her neck; criminals were then allowed to wander the land in such a manner for the rest of their lives, begging for sustenance.

Another form of punishment favored in Tibet was torture and mutilation. Buddhist belief precludes the taking of life, so that whipping a person to the edge of death and then releasing him to die elsewhere allowed Tibetan officials to justify the death as "an act of God." Other brutal forms of punishment included the cutting off of hands at the wrists; using red-hot irons to gouge out eyes; hanging by the thumbs; and crippling the offender, sewing him into a bag, and throwing the bag in the river.[61]

A British woman who visited Gyantse in 1922 witnessed a public flogging and reported that the victim was then forced to spend the night exposed and tied down on the top of a mountain pass where he froze to death overnight. A British resident of two decades reported seeing countless eye gougings and mutilations, while another resident in the late 1940s reported that "all over Tibet I have seen men who had been deprived of an arm or a leg for theft." The most graphic evidence readily available of a public torture can be seen in *Life* magazine, which carried photographs of a whipping (200–250 lashes) that occurred right in the middle of Lhasa in 1950.[62] Even after the Chinese government re-exerted its control over Tibet in 1950 these practices evidently continued. A Lhasa resident who lived directly across the street from the only police station until the mid-1950s reported that

> flogging and confinement in dark dungeons were still generally employed as deterrents to evildoers. . . . [And] despite the harshness of the penal system there was never a lack of petty evildoers.[63]

Religion

It would be impossible to exaggerate how deeply religion permeated *every* aspect of Tibetan life, particularly during the past few hundred years with the establishment of a theocracy. Tibetan Buddhism had many visible manifestations—there were prayer flags, stupas, religious monuments, stones carved with prayers, charm boxes, prayer wheels, and rosaries. The most visible evidence of Buddhism were the monks. Estimates put the number of monks at several hundred thousands, anywhere from 20 percent to 33–1/3 percent of the male population (see Appendix A). A comparable percentage for the United States would result in about twenty-five million monks; for the United Kingdom, six million. There were also an estimated 27,000 nuns in 1959.[64]

Originally, Tibetans practiced a folk religion (*mi-chos,* "the law, or religion, of men") which gave way to *Bon (bon-chos,* "the Bon religion"). But Tibet is best known for its Buddhism (*iha-chos,* "the divine law").

The Buddha was born Siddharta Gautama about 560 B.C. in northern India into a wealthy and privileged noble family. Feeling guilt about his status and feeling a lack of fulfillment in his life he secretly set off one night at the age of twenty-nine (leaving a sleeping wife and son) to search for a more meaningful life. He was to die around 480 B.C., at the age of eighty.

The religion that was to be founded upon his teachings was largely based on the Buddha's reaction to the Hinduism of his day, which had become ossified into a rigid set of rituals and traditions and was headed by an elite and uncaring Brahmin caste. As a result he preached against authority, ritual, and meaningless traditions in the vernacular rather than the Sanskrit of Hinduism that was unintelligible to all save a small, educated elite. He preached the sanctity of all living beings and was against killing. He stressed self-help and attacked supernatural beliefs ("by this ye shall know that a man is *not* my disciple that he tries to work a miracle" [emphasis in original]).[65]

Four principal sects emerged in Tibet, all somewhat different in their methods and political persuasions but not in their reverence for and allegiance to the basic Buddhist doctrines. The sects, often distinguished by the color of the headdresses worn for ceremonial occasions, are called Nyingmapa, Kargyu, Sakya, and Gelugpa. All enjoyed varying periods of predominance in Tibet; but it was the Gelugpa, or Yellow Hat sect, that maintained absolute political power from the eighteenth century until 1959. All Tibetans, except for the very small number of practitioners of an earlier religion known as Bon and a handful of Moslims, consider themselves Buddhists, believing in the "Four Truths" of Buddhism and agreeing on the five universals necessary for release from the endless suffering of the cycle of birth and rebirth.

But Tibetan Buddhism was heavily influenced by the environmental realities of living in such a harsh land: the severe cold and winds, the effects of the rarefied air (Tibetans suffering from the lack of oxygen attributed their discomfort to "poison gas"), the almost complete isolation from the rest of the world, and the resulting lack of scientific knowledge (many Tibetans believed—as late as the 1950s—that the earth was flat),[66] and the high incidence of early mortality. It is not surprising, therefore, that there was a strong belief in the supernatural.

The process of evolution undergone by Tibetan Buddhism adapted to the nature of life on the Tibetan plateau. As Guiseppe Tucci, the West's foremost Tibetologist, has so aptly pointed out, "the entire spiritual life of the Tibetan is defined by a permanent attitude of defense, by a constant effort to appease and propitiate the powers whom he fears."[67] But, as Tucci has demonstrated elsewhere, this created contradictions with the original nature of Buddhism, resulting in Tibetan religion being

> shot with a certain ambiguity: on the one side the fear of capricious spirits that was inherited by Lamaism from the country's original religions and, on the other, the conviction that man possesses the means to control these dark vengeful forces demanding propitiation. Magic, ritual, acts of piety, liberality towards monasteries and teachers, exorcism, liturgical technique, all come to his aid. And the human victim he was at the outset, at the mercy of a thousand invisible forces, is able to become their master.[68]

The theory, however, does not always work as expected in practice. While Tibetans believed—as Buddhism taught—that they could have control over these forces, they never believed they had actually gained the upper hand.

Buddhism proscribes the killing of any living thing, without exception. But Tibet is a land with a harsh climate, little arable soil, and no textile industry. As sources of protein and clothing, animals had to be killed. The solution was not difficult to find: create a separate class of butchers. These butchers "who slaughtered the animals were regarded as sinners and outcastes."[69] Sometimes Moslims were used as butchers. There is no actual admonition against eating meat in Buddhist dogma—only against taking life. There was even a way in which merit could be acquired by buying an animal from a butcher, having it consecrated with the appropriate ceremony, tying a ribbon around its neck, and releasing it. No one would then kill that animal, and the "savior" would be granted the stipulated merit.[70]

Another curious manifestation of the evolution of Tibetan Buddhism was the belief in the merit of quantity over quality in religious practices. In circumambulations of shrines, for example, the amount of merit received depended on the number of circuits performed. Prayer wheels were particularly important reflections of the premium placed on repetition.

> There are table wheels turned by the fingers; portable wheels turned by hand; tiny wheels turned by the winds; larger wheels propelled by manpower; and the largest wheels of all, driven by hydraulic power. Wheels within wheels,

whirling round and round. Imagine all the Tibetans muttering scriptures, continually walking around their monasteries, their cities, and their country where hundreds of thousands of such wheels are perpetually in motion. So this is Tibet.[71]

In addition to turning wheels, Tibetans recited scriptures and continuously chanted the mantra *Om Mani Padme Hum* (Hail to thee, the Jewel in the Lotus). They put up countless prayer flags and some spent their lives "printing" the image of Buddha—in a running stream (repeatedly dipping a piece of wood with the image of Buddha carved onto it).[72] Since quantity was desirable, the wealthier a family was the more religious paraphernalia could be employed on its behalf. The wealthiest could pay a monk to live in their house as a "resident chaplain," to spend his whole life acquiring merit for the family in the appropriate ways.

Pilgrimages and visits to shrines were also significant to the average Tibetan. Some shrines were good for specific purposes—one particular shrine was noted for helping predetermine the sex of an unborn child. Pilgrimages also played an important social function, for the gatherings of people from different areas of Tibet allowed for the opportunity to engage in trade, catch up on news of recent events, make new contacts for future trade possibilities, and afforded monks and women some escape from the monotonous routines of daily life.

For the orthodox Tibetan, simply traveling to the desired location in conventional ways was insufficient. It was not uncommon to see devoted pilgrims prostrating themselves the entire distance. The routine way to go about this was to lie down completely flat in the required direction. Then, laying a stone at the point where the body ended, to stand up at the point of the stone and repeat the process. The more devout resorted to lying widthwise, moving ahead only the width of their body—rather than the length—at each prostration. This would be repeated for hundreds of miles and could take years. To prostrate oneself around the Lingkhor—a circular road around Lhasa, about 8 km. (5 mi.) long, popular for circumambulations, could take a pilgrim three days, prostrating the body lengthwise, and five days, prostrating widthwise.

Tibet abounded in itinerant mystics who, more often than not, exploited the gullibility of the people. Hermits were also plentiful. Entire towns of hermitages were said to exist, where monks were completely enclosed in caves—save only a small hole through which food was passed once a day—from short periods of their life, to their entire remaining life span. Astrologers and fortune tellers also plied their trade, much as they do today on some modern city streets.

Oracles were common in Tibet. There were hundreds of them, specializing in telling the future of exorcising specific evil spirits. The method employed was simple enough. They went into a trance and began to speak in a strange language that was only understood by a trained assistant. During this period their bodies were allegedly taken over by a spirit. The current Dalai Lama has been quoted as saying that oracles have "nothing to do with Buddhism. . . . They should be looked upon as a manifestation of popular superstition."[73]

The Nechung Oracle was the official government oracle who was called upon to help reach important decisions concerning all of Tibet. But life as an oracle was not carefree, for, as one Tibetan official advised "an oracle had better not make mistakes and give wrong answers. Several have been degraded and thrown into jail for having uttered false prophecies."[74]

The aspect of Tibetan Buddhism that has received the most attention in the West is the complex set of rituals based on a canon entitled the *Bardo-thödröl,*

> the book whose mere recitation, when heard by the dead man during the period of his intermediate existence between the life he has left and the one he is to enter in forty-nine days' time, will lead him to salvation.[75]

(In the West, this text is more commonly known as *The Tibetan Book of the Dead.*[76])

Tibetans believe that after a person dies there is a critical period of forty-nine days before the beginning of the next rebirth. A proper rebirth requires the conduct of certain prescribed rituals during this interim period. Upon a death, monks are called in to perform these rituals. If it can be afforded, these monks will stay with the body, in shifts, throughout the forty-nine days. The body is removed from the house only when an astrologer has determined the most propitious time.

It is believed that if the proper rituals are not performed, the soul may reenter the body and run wild. Tibetan homes have traditionally had low doorways and high stairs in order to prevent these types of reactivated corpses from chasing a living being. These corpses are called *ro-langs* or "zombies" and are believed to be sometimes activated by necromancers for their own supernatural purposes.[77]

Tibetan funeral practices are also unique—again, probably for environmental reasons. The ground is frequently too hard to bury people and wood is a scarce commodity in most areas. Poor people were often just thrown into a river, while important monks could count on being cremated. Dalai Lamas and the most important incarnations were usually embalmed. The most common practice, however, was the cutting up of bodies and the grinding of the bones mixed with some grain. These remains were left on hilltops for the vultures. Burial was usually reserved for infants and people with contagious diseases.[78] Some Tibetans believed that if a person did not receive a proper burial he or she risked the danger of being reincarnated as a locust.[79] The strength of Tibetan beliefs in the death ritual is documented by the work of an anthropologist in Nepal. Tibetans in Tibet greatly feared being unable to find someone to perform the proper death rituals (for political reasons explained below). From the mid-1960s to the late 1970s, consequently, these Tibetans regularly (and secretly) sent money and instructions to Tibetan monks in Nepal—via the traders who crossed the frontiers—in order that the necessary rituals be performed *in absentia.*[80]

Two kinds of evidence are frequently used to demonstrate that human sacrifice was an accepted practice in Tibet. First, visitors are shown the many ritual objects of human skulls and bones, particularly the human thigh-bone. These objects do exist and were used in religious rituals;[81] the Chinese however, seem to imply that people were deliberately killed in order to make use of their needed parts. There is not a trace of evidence to support this. It is probably safe to say that these bones were gathered during the unusual mortuary practice described above that allowed vultures to pick away at the body after death. This may be grisly to some, but it is a far cry from purposely killing someone for their bones.

The other "evidence" is the alleged practice of burying live children in the cornerstones of houses and/or monasteries for some undetermined religious purpose.[82] This form of human sacrifice is said to have been practiced right up until 1959.[83] Indeed the Chinese claim to have the testimony of the relatives of twenty-one individuals who were ordered to be killed in 1948, by the authorities in Lhasa, for the sole purpose of using their organs as "sacrificial offerings" in an attempt to have the spirits prevent the Communists from gaining control of Tibet.[84]

But are these accounts, as the refugees claim, mere fabrications? To begin with there appears to be some evidence indicating that the ancient kings of Tibet had live people entombed with them when they died.[85] This was not an unusual practice in other cultures in pre-medieval times. We also know that the older Tibetan religion sanctioned human sacrifices and, at a later date, practiced animal sacrifices.[86]

In twentieth century Tibet, the practice of human sacrifice evolved into animal sacrifice and the self-infliction of wounds for religious purposes. There are frequent accounts of visitors to areas inhabited by Tibetans having witnessed animal sacrifices and such activities as burning the fingers and the ritual breaking of a stone on a man's chest.[87]

But the question of the continued practice of human sacrifice still remains unresolved. In 1915 a British visitor to Gyantse was told that in certain rituals in previous times, babies had been sacrificed in the monastery there, indicating that this practice was not totally alien to Tibet.[88] We also have the testimony of Robert Ekvall, an American missionary and anthropologist who was born in China and spent at least eight years of his adult life in the regions inhabited by Tibetans. He reported that although animal sacrifices were more common, there were some instances of human sacrifices.[89] The most convincing clue we have comes from Sir Charles Bell. Bell wrote that he once visited a spot on the Tibet-Bhutan border where he saw a stupa called *Bang-kar Bi-tse cho-ten* that contained the bodies of an eight-year-old boy and girl "who had been slain for the purpose" of some *religious ritual.*[90]

Evidence of human sacrifice is circumstantial, at best. I would venture to say that in the more remote areas human sacrifice probably did occur. However, it could not have been practiced with great frequency, for an extensive search for accounts by travelers and foreign residents of Tibet turned up only the examples cited above.

No discussion of Tibetan Buddhism would be complete without some mention of the notion of *karma*. One former high incarnated lama defined it the following way:

> according to the Buddhist doctrine of karma . . . any prosperity that we may ourselves enjoy will be the result of our generosity in the past, as poverty is caused by miserliness.[91]

This definition corresponds to the Dalai Lama's notion as well:

> the idea of karma [is] that what comes to us is not only inevitable but also the result of our actions in this life or in others we have lived. Therefore, we have to accept it.[92]

From a purely secular point of view, this doctrine could be seen as one of the most ingenious and pernicious forms of social control ever devised. To the ordinary Tibetan, the acceptance of this doctrine precluded the possibility of ever changing his or her fate in this life. If one were born a slave, so the doctrine of *karma* taught, it was not the fault of the slaveholder but rather the slaves themselves for having committed some misdeeds in a previous life. In turn, the slaveholder was simply being rewarded for good deeds in a previous life. For the slave to attempt to break the chains that bound him, or her, would be tantamount to a self-condemnation to a rebirth into a life worse than the one already being suffered. This is certainly not the stuff of which revolutions are made; it is not, therefore, surprising that there were few peasant revolts, for this idea of *karma* was universally accepted. Indeed, Tibetans in exile continue to accept these teachings. It was recently reported that Tibetan peasants in southern India do not go to a doctor when they feel ill because they accept their sickness as the inevitable result of their *karma*.[93]

In the final analysis it could not be stressed strongly enough that Buddhism was almost universally accepted and that the people of Tibet found it met their spiritual needs, partly because there was no alternative and partly because it helped them find answers to the complexities of their lives while also serving to protect them in their future lives.

Monasteries

With Buddhist belief so pervasive, it followed that the protectors and propagators of Buddhism would play a powerful and influential role in Tibetan society. The role of the clergy was not only spiritual but also economic. Spiritually, popular belief had it that monks were essential, for even if a lay person were able to learn the hóly books, a monk had to interpret how to use the learning and how to perform the rituals. Economically, their extensive land holdings were tax exempt, while the lay population waś expected to supplement the monks' income. To give but one example, Sir Charles Bell cites the financial records for 1917. In that year the government in Lhasa received an income of £720,000, while the church received £800,000. However, as its contribution, the government gave the church an additional £274,000 from its own funds.[94]

The huge number of monks was clearly the backbone of the church's power. A tradition evolved of sending at least one son from each family into the clergy to ensure him some dignity and more than likely guarantee his livelihood. As one mother put it, a monk's life was good "because [there was] no work, plenty to eat, and [it would be] without sin." The monastic orders also provided a safety valve when a family had too many sons and not enough property to divide reasonably. Occasionally the aristocracy would send a son to the monastery to help maintain a position of power and influence for that family through the acquisition of a post within the hierarchy.[95]

The power the church had was wielded through the monasteries to which every monk belonged. The English term is somewhat misleading, as these "monasteries" were not like the Christian contemplative monasteries with which Westerners are familiar. The bigger monasteries in Tibet were, in fact, entire towns—with large plots of agricultural lands, pastoral lands, thousands of serfs, market centers, banking and lending institutions,[96] and military warehouses for the armies raised from among the monastic population. This last was important since whole monasteries would be turned into military forces if the need arose. They were also centers for publishing, art galleries and even governmental, administrative bureaus in the more remote areas. In nomadic areas they served important functions, supplying essential skilled crafts and providing a place where the nomads could store their valuables and have a neutral ground in times of conflict.

Some monasteries were very large. In 1959 the three major monasteries in Lhasa held 16,500 monks (Drepung, 7,700; Sera, 5,500; and Ganden, 3,300).[97] Their power lay, however, not only in their size but in their influence. Each "parent" monastery was in charge of dozens, if not hundreds, of "children" monasteries. The "parent" provided operating funds, trained elites to govern, and gave the "children" membership in a powerful institution. In return the smaller monasteries extended the power and trade capabilities of the "parent" into remote areas, while supplying shelter and guards for the carrying out of that trade.

While it has generally been assumed that all monks received a formal education, this was true only to a very limited extent. The vast majority of the monks learned to memorize lengthy religious liturgy and little else, and were referred to as "nonreaders." Those monks privileged enough to acquire literacy were referred to as "readers." One scholar estimates that 90 percent of the monks at the three major Lhasa monasteries were "nonreaders,"[98] while another estimate puts their numbers, in general, at 75 percent.[99]

When a Tibetan boy joined the monastery he did not cut his ties with his family. Indeed, quite the contrary was required, for the monastery itself provided only the barest sustenance for the monks. In order to advance, learn a skill, or achieve a higher standard of living, a monk was not only required to maintain his family ties but also to engage in some sideline activities. Such activities included performing religious rites for a fee, begging for alms, engaging in trade, or becoming the "resident chaplain" for a wealthy family.

The social classes within the monastery were almost as rigidly enforced as without; social mobility was the exception rather than the rule. Monks from wealthier families hired the best tutors for the children of the family; supported them in the manner to which they were accustomed; *bought* them official positions (even at times the position of "incarnated lama"); and, as one former lama has confessed, hired stand-ins to complete examinations necessary for higher advancement.[100] Wealthier monks dressed better, ate better, and were better cared for. One former lama reports having three guardians: one responsible for his legal affairs, one for his spiritual affairs, and one as a servant in charge of food and clothing.[101] During the first eight years of residence in a monastery, all monks were expected to perform certain kitchen duties; however, exceptions were made for high incarnations and *chogzeds* ("monks who gain privilege by offering gift ceremonies").[102]

Although considered sinful, homosexuality appears to have been widespread among the clergy and almost unknown among the lay population. Within the Gelugpa sect there seems to have been a tendency toward homosexuality; some reports indicate that this was encouraged as evidence of "celibacy"—defined as abstinence from sexual relations with women. There were exceptions; some Gelugpa monks—for example, those who were also government officials—did have heterosexual liaisons.[103]

One of the more unusual features of the Tibetan priesthood was the existence of "priest-rebels," at times numbering some 10–15 percent of the monastic populations. These were monks who had committed sins (such as killing in battle) and as a result had been released from their religious vows and duties in order to engage in military and economic activities on behalf of the monastery, while maintaining their residence there.

> They engage in such activities unhampered by monkish scruples and are often shrewd, ruthless and even swashbuckling characters who still wear monkish robes . . . while they rule and make war like robber chieftains.[104]

The "police" were in charge of enforcement. They were permitted to grow their hair long (other monks have to shave theirs), chant their own prayers, and conduct secret rituals. In order to make themselves appear more fearsome they tore their robes and smeared their faces with soot and grease. However, their appearance was probably not as frightful as the concealed swords, large keys, and iron bars they carried.[105] These "police," or "Iron Bars" as they are sometimes called, were also feared for their practice of kidnapping boys for homosexual activities—an occurrence common enough to encourage boys to walk in groups to prevent being victimized.

The evidence indicates that Tibet, as of 1950, was neither a mythical "Shangri-la" nor a "hell on earth." Tibetans led a difficult and harsh existence in which some benefited more than others. Tibet was a medieval society that somehow survived into the second half of the twentieth century. An anthropologist who interviewed many of the poorer refugees reported that they viewed the old society with some sense of shame and discussed it with outsiders only with extreme reluctance; he reported that "a number indicated to me that they would prefer to remain in Mysore [India] rather than return to Tibet as it was under the old system (serfdom)."[106] Even prominent refugees are coming to perceive the consequences of the old system, although they couch their reservations in milder tones.

> It has become increasingly evident that the system of government which had hitherto prevailed in Tibet has not proved sufficiently responsive to the present needs and future development of its people.[107]

If conditions were so harsh, why was there no general revolt of the serfs? And why did so many hundreds of thousands of youths obligingly troop off to the monasteries and rarely leave? The most frequently offered explanation is that the Tibetan people were "happy" and had no reason to rebel. This argument may well confuse "happiness" with resignation. Witnessing smiling faces and friendly people, which literally every traveler did, could as easily have been an indication of Tibetan stoicism.

I believe that the poor were not necessarily satisfied with their condition but resigned to it. The belief in *karma* was a convincing argument for being content with one's present life for the benefit of one's future lives. *Karma* was only one of the many religious concepts that reinforced the status quo. Isolation from other societies meant that Tibetans could neither experience, nor even learn, of any alternatives to their own society. The system also provided some safety values for those who may have been unhappy. For example, the availability of "human lease" provided, in theory at least, a means of petitioning higher authorities to redress perceived wrongs. And for men, monkhood offered a life of some prestige, escape from the obligations of serfdom, and a modicum of economic stability.[108]

And, so, in this condition Tibet was about to be opened to the world of class struggle, modern industry and communications, revolutionary ideology, and international diplomacy. As I will attempt to show, it was not prepared.

2

The Early History

Writing a history of Tibet is fraught with particular difficulties. The first obstacle is the absence of a formal and widely accepted written language before the seventh century. This lack is remarkable for a society sandwiched between two of the oldest civilizations in the world: China and India. By the seventh century the Chinese Empire was at least 2,300 years old, while the Indian tradition was only slightly younger. Moreover, these dates reflect only periods for which we have solid archaeological evidence; that leaves open the real possibility that new findings may push those dates back even further. The second problem for the would-be historian results from the ascendancy of Buddhism in Tibet. Its worldview required a rewriting of previous history to bring it into proper alignment with the new Buddhist ideology.[1] A third problem arose in the early years of the twentieth century, when Tibet was a pawn in the power struggles of Great Britain, Russia, and Imperial China. The events of that era led to a dramatic polarization of political ideologies, later exacerbated by the establishment of the People's Republic of China. The consequences have been a continual rewriting and reinterpreting of historical events.

On the credit side, early Chinese chronicles, though biased, tend to be fairly comprehensive and are important as sources of corroboration of historical dates. A positive development, and perhaps the most important for the future of Tibetan historiography, is the dispersal of Tibetans outside of Tibet and the fact that some are obtaining an advanced secular education. The result has been a comparative avalanche of published historical material on Tibet based on serious scholarly research.

In the Beginning

Although there is some circumstantial evidence that a political entity existed earlier, solid historical evidence does not predate the late sixth century, when a tribal chief named Namri-songsten (c. 570–620) exerted his power over the neighboring tribes in an attempt at unification. This task was completed by his son, Songsten Gampo (c. 620–649),[2] who is recognized as the first true unifier of Tibet. But he was far more than simply a conqueror. Sensing that as his empire expanded he would have to come to terms with his neighbors, he dealt with the problem in an enlightened way.

He began in 641 by marrying a princess (Wen Cheng [Wen-ch'eng]) of the ruling Chinese Tang (T'ang) dynasty, thereby establishing the first formal relations between the rulers of the Han people and the rulers of the Tibetans and assuring an alliance with his most powerful neighbor. Most historians also credit Songsten-gampo with having married a princess from the ruling house of Nepal. However, some scholars question the existence of this marriage since the documentation is unclear.[3] Although some evidence exists that Buddhism was not totally unknown in Tibet at the time, it was the influence of the Han princess upon her husband that was to be a spur to its wider dissemination. While no proof exists that Songsten-gampo ever personally adopted Buddhism, or that he actively pursued its propagation, his interest in it and his tolerance of those who did proselytize had profound effects upon the Tibetan people for the next twelve centuries.

Princess Wen Cheng brought with her religious artifacts and is credited with having introduced into Tibet the use of butter, tea, cheese, barley, beer, medical knowledge, and astrology. She is said to have encouraged the sending of the sons of tribal chiefs to Changan (present-day X'ian [Sian]), the Chinese capital, for education and to have encouraged the sending of a minister, Thonmi Sambhota, to Kashmir (a major center of Buddhist learning at the time) to bring back a written script for the Tibetan language based on Sanskrit. Moreover, Songsten-gampo is said to have allowed Buddhist missionaries from India, China, and Nepal to travel freely and seek converts while at the same time establishing an indigenous priesthood and promulgating the first set of Tibetan laws.[4]

Like Songsten-gampo, his successors came to power as minors. This period (649–755) was marked by bloody struggles between the adherents of the old Bon religion and those of Buddhism, and a series of Tibetan military conquests. These came to an end during the reign of King Khride-tsang (reign 704–755), who married a Han princess, Jin Cheng (Chin-ch'eng), in 710. The marriage was devised by both parties to bring an end to the military activities against China. Tibet remained a powerful force in central Asia until well into the ninth century. An added bonus to the Tibetans were the several Buddhist temples the princess had built during her reign in what is now Lhasa.[5]

For over a century and a half Buddhism slowly permeated Tibetan society in the struggle of its adherents to dominate their Bon rivals. This feat was finally accomplished in the eighth century with the enthronement of King Trisong Detsen. He was such an ardent Buddhist that he declared Buddhism the official state religion while, following the Indian custom, he awarded estates and serfs to the Buddhist monasteries and exempted them from taxes and corvées.[6] To guarantee the security of the clergy, the king promulgated a code designed to protect them.

> He who shows a finger to a monk shall have his finger cut off; he who speaks ill of the monks and the king's Buddhist policy shall have his lips cut off; he who looks askance at them shall have his eyes put out; he who robs them shall pay according to the rule of the restitution of eighty times (the value of the article stolen).[7]

Nevertheless, the lay nobility and the Bon clergy continued to wield considerable influence and it is highly probable that the king's embrace of Buddhism had as much, if not more, to do with finding a counter to his enemies—who were largely followers of the Bon religion—as with his belief in the superiority of Buddhism. The opposition was able to oust a famous Indian Buddhist teacher whom the king had invited and was powerful enough to count the king's principal wife as an ally.[8]

In 797 King Trisong Detsen was succeeded by his second son, Muni Tsenpo. Tibetan chronicles relate the story of how this monarch attempted, on three occasions, to redistribute wealth evenly among the entire Tibetan populace—only to discover that the wealthy continued to get wealthier and the poor, poorer. When the king complained about his inability to carry out his plan, the sorcerer Padmasambhava is alleged to have said to him, "Our condition in this life is entirely dependent upon the actions of our previous life and nothing can be done to alter the scheme of things."[9] The story is probably apocryphal, intended as a lesson to whomever might question his or her lowly social status and to reinforce the notion that struggle for change would be fruitless. In the end the king was poisoned by his own mother.[10]

Despite the small victories of the forces of Bon, Buddhism continued to make major strides, particularly during the reign of King Ralpachen (c. 815–838). This period is noted for the rise of the Buddhist clergy to positions of major political power. The priesthood expanded, temples were built (with craftsmen from China) and Buddhism was zealously propagated. In Ralpachen's efforts to create a strong Buddhist clergy as a counterweight to the Bon and noble elite he ordered that every seven families in Tibet must financially support one Buddhist monk, and he elevated a monk to the position of Chief Minister. It was this latter measure that finally spurred the opposition into action, leading to Ralpachen's assassination by his brother Langdarma.[11] It was during the reign of King Ralpachen that the Han Chinese and the Tibetans signed their first treaty. Called the treaty of "Uncle and Nephew," it was negotiated by Buddhist monks on both sides to end some military engagements. The treaty was carved on a pillar (erected in 832) and stands to this day outside the Jokhang Cathedral in Lhasa.[12]

Langdarma represented the forces that opposed the propagation of Buddhism, and scholars cite the beginning of his reign (c. 838–842) as the end of what is commonly known, somewhat inaccurately, as the "first diffusion of the doctrine." The pendulum then swung to the opposite extreme, introducing a period characterized by widespread and vicious persecution of Buddhism and its followers. Temples were destroyed, monasteries sealed up, monks forced to convert or even killed, and non-Tibetan Buddhist teachers deported. The adherents of Bon and their allies were able to make a dramatic return to power after almost two centuries. But these events should not be seen as merely a struggle of contending religious persuasions; religion was used primarily as the most overt symbol of two contending power groups. While Langdarma's attacks on the Buddhist monasteries certainly helped the growth of Bon, they also went a long way to curb the growing political and economic forces aligned with the Buddhist clergy. Indeed, one widely respected scholar has argued that Langdarma was not as openly hostile to Buddhism as he has been depicted, but tacitly went along with the anti-Buddhist activities, knowing full well that they aided the rise to power of his faction.[13]

The winners of this latest power struggle, however, were unable to consolidate their power. Langdarma's death, allegedly at the hands of a Buddhist monk,[14] resulted in yet another struggle between two of his sons, subsequently ending the unification Tibet had enjoyed for over two hundred years. Tibet dissolved into numerous tribes, principalities and regional hegemonies that were constantly at war with each other. Songsten-gampo's empire had come to a bitter end.

Coincidentally, similar events were unfolding in China. The end of the Tang dynasty in 907 saw China dissolve into countless warring states, and strong central rule was not to return to Tibet or China for some time. During the Tang dynasty there had been one hundred fifty missions between the two capitals, and eight treaties were signed during a period when Tibet was absorbing Chinese culture.

The fifty-three years that followed in China are known to historians as the period of "Five Dynasties and Ten States," out of which the Song (Sung) dynasty (960–1279) finally emerged. The Song leaders were, however, so preoccupied with military engagements in the south, west, and southwest that little attention was paid to Tibet. One researcher reported that after combing through the Song chronicles he was unable to turn up any significant contacts between Beijing and Lhasa except for the occasional tribute mission from individual tribes in Tibet to the Chinese capital and the deployment of armies by the Song to put down rebellious tribes in, or near, Tibet.[15]

From 842 to 1247 AD there was no central rule in Tibet. While Buddhism was in decline during this period there were two Tibetan areas, geographically widely separated, where Buddhism managed to survive and hold its own. Buddhism managed to survive surreptitiously in the east, in Kham, and in the west where it finally coalesced at the Samye Monastery.

During the tenth century, a local monarch named Chanchup-ö initiated a revival of Buddhism (known now as the "second diffusion of the doctrine") by, among other actions, inviting noted Indian scholars to teach Buddhism in Tibet. One such visitor, Atisá, was responsible for the creation of several new Tibetan religious orders because of his belief that Buddhist practice had degenerated in Tibet under the followers of the Nyingmapa ("One of the Old") order. Astisá's followers established the reformed Kadampa ("One of the Doctrine") order and the less strict Sakya and Kagyupa sects.

This period saw the genesis of what would soon become the monastic monopoly on religious and lay power in Tibet. Monasteries began to acquire large tracts of land, build political power bases, make alliances with wealthy lay patrons, and muster monk armies to protect this newly acquired position in Tibetan society. This monopoly of power would last over nine centuries.

The Mongol Connection

At the turn of the thirteenth century, Moslim armies descended on India and in many areas, particularly in Bengal, began to persecute adherents of other religions. The Buddhists in Bengal gathered their sacred objects and fled north to Tibet, bringing with them such tales of woe that the Tibetans attempted to seal their border with India. But Tibet was no match for the Moslim legions and an alliance with a stronger power was essential. Word spread in Tibet only a few years later that the Mongol armies of Genghis Khan (1162–1227) were conquering the areas of China we now know as Gansu (Kansu) and Qinghai provinces. Partially to preclude a Mongol invasion and partially to acquire an ally against the threat from the south, the Tibetans sent a delegation of submission to the Khan, seeking a formal alliance.

Nothing official came of these efforts until almost the middle of the thirteenth century when Genghis Khan's grandson, Prince Godan (?–1251), dispatched an army that halted only sixty miles short of Lhasa. One of Godan's duties was to gather intelligence about neighboring peoples for the Mongol court in Karakorum. His army discovered that the major centers of power in Tibet were the monasteries and that there was no unity among them. His agents further informed him that the most powerful monastery of the day was the one at Sakya.

Armed with this information, Godan "invited" the head of that monastery, the Sakya Pundita (Kunga Gyaltsen, 1182–1251) to visit him in Lanzhou (Lanchou). The monk arrived in 1245, with his nephew and heir apparent, Phagpa (Lodo Gyaltsen, 1235–1280). After some enforced negotiations the Tibetan delegation agreed to recognize Mongolian suzerainty over Tibet and to pay a regular tribute. They further ingratiated themselves with their hosts by writing letters back to the other factions' in Tibet, urging compliance with the agreement. The Tibetan lay nobility, however, refused to comply and Godan reverted to force. In 1251 he dispatched a Mongol army to Tibet and placed, for the very first time, Buddhist clerical figures in positions of secular political power over all Tibet. It had been four hundred years since King Ralpachen first entrusted Buddhist clergy with a modicum of political power.

The Sakya Pundita died in Lanzhou in the same year as the invasion, and his nephew immediately succeeded him. The Mongols and Tibetans forged a unique "priest-patron" relationship, the meaning of which is debated to this day. For the Mongols, the presence of the Tibetan lamas amongst them meant an introduction to a more formalized culture, a written script, and a hegemony over Tibet that guarded their entire southern flank. Tibetans, by acting as priests, provided spiritual sustenance to the Mongols and served as guides to Tibetan Buddhism. For the Tibetans, especially the clerical elite, it meant the acquisition of supreme power in Tibet and the ability to maintain that power with the help of a strong ally. Thus the Mongol armies acted as their "patrons."

Prince Godan was succeeded by Kublai Khan, who maintained the priest-patron relationship by appointing Phagpa the ruler of the central Tibetan provinces of U and Tsang and naming him "Imperial Preceptor." While this era solidified this special relationship, it also marked the beginning of its inevitable decline. For the Sakya monks the enormous wealth and power showered upon them by the Mongols led to internal dissension, resulting in the murder of a chief lama by his own minister. No powerful leader emerged to end the internecine bickering. Other Tibetan sects were unwilling to sit by and wait patiently for the Sakyas' monopoly on power to dissolve of its own accord. These sects sent several missions to Beijing in vain attempts to seek favor with the Mongol occupants of the Dragon Throne (official seat of the rulers of China).[16]

With the death of Phagpa in 1280 and of Kublai Khan in 1295, the fortunes of both the Sakyas and the Mongols declined. The denouement came with the fall of the Mongol's dynasty in China and the emergence of a new ethnic Han dynasty (the Ming) in 1368. After nineteen successive rulers from 1251 to 1358, Sakya rule finally succumbed. From that time until 1642, Tibet was to be ruled by a succession of lay nobility in conjunction with various sects of Tibetan Buddhism (but with the former clearly in charge). In spite of the Mongols' fall from power over all of China, however, they continued to play a crucial role in the mainstream of Tibetan politics through their sponsorship of various sects.[17]

When the Ming rulers consolidated their power in China they followed the policies of their Yuan dynasty predecessors toward Tibet by inviting leading clerics to visit the imperial court in Beijing. Not many went as readily as they had in the past. From 1566 to the fall of the Ming in 1644, political relations between Beijing and Lhasa were characterized by diplomatic missions, the bestowing of honors and titles, but little, if any, actual political control by the Chinese.[18]

The Buddhist Reformation

During the early years of Ming rule there lived, in Tibet, a man who was destined to change the face of Tibetan culture and history. His name was Tsongkhapa (1357–1417), and he was known as "The Man from the Land of Onions." At the height of his fame, the Chinese Emperor Yong Luo (Yung-lo [r. 1403–1424]) repeatedly invited him to Beijing. Claiming ill health, Tsongkhapa refused, but sent a disciple, Jamchen Choje, in his place. The disciple was honored with the title "All-Knowing, Understanding and Benevolent Peacemaker of the World, Great Loving One, Worshipped by All, Great Prince and Lama from the Happy Steadfast Kingdom of the West, Jamchen Choje, the Great Lama of the Emperor."[19]

Tsongkhapa looked around and saw that the Buddhist church had degenerated in its religious practice and had, in his opinion, far removed itself from the benevolent and compassionate teachings of the Buddha. Like Martin Luther a century later, Tsongkhapa set out to reform his religion. He founded a sect known as Gelugpa ("those who follow the path of perfect virtue") and in 1409 established his first monastery, called Ganden ("place of joy"). He demanded strict discipline from his monks, absolute celibacy, and a return to basic Buddhist teachings. Tibetans flocked to him. Soon Ganden had 3,300 monks, and other monasteries had to be established. In 1416 Drepung was built and housed 7,700 monks. In 1419 Sera was founded for 5,500 monks. All three of these monasteries were in the Lhasa area and were to become pre-eminent in the ruling of Tibet. After Tsongkhapa's death, his disciples spread his teachings across Tibet, founding the monastery at Qamdo (Chamdo) in eastern Tibet in 1437 and ten years later opening the Tashilhunpo Monastery near Shigatse.[20]

Almost immediately, the Gelugpa were faced with a serious difficulty—the question of continuity of leadership. Opposed to hereditary rule, and trying to avoid a dependence on the lay nobility, the Gelugpa elite were hard-pressed to develop a system that would keep questions of succession in their hands and at the same time the concentration of power in the hands of a select few. Tsongkhapa decided to use the concept of reincarnation (*tulku*) to establish succession. The rightful leader was considered to be a reincarnation of Chenrezig, the patron deity of Tibet, and of the Buddha himself.[21] Although long a part of Buddhist teachings, this was the first time reincarnation—as a political function—was institutionalized.

The Gelugpa elite could now decide who the new ruler would be, effecting a peaceful and orderly transition of power. By selecting a young boy as the reincarnation, the clergy prevented noble families from perpetuating hereditary rule. Moreover, since the incarnation was chosen at an early age and was raised exclusively under the tutelage of the Gelugpa elite, the child would be properly socialized into the required ideological perspective. By insisting that the chosen child was in fact the same individual who had just recently died, opponents would be silenced (the faithful could be relied upon to flock to the defense of the child).

The Gelugpa became known as the "Yellow Hat" sect, while the others were commonly grouped under the rubric of "Red Hats"—names that derived from the colors of hats worn during ceremonial rites.

When Tsongkhapa died, inexplicably no incarnation was chosen. In fact the system of reincarnations began to be employed only after the death of Tsongkhapa's most famous disciple, the founder of the Tashilhunpo Monastery, Gedun Truppa (1391–1472).[22] His incarnation was named Gedun Gyatso (1475–1542), who was followed in turn by the incarnation Sonam Gyatso (1543–1588). It was during the latter's reign that the chieftain of the Khoshot Mongols, Altan Khan (1548–1581), summoned the Gelugpa leader to Mongolia. The lama arrived in the summer of 1578 and preached Buddhism with such success that he converted the Khan himself. In return, the lama was given a series of titles, including the familiar "Dalai Lama Vajradhara": *dalai,* Mongolian for ocean; *lama,* Tibetan for priest; and *vajradhara,* Sanskrit for holder of the thunderbolt.[23] In other words, "a priest with ocean-like wisdom and the holder of the thunderbolt." Tibetans are totally unfamiliar with this title; they usually call their leader "Gyalwa Rinpoche" (Victorious One), "Kyabngon Rinpoche" (Precious Protector), or the "Wish Fulfilling Gem" who never dies but "goes to heavenly fields for the benefit of other living creatures." While Sonam Gyatso was the first to be known as the Dalai Lama he is officially considered the third incarnation, with the title of first Dalai Lama going posthumously to Gedun Truppa and of second to Gedun Gyatso.

The fourth Dalai Lama, Yonten Gyatso (1589–1617), best symbolizes the relationship between the Mongols and the Tibetans. A Mongol, from the family of Altan Khan, the fourth Dalai Lama was educated and brought up in Mongolia. His selection assured the Gelugpa sect of continuing Mongol patronage and inaugurated a four-century monopoly of power in Tibet.

To this point in Tibetan history, the Dalai Lama was the undisputed leader of only one and not the most powerful sect, the Gelugpas. He held no temporal power. However, his close alliance with the Mongol military gave him the best opportunity to win that power. But first the ideological foundations of a theocracy had to be laid. The Dalai Lama was portrayed as an individual who had broken the cycle of birth-rebirth and could aspire to ultimate peace in *nirvana.* But his selflessness motivated him to submit himself, voluntarily, to the dubious pleasures of earthly life in order to help others achieve their ultimate goal. It is his selflessness and the belief that he is the direct incarnation of the patron deity, Chenrezig, that make him so holy to the faithful. This devotion did not, however, become widespread, nor did it become a political force, until the fifth Dalai Lama was at the height of his power.[24]

The Rule of the Dalai Lamas

The fifth Dalai Lama, Ngwang Lozang Gyatso (1617–1682), came to power at a time of ongoing warfare and intra-Buddhist rivalry. In 1618 the Karmapa sect from Tsang attacked Lhasa and left the hill around the Drepung Monastery "littered with the bodies of slaughtered monks."[25] For the next two decades the Karmapa were to reign supreme, even forcing many Gelugpa monasteries to convert.

When the Dalai Lama gained his majority, he called upon the leader of the Koshot Mongols, Gushri Khan (1584–1656), to aid his fellow Gelugpa adherents win power in Tibet by destroying their rivals. Gushri arrived in Lhasa in 1638 and finally subdued Tsang in 1641–1642, turning that province over to the Dalai Lama to rule. The relationship forged so many years earlier had now come to fruition—the Mongol leader placing a Dalai Lama in a position of total religious dominance over all Tibetan sects and temporal dominance over an area that stretched from Tachienlu in the east to Ladakh in the west.

Gushri took the title of "Religious King of Tibet" (*Po Gyalpo*), and reserved all military power for himself. Since Gushri was not overly fond of Tibet he did not live there; consequently his power to influence temporal affairs waned, although the position of *Po Gyalpo* survived until 1717. The fifth Dalai Lama was the first notable of his line; and to this day he is known fondly to all Tibetans as "The Great Fifth." He began the construction of the Potala, the great winter palace of the Dalai Lamas, in 1645. He preached religious tolerance toward other sects despite his early efforts to force others to convert to the Gelugpa sect. He is also especially remembered for having begun the line of Panchen Lamas ("Great Scholar"). The first so named was Lozang Chosgyan, a teacher to both the fourth and fifth Dalai Lamas.

Among his other attributes, the fifth Dalai Lama was politically astute. In 1642, two years before the Manchus were to come to power in China, the Dalai Lama sent a mission to Mukden (the Manchu headquarters, now Shenyang) to establish friendly relations with the leaders of this rising power.[26] When the Manchus came to power in 1644, one of their first actions was to invite the Dalai Lama to visit. In 1646, and again in 1647, the Dalai Lama sent missions to the Imperial Throne but did not undertake the trip himself until 1652. Tibetan accounts claim that Emperor Shun Zhi (Shun-chih) came out of Beijing expressly to meet the Dalai Lama; if true, this extraordinary act would have conferred on the Tibetans a degree of equality with the Han Chinese. Chinese accounts relate that the emperor was out hunting when he met the Dalai Lama's party coincidentally. Both accounts agree that the Dalai Lama was exempt from the traditional *kowtow* symbolizing total subservience; he was, however, required to kneel before the emperor.

This was the beginning of a long period of ambiguity in Tibet's status vis-à-vis China. It is unclear just how Tibetans of that day saw the relationship, although Beijing's position is quite clear. To Beijing, Tibet was an important part of its greater empire. Buddhism was fostered in the hope that its nonviolent culture would act as a force of moderation on the militant Tibetan and Mongolian cultures, thereby making rule somewhat easier for Beijing. Moreover, Beijing understood that friendly ties with the Gelugpa leadership in Tibet would also act to mollify the Mongols.

When the Dalai Lama died, the regent kept the news secret for over a decade, employing a monk look-alike for public occasions. History relates that the double so disliked his role that the regent was compelled to bribe and beat him.[27] So obsessed was the regent that no one find out about his ruse that he used to roam Lhasa's streets at night, disguised as a commoner, making sure that there were no rumors that the Dalai Lama had died. He was forced to confide in the state oracle, seeking aid in his search for the sixth incarnation. But the regent was so mistrustful, even of the oracle, that he visited the oracle's mother in disguise; and when the old woman related the sad news of the Dalai Lama's death to him in confidence, he had the mother and son killed.[28] Meanwhile, he managed to get the Potala (winter palace) completed and fought a war with Ladakh in 1683, setting a boundary that—for all intents and purposes—remains in effect to this day.

The regent continued to rule Tibet as the absolute dictator until the recognition and enthronement of the sixth Dalai Lama in 1697. Of all the Dalai Lamas, the sixth was surely the most unusual. Tsangyang Gyatso (1683–1707) has come to be known among Tibetans as the "Merry One," and not without just cause, for he devoted himself more to debauchery than to religious pursuits. By 1702 he had renounced his vows, retained some modicum of temporal power, and spent his time in hedonistic pursuits. He is fondly remembered for his poetry, which constitutes almost the entire nonreligious literature of Tibet (excepting oral folk tales).[29] Not surprisingly, the Dalai Lama's behavior created difficulties within and without Tibet. The regent, Samye Gyatso, was so disturbed by events that he had the Dalai Lama's closest confidant killed in the belief that the monk was acting as the liaison in the Dalai Lama's amorous affairs. The angry Dalai Lama forced the regent's resignation in 1703.

In 1706, in response to an invitation from Beijing, the sixth Dalai Lama set out from Lhasa under escort of Mongol troops. He died en route, just south of Kokonor. While most historians say that his death occurred under "mysterious circumstances," both Chinese and Tibetan sources attribute the death to illness.[30]

Back in Lhasa, early in 1707, the Khoshot Mongol leader, Lajang Khan, who had decided to intervene in Tibetan affairs, announced the discovery of the "real" sixth Dalai Lama—a young monk named Ngawang Yeshe Gyatso (1686–1725), rumored to be Lajang's natural son. The emperor in Beijing thought this turn of events rather peculiar and dispatched an envoy to investigate. He Shu (Ho-shu) thus became the first Han magistrate to be sent to Lhasa, and the event is chronicled in Chinese history as one that "marks the beginning of the setting up in Tibet of an office to manage (Tibetan) affairs."[31] He Shu stayed in Lhasa from 1709 to 1711, conferring the emperor's seal of approval on Lajang's Dalai Lama in 1710 and bestowing upon Lajang the title, "Religious and Devoted Khan."

Almost all historians record that the people of Tibet did not accept Lajang's lama and that in spite of the sixth Dalai Lama's improper behavior, he had been more acceptable to the populace because he had been chosen in the proper fashion.

It was also about this time that rumors began to spread about a boy born in Kham in 1708 who, it was said, showed all the necessary signs proving him to be the incarnation of the sixth Dalai Lama. Lajang immediately dispatched two investigative teams—both of which returned, claiming lack of substantiating evidence. Even the Panchen Lama wrote to the emperor in 1712, disavowing the boy. The matter was not resolved, however, because the state oracle claimed to have had a vision that the boy was indeed the incarnation and the Dzungar Mongols saw in the controversy an opportunity to challenge Lajang's power. Fearing for the boy's life, his father spirited him away to the Kumbum Monastery, in 1715, where he could live under the protection of the Mongols who recognized him as their spiritual leader and where the politically astute father could be afforded the opportunity for further lobbying for political and military support.

In 1714 the abbots of the three big monasteries appealed to the Dzungars to overthrow Lajang and bring the alleged seventh Dalai Lama to Lhasa with them; the Dzungars agreed and a clever plan was devised. In November 1717 the Dzungars attacked Lhasa and gained an easy victory, thanks to help from the monks inside the city who opened gates and dropped ladders over the walls. Lajang was soon killed in hand-to-hand combat.

The Dzungar welcome into Lhasa quickly turned sour, as the Mongols and their monk allies quickly turned from liberators to conquerors. Lhasa was pillaged, and the Tibetan monks distinguished themselves as the "most greedy and cruel robbers."[32] Monasteries and homes were looted and people flogged until they revealed the whereabouts of their hidden wealth. The Lajang lama was deposed and sent into exile while the Panchen Lama, who had been in Lhasa supporting Lajang, hurriedly left for Tashilhunpo (his monastery near Shigatse) to disassociate himself from the activities in the capital.

Tibet as Part of China

These events proved to be not exclusively a Mongolian-Tibetan fracas, for just prior to his death Lajang had sent an urgent appeal for aid to the emperor in Beijing. The letter arrived in March 1718, three months after Lajang was killed. The emperor, unaware of recent events, dispatched an army that was only to find itself halted en route upon learning of Lajang's defeat. In Lhasa, a civil war of sorts broke out; the Manchu leaders, seeing an opportunity to end Dzungar power with a decisive victory, ordered the army to continue on its way through Sichuan. At the same time, they ordered another army that had been victorious over the Mongols at Kumbum to proceed toward Lhasa. The first arrived in September 1720 and the second a month later. Without local support the Dzungars were easily overcome.

Arriving with the child Dalai Lama, whom they had picked up at Kumbum, and, according to a Christian missionary who witnessed it, treating the local populace "with great moderation,"[33] the Chinese armies were welcomed in Tibet. They immediately went about setting up a military government under General Yenshin (Yen-shin) and consolidated their power to the point where, in the words of the missionary quoted above, they "had absolute dominion over Tibet." The Chinese restored order; arrested Dzungar collaborators; pulled down the walls around Lhasa; incorporated Kham into Sichuan, making the new frontier the Yangzi River; and stationed a 3,000-man (Han, Mongol, and Manchu) garrison in the Tibetan capital.[34]

The boy from Kham became the seventh Dalai Lama, Kelzang Gyatso (1708–1758), and was officially enthroned in 1720. But, although properly ensconced in the Potala, he remained without temporal power. Beijing now instituted certain administrative changes. The office of the regent (*desai*)—formerly a co-ruler with the Dalai Lama—was abolished and, from that point on, the office of regent referred to a monk who ruled in the Dalai Lama's name, particularly during the latter's minority. Equally important, a Ministerial Council was established with four members to act as a Cabinet.

The division of power inevitably led once again to internecine conflicts which, in 1728, led in turn to the summoning of a Chinese army to restore peace.

The Dalai Lama and his father were exiled to Kham for seven years. Out of this conflict, a junior government minister, Polhanas, came to absolute power in close alliance with the imperial government of China, and Tibet went on to enjoy a relatively long period (nineteen years) of peace. The Manchus established a permanent presence in Lhasa through an official known as the "amban." The office of amban was to last, uninterrupted, until 1911; at times two ambans served simultaneously.[35] Moreover, a garrison was assigned to Lhasa, numbering two thousand. This Beijing-Lhasa relationship was to continue for almost two centuries.

Within a few years, Polhanas had so succeeded in pacifying the Tibetans that in 1733 he was able to persuade the emperor to reduce the Lhasa garrison to a mere five hundred, and a few years later to one hundred. In its stead, Polhanas created Tibet's first standing army: well-fed, well-equipped, disciplined, and well-treated. In 1735 the Dalai Lama was permitted to return to the capital after having been sent into exile in Kham in 1728 for his part in the political intrigues of that period.

The closing years of Polhanas' rule were marked by growing unrest among the nobility, particularly in the centuries-old rivalry between the noble elites of U and those of Tsang. Moreover, the clergy began to assert itself, demonstrating a growing overt resentment to the few resident Christian missionaries in Lhasa (their movements were restricted) and to the handful of converts, who were subject to arrest and flogging. The dissension came into the open after the death of Polhanas in 1747; this was not surprising since the ability to maintain peace in

Tibet depended largely on Polhanas' strong personality and close alliance with the Chinese emperor.

In 1750 Polhanas' second son began to communicate with the Dzungar Mongols and secretly prepare a coup d'etat against Polhanas' successors. The two ambans resident in Lhasa somehow discovered the plan and found themselves faced with a serious dilemma: how to prevent the coup without a garrison at their command. They lured Polhanas' son into their residence and killed him along with his servants. In retaliation a mob attacked and killed the two ambans.

In the ensuing riots the Dalai Lama opened the Potala to all the Han and Manchu residents of Lhasa, while at the same time writing to the emperor for aid against the dissidents. The emperor responded; and an army of five thousand marched into Lhasa, easily rounding up the ringleaders who offered no resistance.

As a reward for his support, the Dalai Lama, for the very first time, was given extensive temporal power. Not since the tenure of the fifth Dalai Lama, a century earlier, had the office wielded such widespread power. Restrictions were put on the lay nobility—they could not hire their own staff and could hold meetings only in designated locations. A concerted effort was made to end the constant internecine struggles that had been so characteristic of the history of the Tibetan upper classes.

During the reign of the eighth Dalai Lama, Jampal Gyatso (1758–1804), external affairs played the most important role—particularly in the form of warfare. This time, however, the wars were not with the Mongols to the north, but rather with the Gurkhas and the British to the south—peoples with whom there had been almost no previous contact.

In 1769 the Hindu tribe of Gurkhas conquered Nepal and looked northward, tempted by the vast monastic wealth. Finding encouragement for invasion from the anti-Gelugpa forces, the Gurkhas first ventured into Tibet in 1788. At this time they were persuaded to return south by the Tibetan authorities, who promised to pay tribute in exchange for their retreat. When the payments stopped after the first installment, the Gurkhas attacked again in 1791 and marched as far north as Shigatse, where they looted the Tashilhunpo Monastery.

The Chinese emperor once again came to the Tibetans' aid—this time dispatching an army of 10,000 to 15,000 men (accounts differ) which not only succeeded in pushing the Gurkhas south of the border but also managed to fight its way to within about twenty miles of Kathmandu itself. The Gurkhas surrendered and promised to pay tribute to the Chinese emperor every five years in return for the withdrawal of Chinese forces.[36]

To tighten its control over Tibet, China greatly strengthened the power of the amban; they were now considered on a par with the Dalai and Panchen Lamas, in absolute charge of financial, diplomatic, and trade matters. Most significantly, the two lamas were now prevented from directly memorializing the throne in Beijing—all correspondence had to go through the amban, precluding any possibility of criticism or complaint about Chinese officials. Reforms were also introduced, particularly reform of the *ulag* system (corvée labor)—an almost constant preoccupation of Chinese officials. The officials handed out grain and money to the poor and brought some experts in to build Tibet's first mint.

The most controversial reform was introduced in 1793, when the Chinese imperial authorities presented Tibetan officials with a golden urn. This urn was to be used in the selection of a Dalai Lama whenever a dispute arose; it therefore had direct bearing on Tibetan autonomy from China. In disputed cases, the selection was to be done by the amban after the names of the candidates had been placed in the urn. There is general agreement that the ninth, thirteenth, and fourteenth Dalai Lamas were *not* chosen by this method but rather selected by the appropriate Tibetan ecclesiastical officials with the selection being approved after the fact by the emperor. In such cases the emperor would also issue an order waiving the use of the urn. There is also general agreement that the tenth, eleventh and twelfth Dalai Lamas were chosen by the lottery method.[37]

The ninth through the twelfth Dalai Lamas (1805–1875) lived very short lives and died, as historians are fond of saying, "under mysterious circumstances." This period also marked a time when

> the country withdrew into ever-deeper isolation and fossilized under the leadership of the rigid monastic hierarchy: this was now subject to foreign [sic] supervision, but at the same time jealously guarded ancient tradition and was reluctant to admit change of any sort.[38]

Today, Tibet's past isolation in those years is viewed—in retrospect—as having been detrimental; at the time, however, it benefited both Beijing and Lhasa. It was beneficial to Beijing in its efforts to prevent invasion and imperialist encroachment, thereby avoiding the major expense of sending another army that great distance; it was equally beneficial to the clerical figures in Tibet—the Dalai Lamas and the regents, included—who viewed the exclusion of opposing and conflicting ideas as a safeguard in maintaining their traditions and their monopoly of power over the Tibetan people.[39]

3

Early Foreign Contacts

The Earliest Contacts

Tibetans' first contacts with those beyond their neighboring areas were with Christian missionaries. These contacts had no long-term significance because they were brief and the missionaries left few converts. The contact that was to have the most significance began in the eighteenth century and was with the mighty British empire.

The first meeting, in 1772, resulted from an attack by the Bhutanese on neighboring Cooch Behar. Since the British felt the attacked territory to be under their rule, Warren Hastings (Governor-General of Bengal) responded by engaging his army against the Bhutanese. Just before war could break out, the Panchen Lama intervened, offering to mediate the dispute.[1] The offer was gladly accepted and a pact was signed in April 1774.

The British were attempting, unsuccessfully, to open the China coast for trade through Guangzhou (Canton). Hastings saw this alliance with the Panchen Lama as a way to help British trade interests by influencing the clerical leader to sponsor trade through Tibet to China. Hastings therefore dispatched George Bogle and Dr. Alexander Hamilton to Shigatse in 1774–75 for the purpose of establishing a more cordial relationship with the Panchen Lama.[2] But it was to no avail. Bogle reported that the representatives of the regent in Lhasa had told him that "[the regent] and all the country were subject to the emperor of China."[3] The emperor was unwilling to permit trade; all contacts had to be through Beijing.

Hastings, however, was not to be put off so lightly; and even after the death of the Panchen Lama in 1780 and Bogle's death the year after, he continued his pursuit. In 1783 he commissioned Captain Samuel Turner and a Thomas

48

Saunders to visit the newly-found child incarnation in Shigatse.[4] But Turner suffered the same fate as Bogle and reported,

> the influence of the Chinese officials overawes the Tibetans in all their proceedings, and produces a timidity and a caution in their conduct more suited to the character of subjects than allies.[5]

Meanwhile, the Chinese Empire had begun its final decline. The last strong emperor, Qian Long (Ch'ien-lung), died in 1799. In Tibet the last strong amban, Kui Huan (K'uei-huan), left in 1793; his successors proved to be weak and corrupt—one was noted for accepting a bribe of ten thousand taels of gold in exchange for an appointment to the *Kashag* (the Tibetan cabinet).

The nineteenth century saw two invasions of Tibet: one from Kashmir and another from Nepal. The first occurred in 1841–42, when an army from Kashmir led by General Zorawar Singh made an unsuccessful sweep into western Tibet to expand his control of trade in that area. This was the first major invasion that the Tibetans were able to turn back without substantial aid from their Chinese patrons. The Dogra invasion coincided with the first Anglo-Chinese War of 1842 (the so-called Opium War), which put an enormous strain on Chinese military forces, making the deployment of Chinese troops to western Tibet impossible.[6]

In 1856 the Gurkhas swept north again from Nepal on the pretext of trade violations; but, by then, China was being ravaged by civil war and weakened by the European imperialist powers. Tibet, unable to defend itself against a superior force and unable to rely on its patron, was forced to sign a humiliating treaty that relegated some minor border regions to Tibet—but only in exchange for a promise of tribute to Nepal and extraterritoriality (recognition that foreign nationals living in China are subject only to the laws of their own country) for all Nepalese.

Western expansion reached its zenith in the nineteenth century in an era of exploration and conquest. The failure of the Bogle and Turner missions did not deter the persistent British in their quest for greater glory and empire. A few short years after Turner's return, the British attempted another mission to Tibet—this time to the west. The leader, Lt. Col. Charles Cathcart, died en route in 1787 and the mission was aborted. In 1811 they tried again. This time Thomas Manning managed to reach Lhasa, disguised as a Chinese gentleman, and is even reported to have obtained an audience with the infant Dalai Lama. In the following year a William Moorecroft led yet another expedition, which was also abandoned en route. In the 1840s Britain's first ambassador to China, Sir John Davies, made several unsuccessful efforts to secure Beijing's permission for expeditions to Tibet.[7] Others, like the Marquis of Dalhousie, devised their own harebrained schemes, such as blasting roads into Tibet.[8]

In spite of, or perhaps because of, repeated failures to open any communication link with Lhasa, the British trained one hundred thirty Indians for the Survey of India (a government agency). They traveled through Tibet disguised as monks, traders, and pilgrims. Their real mission was to conduct geographical surveys by measuring distances with their rosary beads, hiding surveying instruments in their prayer wheels. Those Tibetans who were found to have aided the Indians were severely punished; a high incarnated lama was even beaten to death.[9]

British colonial officials were not the only ones to find Tibet intriguing. From the 1850s to the 1910s the Russians sent such distinguished explorers as Prejhevalski, Roborovski, Koslov, and Orucheff to search out the mysteries of Tibet. The Englishmen Brower and Welby explored western Tibet from Ladakh. The Swede Sven Hedin made eight trips through northern Tibet in the early 1900s, only to be denied his lifelong dream of setting eyes on the Potala. Sir Aurel Stein roamed Central Asia. The Frenchmen Dutreuil, de Rhins and Fernand Grenard traveled eastern Tibet; the American scholar/diplomat William W. Rockhill traveled the periphery of Tibet extensively—as did countless Christian missionaries.[10]

Tibet as a Pawn

There is no doubt that many of the explorers who risked their lives for an opportunity to glance upon the Potala did so in the interests of science and adventure; others, however, were to pose a threat to Tibet's isolation, for their missions were of a political nature. Tibet, at the end of the nineteenth and beginning of the twentieth century, found itself at the junction of the world's three great empires: the British, the Russian, and the Chinese—each of which either considered, or desired, Tibet to be in its exclusive "sphere of influence."

The British Empire was at its pinnacle, with colonies stretched across the globe and nowhere more solidly entrenched than in the lands south of the Himalayan range. Imperial Russia, on the other hand, was a relative newcomer to the play for Asia, making up for lost time by advancing rapidly east toward the Pacific and south toward the frontiers of the British empire. Conversely, the Manchu empire was in its declining years. Corruption, social decay and external pressures had led to internal strife and chaos that were to bring about the final collapse of the once-unrivaled Dragon Throne.

Before the 1890s, Tibet was the exclusive preserve of China. But from 1895 to 1911, Tibet was to become a pawn in the struggle for world domination between London and St. Petersburg. The Anglo-Russian rivalry that was to propel Tibet out of its isolation began in earnest in the 1840s, at a time when Britain was the undisputed European power in Asia.

At the same time as Britain was forcibly wringing concessions out of China along its east coast, it was also nibbling away at China's tributaries in the southwest. In 1815–16 Nepal was defeated and made into an informal British protectorate, along with the adjacent northwest Indian hill states; Darjeeling was annexed in 1835; Kashmir and Ladakh in 1846; Sikkim was made a protectorate in 1861; Bhutan a protectorate in 1865; and Assam annexed in 1886.

For its part, Russia set the limits of its eastern expansion when it sold the Alaska territory to the United States (1867) in order to prevent British influence there and turned its attention toward Mongolia and Central Asia. Russo-Tibetan relations can be traced back three hundred years, but were almost exclusively religious as they were carried on between Lhasa and Russian Buddhists (Torgut Kalmuks and Buriat Mongols). Russia's "forward policy" was now designed to check British gains for the "aggrandizement of Russia." A Russian general summed it up best when he noted that "the stronger Russia is in Central Asia, the weaker England is in India and the more conciliatory she will be in Europe."

One of Britain's aims at this time was the opening of three trade routes to China: Burma-Yunnan, Kashmir-Chinese Turkestan (present-day Xinjiang [Sinkiang]), and India-Tibet-Sichuan. While exploring the first of these routes, a British official was killed. The incident was used by London to force China to sign the Chefoo Convention of 1876. One of the many terms of this pact allowed the British to mount an expedition into Tibet. In 1885 the Macaulay Mission was organized for just that purpose. The Tibetans, however, were uncooperative and prevented the members of the mission from completing their journey. The Tibetans were resentful that they had been excluded from the negotiations leading to the Anglo-Chinese agreement and were already highly suspicious of the British following the clandestine activities of the Survey of India. The following year the British agreed to forget the mission if China would acquiesce to the British annexation of northern Burma. China had little leverage in these further talks for it had just been defeated in yet another war, this time by the French.

China had not informed Tibet of the 1876 pact or of the agreement to abandon the Macaulay Mission. The Tibetans therefore took the British disbanding of the mission as a sign of weakness. Several years later, in 1887, the Tibetans decided to set up a checkpost at a settlement called Lingtu, eighteen miles south of their frontier with Sikkim. This challenge to the British led to border skirmishes and ended in an attack by two thousand British troops. The subsequent British victory led to two more treaties (the Calcutta Convention of 1890 and the Anglo-Chinese Agreement of 1893) that compelled China to recognize British rights in Sikkim, demarcate the border, allow the British to open a market in Yadong (Yatung), southern Tibet, and extend extraterritoriality to the British in Tibet, while denying the same right to Tibetan traders in Sikkim.[11]

In 1893 the first Dalai Lama in over a hundred years reached his majority and took power. When this Dalai Lama, the thirteenth, had been found, Lhasa informed Beijing of the discovery and the Emperor Guang Xu (Kuang-hsü) responded by officially naming the boy the Dalai Lama and giving the authorities in Lhasa permission to enthrone him in July 1879. This procedure was clearly ceremonial—yet significant in its affirmation of a close relationship between the two governments.

When the Dalai Lama finally reached adulthood, he quickly consolidated his power by replacing officials who aspired to be his rivals. According to his official biography, when the Dalai Lama took over from the regent in 1895 a plot was hatched against him, only to be discovered by the Dalai Lama himself through a dream. The plotters were said to have included the nephew of the former regent and the amban.[12]

Curzon and the British Invasion

The complete cast in this unfolding drama was finally in place when George Nathaniel Curzon was named Viceroy and Governor-General of India in the autumn of 1898. The stage was set for Tibet to find itself at the center of the "Great Game"—if only briefly. In 1899, at the start of Curzon's administration, Tibet was almost invisible to British foreign policy planners. But Russophobia was to be the catalyst for change. This would not be a first, for two earlier British wars with Afghanistan—in 1841 and 1880—had been caused by worries about Russian aggression.

The leading actor in this play was to be Curzon, the architect of British policy toward Tibet from 1899 to 1905. Young, brilliant, aristocratic, self-confident, and arch-imperialist, Curzon had been arguing for an anti-Russian policy in Asia since the early 1880s. The essence of his thinking can be summed up in two quotes:

> Chinese suzerainty over Tibet is a fiction, a political affectation.[13]

> If we do nothing in Tibet we shall have Russia trying to establish a protectorate in less than ten years. This might not constitute a military danger, at any rate for some time, but would be a political danger. The effect on Nepal, Sikkim and Bhutan would constitute a positive danger.... We can ... stop a Russian protectorate over Tibet, by being in advance ourselves.[14]

These two concepts were at the core of British policy in the Himalayan region. Curzon was right about China's growing inability to control the actions of Tibetan officials, particularly after the consolidation of power by the thirteenth Dalai Lama; and if China no longer controlled Tibet, there should be a struggle to establish who would fill the political vacuum, for Curzon did not believe that Tibet could exist as an independent entity. Curzon also correctly diagnosed Russia's inability to pose a military threat to India. The terrain of the Himalayas and the necessarily long supply lines made invasion unlikely. But the Indian viceroy was concerned that Russian influence might endanger British power, prestige, and interests. With China impotent and Russia solely a political threat, Curzon decided that he could achieve his aim of British dominance in Tibet by placing a permanent British official and garrison in Lhasa to protect London/Calcutta interests.

While worries about Russia and a British desire for further imperial glory were the major motivating forces behind Curzon's actions, it would be wrong to ignore the economic aspect. There were many who saw Tibet as an important market for the fledgling Indian tea industry. There is even some confirmation that the Chinese perceived an economic threat, for in the early years of the twentieth century the Manchu official, Zhao Erfeng (Chao Erh-feng), ordered a prohibition against growing tea in Tibet and a tightening up of border control to prevent the British from getting a foothold in the market.[15]

Curzon sent London a lengthy dispatch on 3 January 1903 outlining his concerns and proposing a tripartite (Britain-Tibet-China) conference in Lhasa for the spring of that year. He further proposed that at the end of the talks, the British delegation should leave behind a resident with a guard large enough "to overawe opposition." What followed was an intense struggle between the Balfour government and Curzon. London tried to keep the Tibetan matter in perspective, ever concerned about possible Russian retaliation in the event of any drastic British action. Preferring not to send a mission to Tibet, the home government suggested engineering a Nepalese incursion into Tibet. This would force Tibet to come to terms and resolve some of the border questions without the involvement of British soldiers or money. Curzon refused and the British government finally authorized a very limited delegation to Tibet, with permission to negotiate solely on "trade relations, the frontier, and grazing rights."

Neither China nor Tibet agreed to a meeting at first; but later, under pressure from Curzon, they accepted the idea—on the condition that it take place at Yadong, where according to the terms of the 1893 Anglo-Chinese Agreement the British had the right to open a trade market. The vehement opposition of both the Chinese and Tibetans to holding talks was futile because of the superior strength of the British forces. The only substantial opposition to Curzon's grandiose plans was in London—far enough away to be open to manipulation by an intelligent and determined man.

Curzon had some justification for fearing Russian influence in Tibet. Lhasan officials felt closer to St. Petersburg than to Calcutta. An example of the Dalai Lama's attitude toward Britain is expressed in a letter he wrote to a friend, the Maharaja of Sikkim, in 1900.

> Why do the British insist on establishing trade marts? Their goods are coming in from India right up to Lhasa. Whether they have their marts or not, their things come in all the same. The British, under the guise of establishing communications, are merely trying to over-reach us. They are well practiced in all these political wiles.[16]

This suspicion of British intentions was further heightened by stories of alleged atrocities committed by Christian missionaries emanating from the Tibetan borderlands and India.

Curzon knew of the long-standing friendly relations between Lhasa and St.

Petersburg and events in the early part of this century appeared to fulfill his most dire prophecies. By 1900 Russia had annexed all of Central Asia north of Persia (present-day Iran) and Afghanistan, while building a railway as far south as Tashkent and, by 1901, as far east as Vladivostok. There were rumors that Tibet would rely on Russian assistance if the British opened a trade mart at Yadong and also that the Russian war minister planned "to seize Manchuria and proceed toward the annexation of Korea; he also [so the rumor went] plan[ned] to take Tibet under his rule.' [17]

But Whitehall demanded more concrete proof of Russia's aggressive intentions before it acted. This was to be supplied by a rather enigmatic Buriat Mongol monk named Agvan Dorjieff. He first arrived in Lhasa around 1880, when he joined the prestigious Drepung Monastery and proved to be an exceptional student. His brilliance was reported to the Dalai Lama who appointed him as a royal adviser; it was not long before he became the cleric's most trusted confidant. Stories were prevalent at the time that he was a trained member of the Russian intelligence. Dorjieff made his first trip to St. Petersburg in 1898 (to be followed by at least two more before 1901) ostensibly to raise money for his monastic college. (This was a common practice, as Buriat Mongols had been crossing Central Asia unhindered for centuries.)

Curzon discovered that while he could not even get a written dialogue going with Lhasa, Lhasa had been in communication with St. Petersburg (through Dorjieff). Dorjieff had twice passed through India without Curzon's knowledge. While in Russia the Tibetan missions were being personally entertained by the Tsar and Tsarina. Perhaps most humiliating to Curzon, this information was all gleaned through the Russian press and not his own intelligence channels. Curzon was understandably furious. One rumor that caused great consternation in London was about an alleged secret Sino-Russian Treaty of 1902. The treaty was supposed to provide for the assurance of Chinese territorial integrity in exchange for Russian freedom of action in Tibet, Mongolia, and Xinjiang. Although both Russia and China vehemently denied the existence of any such treaty, Britain was never fully convinced. The British government viewed the treaty as potentially a greater threat than Dorjieff's escapades. In London's view, if it truly existed, it had to be diplomatically countered and protested. Curzon's comments on the treaty were in keeping with his long-standing suspicions and were to foreshadow future events.

> I am myself a firm believer in the existence of a secret understanding, if not a secret treaty, between Russia and China about Tibet: and as I have before said, I regard it as a duty to frustrate this little game while there is still time.[18]

While Russia did have interests in Tibet, it is unlikely that it was willing to exert much effort to pursue them; Tibet was simply not important enough. Russia was probably stirring up trouble in Tibet to anger Britain and distract it with worries about its Himalayan frontiers, hoping it would neglect other more strategic areas. Whether any of the described events actually had ominous meaning for Britain or not, Curzon became convinced that he *had* to act.[19]

British Invasion

The British mission to Khama Dzong—led by Colonel Francis Younghusband—was officially called the Tibet Frontier Commission. Although the Chinese and Tibetan delegations urged them not to cross the frontier, the British mission persisted and reached its destination—Khama Dzong (Khamba Fort)—on 7 July 1903. They settled in there to wait for high-level Tibetan plenipotentiaries and the amban. The Tibetan/Chinese position remained constant throughout this ordeal: there could be no negotiations while British troops occupied Tibetan/Chinese territory illegally. Younghusband could do nothing but wait for further instructions. While he waited, the Tibetans sent three lamas to pitch a tent opposite the colonel's, and they proceeded to spend an entire week cursing the invaders in an apparent attempt to exorcise them.[20]

Unilaterally calling a tripartite conference, invading a sovereign nation without prior provocation, and then having no one to confer with put London in a very embarrassing position. The British were being snubbed; but retreat would amount to an admission that they were in error—a fate the British empire felt it could not endure. To add to the problems, winter was setting in and no one was sure whether or not the mission could survive camping in Tibet through its harshest season.

The London-Calcutta disagreement now began to heat up. Curzon was not above deception. His desperate desire to force London to invade Lhasa was such that he claimed as verifiable rumors that two Sikkimese had been caught spying for the British in Shigatse, then tortured and killed. Curzon demanded permission to retaliate. (In fact the two Sikkimese in question were subsequently released from prison in good condition.) London had partially given in to Curzon on 10 October when the Balfour cabinet authorized the occupation of the Chumbi Valley and the advance of the expeditionary forces as far as Gyantse if negotiations were unfruitful. Before these new orders could be implemented, a new man took over at the India office. St. John Brodrick immediately asked for a complete reappraisal of the plans. He approved them on 16 November but only on the condition that they were "for the sole purpose of obtaining satisfaction, and as soon as reparation is obtained, a withdrawal should be effected."[21]

In spite of the new concessions, London retained deep reservations about the mission—reflected in the vague wording of Brodrick's instructions. On the day the orders were cabled to India, the British Foreign Office assured the Russians that the mission was sent simply to settle mutual problems and that London had no intention of annexing any Tibetan territory. British officials felt they needed a symbol to demonstrate to the Russians that Britain had interests in Tibet; but they did not want that symbol to alarm Russia into any retaliatory action. It was felt that the ideal solution would be to establish a trade mart deep in Tibet; Gyantse seemed perfect.

Curzon and Younghusband were so anxious to act that the plans called for marching in December rather than waiting for the spring. The total force now consisted of 1,150 soldiers, 10,000 unskilled laborers, and thousands of pack animals. One account asserts that the expedition required 18,182 kg. (40,000 lb.) of supplies and ammunition *each day*.[22] London insisted on the fiction that this was purely a commercial mission, accompanied by a military escort. Younghusband was officially merely the head of a political commission that consisted of a few civilians and a handful of "off-duty" soldiers for protection. The remaining troops assembled under the rubric of the "Tibet Military Escort" and were led by Col. J.R.L. MacDonald. London did not publicly acknowledge the extra hands attached to the expedition such as surveyors, geologists, botanists, insect collectors, and "a committee too of licensed curio hunters, who collected curios with much enterprise and scientific precision for the British Museum."[23]

The force assembled and then spent three winter months regrouping and preparing for the march to Gyantse. In London the waiting time was marked by a growing discomfort over the whole affair; but, just as opinion seemed to be turning against the mission, a quirk of fate was to save it. In the spring the Tibetan army mounted a series of attacks that were met with British counterattacks. In spite of the fact that there were few British casualties, Brodrick authorized the issuing of an ultimatum to Lhasa and Beijing, threatening that the expeditionary force would be compelled to drive through to Lhasa unless negotiations were held within a month.

The Chinese and Tibetans remained adamant. They repeated their willingness to negotiate as soon as the last British soldier had retreated across the frontier back to India. It was an impasse. The British expeditionary force continued to fight battles as it moved north, finally reaching the outskirts of Lhasa on 2 August 1904.

The situation now proved to be far more complex than Younghusband could ever have imagined. The Dalai Lama had fled the Tibetan capital; or, as the imperious Younghusband saw it, "was ungracious enough to depart when I went to Lhasa."[24] Without a military force, the amban was powerless. A rift had developed between MacDonald, who wanted to return immediately, and Younghusband, who felt they had overcome too many obstacles and suffered too many hardships to leave without getting what they had come for. The predicament was best summed up by British Prime Minister Arthur Balfour when he observed

> the troops ought to return for climatic reasons in a few weeks. The Dalai Lama has fled . . . yet we cannot retire without striking some blow at [the] enemy. . . .

If the lama refuses to even consider our very reasonable and moderate offers, we have no choice but to turn the expedition from a peaceful into a punitive one; and . . . to destroy such buildings as walls and the gates of the city and to carry [off] some of the leading citizens as hostages.[25]

Since Younghusband found the option of returning to India empty-handed untenable, he proceeded to draft a treaty unilaterally, and have it signed in the Potala by the regent, Ganden Tri Rinpoche, and any other Tibetan officials he could gather together as an ad hoc government. The Kashag ministers whom Younghusband dealt with had apparently, unknown to him, just been appointed to their posts. The regular ministers had been imprisoned for suspected pro-British leanings and it was feared they would be too accommodating to Younghusband. (Most were not reinstated until 1907.) That done, the British expeditionary force left Lhasa on 23 September 1904.

Younghusband found no traces of Russian aid, assistance or arms, thereby negating the major justification for the invasion. He was forced to create his own Tibetan "government" in order that some other party be available to sign the treaty he had written. The amban refused to sign, compounding the illegality of it all. As one critic of the period wrote,

the worthless signatures and seals were all duly attached to the "convention" in imposing array, but they have no more binding effect than if the Archbishop of Canterbury and the Chairman of the London County Council were to sign a new treaty with France.[26]

The treaty provided for trade marts in Yadong, Gyantse, and Gartok; required an exorbitant indemnity from Tibet; stipulated that Tibet recognize the Sikkim/Tibet border; and established restrictions on Tibet's ability to negotiate with any "Foreign Powers." In a separate article, it was further agreed that the Gyantse Trade Agent could travel to Lhasa from time to time.

For all intents and purposes the treaty made Tibet a protectorate of the British empire and Younghusband had obviously exceeded his mandate. The Acting Viceroy, Lord Ampthill, tried to undo some of the damage by issuing orders on 11 November that canceled the separate article, cut the indemnity by two-thirds, to be paid in three installments, and promised that the occupation of the Chumbi Valley would end in three years, providing all the other provisions of the pact were met.

Britain's differences with Russia and the Dalai Lama were to pale in comparison with the difficulties with China. In 1890 Britain had signed a previous treaty recognizing Beijing's right to negotiate on Tibet's behalf. Hence the lack of a Chinese official's signature on the 1904 pact constituted a *de jure* change in Tibet's status. Neither China nor Russia, who opposed any change beneficial to Britain, looked upon this fundamental change with favor. Moreover, this disagreement begged the question of whether China was to be considered a "Foreign Power" in the context of the Lhasa pact. London found itself in a bind. To apply the Lhasa pact as it stood was to risk the wrath of both Beijing and St. Petersburg and possibly risk some form of retaliation. To repudiate it would admit guilt on London's part and reaffirm Tibet's status as part of China. That would allow all the Western nations and Japan equal access to Tibet, since these nations operated in China under an agreement ("most favored nation") that they would all enjoy equal privileges throughout the Chinese empire.

Most historians contend that the Tibetans seemed to like their invaders—mostly because of British "good behavior and courtesy of [the] troops."[27] And, indeed, British largesse produced enough Tibetan collaborators to result in the following popular lyric.

> At first, they speak of "Foes of Our True Faith,"
> And next the cry is "Foreign Devildom,"
> But when they see the foreign money bags,
> We hear of "Honourable Englishmen."[28]

However free the British may have been with their funds, their actions can hardly be termed "benevolent." The expedition was accompanied by a host of specialists whose function it was to gather both scientific and military information. Stripping Tibet of treasure was also an important task, as it had been in earlier British adventures in Egypt and eastern China. One officer said his orders were to "obtain a representative collection of such *objets d'art*, books and manuscripts as would prove of interest to Western scholars." He was quite successful too, managing to collect four hundred mule-loads of treasure for Indian museums, the British Museum and for the private collection of the commander of the army in India, Lord Kitchener.[29]

In the final analysis, the death and destruction were pointless, for while the Younghusband expedition proved to be a military success, it was a political blunder. London regretted the whole affair from the start and spent the next few years trying to undo its damage. China had been humiliated—its weakness preventing it from keeping the British invading army from its territory. The confrontation seemed to have a jolting effect on at least some officials in Beijing, for their energies in the final days of the Manchu dynasty were devoted to regaining at least some of that lost power and prestige in the most remote part of their empire.

Invasion's Aftermath

The year 1905 was a turning point for Russia, as an abortive internal revolution and the débâcle of the Russo-Japanese War effectively eliminated it as a power in Central Asia. That is not to say that Russia pulled up stakes and left the region entirely; but for many years it would not be capable of pursuing its goals militarily. Powerless as it was, the door to Tibet remained ajar; and in this area, at least, Russian intrigues continued apace. In March 1905, while at Urga (present-day Ulan Bator, capital of Mongolia, where he had fled during the British invasion) the Dalai Lama appealed to the Tsar to "assume protection" over Tibet.

The Dalai Lama was anxious to leave Urga and return to his capital; but British and Chinese officials, while eager for him to leave Urga and get away from the Russian influence he was under in that city, were not anxious for him to return to Tibet. Both would have preferred to have him under their influence. A compromise was worked out, whereby the Dalai Lama was permitted to travel as far as the Kumbum Monastery on the Gansu-Tibet frontier.

A new British Liberal government came to power at the end of 1905. Anglo-Chinese and Anglo-Russian relations were given priority over Anglo-Tibetan relations; there was a new willingness to compromise over Tibet. The first evidence of change came with a 1905 Anglo-Chinese conference that had broken down over such seemingly insurmountable problems as the question of Chinese "suzerainty" or "sovereignty" over Tibet. In January 1906 the Chinese delegate, Tang Shaoyi (T'ang Shao-yi), offered to reopen the negotiations with the new British government. The Chinese position had not changed, but the British one had—for John Morley, the new head of the India office in London, was set on improving Anglo-Chinese relations. The Chinese demands were now met, and a treaty—called the Adhesion Agreement of Peking—was duly signed on 27 April 1906.

China agreed to pay the 1904 Tibetan indemnity, recognized the validity of the Lhasa Convention, and permitted Britain to keep the telegraph line it had built from India to Gyantse. The Chinese government agreed to refrain from using European employees of the Imperial Maritime Customs in Tibet. Britain agreed to recognize Chinese "suzerainty" over Tibet and to admit that China was excluded from the term "Foreign Power" as used in the Lhasa Convention. In other words, Tibet was a part of China; and Britain—but only Britain—had special interests and privileges there. Both sides had achieved their aims.

In response to evidence of Russia's renewed interest in Tibet, Morley suggested an Anglo-Russian Entente. This solution would have been unrealistic before the new attitude to Tibet in London had evolved and before the Russian weakness brought about by the revolution of 1905. A pact was duly signed on 18 August 1907. This settled all the outstanding Anglo-Russian disputes in Persia, Afghanistan, and Tibet. Both nations officially recognized Chinese suzerainty over Tibet and pledged not to interfere in Tibetan internal matters. Both also agreed not to send any representatives to Lhasa, although Britain's special trade interests were recognized. To the best of my knowledge, this treaty marks the first official use of the term "suzerainty," in this particular context. Suzerainty became a diplomatic term used to denote a condition under which a dependent state (in this case Tibet) enjoyed local autonomy over domestic matters, while living under the rule of a more powerful entity (in this case China) that exercised control over external affairs and defense. "Sovereignty," on the other hand, describes a situation in which one state exercises *total* control over another.

China's Response

China embarked on a policy designed to regain control in Tibet (and to a lesser extent in Mongolia and Xinjiang). Perhaps to bolster itself against the deteriorating political situation in Central Asia—traditionally a harbinger of the fall of a dynasty—the Qing dynasty's policy could be summed up as: to gain military control of the area west of Sichuan, to "modernize" the Lhasa government, to bring the Dalai Lama back to Lhasa to support Chinese reforms and to reclaim suzerainty over Nepal and Bhutan, thereby undermining British prestige in the area.

Late in 1906, Zhang Yintang (Chang Yin-t'ang), a Han, was named Imperial Commissioner in Tibet and entrusted with the task of restoring Chinese control.[30] Zhang's tactics led to the calling of a tripartite conference in Simla in August 1907. Significantly, the Tibetan, Tsarong Shape, was termed a "delegate," while the Englishman, Sir Louis Dane, and Zhang were termed "plenipotentiary."

Britain appeased China, acceding to demands to restore China's full rights in Tibet, China's repossession of the India-Gyantse telegraph line and the removal of the military escorts assigned to the British Trade Agents.

Zhang left the scene in autumn of 1908, but not before initiating a series of developmental projects, and forcing the officials to a higher level of productivity by having them work harder. Specifically, Zhang and the amban, Lian You (Lien Yu), attacked corruption and "monastic idleness," founded a four thousand-man Tibetan army, secularized the government in Lhasa, opened schools, improved agriculture, and founded a military academy. While none of these reforms lasted very long, they did go some way toward winning the allegiance of the people and the enmity of the ruling elite. Even as anti-Chinese an official as Charles Bell was forced to admit that

> the Chinese officials of the modern school, who came in now, lessened the bribes taken by the Tibetan officials from the poorer classes, and ... gave straighter justice than that dealt out by the Tibetan magistry. There is no doubt some foundation for the Amban's claim that the poorer classes in Tibet were in favor of China.[31]

At the same time, China was also trying to achieve its military aims in eastern Tibet. In 1904, Feng Chuan (Feng Ch'uan) was named as Assistant Amban, stationed at Qamdo. His oppressive policies led to his murder and subsequent uprisings throughout the region. His successor, Zhao Erfeng, was unlike most elite Chinese; he possessed qualities of bravery, honesty, loyalty, and—although ruthless—showed a lack of concern for personal hardships. With Batang as his headquarters, he created a well-trained army of six thousand; and during the following two years pacified most of eastern Tibet, introducing extensive administrative, economic, land, and tax reforms. He abolished corvée labor (*ulag*), threatening offenders with decapitation. He established inns for travelers; appointed school officials; introduced compulsory education; established mining, tanning and agricultural enterprises, and even built a steel bridge across the Ya-lung River. A British official who resided in Chengdu (Cheng-tu), Sichuan's capital, during Zhao's tenure, had this to say of him:

> Though he is known among the Szechuanese by the nickname of "Butcher Chao" [a name that survived until at least the 1950s] owing to his alleged tendency towards wholesale executions, and although his proceedings were doubtlessly at times characterized by great severity by the unfortunate Tibetans who objected to submitting to the Chinese yoke, his reputation was nevertheless that of a just man; and while he did not hesitate to behead a recalcitrant Tibetan Chief or Headman, he was equally ready to decapitate offenders among his own officers and men. A remarkable man, of commanding personality, Chao Erh-feng's justice and fair dealing are remembered today [1922] in Eastern Tibet as well as his severity. . . . Among the lamas, however, his name is universally execrated as the arch enemy.[32]

After a year, in March 1908, Zhao was appointed Imperial Commissioner for the Tibetan Marches; while his brother, Zhao Erxun (Chao Erh-hsün), was named to the post of Governor-General of Sichuan. Now the military advance westward into Tibet could begin. In early 1910, Zhao captured Qamdo and was ready to move on to Lhasa; but the Dalai Lama was also on his way to the holy city, finally bringing his exile to an end. Zhao asked the British for permission to transport 2,000 to 3,000 men to Lhasa via India, a route much faster than that from Qamdo. The request was immediately denied; and hence, a force of 2,000, under Zhong Yin (Chung Ying), was marched toward Lhasa with an advance party of 240 entering the city on 12 February 1910.[33]

The Thirteenth Dalai Lama's Travels

After the Anglo-Russian Entente, the Dalai Lama attempted to reconcile his differences with the Chinese throne. He traveled to Beijing with the omnipresent Dorjieff. Qing dynasty accounts show that the Dalai Lama was at odds with the Hututhku (the highest Buddhist incarnation in Mongolia) in Urga and had appealed for Chinese aid to effect the Tibetan leader's departure from Mongolia.[34] On his way to Beijing, the lama met with several foreign delegates, including the Russian Ambassador Korostovetz. American Ambassador W.W. Rockhill encouraged him to forge closer ties with the British, while the Japanese sent monks bearing gifts and a military attaché bearing arms for his use.

In Beijing the Dalai Lama tried to upgrade his status. But when he was granted an audience with the Empress Dowager, he was excused from the customary *kowtow* but was compelled to kneel in front of her. In return, the Empress bestowed upon him the title of "Our Loyal and Submissive Vice-Regent" and a yearly stipend of 10,000 taels. His status was further lowered when the personal caretaker assigned to him proved to be a lowly shoemaker—a symbolic humiliation.[35] But the thirteenth Dalai Lama was nothing if not politically shrewd, persistent and opportunistic. If he could not look to the Manchus for aid then he would search elsewhere; and his time in Beijing was marked, in the words of the British Ambassador Sir John Jordan, by "a very heated intrigue indeed." He had asked the British for aid and spent a week at the Japanese Embassy undoubtedly for the same purpose; meanwhile Dorjieff continued to pursue his Russian connection. The comings and goings were so numerous that the Chinese assigned the Dalai Lama a "secretary" to screen all visitors; whereupon the visits largely ceased.[36]

With the failure of all his efforts to gain foreign support, the Dalai Lama decided, in December 1908, to leave Beijing for Kumbum and proceed from there to Lhasa. Dorjieff was sent on yet another mission to St. Petersburg. The Dalai Lama returned to his capital on 25 December 1909—one year after leaving Beijing. During his five year absence his expenses for travel, food, lodging, interpreters, and his retinue were paid for by the Chinese government through an annual stipend from the Sichuan treasury.

After staying in Lhasa less than two months, the Dalai Lama became alarmed by the approach of Zhong Yin despite the amban's assurances that the soldiers were only there to protect British trade agents and that the contingent consisted of only one thousand men. The Dalai Lama was not reassured, and as Zhong Yin's advance party entered Lhasa through one gate, the Dalai Lama fled south by another. He reached India on 21 February and was "deposed" on 25 February by an official degree from Beijing observing that

> he has shown himself proud, extravagant, lewd, slothful, vicious and perverse, without parallel, violent and disorderly, disobedient to the Imperial commands and oppressive to the Tibetans. He is not fit to be a reincarnation of Buddha.[37]

As soon as the lama arrived in India, frontier officers—notably Charles Bell—called for immediate British aid. Morley, of course, would not hear of it; he stated that His Majesty's Government "regrets that it is unable to interfere between Dalai Lama and his suzerain."[38] Writing about Morley's refusal of aid, Bell confirmed the high expectations the Dalai Lama had held:

> When I delivered the message to the Dalai Lama he was so surprised and depressed that for a moment or two he lost the power of speech. He could not, or would not, realize the extent to which we were tied and the attitude of the Home Government.[39]

Until the Chinese Revolution in 1911 the Dalai Lama petitioned Indian and Russian officials for aid, while rebuffing the efforts of Chinese officials and the Panchen Lama to persuade him to return to Tibet. His refusal was probably on the advice of Bell and other British officials in India. Although these officials continued to argue for an aggressive policy toward Tibet, Britain negotiated exclusively with China on any new arrangements with Tibet. Ironically, at the time of the Manchu Empire's greatest weakness, it had successfully regained its lost power and prestige in Tibet.

In the course of Zhao Erfeng's military successes in eastern Tibet, he pushed his armies south to Zayul and Pome, just north of what was later to become the McMahon Line. At the time, the Indian boundary (Assam) ran to the so-called "Outer Line"—a horizontal line along the foothills of the Himalayas. That line was to shift as a result of a change in British policy brought about by the growing Chinese presence in the region, and especially the increasing pressure from private British timber interests in search of further forests to exploit. The opportunity to advance the frontier came about in 1911 when British official Noel Williamson was killed while spying north of the "Outer Line"—in direct contradiction to his orders.

London never acknowledged Williamson's violation of his instructions, but demanded some form of reparation. In 1911 and 1912, three missions were sent north of the "Outer Line," ostensibly to avenge Williamson's death but in fact to survey and explore the area. London's policy became one of extending the northeast and northwest frontiers, while keeping the hill tribes under "loose political control." The plan was to make Tibet a buffer state between China and India as it had become between Russia and India in the 1907 pact. In the northeast, the "Outer Line" was surreptitiously moved sixty miles north from the foothills of the Assam Himalayas to their crest. This was done covertly, as the Indian government and the India office in London conspired to keep the public and Parliament misinformed, assuring them that the new frontier was actually the same as the old.[40] The *Times* of London took a different tack, arguing editorially that the frontier had indeed been altered and as a result the old treaties were invalid—even if the altering had been done unilaterally and secretly. It went on to urge intervention if the new situation was unacceptable to the peoples on whom it had been imposed.[41]

Meanwhile the 1911 Chinese Revolution had spread to Tibet where the Chinese garrison rebelled, deposing the Manchu amban. In eastern Tibet, the beheading of Zhao Erfeng in December 1911 proved to be the signal for widespread fighting. By March 1912, there were battles ranging in Shigatse and Gyantse as well as Lhasa—with some Tibetans and members of monasteries fighting on both the Republican and Manchu sides. The resulting chaos became so serious that all the involved parties began searching for a truce. The new Chinese President Yuan Shikai (Yuan Shih-k'ai) dispatched a relief column for Lhasa in July 1912 that got bogged down in heavy fighting around Qamdo. The

Dalai Lama feared the effects of a civil war on his land, while the British saw the fighting adversely affecting their trade.

Yuan's efforts for peace consisted of a declaration that Tibet should be "regarded as on an equal footing with the provinces of China proper." To that end, the white bar in the new flag of the Chinese Republic was said to represent Tibet. Tibet was also permitted representatives in the new National Assembly, and the Dalai Lama's titles were restored in November 1912. However, all these efforts were more show than substance. The Chinese government had dissolved into anarchy and could not possibly enforce its rule over Tibet. In autumn 1912 the Nepali Resident in Lhasa, Lal Bahadur, had negotiated a truce; and all Han soldiers, with the exception of the amban's personal guards, left Tibet via India. By April 1913 the remaining Han left as well, and, for the first time in centuries, there were no Chinese in Tibet.

During the course of all these events, the Dalai Lama was living in Darjeeling. When he decided to return to his holy city he was met at the Tibet-Indian frontier on 24 July 1912, by the peripatetic Dorjieff and a Japanese named Yasujiro Yajimo, who was promptly appointed military adviser to the Tibetan government. Yasujiro's appearance did nothing to calm British apprehension about Japan's growing economic presence throughout East Asia. These apprehensions were later translated into a clear change in attitude and policy reflected in the following two statements. The first, written in 1910, was part of a cable from the Secretary of State for India to the Governor-General in India. "Definite information should now be made available to the Dalai Lama that there can be no interference between Tibet and China on the part of HMG [His Majesty's Government]." But, by July 1912, as the Dalai Lama was leaving India,

> the Government of India wish[es] the Dalai Lama a safe and prosperous journey.... The desire of the Government is to see the internal autonomy of Tibet, under China's suzerainty, maintained without Chinese interference so long as treaty obligations are duly performed and cordial relations preserved between Tibet and India.[42]

The Simla Conference

Instability in the region led London to initiate a new set of Anglo-Chinese negotiations. China was attempting to do the same with Tibet. These efforts continued throughout the latter part of 1912 and the early part of 1913, spurred on by two treaties that appeared during this period. In November 1912, the Russo-Mongolian Agreement and Protocol was signed in Urga. Russia pledged to support Outer Mongolia and to make Mongolia into a Russian protectorate. To prevent any Chinese reaction to this encroachment on an area traditionally in China's sphere of influence, Russia signed a pact with China in 1913, accepting the latter's nominal suzerainty in return for recognition of the earlier treaty.

The parallel between Russian gains in Mongolia and British imperialist goals in Tibet was not lost on everyone. On 3 December 1912, the *Times* of London editorialized:

> the analogy between the Tibetan and Mongolian cases is close. Over both territories Chinese claims were shadowy ... Great Britain and Russia have both said practically the same thing in regard to Tibet and Mongolia respectively—no interference with their autonomy.[43]

One further factor added to the incentive for negotiations—the alleged Tibetan-Mongolian Treaty of January 1913. It was said that Dorjieff had met with the Hututhku in Urga and signed a pact in which Tibet and Mongolia had agreed to recognize each other as being "independent." The text of the "treaty" first appeared in a book published by two British officials who said they obtained the copy from Russian officials in Mongolia in 1913.[44] There was not, at the time, nor has there been since, any official publication of the text by either party. The text does not appear to have been published in any language other than English. Moreover, a high Tibetan official pointed out years later that, "[t]here [was] no need for a treaty; we would always help each other if we could."[45] According to Charles Bell, Dorjieff may have negotiated this treaty on his own based on a letter he was carrying from the Dalai Lama. However, the Dalai Lama denied his letter authorized Dorjieff to negotiate a treaty and, besides, neither the cleric or his government ever ratified the treaty.[46] Whatever the case, to the Chinese it was a real possibility that Russia would come to Tibet's aid with military assistance through Mongolia.

In China proper the situation continued to deteriorate. The 1911 Revolution had ended dynastic rule after two almost uninterrupted millennia and left a political vacuum. The abolition of Confucian education a few years earlier had left a cultural and social vacuum as well. Warlords emerged to fill the vacuum; some proved benevolent and others ruthless to an almost unimaginable degree. The rural areas, in particular, were made to suffer. From the ethnic Tibet-Han border, an American missionary wrote to a Shanghai newspaper.

> There is no method of torture known and not practiced on the Tibetans, slicing, skinning, boiling, tearing asunder and all. . . . To sum up what China is doing here in Eastern Tibet, the main things are collecting taxes, robbing, oppressing, confiscating and allowing her representatives to burn and loot and steal.[47]

In Tibet the Dalai Lama declared independence for Tibet and then began a purge of his opponents. Pro-Han elements were sought out and punished, including thousands of monks at Drepung Monastery. Monks were expelled from the Tengyeling Monastery, their estates confiscated and the monastery completely disbanded. Lay nobility in opposition were unceremoniously dumped into the dungeon under the Potala. The Dalai Lama turned to the British and the Japanese for advice. Charles Bell became an influential adviser, as did Tada Tōkan, a former Japanese soldier, military instructor and Buddhist monk who described himself as the Dalai Lama's "unofficial foreign adviser."[48]

The Dalai Lama tried to introduce some reforms. He attacked smoking, opium use, gambling and cruel punishments. He created an eight thousand-man standing army, tried to reform the penal and *ulag* systems, and began giving officials predetermined salaries, eliminating their dependence on the extortion of the peasantry. Unfortunately, this enlightened approach had only a momentary, if any, effect on life in Tibet. In spite of all the Dalai Lama's efforts, the end of direct Chinese influence in Tibet was "far from obtaining the unanimous approval of the Tibetan population."[49]

Britain was displeased by the turn of events and suspicious of continuing Tibetan links with Russia. It was determined once and for all to rid Tibet of all residual Russian influence, set the boundaries, make Tibet a buffer state and place a resident in Lhasa. London first attempted to achieve these aims by delivering an ultimatum to Yuan Shikai on 17 August 1912. The terms were that Britain would accept Chinese suzerainty over Tibet if Yuan would repudiate all statements implying that Tibet was an integral part of China, and that—with the exception of the amban and his guard—there would be no Chinese troops or officials in Tibet. Furthermore, Britain would not even recognize the new Chinese Republic unless these two conditions were met. The note went on to say that until the conditions were met the Indian-Tibetan frontier would be closed to all Chinese with the exception of retreating soldiers.[50]

London began pressing for Sino-British negotiations in India, and the Dalai Lama suggested the proposed Sino-Tibetan talks also be held in India; thereby a tripartite conference would be created. London and Calcutta agreed; Beijing, however, did not. It was opposed to the conference and grew angry over the British ultimatum. Its opposition only increased when it learned that the Tibetan delegate, Lonchen Shatra, would be recognized as a "plenipotentiary," equal in rank to the British and Chinese delegates. China's anger was not tempered when its proposal that the Sino-British talks take place in London was countered with a British proposal that Darjeeling be the site. China at first refused to attend and then agreed only after the British threatened to go ahead with the Tibetans alone. As a Chinese official put it,

> our country is at present in an enfeebled condition: our external relations are involved and difficult and our finances are embarrassing. Nevertheless, Tibet is of paramount importance to both Szechuan and Yun-nan and we must exert ourselves to the utmost during the conference.[51]

The conference opened in October 1913 with Chen Yifan (Chen I-fan [Ivan Chen]) representing China, Lonchen Shatra from Tibet, and the Indian Foreign Secretary, Sir Henry McMahon, from Britain. The site was changed to Simla (in northwest India) so that, in the words of Viceroy Sir C. Hardinge, "we could exercise more effective control over the proceedings while the Tibetan delegates would not be so exposed to Chinese intrigues as at Darjeeling."[52]

From its inception, there could be no doubt as to who was conducting the conference and for whose benefit. During the entire six months of the talks, British and Tibetan officials were meeting secretly to discuss trade matters and the demarcation of the frontiers. Not only were the Chinese delegates not invited to these talks, they were not even informed of their existence. Moreover, the British were secretly monitoring all the cable communications between the Chinese delegation at Simla and their government in China. In the end, Britain pressured Chen into initialing the pact prior to his government's approval, threatening to omit any mention of Chinese suzerainty over Tibet if he refused. Chen agreed, but only after making it clear that there was a considerable gulf between initialing and signing and that the latter could only be done by the government in Beijing.[53] Chen revealed in private letters to friends that he considered himself to be among enemies. The Chinese naturally enough denounced the pact. They had nothing to gain by signing it except a reaffirmation of their suzerainty. This they felt to be unnecessary since it had been assured in so many previous pacts.

Even the signing was shrouded in controversy. The initialing took place in April 1914. On 1 July the India office in London cabled McMahon with instructions that if the Chinese refused to sign the agreement, he should abandon the talks, promising the Tibetans "that if the Chinese aggression continues Tibet may count on diplomatic support of His Majesty's Government and on any assistance which we can give in supplying munitions of war."[54]

The following day McMahon cabled back that the Tibetans would be satisfied with the initialing only. London immediately responded with an order to McMahon not to sign solely with the Tibetans, but to act as instructed in the 1 July cable. This reply, however, reached Simla too late, for McMahon had gone ahead with the signing on 3 July. The pact that was signed was somewhat different from the one initialed in April. Chen was not permitted in the room when the treaty was signed and was not informed of the changes.

The Simla Convention canceled the 1893, 1906, and 1908 pacts, while dividing Tibet into two parts: inner and outer. It set the India-Tibet frontier, east of Bhutan, along the crest of the Himalayas, in what came to be known as the McMahon Line; and resulted in the acquisition of two thousand square miles of territory for the British empire. (As mentioned before, extensive surveying had gone on above the original boundary, the "Outer Line," after the death of Noel Williamson. The surveying continued while the conference at Simla met, and the new boundary continued to creep farther north on British maps *during* the conference, unbeknown to the Tibetan or Chinese delegations.) In addition, Britain obtained exclusive trading rights, extraterritoriality and the right to station a resident in Lhasa (although the first one was not sent until 1937).

Tibetan motives for signing a treaty were unclear. Tibet gave up territory and switched suzerains from China to Britain. It certainly did not achieve "independence"—unless the state of independence is judged solely by the right to sign treaties with other nations. Moreover, the treaty forced Tibet to give up territory, forced Tibet to agree there were two Tibets—inner and outer, with Lhasa controlling only the former, and put Lhasa on record as being willing to admit to *de jure* Chinese suzerainty. Indeed, it can as easily be argued that Tibet's signing was an example of its *lack* of independence. Tibet, after all, had no choice but to acquiesce to British demands and the treaty offered no gains to Tibet whatsoever—except to escape the formal suzerainty of China.

British officials managed to achieve some legality for their imperialist intentions, but were compelled to do so by resorting to the most underhand means. Indian officials knowingly deceived their superiors in London. They had no more interest in finding a compromise solution to the issues than they had in sponsoring an authentically independent Tibet. The conference provided a convenient façade for the pursuit of British interests in Tibet. Chinese participation provided a convenient way to dispel Russian apprehensions and obscure the fact that the new pact deliberately violated the Anglo-Russian Entente and several other treaties.

The major British participants at Simla were well aware that their actions were questionable. For example, Bell understood that the Tibetans could not comprehend the manipulation of the frontier. "The Tibetans couldn't make maps," he was to write years later.[55] As to the treaty itself, in 1915 Hardinge felt the advantages gained by Britain were "purely academic since it [had] not been signed by the Chinese government or accepted by the Russian government and [was], therefore, for the present invalid."[56] Sir Henry McMahon agreed, lamenting "it is with great regret that I leave India without having secured the formal adherence of the Chinese government to a Tripartite agreement."[57]

Indeed, Britain did not even act as though the treaty was in force; although Bell later (1924) reversed himself and argued that it was—citing the McMahon Line as a example. But in fact the McMahon Line was not the border; and official British publications continued to print the old frontier until some two decades later when a colonial official, Sir Olaf Caroe, persuaded British officials to recall all of its relevant publications and replace them with identical copies—except for the altered borders along the McMahon Line. This little bit of *post facto* historical manipulation was uncovered only because London was unable to recall all of its original texts. As Hugh Richardson, one of Caroe's colleagues, put it,

> in 1936 he [Caroe] discovered that the exact position and nature of India's frontier was more or less unknown. . . . And it was due to Sir Olaf that the frontier was revived and was made very much a reality.[58]

The Simla Convention, therefore, was for many years after its signing in disrepute and unimplemented. Only decades later would history be rewritten in an attempt to show that the proceedings and their outcome were acted upon. Summing up the Convention, an international lawyer who has studied the matter at some length wrote,

> the documents reveal responsible officials of British India to have acted to the injury of China in conscious violation of their instructions; deliberately misinforming their superiors in London of their actions; altering documents whose publication had been ordered by Parliament; lying at an international conference table; and deliberately breaking a treaty between the UK and Russia.[59]

Although blatantly illegal, the Simla Convention did help to achieve Britain's short-term aims. Tibet, for all intents and purposes, became a British protectorate; China and Russia were effectively forced out of the area. By 1914 Britain had shifted policy once again, successfully acquiring all that Curzon and Younghusband had struggled to achieve ten years earlier. Only now the spoils were to prove illusory, for the world was about to undergo a dramatic transformation and Britain was now concerned with matters closer to home.

4

The Modern Era

With the outbreak of war in Europe only one month after the Simla talks ended, British attention was diverted from Tibet. That is not to say that all ties were cut. Soon after the war erupted the Dalai Lama offered one thousand Tibetan soldiers, but Britain politely thanked him, shipped the troops more than five thousand modern bolt rifles, and informed Lhasa they would be called upon if needed. The troops were kept ready throughout the war but never used.[1]

Although his Japanese adviser recalls that the Dalai Lama spent the years 1918–21 in contemplation, locked in the Norbulingka,[2] some evidence exists that during this period he continued to forge closer ties to the British. Charles Bell was invited to Lhasa at least once each year between 1915 and 1919 but was instructed by London not to go. The reasons are unclear; although the refusal may have been connected with secret talks going on with the Chinese. According to the British ambassador to China, Sir John Jordan, the talks were initiated by the Chinese and by 1919 had come "within an ace of being settled" and broke off only "through reasons not connected with Tibet at all."[3]

After the war, Bell again tried to persuade London to allow him to accept an invitation from his old friend the thirteenth Dalai Lama. Permission was finally granted and Bell arrived in Lhasa in November 1920 for a one-year stay. Bell's objectives were obvious enough: to bring Tibet into the British sphere of influence, while making it as dependent as possible. China may have been a toothless tiger, but there were other dangers threatening the British Empire.

> Far and near in Tibet at this time one could notice a growing admiration for the other Island Empire, the Empire of Japan. It was felt that Japan had aided Mongolia against the Bolshevists, that she was a strong Power, and that she

was steadily advancing nearer to Tibet. Mongolia was flooded with Japanese rifles, cheap and serviceable. If the British rifles were held back, let the Japanese be obtained.[4]

Bell proved to be persuasive; and no doubt the Dalai Lama remembered how well the British had treated him during his exile in India a decade earlier. The treatment had differed markedly from the humiliation he had been forced to suffer while at the Manchu court the previous year. At Bell's suggestion the Dalai Lama increased the Tibetan army from five thousand to fifteen thousand; a telegraph line was constructed from Gyantse to Lhasa; a small hydro-electric plant was built in the capital and a police force established with the aid of Sikkimese police officers. A British-style school was set up in Gyantse in 1924. But perhaps the most remarkable accomplishment was the acquisition of permission for Henry Hayden (the geologist on the Younghusband expedition) to spend the year 1922 conducting geological surveys throughout Tibet. Although Hayden's findings were to be of no value to the Tibetans, Bell had persuaded the Dalai Lama to allow a British agent freedom to roam Tibet.

British suzerainty was probably far more benevolent than Chinese would have been, and being under the British umbrella offered the Tibetan nobility the privileges and pleasures of an advanced material technology. So enamored of Britain was the Dalai Lama that he told Bell "all the people of Tibet and myself have become of one mind and the British and Tibetan have become one family."[5] To confirm Bell's success and mislead the Chinese as to his activities, London sent an official message to China in 1921 stating flatly that the British government saw Tibet as "an autonomous state under the suzerainty of China."[6] But even as Bell was leaving Lhasa he knew that among the Tibetan nobility there was a growing sentiment for closer ties with China due to mistrust of British intentions, traditional ties, and economic interests in China. Bell was also deeply troubled by the cruel and despotic rule of the Tibetan aristocrats and by the Dalai Lama's lack of interest in true reform.[7] Even among the most ardent supporters of the British ties there was little wish for a complete break between Tibet and the government of China.

But during the mid-1920s the British government saw little reason to maintain its close contact with Tibet. With British influence in decline, the Russians—now the Soviet Union—re-entered the picture briefly, testing the political waters. In 1927, and again in 1928, Soviet Mongolians visited Lhasa—taking photographs, distributing money to the various monasteries and selected nobles, and collecting information. Both delegations were granted audiences with the Dalai Lama, who treated them with courtesy and undoubtedly inquired about the possibility of closer relations in the future. But internal economic and political difficulties in the Soviet Union precluded any further efforts in a region seen as being of only the most peripheral interest to the leaders in Moscow.

The irony that the Russian delegation was being fêted in Lhasa a mere quarter of a century after the British expedition fought its way there to prevent exactly that was certainly not lost on any of the participants.

Eastern Tibet

During these years other regions of Tibet were in turmoil, particularly Kham and Amdo. These areas are largely populated by fierce and independent nomads. Lhasa had only the most nominal control over their activities. Tibetan officials were reluctant to accept assignments to those regions, and the Tibetan army had a reputation for looting and general disregard for the people it was sent to protect and aid.

From 1911 to 1935 there were four hundred to five hundred "major battles" in the Xikang (Sikang)-Sichuan area (roughly Kham); one American visitor compared the district to the Wild West in his own country.[8] The local people fought equally against rule from Lhasa and rule from Beijing; they also often fought among themselves.

The most notable troubles occurred immediately after the death of the thirteenth Dalai Lama in 1933. This was an uprising—ultimately unsuccessful—intended to create a separate Kham state independent of Lhasa and Beijing. It was led by Rapga and Topgyay Pangdatsang, the "most loved and most feared of all the Khampas and their wealth and power were immense ... they ruled like feudal barons."[9] They attacked the local Lhasa garrison and achieved a short-lived victory but were quickly repelled by a combined Han and Tibetan force.[10]

Political Intrigue at the Highest Levels

The Dalai Lama's death (perhaps unnaturally)[11] in 1933 necessitated a search both for an incarnation to be named the fourteenth Dalai Lama and for a regent. The latter had to be chosen first. Three names were written on pieces of paper, inserted into three identical balls of tsampa (roasted barley flour), and placed in a golden urn donated for this purpose by a past emperor of China. The urn was rolled on the floor until one ball fell out. The one that did bore the name of the nineteen-year-old abbot of Reting Monastery, who immediately became Tibet's regent.

We know that the Reting Rinpoche was a young man devoid of any political experience and noted as a bon vivant who cherished luxury items from the cities of China. One wealthy Tibetan fondly remembered the "Reting Era" as one of few restrictions, gaiety and frivolity for himself and his peers.[12]

In 1941, the regent, in a surprise move, abdicated his position in favor of an elderly man known as the Taktra Rinpoche. It was discovered later that the two men had made a secret agreement to make the regency a rotating position. However, when the time came for the Taktra Rinpoche to relinquish his turn, he refused, causing considerable animosity among the followers of the Reting Rinpoche. The Taktra Rinpoche managed to hold on to the position until the fourteenth Dalai Lama officially took over in 1950.

The hostility felt between the followers of the two men came to a head in 1947 with the explosion of a bomb in a package addressed to the Taktra Rinpoche.[13] The Reting Rinpoche was arrested, along with his attendants, and heavy fighting broke out. Martial law was declared and aristocratic women were sent into heavily guarded hiding places. The fighting ended in three weeks with estimated casualties in the hundreds. At Sera Monastery alone three hundred monks were "butchered" while others were subject to as many as two hundred sixty strokes of the lash. Survivors fled to China proper while other monks looted their deserted quarters.

Reting Rinpoche was imprisoned in a Potala dungeon, which was "like the Tower of London for high ranking officials."[14] He died soon after.

The Guomindang (GMD [Kuomintang]) government of China "demanded" an explanation and were told by Lhasan officials that the Reting was suspected of communist leanings, of ties with the Soviet Union and of heading a ring of communist agents among the monks of Sera, Drepung, and Ganden Monasteries. It is highly unlikely that anyone believed these accusations, and the Indian government quite rightly felt that stories were concocted to placate the stridently anticommunist Chinese government.[15]

In 1944, the United States Office of Strategic Services (OSS) prepared a secret report on Tibetan sectarianism, which succinctly summed up the situation. The largest group was the one that controlled the army and was supported by the British. Another group in Lhasa was closely tied to the first and also to Britain, its members having been largely educated in India. However, this faction held no power. A third group, smaller than the other two, supported closer ties to the Han; while a fourth, made up largely of people in Shigatse and supporters of the Panchen Lama, also favored closer ties to the Chinese government. The fifth group was in Kanting, Kham, and was unrelentingly opposed to Lhasa, Britain, and China in its aspirations for local autonomy. The leaders of this last group, the Pangdatshang brothers, were not above seeking aid from the GMD government of China.[16] The final group, the smallest of all, consisted of followers of the Panchen Lama who largely resided in Xikang Province and had no influence over anyone.[17]

The Panchen Lama

The Panchen Lama—spiritual head of the Tashilhunpo Monastery in Shigatse—was a long-standing rival of the Dalai Lama. There were times when the Panchen Lama and his followers made unsuccessful attempts to enlarge the area over which they exercised temporal power beyond the immediate area of Shigatse. Various Panchen Lamas tried to establish unilateral contacts with the colonial British government in India, while also being accused of maintaining close links to the governments of China. The rivalry between the two clerics intensified during the nineteenth century. The ninth to twelfth Dalai Lamas lived short lives compared to the Panchen Lamas, whose relatively lengthy lives enabled them to consolidate their political positions, emboldening them to take political risks.

When the thirteenth Dalai Lama returned from India in 1912 he ordered the Panchen Lama to meet him along the road to Lhasa. The latter, having worked with the Chinese authorities during the former's exile, was fearful of retribution for his actions. He refused the "request" and appealed to the British to serve as mediators. David MacDonald—a half-British, half-Sikkimese colonial official who spent more than two decades in Tibet and who, in 1912, was the British Trade Agent at Yadong—arranged for the two lamas to talk on a telephone hook-up and helped to set up a meeting on the Gyantse-Lhasa road.[18] The meeting only temporarily allayed the suspicions between the two men.

The rivalry flared up again during the 1920s when the Dalai Lama, to pay for a newly created standing army, raised the taxes for the nobility and imposed some on the major monasteries. The Panchen Lama refused to pay his share, believing it to be inordinately high as punishment for his close ties to the Chinese. In retaliation the Dalai Lama seized three of the Panchen's ministers, throwing them into the Potala dungeon. The Panchen Lama had been assessed at about 25 percent of the entire cost of the army—an amount, he confided to David MacDonald, he did not have.[19]

Once again the Panchen Lama turned to his friends the British to intervene; but rather than wait for a solution to be reached, he fled Tibet in 1923 never to return. He did not leave empty-handed, however, taking along a caravan of fifty mules and ponies carrying U.S.$2,000,000 in gold and musk. He received additional gifts along the way, such as U.S.$3,000,000 in exchange for spending six weeks in the Kumbum Monastery.[20]

Throughout the Panchen's exile, he was in written communication with the Dalai Lama in Lhasa. The major topic of these communications was the terms under which the Panchen could return. The disagreement between the two incarnations centered on the Dalai Lama's conditions that the Panchen Lama return with only an immediate escort and agree to pay the military tax that had precipitated his flight in the first place. The Panchen wanted an exemption from the tax and the permission to return with an escort of Chinese troops.[21]

It became a moot issue when the Dalai Lama died in 1933. The years it would take to find a new Dalai Lama gave the Panchen an opportunity to return to Tibet and exert his influence. The GMD began paying the Panchen a monthly stipend of Ch.$40,000. Others also started to woo the lama. He began receiving letters from Lhasa "beseeching" him to return. The new Political Officer for Sikkim, Basil J. Gould, visited Lhasa in 1936–1937 with authorization from his superiors to travel to the Panchen's base at Jyekundo and escort him back to Lhasa—provided the lama would maintain close ties to the British. Hugh Richardson contends that Gould had no such instructions, yet another participant, Frederick S. Chapman, has written that Gould did, indeed, have instructions to proceed to Jyekundo if necessary. Richardson does acknowledge a change in

British neutrality, arguing that it was in direct response to Chinese threats to restore the Panchen to Tibet.[22]

In the spring of 1937, with the GMD's blessing, the Panchen Lama left Jyekundo, traveling in the direction of Lhasa and accompanied by a GMD military escort. In July, however, he was recalled to Nanjing (Nanking, the GMD capital); the Japanese had openly attacked China after the "Marco Polo Bridge Incident" and the Second World War had begun in Asia. Deeply disheartened, the Panchen Lama died at Jyekundo in December of 1937. His followers split into several factions, all of which continued to receive GMD subsidies and all of which eventually found boys they alleged to be the new Panchen Lama.

The Chinese and the British Vie for Links with Tibet

There are several examples that demonstrate how important the link with Tibet was to the Chinese government. In 1912 the newly inducted President of the Republic of China, Yuan Shikai, and the Dalai Lama had corresponded. In 1919 and 1920 provincial delegations from Gansu Province made official visits to Lhasa, while up to his death the Dalai Lama continued to send learned lamas to the Buddhist temple in Beijing. These exchanges kept the door open. The first serious attempt at reconciliation came in 1930 when the GMD sent a mission to Lhasa headed by Liu Manqing who was born in Tibet of mixed Han-Tibetan parentage. Liu, a government civil servant, met with the Dalai Lama during her four months in Lhasa. Although there was no evident change in the relationship[23] the talks must have been fruitful, for the following year another mission was dispatched by the Chinese government, only to be aborted when the leader died along the way. The Dalai Lama personally performed rites at the man's funeral in Lhasa, which encouraged the GMD to further their efforts. Chinese records indicate that just prior to his own death the Dalai Lama agreed in principle to allow the GMD to establish an office in Lhasa and thereby give the Chinese government an official presence in Tibet for the first time since 1913.[24]

Nanjing had its opportunity to do just that in 1934 when a Han delegation arrived in Lhasa led by General Huang Musong (Huang Mu-sung). Ostensibly, the mission was sent to pay respects to the late Dalai Lama; however, the group had a wider purpose—to firmly and officially establish closer relations between Nanjing and Lhasa. Huang began extensive negotiations with Tibetan officials over border issues, trade, and the status of the Panchen Lama and got as far as writing up a draft agreement. When Huang left Lhasa he left behind two members of his delegation with a radio transmitter to continue the negotiations.[25] On receiving the news of the Huang mission, the British immediately dispatched the Assistant Political Officer for Sikkim, Rai Bahadur Norbu Thondup, to Lhasa to keep an eye on the Han delegation. In 1938 one of the two Han left behind died. The remaining official, Zhen Weibei (Chen Wei-pei), established the "Office of the Commission of Mongolian and Tibetan Affairs" in Lhasa in April 1940 by a unilateral action on Nanjing's part meant to present the Tibetans with a fait accompli.[26]

But Huang and Thondup were not the only visitors to Lhasa in these years. In 1936, at a time when the imminent return of the Panchen Lama was expected, the current Political Officer for Sikkim, Frederick Williamson, traveled to Lhasa to offer his good offices to prevent any conflict that might arise upon the Panchen's return. Williamson was liked, as he was a strong proponent of British military aid and training for the Tibetans. While in Lhasa, however, he fell ill and died of uraemia; the Tibetans forbade the sending of a plane for him from India, deeming such an action as "inauspicious."[27] His successor, Basil J. Gould, arrived in Lhasa, on the first of three visits, soon after Williamson's death.

To the British it looked as though the Chinese government was about to reassert its control in Tibet. They had a mission in Lhasa. The thirteenth Dalai Lama, who had preferred British ties to Chinese ties, was dead; and the Panchen Lama was about to return at the head of a Chinese military escort. The British had to take steps to maintain some influence in the holy city. Gould, in 1936, brought along a military adviser and the new British Trade Agent in Gyantse, Hugh Richardson. He was authorized to offer military training and to "be cautious in sounding out the Tibetan government regarding permanent British representation at Lhasa." Since Nanjing had a more or less permanent resident in Lhasa, the British wanted one as well; but the Tibetans were not amenable to that suggestion, seeing it as a further entanglement in foreign affairs and inimical to their traditional isolation. Gould then decided to ignore the Tibetan interests and find a way of tricking them. "My chief aim," he wrote his superiors, "is to produce the impression of normality and immobility." Gould purposely raised an issue with the Tibetan Cabinet that he knew could only be resolved by protracted negotiations. When the Tibetans pointed this out to him, Gould replied that they need not concern themselves since he had decided to leave Richardson in Lhasa "indefinitely" to conclude the negotiations. Gould wrote years later, "the Cabinet swallowed this and Hugh stayed on," with—it should be pointed out—a radio transmitter so as not to be outdone by the Han.[28] (Hugh Richardson quite strenuously disputes this interpretation. He contends that the Tibetans welcomed a British presence and Gould's sole problem was finding a way of conveying the establishment of such a presence to the *Kashag* in a formal way. In no way, he argues, was this a form of trickery. With all due respect to Mr. Richardson's views, I believe the evidence shows otherwise.)

The Fourteenth Dalai Lama

Meanwhile, following the death of the thirteenth Dalai Lama, top Tibetan officials had been spending much time looking for the fourteenth incarnation. The current Dalai Lama was born into a relatively wealthy peasant family in 1935[29] in a small village just south of the Yellow River, in what is now the Huangnan

Tibetan Autonomous Zhou. His oldest brother—now known as Thubten Jigme Norbu—had, for the seven years prior to the Dalai Lama's birth, been considered a high incarnated lama at Kumbum Monastery, not far from the family village. A few years later, yet another brother was selected as a high incarnated lama and also moved to Kumbum.

Although the discovery of the boy was supposed to remain a secret (the Panchen Lama told the search party "he had found three boys"), rumors were so widespread that by 1938 press photographers were appearing in his village and the family was sitting for group photographs. The rumors also reached the warlord of Qinghai, General Ma Bufang (Ma Pu-feng), who advised the Dalai Lama's parents to place the boy in the Kumbum Monastery with his two brothers for safekeeping after conducting his own tests to determine whether or not this particular youth was really the incarnation. Legend has it that when Ma first inquired about the discovery, the lamas had told him that several boys were being considered; therefore, he summoned them all. After some preliminary questioning he offered the boys sweets; some were afraid to take any, others grabbed greedily, while the youth destined to become the fourteenth Dalai Lama ate a few discreetly. In this way, Ma was supposed to have learned which youth was the true incarnation. Legend aside, we know that the official search party stayed with the Panchen Lama's representative in Xining (Sining) who made formal arrangements for the party to meet with Ma. Moreover, the search party was in communication with Lhasa via telegrams in code, and it is possible Ma knew about this route of communication.

The general knew he had a valuable commodity under his control as did the lamas of Kumbum; hence both demanded, and received, considerable sums of money before they would allow the Dalai Lama-designate to depart for Lhasa. The search party had already confirmed with Lhasa as to which boy was the next Dalai Lama although they tried to keep that secret, continuing to assert that several boys were still candidates. While there was some discussion between Tibetan and GMD officials over the procedures to be used to select the right candidate, it is clear that the Tibetans did this only for form because they had known for some time which boy was to be ordained. The boy and his entourage traveled to Lhasa with a caravan of wealthy Moslim traders who had lent them money required for the "ransoms." This amount was supplemented with a gift to the Dalai Lama from the GMD government (of a disputed amount) to cover "traveling expenses."[30]

In September 1938 the GMD government, situated in their wartime capital of Chongqing (Chungking), and physically as close to Tibet as any Chinese government had ever been, received a cable from Lhasa that three boys had been selected as possible incarnations of the thirteenth Dalai Lama. The message asked that a delegate be sent to choose the proper candidate, using the golden urn, in a ceremony to be conducted jointly with the regent. Chiang jumped at this opportunity, immediately sending General Wu Zhongxin (Wu Chung-hsin), the Chair of the Commission on Mongolian and Tibetan Affairs, who arrived in

Lhasa with a nine-member delegation in December of that year. Chongqing had acceded to the Tibetan request not to send anyone who had previously dealt with the Tibetans.

When the delegation arrived they discovered that two of the candidates had been eliminated and that the Dalai Lama had already been picked. The Tibetans argue that this fait accompli was planned all along. There is no reason to doubt them.

Attempts to Exert Independence

While World War II was raging the Tibetans saw an opportunity to further demonstrate their "independence," creating a Bureau of Foreign Affairs in 1942. The feeling was that if relations with countries around the world could be formalized, these nations would, in turn, recognize and support Tibet's claim to sovereignty.

Lhasa also appears to have made an effort to reconcile differences with the newly selected Panchen Lama. Secret American diplomatic communications indicate that in early 1947 several monks from Tashilhunpo Monastery arrived in Xining to try to escort the young Panchen back to Tibet. Apparently this action was sanctioned by the nobility in Lhasa but was prevented by Chinese soldiers who were protecting him.[31]

An example that is prominently featured in the literature espousing Tibetan independence is the nonofficial Asian Relations Conference held in New Delhi in March/April 1947. Tibet was invited to send a delegation; their flag was flown along with those of other nations; and the maps used indicated that Tibet was separate from China. Since the conference was not government-sponsored, these actions had no diplomatic significance; nevertheless, the Chinese ambassador in New Delhi protested. The maps were altered, the flag was lowered, but the delegates remained until the end. One other small incident occurred that demonstrates the sensitivity of this question to the Chinese government. In the autumn of 1948 the diplomatic corps in New Delhi was shown a film on Kashmir that included, for the briefest moment, a map depicting Tibet outside the boundaries of China. This was cause for yet another formal protest from the Chinese ambassador.

In August of 1947 India achieved its long-fought-for independence and immediately found itself assuming all the colonial privileges and duties willed it by the retiring British empire. India signed treaties with Sikkim and Bhutan that, in effect, perpetuated former British privilege and obligations of suzerainty over these two small princely kingdoms. In Tibet, India took over the British Mission in Lhasa and the trade agencies in the other population centers. Hugh Richardson, who on 14 August was a British civil servant representing Britain in Lhasa, became, on 15 August, an Indian civil servant representing New Delhi in Lhasa. Indeed, the only change was in the flag that flew outside the mission, and Richardson himself recalls that "the transition was almost imperceptible."[32] India felt no shame in accepting the privilege of extra-territoriality for its citizens in Tibet as well as permission to station its troops there (150 by one count). It was not until a year later that India sent a doctor to replace the British one and an Indian representative to learn the ropes from Richardson in preparation for taking over. Given Nehru's posture of anticolonialism, his actions on Tibet and the frontier area hardly supported his public rhetoric.

The contradiction between Nehru's words and his deeds was made explicit by Richardson's recollection that immediately after India's independence Lhasa appealed to New Delhi for a return of territories pried away by British colonial expansion. These areas included Sikkim and the town of Darjeeling. India reportedly claimed that it intended to follow the policies set by the previous government (British) and barred any discussion of the matter.[33] This intractable attitude was to cause New Delhi considerable difficulty with China some fifteen years later.

In China the GMD was fast crumbling under the onslaught of the People's Liberation Army (PLA). In a last-minute gesture, for reasons that remain unclear, the GMD recognized the boy Panchen Lama as the official incarnation in August 1949. It had not done so earlier (the boy was "discovered" in 1941), still hoping to wield some influence in Lhasa and not antagonize Tibetan officials in any way. It may have been a last, defiant gesture as the government of China. The gesture did not help the GMD, of course, and in September the Communists took Xining—and with it the city's most famous occupant, the child Panchen Lama.

It was at this juncture, with the GMD in full retreat and the communists still consolidating their victory, that the Lhasa government made its most daring gesture in asserting its independence: it ordered the Chinese mission to leave Lhasa. This event is shrouded in some mystery. The accepted interpretation has been that the Lhasa government, of its own accord, ousted the entire Chinese delegation. The Chinese claim that it was engineered by the British. Richardson's office was said to be "extremely active" and "unusually frequented by visitors."[34] The Chinese newspapers of the day echoed the same theme.[35]

Richardson was most certainly involved in some manner. He appealed to the government in India to accept three hundred Chinese nationals who were (1) communists; (2) officials who associated with communists; (3) other Chinese officials; and (4) other Chinese citizens. New Delhi agreed to accept individuals who fell into the first two categories but not the final two,

> lest [the] impression be created in China and elsewhere that it approved apparent policy [in] Tibet to take advantage [of the] present situation [in] China to rid itself once [and] for all [of] Chinese influence.[36]

But this begs the question of whether Richardson played a greater role than simply relaying messages between Lhasa and New Delhi. Years later Richardson was to write that the actions of the Tibetans took him by surprise[37]—a position he maintains to this day.

Richardson's cables to his superior indicated that Lhasa had suspicions that the official 133-member Chinese mission included some communist sympathizers. The Tibetans had asked Richardson what to do. Richardson, according to his own account, advised them to expel the suspicious ones. He may have been surprised that they requested the expulsion of the entire Han population; although the possibility exists that had Richardson not mentioned expulsion it would never have occurred to the Tibetans. It is difficult to determine the dates on which the Lhasa government made its decision and when they first spoke to Richardson about this affair. Richardson steadfastly maintains that he was consulted only *after* the expulsion decision had been made by the Tibetans. The diplomatic cables do not mention dates; although they give the impression, intentionally or not, that Richardson was actively participating in the decision-making.

That he was more involved in the decision-making than he likes to admit would not be surprising for Richardson was so fervent a supporter of the Tibetan elite that a diplomatic colleague felt compelled to warn Whitehall to use caution when interpreting Richardson's cables. Richardson had also managed to gain some influence among the Tibetan clerical elite through the distribution of funds, considering it "money well spent."[38]

Another clue to what happened was in a cable from American diplomats in India reporting a discussion held with Major Kaishar Bahadur, the Nepali representative in Lhasa from 1946 to 1949. The major reported that the Chinese delegation was in dire straits because the civil war raging in China had resulted in the passage of several months without pay. The major went on to report that Lhasan officials had inquired of the Han whether or not they would accept funds from a Chinese government that was communist; they replied in the affirmative. This may very well have been the total basis for Lhasa's suspicions about the delegation's alleged communist leanings. In any case, the radio transmitter was confiscated and a large farewell party was held in honor of the Chinese just prior to their departure.[39]

Lhasa's ability to so easily oust the Han delegation is yet another frequently cited "proof" of Tibetan independence. But China had no leadership at the time; a civil war was raging and the delegation was cut off from its government—dispirited and unable to resist the slightest pressure. The departure was obviously more a result of China's weakness than Tibetan strength.

One factor in Lhasa's preparations to maintain its *de facto* independence during these turbulent times was its army. The modern army was established by the thirteenth Dalai Lama and initially trained by Japanese, Chinese, and British advisers. The British system won out in the end, and some Tibetans went to India for further training. So pervasive was British influence in this sector that as late as 1950 the officers issued all their commands in English while the army band was only capable of playing such traditional "Tibetan" tunes as "Auld Lang Syne," "God Save the King" and "It's a Long Way to Tipperary."[40]

In reality, though, the army was hopelessly ill-equipped and undertrained. The

British, while wanting to have an army in Tibet to protect them from possible Chinese attack, were at the same time reluctant to adequately train and equip it for fear that Tibetan nationalism might grow so strong that one day it might use this army to march south. So the Tibetan army was little more than window dressing.

With no illusions about its defenses, Lhasa began sending messages to New Delhi appealing for military aid as the communist victory drew ever closer. The British encouraged the Indians to provide aid—not believing that it would help militarily but for its psychological, morale-boosting value. India complied, sending arms but no troops.[41] Tibetans and their supporters looked elsewhere as well. Lhasa appealed directly to the American Secretary of State, Dean Acheson, calling for "extensive aid" in April 1949.[42] But the futility of it all must have been obvious, for by November 1949 Lhasa's letters were being addressed to Mao Zedong appealing for "assurance that no Chinese troops would cross the Tibetan frontier from the Sino-Tibetan border."[43]

As the second half of the twentieth century dawned, Hugh Richardson finally left Tibet for his long overdue retirement, while his colleague Reginald Fox was compelled to go to India for medical reasons after fourteen consecutive years in the Land of Snows. That, to the best of my knowledge, left five foreigners in Tibet. A Russian electrical engineer named Nedbailoff worked for George Tsarong. The Austrians Peter Aufschnauter and Heinrich Harrer were employees of the local government, as was the Englishman Robert Ford, who staffed a radio station in Qamdo, Kham. The fifth foreigner, Geoffrey Bull, was a former British bank clerk turned evangelical missionary, living in Kanting where he had first arrived in 1947 with a Scottish colleague named George Patterson. By 1950 Patterson had departed for India and the era of Tibetan isolation was drawing to an end.[44]

5

Foreign Intrigues: I

Tibet: insular

The image of Tibet as a "hermit" among nations is not completely accurate. Lhasan authorities did have relations with other governments; moreover, during the first half of the twentieth century, the Tibetan nobility had sent their children to British-style schools in India. But Tibetan society was insular, especially among the elite. There was a marked lack of desire to bring about any change or reform. Knowledge of the outside world or of any of the technological changes occurring elsewhere was not disseminated beyond the small ruling class.

What foreign contacts did exist had little political impact on Tibet. Relations with the Mongolians were mostly of a religious nature; but what minor political ties there were proved to have little impact on the course of events. The relationship with Russia was equally insignificant, except for the briefest moment. For a short time there was a relationship with Japan, which began in the religious sphere, and only incidentally carried over into the political arena. In the late 1930s Japanese monks studying in Tibetan monasteries caused some concern to the Chinese, who were then waging a life-and-death struggle against the Japanese empire. The years of World War II even saw a momentary Tibetan involvement with Hitler's Germany, when a German delegation visited Lhasa in 1939—possibly for the purposes of intelligence gathering. The relationship with Nepal had no perceptible effect on the course of Tibetan history.

There were only three relationships of significance to Lhasa: with the rulers of China, with Anglo-India, and with the United States. This chapter will examine the early years of the third of these relationships, which—as it turns out—proves to be most elusive to understand. Both the United States and Tibet have been, and continue to be, extremely reluctant to discuss the subject. This is unfortun-

82

ate, for I believe that understanding the United States-Tibetan relationship is most crucial for understanding the history of Tibet over the past three decades.

Earliest United States-Tibet Ties

America's first official connection with the authorities in Lhasa came in the early twentieth century when explorer, scholar, author, and American Ambassador to China William Woodville Rockhill began exploring the areas populated by ethnic Tibetans.[1] In 1908 he met with the thirteenth Dalai Lama, then in self-imposed exile in Shaanxi (Shensi) Province, reportedly to discuss the Dalai Lama's request for American aid for his efforts to return to power in Lhasa. History records that nothing came of this meeting and that United States-Tibetan relations ended as abruptly as they had begun, not to resume for almost four decades.

In May 1942, Chinese forces under the command of American General "Vinegar Joe" Stilwell took "a hell of a beating" at the hands of the invading Japanese forces in Burma, resulting in the closing of the legendary Burma Road. While the total amount of goods carried over the road into China was important, more significantly, the closing of this artery dealt a deep psychological blow, cutting China off from any land access to military supplies from its allies. Alternatives had to be found immediately if the war was to be turned around. Cargo flights were initiated from the northeastern corner of India, across the Himalayas to air bases in southwestern China. One of these flights, of which there were thousands flying under the most hazardous conditions, ended suddenly in Tibet when it hit a mountain about 96 km (60 miles) southeast of Lhasa. The entire crew of five American servicemen survived the crash, were helped by friendly Tibetans and taken to Lhasa. There they were treated most hospitably and escorted to India.[2]

But these flights strained the capacity of the United States Air Force, while bringing into China only a fraction of what was required to carry out an effective war effort. An alternative land route across Tibet was suggested. Discussions were held between the British government in India and the Chinese government (then in their wartime capital of Chongqing). As a result, in August 1942 the British approached Lhasa about the possibility of establishing a trade route. While the Chinese had agreed—in principle—to the idea, they had demanded some conditions be met before they would cooperate fully. The Chinese wanted to place their troops along the route, ostensibly to protect the traded goods but, undoubtedly, also to help bolster their claim to sovereignty over Tibet. Just in case the Tibetans proved recalcitrant, Chiang Kai-shek threatened them with invasion if they did not agree.[3]

Like many of Chiang's proclamations in those years, this threat was nothing more than bluster, not even eliciting a reaction. The Tibetans were not enamored of the scheme and reluctantly agreed to go along only if the goods being transported were not for military purposes. They also asked for a tripartite (British-

Chinese-Tibetan) agreement that would have permitted Tibet to bolster its claim that it represented an independent nation state. China, of course, would no more agree to Tibet's conditions than Tibet would to China's, resulting in a stalemate. But India was persistent in working for a compromise. China agreed to place "agents" along the road, while Tibet agreed to a broad definition of goods "not destined for military use."[4]

While secret negotiations were being carried out to unravel the diplomatic tangles, the American OSS (Office of Strategic Services, the forerunner of the Central Intelligence Agency [CIA]), assigned Captain Ilia Tolstoy (the Russian novelist's grandson) and First Lieutenant Brooke Dolan to undertake a mission to Tibet. They were instructed to travel by land from India, through Tibet, to China proper—presumably to determine the feasibility of an overland alternative to the Burma Road. The OSS arranged the journey entirely through British officials in India without consulting China—even London was uninformed.[5]

Tolstoy and Dolan reached Lhasa on 12 December. They carried with them 100 kg. (220 lb.) of equipment, including "vital instruments." They left Lhasa on 19 March 1943, after delivering several gifts from President Franklin D. Roosevelt to the Dalai Lama. Much of their time in Tibet was spent collecting information. They reported on weather conditions, possible sites for airfields, the price fluctuations of the chief commodities in the Lhasa bazaar, Japanese spies (they could not find any and were told the last Japanese monks had left in 1940, although United States officials reported that at least eight were in Tibet as late as 1943),[6] the state of the Tibetan army, the state of the GMD representatives in Lhasa, and a host of other subjects that had nothing to do with an alternative to the Burma Road. Indeed, the British resident in Lhasa complained that "Tolstoy betrayed no interest, or very little, in transport."[7]

The report is notable for the absence of any mention of a possible supply route—the trip's intended purpose. In addition, Tolstoy and Dolan spent one month with British officials in Gyantse and three months (an exceptional length of time) conferring with British officials in Lhasa and with members of the Lhasan nobility; yet the report contains not a single reference to any political matter pertaining to the Tibetan government. One major purpose for the residence of British officials in Tibet was the monitoring of the Tibetan internal political situation and, since the British colonial officials had arranged this visit for their closest allies, it is hard to imagine that they did not share at least some political information with them.

Even the British seemed somewhat confused over the actual purpose of the mission and probably more than a little concerned about possible American encroachment into what was then an exclusively British sphere of influence.[8] In any case, after some communication between London and Washington over the issue of Tibet, the United States government felt compelled to ease the minds of British officials, stating their position on Tibet, unequivocally, in a diplomatic note dated May 15, 1943.

For its part, the Government of the United States has borne in mind the fact that the Chinese Government has long claimed suzerainty over Tibet and the Chinese Constitution lists Tibet among areas constituting the territory of the Republic of China. This Government has at no time raised a question regarding either of those claims.

British policy-makers were less sure, caught between their contradictory views that China had suzerainty over Tibet while Tibet was an "autonomous" state. It was best summed up in 1943 in a War Cabinet memo:

> We have promised the Tibetan government to support them in maintaining the practical autonomy of Tibet, which is of importance to the security of India. . . . On the other hand our alliance with China makes it difficult to give effective material support to Tibet . . . at some stage discussion . . . is probably inevitable . . . [since] our recognition of China's suzerainty over Tibet is a handicap, in that the Chinese Government can argue that suzerainty involves some degree of control.[9]

Since the United States was closely allied to Chiang Kai-shek in pursuit of the war against Japan and since Washington had not formulated an official position on the status of Tibet, it remains a mystery why it would risk alienating Chiang with an unnecessary mission. An aerial reconnaissance or discussions with British officials in Lhasa could have shown that a new route was untenable. Moreover, there already was a trade route of sorts from India to Lhasa and another from Lhasa to Kham/Xikang Province which could carry up to three thousand tons of goods each year. In contrast, the United States Army Air Corps were flying three thousand tons of supplies each month over the Hump. Although nothing concrete came of the mission, it was symbolically important to the Tibetans—after all, the Dalai Lama exchanged gifts with the American president.

Yet another curious aspect of the Tolstoy/Dolan mission is that while the pair was in Tibet, negotiations for a supply road were progressing—albeit with considerable wrangling—between Chongqing, New Delhi, and Lhasa. These negotiations, initiated by Frank Ludlow (the British representative in Lhasa at the time), were successfully concluded in May 1943, and then abandoned when it was concluded that the idea was impractical, allowing for only eighteen hundred tons of goods a year. The Tibetans agreed to define the term "military goods" broadly when it came to deciding what could not be transported; American Lend-Lease goods were specifically mentioned. The route was for goods intended solely for civilian use in China proper.[10] This maximum weight of goods was certainly not worth an OSS mission.

The Tibetans decided to take advantage of U.S. interest by asking Tolstoy for three fully equipped, long-range radio transmitters "for use for broadcasting within Tibet." "Wild Bill" Donovan, the Director of the OSS, strongly supported the sending of the radios, believing them to be helpful to the war effort.[11] Donovan pointed out that the radios were readily available and cost a mere U.S.$4,500. In return the radios "would open all Tibet regions 1,200 miles [1,900 km.] east and west for Allied influence and further modernization of territory which [would] be strategically valuable in the future."[12] These words were written only four weeks after Tolstoy and Dolan had left Lhasa and could be the key to understanding the original rationale for the mission. In spite of Donovan's zeal, however, the United States Department of State was more cautious, opposing the sending of radios to Lhasa on the grounds that this gift might prove "politically embarrassing and cause irritation and offense to the Chinese." The State Department recommended instead that the OSS send a more innocuous gift. In the end, however, the OSS won out and the radios reached Lhasa in November 1943.

Tolstoy's involvement did not end with the radios; in 1944 he again advocated that military supplies be dispatched across Tibet. Recognizing that the amount transportable would be insignificant for the Chinese war effort, Donovan argued to the State Department that these supplies "would be of great value to the OSS operations in China." This plan would double the monthly allocations of supplies provided for the OSS on the flights "over the Hump." Moreover, Donovan argued, it should be "evident that the intelligence byproduct of such a route [was] not to be ignored."[13] Donovan reiterated his belief that Tibet could be strategic and important for future United States intelligence. This proposal was also vetoed by the State Department for having political implications that outweighed all other considerations. This time the State Department won the argument.

In 1945, at the end of the war, Tibet found it was no longer considered a strategically located area of major interest to either the OSS or the State Department. In Lhasa, however, concern grew that the GMD—no longer burdened with a war against the Japanese—would turn its attention westward, seeking to regain influence in Lhasa. Given the limited circles in which the members of the Tibetan elite traveled, they no doubt placed inordinate faith in British and American support.[14] The Tibetans dispatched a mission carrying messages of congratulations to the British and the Americans on winning the war against Japan. The delegation never made it past New Delhi because of the reluctance of London and Washington to grant visas. Letters addressed to President Harry S. Truman were presented at the United States Embassy in New Delhi in March 1946. The letters mentioned that the generators sent in 1943 to run the radio transmitters were ineffectual since they could not function in Tibet's rarefied air. The United States army was instructed to procure three diesel generators (the original ones ran on gasoline). In December 1946 these generators were sent from Calcutta to Kalimpong, where they were handed over to the Tibetan representatives.[15]

To American policy-makers the new generators were seen as token gifts—of limited expense and readily available technology—that could easily be shrugged off if the Chinese complained. But to the Tibetans—to whom electricity had only recently been introduced, and then only in Lhasa for a few hours a day—these gifts had symbolic value far surpassing their technological value. They were seen as symbolic of American concern and support for the government of the infant Dalai Lama in Lhasa.

Political changes came quickly in the east of Asia. In China, civil war broke out again after the temporary hiatus created by an alliance, albeit shaky, between the feuding sides during the war against Japan. In India, in Burma, in Vietnam, in Indonesia, and in the Philippines efforts were under way by the indigenous peoples to win independence from the colonial powers. Japan was under U.S. military occupation, and U.S. foreign policy was undergoing a major shift, adjusting to a new world order. As to Tibet, a considerable gap existed between the attitude of American diplomatic officials stationed in India and that of the policy-makers back in Washington.

In January 1947 the Chargé d'Affaires of the United States Embassy in New Delhi, George R. Merrell, sent a lengthy cable to Washington expressing his view that the 1946 Tibetan Goodwill Mission (the one congratulating the United States for having won the war) should be reciprocated by a mission to Lhasa. Good relations are important, he argued, for "Tibet is in a position of inestimable strategic importance both ideologically and geographically." As a result, he continued, it would be in an excellent position to act as a buffer against Soviet influence. Moreover, Merrell believed, there was a real possibility that hostile governments might come to power in India, China, Burma, or Indochina. Faced with the possibility of anarchy in East Asia, Tibet and its highly conservative people could act as "a bulwark against the spread of Communism throughout Asia . . . an island of conservatism in a sea of political turmoil . . . [and, moreover,] in an age of rocket warfare might prove to be the most important territory in all Asia." Anticipating Washington's reply, Merrell concluded by arguing that the benefits from such a gesture of friendship toward Lhasa would easily outweigh any political difficulties it might cause with Chiang Kai-shek.[16]

The State Department was less than enthusiastic about the plan. Acting Secretary of State Dean Acheson replied that the U.S. army's assessment was that Tibet would not be a suitable launching pad for rockets and that a visit at this time would be of no use. However, the United States did want to keep communications with Lhasa open and would be "disposed to regard with favor" trips to Tibet by Foreign Service officers if these trips could be kept "unobtrusive and unofficial." The caution was duly noted in New Delhi, and the United States ambassador there informed Washington that in order to avoid any future conflicts over the issue of Tibetan independence all future correspondence to Lhasa would be addressed to the "Foreign Bureau" rather than the "Foreign Office"—as the Tibetans called it—indicating official U.S. acknowledgement that Lhasa's office was merely a component of the Chinese Foreign Office and did not represent an independent nation.[17] Although this subtlety is little noted in the historical literature, much has been made recently of Washington's communications with the Tibetan "Foreign Office," symbolizing U.S. acceptance of Tibetan independence (see Appendix B).

The Tibetan Trade Mission

In 1947 the Tibetan government decided to send a "Tibetan Trade Mission" to India, Britain, the United States, China, and several other countries.[18]

Tibet indeed had trade difficulties. Traditionally the only significant trade carried on was with the Chinese interior and India. The imports from China were the most crucial since they consisted of an estimated yearly total of ten million tons of tea. Other imports from that area included silk, cotton goods, brocades, and satins—all in insignificant amounts compared to the tea. Exports included wool, yak tails, hides, furs, musk and deer horns. From India, Tibet imported Western-manufactured consumer goods such as soap, matches, buttons and needles, while exporting the same items as those sent to China.

The key for Tibet, apart from the tea, was the export of wool. The wool, coarse and dirty, was shipped through India to the United States for use in manufacturing automobile rugs. Before World War II this trade amounted to about three thousand to four thousand tons per year.[19] Since 1941, however, because of the war, the United States had not purchased any; the wool had been stored in Kalimpong and was beginning to rot. The Tibetans were also having difficulties with officials in India who were allowing the Tibetans to use the port of Calcutta to export their wool but prohibiting the Tibetans from acquiring the hard currency these exports generated. The Indian government received the U.S. dollars and exchanged them for Indian rupees, which were then handed to the Tibetans. To add insult to injury, the Indians charged the Tibetans customs duties on goods imported through the port at Calcutta. Since Tibet is landlocked, and without commercial airports, railroads, or roads, Lhasa was at the mercy of officials who were, by their actions, hardly affirming their stated beliefs that Tibet was an independent state.

Even with these difficulties the "trade" mission was not all it seemed to be. Tsepon W.D. Shakabpa, the leader of the delegation, claimed some two decades later that the purposes of the trip were to obtain aid for their efforts to ease Indian restrictions on Tibetan trade, to expand Tibetan trade—especially with the United States, to purchase some gold bullion to back up the Tibetan currency, and "to demonstrate Tibet's independence and sovereign status."[20] Not everyone agreed.

Arthur J. Hopkinson was the British/Indian Political Officer for Sikkim from 1945 to 1948. As the latest successor to Sir Charles Bell his job included keeping abreast of matters in Tibet, especially those relating to the ruling elite. Hopkinson believed that the sole purpose of the mission was to buy gold and silver, a feat Shakabpa had been attempting to accomplish for over a year—mainly "for the joy of the chase."[21] Hopkinson also believed that the mission was the brainchild of Rimshi Pangdatsang, eldest of the three Pangdatsang brothers of Kham fame and scion of the family, who was the richest trader in Tibet and a member of the delegation. This suspicion was shared by the Indian government—by now the independent one of Prime Minister Jawaharlal Nehru. Officials in New Delhi informed the United States ambassador that, in their opinion, the mission's sole purpose was the enrichment of the delegates and that they were concerned that any gold purchased would find its way back to India from Tibet to be resold at highly inflated and profitable black-market prices.

The delegation (four officials and an interpreter) traveled from India to Nanjing, where they arrived early in 1948 and met with Chiang Kai-shek. From China it went on to the United States, Britain, the European continent, and finally back to India over a year later. The Chinese governmental position on the trip was predictable—the mission was unofficial and purely private, and the Tibetan "passports" the delegates carried were invalid and worthless. The Chinese had no objections to the mission itself and expressed the desire to make it "official" if the Tibetans consented to carrying Chinese passports.[22] Of course, the Chinese could, in fact, neither help nor hinder the delegation as China had no power over Tibet at that time.

The Tibetan view of the mission was put quite succinctly by Shakabpa himself:

> Throughout their entire journey abroad, they carried Tibetan passports and travel documents, which were recognized and accepted by all the countries they visited; thus, they established another precedent supporting the independent status of Tibet.[23]

Recently declassified U.S. government documents reveal that this, in fact, was not the case, and Shakabpa had been so informed. It is, however, conceivable that, given his lack of diplomatic experience, his statement is an expression of what he believed to be true. The group did not need passports to travel to India, as there had been a long-standing agreement that Tibetans could travel south of their border without formalities. However, they traveled to Nanjing on Chinese passports.

As for British officials, they debated the real purpose of the mission but in the end agreed to give the Tibetans visas "as individuals" and not as representatives of an independent country. In January 1948 the British government informed its counterpart in Washington that the Tibetan Trade Mission would be received in England as "a private commercial affair, not in any official capacity"[24]—even though a banquet was given in their honor and they were received by the Prime Minister at 10 Downing Street. Despite the fact that the Tibetans regarded themselves as an official government deputation, traveling on official government-issued passports, they raised no political issues while in Britain and discussed only personal business. Their British visas were to facilitate travel and were not meant to imply recognition of the passports. "Tibet has *some* international status" according to Whitehall but, "we do not necessarily imply that she is fully sovereign" [emphasis in original]. The British government kept the Chinese embassy fully informed the whole time. In Switzerland the situation must have been similar. During the five days the Shakabpa mission was in Geneva, it was accompanied everywhere by a secretary from the Chinese embassy—a condition that could only have been forced on the Tibetans by the Swiss government. None of the newspapers in Switzerland mentioned the visit.[25]

That left the United States to be considered. In spite of Shakabpa's later claims to the contrary, the Department of State was prepared for the disputes the passport issue was bound to stir up. In December 1947, immediately prior to the mission's arrival in New Delhi, the American Embassy there was informed that if the delegation arrived without *Chinese* passports, then visas were to be issued on Form 257—"standard procedure [in] cases where applicant presents *passport of [a] Government [the] United States does not recognize*"[26] (emphasis added). To avoid any misunderstandings, the United States Embassy in Nanjing was instructed to inform the Chinese government, which it did in July 1948, that there should be "no reason whatsoever to believe issuance of visas indicated any change in American policy on [the] question of sovereignty over Tibet."[27] This message was also delivered to the Chinese Ambassador in Washington, Wellington Koo. In light of this policy, the Department of Commerce assured the Department of State that the Tibetans would be treated equally by all arms of the American government. The Department of Commerce was committed to treating the delegation as private businessmen and to dealing with them only on commercial matters. Since Tibetan exports to the United States totaled only $2 million a year, and Tibetan imports from the United States were "almost infinitesimal,"[28] it is hard to justify the delegation on wholly commercial grounds.

The implication of all the diplomatic cable traffic was clearly that Shakabpa had been, on more than one occasion, apprised of the official American position on his group. However, this knowledge did not deter him from writing years later that

> most significant of all is the fact that Tibetan delegates traveled around the world on *Tibetan* passports, which were accepted as legal documents by the United States, the United Kingdom, and other countries.[29] [emphasis in original]

Diplomatically the mission did not fare too well. Not only were the passports not recognized by the major nations visited, but one of the major goals in the United States was not realized. The delegates were very anxious for a personal meeting with President Harry S. Truman, bringing along letters and gifts for him from the Dalai Lama and the Tibetan Cabinet. In Washington, the request for such a meeting hit a snag when the Department of State agreed—on the condition it be conducted with the approval of, and under the auspices of, the Chinese government.

Ambassador Koo had been kept informed of all United States-Tibetan contact throughout the entire mission—probably without the knowledge, and certainly without the consent, of the members of the Tibetan delegation. While Washington was insisting that "the United States government [had] no intention of acting in a manner that would call into question China's *de jure* sovereignty over Tibet," common courtesy forced it to reciprocate the Tibetans' demonstrated kindness to American visitors in years past. After some negotiations, Koo and the State Department worked out a compromise whereby the Chinese government would formally request a meeting with President Truman (the request was sent 31 July 1948) and Koo would accompany the Tibetans to the White House.

Washington officials, pleased with the compromise, informed both the Tibetans and Koo that they wanted the meeting to take place and that, indeed, President Truman himself had expressed an interest in such a meeting under the plan worked out with the Chinese. But the plan fell through when the Tibetans refused to see Truman in Koo's presence. As a consolation, they were permitted to meet Secretary of State George C. Marshall without Koo. At that meeting Shakabpa asked Marshall for help with the Tibetan-Indian trade difficulties and also permission to purchase 1,420 kg. (50,000 oz.) of gold (U.S.$1,750,000). Marshall refused to interfere with India in any way; however, he did agree to allow the gold purchase.

The Department of State, aware that such a transaction might be considered symbolic of a change in United States policy toward Tibetan independence, informed the Department of Treasury that State "does not intend that such a sale would affect the continuation of this Government's recognition of China's *de jure* sovereignty over Tibet."[30] In spite of granting Tibet permission to purchase gold, America's political position did not change. The Secretary of State instructed the United States Ambassador in New Delhi to tell Indian authorities that "the willingness of the United States to sell gold to the Tibetan authorities does not constitute recognition of the Tibetan administration as a sovereign government."[31]

The Indian government released U.S.$250,000 in U.S. currency, allowing the Tibetans to buy U.S.$400,000 worth of gold. After much wrangling, New Delhi agreed to allow the Lhasa government to import goods through Calcutta without duty and to keep foreign exchange earned through exports. Individual entrepreneurs, however, remained under the old restrictions.

The Cold War Heats Up

Until 1949, American policy and attitudes toward Tibet were unequivocal. As far as Washington was concerned Tibet was, in some form or other, a part of China—albeit while enjoying an extraordinary amount of independence from the central Chinese government. This independence, and possible future strategic importance, encouraged Washington to maintain at the very least some loose, friendly ties to Lhasa while simultaneously supporting China's position on Tibet's status. But, by early 1949, the Chinese civil war was going badly for the American-backed GMD armies; an impending communist victory called for a quick reappraisal of United States policy toward the region.

The reassessment of policy apparently began with a lengthy review of American attitudes by Ruth E. Bacon of the Office of Far Eastern Affairs, Department of State. Ms. Bacon argued in 1949 that, with a communist takeover in Tibet, that area would "assume ideological and strategic importance." She further argued that, in the eventuality of a communist victory in China, the United States should no longer consider Tibet under Chinese authority and urged a prior establishment of covert relations by sending United States officials to Lhasa immediately but "inconspicuously" cautioning against "giving rise to speculation that" the United States might "have designs upon Tibet."

Directly after this report was filed, United States Ambassador in New Delhi, Loy Henderson, concurred with Ms. Bacon's analysis, describing the possibility of communist rule in Tibet as "disastrous." Seeing no action in the ensuing weeks, Henderson again urged haste in sending a covert mission to Lhasa and leaving some Americans there for an indefinite period. This was in June. A week later the American Ambassador to China, Leighton Stuart, agreed to the urgency of the matter. Washington was apparently convinced and informed its ambassadors, on 28 July, that it was "considering . . . [a] . . . covert mission." The plan called for the Second Secretary in the Embassy in New Delhi, Jefferson Jones, to travel to Tibet with either his counterpart from the British High Commission or with an American "explorer-scholar" such as Schuyler Cammann. The mission never left the drawing board because, upon some investigation, Henderson discovered that the British attempt at a similar mission the year before had been discouraged by the Indian government. Indian concurrence was considered essential, since India—in the words of Henderson—had a "practical monopoly on Tibet's foreign relations."[32]

Washington policy-makers were confused in their actions toward Tibet. They had historically supported the position that Tibet was a part of China, however anomalous that situation might have been. Nothing had happened to warrant an about-face in U.S. policy. On the other hand, there was a growing fear of communism in the United States; and it was quickly becoming gospel that *anything* was acceptable if it helped to combat that alleged evil. The confusion is best illustrated by two cables issued within three weeks of each other. Both were to Henderson in New Delhi. The 28 July cable, quoted above, acknowledged that Washington was considering a covert mission to Tibet; but only three weeks earlier Henderson had been instructed that

> the Department does not consider that any of the courtesies extended to the Tibetan Trade Mission while in the United States have the effect of altering the *status quo* among China, Tibet, and the United States.[33]

This period—just prior to the communist victory in China in October 1949—was a busy and nervous one for officials in Lhasa. While there was modest support from the British and the Americans, this support was not be translated into material assistance. Never before had Tibet's isolation been so much of a handicap. The Tibetan government, attempting to win more widespread support for its cause, had begun to allow visits to Lhasa by foreigners. As early as 1944 Arch T. Steele, a foreign correspondent for the *Chicago Daily News,* was permitted to visit Tibet for three weeks. If Steele's function was to favorably publicize the notion of an "independent Tibet" then the trip served its purpose.[34]

The most important visit came in autumn 1949 when American journalist, explorer, author, and broadcaster Lowell Thomas and his son managed to get Lhasa's permission to visit through the good offices of Loy Henderson and India' Minister of External Affairs, Sir Girja Sharkar Bajpai. Both men were friends of Thomas, and they interceded on his behalf through none other than Tsepon Shakabpa. As Lowell Jr. was to write a decade later,

> our Tibetan hosts implored us to tell their story to the world. This my father did through his daily taped broadcasts from Tibet. For my part I hope I did not disappoint them with *Out of This World.*[35]

When the Thomases returned to the United States they held an airport news conference calling for American aid against the communists in China, advice on guerrilla warfare for the Tibetans, and the immediate dispatch of an American mission to Lhasa.[36]

With the declaration of the People's Republic of China on 1 October 1949, Tibetan officials panicked, sending out urgent appeals to Britain, the United States, and India for military aid. The British reply, while sympathetic to the aims of the Tibetan ruling elite, was negative; Tibet was seen as too insignificant to risk antagonizing China. The British supported India's policy needs, recognizing that India was most directly affected because of its proximity to Tibet. Britain encouraged India to offer the Tibetans small arms to boost morale, while acknowledging that they would be of little military significance against the vastly superior People's Liberation Army (PLA). They even offered to secretly replace whatever arms India sent. However, London was adamant that this arrangement be kept secret, wanting no public acknowledgement of relations with Tibet.[37] Also in secret, Washington and London conferred frequently and shared all diplomatic communications regarding Tibet.[38]

The Indian government was caught in a dilemma. Prime Minister Jawaharlal Nehru thought it important to maintain Tibet as a buffer state, continuing to exercise some meaningful control as he had been doing since Indian independence in 1947 and as he continued to do in Sikkim and Bhutan. On the other hand, Nehru also wanted a close relationship with the new government in Beijing in keeping with his policy of nonalignment. He decided to pursue both objectives: recognizing Beijing's suzerainty over Tibet, while covertly supplying the Tibetan army with Indian army "advisers" and some limited military supplies. It remains unclear just how Nehru thought he could carry out these contradictory policies. Few Indian politicians were happy with the situation.

Since the Tibetans seem to have been unaware of British covert support for their cause, and since Indian aid was largely symbolic, the Tibetans turned to their last hope—the Americans. On 19 November 1949, American diplomats in New Delhi met with Surkhang (a Tibetan Cabinet official) and with a representative of the powerful Pangdatsang family. Surkhang told the group that America was the "greatest and most powerful country" and Tibet's only hope.[39] American Ambassador Henderson was instructed to tell the Tibetans that the United States was sympathetic to their predicament although it could not publicly demonstrate any concern or involvement. Secret talks between the Americans and the Tibetans continued throughout 1950 and 1951, often with George Patterson acting as the liaison.[40] But no aid was actually sent, according to the available documentation.

The three nations found themselves in a serious diplomatic quandary. Tibet's ambiguous status only contributed to the uncertainty. All three governments recognized that whoever ruled China would wish to control Tibet. They were aware that the slightest evidence of overt support for the Tibetan elite in their advocacy of an independent Tibet could trigger a PLA attack. This eventuality had to be avoided at all costs. On the other hand, Tibet, the United States, and even India—albeit to a lesser extent—were all anticommunist. Their activities worldwide were designed to deny any territorial gains to any communist regime. It should also be kept in mind that in 1950 it was generally accepted that Moscow controlled the communists in Beijing. To allow Moscow to come as far south as the northern boundary of India, after having just "gobbled up" China, would be seen as allowing a dangerous tipping of the balance of power toward the Soviets. But the geographic realities of Tibet made any major military incursion highly impractical. Then, as if all the prophets of doom were correct in their assessment of the Soviet Union's plan to control the world, the Korean War broke out in June 1950.

In the middle of 1949 the Tibetan aristocracy became increasingly worried. In Lhasa, Reginald Fox was asked not only to maintain radio communication with Robert Ford in Qamdo but also to establish a Radio Lhasa to broadcast its views to the world in Tibetan, Chinese, and English.[41] The clandestine transfer of privately owned jewelry and other valuables to Sikkim and India was accelerated. There were even reports circulating in India that several pilots had been approached about the possibility of flying to Lhasa to evacuate the nobility if that became necessary. It was during this period that the Indian Political Officer in Sikkim, Harishwar Dayal, visited Lhasa and arranged for the transfer of small arms as well as the visit of the Thomases and the aborted aid missions to several nations. To add to the confusion, the Chinese were expelled from Lhasa during the summer months.

Washington's equivocation reflected changes in attitude toward the events in China itself. The United States had become exasperated with the Guomindang and the Truman administration had made a decision late in 1949 that the United States would no longer participate in the Chinese civil war. As early as October 1949, a matter of days after the communists announced their new government, Chiang Kai-shek was informed that "the United States Government does not intend to commit any of its armed forces to the defense of the island [Taiwan]."[42] This was followed up with a public statement by Truman on 5 January 1950, in which he said that "the United States Government will not pursue a course which will lead to involvement in the civil conflict in China."[43]

That is not to say that there was unanimity about this policy—indeed, the administration came under intense pressure to support *all* anticommunist forces. In the case of Tibet, the *New York Times* reported in October 1949 that some United States officials were considering recognizing an independent Tibet because of its strategic location. But Truman seemed to hold his ground, for even when U.S.$75 million was allocated for anticommunist activities in the "general area" of China by the Congress under the Defense Assistance Act of 1949, the Truman administration did not officially appropriate it until after the Korean War broke out. According to a recently declassified history of the Joint Chiefs of Staff (JCS), the money was never in fact spent.[44]

There was a drastic change of policy following the outbreak of war in Korea in June 1950. The hostilities were taken as evidence that the worldwide "Soviet Communist conspiracy" was not to be satisfied with China alone. The 1 January 1950 declaration from Beijing that it still had to liberate Tibet, Taiwan, and Hainan Island had to be taken seriously. Previous JCS recommendations for military aid to Taiwan and anticommunist guerrilla forces that had originally been refused were not approved, and an attempt was made to create a worldwide anticommunist resistance that would be linked together in coordinated actions. As a top secret report to the JCS succinctly stated, "any such successful challenge to the myth of Communist invincibility might importantly strengthen the will to resist among the peoples of Western Europe."[45]

The new attitude on the part of Washington policy-makers was not based on any moral commitment to Tibetan "independence." The very notion of an independent Tibet is conspicuously absent from the many documents that are available from this period. Rather, the United States saw the Tibetans as just another partner in an anticommunist crusade designed, at the least, to bring pressure to bear on China and, at the best, topple the communist government.[46]

The United States found itself in a position of leadership vis-à-vis Tibet, partially as a result of British and Indian resolve not to get too deeply involved and partially to fulfill Washington's self-image as the "policeman" to the world (especially when it came to China, which it had "lost" to communism). India was sympathetic to the Tibetan aristocracy, favoring British colonial policies in the area; but Indian sentiments were not strong enough to compel New Delhi into actions that might precipitate a war with China. India officially recognized the communist government in Beijing in December 1949. American intelligence reported that the "Indian Government is attempting [to] dissociate itself from the Tibetan efforts to retain autonomy."[47] Earlier Indian threats that it would withdraw its support of Beijing's efforts to win its seat in the United Nations if PLA soldiers marched into Tibet were forgotten.

London also adopted a "hands off" policy toward Tibet. In June 1950 the British Foreign Office telegraphed the American ambassador in London that India had inherited Britain's interest in the area. Moreover, "any attempt [to] intervene would be impracticable and unwise. United Kingdom [is] not sufficiently interested in area to warrant embroiling itself with China."[48]

By default, the task of aiding the Tibetan elite was left to the United States (although at one point Tsepon Shakabpa did threaten to go to the Soviet Union if aid from the West was not forthcoming, but the Americans quite correctly saw that as nothing but a bluff). In June 1950, sixteen days before the outbreak of the Korean War, the Tibetan delegation, en route to Beijing, met American diplomats in New Delhi and hinted that they might request aid against the communists. On 16 June Secretary of State Dean Acheson cabled Ambassador Henderson that the United States and the United Kingdom were discussing ways to "encourage Tibetan resistance to Commie [sic] control."[49] But the telegram quoted above, in which the British effectively washed their hands of the whole affair, came a week after Acheson's cable to Henderson; in the end the Americans were really on their own.

In July Henderson informed Washington that while the Korean War might have brought about a substantial change in the attitude of the United States toward the region, New Delhi's views had not changed. Nonetheless Henderson asked his superiors for permission to promise military aid to the Tibetan elite and urged Washington to try to change the British position on future involvement. Acheson replied that in his opinion India would not be agreeable to American involvement since India was currently at odds with the United States over both the Korean War and the seating of China at the United Nations. In spite of this, Acheson cabled that the "Department [was] now in [a] position [to] give assurances [to the] Tibetans re U.S. aid to Tibet." The plan called for Henderson to tell the Tibetans that the United States was "ready to assist procurement and financing."

There was a catch, however—a stipulation that India had to agree to the plan first. If India refused to aid the Tibetans, Washington instructed the Tibetans to ask New Delhi for permission to transport aid across India from a third party (the United Sates). Shakabpa, when informed of these plans, asked for clarification on the type of aid to be expected. Were they getting American troops and planes, he wanted to know. No, the Tibetans should expect only "war materials and finance."

Initially these negotiations were kept secret from India but not from Britain. Only at London's urging did the Americans inform New Delhi. In September the Tibetans sent a delegation to New Delhi with instructions to travel on to Beijing to take part in the negotiations. While in New Delhi they discussed military matters, while publicly saying that they were discussing trade matters. The delegation, including Shakabpa, had been biding its time in India because Britain would not allow it transit to Beijing via Hong Kong. However, in October the PLA entered Qamdo and Lhasa sent word to the delegation to hasten on to Beijing to negotiate a peaceful solution with the Chinese officials. The Indians were now, more than ever, opposed to covert assistance for Tibet; and Henderson cabled Washington that it was a moot issue. But Acheson was not fully convinced, for he replied to Henderson the following day, urging the diplomat to continue in his attempts to persuade the Indians.[50]

The Tibetans then turned to the United Nations in a final desperate appeal for aid. The issue was sponsored by El Salvador, the only country willing to put Tibet on the agenda. Washington instructed its representative to urge his Indian counterpart to vote in support of the Tibetans, promising that the United States would follow suit. The crucial issue, as seen from the American perspective, was not necessarily Tibetan independence but, in Acheson's view, to convince the Indians of communism's "true nature," thereby compelling them to disavow their proclaimed neutrality in world affairs.

On 24 November 1950, the UN voted unanimously to postpone the vote on the Tibet question—in effect killing it. India's vote for postponement was crucial. According to their UN representative, Sir Benegal N. Rau, Beijing had showed a softening of its attitude toward Tibet, witnessed by the signing of an agreement (discussed in the next chapter) through negotiations. Britain concurred, and its representative went on to note the "obscurity of [Tibet's] legal situation." Neither the United States nor Britain could afford to openly involve itself in an area of the world in which the stakes seemed low—especially in this post–war period, when the flames of anticolonialism were burning so brightly throughout Asia and Africa.

But Washington was not to be deterred. Henderson was ordered to continue pushing for an Anglo-U.S.-Indian joint effort to aid the Tibetan elite. As late as June 1951, and perhaps later, Fraser Wilkins, the first secretary of the United States embassy in New Delhi, met with prominent Tibetans in India on such issues as the further release of gold by the United States and the continued purchase of Tibetan wool. George Patterson was once again the liaison.[51]

In December 1950 the Dalai Lama fled Lhasa for a Tibetan town just north of the Indian border. A month earlier Washington and New Delhi had discussed sending an American pilot to Lhasa to fly the Dalai Lama out.[52] New Delhi let Washington know that he would be welcomed in exile, although he would not be permitted to live near the Tibetan frontier. New Delhi also informed the United States that it did not expect the Chinese to have much trouble regaining control over Tibet. While diplomatic communications indicated that India was fairly sure on this matter, there are hints that a debate was raging within India's ruling circles. Sometime in 1950 a meeting was held in India and attended by the

Indian Foreign Secretary, the Indian Ambassador to Beijing, B.N. Mullik of the Intelligence Bureau, and the Chief of the Indian Army Staff, General Cariappa. Interestingly, all but Cariappa favored Indian military intervention despite the geographic obstacles. In the end it appears that cooler heads, such as Nehru's, prevailed.

The secret U.S.-Tibet talks lasted to at least 1952 when it appeared that at this point the Department of State handed over the Tibet issue to the Central Intelligence Agency whose files remain classified. The United States used such intermediaries as George Patterson, Heinrich Harrer, Surkhang Rimshi, and especially Tsepon Shakabpa of whom the Americans were wary. American diplomats were sent to Kalimpong on "vacation" with their families while secretly acting as liaisons between the Lhasa government and Washington. At first the United States wanted to spirit the Dalai Lama out of Lhasa. After the Tibetan leader voluntarily fled to Yadong, U.S. policy was to lure him across the Indian frontier. Yet this failed as well for America's Tibetan allies were "unable to counterbalance the tremendous weight of superstition and selfish officialdom, including delegates from monasteries, oracles of incredible influence, and the misguided wish of the Lhasa Government itself to preserve ... the religious integrity of Tibetan life as personified and symbolized by the Dalai Lama." So wrote an American diplomat accusing the Tibetans of putting their own culture above the interests of Washington's worldwide anticommunist crusade.

In their efforts to enlist the Tibetans, Washington frequently appealed for assistance from Britain asking them to intervene with the Tibetans and the Indian government. But Britain was not part of the anticommunist crusade and it looked at the situation with a somewhat less jaundiced eye. It did not like the Tibetan representatives: Pangdatsang "from personal experience," was regarded in Whitehall as "an unscrupulous rogue"; Shakabpa was a "slippery customer" who feared reprisals from the Chinese for his especially brutal treatment of his serfs; Surkhang was "a complete cipher and an opium eater." Whitehall was also dissatisfied with Washington's tactics. They felt the Dalai Lama's denunciation of the Seventeen-Point Agreement would be nothing but a "propaganda stunt" and meaningless to Tibetans. Moreover, London argued that the Dalai Lama's influence was exclusively within the boundaries of Tibet and that his departure would be more harmful than beneficial.

When the Dalai Lama returned voluntarily to Lhasa, Washington continued to pursue him, laying out a plan for him to follow in a secret letter in 1951. The Dalai Lama would have to "disavow" the agreement with Beijing and appeal for aid from the United Nations and the United States. The United States would then publicly support him and arrange for his exile in Thailand, India, Ceylon, or the United States. When he had arranged for resistance to Chinese rule, the United States would be "prepared to send ... light arms through India" and money directly to him. Lastly, arrangements would be made to have Thubten Norbu travel to the United States.[53]

Meanwhile the Tibetan elite pursued their anti-Chinese activities, undoubtedly spurred on by American expressions of support despite an absence of concrete results. One of the Dalai Lama's older brothers, Gyalo Thondup, went off to Taiwan to confer with the GMD. Another older brother, Thubten Norbu, "slipped quietly into Kalimpong" with a letter authorizing him to negotiate on behalf of the Dalai Lama. He began almost immediately to meet secretly with the Americans. In fact a deal appears to have been struck. The Americans agreed to raise the Tibet issue at the UN and provide funds for the struggle against Beijing, on the condition that the Dalai Lama repudiate the recently signed Beijing-Lhasa agreement. The question of military aid would be left to discussions with the Dalai Lama when he arrived in India where he would be expected to first ask India for aid and then, if turned down, ask for permission to approach another nation. Norbu presumably sent the message on and then promptly flew to the United States under the auspices of the American Committee for Free Asia, a CIA-funded anticommunist organization.[54]

Imperialist Threat?

In April of 1949 the American Secretary of State, Dean Acheson, cabled his ambassador in New Delhi that Washington would like to see the "Tibetan military capacity [to] resist quietly strengthened."[55] However, there is nothing to demonstrate any evidence of U.S. military assistance throughout the rest of that year or the early 1950s. Hints of such assistance remain uncorroborated. For example, an article appeared in the Soviet newspaper *Pravda* on 13 May 1950, datelined Prague. A Czech correspondent in Calcutta had reportedly observed U.S. officials arriving in that port city to supervise the unloading of a shipment of arms destined to travel by special train to Darjeeling and then by trail to Lhasa. The correspondent further reported that the plan called for American soldiers to escort the shipment as far as Darjeeling.[56] On the same day that the *Pravda* article appeared, Radio Peking reported an alleged pact between Prime Minister Nehru and Ambassador Henderson, calling for the supplying of U.S. arms to the Tibetans.[57] This radio report was probably based on information provided by the same unnamed Czech correspondent. One other clue comes from an Indian source, claiming that Truman had agreed to supply sufficient military transport for one brigade of troops—presumably Indian—considered the minimum necessary for the defense of Tibet.[58]

Whether the American government had begun to supply the Tibetans this early or not, Washington's attitude toward Tibet was undergoing a dramatic change because of its position on the frontiers of communist "expansion." Henderson's urging of U.S. support for the Tibetan oligarchy began to be heard with more sympathy back home. In the summer of 1950 instructions were given to the Office of Policy Coordination, the bureaucratic arm officially in charge of covert operations, "to initiate psychological warfare and paramilitary operations against the Chinese Communist regime."[59] The purpose—in the words of a National Security Council memo of a year later—was to "foster and support anticommunist elements both outside and within China with a view to developing and expanding resistance in China to the Peiping [Beijing] regime's control, particularly in South China."[60] Or, as succinctly expressed by an American involved in the clandestine Tibetan operation, "the theory was that by creating chaos in China's rear we could blunt Chinese aggression elsewhere."[61]

It was also during this period, and most likely a result of this attitude, that an unusual pamphlet appeared, entitled *Armed Forces Talk No. 348: Tibet—Roof of the World.* It was published by the United States Department of Defense and "intended as a lesson plan for military unit commanders or their representatives to use in conducting troop education and information programs," and, according to Washington sources, was a "part of a continuing program on international awareness."[62] The files on this rather bizarre publication that could answer such questions as why it was written, who wrote it, and what its purposes were, are now lost or destroyed, according to the Defense Department. It seems odd that the United States should have felt the need to educate its soldiers about Tibet when the nearest GI was thousands of miles away. A copy of this pamphlet made its way to Kalimpong and was reproduced in the only Tibetan newspaper at that time, the *Tibet Mirror.* Undoubtedly, a copy also turned up in Beijing.

We are left with the question of when the American government actually began covert operations in Tibet and/or with Tibetans in India. The answer to this remains hidden. One observer has estimated that covert support began as the Korean War was winding down and resources were being freed for other purposes.[63] This contention is supported by testimony given to a Congressional committee in early 1954. The witness was Assistant Secretary of State for Far Eastern Affairs, Walter Robertson, who stated "our hope of solving the problem of the mainland of China was not through attack upon the mainland but rather by actions which would promote disintegration from within."[64]

In recent years we have discovered that this indeed was official U.S. policy. Countless covert operations were planned and executed against the PRC in a vain attempt at "destabilization." These operations included the training, from 1950 to 1953, of one hundred Chinese agents who were then clandestinely returned to China for purposes of sabotage and the recruiting and training of dissident minority peoples and GMD soldiers for clandestine activities along China's southern rim from northeast India, through Burma, and Laos. At one point during these years there were so many American agents posing as Christian missionaries in northeast India's Assam Province that the provincial government felt compelled to expel *all* American missionaries. In another instance the provincial government of Uttar Pradesh publicly complained that U.S. experts who visited sensitive areas purportedly to verify how U.S. aid was being utilized were actually taking photographs and drawing maps. They also complained about the missionaries in their province who possessed radio transmitters. This theme was taken up by the press, with the *Hindustan Standard* asserting that the Indian government had irrefutable evidence of the spy activities of certain missionaries. It is within this context that the nature of American support for the Tibetan aristocracy must be assessed.

Washington's official views and actions were no doubt encouraged by influential individuals who had enlisted in the anticommunist crusades. These were people such as Supreme Court Justice William O. Douglas, who—in spite of his later reputation as an archliberal—was in the early years of the Cold War a "self-appointed, one-man research project on Communism."[65] Douglas happened to be climbing in the Himalayas during the summer of 1951 when the Dalai Lama fled to Yadong. He saw the whole episode as "Soviet Russia, acting through Red China," making moves on "the international chessboard" to conquer the "Buddhist world." Douglas rushed toward Yadong, where he had made arrangements to meet the Dalai Lama,[66] hoping to persuade him to flee to the United States where he could be used as the symbolic head of a worldwide Buddhist, anticommunist crusade. But by the time Douglas arrived on the Tibetan frontier the Dalai Lama had returned to Lhasa.

In late 1950, a series of articles appeared in the *New York Times*. Written by a veteran correspondent, Robert Trumbull, these articles claimed that the Soviets had sent numerous agents into western Tibet where they traveled disguised as monks carrying tools and instruments hidden in hollow statues of the Buddha. Their purpose, according to Trumbull, was to prepare for a drive into India by communist armies and in the meantime survey for mineral wealth. Acheson did his part by telling the paper that he had no reason to doubt the authenticity of these stories; while Lowell Thomas proclaimed on CBS radio that this story was "one of the most important . . . of the year, possibly one of the most important I have put on the air . . . a notable scoop."[67] After thirty years not a hint of corroboration of this charge has surfaced.

Newsweek magazine reported that Trumbull had paid U.S.$1,000 to American and British intelligence for the story. Trumbull claimed the Soviets were in Tibet in April–June 1950. However, a "Top Secret-National Intelligence Survey" prepared by the American government in November of that Year (eleven days before Trumbull's article first appeared) surveyed Soviet capabilities and intentions around the world. In the case of Tibet, which was discussed several times, none of the incidents Trumbull reported were even hinted at. Trumbull informed the author that he was approached by a "British Himalayan enthusiast and Tibetophile" who sold the story to the North American Newspaper Alliance, through Trumbull, for U.S.$2,000. Trumbull went on to say that Indian intelligence officials doubted the story although he remains convinced of his informant's "good faith."[68]

The new government in Beijing was undoubtedly gravely concerned by perceived threats to its southwest flank from outside powers determined to wrest Tibet from China. It has been argued, by political opponents of the government in Beijing, that Chinese communist cries of "imperialist intrigues" were disingenuous—meant simply to justify military operations in Tibet. It is correctly pointed out that there is little or no evidence demonstrating any concerted efforts to prevent the integration of Tibet into the People's Republic of China. While factually this may be the case, it largely misses the point. It fails to place the Tibetan situation into the larger context of a government coming to power only after a protracted civil war in which its opponents were aided by the strongest world power. It also ignores the fact that while the communists were attempting to consolidate their victory, the United States became a sworn enemy committed to the overthrow of the government so recently installed in Beijing. This was no empty rhetoric, for American troops were advancing on the Yalu River border between China and Korea. At the same time the American Seventh Fleet had entered the Taiwan Strait, protecting the Chinese Communist Party's (CCP) major rival. Moreover, the United States committed itself to aiding and abetting counterrevolutionary activities aimed at the Chinese mainland. And furthermore, America's successful efforts to enlist support in this cause—manifested in a worldwide economic blockade of China and the exclusion of Beijing from its seat at the United Nations—could not have done much to allay fears of "imperialist intrigues" among the leadership in Beijing.

There is amply evidence of Beijing's concern. A mere seven weeks after the revolutionary victory, Radio Beijing broadcast a scathing commentary against the American appropriation of U.S.$75 million to be used for anticommunist activities in the "China area" as well as alleged American plans to build military and air bases in Tibet.[69] Radio Taipei ("Voice of Free China") confirmed these fears a few weeks later when it reported that the communist authorities were highly suspicious of all Americans still remaining in China and were attempting to question them.[70] In America, at this time, the McCarthyite movement was just beginning to gain momentum. The forces on the political right were looking for scapegoats, demanding the heads of those responsible for the "loss of China" and calling for the encirclement of China in order to force its government to capitulate.

There is a growing body of evidence showing that, throughout the 1940s, the Chinese Communist Party attempted to maintain friendly and cordial relations with the government of the United States, and that in fact it wished to pursue a policy of what could only be called moderation after it had taken power in Beijing. This policy of moderation lasted right through 1949, as demonstrated by American diplomatic papers;[71] but the response from Washington was continually negative. Future historians of this period may very well lay the blame for the close ties between Beijing and Moscow during these Cold War years on Washington. In any event, there will always be some who refuse to believe that Beijing is capable of moderation. In a remarkably revealing dispatch to the *New York Herald Tribune* in 1949—before Beijing took any actions against Tibet—a correspondent in Tatsienlu (Kanting) reported that he had been told by several communist Chinese officials that Beijing's policy toward Tibet was to bring abut change as slowly as possible, while at the same time respecting Tibetan customs. However, these officials continued, they believed this policy would change if Anglo-American intrigues were perceived as being a major threat to future Chinese rule over Tibet. Zhou Enlai (Chou En-lai) repeated almost the same policy to the Indian Ambassador to the PRC, K.M. Panikkar, in August 1950, when the latter expressed his government's concern abut the situation in the Himalayas.[72]

This produced a vicious circle, with the American "right" calling for the obliteration of communism in Beijing and the communists in Beijing interpreting that as a direct threat to their existence and acting accordingly. The Americans then used these actions as evidence that their dire predictions were coming true and thereby stepping up their anticommunist activities; this in turn bringing a stepped-up response, and so on. Voices of reason were simply drowned out. And so it was that in November 1950 *Xinhua* (New China News Agency) announced,

> Chairman Mao Tse-tung of the Central People's Government and Commander-in-chief Chu Teh of the People's Liberation Army are deeply concerned about the prolonged oppression of the Tibetan people by British and American imperialism and by Chiang Kai-shek's reactionary government and have accordingly ordered their Army to move into Tibet to help the Tibetan people shake off this oppression forever.[73]

Until World War II—while Britain maintained Tibet comfortably under its wing—there was little interest in Tibet in the United States. After 1937 both Chinese and British representatives resided in Lhasa; and both had radio transmitters, the only ones in all Tibet, with which to communicate with the outside world. The Tolstoy/Dolan mission, which, as I have mentioned, conducted intelligence activities, such as surveying for potential airfields, brought the United States into the picture by its collaboration, as the Chinese saw it, with the British.

Soon after Tolstoy and Dolan left Tibet, the American gift of three radio transmitters arrived. Although ostensibly given in secret, they had to pass through Kalimpong on their way to Lhasa; it is highly unlikely that they went unnoticed there. Then came the Tibetan Trade Mission, which was welcomed and treated hospitably even if not as official representatives of an independent sovereign state. There was sufficient public speculation that the mission's major purpose was the acquisition of material aid to be used against the Chinese for Beijing to have believed that the purpose of the mission was not solely to promote trade. Soon after the delegation returned to Lhasa, the Chinese community there was compelled to leave. Beijing certainly saw some connection between the two events; although it is not possible to determine how much Lhasa's feeling of assurance of Anglo-American support for their cause was a factor emboldening them to deport the Han Chinese.

Then, on top of all these activities, Lowell Thomas turned up—"the traveling salesman for American weapons, who functions as a radio commentator"[74]—on what is perceived as a semi-official visit. Thomas, well known for his outspoken, anticommunist views, left Tibet calling it "the most anticommunist country in the world," publicly appealing for American military aid for the oligarchy along with training in guerrilla warfare and the establishment of an American diplomatic mission in Lhasa.[75] He was also offered the opportunity to express his views to President Truman in a personal visit and wrote to the Dalai Lama that the president was sympathetic to his cause. After Thomas, former OSS officer Leonard Clark showed up in Amdo, ostensibly to climb mountains but, according to one scholar, actually to investigate the possibilities for future anticommunist activities in the area.[76]

As Lhasa was becoming a "tourist attraction," the word spread that weapons were being supplied to the Tibetan army for eventual use against the PLA. One British journalist wrote:

> I have recently returned from the Tibetan border where I saw between 500 and 2,000 mule loads laden with boxes of grenades and cartridges daily struggle along precipitous mountain paths that lead over the 14,000 foot pass of Nathu La to Lhasa. All the materials are American disposals.[77]

The last sentence is revealing. We know, from the American diplomatic papers, that the Indians were supplying small arms to the Tibetans at this time. It would be logical to assume that the equipment was American war surplus (supplied to India in the areas where U.S. troops were stationed, such as northeastern India). What remains a mystery is whether the United States played an active role in supplying these materials directly for the purposes of the Tibetans.

But arms were not the only supplies that worried the Chinese—there were also those radio transmitters. At first there were only the ones owned by the British/Indian and Chinese missions in Lhasa. The American OSS then sent three more transmitters. In 1948 the Lhasa government hired two British citizens, Reginald Fox (who, since 1947, had been living in Lhasa, acting as the radio operator for the British mission) and Robert Ford. Their first instructions were to establish a Radio Lhasa. Fox had his own radio equipment, and Ford brought along two more transmitters from India. By 1949–50 there were six radio transmitters in all—none of them owned by the Chinese, who had been expelled from the area and who had had their radio confiscated.[78]

In the earliest maneuvering over Tibet, the CCP found considerable resistance from Lhasa to the Chinese suggestions for negotiations. This reluctance to talk was coupled with actions clearly meant to anger Beijing and heighten suspicions. The Dalai Lama's two oldest brothers were not to be trusted. Gyalo Thondup first fled to Taiwan, where he met with Chiang Kai-shek, then traveled to the United States, returned to Lhasa, and then fled again to India ("he had found it difficult to get used to the new conditions prevailing [in Tibet]".[79] The older brother, Thubten Norbu, fled to the United States, where he came under the wing of the arch anticommunist movement.

As the communist forces approached eastern Tibet, Lhasa's response was twofold. Delegations were sent to other nations to appeal for assistance. Tibet also appealed to the United Nations—the very organization that had declared war on China's Korean frontier, while refusing China membership. India intervened, threatening to end its support for China at the United Nations if military forces were deployed in Tibet, claiming "that the military operations of the Chinese government against Tibet had greatly added to the tensions of the world and to the drift toward general war." China was furious at this "external obstruction," accusing New Delhi of interfering in its internal affairs and of purposely delaying the Lhasa delegation in New Delhi then heading for Beijing to begin negotiations. China also believed that the Tibetan delegation's reluctance to travel to Beijing for negotiations also was the result of outside interference.[80]

A picture emerges of sufficient circumstantial evidence to clearly demonstrate foreign involvement. This involvement could easily be construed as threatening to China's territorial integrity. When these developments are seen in the light of other world events—the Korean War, American military occupation of Japan, assistance to Taiwan, and aid to the French colonial government in Indo-China and the persistent public statements of prominent McCarthyites in the United States—China's reactions became comprehensible. Still, the question remains: how real were these perceived threats?

There is no proof that any of the visitors, except of course Tolstoy and Dolan, were traveling in any official capacity to initiate relations between Lhasa and Washington or Lhasa and London. The Lowell Thomas trip was the most bitterly attacked—probably because of the vast publicity it received and Thomas's personal notoriety and bitter anticommunism. But his son claimed unequivocally that,

> not only had there been no consultation with officials in Washington previous to our journey, but in my father's haste to get off he failed to ask President Truman if he wanted to send a gift or letter to the Dalai Lama. Ours was decidedly *not* a government mission, but we had every intention of openly informing the American people of whatever we could learn about the growing crisis with which Tibet was confronted—and with Tibet, the nations of the free world. (Emphasis in original.)[81]

His is certainly a plausible description, and there are reports that the Lhasan officials were angered to learn that Thomas was not an official emissary.[82] The government documents concerning this event remain classified, and Lowell Thomas Sr. vehemently denied to the author that his trip had any official function.[83]

As to the weapons being supplied by the Indians (Americans?) they were small weapons; and no one in India, Britain, or the United States ever believed they would make a significant difference. In fact, the American diplomatic papers are replete with references to the weapons being used largely to boost morale, since nothing could stop the PLA if they were determined to March into

Tibet. Militarily, then, the weapons were not a threat; but they were certainly a provocation, adding to Tibetan hopes for resistance against the Chinese.

As the weapons were "paper tigers," so were the radios that had begun to multiply. While it may have been disconcerting to find a British citizen (Robert Ford) in Qamdo relaying news of Chinese troop movements back to Lhasa, and perhaps to the Indian mission as well, a single individual could not have been that significant. There were only three foreigners in Lhasa's employ in 1950 and only two other foreigners in the vicinity. If indeed there were more, Beijing has not produced any evidence to prove that allegation.

The travels of the Dalai Lama's brothers can be seen in the same fashion. They did not produce any substantive results—at least as far as we are able to discern to date—but acted rather as another irritant and symbol of possible provocation against Beijing. They were talking to China's two greatest enemies—the United States and Taiwan—and no doubt relaying their findings back to Lhasa. Although China was aware of the brothers' travels to Taiwan,[84] nothing concrete seems to have come of the traveling, at least in the early years of the 1950s.

The desperate appeals to other nations by the Lhasan oligarchy were a last-ditch effort to protect their positions in society—to maintain the status quo. The appeal to the United Nations, where the matter never came to a vote, the attempt to send delegations to other countries, doomed to failure from the beginning and the crude attempt by India to intervene between Lhasa and Beijing, all added up to more provocation in the eyes of the Chinese government. Again, little of any concrete value came of these efforts. Immediately after the signing of an agreement between the Dalai Lama and Beijing, India recognized Tibet as a part of China. Overt diplomatic activity ceased between Indian and Tibetan officials.

While individually these actions did not appear to have any substance—borne out historically—coming together as they did in the midst of other serious world problems, the total sum of the events was understandably perceived as a serious attempt by the United States (and secondarily by Britain) to "destabilize" (the CIA's euphemism for overthrow) the government in China.[85] China saw itself threatened in Tibet and reacted accordingly. If there is any surprise it is that Beijing did not act more quickly and with more severity.

6

The 1950s: The Honeymoon

In July 1949 all the Han residents in Lhasa had been expelled from Tibet—partially to counter the possibility of "fifth column" activity. As an additional precaution against the communists, the Lhasan authorities called upon the aid of spiritual forces by instructing the monks to hold public services, install new prayer flags and prayer wheels, and to bring out rarely used amulets thought to possess great power.

Among the elite (there is no way of determining how the average serf or shopkeeper felt) these major efforts combined with ceaseless rumors and discussions created an atmosphere so tense that even natural occurrences, such as an earthquake that struck southeastern Tibet in August, were interpreted as a celestial sign of foreboding. As a result, one resident recalls that "the people were beside themselves with terror."[1]

On the Han side there was never any doubt about the future of Tibet; the only question was one of timing. In September 1949, only weeks before the communists were to achieve their final victory, *Renmin Ribao* published an article by an ethnic Tibetan named Tian Bao, entitled "All Tibetans Ready to Welcome Victorious Liberation."[2] Propaganda aside, the communists were acting on their promises when, on 24 November 1950, they announced the establishment of the East Tibetan Autonomous Region headed by Tian Bao and encompassing a population of 70,000 (80 percent Tibetan, 20 percent Han and Yi).[3]

In retrospect it appears that initially the new Chinese government had not planned to march their soldiers into Tibet, although, given their military superiority, this was certainly possible. Beijing had devised another plan, identifying ethnic Tibetans who agreed with their communist ideology and through these individuals finding other Tibetans willing to compromise with Beijing and work alongside its cadres. In January 1950 the Chinese press gave much space to meetings between these "democratic personages" and PLA commander Zhu De (Chu Teh).[4] Beijing sent another high incarnated lama, "Living Buddha" Ge-da, to Lhasa to try personal intervention. He got as far west as Qamdo, where, while awaiting permission to travel on to Lhasa, he was murdered in August 1950.

The death of Ge-da, a lama who had been acting as intermediary, apparently hardened Beijing's attitude—undoubtedly already soured over Lhasa's lack of response to earlier appeals for peaceful negotiations. Beijing demanded that Lhasa's official representatives arrive in the Chinese capital by 5 September; and when they did not, the PLA was ordered to attack. The order went out on 7 October, and the army reached Qamdo four days later. Robert Ford, whose position in Qamdo afforded him the unique opportunity to witness these events, frantically radioed Lhasa of the approaching soldiers; but the response was slow in coming for the Lhasan nobility were, at the time, busily engaged in yet another round of endless partying.[5] The Tibetan government forces were also unable to rely on aid from the local Tibetan population. The Khampas were anti-Lhasa and consequently helped the Chinese forces obtain transport and worked as guides and interpreters.[6] In a few days the fighting in Qamdo was over. The number of casualties totalled 180 Tibetans killed or wounded, 898 Tibetans taken prisoner, and 4,317 Tibetans having surrendered. Among those surrendering was Ngabo Ngawang Jigme, an aristocrat and a member of the Tibetan Cabinet who, just days before, had arrived in Qamdo to take up the position of governor of East Tibet.

Throughout this time Lhasa was determined to pursue its own course, not relying solely on the supernatural. Lhasa had not responded to Beijing's entreaties, using various strategies to avoid having to sit down with Chinese officials. In the closing days of 1949, Tibet tried to send a delegation to Nepal, India, the United States, and Britain to appeal for aid against the Chinese. Beijing publicly protested. The nations involved responded by refusing to receive the Tibetans, who, in the end, never left Lhasa. In February 1950, having exhausted their options, the Tibetan leadership authorized Tsepon Shakabpa and Tsecha Thubten Gyalo to travel through India to Beijing via Hong Kong.

This plan, too, went awry as the British equivocated about issuing Hong Kong visas. When the new Chinese ambassador arrived in New Delhi the Tibetan pair held a series of talks with him. They disagreed on two crucial aspects: Beijing's position that Tibet should acknowledge itself to be a part of the PRC and Tibet's acquiescence to China's taking control of Tibet's external and defense policies. Officials in Lhasa, after discussing these issues, cabled Shakabpa to refuse. According to Shakabpa, before he could reply to the Chinese diplomats the PLA attacked Qamdo.

Shakabpa felt he was left with only one recourse—to appeal to the United Nations. There, only El Salvador (the "pocket satellite" of the United States, as the communist press referred to it) was willing to raise the issue on behalf of the

Tibetans, and the issue was dropped without a vote being taken. The British representative called Tibet's status ambiguous, the Americans said it was largely an Indian concern, the Soviet Union condemned UN intervention in a Chinese internal matter, while the Indians voiced their hopes for a peaceful resolution.[7] None of the major countries concerned was willing to openly discuss the issue.

Beijing's perception of threat from its bitterest foes—having Tibet discussed at the UN, the outbreak of the Korean War, and the subsequent shift in American policy toward China—spurred it to action. On November 8, 1950, the Chinese Southwest Military Administrative Committee and Military Command proceeded to "order the People's Liberation Army to enter Tibet for the purpose of assisting the Tibetan people to free themselves from aggression forever."[8]

In Lhasa, confusion continued to prevail although the situation was to change quickly. After the news of the PLA victories in Qamdo all the notable oracles were called together and asked for advice. After performing the requisite rituals, they agreed among themselves that the Dalai Lama should be officially enthroned—even though he was only sixteen years old, two years short of his majority. This was hastily done. At just about this time the Dalai Lama's brother, Thubten Norbu, arrived in Lhasa. Following discussion, the Dalai and his court fled from Lhasa for the town of Yadong, just north of the Indian frontier.[9]

The decision to go to Yadong could not have been an easy one to make. If the ruling elite had decided to elevate the cleric to power at the age of sixteen in order to bolster the people's morale, as they have argued since, then fleeing from Lhasa—an action likely to undermine morale—would be ill-advised. Indeed, the Dalai Lama recalls that he was opposed to the move. So concerned about this contradiction was the leadership that the trip was intended to be a secret. But not only did the Dalai flee, so did hundreds of pack animals loaded with wealth and treasure to be deposited in Sikkim. Moreover, a good part of the Lhasan nobility also fled with their treasures.

In Yadong, a provisional government was established. But even in Yadong the dispute over where the Dalai Lama should live continued. His court was constantly visited by delegations of Tibetans beseeching him to return to Lhasa.[10]

Before his departure from Lhasa, the Dalai Lama sent a message to the PLA in Qamdo indicating that he "sincerely wanted to restore the friendship" between the Tibetans and Chinese. Moreover, he authorized two delegations (one from Qamdo, one from Lhasa via India) to travel to Beijing to finally begin negotiations. The Tibetans arrived in Beijing within days of each other. On 23 May they signed the "Agreement of the Central People's Government and the Local Government of Tibet," or, as it is commonly known, the Seventeen-Point Agreement.

On 14 July 1951, PLA General Zhang Jingwu (Chang Ching-wu) arrived in Yadong and immediately plunged into a round of talks with Tibetan leaders culminating in the decision to have both General Zhang and the Dalai Lama travel north to Lhasa. With the Dalai Lama's return, the bulk of the aristocracy returned as well.

On its face, the Dalai Lama's return may seem odd. According to George Patterson, who claims to have been a participant in these events, the Dalai Lama was "desperate" to leave Tibet for Indian exile. His belongings had already been sent ahead; his family was anxiously awaiting him in Kalimpong, India; and Heinrich Harrer had even drawn up a map of the route to be traveled south.[11]

Major Kaishar Bahadur, Nepal's representative in Lhasa from 1946 to 1949, believed the return resulted from clerical pressure on the lay leadership for selfish, not nationalistic, reasons.

> The monks . . . are so firmly entrenched in a system which perpetuates their power and idleness, that they would go to any lengths to maintain their dominating position in the country and to keep their life of relative affluence. The monastic centers are like college towns with as many as 10,000 monks in one place, whiling away their time, spending the mornings in droning mechanical prayer, supported in parasitic luxury on the meager resources of the country. Many of the monks, if they believed their system would not be disturbed, would put up no effective opposition to Chinese Communist influence. They would be principally concerned in maintaining themselves in power even at the expense of the country.[12]

The Dalai Lama admitted that his advisers were split into two factions—one advocating return to Lhasa and cooperation with the Han and one advocating exile and struggle for complete Tibetan independence—although he contended the split was not along lay-cleric lines.[13] The former faction won out by arguing that the Seventeen-Point Agreement would ensure a peaceful arrival of the Chinese. Moreover, this group, led by the abbots of the three major monasteries in Tibet, was chiefly concerned with maintaining the status quo, which specifically meant, as Major Bahadur so astutely observed, conserving their power and positions.

During these difficult and confusing times, Thubten Norbu had "slipped quietly into Kalimpong" with, according to some sources, a letter authorizing him to make a deal with a foreign power on behalf of his younger brother. Though Norbu met with Chinese diplomats in Calcutta, he negotiated largely with the Americans. He eventually traveled to the United States under the auspices of the CIA, declining Prime Minister Nehru's offer of political asylum. While Norbu has never, to my knowledge, publicly acknowledged any agreements with the Americans, the man who acted as his liaison has. George Patterson admits that a four-point agreement was reached:

> —Washington would sponsor the Dalai Lama and one hundred twenty followers in any country they chose;
> —Washington would agree to raise the Tibet question at the UN;
> —Washington would provide funds for military actions against the Chinese; and
> —Washington would consider providing other military assistance.

But, all of these commitments were predicated on the condition that the Dalai Lama leave Tibet and publicly repudiate the Seventeen-Point Agreement.[14] The American government, therefore, tacitly recognized the agreement as a valid legal document.

During the latter half of 1951, PLA units continued to arrive peacefully in Lhasa and other major Tibetan population centers. The Indian government protested but China admonished New Delhi not to interfere in an internal matter. India could do little else but drop the issue, for it had recognized the communists as the official government of the PRC, and the Dalai Lama voluntarily returned to his capital and publicly sanctioned the Seventeen-Point Agreement.

In Tibet there were threats to the peaceful implementation of the Seventeen-Point Agreement. No less an authority than the Dalai Lama confirms this fear, for he recalls how the Chinese were obsessed with "nonexistent 'imperialists' " and regarded his two older brothers as the chief culprits.[15] In August 1950 Prime Minister Zhou Enlai expressed some of those concerns when he asked the Indian Ambassador to Beijing, K.M. Panikkar, if there was any truth to the rumors concerning Nepali offers of troops to the Tibetan leadership.[16]

The Seventeen-Point Agreement

The Dalai Lama and his followers outside of Tibet have contended, since 1959, that the Seventeen-Point Agreement was of dubious legality. They believe that the delegates were compelled to sign the document, using facsimiles of Tibetan seals manufactured in Beijing (when the Tibetans refused to use the originals). As the Dalai Lama himself wrote,

> this was presented as an ultimatum. Our delegates were not allowed to make any alterations or suggestions. They were insulted and abused and threatened with personal violence and with further military action against the people of Tibet, and they were not allowed to refer to me or my government for further instruction.[17]

Indeed, the Dalai Lama says he first heard of the agreement over Radio Beijing.

In recent years the Chinese government has publicly presented its version of events asserting that the Tibetan delegates went to Beijing voluntarily, argued their case, and agreed to the provisions of the pact only after discussions with their Chinese counterparts and consultations with their government in Yadong. Moreover, the Chinese argument continues, the Dalai Lama voluntarily returned to Lhasa after the signing of the agreement and, of his own volition, sent a cable to Beijing that read, "the local government of Tibet and the Tibetans, lamas, and laymen, unanimously support the agreement."[18]

The policy of the CCP in Tibet was not difficult to discern. It was to work with the Tibetan elite in a "united front." The Chinese made extraordinary efforts to win them over. Tibetan aristocrats were taken on all-expense-paid tours of China and even northern Korea to witness the massive destruction caused by American bombing there. Zhou Enlai concerned himself with homesick Tibetan students in Beijing. The policy was clearly laid out in a remarkable directive from the Central Committee of the CCP. It was a two-fold policy—based on a military presence and economic stability in Tibet.

> We depend solely on two basic policies to win over the masses and put ourselves in an invulnerable position. The first is strict budgeting coupled with production for the army's own needs, and thus the exertion of influence on the masses; this is the key link. . . . We must do our best and take the proper steps to win over the Dalai and the majority of his top echelon and to isolate the handful of bad elements in order to achieve a gradual, bloodless transformation of the Tibetan economic and political system over a number of years; on the other hand we must be prepared for the eventuality of the bad elements leading the Tibetan troops in rebellion and attacking us, so that in this contingency our army could still carry on and hold out in Tibet. . . . The second policy . . . is to establish trade relations with India and with the heartland of our country and to attain a general balance in supplies to and from Tibet so that the standard of living of the Tibetan people will in no way fall because of our army's presence and will improve through our efforts. . . .

> As yet we don't have a material base for fully implementing the Agreement, nor do we have a base for this purpose in terms of support among the masses or in the upper stratum. To force its implementation will do more harm than good. Since they are unwilling to put the Agreement into effect, well then we can leave it for the time being and wait. . . .

> Let them go on with their insensate atrocities against the people, while we on our part concentrate on good deeds—production, trade, roadbuilding, medical services, and united front work (unity with the majority and patient education) so as to win over the masses and bide our time before taking up the question of the full implementation of the Agreement. If they are not in favor of the setting up of primary schools, that can stop too.[19]

The directive clearly stated that the Chinese would not force implementation of the Seventeen-Point Agreement, although the Dalai Lama claims that is exactly what they did. When the first civilian cadres were on their way to Tibet, they were addressed by Deng Xiaoping in Chengdu and told to avoid mention of class struggle and socialism for it would not be understood. They should limit themselves to helping the Tibetans.[20]

The Chinese government understood full well that the Tibetan leadership were not in favor of the agreement, and understood that force would only alienate them further.

The Chinese version is unequivocal.

> The facts are that this agreement was concluded after repeated negotiations and *full consultation between the representatives* of the Central People's Government and the Tibet Local Government lasting from late April to May 1951. After the signing of the agreement, in his October 1951 telegram to Chairman Mao Tse-tung, the Dalai Lama referred to the agreement as one concluded "by the delegates of both parties on a friendly basis." [emphasis added][21]

As usual both sides overstate their case. The delegation was sent to Beijing because the *Kashag* had turned down the opportunity to negotiate in Lhasa, which the Chinese had originally agreed to. The delegation was empowered to discuss everything except Chinese sovereignty over Tibet, and it was instructed to keep in touch with the Tibetan government, which it was able to do through a wireless system established for this purpose. While there was no outright coercion, the Tibetans were fully aware that they were negotiating from an extremely weak position in that they were glaringly overmatched militarily and that there was no hope of serious outside intervention on their behalf.

The delegation in Beijing cabled the *Kashag* that it would be impossible to prevent Chinese troops from entering Lhasa. The *Kashag* replied that, in that case, they were authorized to agree to have the Tibetan army incorporated into the Chinese army and to allow the former to be in charge of defense. The delegation head, Ngabo, believed that now that the *Kashag* had changed its mind on the single item he was not originally authorized to negotiate, he no longer had to consult with them on every point.

The negotiations went on for about a month and there were many disagreements. At times the talks broke down. Nevertheless, it was clear to the Tibetans that Beijing would not allow any significant changes in its original proposals. In addition to the Seventeen-Point agreement, there was an additional Seven-Point Agreement, kept secret until quite recently, which allowed for, among other things, the Dalai Lama to retain his position if he was out of Tibet for a number of years, for the Tibetans to maintain a police force, and for the Chinese military commission to include two members of the *Kashag*.

When the negotiations ended, Ngabo told the Chinese he had the authority to sign but did not have his official seals. The Chinese asked if their duplicates would be acceptable, and the Tibetans agreed to that arrangement.

The *Kashag* was horrified by the agreement when they learned of its provisions. Nevertheless, the Dalai Lama returned to Lhasa and in September the National Assembly met and listened to Ngabo explain his actions and the terms of the agreements. After some deliberation the National Assembly recommended that the Dalai Lama accept the agreement and make a public announcement, in effect officially ratifying the Seventeen-Point Agreement and its secret codicil.[22]

The agreement itself restated Beijing's position that Tibet was a part of China and denounced both "imperialist intrigues" and the GMD oppression of previous decades.[23] The political incorporation of Tibet into China had been accomplished. Further, in line with communist practice of having a parallel CCP structure for every administrative one, the Work Committee of the Chinese Communist Party for the Tibetan Area was established in 1951. Zhang Jingwu was named secretary, with deputies who included General Tan Guansan (T'an Kuan-san), Zhang Guohua (Chang Kuo-hua), and Fang Ming. No ethnic Tibetans held any leadership positions or membership.

With the formal signing of the Seventeen-Point Agreement, Beijing authorized the dispatch of thousands of Han soldiers and civilian cadres to Tibet. The first Han to arrive in Tibet, most of whom walked from Kham, were met along the way by Tibetans expressing cautious suspicion—little or no overt welcome or opposition. The trip was extremely difficult; many suffered from the cold and from the lack of oxygen (because of the altitude). But even those difficulties were dwarfed by the lack of food. The Chinese could carry little food themselves and could obtain little more from the barren lands they passed through. Food had to come by air drop from planes flying out of an airfield near Kantze. A severe shortage of parachutes and the inability of pilots to judge the targets accurately meant that many packages were destroyed on impact or lost in inaccessible ravines or gullies. The results were incredibly low daily rations of only 187.5 grams (6.5 oz.) of food for each individual.[24]

The Seventeen-Point Agreement was to be a major turning point in Tibetan history. Beijing clearly believed Tibet to be a very special case for why else would it insist on a pact of incorporation; no other part of China was subject to such a condition. Moreover, the incorporation of Tibet in 1951 fundamentally altered the Sino-Tibetan relationship for Tibet was now a part of China in a manner it had never been before—total consolidation into the Chinese state.

The Economy

The most immediate problem Lhasa and Beijing had to face was the American boycott of Tibetan wool, resulting from a United States policy forbidding trade with any "communist" nation (which Tibet had become). Beijing's response was to purchase Tibet's entire wool production at three times the market price. This would have been in line with their policy of winning the support of the Tibetan people, benefiting both the serfs responsible for raising the sheep and the nobility who profited from the sale.

While the wool problem was quickly and easily rectified, inflation was quite another matter. This was the result of the influx of a large number of PLA soldiers and civilian Han cadres with money and the money that was dispensed to the peasantry in the form of grants and loans. Steps were taken to combat it. The PLA had established their own farms on unused land causing resentment among the peasants who were not permitted to do the same. Their production was further supplemented by large purchases of grain from Lhasa government storehouses, which, according to a Chinese eyewitness, were quite substantial.

Although Russian sources claimed, at the time, that food prices in Tibet had fallen by about one-third by 1952,[25] Hungarian visitors reported meat prices up 50 percent and salt 800 percent until the central authorities stepped in during 1954–55.[26] This intervention was said to have led to the doubling of food imports in the period 1954–57. The Chinese failed to get inflation under control until the latter part of the decade.

Support or Opposition?

By most accounts there were some Tibetans who were pleased to see the Han in Tibet. Peter Aufschneiter told British diplomats in Kathmandu that ordinary Tibetans liked the Han because they were honest and they distributed land. Among the younger generation of the nobility it was seen as an opportunity to make some positive changes. Many who had been previously studying in British-style schools in India voluntarily transferred to the Central Institute for National Minorities in Beijing.[27]

Among their more outspoken elders, resistance to the Han manifested itself not only in actions such as food hoarding but also in the creation of a group called the "People's Council" (*Mimang Tsongdu*) in early 1952. This group held meetings, put up posters, and propagandized among the populace of Lhasa, in an effort to demonstrate popular displeasure against the presence of the Chinese. On 31 March 1952, they

> took advantage of a religious activity to call a "people's conference" and to send a so-called "people's delegation" to present us [Han cadres] with a petition. On the night of 1st April, they openly mustered more than a thousand Tibet troops, lamas, and ruffians

to march in groups on various PLA and civilian administrative offices, shouting slogans such as "PLA, Get Out of Tibet" and "The System in Tibet Cannot Be Changed." Chinese who were in Lhasa in the early 1950s confirmed that the streets were unsafe for the Han. Civilian cadres could not leave their residences without passes that were constantly checked on the streets by military police. Even then they were restricted to well-traveled routes.

General Zhang Jingwu visited the Dalai Lama in an effort to have the two most prominent leaders of this dissent (Losang Tashi and Lukhangwa) ousted from their positions as co-prime ministers.[28] The Dalai Lama alleged that Zhang used force (but Zhang's wife, some three decades later, while acknowledging that the visit took place, denies that any coercion was used). But the uncompromising and harsh manner in which Chinese officials in Tibet dealt with this matter did not augur well for the future.

To understand the unfolding of events in Tibet it is crucial to ascertain who was making policy in Beijing and how policies were being carried out. Although during the Cultural Revolution Deng Xiaoping was portrayed as the architect of Tibet policy, a highly reliable Chinese source asserts that it was Mao himself who planned and dictated that policy. Throughout the 1950s, according to this source, every decision made in Tibet by Zhang Jingwu had to be personally cleared through Mao in Beijing. Indeed, among the Han in Tibet, Zhang was known as the "representative of Mao's office."

While some of the internal opposition to Beijing's reassertion of rule stemmed from a genuine belief that Tibet was an independent nation state, some resulted from a fear that the privileged lifestyle enjoyed by the upper strata would somehow be diminished. There is no disagreement that radical reform was long overdue. The Dalai Lama himself claimed in later years that in 1949 he unilaterally established a reform committee (*Legchoe Lekhung*). The Dalai claims that the Chinese were opposed to this committee because the reforms were not radical enough. Moreover, he asserts, they didn't want anyone but themselves to get credit for societal improvements. His brother Gyalo Thondup told American diplomats that the reforms were initiated by the Tibetans to "beat [the] commies at [their] own game."[29]

The Dalai Lama strains credibility by omitting mention of the obvious source of opposition to such reforms, regardless of who was instituting them—the ruling oligarchy. The nobility had historically resisted efforts to dilute their extravagant lifestyle. Ironically, at this time, they had the support of the government in Beijing that was insisting on the maintenance of the status quo. Indeed, a former Tibetan official and Indian diplomats in Lhasa agree that while the Dalai Lama was in favor of reform, his chief opposition came from among his own officials.[30] In 1954 the Dalai Lama accepted an invitation to visit Beijing in spite of a widespread fear among his followers that he would not be permitted to return. These fears were somewhat allayed by radio broadcasts he made from Beijing, assuring his people that he was safe and would be returning shortly.

The Dalai Lama stayed in Beijing for several months, where he grew to like Mao Zedong but not Zhou Enlai.[31] He assured Mao that his brothers had no foreign connections (either a deliberate lie or the honest result of a lack of information) and that he was considering the repatriation of his treasures from Sikkim where they had been sent for "safekeeping" in 1950. While in the Chinese capital, the Dalai wrote an extraordinary poem to Mao that he has only recently acknowledged, contending that the composition of poetry was a common practice in Tibetan culture. The unabashed adulation in the poem hardly demonstrates someone unhappy with the Chinese presence in Tibet.

O! Chairman Mao! Your brilliance and deeds are like
those of Brahm and Mahasammata, creators
of the world.

Only from an infinite number of good deeds can such a
leader be born, who is like the sun shining
over the world.

Your writings are precious as pearls, abundant and
powerful as the high tide of the ocean
reaching the edges of the sky.[32]

It is possible that the Tibetan attitude toward China was based on a realistic
assessment of the situation. There was little active resistance during the early
half of the 1950s. The American and British governments had apparently chosen
not to be involved in the area; and India, the main hope for the upper strata
dissidents, had also demonstrated its unwillingness to support an illusory independence in Tibet. In December 1949, New Delhi had officially recognized the
PRC and on 15 September 1952 announced that henceforth any relations with
Lhasa would be conducted solely through Beijing. Furthermore, the Indian diplomatic mission in Lhasa became a consulate general, while the Trade Agencies
(in Gartok, Gyantse, and Yadong) were to come under the jurisdiction of the
Consulate, thereby recognizing that Tibet was a part of the PRC.

On 31 December 1953, the Indian and Chinese governments began a series of
negotiations, culminating on 29 April 1954, in an "Agreement Between the People's
Republic of China and the Republic of India on Trade and Communications Between the Tibet Region of China and India." This was followed in October by a
trade agreement meant to preserve the traditional Indo-Tibetan trade. Indian officials, however, predicted correctly that the integration of Tibet into China and the
construction of roads would eventually encroach on that trade.

The treaties had far-reaching consequences. They put India on record as accepting Beijing's rule over Tibet while limiting Indian influence by the repatriation of Indian troops and the ending of extra-territoriality for Indian nationals in
Tibet. (In August 1955 Nepal and China signed a similar pact.) The initial treaty,
which expired on 2 July 1962, also set the "Five Principles of Peaceful Coexistence" (*Panch Shila,* as they came to be known in India) that became the bench-
mark for foreign relations among the nonaligned and newly emergent nations of
the day. The five principles were:

1. mutual respect of each other's territorial integrity and sovereignty,
2. mutual nonaggression,
3. mutual noninterference in internal matters,
4. relations to be based on equality and mutual benefit, and
5. peaceful coexistence.

Administrative Changes

When the new communist government took over it divided ethnic Tibet into
various administrative units. The Amdo region came directly under Beijing's
rule, where—for all intents and purposes—it had always been. Historically,

Lhasa exerted little secular authority over the disparate and sparsely populated villages, monasteries, and tiny feudal principalities in Amdo. The Kham area was designated as a separate administrative unit run from Qamdo. Here again was an area marked by Lhasan control in parts and complete lack of control in other parts. The Panchen Lama was returned to his traditional seat in Shigatse from which his predecessor had fled some three decades earlier. The final and largest administrative unit was centered in Lhasa and led by the Dalai Lama.

While these divisions conformed to historical realities, the *official* delimitation and Beijing's support effectively created potential rivals to the political power of the Dalai Lama and his administration. Both the Panchen Lama and the Khampas had been politically impotent just before the Han arrival. By re-establishing both groups on a par with Lhasa as *de facto* and *de jure* administrative areas and by assuring that officials were put in to effectively run these areas, the monopoly of power enjoyed by the Lhasan oligarchy was diluted. It remains unclear if China's officials fully comprehended the consequences of their actions, but we can be sure resentment must have resulted among the leadership in Lhasa.

Beijing's long-term goal was to integrate Tibet into the PRC under a Tibet Autonomous Region (TAR)—an area with more local autonomy than the predominantly Han provinces of China but by no means an independent state. But an intermediate stage was necessary to pave the way to integration. This began while the Dalai Lama was still in Beijing with the establishment of the Preparatory Committee for the Autonomous Region of Tibet (PCART) on 9 March 1955.

Originally made up of 51 members (46 Tibetans and 5 Han), it later grew to number 55 (50 Tibetans and 5 Han). Its major tasks were:

1. to gradually assume more and more responsibility for the governance of Tibet,
2. to spur local industrial development and see that it fitted into the central plan,
3. to bring the classes of people closer together and promote class cohesion,
4. to promote education,
5. to guard against excessive zeal in the imposition of reforms, and
6. to protect the freedom of religion and the monasteries.

The Dalai Lama was named chair of the PCART and the Panchen the vice-chair. The composition of the rest of the group (14 representatives from Lhasa, 10 from Shigatse, 10 from Qamdo, 14 prominent lay and clerical leaders, and 5 Han) was aimed at democratic representation of the various factions. This was good in theory, but failed in practice. The PCART regulations clearly stipulated that all substantial decisions *must be* approved by the State Council (China's version of a Cabinet). This left Beijing with effective veto power, sharply curtailing any power the PCART may have had on paper.[33]

The creation of the PCART was seen as sufficiently significant by the Chinese for Vice-Premier and Politburo member Chen Yi to travel from Beijing to Lhasa, accompanied by a party of eight hundred, to participate in inaugural festivities. The festivities were on a grand scale—so grand that officials were later criticized for extravagance. Chen Yi didn't speak, but the Dalai and Panchen did. The speeches, naturally enough, were all laudatory. The Dalai Lama praised the Han in Tibet:

> During the past few years, the PLA units and the workers in Tibet have strictly adhered to the policy of freedom of religion, carefully protected the lamaseries and respected the religious beliefs of the Tibetan people. They have also donated much to the Tibetan monks each year. All this has greatly helped to remove the apprehensions that previously prevailed among the broad masses of Tibetans, particularly among the lamas, as a result of the rumors and instigations made by agents of the imperialists.

But in the midst of all the praise there were discernible hints of impending difficulties. For example, the Dalai Lama noted that, "recently some news from neighboring provinces and municipalities where reforms are being carried out . . . has reached Tibet and aroused suspicions and anxieties among some people here."

Then Zhang Guohua offered reassurance:

> Some people suspect that the present cooperation between the Chinese Communist Party and the upper sections of the people is only an expedient for exploitation and that after the reforms, there will be no further cooperation. This is absolutely a misunderstanding.

When Chen Yi returned to Beijing, his official report cautioned that

> reform must be carried out by the leadership personnel and the people of Tibet, that the Han cadres could only assist and not monopolize things and that the Central Government could not order the compulsory implementation of the reforms.[34]

The Lama's Travels

Early in 1956 the Maharaj Kumar of Sikkim, in his capacity as president of the Mahabodi Society, invited the Dalai and Panchen to travel to India for the Buddha Jayanti, the celebrations marking the 2,500th anniversary of the Buddha's birth. According to the Dalai, the Chinese initially opposed the idea, urging him to send a deputy, but in November, however, they gave their approval.

On 26 November 1956 the Dalai Lama and his retinue arrived in New Delhi. The Panchen Lama, his retinue, and a number of high officials such as Ngabo Ngawang Jigme went with him. In India the Dalai Lama enjoyed a high degree of freedom—taking part in the Buddhist celebrations, making pilgrimages to holy sites, visiting major cities, attending a UNESCO meeting, and spending considerable time with brothers Gyalo Thondup and Thubten Norbu as well as former dissident ministers Tsepon Shakabpa and Lukhangwa. According to the Dalai these four were the core of a group that, in frequent heated discussions, urged him to remain in India to take advantage of this "golden opportunity," as Shakabpa called it.

The efforts of this group of self-exiled Tibetans to prevent the Dalai's return to Tibet appear at first to have been successful. The Dalai informed Nehru that he had no desire to return to his homeland, asking for either political asylum in India or assistance in acquiring similar status in any Buddhist nation.[35]

Nehru, displeased by this turn of events, tried to convince the Tibetan that he would be more useful in Lhasa, working closely with Beijing and sustaining the morale of his people. Nehru arranged for the Dalai to meet with Chinese Premier Zhou Enlai as he passed through New Delhi on one of his frequent trips abroad. Zhou listened intently to the Dalai's complaints and assured him that a transition to communism would not be imposed against the Dalai's will. Apparently Zhou was sufficiently reassuring. The Dalai decided to return to Lhasa—ignoring pleas to the contrary from his small group of advisers—on the condition that changes would be implemented immediately.

On 27 February 1957, Mao Zedong made a speech to the Eleventh Session (Enlarged) of the Supreme State Conference.

> In some areas, both Han chauvinism and local nationality chauvinism still exist to a serious degree and this demands full attention. . . . Democratic reforms have not yet been carried out in Tibet because conditions are not ripe. According to the seventeen-article agreement reached between the Central People's Government and the local government of Tibet, the reform of the system *must* be carried out, but the timing can only be decided when the great majority of the people of Tibet and the local leading political figures consider it opportune, and we should not be impatient. It has now been decided not to proceed with democratic reforms in Tibet during the period of the Second Five Year Plan [1958–1962]. Whether to proceed with them in the period of the Third Year Plan can only be decided in the light of the situation at the time. [emphasis added][36]

The Dalai Lama agreed to return to Lhasa, arriving 1 April 1957. He said that one of the reasons he returned was that while third party aid (GMD/CIA) *may* have been discussed—he claims not to recall exactly, twenty-five years after the fact—there were no absolute guarantees of assistance from other nations.[37]

Along the route home, the Dalai told Han officials he would now be both more critical of the shortcomings of the Chinese regime and more helpful in resolving disputes. He then proceeded to make public speeches telling his people that the Han had come to Tibet to aid them and not to oppress them, and that they should feel free to criticize China's mistakes. He made these speeches voluntarily—free from coercion from either the Indians or the Chinese.

The Chinese were true to their word. By August the *Xizang Ribao* (Tibet

Daily) reported that 91.6 percent of the Han cadres scheduled to be recalled had already left Tibet. In the same month the Communist Party branch in Tibet launched a "Program for Propaganda on the Non-Institution of the Democratic Reforms in the Tibet Region During the Period of the Second Five Year Plan." While these efforts did allay the fears of the Dalai Lama and the majority of the ruling elite, they did not have the desired result of quelling a growing rebellion. According to the Dalai Lama, this was partially because the Chinese cadres were "deaf" to the constructive criticism offered by the Tibetans. The Chinese press over the next two years was full of articles about the approaching storm.

Economic and Social Development

In 1950 Tibet was a primitive land with a feudal social structure and a pre-industrial economy. The Han referred to it as a land of "three great lacks" (fuel, communication, people) and of "three abundances" (poverty, oppression, terror of the supernatural). The first tasks the Chinese set themselves were to survey the land, restructure the local governing organs, and establish a network of transportation and communication facilities.

The administrative changes in the early years were not felt in the areas controlled by the Dalai and Panchen Lamas but rather beyond, on the periphery of what was later to be known as the Tibet Autonomous Region. For the most part, China is divided into provinces, counties (xian), and districts (zhou). Where non-Han ethnic groups make up the majority of the population, the areas were given a special designation—"autonomous." This "autonomy" was interpreted as local autonomy, exercised by the leaders of the non-Han ethnic majority. The first such area—called the East Tibetan Autonomous Region—was established in November 1950 in what was then Xikang Province.

Transportation

The most crucial development in these early years was the construction of the very first roads in Tibet's history. Economically and militarily the roads were to become the greatest harbinger of change. Formidable obstacles had to be overcome and Soviet experts were consulted. The first artery (Yaan, Sichuan to Lhasa) stretched over fourteen mountain passes, for a distance of 2,400 km. (1,500 miles) and took four years and nine months to complete. It was officially opened for traffic on 25 December 1954, the same day as the 2,100 km. (1,300 miles) long Qinghai-Tibet Highway. The third major link was opened in October 1957 from Xinjiang Province through the disputed (with India) Aksai-Chin area, totaling 1,200 km. (750 miles).[38]

Economically the roads succeeded in cutting the price of some key goods from the Chinese interior; the price of tea dropped by two-thirds in two years. The roads allowed one truck to transport, in two days, the same quantity of goods previously carried by sixty yaks in twelve days. The roads, all from the interior of China, also aided Beijing's plans to shift most of Tibet's trade away from its southern neighbors, toward the Chinese interior.[39]

The enormous cost of building these roads and keeping them open under severe climatic conditions and sabotage by dissidents was rarely appreciated outside of China. China admits willingly that the roads were a "military necessity" but blames Tibetan dissidents for preventing further expansion. China's opponents simply argue that the roads are of no economic value whatsoever and are of "no practical use to the Tibetans and their country."[40]

It is true that the roads themselves are insufficient to promote major industrial development. The lack of fuel supplies in Tibet meant that in every convoy of ten trucks, three were needed to carry fuel. From the beginning, it was clear to Chinese planners that only a railroad could bring Tibet firmly into the industrial age. But, while the obstacles to road-building were formidable, those to the construction of a railroad appear to have been insurmountable. A 1976 CIA study optimistically estimated that a railroad was at least a decade away.[41]

In June 1979, Xinhua reported that a railway bound for Tibet, connecting Lhasa to Xining and Lanzhou had been begun in 1974. In five years it reached Golmund in central Qinqhai where it is today still 1,000 km. (625 miles) from Lhasa, as the crow flies.[42]

Other Reforms

While major reforms were not attempted, efforts were made to reduce the use of *ulag* and to strip local Tibetan officials of the power to tax their subjects and to hold their own courts. In spite of the early failures of these efforts the Han introduced new disturbing elements into the Tibetan social system. Telephones and telegraphs arrived in 1952, with banks (branches of the Bank of China). There followed newspapers, radio programs, and the modern printing of books and pamphlets in Han and Tibetan languages. Hospitals and health units were established, medical workers trained, and veterinarian stations built. Airline service was inaugurated in 1956, while a nascent industrial base was created with the opening of Tibet's first coal mine in 1958 and its first blast furnace in 1959.

To the Tibetans these introductions to the twentieth century technology were significant; but to the Han they represented only minor efforts, leaving the most sensitive areas of Tibetan life intact. The Dalai Lama still ruled from the Potala, and the aristocratic elites remained in their official offices. Furthermore, the most crucial and vital aspect of Tibetan life—religion—continued to flourish. Not only were no religious reforms introduced, but the monasteries were actually given additional subsidies by the Chinese government.[43] So unaffected was religion, that in 1956 the British communist journalist Alan Winnington noted on a visit to Lhasa he "never met a Tibetan who cast any doubt on religion."[44] The Chinese government actually allocated U.S.$500,000 to renovate the Buddhist temple in Beijing; additional funds were granted to Tibetan Moslims for a *haj,* a pilgrimage to Mecca, in 1957.

To spread the revolutionary message and Marxist ideology the Chinese established political associations, bringing people of similar backgrounds together for the purposes of political consciousness raising. These groups included the Democratic Youth Federation, the Woman's Patriotic Association (headed by the Dalai Lama's elder sister), the Young Pioneers, the Chinese Buddhist Association, and the like. Moreover, public criticism meetings (*thamzing*) were introduced only to become one of the most hated components of Chinese rule. These meetings— common throughout China—were used to weed out nonconformists, uniting groups against common enemies by publicly identifying them. Formal schools for secular education were established, especially after 1955. Supplies, books, and tuition were, for the most part, provided by the state. By July 1957 there were 78 primary schools, with 6,000 pupils; 1,000 other students were studying in nationalities institutes in other parts of China (the ten nationalities institutes graduated 94,000 students—from all fifty-plus minorities—in the years 1950– 78). These schools were confined to urban areas.

Chinese leaders faced a major contradiction in not wanting to create alienation and resentment by altering Tibetan society, on the one hand, but feeling they had to offer some relief to the masses in order to gain their allegiance, on the other. This difficulty was summed up by an Indian diplomat living in Lhasa: "While most officials live smugly in their ivory towers, leading much the same life of idle dissipation, the common people find the heavy burdens imposed on them insupportable . . . they have derived little comfort from the alliance which the Communists have forged with the ruling aristocracy of Tibet."[45]

Two scholars who examined the changes initiated during the decade of the 1950s summed it up this way:

Of course the building projects and the economic reforms sponsored by the Chinese from 1950 to 1959 did have an appreciable impact on some segments of Tibetan society. Yet, most of the effect was informal and indirect and much of it concerned only the fringe areas of Tibetan life, without penetrating the inner recesses of the communities' traditions. It is symptomatic, for instance, that in all the years no truly basic changes were introduced in the patterns of Tibetan socioeconomic relations. Although many of the more barbaric and objectionable aspects of Tibetan customary law and justice were discouraged and in actual practice abandoned, the main body of Communist China's statutory law was never enforced in Tibet.[46]

Tibetans Outside the TAR

The policy of moderation and gradual reform was reserved exclusively for the inhabitants of the area termed the TAR. Ethnic Tibetan areas (Kham and Amdo) outside the political boundaries of the TAR appear to have been destined for a different fate. While China agreed, in 1956, to cut back on even the most superficial reforms within the TAR, there was a simultaneous decision to introduce "democratic reforms" in the various autonomous *zhou* and *xian* of China. These reforms would bring about basic changes that would alter the socioeconomic structure of the community by ending feudal ownership of land and serfs, carrying out land reform, collectivizing production, and de-emphasizing religious influence.

It is not just coincidental that open rebellion broke out against Beijing's rule precisely where and when these reforms were being introduced. The Chinese readily admitted to the difficulties they were encountering. The Chair of the Committee of Nationalities Affairs told an Indian journalist that a revolt had broken out in Kham in February 1956 but had been quickly suppressed.[47] And, in 1958, an official of the Qinghai CCP Provincial Committee observed that the "great socialist revolution in the pastoral areas has been a very violent class struggle of life and death."[48]

There are currently two interpretations of the motivations behind these revolts. The first, appearing in *Renmin Ribao* in June 1956, blamed "a few feudal lords" for setting nationalities against each other because they felt their own political and economic power threatened.[49] The second view is offered by Dawa Norbu, a highly articulate and thoughtful Tibetan refugee:

> With regard to ethnic Tibet the Chinese policy was based on a rigid legality and lack of realism: treat the ethnic Tibetans living in China . . . as both *de jure* and *de facto* Chinese, since they were not under the jurisdiction of Lhasa . . . but no matter how far away from Lhasa or even how relatively close they were to the Chinese provinces, they behaved and acted like any other Tibetans. . . . [50]

Norbu is criticizing the Chinese treatment of Tibetans outside the political boundaries of the TAR—a treatment that ignored the social, economic, religious, and ethnic similarities of Tibetans on both sides of the arbitrary boundary. To demonstrate the rigidity of the Chinese view, Norbu cites a conversation he had with a refugee from the eastern principality of Derge, split in two at the Drichu River by this political boundary. The western half was ruled by Lhasa and the eastern by Beijing. The refugee related that while the eastern half was subjected to reforms and the imposition of Chinese law, the western part was left untouched. People there could "do anything [they] like: including kill Chinese and get away with that."[51] This represents testimony as to how arbitrary the Han cadres could be; also how far they were willing to go to avoid interference with the Lhasa administration. The two explanations are not mutually exclusive. Norbu is correct in noting that inhabitants on both sides of the boundary remained Tibetans—indistinguishable one from the other in their actions, beliefs and lifestyles. However, the rebellion was by no means a popular uprising of the serfs and herdspeople. It was initiated and led by the chiefs of the clans and wealthy traders[52] who were certainly encouraged if not covertly aided by contacts with some outside forces. In any event, in the words of Dawa Norbu, "let there be no doubt about this. The Tibetan Rebellion was in defense of Tibetan Buddhist values, and the political and sacred institutions founded upon such values."[53]

The problems of the Chinese regime did not begin and end with the mechanical application of reform policy. There are accounts of Han cadres who were dismissed for being critical of these policies. There was, in addition, the open disaffection among Han workers in Tibet who suffered from the harsh working conditions, low pay, and susceptibility to illness.

The most curious policy was toward nomadic life. The CCP official view stated that, "in short, a nomadic life is neither beneficial to the development of animal husbandry, nor to the prosperity of the human population."[54]

A negative opinion of the nomadic existence is common among those raised in a sedentary agricultural society who see nomads as shiftless and difficult to control. This view could have been expressed as easily in Lhasa as in Beijing. The Chinese clearly understood the impossibility of instituting reforms to end nomadic life, in the short term, and lamented the inability of cadres from sedentary areas to fully comprehend the situation in the pastoral areas. Nor was this a new revelation.

Despite this understanding on the part of the Han, the introduction of veterinarian stations, experimental breeding stations, schools for children, fixed areas for economic support (e.g., winter feed areas for animals, banks for loans), and similar innovations led to a marked decrease in the mobility of the nomad population. Further alienation came from the forced confiscation of weapons—a nomad's most prized possession—and the apparently random humiliation of revered clerical figures in a vain effort to diminish their prestige, and hence their power, in the eyes of the general population.

Beijing's willingness to suspend reforms was not solely designed to lure the Dalai Lama back from India. The policy was also a response to the instability plaguing the areas on the TAR's periphery. Difficulties within the TAR persisted as well. These could be roughly classified into two categories: (1) the improper carrying out of policies by local officials and (2) "Great Hanism."

The Chinese were aware of these problems. In 1957 *Xizang Ribao* admitted that only a few of the aristocracy supported communism, "while the majority still harbor varying degrees of doubt and are actually against it . . . [and] the large portion of the masses still lack such enthusiasm [for communism]."[55] Confirmation of this view came from none other than the CCP Central Committee, who understood that

> since neither our lack of a material base nor their [the Tibetan elites] advantage over us in social influence will change for the time being, neither will the unwillingness of the Dalai's clique to carry out the Agreement fully. At present, in appearance we should take the offensive and should censure [the anti-Han activities] . . . but in reality we should be prepared to make concessions and to go over to the offensive in the future (i.e., put the Agreement into force) when conditions are ripe.[56]

The Chinese leadership was also aware that support from the Dalai and Panchen Lamas would only come about under certain conditions. General Zhang Guohua outlined the conditions as a desire of the working people for reforms, the existence of a plan based on "scientific investigation" and an "appropriate number of cadres of Tibetan nationality."[57] The Chinese press had abundant criticisms of Tibet on inflation, the improper implementation of policies, the danger of reforms, and ethnic clashes.

The communist authorities were not blind to the realities they were facing in Tibet; although, unfortunately, this insight was soon forgotten. At the time, however, Beijing's views were close to those of the Dalai Lama himself as he spoke at the inauguration festivities for the PCART.

> Tibet has no other way to travel but the way of Socialism. But Socialism and Tibet are still very different from each other. A gradual reform has to be carried out. . . . This will depend on circumstances and it will be carried out by the leaders of the people of Tibet and will not be imposed on them by force by other people.[58]

Han-Tibetan Relations

Crucial to an understanding of events from 1950 through 1980 is a comprehension of the relationship between the Tibetan and Han peoples. Historically that relationship has been abysmal. The Han have always considered themselves superior: culturally, politically, and militarily. Little or no attempt was made to further understanding on either side. Attitudes of cultural superiority led to policies that only further exacerbated the hostility.

The communists took this situation into account; long before assuming power there was an attempt to accommodate it (see Appendix B). But Tibet in 1950 presented some unique problems that the CCP could not have foreseen. The CCP had been unable to establish a base of any significance there, and they had virtually no contacts among the people within the TAR, only with ethnic Tibetans from the peripheral areas. Further, they lacked trained personnel who understood Tibetan society or spoke the language.

Chinese Communist policy toward the minorities was implemented through the Nationalities Affairs Commission (NAC). The NAC (with twenty-two members, only three of whom were Han) was meant to pursue a policy of uniting with "patriotic bourgeois nationalities' upper strata" in carrying out reforms and economic development. This policy was followed—even in the midst of major political campaigns urging class struggle, antirightist activity, and the Great Leap Forward. These were all political campaigns from which the Tibetans were almost exclusively exempt, probably in an attempt to preserve the fragile "united front" there. Han cadres, at the local levels, went through a "do good things movement" and were urged to "work together, eat together, live together." The ideal cadre, the Chinese press suggested, was one who spent his days helping and his nights entertaining, learning the local language, and propagandizing.[59] In spite of Beijing's difficulties in finding cadres willing to work in such harsh conditions, China's most acerbic critics were forced to admit that during the 1950s the Han soldiers and civilians for the most part acted in an exemplary fashion. Tibetan nobles and former officials currently in exile now admit that, in comparison, the behavior of Tibetan officials left much to be desired.[60]

China tried to prepare its people before they ever got to Tibet. They were taught to respect local customs and etiquette, never to defile temples and holy sites, and to never criticize the Dalai Lama or religious practice. They were told not to bring up communism and class struggle. They arrived carrying whatever provisions they could, and paid for everything they purchased. They paid wages to the Tibetans who worked for them and practiced egalitarianism among themselves to set an example. For those who strayed from these regulations heavy penalties were imposed. Fraternization with Tibetan prostitutes brought especially severe treatment.[61]

When the communists first arrived in Lhasa, only a few of the aristocracy joined them enthusiastically. In Kham, however, the upper classes welcomed them as potential liberators from the strongly disliked Lhasan officials. As Robert Ford saw it in Qamdo:

> There was no sacking of monasteries at this time. On the contrary, the Chinese took great care not to cause offense through ignorance. They soon had the monks thanking the gods for their deliverance. The Chinese had made it clear they had no quarrel with the Tibetan religion.[62]

When the PLA captured Qamdo they released all their Tibetan prisoners with pocket money, safe conduct passes, and a short lecture on the dangers of Anglo-American imperialism.

Individual Han of course continued to harbor feelings of superiority toward Tibetans and believed that they should learn from "the more advanced nationality." (Constant attention in the press to ending Hanism was a sure sign that the problem continued to exist.) There were also a few defections of disgruntled PLA soldiers and civilian cadres, but no evidence that the total number of defections was more than a handful.

As early as October 1951, Zhou Enlai stated that difficulties would increase if Han cadres were not educated against chauvinist attitudes. At the same time he attacked "narrow nationalism," i.e., nationalistic sentiments on the part of the minority peoples.[63] The foremost analysis of nationalities work in the early 1950s described the attitude as follows:

> Only when all national autonomous organs are staffed by cadres of the nationalities and they are assisted in their work to the point that they can assume

responsibility, only then will a close relationship develop between the masses of the nationality and the organs of local self government, the real situation be understood and the success be scored in comprehending the sentiments, emotions and sufferings of the people of the nationalities. Han cadres cannot take the place of nationalities cadres in this kind of work. . . . [Furthermore, the minority cadres] must be encouraged to dare to reflect the actual situation and to risk putting forward unconventional ideas. . . . The alternative is to allow nationalities cadres to acquire from the Han cadres a tendency to become overtimid[sic] and to ignore the natural feelings of people of the nationality in question. This would reduce the potential helpfulness of the nationalities cadres and finally lead to the casting off of the broad masses of the nationalities. . . . It is essential, moreover, to seek out and grasp their views, develop a cohesive force among them and to let them carry things out on their own. This is their right. We must have unlimited faith in the people of the national minorities.[64]

The authorities in Beijing had analyzed the situation correctly. The policies of slowly introducing reforms in Tibet and working through existing administrative structures were most threatened by two factors: "local nationality chauvinism" and "Great Hanism." Economic and social differences could have been more readily resolved if these conflicting attitudes could have been reconciled.

The Chinese leaders also understood, from the very beginning, that "Great Hanism" presented the more troubling stumbling block to improved Han–Tibetan relations. So much so, in fact, that in 1953 the Central Committee of the CCP, alarmed at its prevalence, ordered investigators sensitive to the problem be dispatched. Their visits—the CCP asserted—"should not be those of 'looking at flowers on horseback' " (i.e., superficial). The committee demanded that "newspapers should publish more articles based on specific facts to criticize Han Chauvinism openly and educate the Party members and the people."[65]

These directives apparently were implemented; the Chinese leadership's willingness to postpone reforms in 1956 showed an attempt to rectify the conflict. But the second half of the 1950s was also a time of dramatic shift in policy in Beijing. By 1957 Great Hanism was no longer considered the greatest threat; that was now local nationalism. The change of line eased pressure on the Han cadres, placing greater blame for the difficulties on the shoulders of the Tibetans. This, in turn, no doubt led to a subtle, but perceptible, increase in Great Hanism.

China has never explicitly acknowledged this shift; consequently, searching for an explanation in the Chinese press is fruitless. Anonymous Chinese officials attribute the change to the "antirightist" campaigns in 1957 that followed the Hundred Flowers movement. According to these sources, Mao was, at the time, under some criticism; he, in turn, criticized China's "intellectuals." In the minority areas, the only "intellectuals" were the ethnic upper strata, who now became the targets of this campaign.

Misunderstandings on both sides, based on lack of comprehension of each other's customs, were coupled with a deep-seated mutual distrust. The key to

Han-Tibetan conflict comes from cultural misunderstandings. The average Tibetan could not have helped but be overwhelmed by Chinese political and technological innovations. A Tibetan refugee put it best: "So many things, the likes of which we had never heard before, were said that it left us thoroughly confused."[66]

Misunderstandings abounded. When Radio Beijing began broadcasting in Tibetan in 1949–50 it could not help communication much since only a handful of Tibetans had radios. Moreover, the programs were broadcast at 10:00 P.M. local time, when all Tibetans had long since retired for the night. Another example is the PLA's strict adherence to the orders prohibiting burdening the local populace. Instead, to supplement their diet, many caught fish and killed small game— ignoring Buddhist proscriptions against killing. A fortuitous misunderstanding arose when the PLA first arrived. They were pleased to be met by handclapping Tibetans, as clapping is a gesture of welcome in Han culture; however, in Tibetan culture, the same gesture is used for driving away evil spirits. Census-taking among the nomads in Kham was construed as being a precursor to future mass arrests. Doctors trained in modern medicine had to watch for charges of anti-Buddhism if they tried to rid Tibetans of lice and spoke of killing germs for hygienic purposes. Han residents objected to the Khampa's propensity for expensive clothing, singing, dancing, and promiscuity and held the Lhasan officials responsible. However, Lhasan officials had as little control as the Han over the conduct of the nomadic population. Public criticism of monks were interpreted by the Tibetans as gratuitous ridiculing of their faith. There were unintentional desecrations of holy sites by affixing radio antennae. Individually, these incidents could be shrugged off as minor cultural *faux pas;* but taken together, over a period of time, they led to resentment. Rumors of allegedly heinous crimes committed by the Han became prevalent, as did stone throwing by children and pejorative name calling.

In the final analysis, the Chinese authorities failed to comprehend that *any* change—regardless of how small and seemingly insignificant—could not help but have a profound effect on such a rigid and ossified feudal society. By installing the Panchen Lama at Tashilhunpo Monastery in 1952 the Chinese had rekindled a centuries-old rivalry. By paying wages to Tibetans for building the roads they disrupted the practice of *ulag.* By paying Tibetan children to attend school (Dawa Norbu remembers being paid U.S.$11 to $15 each month in silver coins) they gave the serfs added economic leverage and disrupted age-old work practices. By providing the most modest training for Tibetan cadres they created alternative avenues of social mobility for serfs.

At times the Chinese were forced into difficult decisions. In 1956 or 1957, a landlord beat one of his serfs for failing to provide the required *ulag.* The serf, coincidentally, was a part-time communist cadre. If the incident went unreprimanded it would have encouraged other feudal lords to prevent their serfs from joining forces with the Han. Conversely, to intercede would mean a major change in the *ulag* system. The Chinese decided to intercede, abolishing *ulag* responsibilities for all Tibetan cadres. This encouraged serfs to volunteer more readily for positions as cadres, thereby further disrupting Tibetan society and further alienating its feudal elite.[67]

It was, then, a combination of factors that appears to have doomed Beijing's original plans for Tibet: misunderstandings of the nature of Tibetan society, a lack of consistency in Beijing's political line, persistent Chinese chauvinism, and an inability to respond adequately to growing resentment on the part of the Tibetan populace. While relations were not totally soured by the latter half of the 1950s, they were not totally amicable either. One sure sign that the situation had not irremediably deteriorated was that the Tiber-India/Nepal frontier remained open throughout the decade, as Tibetan, Sikkimese, and Bhutanese traders and aristocracy routinely and readily crossed back and forth.

Yet, the seeds of dissension had been sown. Unfortunately, as problems festered—exacerbated by hostile forces on the outside—an explosion was imminent and perhaps, in hindsight, unavoidable.

The roof of the Jokhang Temple in central Lhasa. One of the most sacred buildings in Tibetan Buddhism. The city of Lhasa was originally built around it.

Young monks at the Jokhang Temple.

The Potala in Lhasa.

PLA soldiers are a common sight in Lhasa. This one walks around the Barkor, an important commercial and religious street which circles the Jokhang.

Elderly pilgrim asking for alms along the Barkor.

Entrepreneurs from all over China bring in manufactured goods for sale on the streets of Lhasa.

As nationalist feelings have come to the fore, more PLA troops have been sent to Tibet. This truck full of soldiers is in Lhasa.

Tibetan children with homemade toys. The child in the center is wearing a version of a Chinese military uniform.

Han Chinese have moved into Tibet, especially Lhasa, and set up small private business ventures. Here is a Chinese restaurant in Lhasa which caters to, among others, foreign tourists.

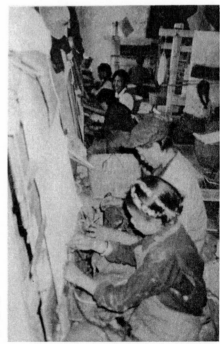

Traditional Tibetan carpet weaving continues to be practiced in Shigatse. This is in a private, Tibetan owned, firm.

The Tashilhunpo Monastery was largely spared the destruction wrought on religious buildings all over Tibet.

Tashilhunpo monastery in Shigatse, the home of the Panchen Lamas.

Chinese-owned shops in Tsedang.

Dentists set up shop on the main street of Tsedang (Zetang).

Tibet is no longer isolated. Michael Jackson poster in a shop window.

Chakpori Hill upon whose summit the only Tibetan medical college once sat before its destruction during the Cultural Revolution. Now there is just a radio tower. At the base of the hill is the Palhalupuk Temple.

Horsemanship at a harvest festival
not far from Lhasa.

A rebuilt monastery.

The devout place prayer flags at the top of mountain passes.

A monk artist displays his mural depicting the two faces of religion in the old Tibetan society, "preaching benevolence on the one hand and oppressing and killing people on the other." [1965] (*Caption and photo by Israel Epstein*)

The traditional and the new intermingled after 1959. This is a pre-harvest festival participated in by Tibetans—mainly ex-serfs and slaves—expressing gratitude to Mao Zedong and the communist party for the abolition of feudal land ownership and servile status. [1965] (*Caption and photo by Israel Epstein*)

7

The 1950s: Revolt

The Chinese leadership have admitted that covert acts of sabotage against them began almost simultaneously with their arrival in Lhasa,[1] although these incidents seem to have been unorganized and spontaneous. The first *organized* protests began with the establishment of the "People's Council" (*Mimang Tsongdu*) by two prominent Tibetan officials: Lukhangwa and Lozang Tashi. Initially, at least, the People's Council confined itself to anti-Han demonstrations, putting up posters, and circulating petitions and leaflets.

At the time, the Chinese media portrayed these activities as isolated and without wide support. The CCP Central Committee, however, knew better.

> The recent demonstration in Lhasa should be viewed not merely as the work of the two Silons [officials] and other bad elements but as a signal to us from the majority of the Dalai clique. Their petition is very tactful because it indicates not a wish for a break with us but only a wish for concessions from us. One of the terms gives the hint that the practice of the Ch'ing [Qing] Dynasty should be restored, in other words, that no Liberation Army units should be stationed in Tibet, but this is not what they are really after. They know full well that this is impossible; their attempt is to trade this term for other terms. The Fourteenth Dalai is criticized in the petition so as to absolve him from any political responsibility for the demonstration.[2]

The majority of the upper strata (70 percent according to Ngabo) was supportive of the dissident faction; although it is impossible to tell what, if any, support came from the people. Reports from sympathizers put the number of supporters anywhere from 35,000 to 300,000.[3] The group had close connections to the Tibetans living in self-imposed exile in Kalimpong, particularly after its leaders were expelled into India. While in India in 1956, the Dalai Lama met with these individuals and overrode their entreaties that he remain in exile.

The area in which the arrival of the Han caused the greatest resentment—and later was the source for the greatest dissension—was eastern Tibet. It remains unclear precisely when open revolt began. There are reports of rebellious activities as early as 1951–1952. These seem to have ended upon the PLA's quick actions taken to alleviate the precipitating problems and in response to appeals for peace from the Dalai Lama. It is possible that these early revolts were caused by GMD remnants, known to have retreated into the area, who steadfastly refused to negotiate with their communist counterparts. These early activities, by all accounts, were unorganized and sporadic. It was not until 1956 that resistance took on a more organized shape; then it was led by, in the words of one former rebel leader, "big traders in Lhasa and the heads of the Kham monasteries."[4]

The rebellion in the east was led by the fierce and feared Khampa nomads, whose exploits were to inspire so many anti-Han exiles and their supporters in later years. The urge to revolt smoldered during the first half of the 1950s. The Dalai Lama appeared to disapprove of revolt when he traveled through Kham in 1954–1955 on his way to and from Beijing. He did speak to rebel leaders and, according to a former Tibetan official, offered them food.[5] According to American intelligence sources the incident that touched off an open, full-scale rebellion came in March–July 1956 and was precipitated by Han interference in religious activities and the confiscation of weapons. Many believe it began at Lithang Monastery when Tibetans objected to the Chinese making an inventory of the monastery's holdings. The subsequent actions led to a twenty-six-day siege of the monastery by the PLA and its eventual destruction followed by a massacre of the monks and their lay supporters. The Tibetans were said to have retaliated by attacking PLA units and consequently suffered "savage" reprisals.[6] The interference in religious activities may very well have been a localized phenomenon confined to those monasteries in open revolt. One lama, who later moved to the United States, remembered traveling extensively through Kham up to 1959 and never once having his religious activities or studies interrupted.[7]

We can be certain that from 1956 there was open, and considerable, rebellion in Kham. The Tibetan rebels used religious festivals as covers for recruiting and meeting; they used the monasteries to store food and arms.[8] But this was all in Kham. Lhasa was a world away. The Dalai Lama's chamberlain had been informed of what was happening at least as early as 1957.[9] We do not know precisely how informed the Dalai himself was. We do know that his advisers were split as to the best way to handle this delicate situation. The group that had the Dalai's ear urged moderation and preservation of the status quo; another group covertly supplied the rebels with arms, ammunition, and food originally collected prior to 1950 in anticipation of a Khampa attack on Lhasa.[10]

In June 1958 the rebels claimed they had brought twenty-three separate groups together to establish the Volunteer Freedom Fighters (VFF) or the National Volunteer Defense Army (NVDA)—led largely by the Chushi Gangdrug (four rivers, six mountains, an ancient name for Kham)—in the Loka region, 25 to 30 km. (16–19 miles) south of Lhasa. While some rebel leaders admitted that there were many poor Tibetans happy to see the Han, they argue that most were opposed to their presence and were willing to bear arms against them. But it is difficult not to wonder how much "volunteering" there really was if the rebel leaders were feudal nobles. One wealthy rebel leader admitted donating to the cause forty-six "employees," along with their weapons and horses, as well as other supplies such as one hundred pack horses and mules.[11]

The very first rebels were indeed the lawless Khampa nomads, who thought nothing of unleashing a "scorched earth" plan that "disrupted communications; they plundered the people and engaged in rape, arson, and murder; they attacked agencies and army units of the Central People's Government."[12] While these rebels probably inspired fear in most Tibetans, they also articulated the grievances of the populace. As they moved farther west, they encountered populations far less discontented, having been subjected to fewer changes. Rebel supporters report that bandits who disguised themselves as rebels engaged in looting and plunder. It was easy to confuse the bandits with rebels, since the rebels also took goods from the people. The rebels, however, issued receipts—much like the communists did during their Long March—redeemable "when Tibet becomes free again."[13]

The creation of the Volunteer Freedom Fighters did not solve the myriad problems faced by the rebels. The Dalai Lama's advisers remained split; the VFF failed to produce any single, or group of, easily discernible spokesperson(s). Both the absence of communications facilities and the vast distances that had to be covered on horseback or foot hampered the rebels' ability to mount military actions against the Chinese. Yet rebel activity spread perceptibly during the final years of the 1950s. Beijing readily admitted that revolts had broken out but characterized them as isolated events, outside the TAR, kept up only through the efforts of the upper strata.

The authorities in Beijing never publicly acknowledged the extent of the discontent felt by the Tibetan people nor how extensive was the area of the TAR through which the rebels roamed. The possibility exists that the authorities were simply unaware. Perhaps the Chinese leadership's fervent desire not to add to growing dissension in Tibet explains Beijing's tolerance. As long as the Dalai Lama continued to work with the Chinese leadership, and as long as the rebel activity remained at a tolerable level, a hands-off policy might have been adopted.

While the extent of the revolt remains hazy so do the figures of alleged casualties for the period 1956–59. Estimated numbers of rebels are also unreliable. Casualty figures for Han alone run as high as 40,000 and for Tibetans up to 65,000. One source claims that 65,000 Tibetans were killed in Kham, alone, in the single year of 1956. Rebels are estimated at anywhere from 50,000 to

200,000. A secret U.S. State Department study called all such figures wild exaggerations, although it declined to make any estimates on its own, arguing convincingly that the truth would never be known. (Parenthetically, the report blamed Gyalo Thondup for the inflated accounts.)[14]

1959[15]

It is evident that the burgeoning rebel forces were bound to clash eventually with the Chinese administrators, whose patience was beginning to wane. By August 1958, the rebel leaders, who had been moving slowly westward toward the holy city, began actively recruiting within Lhasa itself. Throughout the remainder of that year and through the earliest weeks of 1959, Lhasa filled with refugees from the fighting in Kham and, simultaneously, with pilgrims making their annual trek to celebrate the Lunar New Year. The atmosphere in Lhasa grew increasingly tense. The Dalai Lama's advisers continued to disagree over appropriate action. Consequently, the Lhasan administration neither fully supported nor fully opposed the dissidents. Those who advised opposition to the rebels continued to have the support of the Dalai; therefore, when the rebels appealed for support on February 16, 1959, they were told to return to their homes and cooperate with the Han.

The conflagration was ignited by a relatively minor incident. According to the Dalai Lama, on 1 March he was approached by a Chinese emissary inviting him to attend a theatrical performance at a PLA camp near Lhasa. He later wrote that he was preoccupied at the time with studies for a series of forthcoming religious examinations and, as a result, failed to reply. On 7 March, he continued, he was approached once again and pressed to pick a date on which he could attend the performance. March 10 was selected. The Dalai said that he was immediately suspicious of the invitation since the request did not come through the normal channels. Also he had been specifically requested to forego his usual retinue and come to the camp with only a handful of unarmed bodyguards. The visit was to be kept secret. He wrote:

> A rumor spread at once throughout the city that the Chinese had made a plan to kidnap me. During the evening and night of the 9th of March excitement grew, and by the morning most of the people of Lhasa had decided spontaneously to prevent my visit to the Chinese camp at any cost.[16]

The crowd that gathered around the Norbulingka (the Dalai Lama's summer palace, where he happened to be at the time) on the morning of the tenth has been estimated at from ten thousand to thirty thousand and included the entire Tibetan army. Beijing asserted that the rumors were spread by the dissident leaders, hoping the crowd would put "the Dalai Lama under duress."[17] In the meantime, the rebels roamed Lhasa, seizing Tibetan cadres and surrounding

Chinese administrative offices while shouting slogans such as "Drive Away the Han People" and "Independence for Tibet."

The mood of the crowd around the Norbulingka can be discerned from the actions they took against two Tibetan officials who arrived at the palace attempting to defuse the situation. The monastic official was stoned to death, while his lay companion was badly injured.

As the day wore on, the Dalai Lama instructed his chamberlain to call the Chinese camp to tell them he would be unable to attend the theatrical event. Han officials replied that he had made the wisest decision, considering the circumstances. The Dalai Lama then assured the crowds outside that he would never venture into the PLA camp. To alleviate Chinese concerns, he dispatched three ministers to meet with the Chinese general in charge and inform him that the absence of the Dalai from the show was a result of the crowd reaction and did not reflect any lack of desire to attend on his part.

As evening fell, part of the mob dispersed, only to reassemble in other sections of Lhasa for additional meetings and demonstrations. At 6:00 P.M. a meeting was held outside the Norbulingka, attended by about seventy representatives of the Tibetan government, the Dalai Lama's bodyguard; and rebel leaders. It was resolved to renounce the Seventeen-Point Agreement and call for the expulsion of all the Han from Tibet.

That evening was also the occasion of the initiation of a remarkable correspondence between General Tan Guansan (Political Commissar of the Tibet Military District) and the Dalai Lama. Tan wrote first, suggesting that "it may be advisable that . . . [the Dalai] . . . not come for the time being." The Tibetan replied the following day, saying "reactionary, evil elements are carrying out activities endangering me under the pretext of protecting my safety." He expressed his "indescribable shame" at this turn of events. On the same day, the eleventh, Tan replied, telling the Dalai that rebel fortifications and machinegun emplacements were disrupting the normal flow of communication. Further, the Tibetan Cabinet had been asked to intervene with the rebels to head off possible PLA intervention.

The Dalai next wrote on the twelfth, informing Tan that he had instructed the Cabinet to comply with the request for intervention with the rebels. Once again he expressed sorrow at the crisis, stating that the "unlawful actions of the reactionary clique break my heart." Tan's final letter, written on the fifteenth, clearly demonstrated his exasperation over the continuing crisis.

> The traitorous activities of the reactionary clique of the upper strata in Tibet have grown into intolerable proportions. . . . The Central People's Government had long adopted an attitude of magnanimity and enjoined the Local Government of Tibet to deal with them seriously, but the Local Government of Tibet has all along adopted an attitude of feigning compliance while actually helping them with their activities with the result that things have now come to such a

grave impasse. . . . [If no action is taken, the] People's Government will have to act itself to safeguard the solidarity and unification of the motherland.

Tan offered the Tibetan leader the option of moving to the PLA camp to assure his safety, cautioning that "as to what is the best course to follow, this is entirely up to you to decide."

The day before, the Dalai Lama had called some of his ministers together to plead for a peaceful solution based on compromise. After receiving Tan's letter of the fifteenth he replied, the next day, saying:

> I am trying skillfully to make a demarcation line between the progressive people and those opposing the revolution among the government officials. . . . A few days from now, when there are enough forces that I can trust, I shall make my way to the Military Area Command secretly.[18]

The picture of an improving situation painted by the Dalai Lama was inaccurate. The mob refused to disperse or remove the barricades they had erected on the roads around Lhasa. Some of their leaders had moved their center of operations to a nearby village, thereby lessening the influence the Dalai—a virtual prisoner in his palace—may have had on them.

Tan's letter of the fifteenth is alleged to have been delivered along with an additional note from Ngabo, who was staying with the Chinese throughout this time. Beijing has never verified the existence of this particular note, but the Dalai has written that it revealed rumors of rebel plans to kidnap him and urged him to refuse to go along but rather to move into a separate building within the palace grounds along with a few highly trusted advisers. The Dalai was then to let Ngabo know which building he was in so it would not be damaged.

By the sixteenth Lhasa was rife with rumors that the PLA were preparing to shell the Norbulingka and that new Chinese troops were arriving from other parts of the country. On the seventeenth some Tibetan Cabinet ministers sent a letter to Ngabo, requesting his aid in helping to move the Dalai Lama to the PLA camp. Ngabo acknowledged receipt of the letter and promised assistance. Then, suddenly, at 4:00 P.M., the Dalai Lama claims to have heard two mortar shells fired from the direction of the military camp, only to splash harmlessly into a marsh in the palace compound. A state of near panic ensured, since it was assumed—although never verified—that the Chinese, finally having come to the end of their patience, had decided to attack. The Dalai Lama recalled that at this point the hasty decision was made that he would have to flee. By 10:00 P.M. that evening he was gone, dressed as a simple monk. He left so quickly that "all [he] could take was one or two changes of lama robes."[19] By 2:00 A.M. of the twentieth, according to the Dalai Lama, the PLA began to freely shell the Norbulingka. This was fifty-two hours after he had fled, but before, or so he says, the Chinese knew he was gone. "By the end of the first day . . . the Norbulingka was a deserted smoking ruin full of dead."[20] On the way to India, the Tibetan party paused briefly to establish a provisional government in the town of Lhunste

Dzong, continuing on to cross the Indian frontier on 31 March.

This version of events, coming entirely from the Dalai Lama and written fewer than two years after the fact, has become the official, unquestioned account used for two decades by journalists and scholars alike. An examination of the available Chinese—and other—sources, including a new autobiography by the Dalai Lama, confirm some aspects of the story, yet question others.

China concedes that the theatrical performance was set for 10 March, but emphatically denies that the Dalai Lama was coerced in any way to set that date. Beijing has maintained, in fact, that it was the Dalai who set the date and, indeed, had done so *one month earlier*. For years this claim was roundly ridiculed as "communist lies and propaganda" until Dawa Norbu publicly acknowledged that a former Tibetan official had confided in him that the Chinese account was correct. When confronted with this contradiction in 1981 the Dalai Lama admitted that his original story was incorrect, agreeing that he had selected the date several weeks prior to the event. However, he continued to maintain that the invitation was unusual because in the days prior to the event the Chinese had set new stipulations such as the absence of his usual retinue.[21]

China maintains that the populace was forced to gather around the palace under threats of fines and physical punishments. The Chinese further allege that the mysterious mortar shells referred to above were fired by the Khampas and that the Dalai fled, on the evening of the seventeenth, but under duress. The rebels were said to have then openly attacked the PLA at 3:40 A.M. on the twentieth with the Chinese holding off on retaliating until 10:00 A.M. of that day. Within forty-seven hours all was calm again in Lhasa and the shops and businesses again open.

Not surprisingly, the Chinese accounts contradict and ridicule those of the Dalai Lama, and vice versa. The Western and Taiwanese press made much of the alleged damage in Lhasa. The Norbulingka was said to have been "razed," the Potala "badly damaged," Drepung and Sera monasteries "reportedly were reduced to ruins." A reporter from a highly respected Calcutta periodical told his readers,

> my source, who I am reluctant to disbelieve, told me, on the best authority, that Norbulingka with its 200 buildings, its two-mile wide and half-mile broad compound, has been reduced to shambles by heavy Chinese artillery.[22]

Beijing categorically denied firing upon the Norbulingka and told anyone who would listen that the PLA were under *strict* orders not to fire on the Johkang Cathedral or the Potala. The summer palace was said to have suffered some limited damage caused by the rebels, such as the punching of holes in the walls of buildings through which to fire their rifles. Twenty-one years after the fact the Chinese admitted that the Potala "suffered serious damage"but did not specify who caused the damage.[23] As to the Norbulingka, the stories of its destruction were meant primarily to incite public sentiment against the Chinese. British visitors in 1962 confirmed that the palace had suffered little damage and there was no evidence of rebuilding. A Tibetan who left in 1969 asserted that as late as 1964 the Norbulingka remained intact.[24]

Taiwan had a slightly different version of the events—that the PLA fired on the Norbulingka only after the Dalai had fled. This backs up the story told by their arch-enemy, the communists. However, Taiwan went on to claim that the uprising was not limited to Tibet alone, but was an integral part of a China-wide, anticommunist (but not anti-Han) crusade.[25] Anticommunist elements in the United States believed:

> the Tibetans have a kind of sentimental regard for a tradition of fairly decent neighborly relations with China over a great many centuries, and really did not want a total break of relations forever with China. . . . They do want to be totally independent of this godless, overbearing and merciless Red regime.[26]

When it comes down to it, the Chinese version seems the most plausible, however stilted the language.

> These traitors have used their legal status . . . to muster reactionary forces from among the upper strata, collaborated with the external enemy and actually directed some of the most reactionary major serf owners in Sikang and Tibet to organize armed rebel forces in certain regions east, north, and south of the Tsangpo River to oppose the Central People's Government and betray the motherland. Their rebellion was engineered by the imperialists, the Chiang Kai-shek bands and foreign reactionaries. Many of their arms were brought in from abroad. The base of the rebellion to the south of the Tsangpo River received air-dropped supplies from the Chiang Kai-shek bands on a number of occasions, and radio stations were set up there by agents sent by the imperialists [the U.S.] and the Chiang Kai-shek clique to further their intrigues.[27]

The revolt was, in the final analysis, highly localized—confined almost exclusively to Lhasa and the Loka region. One refugee reported that the people of Sakya, an important center only a few days' travel from Lhasa, only learned of the revolt when the PLA arrived there in April.[28] About ten thousand Tibetans were arrested and sent to the Ngchen Hydroelectric Plant "to repair some of the damage they had done." Most were released after eight months and the plant itself fully completed—no doubt earlier than anticipated as a result of the extra, unplanned labor—by April 1960.

As for the flight to India, the Dalai Lama remembers it as being largely uneventful, with some weather difficulties and minor illness near the end. China announced his arrival in India before anyone else, causing acute embarrassment to Prime Minister Nehru's government, which did not publicly acknowledge the Lama's presence in the country until two days after his arrival. Indeed, the Chinese now say that it was Mao who personally ordered the PLA to allow the Dalai Lama to cross the frontier. "If we had arrested him," Mao told the Soviet ambassador in Beijing, "we would have called the population of Tibet into rebellion." As it is, Mao continued, without the Dalai Lama in Tibet, the Tibetans would be less resistent to revolutionary changes.[29] The Dalai eventually established his headquarters in Dharamsala, northwestern India.

Aftermath

China's response to the revolt was sure and swift. From the Chinese perspective the Tibetan aristocracy had betrayed the Seventeen-Point Agreement, repudiating the policy of working for gradual reform through a coalition. On 23 March a form of martial law was declared, establishing Military Control Committees throughout the TAR (with the exception of Shigatse). On 28 March the State Council dissolved the Tibet Local Government, elevating the PCART "during the period of the Dalai Lama's abduction," while the eighteen members of the body who fled to India were officially relieved of their posts and replaced.

On 23 April, *Xinhua* (New China News Agency) reported that in the Loka region rebels had been defeated after ten days of fighting. Unconfirmed reports circulated outside Tibet that in Lhasa some Han were arrested for "unreliability" and that morale among the rest was low. Since low morale was already a problem among the Han cadres, at least some might have taken advantage of the revolt to express their dissatisfaction. Meanwhile, the Tibetans once again appealed to the United Nations and found that the Republics of Eire and Malaysia were willing to sponsor a resolution calling upon China to respect "the fundamental human rights of the Tibet people and . . . [their] distinctive cultural and religious life." The General Assembly passed the resolution by a vote of forty-nine for, nine against, and twenty-six abstentions.[30] During the debate, Nepal's ambassador expressed his government's caution in rushing to judgment.

> In Asia today a call for reverting to the traditional way of life may amount practically to a call for the maintenance of the social status quo when this status quo is no longer desirable and can no longer be maintained. . . . [W]e are not inclined to accept tradition as an end in itself, as a sacred absolute thing which should never be molested.[31]

Yet China was not even permitted a seat at the UN (Taiwan holding the Chinese seat); the resolution was therefore only an exercise in diplomatic futility. The Dalai Lama turned his attention to Washington. On 5 January 1960, he wrote to the U.S. Secretary of State, Christian A. Herter, thanking him for U.S. support at the UN. The Dalai was perhaps hoping for a pledge of further overt assistance, but the reply he received was far from that.

> As you know, while it has been the historical position of the United States to consider Tibet as an autonomous country under the suzerainty of China, the American people have also stood for the principle of self-determination. It is

the belief of the United States Government that this principle should apply to the people of Tibet and that they should have the determining voice in their own political destiny.[32]

Neither "autonomous country" nor "suzerainty" is ever defined, let alone their seeming contradiction. And, what was most disappointing for the Dalai Lama, nothing was said about openly aiding his cause.

Next to Tibet and China, India was the nation most affected by the revolt. Initially, New Delhi closed the frontier with Tibet barring refugees from crossing. The flood of people who followed, however, quickly changed the situation. India accepted the fleeing Tibetans; but on a political level, however, India demonstrated considerable restraint. A spokesperson for the Indian Foreign Ministry told the press:

> The Government of India wants to make it clear that it does not recognize any separate Government of Tibet and there is, therefore, no question of a Tibetan Government under the Dalai Lama functioning in India.[33]

The Dalai Lama himself was warmly welcomed but kept, for the most part, in isolation from individuals not approved by the Indian authorities. This so incensed some of his supporters that they grossly exaggerated his suffering, calling the barbed wire around his compound

> painfully reminiscent of the outer wall of a German concentration camp.
> The most lurid stories of one's school days cannot equal the activity of India's security police to ensure that no one comes near the Dalai Lama.[34]

When the Dalai Lama first arrived in India he made a statement in the Indian town of Tezpur, repudiating the Seventeen-Point Agreement, renouncing Beijing's rule over Tibet, and calling for worldwide recognition of Tibetan independence. A controversy immediately arose. China called the statement "a crude document, lame in reasoning, full of lies and loopholes." The Chinese pointed out that it was contradictory to his 1951 telegram to Mao Zedong in which he praised the agreement. The Chinese argued that the Dalai Lama never once brought up the subject of Tibetan independence—even in his meetings with Zhou Enlai in India where, presumably, he could speak freely. Tibetan leaders who remained in Lhasa questioned the authenticity of the style and language of the statement. They wondered why he used the pronoun "he" rather than "I," indicating a "European or a near-European style,"[35] rather than a Tibetan one. In his analysis of this controversy, British scholar and journalist Neville Maxwell pointed out that the Dalai Lama indicated the exact point of his crossing into India (Khinzemane). This is seen as a curious observation, since Tibetans are usually vague about the frontier. The preciseness—especially during such a traumatic time—indicates, at the very least, some coaching.[36]

The Dalai Lama appeared surprised by the criticism; a few days later he issued another statement emphatically standing behind his previous one, which was, in his words, "issued under my authority and indicated my views and I stand by it."[37] Interestingly enough, he did not actually assert that he had personally written the initial statement.

Two secret CIA documents contend that when the Dalai Lama met Indian officials they had a significant difference of opinion. The Indians urged the Tibetans not to denounce the PRC and to strive for some measure of internal autonomy for Tibet, not outright independence. The intelligence report goes on to state that there was considerable wrangling between the Tibetans and Indian government representatives over the Dalai Lama's statement. The Indian's initial draft used the third person and the Tibetans wanted the first person used. The Indian view appears to have prevailed. Although the Dalai Lama had prepared a statement before his arrival in India, he was compelled to read the Indian statement.[38]

Some Thoughts on the Revolt

More than any other event in modern Tibetan history, the events of 1959 have been marked by hyperbole, as reflected in the two statements below.

> Thus the Lhasa Rebellion became more than a general opposition to Chinese invasion. Simultaneously, as never before in history, a nation stood up to oppose both feudalism and communism, the two extremes of the political spectrum. It was a double revolution: first, the long overdue revolution against aristocratic privilege and the religious tyranny of the great abbots, and also against the equally dismal tyranny of imperialistic Chinese communism; the Hungarian and the French Revolution combined.[39]

> The truth is that the 10th March 1959 was the culmination of the resistance of the Tibetans to an alien rule imposed on them since 1949 [sic]. It has national dimensions in that Tibetans from all over the country had gathered in Lhasa for the annual Monlam (Great Prayer Festival) and also there were many volunteers of the resistance groups who had been waging guerrilla war in eastern Tibet. It was spontaneous in nature and nationalistic in content, sparked by the fact that the Chinese had designs to kidnap His Holiness the Dalai Lama to China.[40]

The claims made in these two statements are easily disproved by the facts. From the very beginning, the Dalai Lama's private and public communication with Han officials remained friendly and supportive. He willingly returned to Lhasa from Yadong in 1951 and later from India in 1956. When he complained of difficulties in 1956 he received an immediate response from Chinese authorities. In return the Dalai expressed his most effusive support for China in speeches and articles as late as January 1959 (published in *Xizang Ribao*).[41] In 1955, after meeting Mao, he was quoted as saying, "from the time I left Lhasa, I had looked forward to our meeting. I was overjoyed to see him [Mao] face to face, and felt he was a dear friend to our people."[42] And, further,

I have heard Chairman Mao talk on different matters and I received instructions from him. I have come to the firm conclusion that the brilliant prospects for the Chinese people as a whole are also the prospects for us Tibetan people; the Path of our entire country is our path and no other.[43]

The Dalai Lama has never repudiated the fact that he was on friendly terms with the Han for almost a decade, but now argues that his conciliatory attitudes were solely meant to avoid an outbreak of violence, playing for time in the hope that moderate solutions could be found. China cannot be blamed for thinking this explanation too convenient and too much the beneficiary of hindsight. Can Chinese officials be blamed for believing the Dalai Lama was forced to leave Tibet against his will, or that the Tezpur statement was not his own? All the evidence supported those points of view. The disbelief with which China's version of events was received in the West only reinforced Chinese xenophobia and distrust of the world's news media.

There was the claim of official support from the Tibet local government for the rebels. The Dalai expressed his antipathy toward them: "I am a steadfast follower of the doctrine of nonviolence. . . . So from the very beginning I was strongly opposed to any resort to arms as a means of regaining our freedom."[44] In 1973 he told an interviewer that the rebel cause was futile, like "jumping off a cliff when you have eyes to see."[45] But at least some high Tibetan officials were active supporters of the rebel cause and not inconceivably they may have misrepresented themselves as acting on behalf of the Dalai. At least publicly, China contends—to this day—that the Dalai Lama had nothing to do with the dissidents.[46] But the fact remains that the rebels were the only Tibetans actively striving for Tibetan independence; and by not openly condemning them, the Dalai Lama implicitly encouraged them. After 1959 he appeared more willing to be seen as publicly supportive, at one point rewarding a major rebel leader with the rank equivalent to general for his rebel activities.

There is also the matter of the decision to leave the Norbulingka and the actual execution of the flight to India. As described above, the Dalai Lama has written that the revolt was a spontaneous outpouring of support from the Tibetan masses in response to the unusual circumstances under which he was invited to the Chinese camp. Furthermore, he alleged that the situation became progressively worse, climaxing with the explosion of two mortar shells near his palace that precipitated a hasty departure. So hasty, in fact, that he fled with only the clothes on his back.

The story has a romantic ring to it. But close scrutiny raises serious doubts. We now know that the Dalai Lama himself picked the date for the theatrical performance, long in advance of the event; and, from former Tibetan officials, that the circle around the Dalai knew full well there was little or no chance of his being kidnapped by the PLA.[47]

On 2 March 1959—only days before the revolt broke out in Lhasa—the Calcutta paper the *Statesman* published a remarkable article by an unnamed author. This author, proving to have exceptional sources and insight, uncannily predicted the possible course of events in Tibet in coming days. He wrote that the Khampas and refugees, alike, in Lhasa would agree that the Chinese soldiers presented little threat to the Tibetans in the holy city. In spite of this, the rebels would begin cutting off all the roads leading into the city in the event that fighting broke out. Moreover, the author surmised, the Dalai Lama would be unwilling to leave Lhasa; in order to convince him to leave, the Khampas would have to create some disturbance.[48]

This report puts the claims of trouble in a more dubious light. One resident of the city recalls rumors that the Norbulingka was reduced to ruins and that the Han were machine-gunning helpless monks—rumors designed to arouse the anger of every Tibetan, encouraging all to join the anti-Han rebellion. The questionable nature of the rumors also raises doubts about the alleged spontaneity of the revolt.

The most likely explanation for the conflicting stories lies in the unique position of the Dalai Lama. He is cut off from his people, and at the mercy of his advisers—his sole source of information. It is possible that the Dalai Lama did not know precisely what was transpiring. "My contact with the world was slight," the Dalai Lama recently recalled, "and most of my information about it came from dismal reports brought to me by my sweepers and various officials."[49] Rather, he was a victim of circumstances—a symbol being used by both the rebels and the Chinese to give legitimacy to their respective actions. Having been brought up to trust his advisers implicitly, he did so then, and still does to this day. He was told that the mortar shells came from the Chinese camp, and he believed he had been told the truth. He was writing to General Tan, informing the Chinese of his support and of his plans to move to their camp. Why would the Chinese have fired shots, thereby precipitating a crisis? On the other hand, the rebels, undoubtedly disturbed by the Dalai Lama–Tan correspondence, needed some grand gesture to get the Dalai to finally break with the Chinese. Logically, the mortars could have come from the rebels. The Dalai Lama may, indeed, have believed the plans for his departure were hastily drawn up. This belief is maintained to the present.

The groups that emerged from this crisis with the most blemished record were the Western and Indian press corps. Their doctrinaire anticommunism led them to glorify the Dalai Lama and life in Tibet, while reacting to every explanation offered by China—even when documents were produced—with scorn and ridicule. The American press led the way, glorifying the Dalai Lama's flight to India by describing the "howling winds that cut like a sword" and the "bitter cold" that he had to face.[50] Their British colleagues were close behind, calling the cloudy weather conditions that prevailed during most of March "sublime mysticism." No less an authority than the prestigious, and usually hardheaded journal, the *Economist,* proclaimed, "the cloud that really helped the Dalai Lama in his remarkable escape was evidently the unity of the Tibetan people in their hatred of Chinese military rule."[51] The Indian press, in particular, seemed enthralled with this "cosmic cloud" theory, regaling their readers with accounts of how the cloud prevented air reconnaissance and how they mysteriously broke only on the very day the Tibetan leader stepped on Indian soil. To his credit, the Dalai Lama rejected such explanations.

While the notion that the Dalai Lama had been abducted was considered unworthy of serious attention, so were the Dalai–Tan letters. Both Nehru and *Time* assured their respective audiences that the letters could not be anything but the cleverest of forgeries. This rush to judgment caused considerable embarrassment when China published photocopies of the letters, half of them in the Dalai's handwriting, whereupon the cleric was obliged to verify their authenticity.

So distorted was the press's collective judgment that stories were even circulated that the revolt was planned in Beijing as an elaborate, Machiavellian scheme to rid Tibet of the Dalai Lama. This theory maintains that the scheme failed when he safely reached exile. The Western press is not alone in its capacity for flights of fancy. The Soviets, in recent years, have echoed the very same theory. The propaganda blitz seemed to work, for it is difficult to find even a trace of support for the Chinese position—even among seeming supporters of China such as left-wing groups in Asia (although the Soviet Union remained a staunch supporter of the Chinese at that time).

There were a few voices of reason, such as the Indian Ambassador to China who attacked the "sensational reports of the American correspondents and the blood-curdling stories raised from Hong Kong by Taipai [*sic*] agents."[52] And there was also David S. Connery, editor-in-chief of the *Time–Life* Bureau in New Delhi. Writing in the *Atlantic* (significantly not in *Time*), Connery described how Kalimpong became deluged with journalists from around the world,[53] who were inundated with phone calls from frantic editors pleading for colorful, descriptive accounts of burning monasteries. So relentless was this pursuit of "information" that one reporter from a major British newspaper was heard to declare in exasperation, "Fiction is what they want. Pure fiction. Well, by God, fiction is what they are going to get."

And fiction *is* what they got. Stories circulated of two thousand to one hundred thousand Tibetans killed. Elaborate descriptions of the villages the Dalai Lama was alleged to have passed through were openly plagiarized from a book on village life in the Indian Northeast Frontier Area (NEFA). The *London Express* reported that the Dalai Lama had arrived at 9:00 P.M., "under a brilliant starlit sky," when in fact he arrived at noon the following day. The *Daily Mail* reported that the Dalai Lama was met by "monks in bright yellow robes," when Tibetan monks' robes are maroon-colored. The *Daily Mail* had also dispatched Noel Barber to the area who, it turns out, chartered a plane to fly over the NEFA areas to search for the Dalai's as yet unseen party. In fact, in order to scoop his fellow journalists, he filed his story *before the flight was even scheduled to leave.* Weather conditions prevented the plane from ever leaving the ground. This was a minor technicality that did not prevent him from filing his story. Neither did it keep his paper from printing it under the heading, "Noel Barber Moves Up to the 'End of the Line' as Dalai Lama Prepares for Next Lap to Freedom."[54] Given this enormous media campaign it is hardly surprising that China appeared the villain.

The Indian Response

The Indian response to the upheaval was tempered by a recognition that they could do little about it. Perhaps they were also chastened by their own covert involvement in getting the Dalai Lama out of Tibet (see chapter 8). The Lhasa government, however, did not lack support among influential Indian officials. From as early as 1947 support existed for the Tibetan oligarchy, not the least of which came from Harishwar Dayal and Aba Pant. They were the Indian Political Officers for Sikkim—a position vital in influencing New Delhi's attitude toward Tibet.

Also at the time a widespread, and sometimes vitriolic, debate ensued in India over New Delhi's best course of action. Only the Communist Party of India supported China. The press campaign described above, and a prevalent notion that China had "expansionist" designs on the subcontinent, combined to the point that emotional reaction overrode reason. Nehru found himself under considerable pressure to act concretely against the PRC—even if that action was purely symbolic.

Nehru, however, did not act—not only because he was unable to change anything, but also because he kept a wider perspective on the issue. Nehru was in the forefront of world leaders committed to uniting newly independent nations and finding peaceful solutions to world problems. Moreover, he was a fervent believer in the noninterference in the internal affairs of other nations. His willingness to sign the 1954 Sino–Indian Agreement on Tibet, for which he also came under heavy political fire, is best seen in the context of the Geneva Conference on Indo-China of that same year and the Bandung Conference of Nonaligned Nations the following year. These larger efforts, Nehru almost certainly knew, would have been badly damaged if he was perceived as being unable to resolve peacefully a small matter on his own frontier.

The Soviet Response

Before the formal break between China and the USSR in August 1960, Moscow's public views echoed Beijing's.[55] By March 1959, however, Beijing–Moscow relations were definitely cooling. There resulted a slight, but discernible, change in news reporting. It began with Soviet accusations of covert aid to the Tibetan rebels from other countries. Mention of Indian complicity was dropped; only Taiwan and the "imperialists" (the Americans) were considered the guilty parties. When a small border clash left nine Indian and one Chinese dead, the Soviet press maintained neutrality despite China's attempts to persuade Moscow to condemn the Indians.

Throughout the period of criticism, Moscow never raised the fundamental issue of Chinese sovereignty over Tibet. Perhaps Russian leaders were mindful of the volatile and communicable nature of "local nationalism"—a condition not unknown in the Soviet Union. Until its demise, the Soviet Union's explanation of events in Tibet was that Tibetans were not rejecting communism, *per se*, but only the Chinese variation of it.[56]

International Commission of Jurists

Barely weeks after the revolt erupted in Lhasa the International Commission of Jurists (ICJ) established a Legal Inquiry Committee (LIC) to conduct a preliminary investigation as to what had happened in Tibet. The findings, published in July 1959,[57] indicated sufficient evidence to warrant a full-scale investigation. The LIC was authorized to proceed, publishing their findings the following year.[58]

Relying heavily on carefully selected Chinese public statements and interviews with certain refugees, especially with the Dalai Lama, the LIC came to several conclusions. Tibet, they contended, had been an independent state for the better part of its history—especially for the period 1912 to 1950. Further, Tibetan officials were perfectly within their legal rights to repudiate the Seventeen-Point Agreement. There was insufficient evidence to demonstrate an attempt at genocide on the part of the Han against the Tibetans; however, there was evidence to show that the Chinese had violated the Tibetans' "right to exist as a religious group . . . [but not] their right to exist as a national, ethnical [sic] or racial group."[59] This was dubbed "cultural genocide."

For over three decades, now, these reports have been the foundation for the argument proffered by those opposed to China's rule in Tibet. The Committee's findings of "cultural genocide" have been frequently referred to simply as "genocide." The *Christian Science Monitor* acknowledged that the evidence gathered was exclusively from one side, but nevertheless felt no compunction in reporting that the LIC's "examination had been thorough."[60] The American Ambassador to the United Nations, Henry Cabot Lodge, praised the initial report in 1959: "It seems that there is no reason whatsoever for doubting one single fact that the Dalai Lama has stated."[61] Others exaggerated: "This masterly document is based largely on eyewitness accounts of refugees collected under rigorous cross-examination by competent lawyers."[62]

But were the ICJ, the LIC, and the two reports what they appeared to be? Closer examination raises doubts. The ICJ was not an independent grouping of distinguished and objective jurists from every part of the world with the sole aim of exposing violations of human rights wherever they may occur. In reality, the ICJ grew directly from the Investigating Committee of Free Jurists (ICFJ)—also known as the Investigating Committee of Freedom-Minded Lawyers from the

Soviet Zone and the League of Free Jurists. This group was created by American intelligence operatives in 1949 for the purposes of publishing anticommunist propaganda and for recruiting agents in East Germany to work for the CIA and West German intelligence. The evolution to the ICJ came in July 1952, at a conference of the ICFJ, and was later supported by grants of at least U.S.$650,000 from the CIA during the years 1958 to 1964. As the prestigious *American Bar Association Journal* described it, the ICJ was formed as an organization "whose primary purpose is to gather evidence and publish documented reports throughout the world of systematic Communist injustice behind the Iron Curtain."[63]

It should be noted that CIA funding does not automatically mean CIA manipulation. As one ICJ Secretary-General, Niall MacDermott, put it, "I have no evidence to suggest that the CIA had any part in the preparation of the report or the materials in it."[64] Nevertheless, CIA funding, at the very minimum, is sufficient proof that the ICJ was seen by the United States government as a useful ally in the Cold War against communism.

The driving force and chair of the committee was an Indian jurist named Purshottam Trikamdas, a senior advocate at the Indian Supreme Court and a former leader of the Praja Socialist Party. In spite of its name this opposition political party had established links with CIA-funded, anticommunist international groups such as the Congress for Cultural Freedom. In April 1960, *while* the LIC was still completing its final report, Trikamdas felt no compunction about attending the "Afro-Asian Convention on Tibet and Against Colonialism in Asia," where he delivered a blatantly anti-Chinese speech. The conference was characterized by the Indian press as a gathering called to demand the "liberation" of Tibet from China's rule. By its own literature it was supposed to "lend support to the people of Tibet."[65] After the reports were published, Trikamdas saw nothing wrong in violating judicial ethics by publicly advocating the cause of the Dalai Lama, or misrepresenting the findings of the LIC to a press gathering, or writing an anticommunist diatribe.[66]

As to the committee's "rigorous cross-examination," there is certainly no evidence of this in the report itself; all the testimony appears to have been accepted verbatim. At least one journalist who attended the LIC sessions reported that there was no questioning of the testimony, particularly that of the Dalai Lama.[67] Refugee statements must be examined with the utmost caution. While they undoubtedly contain some truth, they tend to be influenced and exaggerated by emotional trauma and a psychological need on the part of refugees to justify their actions to others— and even to themselves. Refugees, especially in the period immediately following their ordeal, tend to be disoriented, frightened of being repatriated, and anxious to please their hosts. Refugee situations only compound the usual subjectivity of oral accounts, for recollections are inevitably biased by the individual's inability to view situations beyond their immediate experience.

Other weaknesses in refugee accounts were best summed up by a British woman whose sympathy for, and firsthand accounts of, the Tibetan refugees resulted in an invitation to write a pamphlet of alleged "atrocity" stories—an offer she reluctantly declined because

> I myself had to collect "stories" from the refugees and failed to obtain one which I could conscientiously pigeon-hole as "authentic." I learned by experience how impossible it is, when talking through an interpreter [as the members of the Inquiry Committee presumably had to do in each instance] to assess all those subtle means which are so vastly important whether or not one informant is describing something which actually happened to himself. The ordinary Tibetan is by nature truthful and honest. But, to rely upon this unquestionable fact without, at the same time, recognizing that his view of "truth" bears no relation to what the West would regard as valid evidence is dangerous. The Tibetan peasant has been accustomed from his cradle to his grave to accepting legend and fairy tale [sic] as literal truth.[68]

There is no evidence to suggest that the committee appreciated these difficulties or that they even seriously attempted to obtain evidence from the Chinese perspective. True enough, the committee did ask China for permission to visit Tibet and complained when they were turned down, but they did not even try to contact the seventy or so journalists who had visited Tibet throughout the 1950s.

Indeed, it is probably safe to say that the committee was well aware that China would never honor their request to travel through Tibet. It is likely that the letters of application were sent to head off criticism of having reported only one side of the story. It is equally safe to surmise that the committee knew what its findings would be even before beginning its investigation. Chinese charges of foreign, covert involvement in the revolt are ridiculed. In the committee's opinion, the allegation that the Dalai Lama was abducted was "obviously untrue" and itself threw "a great deal of doubt on the Chinese version of the uprising." Chinese descriptions of medical treatment provided for the Tibetans were shrugged off in favor of claims of malice from the Chinese, leveled by refugees with no medical knowledge whatsoever. The legal status of Tibet as an independent state was examined only from 1873, while Chinese dynastic sources were simply ignored.

The committee's bias also had an effect on its ability to gauge the reliability of informants. The members accepted as unequivocally true such ludicrous statements as: "It must, therefore, be pointed out that serfdom does not exist in Tibet in any form whatsoever" [Tsepon Shakabpa] and "Almost every Tibetan engaged in [an] agricultural occupation, however poor he may be relatively, has, in his possession a minimum of 5 to 6 cattle, and 30 sheep." [Dalai Lama][69]

The most telling example of the lack of objectivity on the part of the committee is its treatment of sterilizations. The LIC quotes the Dalai Lama as stating that sterilization began in 1957 and was carried out on a "large scale"; "two or three villages were completely sterilized." The Tibetan leader went on to claim that

> the Communist Chinese adopted these measures under the pretext of preventing certain epidemic diseases. They administered certain injections to men and

women in order to make them impotent. They also forced upon them treatments to make the male and female reproductive organs functionless.[70]

In this instance the committee made its charge on the basis of a single complaint:

> expert medical evidence on the details given is that the treatment described is not in accordance with any known method of sterilization. Searching clinical investigations of Tibetans who claimed to have been sterilized produced no proof that this had been done.[71]

The Dalai Lama's promises to produce evidence to back up these charges never materialized. That did not prevent widespread publicity, as though the allegation had been irrefutably documented. In the years following the publication of the LIC's report, the Dalai Lama, Trikamdas, and the ICJ all claimed to have found proof of sterilization; yet they failed to produce a single person who could be clinically examined to verify these claims. One must keep in mind that impotency is a frequent consequence of the ravages of venereal disease, which was rampant throughout Tibet.

So convinced of Chinese wrongdoing was the LIC that one unsubstantiated charge failed to lead the committee members to question the other charges. Niall MacDermott (Secretary-General of the ICJ) pointed out that the reports were not official since they were compiled by the special LIC and not the ICJ staff (the ICJ never repudiated them either) and that "no report published by the ICJ has been compiled in this way, and I cannot think we would do so today."[72]

Conclusion

In trying to sum up the events of the 1950s, the emerging evidence tends to substantiate China's view of events. The Dalai Lama's oft-stated view that China's "colonial" rule was so oppressive and murderous that the Tibetan people felt compelled to rise in one mighty swoop to cut their chains was not quite accurate. However, neither were China's claims of absolute benevolence, harmony, and freedom from feudal oppression ("a joyous liberation was stirring the ends of the land"). Perhaps it can be said that when events were depicted for public consumption, China appears to have fabricated the least.

Because the Chinese were committed to disturbing Tibetan society as little as possible, and because they—especially local Han cadres—could not believe that any Tibetan outside the aristocracy would want to maintain the status quo, they viewed the rebellion as a refutation of their enlightened policies and never fully understood why it happened.

> Neither the political system existing in Tibet nor the original positions and powers of the Dalai Lama have been changed; lama and lay officials at all levels remained at their posts as before; religious activities and the customs and habits of the local people were respected; and the Tibetan currency continued to circulate. The agreement's provisions that the Tibet Local Government

should carry out reforms of their own accord and that the Tibetan Army should gradually be reorganized into People's Liberation Army units have never been carried out. At the end of 1956, the Central Authorities announced to the Tibet Local Government that it was permissible not to carry out democratic reforms before 1962.

In a word, in the past eight years, the political, social and religious customs in Tibet remained as they were before the peaceful liberation. There was hardly any item in Tibetan internal affairs for which the former Tibet Local Government (the *Kashag*) was not responsible.[73]

It is fruitless to look for villains in this historical drama. The Chinese leadership had difficulties containing "Great Hanism" and was unable, or unwilling, to understand the error of their policies in eastern Tibet. Moreover, they failed to understand the pervasiveness of Buddhism in Tibetan life. For their part, the Tibetan oligarchy saw Han-initiated reforms as a direct threat to their power and privilege and worked actively to thwart them. One Tibetan recalls having been encouraged to taunt those Tibetan children who dared attend Chinese schools with such epithets as "You students are two-headed monsters. You eat the shit of Hans."[74] The mass of Tibetans was steadfastly tied to the status quo—without the slightest knowledge of, or experience of, any other way of life. Confused by the new ways offered by the Han, fearful of the Han who simultaneously urged "liberation" of the serfs from the feudal masters while creating alliances with these masters, they did not join their "liberators" in large numbers. Most likely, they preferred the lifestyle to which they were accustomed. Nor can we ignore the effect of foreign, covert activities—discussed in some detail in the following chapter. In the end, however, perhaps it was Jawaharlal Nehru who best summed up the situation when he told his Parliament that the revolt in Tibet was "more a clash of wills . . . than a clash of arms."[75]

8

Foreign Intrigues: II

No description of the events in Tibet during the decade of the 1950s would be complete without an examination of the role played by third parties to the dispute—specifically, the Guomindang regime on Taiwan, the Indian government, and the American Central Intelligence Agency. Admission of assistance from these third parties is difficult for the Dalai Lama and his followers. For years they claimed that the revolt was generated solely as a response to the oppressive practices of the Han and was, as a result, a popular uprising. When news of covert aid began to leak out the questions arose of how important this aid was to the revolt and who actually engineered it.

These remain difficult questions. Refugees are reticent about discussing them; consequently, for a long time—contrary to the evidence—the acceptance of aid was flatly denied. When China accused the rebels of receiving help from the outside, the Dalai Lama retorted that the reports were "completely baseless."[1]

In 1961 he was quoted as saying that "the only weapons that the rebels possess are those they've managed to capture from the Chinese. They have guns but they've even been using slingshots, spears, knives, and swords."[2] In 1974 he reiterated his position.

> The accusation of CIA aid has no truth behind it. My flight was conditioned by circumstances developing in Lhasa because of Chinese atrocities. . . . Originally the plan was to remain in South Tibet and from there contact the Chinese . . . but the Chinese soldiers were let loose upon the innocent peace-loving Tibetans which left me no alternative but to cross over to India.[3]

When the Dalai's brother, Thubten Norbu, was asked by *US News and World Report*, "are you getting any weapons to resist the Chinese?" he replied, "There is nothing at all coming in from the outside."⁴ Every effort by China to raise this charge was rebuffed out of hand. For example, in March 1959 *Xinhua* reported that

> many of the arms were brought in from abroad. The rebels' base south of the Tsangpo river on a number of occasions received airdropped supplies from the Chiang Kai-shek bands and radio stations were set up by agents sent by the imperialists and the Chiang Kai-shek bands for their intrigues.⁵

Instead of investigating these charges, the world's press responded much like the *Economist:*

> Nobody, either in committed or uncommitted countries, would be taken in by the communist allegations that . . . the rebellion was supported by "imperialists, the Chiang Kai-shek bands and foreign reactionaries."⁶

The worldwide rejection of these charges did a disservice to the cause of the Tibetan refugees by making the eventual acknowledgment of aid all the more difficult and embarrassing. The initial covert ties with the GMD were made through the Dalai Lama's brother, Gyalo Thondup, who had been educated in GMD-ruled China prior to 1949 and had married a Chinese woman. In 1950, before settling in Kalimpong he traveled between Taiwan, India, and Lhasa.⁷

By 1956 the GMD was actively involved in aiding rebel forces inside Tibet,⁸ although some evidence indicates that aid may have begun some years earlier.⁹ We do not know if the CIA–GMD–Tibetan rebels contacts were continuous from 1949–50 or whether there was a break. George Patterson, who argues that the association was continuous, was intimately involved as a translator and go-between in India in these negotiations. He reported that in 1953 Thubten Norbu contacted the CIA and was told to take his case to the GMD (from whom he was already receiving covert aid).¹⁰ Patterson also recalled an encounter two years later between Ragpa Pangdatsang and representatives from the Indian and American governments. At this time the United States was supposed to have suggested a ten-year plan of revolt, the aim of which was the eventual overthrow of China's control in Tibet. More recently Patterson had changed the emphasis of his recollections, saying that the talks he was involved in dealt primarily with trade and only secondarily with military matters.¹¹ John F. Avedon, whose recent book can be considered the "official" version of the Dalai Lama view of history, contends that Gyalo Thondup made an agreement with the CIA as early as 1951. It was initially an intelligence gathering arrangement (and one of financial assistance and small arms shipments after the outbreak of the Korean War) upgraded to guerrilla warfare in 1956.¹²

Within a short space of time the United States had eclipsed the GMD as the rebels' prime source of military aid.¹³ By the mid-1960s the GMD seems to have ended its role as supplier to the rebels, devoting its energies to trying to manipulate and divide the rebel forces outside of Tibet.¹⁴ Reports that as late as 1969 the GMD was secretly sending agents into Tibet are probably the result of more wishful thinking than reality.¹⁵

There was a noticeable increase in clandestine activity in 1957 (after the Dalai Lama had returned to Tibet from India and the C–130 Hercules aircraft were added to the U.S Air Force). Arms shipments grew thanks to contacts made by Norbu and Thondup and by Yampel (Rimshi) Pangdatsang. This was done largely by secret air-drops. C–130E aircraft could make the 2,400-mile return trip from Bangkok with twenty-two tons of supplies. One former resident of Lhasa recalls rumors of such flights in 1958;[16] and, sure enough, that very year China complained about just such activity to India and Nepal, but to no avail.[17] The flights were originating in Bangkok, presumably without the knowledge of the Indians or Nepalese.

GMD aid came in several forms: clandestine radio stations inside Tibet, "air-dropped supplies from the Government of the Republic of China [Taiwan] on a number of occasions,"[18] and the training of rebels in guerrilla warfare in Taiwan (mostly Chinese-speaking, ethnic Tibetans from Kham and Amdo).[19] There was also the inevitable propaganda support, complete with such hyperbole as Chiang Kai-shek addressing his "fellow countrymen in Tibet" and promising "direct support" because "Tibet [is] now ablaze with anticommunist fire."[20]

After the 1959 revolt there was a flurry of GMD activity reflecting the hope that this upheaval would mark the beginning of a general revolt all over China. When the Dalai Lama reached India he was met by a representative of the GMD government and a delegation of five Buddhist monks from the island. In return, some Tibetans visited Taiwan in search of further aid (including eight rebel guards who traveled from Lhasa with the Dalai Lama); others were being lured to settle permanently in Taiwan in exchange for monetary rewards.

But, as Thubten Norbu and his brother, the Dalai Lama, were thanking GMD officials for their help, the United States appeared to be applying public pressure on Taiwan to stay out of the conflict.[21] It remains unclear if this was simply a public cover for covert activities or the result of a rivalry between the intelligence agencies of the two allies. A more complete assessment of the GMD role will have to be left for future historians.

The CIA

Understanding the involvement of the CIA is really the key to understanding the rebellion. While the rebellion was purely a Tibetan matter launched in hopes of preserving the traditional culture and lifestyle, when the CIA became interested and involved, as it did in countless rebellions around the world, its goal, everywhere, was to manipulate the rebellion to serve American foreign policy interests. Because the CIA provided the resources, and because the rebels hoped that the CIA would bring all of the power of the United States to bear on the Chinese, CIA officers were able to manipulate the progress of the rebellion. The CIA's involvement began in earnest either in 1955 (with the meeting George Patterson referred to above) or shortly after, in 1956. One rebel leader, Wangdu, recalls leaving Tibet in 1956 and being trained by the Americans somewhere overseas. Later, he was secretly dropped back into Tibet, in the Kham region, where he began organizing rebel activity until his departure for Nepal in 1966.[22]

It was Gyalo Thondup who arranged the first CIA training missions, picking six Tibetans for that purpose. Their story reads like a typical spy novel. They were told to walk out of Kalimpong individually; they were then picked up by Thondup outside the town and driven to Siliguri. There, they were given compasses and told to walk toward East Pakistan (now Bangladesh)—a few hours away. On the frontier they were met by two Pakistani officers, a Chinese-speaking American, and a Tibetan interpreter. They were given turbans and Punjabi pajamas and told to walk to Dhaka. From there they were taken on a five-hour flight (perhaps to Taiwan) and told to don American military uniforms. At this location they were joined by Thubten Norbu; they spent the next four months learning how to read maps and how to use a radio transmitter, a parachute and weapons. They were then parachuted back into Tibet in the autumn of 1957, from a plane flown by an American pilot. They each carried with them a pistol, a small machine gun, an old Japanese radio that had to be wound by hand, U.S.$132 worth in Tibetan currency, and two small vials of poison to swallow if captured. Their mission was to urge the Dalai Lama to publicly appeal for U.S. assistance.

Upon landing they spread out and contacted Gompo Tashi Andrugstang, the rebel leader. In January 1958 they spoke to the Dalai Lama's Chamberlain, Thubten Woyden Phala, in the Norbulingka. The Chamberlain offered no help, telling the rebels that half the cabinet was supportive of the Chinese. He advised them that rebellion was useless and that they should give it up. But Andrugstang was not one to be deterred. He appealed to Washington for further assistance, only to be told that such help would be provided only if the Dalai Lama requested it directly. In May 1958 two of the foreign-trained agents and Andrugstang tried to see the Chamberlain again. This time their lack of success prompted the rebels to move out of Lhasa to the Loka region. The Americans were said to be furious, since they expected the rebels to stay in Lhasa, keeping in close contact with the government officials.

The Khampas wanted to mobilize their people against the Han. The Lhasan bureaucracy wanted to preserve their lifestyle through compromise with the Han. The Lhasans were fearful of what would happen if a rebel force, led by Khampas, was ever successful enough to force the Han out. There was the real threat that the Khampas might very well decide to rule Tibet themselves. It is unclear how much of these internal politics were understood in Washington. What is obvious is that Washington did not want to appear to be aiding rebel forces in Tibet when they did not even have the official approval of their own religious and secular leader—the Dalai Lama. Such aid would almost certainly precipitate a war with China and its ally the Soviet Union. Hence, there was a dogged determination on the part of American intelligence officers to obtain official approval for their activities from the Dalai Lama himself. The rebels' inability to get that approval through peaceful means may very well have been the impetus for the events of March 1959, described below.

Toward the end of 1958 the CIA decided to make its first air-drop of arms, ordering the Khampas to a designated spot with thirty mules and only one trusted individual. When the Khampas pointed out that the spot was directly over a nomad camp (thereby threatening the secrecy of the operation) and that one person could not possibly control thirty mules, the CIA ignored their objections and proceeded with the drop. This shipment included 100 British-made rifles, 20 submachine guns, two 55mm mortars, 60 hand grenades, and 300 rounds of ammunition for each weapon. While the Dalai Lama continues to downplay the significance of the aid provided by the CIA, between October 1958 and February 1959, Civil Air Transport (CAT), one of the CIA's airlines, dropped almost ten tons of weapons and supplies to the rebels.[23]

Meanwhile, training operations for the Tibetans had been shifted from Taiwan to Saipan and finally to Camp Hale, Colorado, although the Tibetans were never told where they were. This last site was a natural: 2,800m (9,300 ft.) above sea-level and far more similar to the Khampas natural environment than the other sites. One of the instructors was World War II marine veteran and legendary guerrilla instructor Anthony Poe[24]—an indication that Washington, at least, felt this operation to be significant.

Despite the cries of innocence on the part of the Dalai Lama, officials in Washington were planning for the events months before that fateful March in 1959. George Patterson maintains that he was told long before then, by his Khampa friends, that there were plans to spirit the Dalai out of Lhasa. The Dalai's denials are scoffed at by an American who was involved in the planning operation, arguing that the logistics of the operation were too complex for the relatively unsophisticated Khampas to have planned and carried out alone. This attitude, widely held within the CIA and government circles in Washington, is a good example of American attitudes of the time, which were a generous mixture of romanticization of the Khampas, disparagement of those not as materially advanced, and a fervent belief that only Americans are capable of performing such tasks.

Not only were Tibetans trained in the use of radio transmitters, but the Dalai Lama was accompanied by a Khampa who had been trained and equipped with a movie camera and sufficient color film to preserve a visual record of the flight. The Americans used a Lockheed C130 aircraft—modified especially for flight over the thin air of Tibet—to drop food and fodder for the Dalai's party and were able to do so thanks to the training other Khampas had in learning how to place distinctive panels in the snow as targets for the pilots. The radio operator joined up with the Dalai's entourage about halfway to India and from that point on was in constant radio communication with the CIA station in Dhaka.[25] One view is that "this fantastic escape and its major significance have been buried in the lore of the CIA as one of the successes that are not talked about. The Dalai Lama would never have been saved without the CIA."[26]

This view is confirmed by Richard Bissell, the former head of clandestine operations for the CIA, who also believed that the Dalai Lama could not have made his escape good without the CIA-trained operatives who accompanied him.[27] As to the Dalai Lama himself, he confirms the constant activity of the Khampas "who came and went, keeping in touch with all the isolated bands who were living in the mountains." This rather interesting admission raises the possibility that the Khampas were also picking up air-dropped supplies in their wanderings and that the Dalai Lama, as on so many other occasions, was not kept fully informed—given his previous aversion to the rebel activity. The Khampas rightly thought they would be better off not telling him. When this interpretation was presented to the Dalai Lama he denied it adamantly, affirming his earlier position that there were no air-drops and that he was only accompanied by a Khampa who had a radio.[28]

Although hints appeared about covert aid—such as a *Washington Post* story that "guerrillas are said to have been well supplied by some mysterious agency with necessary light weapons and ammunition"[29]—most prominent American leaders and the major news media representatives did not believe it. American leaders also, for the most part, publicly urged their government not to make the Tibet issue another front in the Cold War. Mike Mansfield, an Asia scholar and then-Democratic Senator from Montana, was one of the few prominent officials in Washington advocating the recognition of the Dalai Lama's administration as the only rightful one for Tibet. An Indian scholar summed up American opinion:

> Although the United States was not involved in the Tibetan revolt . . . it was frequently mentioned by the Chinese Communists, as well as by the Communist Party of India, as one of its main instigators. . . . However, on no occasion did they bring in any evidence to substantiate their charge. The American press did not take the charge seriously and made no effort to refute it.[30]

But others, like L. Fletcher Prouty, an officer in the air force who worked with the CIA during the late 1950s and early 1960s, point out that physical evidence is not always necessary.

> Although we may have cloaked our activity on the border of India in the deepest secrecy, who in India and who in Russia would believe that such activity was being supported and directed by anyone else than the covert peacetime operational forces of the United States? . . . If the Dalai Lama is spirited out of Tibet in the face of an overwhelming Chinese army of conquerors, are the Chinese going to think he found his support in heaven[?][31]

The Chinese never produced any evidence—because they did not have anything concrete to produce. Before the Khampas were dropped back into Tibet their clothes and equipment were carefully searched to dispose of any markings that may have identified them with the United States. Even the labels of their medicine bottles were removed. But, as Prouty correctly pointed out, it would be foolhardy to believe that the Chinese were not highly suspicious and that their public statements were not simply rote condemnations, but were rather based on some sense of what was actually happening.

In May of 1959 a mysterious Canadian citizen approached the American government, asking to discuss with them covert operations in Laos. He was granted a meeting—ostensibly with only the Joint Chiefs of Staff, but actually with CIA personnel too. As this Canadian talked he proved to be highly knowledgeable about the back roads of Laos and infiltration routes into China from that region. He also began talking about Tibet and how easy he thought it would be to sabotage road transportation there since most of the arteries were built precariously on the mountainsides and that, once sabotaged, it would take weeks or months to repair even the slightest damage. The following month, in a meeting with then Deputy Secretary of Defense Thomas S. Gates, the decision was made to begin concerted covert operations against the Chinese in Tibet. Three C130s were modified by the Lockheed Corporation to withstand the rarefied air and make the long, round-trip journey from their bases in Thailand. Camp Hale was put into full operations (from 1959 to 1962 about 170 Khampas were trained there). The activities were divided in two: one was to take place largely in the north near Lake Koko Nor, designed to sabotage roads and gather information; while the other operation was to take place in the south, designed to keep the Khampas supplied in order to preserve them as a fighting force in selected areas of Tibet.

This major recruiting effort yielded 14,000 Tibetans and some additional tribal people in the field, "entirely dependent on long-range transport and infiltration," and "armed, equipped, and fed by the Agency." By early 1960, however, efforts in this arena began to wane as preparations for the invasion of Cuba and growing involvement in Vietnam and Laos drained CIA resources. Then, suddenly, on President Dwight D. Eisenhower's orders, all clandestine operations—including the flights over Tibet—came to an abrupt halt after the downing of an American U–2 spy plane piloted by Francis Gary Powers. According to Prouty, the CIA people involved in the Tibetan operation were "very bitter" about this turn of events, feeling that the crisis with the USSR had nothing to do with their activities (although U–2s had been flying over Tibet as well as from bases in Pakistan). Soon after, a less satisfactory alternative land route was immediately established.[32] So ended phase one of the CIA's post-1959 plans for Tibet.

After the Cuban Bay of Pigs fiasco, President John F. Kennedy issued two memoranda: National Security Action Memorandum (NSAM) 55 and National Security Action Memorandum 57. These documents announced a presidential decision to change the rules by which intelligence operations were governed. From that point on, all major military operations (clandestine and otherwise) would be under the direct supervision of the Joint Chiefs of Staff (JCS). However, the possibility was left open that small, covert operations "may be assigned" directly to the CIA. Since at this time it was Prouty's job to brief the Chair of the JCS, General Lyman L. Lemnitzer, on these memoranda, he is a good source on how they were interpreted. He is convinced that both Lemnitzer and Kennedy believed this meant an end to the type of operations the CIA was conducting in Tibet, Cuba, Laos, and elsewhere. After Kennedy's death in November 1963, the CIA interpreted the memos to mean that they were free to begin small, covert operations; if these became—advertently or inadvertently— major operations, the military would bail them out.[33]

Major operations, such as flights into Tibet, were no longer possible; the CIA was now restricted to ground operations. The Camp Hale (Colorado) training continued through 1964, with the exception of the year 1962 when the camp was closed down for unspecified reasons.[34] In December 1961, the Colorado effort was almost exposed when a bus transporting Khampas to an airport outside the base had an accident, consequently missing a predawn flight. Workers at the airport arrived to find the place swarming with armed troops; some caught sight of the Tibetans. Defense Secretary Robert McNamara successfully persuaded the Washington bureau of the *New York Times* to kill the story, which was not published until twelve years later.[35]

India's Role

Up to this point the Indian government's role is somewhat mysterious. Prouty was under instructions to keep the Indians out of the whole matter—even to the extent of having the CIA planes avoid Indian air space.[36] This might help explain a 1958 exchange between Nehru and Zhou Enlai. In July, Zhou accused India of ignoring the actions of Tibetan emigrés who were planning a revolt from Indian border communities with the aid of the CIA and GMD. Nehru replied that the charge "must have been based on a complete misunderstanding of the facts" and that "the Government of India will never permit any portion of its territory to be used as a base of activities against any foreign government, not to speak of the friendly Government of the People's Republic of China."[37] A year later, when China reiterated these charges, Nehru again replied that it was "practically impossible" to smuggle weapons across the Indo–Tibetan frontier. China may, indeed, have *assumed* that the weapons and other aid were coming from India. This, in turn, left India feeling itself to be the aggrieved party—that is, if history proves that India was not clandestinely involved in some manner.

India's role is still hazy, more so than even that of the GMD. We know that from as early as 1950 there was considerable support among Indian officials for military action against Tibet. This support was led by prominent individuals, such as Deputy Prime Minister Sarder Patel, and high officials within the External Affairs Ministry.[38] While Nehru and Indian Ambassador to the PRC, K.M.

Panikkar, won the day with their advocacy of Indian neutrality, Nehru appears to have acceded to his critics to at least a limited degree. The Director of India's Intelligence Bureau, B.N. Mullik, has revealed that in 1952 Nehru instructed him to "keep in touch with the Dalai Lama's brother Thondup and all other Tibetan refugees and help them in every possible way."[39] George Patterson recalls being approached by Indian officials at about this time to help bring some Tibetan rebel leaders from Tibet to Kalimpong "to work for Tibetan independence."[40] Mullik hastens to add that the aid supplied by India was not material, but was restricted to moral encouragement. This moral support extended to tacit acceptance of the shipment of material aid from other sources (Mullik cites only Tibetan exiles as the sources) on condition that these activities not be carried out too openly. Moreover, the Indians had their own agents who could

> penetrate deep into Tibet and could go even up to Qamdo, Jyekundo, Gartok, etc. [They] had accurate information about the Chinese positions all over Tibet, the exact strength of their garrisons and quite a lot of details about their armaments, stocks of ammunition and food.[41]

We can assume that moral support extended to the sharing of such information with rebel leaders.

It is possible that the Indian and American intelligence services were not, at this juncture, collaborating. With encouragement from the Indians, which—in spite of Nehru's disclaimers—must have included turning a blind eye to anti-Chinese activities and to material support from America, the Tibetan rebels may have been getting along quite comfortably. That could mean that New Delhi really did not have anything to do with the events of March 1959. Except, on 17 April 1959, the *Bombay Free Press* quoted the Indian correspondent of the London *Daily Telegraph* as saying that his Tibetan sources had revealed to him that there was, in fact, Indian assistance in the Dalai Lama's escape. These sources are said to have revealed that Apa Pant, the political officer for Sikkim, on a visit to Lhasa in 1958, had placed radio operators in the Indian Consulate there and also among the Dalai Lama's household and that these agents played some unspecified role in the escape. New Delhi, of course, angrily denied the story, as did George Patterson who, in 1981, was sure that Apa Pant had not even traveled to Lhasa in 1958. We do know, however, that Nehru was planning a trip to Lhasa for September 1958; although the trip was called off, it is conceivable that Pant could have been sent ahead to make preparations.[42]

While the Americans and the Indians may have been secretly working toward the same ends, without collaboration, that all changed with the outbreak of the Sino-Indian conflict of 1962. Immediately after that conflict, Nehru appealed for additional aid from both the Americans and the British. Both responded positively. The Americans sent a delegation headed by Averell Harriman (then Assistant Secretary for Far Eastern Affairs), Paul Adams (Commander-in-Chief of an American "Strike Force"), and Roger Hilsman (Director of Intelligence for the Department of State). One of the goals of this high-level delegation was "to send the Chinese Communists a signal of deterrence."[43] There can be little doubt that covert aid to the Tibetans was discussed; after Nehru's humiliation at the hands of the Chinese, he was presumably more receptive to clandestine activities against his northern neighbor. According to John Avedon, the Indians got involved in 1962 "under CIA tutelage" by forming a Special Frontier Force (special code name, Establishment 22) under the command of the Research and Analysis Wing of Indian Intelligence. They set up a secret base in Orissa where the Americans, Indians, and Tibetan rebels would meet weekly.[44]

There was other suspicious activity as well. At about this time the "Tibet Welfare Association" was reestablished on Taiwan, and GMD agents again began to openly recruit Tibetans in Kathmandu.[45] The Indians observed new air traffic, leading Nehru to complain to Zhou Enlai about unauthorized flights over Indian territory from the direction of Thailand. Zhou denied that these flights had anything to do with the PRC, inviting the Indian Prime Minister to see for himself by shooting one down. The Indians never did, but the Burmese government did and discovered it was being flown by Taiwanese pilots.[46]

The 1962 conflict ended hopes of a close relationship between India and China. Chinese propaganda attacks on India's alleged covert activities "in" Tibet became more frequent and explicit, albeit exaggerated.

> The Indian Government has long harbored aggressive designs towards China's Tibet. In 1959, the Indian Government instigated a handful of Tibetan serf owners to a counter-revolutionary rebellion in Tibet, China, in an attempt to subvert China's sovereign rights over Tibet. Unwilling to give up its sinister designs after the failure of this counter-revolutionary rebellion, it coerced by force, tens of thousands of China's Tibetan inhabitants going into India creating a so-called question of Tibetan refugees.[47]

Just before the 1962 war, a decision had been made to concentrate the guerrilla forces in a tiny, isolated, semi-independent feudal principality called Mustang, on the Tibet–Nepal border—an eight- to twelve-day walk from Pokhara, with a population of ten thousand subsistence farmers.[48] In 1960 the Nepali Prime Minister, B.P. Koirala, had told a news conference that the authorities had captured Tibetan refugees with arms, ammunition, and walkie-talkies and that he would not tolerate Nepal being used as a base for military operations against China.[49] There is no reason to believe that the activities in Mustang were kept secret from the Nepalese—at least until 1962, when the Chinese informed them and suggested immediate action but nothing appeared to happen. In 1964, or 1965, several Khampas were arrested in Kathmandu with arms and radios after anonymous phone calls to the city's newspapers led to the seizure of several caches of Chinese arms. It was discovered that the arms came from the United States Embassy, resulting in the expulsion of an American diplomat and the forbidding of a USAID mission to use its private plane and two helicopters on their private airstrips.[50]

Meanwhile, in Mustang, the American advisers (some reports say the Dalai Lama) picked a former monk named Baba Yeshe ("illiterate but highly intelligent and extremely ruthless") as the leader of their operation. No longer working through Dhaka, but through the United States Embassy in New Delhi, the CIA had gathered two hundred Tibetans in Mustang in a short time. Referred to as Khampas, these men were mostly from western Tibet and the northern Chang Thang (by this time access to Nepal was easiest for Tibetans from these regions). Unfortunately for the Khampas, it was many months before the CIA started dropping supplies to them. Some were so desperate for food that they resorted to boiling and eating their shoe leather; several died of starvation. When the airdrops began (via a new CIA airline called Air Nepal), the goods were accompanied by four Khampas trained by the CIA; twelve additional trained men soon arrived on foot via India. Their first raid took place in late 1961. A Chinese convoy was attacked; six Chinese were killed, as was one of their own.

A few years later, another raid yielded some documents that carried the first indications to Western intelligence that the Great Leap Forward had created some difficulties for China. As the raids continued, the amount of pay the rebels received began to increase, all of it being sent through Thondup in India: Rs. 5,000 a month, and later Rs. 22,500 every two months.

The raids did not always go well. For example, in 1963 the GMD once again tried to manipulate the rebel forces, using agents recruited largely from Amdo. These efforts resulted in Khampa-Amdowan fighting in spite of pleas from the Dalai Lama for unity and peace.[51] At just about this time, as the competition subsided, George Patterson reappeared, persuading the Khampas to take him and two British cameramen on a raid into Tibet.[52] Patterson reported that there were ten war camps in Mustang and that the local people acted as though the Tibetans were an "occupation force." They were so afraid that another Western visitor had trouble getting guides to travel around the area.[53]

Patterson's foray into Tibet made the CIA understandably furious, since the cameramen had recorded the raid. The resulting unwelcome publicity, brought on by the airing of the film on television all over Europe, caused the CIA to cease funding the rebels for six months. In fact, Patterson's coup and the CIA anger did nothing to make the world aware of the existence of *covert* activities. When yet another report of third-party involvement surfaced in Hong Kong a couple of years later, the media proceeded to shrug it off.[54]

The hiatus after the Patterson affair was only temporary. A few months after Patterson was in Tibet the CIA did a major update of its 1951 weather study of Tibet, which turns out to be remarkably extensive. The report was issued to explain "the effects of meteorological elements upon military operations . . . air, air-ground, and ground-surface." The report goes on to define "air-ground" as "such operations as parachute drops, chemical and biological warfare, tactical support, low-level reconnaissance, and air rescue." The report carried an analysis of the clothes necessary in various regions of Tibet during different seasons and also included extensive maps and charts giving *hourly* analyses of fogs, dust, cloud ceilings, precipitation, and other conditions.[55]

The raids continued sporadically, although the tightening of Chinese border patrols made them exceedingly difficult after 1967. There were at least two more drops (largely anti-aircraft guns) in 1965 and 1966. However, as the decade wore on, the U.S. involvement in Southeast Asia became deeper and deeper, leaving less time, less energy, and fewer resources to expend in other areas—particularly where returns were seen as inconsequential. In the last known raid in 1969, the Khampa raiding party was defeated by the Chinese and all the men were killed.[56]

As the CIA connection began to diminish in direct proportion to its growing involvement in Southeast Asia, the Khampas got a brief second life—with the Indian government playing the role of big brother. While India had been aiding the Tibetans since at least 1962, and possibly earlier, by 1970 CIA money had totally dried up. The CIA had been in radio communication with the Mustang Base through special antennas in Orissa and New Delhi. Moreover, the rebels were meeting weekly with the CIA and Indian intelligence jointly. The Indians placed the entire operation under their Research and Analysis Branch of the Intelligence Bureau, supervising it from the prime minister's office. They established the Indo-Tibetan Border Police, for which Tibetans were recruited as part of the Indian army and trained recruits at Dehra Dun and Agra. While their purpose was, ostensibly, to guard the northern frontiers of India (for which the Tibetans were uniquely acclimatized) the recruits had also been promised that when the time came they would be "used to liberate Tibet." Some were used in the Bangladeshi War, in which forty-one were killed.

One final curious note about American involvement concerns the U.S. army's efforts to train some of its soldiers to speak Tibetan. There are no records of this prior to 1964. We know there were two soldiers studying Tibetan in 1967 and twelve more the following year. The army today claims to have no records that explain why these men were being trained to speak Tibetan or why the leadership felt these skills necessary.[57]

All in all, American involvement did not alter the situation in Tibet in any discernible manner after 1959. George Patterson agrees that the rebel activity was no more than a nuisance to the Chinese. Although he believed in the potential of the rebels, they could never realize it because of the insidious activities of Gyalo Thondup, regional differences that precluded unity, and the fact that many of the air-dropped supplies were lost when the planes missed their targets.[58]

The raids, in the final analysis, did not cause major disruptions, in no way weakened the strength of the central government in China or its hold on Tibet and failed to bring the Dalai Lama any closer to fulfilling his wish of triumphantly returning to Lhasa. Indeed, it can be argued that the opposite was the case. Few, if any, have illusions that the story related in these few pages represents the limits of American and Indian covert activities in the Tibetan "theater." There was another level of assistance of which our knowledge is only fragmentary. This included helping prominent refugees through organizations such as the Asia Foundation and the Emergency Committee for Tibetan Refugees—discussed further in chapter 10.

No doubt there was also some press activity—handing out false stories, aiding propaganda—especially during the 1959 period. As a footnote, the United States Information Service, with the help of Tibetan refugees in Switzerland, produced a thirteen-minute documentary portraying the Dalai Lama's flight from Lhasa. Entitled "Man from a Missing Land," it was ready for release in 1971; however, President Richard M. Nixon's surprising announcement in July of that year that he would be visiting China quashed plans to air the film, and indeed all anti-Chinese propaganda for the time being. Never released, it remains a sad remnant of the Cold War in Tibet.[59]

Meanwhile, back in the field in Nepal, the counterrevolution was, for all intents and purposes, over. There was only the last tragic chapter of the Khampa story left to unfold. What was once a sizable force, with as many as fifteen thousand armed men, supplied with some of the latest technology (for example, radio transmitters powered by solar batteries) by 1970 had been reduced to a sorrowful few, fighting among themselves and surviving in a hostile population that tolerated their presence only because it was "the wish of the Dalai Lama."[60]

Baba Yeshi was forced to surrender his command in 1969 to Wangdu, a nephew of Andrugstang. Yeshi, in anger, defected with 150 of his followers, making a deal with the Nepali authorities that in return for leading the Nepali Army to the Khampas, the defectors would be settled on a piece of good agricultural land somewhere in Nepal. The offer was accepted by Kathmandu, although no immediate action was taken against the Tibetans. With the end of American involvement, the Chinese enlisted Nepal's aid in finally ridding themselves of this Tibetan nuisance—the Khampas. In December 1973 Mao Zedong told visiting Nepali King Birendra that the Khampas were a major obstacle to better Sino-Nepali relations. This seemed to have the desired effect, for in March 1974 a prominent rebel was arrested and an ultimatum was presented to the Tibetans giving them until July to surrender or face the consequences.[61] They didn't surrender. In the autumn of 1974, Gurkha troops were recalled from their United Nations assignments; a major drive was undertaken to ferret out the remaining Tibetan guerrillas. The Dalai Lama, hoping to avoid needless bloodshed, intervened, urging the rebels to lay down their arms. Most did and by February 1975 it was all over. Wangdu and forty of his men, unwilling to surrender, escaped. They ran for a month before reaching the Nepal–India frontier, where they found the armies of both nations waiting for them. While the Indians looked on helplessly, Wangdu and four of his men were slain by the Nepalese; the remainder surrendered. The Royal Nepalese army then began clean-up operations.[62]

In 1979 the final act was played out. Seven former Tibetan guerrillas, who had been arrested in April 1974, were sentenced to life imprisonment on a host of charges—including jeopardizing the sovereignty of Nepal and raising arms against a friendly power (China)—only to be released in December 1980 during an amnesty declared to mark the birthday of the King of Nepal. Tibetans, angered at Nepal's action, accused Beijing of virtually buying the allegiance of the Nepalese by signing a five-year economic and technical cooperation pact in 1972. There can be no question that Beijing must have repeatedly urged Kathmandu to act against the Tibetans, but it would be wrong to assume that Nepal had no interest in ridding itself of these rebels. Nepal gained no benefit from their presence. No nation would be pleased to host an uncontrollable, heavily equipped army of insurgents; especially when the insurgency was aimed at a neighboring country with which the hosts have friendly relations. It is likely that after assurances that the Americans had withdrawn from the operation, Nepal was amenable to punitive actions against the rebels—with or without China's blandishments.

When the Dalai Lama was presented with evidence that members of his staff had, indeed, been in touch with, trained by, and working for the CIA he replied,

> Some points are not convenient for us to comment upon. This kind of report is extremely dangerous, because it implies that the resistance in Tibet was initiated by some outsiders. This is not so. I want to emphasize that the whole policy was initiated by Tibet whether we had CIA/United States help or not; with or without the CIA, Tibetan determination was there from the start.[63]

This represents only a slight modification of his 1974 position denying the existence of CIA air-cover, parachuted supplies, maps, and radios.

Of course he is right. It is useful to note that the CIA's method of operation is to seek out whatever resistance and dissension already exist, then work to become part of that resistance—expand it, manipulate it, take control of it, and finally order it to function for the CIA's interests, whatever its original purposes.

There was Tibetan opposition to the arrival of the Chinese, and there is no reason to doubt that it originated among the Tibetans themselves. But the evidence appears to indicate that the dissension in Tibet was insufficiently widespread to sustain a lengthy, open rebellion.

The Chinese authorities might have acted differently if the rebellion had been allowed to die a natural death soon after 1959. All the indications are that the CIA and the Indians understood full well that the Tibetan rebellion had no chance of success or even of causing any major disruption to the Chinese. The government of the United States was only interested in harassing China's rulers. "It was a flea biting an elephant," recalled one CIA veteran. "Basically Tibet was just a nuisance to the Chicoms [Chinese Communists]. It was fun and games. It didn't have any effect." Besides, Washington's chief ally in the region, the government in Taiwan, vehemently opposed Tibetan independence.[64] It was certainly not fun and games to the Tibetan rebels risking their lives for their cause. Nevertheless, American support continued to raise false hopes. It was a small price for Washington to pay to keep Beijing guessing and worrying, at the same time tying down thousands of soldiers in the TAR. To the Tibetans the private expressions of support, from the days of Lowell Thomas's visit, and the aid held out a promise that others sympathized with their plight and would work for their eventual return to Tibet. Perhaps therein lies the cruelest tragedy and the greatest damage from this outside intervention; the Tibetan refugees will pay the price of two decades of false hope for many years, if not generations, to come.

9

Tibet After 1959

By April 1959 the Tibetan revolt was over. Beijing had abolished the Dalai Lama's administration ("Tibet Local Government") and replaced it with the Preparatory Committee for the Autonomous Region of Tibet (PCART) as the official government of the region. Tibet was reorganized into seventy-two rural counties, seven special administrative districts, and one municipality (Lhasa) in order to dissolve the feudal governing structure. In urban areas, street and local committees were established to look after local security, call meetings, and perform other organizational tasks. In rural areas, Peasant Associations were established.[1]

Less than a month after the rebellion the Panchen Lama returned to Tibet for the First Plenary Session of the newly empowered government. The PCART had added six new departments (Public Security, Public Health, Industrial and Commercial Administration, Communications, Agriculture and Animal Husbandry, and a Counselors Department) to the six already in existence (General Office, Religious Affairs Commission, Civil Affairs Department, Financial Department, Cultural and Educational Department, and Construction).

These administrative changes received official approval about a fortnight later at the First Session of the Second National People's Congress (NPC), China's nominal Parliament. The vote of approval for the changes was accompanied by a warning to the PCART that a distinction had to be made between those nobles who had opposed the rebels or remained neutral and those who had supported the rebel cause. The NPC authorized the PCART to "carry out democratic reform in Tibet step by step, and free the Tibetan people from suffering so as to lay the foundations for the building of a prosperous, socialist New Tibet."[2]

The Second Plenary of the PCART then met in July to decide how to implement the new policies. The policy of working with the Lhasan elite in a united front had met with failure; consequently, Beijing's officials felt they had been betrayed. While they saw their restraint during the 1950s as moderation and benevolence, many prominent Tibetans took their stand as an indication of weakness. The hardliners in Beijing had been vindicated; now nothing could stop an all-out attack on the feudal social structure in Tibet. These changes were dubbed "Democratic Reforms."

In May it was announced that Tibetan farmers would be exempt from taxes and grain sales to the state for the remainder of the year. The PLA distributed interest-free loans in the form of 1,750 tons of seeds and grain. These policies were partly implemented by groups of Tibetan students sent back from schools in other parts of China. These students were accompanied by Tibetan-speaking Han cadres, who took over a number of important administrative positions. By October, 1,200 Tibetans and 200 Tibetan-speaking Han were said to have arrived in Tibet along with 1,000 Han technical advisers.

In June a two-stage campaign was launched. The first part was known as the "three antis and two reductions" (anti-rebellion, anti-corvée, anti-slavery; reduce land rent, reduce interest). The second stage involved the confiscation of land, livestock and tools that belonged to lords who had fled Tibet and the subsequent distribution of this property to the serfs who worked the land. The members of the aristocracy who had stayed loyal to China (500 by one count) were also deprived of their land, tools, and livestock though they were monetarily reimbursed.[3]

In pastoral areas the campaign was somewhat different—there were "three antis and two benefits" (anti-class division, anti-struggle, anti-distribution of property; benefit from the abolition of feudal privilege, benefit from effective measures for everyone). In monasteries it was the "three antis" (anti-rebellion, anti-feudal privilege, anti-feudal system of exploitation and oppression). Those monasteries that had abstained from the rebellion had their land and capital goods redeemed; they were also eligible for government subsidies if they were unable to be self-supporting.[4] By late 1960 it appeared as though the first two stages of the "Democratic Reforms" had been successfully carried out.

The next stage embarked upon was "socialist reform," i.e., the communalization of agriculture. In August 1960 the Chinese press reported that the very first steps toward the creation of rural communes had been taken by 100,000 households, organized into 8,400 mutual-aid teams.[5] Several families jointly worked the land, while each maintained private ownership of their portion. By late 1962 all of Tibet's 166,000 rural households were said to have joined mutual aid teams with their neighbors for a total of 22,000 teams.[6] Since private ownership was still a feature of this process, there was much public fanfare concerning the public distribution of land deeds to the sedentary population and cattle ownership certificates to the nomadic population throughout late 1960 and early 1961. Although these policies were welcomed by many, there were some difficulties. The Panchen Lama himself indicated problems, when in December 1960, he called on the cadres to "recheck" the Democratic Reforms. He also blamed

> a handful of the most reactionary self-owners and their agents who are not
> reconciled to the elimination of feudal serfdom and consequently have resorted
> to various treacherous and vicious means to buy over, inveigle, threaten, harm,
> or murder cadres and active elements among the various nationalities and carry
> on various kinds of sabotaging activities.[7]

In August 1962 the authorities announced the establishment of an election committee to prepare for the formal inauguration of the Tibet Autonomous Region. But the TAR was not set up until September 1965. The delay indicates that problems of continued resistance were plaguing Beijing. While we have evidence that the CIA was busy promoting dissension by encouraging the rebels to continue their endeavors, the success of its efforts is difficult to gauge. Western monitoring of Radio Lhasa revealed that in April 1961 the Fifth Plenary Session of the PCART voted to postpone agricultural socialization for another five years—the time deemed necessary to consolidate the reforms already introduced. The blame for this action was put on rebel activity, the lack of sufficient numbers of adequately trained Tibetan cadres, the lack of a thorough comprehension of the benefits of socialism by the masses and bad weather in 1961–62.[8] It is likely that repercussions from China's economically disastrous Great Leap Forward also played a role.

During the Cultural Revolution, a few years later, Liu Shaoqi (Liu Shao-chi) was blamed for the policy of a five-year "stabilized development" during which time plans for further mutual-aid teams were postponed; collective property was returned to private ownership; the few mutual-aid teams that had taken the next step toward socialization by upgrading themselves to agricultural cooperatives were forced to return to a team status; and a host of similar, backward steps were taken.[9] This was a clear admission by China that, despite the failure of the rebellion and the lack of evidence of mass support for the rebels, Tibetans remained staunchly opposed to rapid socialization. Years later, Beijing was to admit "left" shortcomings ("mistakes") in the implementation of policies and the inability of local cadres to correct them.[10]

In December 1964 the Chinese press began calling the Dalai Lama a traitor, announcing his official dismissal from his position as the chair of the PCART, five-and-a-half years after he had fled to India.[11] China had until now persisted in keeping his titles intact, arguing that he was coerced into fleeing Tibet. But his continued support for the covert activities against China—his support of India in the 1962 Sino-Indian War, the publication of his autobiography, which was strongly critical of Chinese rule in Tibet and, not surprisingly, advocated Tibetan independence, and the promulgation of his "Tibetan Constitution" had exhausted Chinese patience. Only days after the accusations appeared against the Dalai Lama, it was announced that the Panchen Lama had taken the Dalai Lama's lead.

After the Dalai Lama turned traitor, the Panchen organized a counterrevolutionary clique on behalf of the overthrown serf-owning class and engaged in wild activities against the people, the motherland and socialism.[12]

The Panchen Lama

The fall of the Panchen Lama came as a surprise to observers outside China since there had been no indication that he was at odds with the authorities. In 1959 he had supported Beijing's efforts to quell the abortive rebellion, had denounced feudal privileges in the monasteries, and had supported productive labor for the monks who were physically able. He had been a consistent advocate of unity among all rival groups in the PRC and never appeared to be under duress. It is indisputable, however, that he was unable to openly express his views if indeed these views were in opposition to those held by Chinese authorities. According to a 1967 article in the Japanese newspaper, *Yomiuri Shimbun,* wall posters in Beijing quoted accusations made by Zhou Enlai that the Panchen Lama had prevented the secularization of the priesthood in 1960–61 and had written a 70,000-character memo to Mao Zedong in 1962 complaining of conditions in Tibet.[13] Refugee sources confirm the existence of the memo, claiming it was the culmination of a two-year-long effort by the Panchen to bring redress for continuing persecutions of suspected Tibetan rebels, shortages of food, and excessive pressures to curtail religious activities.[14]

The situation came to a climax during a 1964, seventeen-day trial. The Panchen Lama was accused of planning a revolt "on the instigation of the conspiratorial clique in Kalimpong."[15] Reports in India spoke of his being beaten and publicly humiliated. He was found guilty and "sent on a compulsory leave to remold himself."[16] That is, he was imprisoned in 1964[17] and not heard from again until his release in 1978.[18] He was subsequently elevated to a high, if symbolic, post at the National People's Congress in September 1980.[19]

China's Efforts

Throughout the 1960s there was continued opposition to China's rule within and around the TAR. There were three major reasons for this: continued difficulties in Han-Tibetan relations, the role of religion and the religious community and social conditions, particularly food shortages. Despite continued appeals from high officials to remedy these ills, local cadres appear to have been unable to overcome the problems.

After the failed revolt of 1959 China launched an all-out campaign to fully integrate Tibet into the PRC—politically, economically, and socially. The indigenous agents chosen for this task were the poorest Tibetans—the former serf population. Large supplies of agricultural tools and seed were issued to them, either gratis or as interest-free loans. Some former serfs were trained to be industrial workers, some were elected to positions of at least nominal authority and then recruited into the PLA (for which, even China's harshest critics are forced to concede, there was never a shortage of Tibetan volunteers).[20] To ease Han-Tibetan animosity, Tibetan language classes were begun on Radio Lhasa in 1961. It is claimed that these classes were compulsory for all Han in the TAR. By 1964 *Renmin Ribao* reported that 80,000 copies of a Tibetan language study book had been published.

By no means were all the efforts to ease tensions aimed only at the Han. The training of Tibetan cadres for high-level positions was once again viewed as a priority. In 1957 the CCP established the School for Administrative Cadres of the Tibet Autonomous Region, to provide supplementary education for ethnic Tibetans completing their courses at the various Nationalities Institutes in China. The ideal target population was clearly defined:

> When appointing and promoting Tibetan cadres, the Party committees at all levels took care first to select youths of the Tibetan nationality from among the poor serfs and slaves and other laboring people who had high class consciousness, were obedient to the Party and actively willing to work, and were promising. . . . These cadres of the Tibetan nationality from among poor serfs and slaves, heavily oppressed and exploited in the old society by the three major manorial lords . . . felt deep class hatred against the old society and cherished deep class love for the laboring people. They are the readiest to accept the education of the Party, and they would serve the laboring people wholeheartedly. They formed the hard-core strength in the ranks of the cadres of the Tibetan nationality.[21]

But this segment of the population had the least formal education and lacked even the most basic literacy and may have been a factor in the poor administration of policies at the local level.

The following chart, culled from a number of sources (some contradictory), indicates the growth in the number of Tibetan cadres. In most cases the area referred to in the source materials is not indicated, but it is probably safe to assume it refers solely to the TAR.

While the growth in total numbers is evident, on the whole, discrepancies remain. This is particularly true of the last five sets of figures. Figures "l" and "m" were given to different groups of travelers only weeks apart by the very same officials in Tibet. The next two were published in *Beijing Review* and offered in a speech by Yin Fatang (Yin Fa-t'ang), the Communist Party leader in Tibet, also only days apart from each other. The last one was reported in the official Chinese press in 1982. The differences in the numbers are not explained.

The shortage of Tibetan cadres is compounded by the fact that for the most part they have been relegated to low-level positions. By 1975 all district (zhou) level cadre positions, the lowest level in the Chinese administrative structure, were filled by Tibetans.[23] The next level is the county (xian), and the cadres

Date[22]	Number of Tibetan Cadres	% of all Cadres in TAR
a. January 1964	12,000	n.a.
b. November 1964	17,000	n.a.
c. 1965	7,508	30–32.9
d. 1965	16,000	45
e. 1972	20,000	n.a.
f. 1976	27,000	60
g. 1976	36,000	n.a.
h. 1978	40,000	69
i. 1978	40,000	64
j. 1978	20,023	44.5
k. 1980	45,000	n.a.
l. July 1980	47,000	64.6
m. July–August 1980	33,000	56.9
n. May 1981	27,000	52.8
o. May 1981	36,000	60
p. 1982	29,406	54.5

n.a. = not available
(where different figures are cited for the same year, different sources were used)

there remain 58 to 60 percent Tibetan; while at the regional level (TAR), Tibetans represent only 44 percent of the cadres.[24]

These Tibetan cadres found themselves forming a new elite in the society—some apparently abusing their authority to the point that the central authorities launched a campaign in 1972–73 promoting respect for their own people. This problem is confirmed by a former cadre, now in exile in India, who characterized these office-holders as fitting into one of three categories: supporters of Mao, usually poor and largely CCP members; those opposed to feudal Tibet but not fully convinced of the virtues of communism; and those opposed to the Han presence. The middle group was allegedly the vast majority, while the final group was the smallest.[25]

At the same time as the Chinese authorities were recruiting cadres, they were also busy recruiting Communist Party members. The first Tibetan member from the TAR was initiated into the CCP in the mid-1950s; the Chinese press claimed 1,000 Tibetan members by October 1957, with an additional 2,000 Tibetans in the Communist Youth League (CYL). By August 1965, Tibetan members were said to total 4,000 and 10,000 respectively. In 1973, Chinese press reports told of recruitment into the CCP and CYL of 11,000 new Tibetan members; four years later, however, the press was again using the figure 4,000 for Tibetan CCP membership. More recent claims, such as 40,000 CCP members in the TAR, do not differentiate between Han and Tibetan membership. The sudden growth and decline of membership may be attributed to the large-scale recruitment drives of the Cultural Revolution and a subsequent purge following the fall of the "Gang of Four" in October 1976. As of 1982 Tibetans had begun to reach important posts in the CCP, such as the party secretary of the Lhasa city branch.[26]

Religious Life

The greatest area of misunderstanding between the Tibetans and the Han was religion. The Han people's negative view of the Tibetan religious institutions was naturally enough reinforced when many of the monasteries took an active part in the 1959 revolt, at the very least as support bases for the roving rebel bands. The monastic opposition to the Han within the TAR could scarcely have resulted from persecution, since religious practice was barely, if at all, altered in any way prior to 1959. It is therefore more than likely that the anti-Han attitudes of the monks came from stories of Chinese anti-religious activities in eastern Tibet, threats created and fueled by rumors, and undoubtedly on direct instructions from the upper strata monks whose loyalties and ties to the lay aristocracy were unassailable.

The extent of monastic involvement in the revolt can be gauged from a speech made by Ngabo in April 1960. He asserted that in 1959 there were 2,469 (the exiles now argue that there were about 6,200) monasteries, with 110,000 monks and nuns within the TAR; but only a year later the clerical order had diminished to 1,700 monasteries, with a population of 56,000 clerics.[27] Since only about 10 percent of the monks and nuns making up the difference fled into exile, we can speculate that the remainder either left the priesthood or were imprisoned.

Unquestionably, the communists had their doubts about the value of religion and were highly suspicious of its institutions. Those monasteries that participated in the revolt were severely punished, while the others received stern warnings. The retaliation was not as wanton as some accounts may have it. A refugee monk related an incident at a monastery in Kham in late 1958. The PLA arrived one day and shut all the monks in one room while they searched the monastery. Finding nothing, they released the monks unharmed and left them to continue practicing their centuries-old rituals.[28]

The use of force was never publicly debated by the Chinese authorities and the arguments against it are persuasive. At this point, China's policy was to allow religion to continue while simultaneously and peacefully discouraging Tibetans from practicing it by offering incentives for the monks to turn to secular life.

All evidence points to the continued practice of religion in Tibet through the first half of the 1960s.[29] New monks were trained and ecclesiastical examinations were held until late 1965.[30] Even the Moslim mosque in Lhasa was rebuilt at the expense of the Chinese government in 1965. A nun, now living in India, told a journalist that her convent was visited by Han officials in 1961; typifying the prevailing Chinese attitude, the inhabitants were instructed to become productive members of society. She and her colleagues took on part-time work to pay for their upkeep while continuing to shave their heads, wear clerical garb and practice their religion up to 1966.[31] Similar accounts by refugees from varying parts of Tibet have appeared in the Western press.[32]

Several factors were at work in the diminution of the role of the clerical community. Since most monks joined the priesthood involuntarily at an early age, some indeterminable percentage almost certainly resented the action and later in life welcomed an opportunity to leave, although not necessarily to return to serfdom (which would have been the case before 1959). Secular educational opportunities offered an alternative to the previous monastic monopoly. Furthermore, monasteries were financially hurt when mutual-aid teams neglected to allot sufficient provisions in the distribution of their agricultural output. Press attacks on "monastic laziness" must also have had a negative effect. Also, it is important not to underestimate the lure of monetary rewards and the promise of material benefit for those who joined the ranks of the lay worker.[33] Taken as a whole, these factors must have played a considerable role.

Agriculture

It was in the sphere of agriculture that China hoped to win over the majority of the Tibetan population. Equal land distribution would result in an average of 35 *mu* (a little less than 6 acres) to each peasant, along with some agricultural tools and animals. These acquisitions were supplemented with loans (totaling RMB 6,300,000) and the further loans of seed and tools at little or no interest (some seeds and tools were even distributed gratis).

Agricultural scientists were dispatched to Tibet to work on improving traditional, but antiquated, farming methods. They taught deeper planting, systematic seeding rather than scattering, the use of fertilizers, and so on. All these efforts were said to have improved output, and in 1963 *Renmin Ribao* declared that production was 80 percent over the total output of 1959.

The socialization of agriculture in Tibet was markedly different from that in the rest of China, where the stage of mutual-aid teams led to two types of cooperatives, and finally culminated in people's communes. In Tibet the cooperative stage was simply jumped over. The first communes were established in 1965; 50 were formed by late 1966. It was not until 1974 that the Chinese could report that 90 percent of the townships communized; 93 percent were completed by 1975. In this socialization process, opposition from the Tibetans seems to have played a major role in preventing rapid progress.[34]

If religion is the major point of contention between proponents and opponents of China's actions in Tibet, then the question of food must be a close second. From 1960 to 1975 reports from China regularly stressed ever-increasing harvests (except for 1967, acknowledged to be a poor year). In 1974 or 1975, "for the first time in history" Tibet was proclaimed self-sufficient in grain.[35] Until that time, 30 percent of Tibet's grain was imported from other parts of China. China's detractors doubted those claims to self-sufficiency, as did American

Food Distribution in Tibet

Date[38]	Yearly Per Capita Grain Received (kg)	Location	Source of Information
a. pre–1959	349	Lhasa	Tibetan refugee
b. pre–1959	525	Area around Red Flag People's Commune	Tibetan refugee
c. pre-1959	144–180 (ration for workers and officials)	Eastern Tibet	Tibetan refugee
d. Summer 1959	120	Sakya	Tibetan refugee
e. Summer 1959	204	Red Flag People's Commune	Tibetan refugee
f. 1959–66	200	n.a.	Chinese official
g. late 1963	266	Tibetan area of Gansu	Chinese source
h. 1964	120	Shigatse	Tibetan refugee
i. 1964	210	Eastern Tsangpo River	*Xinhua*
j. 1965	179	Red Flag People's Commune	Tibetan refugee
k. 1965	418	Red Flag People's Commune	Foreign visitor
l. 1966	501	Red Flag People's Commune	Foreign visitor
m. 1967	120–188	n.a.	Tibetan refugee
n. 1967	178 (workers and officials) 138 (peasants)	n.a.	Dalai Lama's official
o. 1968–69	156–180	n.a.	Tibetan refugee
p. 1970	35	n.a.	Dalai Lama's official
q. 1972	260	Tibetan area of Sichuan	Chinese source

(continued)

(*Food Distribution in Tibet, continued*)

Date[38]	Yearly Per Capita Grain Received (kg)	Location	Source of Information
r. 1972	190	Lhasa	Tibetan refugee
s. 1973	175	Central Tibet	Tibetan refugee
t. 1974	270	n.a.	Chinese source
u. 1974	120	Western Tibet	Tibetan refugee
v. 1975	150–192	Lhasa	Tibetan refugee
w. 1976	96–120	n.a.	Tibetan refugees
x. 1976	120	Shigatse	Tibetan refugee
y. 1976	141	n.a.	Tibetan refugee
z. 1977	90–120	n.a.	Dalai Lama
aa. 1977	156	n.a.	Tibetan refugees
bb. 1977	211	n.a.	*Xinhua*
cc. 1978	248	n.a.	*Xinhua*
dd. 1978	280	Kesong People's Commune	*Xinhua*
ee. 1979	250	Throughout TAR	Chinese source
ff. 1979	380	Shigatse	Tibetan refugees
gg. 1980	300	n.a.	*Xinhua*
hh. 1980	159 (total for 2–3 member family)	n.a.	Dalai Lama's office
ii. 1980	300–350	n.a.	Chinese source
jj. 1980	315	Nyingchi *xian*	Radio Lhasa
kk. 1981	457	Throughout TAR	Chinese sources
ll. 1982	250	Throughout TAR	Panchen Lama
mm. 1982	231.5	Throughout TAR	*Xinhua*

intelligence analysts who believed that *their* figures showed grain production to have barely kept up with the natural population increase in Tibet.[36]

No sizable amounts of food were imported into Tibet before 1950—with the notable exception of tea, which came almost exclusively from Sichuan Province. The imports that came into the border regions and the luxury food items for the aristocracy were negligible when set against the needs of the entire Tibetan population. Nor were there any appreciable food exports. Why then the need for extra food after 1950? There was, of course, the arrival of tens of thousands of Han, the departure of tens of thousands of peasants with managerial and agricultural skills in the years after the 1959 revolt, the disruptions caused by rebel activities, the opposition to the socialization of agriculture, and urbanization of rural Tibetans in response to the lure of even limited industrialization. All these changes occurred without a concomitant growth in agricultural output by those who remained on the land.

The preceding chart is instructive, though the figures should be treated with caution as they are subject to certain variables not recorded here, such as the variable weights of the traditional Tibetan measure, *khel*, which could be from 11.8kg to 19kg.[37]

It is difficult to compare these figures with food consumption before 1950. There are almost no records for those years although accounts from both former residents and visitors indicate that Tibet had achieved some level of self-sufficiency. We are limited to scant clues such as that offered by the former aristocrat who recalled that on a "small" estate 200 agricultural serfs produced 36,000kg of grain in one year[39]—a per capital output of 180kg. This was then reduced by taxes, animal feed, investment for the following year's crop, and so on.

The 180 kg mark is interesting. In the chart the figures hover most consistently around the 200kg mark. It is most likely that the average Tibetan continued to consume the same amount of food or only slightly more after 1950 as before. The Chinese government's policy in Tibet has been to step in with relief aid when the per capita annual distribution of grain falls to the 163kg mark. This figures for Tibet is somewhat below the "poverty line" in other parts of China—such as in Guangdong (Kwantung) Province where the government intervenes when the per capita distribution falls to 180–200kg.[40]

The 200kg figure corresponds with the per capita availability of grain throughout the rest of China as well. It should be kept in mind that on the whole the Han diet is more dependent on grain (80–90 percent of total caloric intake) than the Tibetan diet which includes large quantities of butter and, when available, meat. While some localities in China report quite high rations (360kg for a sales clerk, 540kg for a coal miner),[41] the urban adult ration in the major cities on the east coast ranges from a low of 180 to a high of 360kg in 1983. Average direct grain consumption peaked at 252kg per capita in 1985. It was down to 235kg in 1991 with people eating more meat, sugar, fruit, etc.[42]

Grain rations in the urban areas and distribution in the rural areas are supplemented by wages that can be used to purchase additional food items. This private sector may represent as much as an additional one-third or more to a peasant's income—RMB 38 in 1981 for peasants and herdsmen. Some reports from Tibet say that wages average from RMB 100 to RMB 252 (U.S.$66–166) each year. In 1979 a report from western Tibet claimed individuals had an average of RMB 150 (U.S.$100) in savings along with 150kg of grain in reserve. By 1984 rural income in the TAR was said to average RMB 280–300 (U.S.$180–200) and urban income about RMB 30 (U.S.$20) above that.[43] In the rest of China, the average annual per capita rural income is thought to be in the vicinity of RMB 83.4 (U.S.$55.60);[44] and for all of China (rural and urban), RMB 208.5 (U.S.$139).[45] There is no reliable way to gauge the extent of other food supplements such as vegetables, dairy products, and meat.

Just as the monetary wage scale in Tibet corresponds to the scale in other parts of China, so does the general figure of 200kg per capita grain consumption. (In 1978, average yearly grain consumption per capita throughout China was 196.5kg.) This 200kg represents 1,800 calories a day. Nutritionists have estimated that 1,600–1,800 calories are needed to maintain the Basic Metabolic Rate (BMR) for an average resting adult for a day. (These figures correspond to those used by the United Nations, which places the minimum subsistence diet for an adult at 180 kg grain, annually.) Over a period of a year, 180kg of grain translates into roughly four bowls of rice/wheat/barley each day.) In other words, the basic ration through China, as well as Tibet, would be just barely adequate if not supplemented with additional food.

Chinese officials have recently been candid about the shortages in agricultural output in Tibet. *Renmin Ribao* reported that "no marked improvement had been brought about in the Tibetan people's livelihood" since at least the years of the GPCR. Yin Fatang, head of the CCP in Tibet, has been quoted as having said "the greatest reality in Xizang was its poverty." This is in spite of grain output increasing 2.5 times and some additional growth in per capita output, which stands around the 250kg mark—at least one-third below the rest of China where the annual average was put at 307kg in 1976.[46]

In sum, it is probably safe to say that for the average Tibetan peasant, living in a small village, the availability of food has increased only slightly since 1950.[47] This small increment takes into account the modest per capita increases in food production, natural population increases, and the arrival of Han soldiers and civilians who account for the consumption of the large food imports.

Education

After 1959 a high priority was set on the development of education, especially toward the end of the Cultural Revolution.[48] The following chart illustrates the gains for the TAR.

Education in Tibet, 1965-81

Date[49]	Primary Schools	Middle Schools	Technical Schools	Tertiary Level
a. 1965	1,600–1,970	7	0	1 (teacher's college)
b. 1976	4,300	n.a.	0	3 (factory-run colleges)
c. 1977	4,900	"50 odd"	0	1 (teacher's college) 10 (factory-run colleges)
d. 1979	6,000	50	22	4 (colleges)
e. 1980	6,600	52	25	4 (colleges)
f. 1981	6,000	70 (middle and technical schools)		4 (colleges)
g. 1981	6,586	55	22	4 (colleges)*

*Tibet Institute for Nationalities; Tibet University (est. 1985); Tibet Medical College; Tibet Institute for Agriculture and Animal Husbandry.

Despite impressive gains, deep-seated difficulties remain. The 280,000 registered students in the TAR's educational system are largely children in the urban areas. In Lhasa, for instance, 80 percent of the eligible children attend school, while in the rural areas 30 percent or less is a common figure.[50] Since there are so few middle schools it is safe to assume that in most of Tibet those children who do manage to get any formal schooling do so only on the primary level.

One of the major reasons for the shortage of middle schools appears to be an acute lack of trained teachers. It is unclear how many of the 78,000 graduates of China's ten Nationalities Institutes (1950–1978) were from and are returning to Tibet or how many would be used as teachers. As described earlier there were no formal schools in Tibet before 1950, except for the two small ones run exclusively for future government functionaries. Through the 1950s the Chinese government only trained 150 Tibetan teachers, in accordance with the policy of introducing only gradual reform to Tibet. Although 1,200 students were enrolled in the Lhasa Teacher's College in 1974, it was necessary to recruit 389 Han teachers to live in Tibet to help offset shortages.[51] New policies adopted in the late 1970s of stressing quality of education and consolidation of educational resources mean that equality of educational opportunity in the TAR will be relegated to a future time and many primary schools in the rural areas may now be closed down.[52]

One of the most sensitive educational issues in Tibet is the language of instruction. In the 1950s and early 1960s the Tibetan language was used widely, particularly in the primary schools. During the Cultural Revolution it was undoubtedly abandoned; there is some evidence of a slight revival in the early 1970s. A Tibetan typewriter was developed, Tibetan-language book publishing flourished (almost exclusively translations from Han works, rather than from the indigenous culture of the Tibetans), films were dubbed in Tibetan, and reports appeared of Han stage actors studying the Tibetan language in preparation for bringing their shows to the TAR. The Dalai Lama's frequently repeated condemnations of China for using the Han language as the medium of instruction in the TAR schools rings hollow, since the medium of instruction in Tibetan schools in India is English.

Health Care

The state of health care before 1950 was appalling, despite the use of herbal medications. The introduction of modern medical care in Tibet (as well as in China proper) is applauded even by China's most truculent critics. The remaining criticism concerns the inequality of health care.

Currently, the emphasis is on the integration of modern and herbal medical techniques. Some previously debilitating medical problems, such as tetanus, are now under control; there are, however, some signs of an increase in the incidence of cancer and problems with dysentery and diarrhea continue to plague the population, especially the children.[53]

The movement to train paramedics—"barefoot doctors"—pioneered by the Chinese government exists also in the TAR, although the actual number of practicing paramedics is a matter of dispute—the latest and largest figure stands at 8,000. As in the rest of China, there were complaints about the inexperience and relative youth of those selected (15 to 19 years old in most cases) and about the lack of formal education received before medical training (from a total absence of any education to only the completion of primary school).[54]

Industry

In the field of industrial development, the emphasis through the 1960s remained on expanding and improving the road system throughout the TAR. Roads to Kathmandu, Nepal, Yunnan Province, and more remote areas of the region, were constructed until the total road grid numbered 90 with an aggregate length of over 21,000km (13,125 miles), reaching into 98 percent of the *xian* and 76 percent of the *zhou,* crossing 400 bridges along the way. Building the roads did not end the headaches for the government, for keeping them open the year round proved difficult.[55]

Industrial development expanded at a much slower rate. By 1964 there were only sixty-seven industrial enterprises (cement, tanneries, lumber mills, motor repair shops) established in the TAR and they were only small and medium-sized. The policy of moving slowly in this sphere during the GPCR was condemned as "revisionist trash" and blamed largely on Liu Shaoqi. The new policy created an upsurge in industrial activity, resulting in 250 new enterprises by 1975, a number of coal mines, and greatly expanded scientific exploration.

Not all this industrial growth was confined to the previous urban areas, for new industrial towns were created. There was Nyingchi on the Sichuan-Tibet highway, which grew from a population of 800 to 15,000 in little over a decade "with the warm support of fraternal workers in the motherland's interior provinces" (Sichuan, Shaanxi, Hubei, etc.).[56] The Shanghai Weilun Woolen Textile Mill moved to Tibet and set up the region's first plant.[57] There was also Shihchuando in the far west along the Xinjiang-Tibet highway.[58]

External Affairs

The repercussions from the events of 1959 in Tibet were felt on external as well as internal affairs. As we have seen, the UN was extremely reluctant to get involved in Tibet, in spite of repeated appeals from the Dalai Lama and the efforts of Hugh Richardson, who traveled to New York at one point to plead the Dalai's case. In 1959 the matter was put off because of the pressure of more urgent business. In 1959, 1961, and 1965 the issue came to the floor of the General Assembly. Resolutions on Tibet were passed, urging that the human rights of the Tibetans be respected.

These resolutions served no practical purpose. None even mentioned China by name, nor did they question the legitimacy of Chinese rule in Tibet (the 1961 resolution did regret, in passing, the depravation of the right to self-determination)—worded, as they were, solely to express regrets over the alleged abuse of "human rights" in Tibet. The UN's denunciations of those who did not act "reasonably" and "fairly" flew in the face of its own actions of denying the PRC membership during this period. It is hardly surprising that the Chinese government regarded these resolutions with little more than contempt.

While the UN resolutions may have given some intangible psychological lift to the Tibetan refugees, the state of Sino-Indian relations was of more importance to them. The major bilateral issue was then, and remains today, the dispute over common frontiers—particularly the area at the western end known as the Aksai Chin and in the east, the Towang Tract. Before 1959 the issue was broached gingerly by both sides and was only superficially touched on in talks between Prime Ministers Nehru and Zhou.

The growing revolt in Tibet in the closing weeks of 1958 and the ensuing political pressures in India compelled Nehru to begin a year-long correspondence with Zhou Enlai, resulting in the clear enunciation of both nations' positions on the frontier issue. India's contention was that a dispute did not exist; the boundaries set by the British colonial administration were legal and acceptable, confirmed by general practice and the lack of previous disputes. With no prior disputes, Nehru argued, there was nothing to discuss. China, on the other hand, felt that the boundaries had been imposed when India was under colonial domination and when China was weak and under fragmented warlord rule. Since both nations were then newly independent, Zhou argued, the boundary issue should be fully discussed among equal parties and a resolution agreeable to both sides reached—even if that agreement did nothing more than confirm the status quo.

The issue might have remained a polite diplomatic disagreement had not the Tibetans risen in revolt in 1959. China assigned much of the blame for the uprising to India: weapons arrived from there, exiles were permitted to operate against the PRC from Indian safe havens and refugees were welcomed, thereby encouraging self-imposed exile. The Dalai Lama, restricted as he was, made provocative statements from India, and New Delhi deliberately overlooked activities such as the celebration of the "Republic of China" National Day by pro-GMD Han and Tibetans in Kalimpong in 1959.

Nehru was in an unenviable position: on the one hand not wanting to alienate his powerful northern neighbors, on the other trying to appease the strong anti-communist political elements in India. His compromises (welcoming the Dalai Lama but restricting the Dalai's political activities, welcoming the refugees but preventing their congregation in communities along the sensitive frontier) did not please or appease either side. Inevitably, relations between New Delhi and Beijing began to deteriorate. China began to interfere with Indian Trade Agency activities and restrict pilgrim traffic to Tibet (an excellent conduit for guerrillas). India retaliated by expelling the manager of the Bank of China as well as several Chinese residents of Bombay and Calcutta purported to have close ties to the Chinese government.[59]

Before conditions deteriorated completely, China made some gestures in a futile attempt to ease the tensions. The holy sites of Kalish (Kang Rinpoche) and Manasarovar (Mavan Tso) were reopened to Indian pilgrims in 1961. Regrettably, the gestures were too little, too late; on 20 October 1962, war broke out. This conflict was short-lived, ending on 21 November. No land actually changed hands, the status quo continued, while Sino-Indian relations soured to a point from which they had not recovered two decades later. The war made China far more wary and security measures were tightened. In India the decision was made to increase covert activities, enlisting the support of Tibetan dissidents.

In March 1963, the Dalai Lama announced the publication of a Constitution for a future Tibet that he hoped to rule. This triggered an official protest from China, and Chinese media attacks on India noticeably increased. Three months later the Sino-Indian Agreement on Trade and General Relations lapsed; no extension was even considered. Nehru told the Lok Sabha that China had offered to negotiate a new treaty; India, however, refused until certain conditions were met, such as the release of two million rupees allegedly owed to Indian traders, the lifting of restrictions on the travel of these traders, and the removal of

Chinese forces from the Aksai Chin. These conditions were quite out of the question for China. The treaty lapsed and China expelled the Indian traders still in Tibet, confiscating the buildings they were using. Displeasure turned to outright hostility. Beijing accused New Delhi of "engineering and supporting" the revolt in Tibet and "using Tibetan rebels who fled to India to carry on subversive activities against China."[60] Nehru responded by lifting the travel restrictions on the Dalai Lama who first ventured to Japan in 1967,[61] and by overlooking overt Tibetan political activities against China. At the UN, India voted for the 1965 resolution condemning China—a shift from its previous abstentions in 1959 and 1961. In 1967 Deputy Prime Minister Morarji Desai began referring to "two Chinas" (the PRC and Taiwan). Finally in 1970 India initiated an appeal to the UN Human Rights Commission to investigate the alleged deprivation of "human rights" in Tibet by the central Chinese government.

The continuing escalation of hostilities had made China and India uneasy enemies, to the pleasure of the Tibetan refugee leadership. India has lost its unique trading position in Tibet and, not inconsequentially, its unique listening post in one of the PRC's most remote and unstable areas. Moreover, New Delhi has lost its chance to influence policies in Tibet when it could have been a moderating force. China lost an important ally in international affairs and increased its security burden along a remote and desolate frontier—a frontier through which both people and information were passing. Only Tibetan dissidents profited from the situation, for it gave their cause added weight.

The Great Proletarian Cultural Revolution (GPCR)

In November 1965 Yao Wenyuan (Yao Wen-yüan) launched an attack on Wu Han, then vice mayor of Beijing. This event marked the beginning of a political and social upheaval of a magnitude equal to the Chinese Revolution of 1949. The initial incident itself was obscure. Wu Han was criticized for having written a play (*Hai Jui Dismissed from Office*) four years earlier. This seemingly innocuous act was the culmination of a struggle among political factions with roots that could be traced back to the years of the Great Leap Forward (1959–1962), and perhaps even to the pre-1949 era.

The official launching of the GPCR was announced in *Renmin Ribao* on 1 June 1966. Students from all over China were urged to leave school and become Red Guards on behalf of the struggle to speed up the advent of communism. This struggle was launched on a sun-drenched August day, as over a million Chinese youths stood in Beijing's Tiananmen Square, waving little red books of Mao Zedong's quotations and shouting "Long Live Chairman Mao." The reasons remain obscured in political rhetoric, but the sharply different political views expressed by two distinct factions in the Chinese leadership must have played a role. On the one hand, there were Liu Shaoqi and Deng Xiaoping, advocating a policy of moderate socialization with a dampening of political and revolutionary fervor. On the other, there were leaders such as Lin Biao (Lin Piao), Jiang Qing (Chiang Ch'ing—Mao's wife) and—almost certainly—Mao himself. This latter group advocated more drastic policies, more decision-making based on political considerations ("putting politics in command") and a speed-up of actions leading to a communist state. The anarchy that developed during these years (now commonly referred to as "the ten lost years") and the subsequent purging of the leadership and denunciation of the GPCR has clouded considerably the issue. In spite of that and in spite of a paucity of material on Tibet during these turbulent years, the outlines of what transpired are discernible.

As early as February 1965, Radio Lhasa was predicting "a protracted, complicated and even violent struggle" to overcome the influences of the old society. By August 1966, only days after the Red Guards had rallied in Beijing, "the Great Proletarian Cultural Revolution had spread to Lhasa, uprooting in its tide the poisonous weeds of the old society and touched the roof of the world." A campaign was immediately launched to eliminate the "four olds" (ideology, customs, culture, and habits) and replace them with the "four news" (also ideology, customs, culture, and habits). Street names were changed to reflect revolutionary themes, tens of thousands of copies of the volume of Mao's quotations were distributed, Mao's portrait began appearing all over Lhasa, compulsory study groups were organized to read and discuss Mao's writings, and illiterate peasants were encouraged and praised for memorizing Mao's exact words.[62] More ominously, the Jokhang Cathedral was attacked by the most militant Red Guards and many religious objects were destroyed.

Throughout the latter half of 1966 the Red Guards began to pour into Tibet. Some even managed to fly, their fares arranged for them by sympathetic officials in Beijing.[63] On the whole the government in Beijing was opposed to these developments. The policy of Beijing toward Tibet continued to be that the region had a special status—that it was an area to be excluded from China's political campaigns. Zhou Enlai ordered the Red Guards to stay out of Tibet in August 1966. When this order was ignored he repeated the instructions in October, again in vain. In November, the State Council explicitly reiterated Zhou's expulsion orders for those already in the TAR, and a farewell banquet was held in Lhasa for the allegedly departing youth. In the end, however, they did not leave. With the intercession of Zhou's political foes in Beijing, they were permitted to continue their rampage through Tibet.[64]

In December 1966 one Red Guard faction established the Lhasa Revolutionary Rebel General Headquarters (Rebels).

> We a group of lawless revolutionary rebels will wield the iron sweepers and swing the mighty cudgels to sweep the old world into a mess and bash people into complete confusion. We fear no gales and storms, nor flying sand and moving rocks. . . . To rebel, to rebel, and to rebel through to the end in order to create a brightly red new world of this proletariat![65]

A month later an opposing group formed the Great Alliance Rebel General Command Post of the Tibet Autonomous Region Rebel Revolution (Alliance).[66] The Rebels, mostly Han who had recently arrived in Tibet, were aligned to the leftist elements in Beijing and claimed a membership of 200,000. The Alliance consisted mostly of Han cadres already living in Tibet; they were allied with Deng Xiaoping and Liu Shaoqi, and claimed a membership of 500,000. Both membership claims are almost certainly greatly exaggerated.

Both groups proclaimed to be supportive of Mao Zedong's ideological instructions. But there were at least two major points of difference between them—differences that apparently reflected the differences between the factions in China's leadership thousands of miles away in Beijing. One concerned the speed with which social and economic innovations should be implemented and the second had to do with the status of the participants in each group. The Alliance attracted the higher-ranking cadres, while the Rebels attracted the lower-ranking cadres and Han workers such as the truck drivers and those who worked on the roads.[67] Fighting between the two began sometime at the turn of the year 1966–67. With the help of additional Red Guards imported from other parts of China, the Rebels seized power in Tibet in January 1967. Having apparently acted without the consent of higher authorities, the young victors were well aware of the implications of their actions as witnessed by a comment made by one Rebel member who had taken part in the seizure of the *Xizang Ribao*. "Various kinds of fighting organizations also acted first, were declared "unlawful" in mid-course by the "reactionary line" and later gained Chairman Mao's approval."[68]

By February there was "beating, looting, and searching"[69] in Lhasa. The fighting continued throughout 1967 in spite of yet another appeal from Zhou Enlai for moderation. The Rebels, having already seized the *Xizang Ribao*, went on to take over the radio station and offices of *Xinhua* (where they arrested the reporters). Wall posters in Beijing indicated that, by March, Zhang Guohua had managed to regain control of the government apparatus in Lhasa. Even if these accounts were accurate, the chaos did not abate; the continued fighting was said, in August 1967, to have "seriously damaged the reputation of our army and the people."[70]

Although the struggle for power seems to have been largely confined to Lhasa, it did spread to the highly sensitive border region in the Chumbi Valley along the Sino-Indian frontier, bringing expressions of concern from at least one of the warring factions. There can be no doubt that both factions were acutely aware of, and nervous about, the possibility that the Soviet Union, the United States, and/or India would take advantage of the turmoil.[71] In early 1968 the fighting had spread to Shigatse while continuing in Lhasa until, according to some reports, sometime in 1969. By late 1969 the worst was over.

It has generally been assumed that Tibetans, for the most part, did not take part in the internecine struggles, but recent reports appear to belie that notion. One Tibetan refugee is quoted as recalling that "large numbers of Tibetans, especially students and Tibetan cadres, took part in the fray."[72] Some reports go further, claiming that it was almost exclusively the Tibetans who were responsible for the physical damage, egged on by their Han colleagues.[73] This implies that the Tibetan youth were unable to control their own actions, behaving as mere puppets for the Han. This contradicts another refugee claim—that Tibetan youth were in continual rebellion against the Han. The young Tibetans were probably caught up in the spirit of the day, just as were their Han counterparts— listening to the same revolutionary speeches, reading the same documents, and involved in the same kind of political groups. Indeed, it would be surprising had the educated youths exempted themselves from the tumult around them.

The disruption these activities caused to Tibetan life was selective. For example, while Nepali trade agencies were closed for a time, the traders' houses were unmolested. And, while there are ample accounts of mindless destruction of religious objects, there are also tales of valuable items being removed before homes and temples were attacked. Some reports claim that before a temple was destroyed it was first visited by experts who marked the precious stones, then by others who marked the precious metals (for removal), and only then it was attacked; the remaining timber and the saved stones were then reused for other buildings.[74] While it is possible that an inventory of religious objects was made and that they were removed before the destruction of the buildings that housed them, an operation such as this sounds too organized for an anarchic time such as the Cultural Revolution.

The damage caused by the wanton destruction and the fighting was awesome. Contrary to the propaganda claims that the Tibetans were "jubilantly" welcoming the Cultural Revolution, the reality was far more cruel. Even if we discount stories of thousands of Tibetans killed (government officials claim fewer than one hundred people died during the GPCR) and of monks and nuns being forced to copulate with each other in public, to smash icons and kill flies, verifiable activities of the Red Guards are terrifying enough. There were killings and people hounded into suicide. People were physically attacked in the streets for wearing Tibetan dress or having non-Han hair styles. An attempt was made to destroy every single religious item. All but a handful of monasteries and temples (the figures range from 2,000 to 6,500) were destroyed, many taken down brick by brick until not a trace was left.

One Tibetan refugee remembers what it was like in her commune.

> In the Red Flag Commune, the Cultural Revolution began at the end of 1966. . . . They showed contempt for the Tibetan script and banned Tibetan songs and dances. Tibetans were made to sing Chinese songs, wear Chinese dress and practice Chinese customs. We were also asked to speak in "Tibetan-Chinese Friendship Language," which was a mixture of Tibetan and Chinese.

> The Red Guards started off by destroying all the small shrines and pulling down the prayer flags. Then they confiscated all religious objects and articles, even prayer beads. They destroyed all religious monuments and paintings in

our area. They took the statutes . . . and sold them to the Chinese antique shops . . . and burnt all the ancient holy scriptures. They cut off the long hair of all the men and women and killed all the dogs.

They came from house to house and forced everyone to buy Mao's portraits and painted his sayings all over the walls. Everybody was required to carry Mao's Red Book at all times. They stopped anyone any time and made them recite Mao's thoughts. If anyone failed, then he was detained.[75]

The physical damage done by the Red Guards is irreparable however tireless are the efforts to repair it. The deaths of countless Tibetans will not be soon forgotten. Perhaps more important are the psychological scars which have created a breach between the Han and the Tibetans which will take decades, if not generations, to heal; and indeed may even prove to be unreconcilable.

Zhou's appeals for restraint and the efforts of some officials to limit the destruction (such as the successful protection of the Drepung Monastery) were insufficient to stop the havoc. The attacks were not only against the Tibetans but also the Chinese leadership which had shaped the moderating policies in Tibet—treating it as a "special case" and "backward," thereby precluding dramatic and sudden revolutionary change. It was an attack on the policy of working with the Tibetan elites and allowing them to maintain their feudal positions in the midst of a socialist society.

There was no question as to whom the Red Guards had identified as the architects of the policies toward Tibet. Deng Xiaoping, Zhang Guohua, Wang Jingwei (Wang Ching-wei) and Zhou Renshan (Chou Ren-shan, first acting secretary of the CCP Committee in the TAR) were collectively accused of attempts "to preach the reactionary nonsense of [their] master, Liu Shao-ch'i . . . and to oppose the decision made by one person [Mao Zedong]."[76]

As the political factionalism of the GPCR approached civil war all across the Chinese nation, the leadership began to dispatch units of the PLA to restore order and establish "revolutionary committees" to rule different areas and industries in China. One of the last regional groups to be set up, presumably because of the continued factionalism, was in the TAR. Taiwanese sources reported that the original date set was May 1968;[77] but continued fighting caused a postponement. In June 1968 the Chinese media carried appeals for peace from the military commander who had led the PLA against the Rebels, Ren Rong (Jen Jung). In September the Revolutionary Committee was finally established, with Zeng Yongyan (Tseng Yung-yen) as its head. Of the total of thirteen vice chairs on the committee, only four were Tibetans. Many prominent Tibetans were jailed; a handful—like Ngabo—managed to escape that fate. He explained: "Then it was difficult for me to work in Xizang. The party and Central Committee cared about me, and Premier Zhou personally sent an airplane to fly me to Beijing."[78] He was not to return to Tibet until August 1979.

Post-GPCR Events

In 1969 the fighting stopped. The major influence on China's attitude to Tibet after that date was the deterioration in Sino-Soviet relations, and the growing Indo-Soviet friendship. While the non-Han population in China at the time represented only 7 percent of the total population, they lived in areas that made up 60 percent of China's land mass. And, most crucially, that 60 percent of land is predominantly along the frontier areas of India and the Soviet Union, as well as Burma and Southeast Asia. With the Soviet Union and India seen as enemies of China—and allied with each other—the threat to China, especially along the frontiers, grew. For self-protection China considered it essential that the minority peoples in those areas not be alienated from Beijing and that they remain loyal to the PRC.

The next event to affect China's thinking was the creation, in 1971, of the independent state of Bangladesh. The Indian government played a major role in the victory of the Bangladeshi forces, naturally raising fears in China that India might duplicate its success—this time along its northern frontier, with Tibetan dissidents. India at the time was recruiting Tibetans into its armed forces. By 1973 the *Economist* reported that the number of recruits had reached ten thousand—about 10 percent of all the refugees.[79] This number is probably exaggerated, but that does not contradict the basic fact that many Tibetans were indeed being recruited and trained by India.

The final event was internal—the death of Lin Biao in mid-1971 and the subsequent purge of his followers such as Zeng Yongyan in Tibet, who was assigned to a lesser post in Manchuria. This led not only to a more moderate policy in China itself but apparently also freed the Chinese leadership to establish ties with the United States, formerly characterized only in the most pejorative terms. Lin's death and China's cautious dismantling of its xenophobic foreign policy also led at long last to China's membership in the United Nations.

For the Tibetans the ties with Washington meant an end to American covert aid to the rebels in India and Nepal. The PRC's admission to the UN meant an end to any more resolutions on Tibet, however ineffective. Moderate policies brought about some dramatic changes in all of China's minority areas. In Tibet the changes were especially dramatic. There was an abrupt end to the attacks on religion and a greater emphasis in the media on the need to respect the special circumstances of minorities. Monasteries that were still standing began to be repaired. At least U.S.$500,000 was allocated for the refurbishment of the Jokhang Cathedral alone. Religious practice seems to have made a cautious return. Although some refugees complained that circumambulation remained proscribed, Nepali visitors reported that the Barkor Road (as the Lingkhor Road mentioned earlier, a path for circumambulation) was being used for just that purpose, as it had been for centuries.

In 1971 the "four basic freedoms" (to practice religion, to trade, to lend money with interest, to keep servants) campaign was launched—scheduled to run for two years. Tibetans were permitted to wear their indigenous clothing once again, allowed to celebrate the Dalai Lama's and the Buddha's birthdays, permitted freedom to travel within Tibet and perform traditional dances. Monks and former nobles were released from prison. Tibetans were once again writing to friends and relatives in India and the United States, and 200 traders were permitted to take their goods to Nepal for sale (all but ten returned). One frequent visitor to Asia commented on how the situation in Tibet had been restored, with the important exception that "at least now you don't see emaciated serfs in rags carrying the litter of a noble dressed in warm clothing, turquoise rings and gold bracelets."[80]

The most interesting aspect of this new policy was the changed attitude toward the Dalai Lama. After having been fiercely condemned during the GPCR period, secret negotiations appear to have been opened between the Dalai and Beijing by either Chinese agents or unidentified go-betweens. George Patterson contends that he was approached by the Chinese while living in Hong Kong and asked to act as a liaison in opening a dialogue with the Tibetans. These secret talks seem to have lasted until 1974 when they were mysteriously and abruptly ended.

Publicly, the Dalai Lama maintained his strident views, rejecting any suggestions of a possible compromise. Nevertheless, rumors of his impending return to Tibet were so widespread during the early 1970s that George Patterson wrote an article in April 1973 that the Dalai Lama was hoping to return to his beloved Lhasa by his birthday in June of that year. These predictions were based on inside information and undoubtedly nurtured by alleged quotes, such as: "I believe firmly there is common ground between communism and Buddhism. . . . It [communism] aims, I am told, at obtaining for the deprived what is due them."[81]

India reinforced this new mood by lessening tensions with China. In 1972 Indian Foreign Affairs Minister, Swaran Singh, stated New Delhi's position without equivocation: "the question of "sovereignty" or "suzerainty" in Tibet was a matter for the Chinese to decide."[82] India, in response to a request from China, agreed to stop referring to the Tibetans in their country as "refugees," thereby making them ineligible for UN refugee assistance. It even took the extreme position in 1973 of preventing the Dalai Lama's annual speech on the anniversary of the 1959 revolt and forbidding the concurrent commemorations and demonstrations against the Chinese Embassy in New Delhi.

But efforts toward a compromise ended without positive resolution and without explanation. After forty Tibetans were issued visas by China to attend a religious ceremony performed by the Dalai Lama in India, the Chinese media renewed its attacks on the Dalai. These attacks were almost simultaneous with a widespread campaign being launched in Beijing, ostensibly to criticize Lin Biao and Confucius. These two became connected when the press tied Lin Biao and Confucius with the Dalai and Panchen Lamas, calling them all "jackals of the same lair."[83]

This period in contemporary Chinese history remains unclear. The extreme leftists (the "gang of four") had assumed power in Beijing, and Deng Xiaoping had been purged a second time. Throughout China more radical policies became obvious. The only curious note is that in 1975 Dr. Han Suyin (born in China, but a long-time resident in Switzerland) became the first non-Chinese resident to be permitted to visit Tibet in over a decade. Other Westerners followed in 1976, but this may have had more to do with the final end of guerrilla activity against China than with the ideological struggles unfolding among the leadership in Beijing.

While the more moderate policies improved the situation in Tibet considerably, there were still difficult problems. In September 1976 *Renmin Ribao* put it quite bluntly when it called on the Han living in the TAR to

> strictly abide by the Party's nationalities policy, respect the habits and customs of the minority nationalities and learn their language . . . [for Han–Tibet unity is an] indispensable condition for making further efforts to build a Socialist New Tibet.[84]

10

The Tibetan Diaspora

The geography of Tibet and an obsessive xenophobia—exemplified in laws demanding severe punishments for any Tibetan found aiding a foreign traveler—were the major factors maintaining Tibet's isolation from the rest of the world. That is not to say that Tibet was able to completely seal itself off, for its lack of total self-sufficiency necessitated a lively and flourishing trade network. The expansion of trade alone brought Tibetans into contact with Mongols to the north, Han Chinese to the east, Indians and Nepali to the south, and Kashmiri Moslems to the west (as well as the Europeans mentioned earlier). However, since Tibetan society, throughout its thirteen centuries of written history, had not been subject to any cataclysmic upheavals, the emigration from Tibet has been negligible. The few Tibetans who left included those who intermarried, participants in religious pilgrimages and children of the aristocracy sent to British missionary schools in India. The Indian hill town of Darjeeling boasted a Tibetan population as early as the mid-nineteenth century, while its neighbor, Kalimpong, saw its Tibetan population grow to about 1,500 before the fateful year of 1959.

Even after 1950 there were so few Tibetans in exile that their presence outside Tibet remained largely unnoticed by the world at large. This situation was to change drastically after the failed uprising in Lhasa in March 1959. The flight of the Dalai Lama was the signal for tens of thousands of Tibetans to flee south. According to all accounts the bulk of the refugees left Tibet in the years 1959 to 1963. Many fewer left from 1963 to 1965. The refugees who left after 1965 constituted only a small number.

One researcher, examining a group of refugees to determine their motives for having left Tibet, questioned 869 families in 1974–1975. He found that the

Tibetans listed their reasons in the following order of descending importance:

> —anxiety over not being allowed to remain practicing Buddhists;
> —rumors of atrocities committed by the Han;
> —rumors of Tibetans being prevented from marrying Tibetans;
> —rumors of Tibetans being compelled to marry Han;
> —the departure of the Dalai Lama; and
> —incessant political meetings, insecurity over the future, and the educating of children to watch and report the behavior of their parents.[1]

When the refugees left Tibet they crossed over mainly into Bhutan and India's Northeast Frontier Area (now called Arunachal Pradesh). Lesser numbers trekked into Nepal, Sikkim, and Ladakh. For the most part they were welcomed, despite the host countries' inabilities to meet the needs of such a large influx of destitute people. But one recalls being prevented from crossing the frontier until bribes were paid to the Indian border officials. This refugee subsequently bitterly complained that in his experience, India's "corruption and bribery [were] every bit as common as they used to be in Tibet."[2]

How Many Refugees?

It is impossible to determine how many Tibetans actually left. Census figures are unreliable, and the situation is further complicated by the fact that it is politically advantageous to the refugee leadership to inflate the numbers of refugees. The greater the refugee population, the more proof that communist rule in Tibet was oppressive and rejected by the populace. Emigrating was seen as an example of people voting with their feet.

The figures most commonly cited for the number of refugees who left Tibet are between seventy-five thousand and one hundred thousand. No accurate census has ever been undertaken, and the question of how many of the refugee population are children born in exile is rarely considered. The confusion is made apparent even within the refugee community and among their supporters, when the same officials will cite widely varying figures at different times. Recently, the Dalai Lama and his followers have been using the figure of one hundred thousand. In 1979 the Dalai Lama used this number to indicate all Tibetans outside of Tibet, including children born in exile. This was at odds with an official publication from his office a year earlier that set the number at eighty-five thousand.[3]

Even ascertaining the refugee monk population is difficult. One Tibetan refugee official observed that "the unbelievable cruel treatment meted out to religious leaders in Tibet has resulted in there being among the refugees a very high proportion of lamas."[4] Since the ecclesiastic population of Tibet prior to 1959 has been estimated at 15–20 percent of the male population, we can assume that the percentage of clerics among the refugees would exceed that. The same official then proceeds to put the total number of refugee lamas at 7,000. That was in

1974. The very same number (7,000) was used in an official publication printed in 1969, indicating—if the figures are accurate—that there was no growth in the clerical refugee population from 1969 to 1974.[5] The very same official, writing elsewhere, put the total number of clergy at exactly 10 percent of the refugee population.[6] Other Tibetan sources cite 5,000 monks in one instance and 6,102 monks and 150 nuns in another.[7]

The following table attempts to estimate the Tibetan refugee population for 1980. My figures are compared with a breakdown provided by an official refugee publication published in 1976.

Tibetan Refugees

Country of Residence	1980 Estimate	1976 Figures
India (including Sikkim)	65,000–70,000	68,748
Nepal	7,000–11,000	8,673
Bhutan	3,000–5,000	3,275
Switzerland	1,000–1,200	1,170
Canada	300	300
Europe (except Switzerland)	200	200 (including Japan)
United States	150–200	180
Taiwan	100	n.a.
Japan	30	n.a. (see Europe)
Total	76,780–88,030[8]	82,546[9]

The 1976 figures were corroborated by the refugee "Minister for Home Affairs" who said, in London, in October 1980, that there were 67,736 Tibetans in India and 11,690 in Nepal.[10]

Keeping in mind that there is general agreement that only a negligible number of refugees left their homeland after 1965, that even fewer returned home and, estimating an annual natural population increase of 3 percent (a little high perhaps, but common for nonindustrialized people—especially recent immigrants), it can be safely assumed that the number of Tibetans who actually fled from Tibet totals 50,000 to 55,000. This is far fewer than figures commonly quoted by refugee organizations and the Dalai Lama's followers. These figures are in line with estimates made by the United Nations High Commissioner for Refugees (UNHCR), whose experts believed that in 1967 the Tibetan population of India, Sikkim, and Bhutan was about 55,000 (refugee figures of the same period referred to 67,000);[11] while in Nepal they estimated that there were about 7,000 (the *New York Times* cited 10,000 at the time).[12] If we assume that the 50,000 to 55,000 figures is accurate, then an annual population increase of slightly better than 3 percent would bring the total of the entire Tibetan refugee population to about the 100,000 mark after two decades in exile. While estimates of those who died from the hardships en route to India run to tens of thousands, this number will never be known.

For years the Chinese told foreign visitors that 30,000 had fled; in 1976 they cited the figure of 40,000.[13] The Chinese have widely publicized the return of prominent Tibetans, such as the scion of the Pangdatsang family, an American-educated refugee who, after his return, wrote the first Tibetan book on life in the United States.

Life in Exile

Emergency camps were set up across the southern rim of the Himalayas. Aid was successfully solicited from a number of foreign countries, and foreign volunteers offered their services. However, for the most part "the sons and daughters of Tibetan aristocrats and wealthy Tibetans studying in colleges or working around Darjeeling, did not come to help."[14]

The situation in the early years of exile was precarious. Special problems existed for the Tibetan exiles: the difficulties of crossing the Himalayas on foot, the unavailability of resources in the host countries, and the problems of adjusting from a meat diet to a vegetarian one, from a cold climate to a warm, and from a sparsely populated region to a densely populated one. To the Indians, accustomed to refugees, this particular situation was eased somewhat by the existence of a single, recognized central authority. Given their previous status in Tibet, it was only natural that the Dalai Lama and the members of his administration in exile would emerge as the undisputed spokespeople for the refugees.

The Indian government initially placed responsibility for the refugees under the authority of the minister for external affairs who worked directly through the Dalai Lama. Nevertheless, the Indian government placed severe limitations on the Dalai Lama's political activities—to this day withholding official acknowledgement of the self-styled "government-in-exile." To the Indians, the Dalai Lama was the spiritual leader and spokesman for his people, but had no legitimate political status. When it became apparent that the Tibetans were in India to stay for some time, the government shifted responsibility for them to the ministry for rehabilitation, later creating a quasi-official office—the Central Relief Committee, headed by J.B. Kriplani—to coordinate and allocate all funds and volunteers involved with Tibetan refugee work.

The first attempt to provide the refugees with a means for economic independence was the establishment of ninety-five road construction camps along the northern borderlands in India. These were areas in which the Tibetans were uniquely qualified to labor. In spite of massive aid from the Indian government and outside sources these road building camps proved to be the most consistent source of income for the refugees. Approximately 18,000 to 21,000 Tibetans were employed in road building, at an average wage of U.S.$0.30 a day. Conditions were so bad that Tibetan refugee officials admitted in 1964 that these workers were worse off than they would have been if they had remained in Tibet.[15] The squalor, low pay, constant threat of illness, and the shortened life expectancy were not all the refugees had to endure. The worst injustice was surely the separation of the children from their families. Five thousand children were taken from their parents to live in permanent refugee camps. Three thousand others were permitted to stay with their parents in the road camps, but only on the condition that those under fifteen would not be allowed to work. Nevertheless, as is so often the case, a few extra pennies are always required; and there were frequent reports of children under the age of fifteen engaged in hazardous work.

Another point of contention is the source of the funds that poured in during the early years after the revolt. One of the first sources was the money the Dalai Lama had invested in Sikkim/India in 1951 when he fled to the south of Tibet. Upon returning to Lhasa in that year, he ordered that several mule-loads of silver and gold be sent across the frontier to be invested for possible future use. There has been widespread speculation as to the value of this haul—one high incarnated lama described it as "considerable wealth . . . invested with the government of India . . . [that had]been accruing interest."[16] One report set its worth at U.S.$3 million.[17] Gyalo Thondup has been quoted as placing its value at 50 thousand rupees (roughly U.S.$7 million). The Dalai Lama's officials have put it at 80 thousand rupees (U.S.$11 million).[18] As recently as 1978 a spokesperson for the Dalai Lama's administration indicated that for almost two decades the Dalai's "principle source of funds . . . has been the "sizable" gold reserves that the government of Lhasa shipped out before the 1959 uprising and stored in Sikkim."[19] A controversy arose over the management of the money. Gyalo Thondup claimed that he was authorized to use it; but he was hastily and harshly rebuked by his brother, the Dalai Lama, who insisted that the money was his and that only he could decide what to do with it.[20]

Foreign Aid

Apart from the Dalai Lama's money, the bulk of the funds came, in the final analysis, from the India federal and state governments, which provided land, food rations, medical assistance, and more general relief aid. The total amount spent on the refugees will probably never be calculated, although we know the Indians had spent over U.S.$6 million by 1962. In the early years the slack was taken up by foreign governments and private relief agencies; however, as these became less involved, the Indian government became more involved. By the end of 1965 U.S.$2,625,000 had been spent on the agricultural settlements; 750,000 rupees (roughly U.S.$11,000) was spent solely on the Bylakuppe Settlement in southern India at a time when its population numbered 3,000.[21]

After the Indian government, the major sources of funds were Western nations—through both governmental and private channels. In the early years (1959–62) organizations such as CARE, the International Red Cross, the YMCA, Catholic Relief, Church World Service, the International Rescue Committee, and Save the Children Fund all participated. In addition, Swiss and American governments and, later on, the United Nations High Commissioner for Refugees (1964–1973) also contributed to refugee assistance. During the first decade of exile, the Tibetan refugees received U.S.$5,300,000 in direct aid from the American government.[22] One estimate of the total amount provided ran to more than U.S.$20 million; this would average over U.S.$400 received for every man, woman, and child. The truth is that although we will never know what the total was, as one refugee publication put it: " . . . no one can dispute that the amount is considerable by any standard."[23]

Added to the official aid and funding were private funds. In 1960 a Tibetan Friendship Group was formed in the United States—followed closely by similar groups in France, Switzerland, England, Norway, South Africa, Australia, and New Zealand. These groups raised and donated funds and encouraged the financial adoption of individual refugees by their members. For the fiscal year June 1975 to June 1976 the American group donated U.S.$5,614.94, not including funds sent independently by their membership.[24]

In the United States, the American Emergency Committee for Tibetan Refugees (AECTR) was hastily formed in March 1959. Under the leadership of journalist Lowell Thomas and Supreme Court Justice William O. Douglas, this agency was to remain in existence only a few months, in order to help the Tibetans get settled in exile. Although the complete story of the committee is yet untold, there remains much speculation and considerable circumstantial evidence that a major source of its funding was the CIA. While the AECTR's literature attributes its genesis to the efforts of Magnus I. Gregerson of Columbia University's College of Physicians and Surgeons, other documents attribute it to the efforts of one Marvin Liebman, the secretary to the anticommunist "Committee of One Million Against the Admission of Communist China to the United Nations." Liebman was a prominent rightist, anticommunist crusader, who, within two weeks of the fighting in Lhasa in March 1959, had consulted with the United States Department of State's Public Affairs Adviser of the Bureau of Far Eastern Affairs, and the AECTR was born.[25] By December that year it was able to send U.S.$200,000 and medical supplies to the refugees in India.[26] By 1961 it had provided a total of U.S.$707,503 in cash and supplies.[27]

Lowell Thomas, Sr. assured me that the AECTR was, from its origins, a privately funded and privately organized group.[28] The committee's annual financial reports demonstrate that Washington was using the AECTR as an official conduit for funds to the refugees. In its nine years of existence the AECTR provided a total of U.S.$2,431,868, of which 31.6 percent was raised through public solicitation and 44.6 percent came in direct funds from the American government (pharmaceutical companies provided 23.8 percent of the total in drugs). This, of course, was in addition to the direct aid and surplus food Washington was providing for the refugees. Curiously, it "mysteriously and abruptly ceased operations in 1967," turning all of its activities over to the New Delhi office of Catholic Relief on March 1, 1968, and leaving many projects that had relied on the AECTR for funding high and dry—without so much as a warning and/or an explanation. Lowell Thomas, Sr. attributed the cessation of operations to the Indian government's "having problems" with the Chinese government and not wanting to offend them.[29]

Other governments appeared to get involved covertly. F.N. Beaufort-Palmer recalls that when he first raised the possibility of forming a Tibetan aid group, in a letter to the *Times* (London), he was approached by " . . . a young man in the Foreign Office [who] came and saw me more than once in a secret sort of way. From him we learnt much about Tibet and who, if we did find a society, would help and, almost more useful information, who would hinder us."[30] Mr. Beaufort-Palmer has rebuffed repeated requests for further elaboration upon his remarks.

Settlements

While the refugees were waiting to "liberate" Tibet from the communists, they needed some immediate relief from the squalid conditions of the temporary camps in which they were compelled to live. At first the Dalai Lama wanted all his people housed together in large concentrations just south of the Tibetan frontier, but for obvious security reasons the Indian government immediately ruled out that possibility. Instead, two temporary transit camps were established (Missamari in Assam State and Buxa in Bengal) until such time as the refugees could be moved to more permanent resettlement areas in different parts of India.

The camp at Buxa was a former British detention camp for political prisoners and was now used exclusively for the Tibetan clergy. At one time there were as many as 1,500 monks there, despite the almost intolerable living conditions. The situation at Buxa was so bad that by 1969, 200 monks had contracted tuberculosis, 80 of whom died.[31] The 900 monks who were still there in 1969–1970 were finally moved south to the Tibetan settlements at Bylakuppe and Mundgod. The camp at Missamari was little better. Conditions were so bad that foreigners were prevented from visiting. According to a Tibetan-speaking scholar, half the Tibetans died from the climate and neglect in the first year.[32] A Swiss refugee group put the population of Missamari at upwards of 8,000 in 1960.[33]

The first school for Tibetan children was established at Mussouri in March 1960. Eventually the Indian Minister of Education formed the Central Tibetan Schools Administration (CTSA), and by 1980 it was operating four residential and thirty day schools for 8,192 students (another 2,000 pupils studied at non-CTSA Tibetan schools). At the same time, thousands of other Tibetan children remained without educational resources. It can be safely assumed that at least 40 percent of the Tibetan exile population is of school age, or approximately 40,000 children. Consequently, the majority of Tibetan children in exile are not being formally educated. (The situation has become more acute since 1975, when the

Indian government ended free access to the residential schools for the Tibetan children born in India.) The Dalai Lama was said to be deeply concerned, but funds were lacking.

In an attempt to help make the refugees self-sufficient, handicraft centers were established. They tended to be small, cooperative enterprises, with severely limited capitalization and resources, which, nevertheless, managed to eke out a living for their members. Carpets and sweaters were the chief products. The woolen sweater industry, in particular, caught on and has become almost an exclusive Tibetan cottage industry throughout the subcontinent. The sweaters are knitted predominantly during the summer months and sold by traveling Tibetan traders during the winter.

Agricultural Settlements

The major resettlement efforts, and without a doubt those that offer the most hope for the future, are the agricultural settlements established especially for the Tibetan refugees. In Karnataka State, alone, there are five such settlements, housing over twenty thousand people.[34] Apart from these there are also settlements in Orissa State, in Arunachal Pradesh, and in northern India—around some of the former British hill stations.

The first agricultural settlement was set up after Prime Minister Nehru, at the Dalai Lama's instigation, appealed to the state governments for allocations of unused land. Mysore State (now Karnataka) responded with an offer of three thousand acres at Bylakuppe for an initial group of three thousand refugees. This was the most advanced settlement, largely because it received much technical assistance from abroad and from official organizations in India. This aid has included the establishment of a dairy farm by the National Christian Council of India, the sending of agricultural experts and trucks by the Swiss, and the founding of a carpet weaving center and setting up a "work center" for the elderly by the AECTR. Today the settlement houses over five thousand, and some have become so well off that

> it has become more common for young, impoverished Indian boys to be taken in by Tibetan families. In return for room and board these Indians would do a variety of household tasks such as hauling drinking water from the wells.[35]

The first five years were so prosperous that bicycles, horses, and gambling began to proliferate, while Tibetans were increasingly able to hire landless Indians for the labor needed in their fields.

In contrast, the settlement at Maniput in Madhya Pradesh State is in very poor condition. Established in 1963, through a government of India grant of 2,132,200 rupees (roughly U.S.$300,000), it had as many as five thousand inhabitants at one time. The major differences between the settlement at Maniput and that at Bylakuppe were the land conditions and the degree of outside technical assistance. The camp at Maniput is in a dense forest, in constant danger from tigers, snakes, and adverse weather conditions—all of which have taken a heavy toll in lives. Help for the community came largely in the form of funds from the AECTR. A hospital was built in 1964, only to be suddenly and mysteriously closed down three years later. The YMCA also sent a volunteer teacher. However, by 1978 there were only 1,100 inhabitants left at Maniput; and they were living without electricity, industry, or irrigation. Morale was very low, and there was little to show for fifteen years of labor.[36]

While the situation at Bylakuppe may be envied by Tibetans living in other agricultural settlements, a closer examination demonstrates that the fruits of success are not evenly distributed. A visit in 1977 by a Tibetan refugee journalist found that after sixteen years the "water and electricity facilities are . . . not very satisfactory," that there were no metaled (paved) roads, and the hospital was inadequate. The available education was so poor that the wealthier families were sending their children to schools in Bangalore, while those who were unable to afford such an expense, but were equally concerned about their children's education, were keeping them at home rather than send them to the Tibetan schools. After sixteen years of technological and financial assistance, the camp's leadership had still failed to establish even the most rudimentary social welfare scheme for the poor under their charge.[37]

In the settlements the day-to-day administration is run by an official appointed by the Dalai Lama; this person becomes the Camp Leader. The Camp Leader "in many respects . . . is considered the king of the settlement. He can virtually command people within the settlement."[38] One anthropologist, upon studying this administrative structure, observed that it put an end to the traditional Tibetan serf/lord relationship, but had replaced it with a "paternalistic hierarchical rule."[39]

There is also the problem of a shortage of land. Back in the 1960s, each refugee received one acre of land. However, no provisions were made for population increases—either through immigration or birth. With land size fixed, the larger the family, the greater the difficulty in providing adequate sustenance. To maintain political loyalty, the camp leaders discourage mingling with the Indians who live in the vicinity—a process aided by the absence of opportunity for the Tibetans to learn the local Indian languages. Women are even worse off than their male counterparts, for they need permission—from a male—to leave the camp; they cannot vote; and they are given second preference when it comes to education.[40]

Education

Education was a top priority for the Tibetan refugee leaders. Except for the teaching of Tibetan language and history—carried out by Tibetan teachers—Indian teachers were employed, using English as the medium of instruction. (In light of this, the Tibetan refugee accusation that the Chinese are destroying

Tibetan culture by using *Chinese* for teaching in the schools in Tibet, rather than Tibetan, is curious.) According to an interview with the secretary of the Tibetan Education Council, most of the curriculum taught in the Tibetan schools is worthless for the students' future vocational needs. One discontented Tibetan claims that his nephew, after nine years of schooling, has yet to read a newspaper or an entire book.[41]

Not all Tibetan children attend school. There are few schools in the agricultural settlements and residential school costs (about U.S.$120 per year) are a formidable expense for the average Tibetan family whose total family income averages U.S.$792–2,400 yearly. These conditions, of course, do not affect the former aristocracy who send their children to exclusive, and expensive, private Anglo-Indian schools or abroad for their education. The Dalai Lama's youngest brother was educated at the prestigious, Catholic St. Joseph's School in Darjeeling where the rector was quoted as having said that the young pupil had "forgotten all that nonsense about being an Incarnation."[42]

Health Conditions

Considerable sums of relief money have been sent to the refugees, but this money has not been managed adequately. Blame must be put with the Tibetan leaders in Dharamsala. Even in the Dalai Lama's own backyard, Dharamsala, where approximately three thousand Tibetans live, the sanitary conditions remain deplorable—with an acute shortage of public latrines and no system for the disposal of garbage, as recently as 1979.[43] An American doctor who worked for several months during 1978 at the Delek Hospital in Dharamsala complained about these conditions and described them as contributing to "a plague of illness."[44] It was not until 1981 that a Department of Health was established; even, at that, only enough money was allocated to run the office in Dharamsala.

Life in the south of India, in the agricultural settlements, is not much better. At Mundgod the original plan called for 4,000 acres of land for 4,000 Tibetans. However, 640 acres are being used for buildings and roads, leaving only 3,360 acres for a population of 7,140 as of 1981. The arable land has no irrigation facilities and drinking water is in very short supply. A recent visitor appealed for additional aid for Mundgod because the children were said to be suffering from malnutrition. Of all the deaths of those under five years of age, 40 percent are attributed to malnutrition. Indeed, the child mortality rate in this camp is 162 per 1,000 live births.[45] As recently as 1980 an American physician, commenting on the general refugee situation in India, termed it "wretched" because the refugees were

living in extreme poverty, in unhealthy settlements on "leftover" land in the poorest areas of India. Most of their energies are devoted to the personal struggle for survival. . .the people sink into poverty, apathy, illness, alcoholism, and despair.[46]

Some of the lack of medical attention is culturally derived rather than the result of an uncaring administration. Visitors to the agricultural settlements have found that even when medical facilities exist they are often underutilized because of a lack of understanding of modern medical practices and the deep-seated belief in *karma*. As one Western physician put it, there is an "inevitable conflict between some traditional Tibetan and modern "western" attitudes to hygiene and the nature of the disease process."[47]

Tibetan "Government-in-Exile"

These problems are only the tip of the iceberg. But there has been little hesitation in establishing an administration paralleling the one that existed in Tibet, at an enormous cost, in order to assure continued control over the Tibetans in exile. Under the Dalai Lama, who retains supreme authority, there is a Cabinet (*Kashag*) and there are nine administrative offices. A Constitution, written with the help of an Indian lawyer,[48] was promulgated in 1963, in an attempt to integrate modern Western concepts of parliamentary democracy with the feudal traditions of Tibet. It is a strange mix at best. It begins with a classic understatement:

> whereas it has become increasingly evident that the system of government which has hitherto prevailed in Tibet has not proved sufficiently responsive to the present needs and future development of the people

and proceeds to guarantee equality before the law, due process of law, right to legal counsel, freedom of speech, assembly, travel, association, and residence. A National Assembly was created, with three-fourths of the membership to be popularly elected, but with limited powers, it has no say over taxation matters. (Interestingly, for a constitution based on Buddhist ideology, there is no stipulation banning "unclean castes" [butchers, tanners, corpse-handlers], a common practice in Tibet prior to 1959.)

The most curious aspect of the entire document must be the functions given to a body known as the Council of Regency. This three-member group is elected by the National Assembly and is expected to rule

> when the National Assembly, by a majority of two-thirds of its total members in consultation with the Supreme Court, decided that in the highest interests of the State it is imperative that the executive function of His Holiness the Dalai Lama shall be exercised by the Council of Regency.

To a Westerner, this statement sounds fairly routine; but it is nothing short of remarkable. To all Tibetans the Dalai Lama is no mere mortal, but the reincarnation of their patron deity. According to Buddhist dogma, no human can ever overrule a Bodhisattva (as a highly literate Tibetan put it, "the masses are over-awed by the very mention of the name of their religious and temporal head.")[49]

Moreover, a major and serious contradiction exists in the "Foreword" of the Constitution that states unequivocally that it "takes into consideration the doctrines enunciated by Lord Buddha."[50] If that statement is to be accepted at face value, then the Dalai Lama can never be deprived of his powers—spiritual or temporal—unless he abdicates. More than one eyewitness in India at the time of the constitution's publication, reported that "among the ordinary refugees the promulgation of the Constitution caused horror and grief and it is repudiated by them as totally unacceptable."[51]

Nothing testifies to the strength of the religious ties among Tibetans more than the hold the Dalai Lama continues to maintain over his people. The relief operations have been bedeviled with organizational rivalry and the intrigues of "unsavory members of the Tibetan ruling clique."[52] Relief supplies, particularly medical supplies, have been found to be on sale in the market in MacLeod Ganj, less than two miles from the Dalai Lama's place of residence. The Dalai Lama's late sister, Tsering Dolma, was widely disliked. In order to control the comings and goings in the nursery that she administered, she instituted a system whereby pairs of children stood guard at all the entrances, regardless of the weather, in order to inform her first of any visitors. Moreover, while the children in her care were frequently on the verge of starvation (a refugee worker recalls an incident in which she was attacked by starving children as she was carrying a plate of breakfast scraps) she was noted for her formal, twelve-course luncheons. Meanwhile, in bitterly cold weather the children were clad in "thin, torn, sleeveless cotton frocks—though when VIPs visit the Upper Nursery every child there is dressed warmly in tweeds, wool, heavy socks, and strong boots."[53] In general the corruption was so bad that the Director of Operations for the UN High Commission for Refugees noted that if all the relief supplies that were sent to India were distributed, every Tibetan should have at least one-and-one-half blankets each. This is in no way meant to give the impression that every Tibetan leader was corrupt; the home established for children in Mussouri by the aristocratic Taring family, is, by every account, a humane, well-run, and property organized model.

Contradictions

The Tibetan leadership is faced with some vexing contradictions. On the one hand, it extols the virtues of being prepared to return to Tibet at a moment's notice. On the other hand, in order that the refugees be able to raise themselves above the bare subsistence level, it is essential that they *do* put down some roots in their current communities and make contact with their neighbors. They cannot do both, and the Dalai Lama and his advisers have been unable to reconcile both needs.

A second major contradiction lies in the relief program for the refugees. One of the major sources of political power for the Dalai Lama is his ability to control relief funds, educational scholarships, and the hiring of Tibetan teachers and bureaucrats. These powers only continue as long as there are many stateless refugees. Consequently, it is to the benefit of the leadership to keep Tibetans in children's homes, transit camps, and temporary facilities—not unlike the situation among the Palestinian refugees. According to a high Tibetan refugee official, as of October 1980 as many as 17 percent (11,402) of the refugees in India and an astonishing 35 percent (4,058) of the refugees in Nepal remained unsettled.[54]

The Tibetan refugee community is not a cohesive single unit. Certainly there is admiration, and even awe, for the Dalai Lama and his spiritual rule. Even among his severest critics, the Dalai Lama himself is rarely blamed, while wrath is heaped on those who surround him. The more obvious divisions are the ones inherited from Tibet. There is dissension between the Buddhist sects as well as regional differences. As one Tibetan noted, "regionalism continues to be the main disease afflicting the Tibetan society in exile." Groups of Tibetans from outside the central regions (U, Tsang) lobby for greater participation in the administration, but while Dharamsala tends to view these groups with "guarded hostility and benign neglect" they continue to make their presence felt. So much so that this regional squabbling led to a suspension of elections of representatives to the nominal Parliament after 1982. For a while the Dalai Lama appointed all delegates unilaterally.[55] The rifts are bound to widen if the leadership does not recognize and resolve them. As relief funds diminish, as younger Tibetans have more contact with, and are more influenced by, the indigenous people among whom they live, as more Tibetans move out of refugee camps, and as the prospect (for the vast majority) of returning to Tibet grows dimmer with each passing year, the power of the Dalai Lama and his ruling group weakens.

Disagreements Within the Ranks

By the year 1972 the clandestine funds for the guerrilla operations against China were used up, relations between China and India were beginning to warm up once again after a decade of correct frostiness, and the Dharamsala group had no bold new plans to lift the spirits and hopes of their followers. Tibetans had begun to voice their opposition to leadership policies. In Bylakuppe those in opposition were not appointed to administrative posts, nor did they receive educational scholarships.

First indications of this trend were in evidence at a student meeting at the Institute of Higher Tibetan Studies in Sarnath during a "Tibetan Freedom Conference," held in July 1972. The meeting which pledged to "launch a mass movement to struggle for the restoration of Tibet's rightful independence."[56] Their unilateral efforts placed the leadership in an awkward position. On the one hand, the leaders could not help but lend support to the causes articulated by the younger generation, since they echoed the rhetoric emanating from Dharamsala. On the other hand, by supporting the young people's efforts, the leaders found themselves supporting an alternative power base that could ultimately threaten their own power.

In January of 1977, President Jimmy Carter took office in the United States, pledging to carry out a foreign policy based on the principle of "human rights" around the world. This led Tibetans to declare that, "it is his special emphasis on the human rights issue that makes him a potential Messiah for Tibetans."[57] In March of that same year, a new government came to power in India—under the Janata Party that had several leaders long committed to the Tibetan refugee cause. These two events—coming, as they did, only months apart—brought great hopes and expectations to the Tibetans.

March 10, 1977, was the eighteenth anniversary of the failed revolt in Tibet. A group of young Tibetans, angered that previous anniversary demonstrations had been placid and routinized, tried to break into the Chinese embassy in New Delhi. Forty policemen and several Tibetans were injured; 209 Tibetans were arrested for rioting, violation of a probationary order, assault and attempted murder. At the same time, a short distance away, a handful of Tibetans launched a hunger strike on the doorstep of the United Nations Information Office. The Tibetan Youth Congress endorsed these actions, saying, in a press release: "if the United Nations chooses to ignore the appeal of the Tibetan people then nonviolence will have been dealt a deathblow [sic], and the Tibetan people will have to find recourse in a more active and positive path of action in their struggle for independence."[58]

The response from Dharamsala was swift. The youth group was ordered to disband—one of the elders calling the Youth Congress "an association of children who though educated have no knowledge of what Tibet was really like."[59] The repressive measures probably came as no surprise to the youth leadership; several months earlier they had warned Dharamsala that it must come to grips with the new situation outside Tibet, for "it was high time Tibetans realized that serving the government in a democratic system is vastly different from serving it in feudal Tibet."[60]

One additional potential difficulty appears in two recent studies by Indian scholars which indicate that a distinct socioeconomic class difference is being reinforced in India by the selection of Tibetan refugees sent to live in the agricultural settlements in the south. While all classes of Tibetans fled Tibet, it appears—if these studies are accurate—that the poorer classes are being relegated to the hotter, more economically depressed, more crowded agricultural settlements where education and employment opportunities are far below those in the northern refugee centers such as Darjeeling, Kalimpong, New Delhi, Dehra Dun, Dharamsala, etc.

One study of Tibetans in the north found that 25.29 percent characterized themselves as previously "very rich," 20.0 percent as "rich," 40.0 percent as "middle," and 14.71 percent as "lower middle." None thought of themselves as "poor." Their jobs were broken down as 14.71 percent state officials, 9.81 percent clerics, 3.40 percent military officers, and 72.08 percent as self-employed (presumably traders). The researcher noted that, of the 40 percent of the families

surveyed in New Delhi, Dehra Dun, and Dharamsala: "The refugees dis-
proportionately represented the monastic hierarchy, upper classes and the active
participants in the Tibetan resistance movement."[61]

Another study in the Mundgod settlement in the south, which canvassed 805
of the 868 resident families, found that almost all characterized themselves in
their former professions as peasants, herders, and in the service of trades. Of the
3,869 people, 2,871 had no schooling, 639 were currently attending school, and
only 18 had completed high school (the remainder probably did not answer).[62]

Politics in Exile

While there is, of course, a wide range of political views among the Tibetans,
three distinct perspectives appear to have emerged as most prominent. The first
group is content with the status quo, assimilating comfortably into new environ-
ments and performing the obligatory activities—promoting the return to Tibet as
ritual with little substance. The second group, understandably much smaller than
the first, has advocated coming to an agreement with the communists based on
some form of effective home rule for the Dalai Lama. This group, in the past,
was minute; but in recent times has been joined by none other than the Dalai
Lama. The final group, the most difficult to quantify, advocates violent means to
regain power in Tibet and the acceptance of aid from any source (including the
Soviet Union) to achieve its goals. Most of the refugees do not openly espouse
any of these political views but, more than likely, lean toward the first.

At the time, the Soviet connection was hardly as fantastic as it might first
appear. Since the Sino-Soviet split of 1959, the Soviets conducted covert activities in the Chinese borderlands, hoping to foment revolt among the ethnic minorities that inhabit those areas.[63] Furthermore, the Soviets found themselves
standing hopelessly by, while a close ally, India, moved to better relations with
its most bitter foe—China. The opportunity to support Tibetan terrorist activities
in India against China and/or against Chinese nationals, buildings, visitors, etc.,
could have proved too enticing for Moscow even though these activities might
have weakened Indo-Soviet relations.

In 1979 the Dalai Lama visited the Soviet Union and Mongolia, returning
with reports about the freedom to practice religion he had witnessed. In addition, the
Dalai also began talking about creating a socialist system in Tibet. When asked in
November 1979 what sort of government would best suit Tibet, he replied: "Broadly
speaking, I think it will have to be socialism."[64] The Dalai Lama was probably
reflecting a politically astute attitude—pretending to lean closer to Moscow in order
to gain greater leverage for bargaining with Beijing in secret talks.

For the first time since the beginning of the twentieth century, at least some
Tibetans find themselves in the midst of foreign entanglements involving several
major powers. Improved Sino-Indian relations are contingent on several outstanding issues—not the least important of which is the Tibetan refugee di-

lemma. Near the end of 1981 China and India began discussing their differences with the aim of reaching an amicable solution. As long as the Dalai Lama insists on recognition of a "government-in-exile," and as long as the younger generation grows increasingly impatient at the inability of the Tibetan leadership to fulfill pledges of returning home, the Tibetans will remain a major irritant to the two Asian giants. The Tibetans understand this only too well and worry about their future. If New Delhi and Beijing reestablish their previous relationship of *Chini-Hindi-Bhai-Bhai* (China-India-Brothers) it is highly unlikely that the Tibetans will be consulted as to what is being planned for them in diplomatic negotiations. It is true that in India the Tibetans and the Dalai Lama himself enjoy widespread support from the media, a number of prominent individuals, and from the government, for the time being. But, perhaps, a harbinger of the future is the quote from an Indian police superintendent who told a correspondent from the *New York Times,* "the Dalai Lama is a liability to us."[65]

Nepal

India is home today for over 80 percent of all Tibetan refugees, with the second highest concentration in the Kingdom of Nepal; their numbers are commonly put at 11,000 to 12,000.[66] Today, while several thousand remain unsettled (refugee officials confirm these numbers—4,058 or 35 percent of the entire Tibetan population), about 5,000 live in fourteen settlements that were, for the most part, established by international relief agencies. The settlements are agricultural, supplemented by handicraft industries. As in India, the conditions under which these people are compelled to live are far from desirable, even after years of overseas aid that included large shipments of U.S. surplus foodstuffs. Disease is rampant; a dispensary nurse reported in 1975 that children were dying needlessly from such readily curable ailments as intestinal worms and dysentery. The Dalai Lama's representative in Nepal has admitted that the international agencies are pulling out, finding that although they have supported the refugees long enough for them to have become self-sufficient, instead "the social problems have increased tremendously." He attributes that increase solely to "a geometric [rise in the] birth rate."[67]

The remaining 65 percent of the Tibetan refugees in Nepal are scattered throughout the mountains and valleys of the majestic Himalayan northern half of this kingdom, mainly near the Tibetan border; some are involved in cross-border trade. It is virtually impossible to assess the conditions of these estimated 2,300 to 3,000 Tibetans, although it would be safe to assume that they also live in difficult and indigent conditions—with little hope for future prosperity.

Bhutan

It should come as no surprise that when the Tibetans fled their homes many chose to go to the tiny Himalayan kingdom of Bhutan. In addition to the geographic similarities to Tibet, the majority population, Drupkas, is ethnically, culturally, and linguistically related. At first the welcome was warm, although Bhutanese officials were concerned about the ecological effects of a large influx of people into their nation of only 1.25 million. As in Nepal, many of the Tibetans continued moving south to India but approximately four to six thousand elected to stay, settling with apparently little friction.

This seemingly successful resettlement was abruptly interrupted in 1973. In April, just months before the official coronation of the current monarch, King Jigme Singye Wangchuck, the government of Bhutan announced the arrest of more than thirty individuals, almost all of them Tibetan refugees. The arrests were said to be in response to a plot that had begun a year earlier with the fatal heart attack of the previous monarch. During the latter years of this king's reign, one of the most influential people was his alleged mistress. This woman, Ashi Yanki, was accused of being the ringleader of a group that had plotted to kill the young heir to the throne, set fire to the capital of Thimpu, and, in the resulting confusion, carry out a coup d'état that would have effectively put Bhutan under the control of Tibetan refugees. The purpose of this coup, it was claimed, was to turn Bhutan into a military camp and a staging area for raids into neighboring China. It was further alleged that Ashi Yanki's major source of support and encouragement was none other than Gyalo Thondup.[68]

There was a noticeable increase in the general mistrust toward the newcomers from the indigenous population. Subsequently, Tibetans were frequently spat at on the street, and the government severely restricted their freedom to move around the kingdom and subsequently tried to settle them in scattered locations, breaking up the concentrated areas in which they had voluntarily congregated. The king told an interviewer that 922 Tibetans were "voluntarily" moved from "restricted" areas after the alleged coup attempt.[69]

Although some suspect the story about the coup is far-fetched, questions concerning the loyalty of some Tibetans to their adopted homelands are plausible.

The Dalai Lama must maintain the absolute and undivided loyalty of the refugees in order to preserve his secular power. He is opposed to assimilation, and is especially opposed to the acquisition of citizenship in the settlement countries. In 1979 it was rumored that representatives of the Dalai Lama were warning Tibetans not to choose Bhutanese citizenship, lest they be barred from any future "independent" Tibet. Whether the Dalai Lama specifically ordered such warnings or whether they were initiated by his local representatives, the admonition conforms with the Dalai Lama's public statements against assimilation. In response, the Bhutanese, wanting all Tibetans to assume citizenship and profess their political loyalties solely to their king, have promised the refugees that they are free to renounce Bhutanese citizenship any time in the future—as are all Bhutanese.

With the Bhutanese administration pressing on one side, threatening to deport all non-Bhutanese citizens to China; and Dharamsala pressing them to remain stateless, the Tibetans were caught in the middle. They are undoubtedly not seriously interested in returning to Tibet, but they remain outcasts in Bhutan. Meanwhile, Dharamsala appealed to other nations to admit these unfortunate people, but for several years no nation agreed. Washington, for example, pointed out that Bhutan was offering all Tibetans citizenship and not automatic expulsion, simply because they were Tibetans. Moreover, Washington pointed out that the Tibetans had lived in Bhutan for twenty years, and citizenship after such a residence was not an unreasonable request.[70] India finally responded, however reluctantly, agreeing eventually to take all the Tibetans who wished to leave Bhutan.

Sikkim

In the tiny principality of Sikkim, which was a semi-independent entity when the Tibetans came and has now been unilaterally annexed by India, the arriving Tibetans also found a people ethnically related. Tibetans have lived in Sikkim and studied in its monasteries for centuries, and of the current Tibetan population of about five thousand, half were resident there prior to 1979. The Dalai Lama's efforts to maintain political control in Sikkim are complicated by several factors. One is the existence of a sect of Buddhism that cooperates with Dharamsala on religious and cultural matters, yet rejects its political authority. Another factor is the extensive influence of the Nepali population, which, largely through immigration, is the majority ethnic group. The wealthy refugees send their children to British-style missionary schools where they are socialized outside of Dharamsala's influence, while the less affluent parents are sending their children to Nepali schools.

Since there was an established Tibetan community here in 1959 when the refugees arrived it was inevitable that the newer arrivals would quickly assimilate and adopt an attitude independent of Dharamsala. Little is written about their life-styles, although for the most part these refugees are believed to be somewhat better off than their compatriots in India and Nepal.

Europe

In Europe, Tibetans have arrived in small groups and have been welcomed in a number of countries. There are a few hundred Tibetans in Britain, France, Germany, the Netherlands, Sweden, and Denmark. It is in Switzerland, however, that they have arrived in the largest numbers. In 1961 the Association for Tibetan Homesteads was established to facilitate the immigration of Tibetans to Switzerland. The Swiss government agreed to permit one thousand Tibetans to come, guaranteeing 75 percent of the costs, although the funding was raised entirely from private sources (since 1975, predominantly the Swiss Red Cross). In the early 1980s the Swiss agreed to allow several hundred more Tibetans to settle there.

While seemingly well off, and immeasurably better off than their compatriots on the Asian subcontinent, Tibetans have found it difficult to adjust to life in their new Europe homes. Because they lack self-sufficiency after almost two decades, the Swiss Red Cross is still compelled to support many of them at an average yearly sum of U.S.$250 each. A Canadian government study of their resettlement in Switzerland concluded that the "prospect for the future is that the Tibetans will require long-term financial and social assistance." This partially results from the adjustments necessary after the upheavals of moving from one culture to another and partially from the erroneous initial assumptions made by the Swiss that led to unfulfilled expectations. For example, "much to the disappointment of local authorities," the Tibetans have tended to favor day laboring and industrial work rather than apprenticeships and farming professions, since the former are higher paying and less strenuous. All this is subject to change, of course, as assimilation leads to further intermarriage. Tibetan parents encourage their children to receive a European education in order to help them better adjust to Swiss life. Currently, 30 percent of the Tibetan population is under sixteen years of age.[71]

North America

There is a marked difference in attitude between the government of Canada and that of the United States toward the Tibetans. Washington has pursued a policy of allowing individual Tibetans into the country—deciding each case as it comes along. This has resulted in a Tibetan population in the United States of about 150 to 200. Canada, on the other hand, conducted a series of studies on how to best accommodate the refugees and on how they had fared in Switzerland. The results of the studies convinced Ottawa to allow a planned arrival of about 300 Tibetans since 1970.

Canadian immigration began to be considered when the Tibetans approached the Canadian Consul General in New York in 1966. Ottawa immediately ruled out the possibility of a large group, arguing that it would hinder assimilation and integration. In December 1968 Prime Minister Trudeau wrote to the Dalai Lama offering to take a small group of people on the condition that employment could be found for them. Two months later the Dalai Lama accepted the offer, and in June 1970 Ottawa authorized a program for 240 Tibetans at a cost of CAN$3,300 per person.

The Canadians, characteristically, chose the refugees carefully, weeding out the poor and uneducated. Of the first 228 to be admitted, 33 percent had monastic careers in Tibet, 15 percent were merchants, 9 percent were civil officials, while 29 percent were dependents. An extraordinary number, over half, had received a secondary-level education. The Tibetans in Canada—as in Switzerland—have spurned agricultural work, gravitating toward light industry and moving near urban centers. Because their small numbers are spread out from Alberta to Quebec, maintaining traditional cultural practices is difficult. A study conducted by the government in Ottawa in 1975 found that only half of the refugee children continued to speak Tibetan at home, while one-third were not receiving any instruction in traditional languages or cultural matters on a regular basis.[72]

In the United States the first suggestions for Tibetan immigration came from Dale Ernest and Col. Ilya Tolstoy, who, in 1959, suggested that yaks be imported with the Tibetans and that they be settled in Alaska. The Whitney Foundation sponsored a feasibility study. The Alaskan project was abandoned when a high incidence of unemployment was discovered in that newly constituted state. Wyoming and Colorado were then studied as alternative sites, but were also rejected. In 1967 the refugees' supporters did manage to bring six Tibetans to the United States to work as loggers in the state of Maine, where a labor shortage existed. Although the Tibetan population of Maine reached thirty by 1971, it fell back to zero soon after.[73]

The only other organized group of Tibetans to come to the United States has been from the Sakya region of Tibet, admitted with the intercession of the University of Washington in Seattle. Sponsored by the Rockefeller Foundation, under a grant for "Free World Scholars," these refugees were used as informants for extensive anthropological studies of life in the Sakya region. The remainder have come as individuals or as family groups, promoting their religion (about 10 percent are clergy) or their political beliefs, or as students or sojourners in search of a new and better life.

It is interesting to note that in the United States, and to a lesser degree in Canada, the Tibetans have been able to successfully gather together large numbers of followers who actively support their political efforts against the Chinese. It is natural that their first allies would be the extreme anticommunist fringe. In addition, these refugees have been highly successful in capitalizing on mass alienation among the young people in the United States. With Buddhist monasteries, study groups, rural communes, and even an accredited college in Boulder, Colorado (established by the late Chogyam Trungpa), they have converted hundreds, if not thousands, to their religious beliefs—thereby creating a large, receptive audience for their political beliefs.

Conclusions

In attempting to assess the conditions of Tibetan refugees, we are immediately faced with doubt as to the credibility of official pronouncements emanating from Dharamsala. The refugee leadership views itself as a small, embattled entity, fighting the world's lack of interest in helping refugees return to their divinely (as they perceive it) appointed places of rule in Lhasa. Given this attitude, it is not surprising that the leadership expended its major efforts in an attempt to regain power—even risking temporary material deprivation of the people. But it is more complex than that. If the leadership had devoted its efforts to securing a better life for the Tibetans, that probably would have contributed to the erosion of the concept that gives their political existence legitimacy—that they constitute a "government-in-exile," preparing the way for a resumption of power in Tibet one day.

In spite of the sacrifice of the well-being of the Tibetan community, the Dalai Lama remains remarkably popular. He seems to be above direct criticism, despite a report from a Christian missionary that while the Dalai was in Mussouri, soon after his arrival in India, his guards intercepted a Tibetan pilgrim with a hand grenade.[74] His spiritual role, uniting the refugees, far outweighs his political functions—at least for the time being.

The promotion of nationalism is particularly important to supporting the belief that Tibet was once an independent country. Some older symbols of nationalism such as a flag and a national anthem were supplemented with a new holiday (10 March the anniversary of the 1959 revolt) and a Constitution. There is also

> a constant effort in the media to retain the ideas of an overriding Tibetan nation by keeping the plight of the Tibetan "brethren" left behind before the people. There has been a steady diet of "eyewitness" accounts of the situation in Tibet by recent refugees, . . . all of which have the theme of how lucky the refugees are in India and how the downtrodden brothers left in Tibet still believe in the Dalai Lama and earnestly desire a free Tibet headed by the Dalai Lama. Concomitantly, the Tibetan media continually expounds on how the Chinese communists are trying to eradicate the Tibetan race in Tibet. It is, therefore, the duty of the refugees, led by H.H. [His Holiness] the Dalai Lama and his government to maintain the greatness and vitality of the Tibetan race and culture-nation.
>
> Underlying these perspectives is the theme of *rgyalzhen* or patriotism to the Tibetan cause. Support and compliance with the DLG [Dalai Lama's Government] is considered patriotic whereas opposition and disagreement is considered traitorous because it allegedly harms the "Tibetan cause."[75]

Continued proclamations that a return to Tibet will occur "soon," ties the leadership to a commitment that is, at best, unrealistic. In addition, the leadership will find it increasingly difficult to prevent further assimilation.

The Dalai Lama has frequently spoken out against both mixed marriages and the acquisition of citizenship in his people's adopted countries. But since being stateless in India means having no legal rights and having to register with the local police whenever one moves,[76] it is not surprising that more and more Tibetans are becoming Indian citizens. In line with Tibetan aristocratic tradition, however, what is preached to the "masses" is not necessarily followed by the elite. Two of the Dalai's brothers are American citizens. It will surprise no one when the practice spreads. By 1978, in Switzerland—where citizenship requires either twelve years of residence or marriage to a Swiss citizen—5 percent of the resident Tibetans had chosen to end their statelessness. This percentage is bound to rise as more refugees become eligible for citizenship.[77]

The longer Tibetans remain refugees, the more reluctant will the international relief agencies be to continue providing aid. Withdrawal of aid will further reduce the Dalai Lama's secular power. Another consequence of continued exile and unfulfilled expectations will be a growing sense of frustration on the part of the younger generation—brought up to believe that their major goal in life was to "liberate" Tibet from the "heathen Chinese." The rift between older and younger Tibetans can only continue to grow if the leadership stubbornly clings to the rhetoric of the last twenty years. Conditions of living will inevitably worsen in agricultural settlements, caught between fixed land allocations and an unremittingly upward population spiral.

While this chapter has concentrated on the difficulties faced by Tibetan refugees, it should be pointed out that there are areas of success. The successes have come not only in the industrial nations of Canada and Switzerland, but also—to a more limited degree—in India, where the general conditions of the refugees is roughly equivalent to that of their Indian neighbors. Many have become educated, some achieving the highest educational honor; many more than would have been possible in the Tibet of years past; furthermore, they are not limited to the upper strata. Certainly the cataclysmic events of the past three decades have reduced the social divisions—both economically and educationally—to an extent hitherto impossible. Also, Tibetan entrepreneurial skills have resulted in a burgeoning middle class. But the harshest reality remains an uncertain future. The successes, attributable more to individual effort than to the refugee leadership, are but a hint of the potential.

11

The Current Situation

In September 1976 Mao Zedong died. Less than a month later his widow, Jiang Qing (Chiang Ch'ing), and three of her cohorts (Zhang Chunqiao [Chang Chun-chiao], Wang Hongwen [Wang Hung-wen] and Yao Wenyuan), dubbed the "gang of four," were arrested in a power struggle that brought the subsequent resurrection of Deng Xiaoping and heralded some of the most significant changes in China since 1949.

The central authorities admitted errors in past policies. As these related to Tibet, they were outlined succinctly:

> 1. "The creation of a large number of unjust, false, and erroneous cases and hurting and implicating many cadres and masses";
> 2. the mechanical implementation of policies such as those used by the model Dazhai (Tachai) Brigade; the forced planting of wheat, the setting of unreasonably high targets for production, and state purchases all leading to the people "having difficulty in their living";
> 3. regional autonomy was ignored and became "a mere formality," and Tibetan culture and religious practices were forbidden ("most temples were destroyed") and
> 4. excessive capital investment was used without regard to actual situations or the availability of supplies leading to poor results and even heavy losses.[1]

The first indications of change in Tibet came when Western travelers were again allowed to visit. Swiss resident Dr. Han Suyin was the first, in 1975; but by 1977 American government officials and members of the diplomatic corps in Beijing were beginning to take what became routine pilgrimages. In August 1979 the Second Session of the Tibet People's Congress met in Lhasa; it elected

Tian Bao as the chair of the TAR, Ngabo as chair of the Standing Committee of the Congress, and another Tibetan, Zi Cheng, as president of the higher people's court.

Although Tian Bao was born in what is now Sichuan, he became the first ethnic Tibetan in a major leadership position since March 1959. Several former members of the upper strata and officials in the Dalai Lama's pre-1959 administration were appointed to high, although largely powerless, positions. Several of these men had just been released from prison where they had languished since 1959.

In late September, a senior vice premier of China, Ye Jianying (Ye Chienying), gave a remarkable speech on the occasion of the thirtieth anniversary of the founding of the PRC which included an admission of guilt on the part of the Beijing government: "It is true that the people's interests have sometimes been seriously harmed as a result of mistakes in our work in certain periods since liberation."[2]

In August 1980 *Renmin Ribao* published a sharply worded editorial indicating new instructions from the highest level of the CCP. To regard minority peoples solely through the perspective of class analysis was now deemed to be an "erroneous formulation" and the result of an "ultra-left line." This line, it continued,

> gravely undermined the Party's economic policies and those toward nationalities, religion, the united front and cadres. Ruthlessly they [Lin Biao and the "gang of four"] brought cases against large numbers of people which were based on unjust, false and wrong charges, striking blows at minority peoples and their cadres as if they were class enemies.

The editorial set out three objectives for which Beijing was determined to strive:

> 1. Introducing national regional autonomy and consolidating the unity and unification of the various nationalities on a democratic basis and on an equal footing.
> 2. Gradually eliminating the political, economic, and cultural inequalities among the nationalities.
> 3. Acknowledging national differences, taking into consideration the special features of the various nationalities and correctly approaching and handling national contradictions.

The last objective was, by far, the most urgent. As "Special Commentator" observed:

> the experiences of the post-liberation years point to the fact that in areas inhabited by minority peoples, there were two different working policies—either running affairs according to the special characteristics of these nationalities and areas, or mechanically copying the policies, tasks, and methods used in the

areas inhabited by the Han people. Which of the two we adopt will determine whether we succeed or fail in our work in this field. To this day there are still many problems in areas inhabited by minority peoples. If we look into their causes, most of them are connected with our working policies.[3]

There can surely be no clearer admission of shortcomings by any government. This August statement came a full seven months after substantial changes had been implemented. Four months later Ren Rong was ousted as First Secretary of the CCP in Tibet; Yin Fantang was named in his stead as Acting First Secretary. Born in Shandong (Shantung) Province, Yin had twenty years of experience working in Tibet and, most significantly, spoke fluent Tibetan—a rare feat among the Han cadres. The CCP organization in the TAR met in September 1979 to formally propose the new policies. Promising to eliminate the "ultra-left influence" they outlined a number of proposals—the most critical of which was that smaller production units (teams composed of twenty to thirty families) rather than the larger communes be the chief accounting units. Decisions about work and production outputs would be made by the teams, giving individual households a greater say in their daily lives. The proposal was made that larger private plots should be allowed. To make it abundantly clear that the government in Beijing would no longer strive for egalitarianism in the foreseeable future, the promise was made "to make the well off richer and help the poor become comfortably off."[4]

In short, the CCP proposed to ease central government control over the local areas; create smaller work groups for added flexibility; and allow these smaller units (in this case production teams) to determine what tasks needed to be done, how they would be handled, and by whom. In addition, it was proposed that each individual household be made responsible for specified output so that larger and/or more ambitious families would no longer be responsible for aiding their smaller and/or less ambitious neighbors. Not an incidental result of these policies was the placing of more power over decision-making in the hands of the peasants themselves.

This was not all, however. In May a high-level delegation arrived in Lhasa on an inspection tour of Tibet. The group consisted of Hu Yaobang (General Secretary of the CCP), Wan Li (a Politburo member and Vice-Premier), Yang Jingren (Yang Ching-jen) (Chair, State Nationalities Affairs Commission) and Ngabo Ngawang Jigme. After the trip the group submitted a report calling for the creation of authentic regional autonomy, exemption from state purchases of grain for "a few years," an increase in state subsidies, "specific and flexible" economic planning, a "revived and developed" Tibetan culture, education and science, and a commitment that fully two-thirds of all the cadres in the TAR be ethnic Tibetans within two to three years. (By the end of 1982, 60 percent were Tibetan.)[5]

A month later, in June, all the criticisms of past efforts and proposals for future efforts were formally incorporated into a series of specific plans. Written and spoken Tibetan was adopted as the primary language in legal matters. Tibetans would enjoy a two-year tax holiday on agricultural and animal products and a five-year tax hiatus on industrial and commercial taxes. The state announced a decision no longer to assign work projects arbitrarily but to contract for needed workers through the individual communes. Commune members would have the freedom to decide what and how much to cultivate, while the production teams would be free to make work assignments. Border trade would be promoted and traders would be free to cross into Burma, India, Bhutan, Sikkim, and Nepal. Private plots and sideline industries would be encouraged. Ironically, the opening of the frontiers and the easing of travel restrictions have created a noticeable rise in the incidence of smuggling; in late 1981 the Lhasa administration was obliged to create an "antismuggling" office.

The situation was so bad that even these dramatic reforms were deemed insufficient. In 1981, it was revealed, the central government was giving direct subsidies to 320,000 Tibetans whose income did not meet even the most minimum requirements. This number represents almost 20 percent of the population.[6] By 1984 the authorities in Beijing admitted that "since 1980 living standards had not improved much."[7]

To counter these failures, a "do-as-you-like" policy was initiated. Communes were disbanded completely; land was allocated to individual households to do with as they wished. There was no mention in the press of the "responsibility system" prevalent in the rest of China where individual households must sign contracts to deliver a percentage of their output to the state in return for the use of the land. Taxes were waived until at least 1990, free markets were established, trade with neighboring countries was liberalized and encouraged, all state sales quotas were abolished and subsidies from Beijing were once again increased. Schooling was made totally free (the only place in China where this is so), tourism was encouraged (6,300 visitors from 1980–1983), temples and monasteries were being rebuilt. In addition, Yin Fatang was replaced as head of the CCP in Tibet by Wu Jinghua (Wu Ching-hua); a curious choice since Wu speaks no Tibetan and is of the Yi nationality from Sichuan.[8]

It will take several years before an adequate assessment can be made of the effectiveness of these latest policies. Historically, one of China's major difficulties has been the inability of the central authorities to ensure compliance with orders given by the local authorities. During the days of imperial China, officials had a saying that "heaven is high and the Emperor is in Beijing," implying that the farther away from the capital they were stationed, the greater was their flexibility to govern as they pleased. This seems to have been just as true over the past thirty years in Tibet. Regardless of the efforts exerted by Beijing, local cadres in Tibet have continued to act according to their own interests. Recent reports from Hong Kong indicate that local cadres in the TAR continue to be an obstacle to the introduction of reform.[9]

The new policies have encouraged Tibetan refugees to return to their homeland, and have allowed families divided by exile to communicate through the mail. Appeals to the refugees to return began as early as 1963. Radio Lhasa claimed that about two thousand Tibetans had visited Tibet—200 of whom had decided to stay permanently during 1978–80. (Dharamsala put the figures for the same period at 200 visitors and fourteen returnees.)[10] The new policies have also included—to the best of our knowledge—the release of most political prisoners in Tibet, including the Panchen Lama.

In recent years Tibetans have been more free to leave Tibet than at any time since 1959. In 1980, 200 Tibetans traveled to India to watch religious ceremonies conducted by the Dalai Lama. A year later over a thousand Tibetans were waiting to meet the Dalai Lama when he arrived at the Buddha's birthplace in Lumbini, Nepal. Beijing is now issuing three-month exist visas to so many Tibetans that refugee publications in India speak of a "spurt of visitors" and "large numbers of Tibetans" arriving in India. It is somewhat more difficult for the refugees to visit Tibet; however, they are also arriving in unprecedented numbers. It has become easy for non-Tibetans—who have considerable incomes—to visit fabled Tibet; tourism for the very rich is flourishing in Lhasa, Shigatse, and Gyantse as well as along the Tibet-Nepali border where a modern air-conditioned, fifty-room, Western-style motel has recently been completed. As for trade, twenty-one trade routes have been opened along the 1,415 km. (2,264 miles) Tibet-Nepali frontier.

The changes have also meant a return to the official pre-Cultural Revolution attitudes toward the aristocracy. China, admitting its errors, has begun investigations of charges against Tibetan cadres, former feudal lords, and traditional Tibetan doctors who were "persecuted and discriminated against for years." Former feudal lords who did not participate in the 1959 revolt will again receive installments of the money owed them for the purchase of their lands and estates. By May 1982, Chinese authorities had paid 1,158 Tibetan households a total of RMB 3,146,500 (U.S.$1,851,000) toward settling these accounts.[11] Even outside Tibet there have been repercussions. In New Delhi, were quite recently Tibetan demonstrators and their Indian supporters were banging on the gates of the Chinese embassy, the ambassador opened those gates, offering tea to members of the Indo-Tibetan Fellowship.

Religion

No changes can be more important for the average Tibetan that those concerning their religious practices. Beijing admits that of the 2,500 or so monasteries [the exiles put the number at over 6,000] and the 150,000 to 200,000 clergy prior to the GPCR, only about ten institutions remained standing—with about 1,000 inhabitants.[12]

> religious freedom was practically nonexistent when Lin Biao and the gang of
> four held sway. In order to restore the Party's religious policy, Article 147 of

the Criminal Law which was promulgated last July [1979] and is to come into force as from January 1, 1980, stipulates:

"A state functionary who unlawfully deprives a citizen of his legitimate freedom of religious belief or violates the customs and folkways of a minority nationality, to a serious degree, shall be sentenced to imprisonment for not more than two years, or to detention."

At the same time, the law does not condone all religious practices; it specifically disallows the practices of the supernatural: "sorcery, witchcraft, fortune-telling, palmistry, phrenology, magic, and so on."[13]

The latest 1982 Chinese Constitution prohibits "discrimination against and oppression of any nationality," while also banning "any acts that ... instigate their [minorities'] secession [from the Chinese nation]." The constitution also allows for "freedom of religious belief" and punishment for those who "discriminate against citizens who believe in, or do not believe in, any religion."[14]

Errors of the past are being redressed. In 1980 RMB 500,000 (U.S.$322,580) was allocated to rebuild the destroyed Ganden Monastery outside of Lhasa. Butter is now being burned again for religious festivals (a 1976 visitor reported that its burning had been banned as wasteful), and in 1979 the Tibetan New Year was celebrated again for the first time in "the past dozen years or so." It is the training of new monks, however (twenty at Drepung as of mid-1980) that especially signals a return to the pre-1959 days. By 1984–1985 monasteries were functioning with fourteen hundred monks.[15] But while temples and monasteries are open to the faithful for prayer and pilgrims are once again pouring into Lhasa, the days on which the facilities are open remain restricted. Furthermore, and, on a more ominous note, in May 1981 the Panchen Lama noted that local cadres continue to interfere with religious practices, stating that "the party's policy on freedom of religious belief has not yet been implemented in some localities." Tibetans have also been warned not to "abandon production to go to worship Buddha," not to "arbitrarily revive" monasteries "without permission" and not to "use religion to carry out sabotage."[16]

Economy

Second only to religion, the economy has suffered the most in Tibet. Attempts to change the nomads into sedentary farmers failed. Efforts to coax Tibetans away from their staple of barley to winter wheat also failed. (This wheat was unsuited to Tibet's soil as it depleted the soil's essential nutrients at a far greater rate than did the native barley—resulting in rapidly diminishing outputs after some initially huge harvests). Moreover, hunting and fishing, coupled with precipitous population growth (created by the introduction of Han civilians and soldiers), have altered the delicate balance of the Tibetan plateau, making large segments of it uninhabitable for perhaps generations.[17] This misuse of the land is the result of several years of poor weather conditions, implementation of erroneous policies, and the refusal of political leaders to heed the advice offered by technical experts.

In early 1980, Beijing dispatched 520 work-teams to the TAR to carry out relief work. They took with them 4,485 tons of grain, 2,830 milk cows, 1,200 sheep, 43,000 quilts, 52,000 household utensils and substantial amounts of clothing. A total of 200,000 tons of food and goods are shipped into the TAR yearly. Beijing also promised to increase state subsidies. By 1980, annual subsidies were said to be running at U.S.$285 million (94 percent of the TAR's budget)—a staggering sum for a population of fewer than 2 million. Moreover, Beijing reported that since 1952 subsidies to the TAR have totaled RMB 6,390,000,000 (U.S.$4,260,000,000).[18] Furthermore, Tibet will also share in a subsidy of RMB 500 million (U.S.$300 million) pledged each year for "economically underdeveloped areas" all over China; this sum was to increase 10 percent each year after 1981. When these subsidies are added to the tax holidays described earlier, the Chinese government is clearly making a substantial monetary investment in Tibet.

Other difficulties should sound familiar by now. Only 10 percent of the Han speak Tibetan, while it is estimated that only 10 percent of the Tibetans have learned to speak Chinese. As in the past this situation only serves to exacerbate the continued unrest that plagues Beijing's rule in Tibet. In 1983 Yin Fatang ordered *all* cadres, officials, and PLA officers under fifty to learn Tibetan. He also ordered that all government documents be in Tibetan. "Great Hanism" continues to contribute to the unrest. The Chinese media reported that in the ten years preceding 1979 this attitude had grown rather than diminished. Discontent among Han cadres had not diminished, either, in spite of a 30 percent cost of living allowance, promises of better food, better housing, more frequent pay rises, and better future employment prospects for their children. All these extra benefits, which taken together mean a 71.82 percent addition to the original salaries, must surely cause resentment among the Tibetan cadres. Moreover, residential patterns and education patterns clearly demonstrate that the Han and Tibetan officials mix and live in separate communities, further exacerbating the separateness.[19]

Dalai Lama

China's new government has not only begun to make changes inside Tibet, but has made very effort to do so quickly. Nothing would hasten change more than the return of the Dalai Lama, supporting the new policies. In early 1979 a proposed visit to Tibet by a group of young refugees was canceled at the last minute because of the insistence of the Chinese embassy that the group members declare themselves "overseas Chinese." However, from August to December 1979 a five-member delegation, handpicked by the Dalai Lama's "Security Department" and his younger brother, Lobsang Samten (an American citizen), traveled via Hong Kong and Beijing on a pre-arranged itinerary. Upon their return they refused to comment publicly except to thank "the Central Government of the People's Republic of China, [which] graciously provided necessary facilities for the tour and placed no restrictions on their movements."[20]

This extraordinary trip offered the first public evidence that Beijing and Dharamsala were in communication—and could come to some agreement. This delegation was immediately followed by two other groups sent by the Dalai Lama—one led by his younger sister, Pemba Gyalpo. There were also private visits by his two older brothers (Thubten Norbu and Gyalo Thondup) and their families. Considering that these two men had spent much of the past thirty years working feverishly against the Chinese, in collaboration with China's greatest enemies, Beijing's permission to them to travel indicates a tolerant attitude. There were so many trips during this brief period that the *New York Times* went so far as to predict that the Dalai Lama's return to Tibet would "not be delayed much past the end of the year [1980]."[21]

It is not yet possible to pinpoint the genesis of this recent dialogue. In spite of overt intransigence, as early as the latter part of 1976 the Dalai Lama was known privately to be leaning toward reconciliation with Beijing. He must have been pleased when, in May 1977, China made its first *public* gesture toward him. It is quite possible that the gesture resulted directly from his private assurances, conveyed to the authorities in China. On May Day Ngabo met with a visiting Japanese delegation in Beijing, telling them that the Dalai Lama would be welcomed back upon agreeing to "embrace the motherland and stand on the side of the people."[22]

The rumors that followed this and other overt gestures from the Chinese, became so persistent that the Dalai Lama felt obliged to publicly renounce them, calling them "systematic propaganda . . . trying . . . to hinder our way to freedom."[23] He also felt the need to write an article (in 1977) that appeared in the *Asian Wall Street Journal*, adamantly declaring that his return was not imminent and was contingent *solely* on proof that the Tibetans in China were pleased with the status quo there. "If those six million Tibetans there are really happy and contented we would be prepared to return and accept whatever status the majority of them are prepared to grant us." He called on the UN to mount a plebiscite and then threw the gauntlet down to China.

> In fact, it would be a reassuring sign to us if the Chinese government stopped being selective about whom to invite. It would also be encouraging if the visitors' itinerary weren't confined to Lhasa and its immediate vicinity.[24]

The Dalai Lama got his wish (China says it was the Dalai Lama who initiated the talks in 1979 and the Tibetans says Deng Xiaoping sent an emissary to Gyalo Thondup "offering an unconditional truce").[25] Beijing allowed three delegations of the Dalai Lama's handpicked representatives, including most of his family, to travel in Tibet. They spent several months in Tibet, traveling not only in the TAR but also in Amdo and Kham. (How free they were, though, is a matter of some dispute.) Moreover, two high level delegations visited Beijing for protracted, secret negotiations on the terms under which the Dalai Lama would visit/return to Tibet. "Let bygones be bygones. Forget the past and look forward," announced Yin Fatang over Radio Lhasa in 1982. As a result Tibetan refugees who are not officials have also been allowed to visit. Many of these are from comfortable, middle-class homes in Europe and North America and are not dispassionate observers. Nevertheless, all the travelers have been met with tremendous enthusiasm by the indigenous population; and all have been universally appalled by the living conditions they have witnessed. The descriptions published to date have some similarities with the earlier descriptions of Tibetan agricultural settlements in southern India—not to mention descriptions of life in Tibet before 1950.

Because living conditions are indisputably poor in Tibet, there are bound to be dissenters. The members of the Dalai Lama's second delegation were made aware of this when they found themselves at the head of a two-thousand-strong Lhasan demonstration in support of the Dalai Lama. Chinese authorities, accusing them of "surreptitiously advocating Tibetan independence," cut their trip short by six days.[26] Since the delegation members were all outspoken advocates of Tibetan independence before they visited Tibet, the charge is hardly surprising; we can only wonder what the Chinese expected in allowing them to visit.

Favorable comments from the Dalai Lama about socialism and his protracted and delicate negotiations with China are not welcomed by all of his followers. When his first delegation left for China in 1979 he felt obliged to keep their departure a secret until their plane had actually left the ground in New Delhi. He even kept it a secret from his cabinet. To shield himself from the inevitable criticism, he arranged to be in Europe and the United States when the delegation was in China. Demonstrations in protest of the trip broke out. In a classic understatement, the *Tibetan Review* told its readers, "reaction of the ordinary Tibetans to the trip continues to be uncharitable on the whole."[27] The Dalai Lama is well aware of growing opposition to his outward willingness to negotiate with the Chinese—as is demonstrated by his statement, "That there are already some Tibetans in exile who find it difficult to reconcile what they call my liberal ideas, my openness to socialism and the good points found in Marxist theories."[28]

International Implications

The Dalai Lama's return to Tibet, if it ever happens, will have repercussions beyond his people in exile and the PRC. Indeed, in 1982 the Dalai acknowledged as much by telling his people that reconciliation between him and the PRC is "an issue that is deeply linked with the changes in the international political scene."[29]

The leadership in Washington has always had a somewhat ambivalent attitude toward the Dalai Lama—supporting his people in exile and voting for him at the UN on the one hand, but for twenty years refusing to let him visit the United States. The Dalai did finally visit the United States in late 1979 and again in mid-1981, but both times with only lukewarm enthusiasm and minimal assistance from Washington.

As far as we can tell, America no longer has any covert relationship with the Dalai Lama or his people. There is little reason to doubt that Washington would be pleased with a Beijing-Dharamsala agreement and a stabilization of the situation in Tibet, thereby preventing any encroachments by the Soviet Union in that area.

New Delhi would be equally pleased with such an agreement, for the Dalai Lama remains an obstacle to diplomatic relations between the once-allied China and India. Over the years, New Delhi's treatment of the Dalai Lama's political position has fluctuated widely. All along, New Delhi has steadfastly refused to recognize the Dalai's "government-in-exile," maintaining that Tibet is a part of China. Even when the most vocal and ardent supporters of the refugees were elevated to positions of power—in several of Indira Gandhi's governments and especially in the short-lived Morarji Desai government—improving relations with China always took precedence over championing the cause of Tibetan refugees. This was never made more explicit than by the February 1979 visit of Foreign Minister Atal Behari Vajpayee to Beijing. Not too many years earlier it had been Vajpayee himself who led demonstrators to the gates of the Chinese embassy in New Delhi, demanding that they leave Tibet. Vajpayee reaffirmed India's position on Tibet and China just prior to his departure—much to the chagrin of the Tibetans in India.

So strong is feeling in India against China that even a minor incident involving a handful of yaks that inadvertently strayed across the Bhutan frontier became, for the Indian press, a full-blown "yak-war."[30] Nevertheless, talks that began in Beijing in late 1981, in an attempt to resolve the long-standing border question between the neighbors, do not bode well for the refugees.

The potential role of the Soviet Union was, until its demise, the largest question mark. The Dalai Lama has long been aware that he had a "Russia Card" to play in his relationship with China. For example, in 1977, when asked about potential support from Moscow, he adroitly replied, "as long as they [the Russians] support our principles and our objectives, support from any quarter is welcome."[31]

For its part, Moscow responded. Its press related tales of how Mao Zedong had purposely precipitated the 1959 revolt. At the UN, during a debate on Vietnam, Moscow's delegate chastised China for its "aggression" in Tibet. In May 1980 a Soviet official told a news conference in New Delhi that his nation would be only too happy to aid the refugees in any way it could. The Soviet press also carried numerous articles recently championing the refugees without much regard to accuracy. At one point, the claim was made that 200,000 Tibetans took part in the demonstration in Lhasa mentioned above—rather than the actual two thousand.[32] It was Moscow's potential support that appeared most ominous to Beijing. Apart from a few activists, however, it seemed unlikely that many Tibetans would have supported a pro-Soviet cause. Certainly none of the refugee leadership did—the Dalai Lama's public statements notwithstanding.

What if the Dalai Lama returns? It is my opinion that—apart from the Dalai Lama and his immediate court—China probably would not welcome large numbers of refugees back. Nepali officials believe that Beijing would like to give Tibet real regional autonomy under the Dalai Lama and make it a showcase for a special relationship that could then be a model for the future reintegration of Taiwan into the rest of China.[33]

I believe that the Dalai Lama wants to return as much as the authorities in Beijing want him to. In his 1982 annual address, marking the failed revolt of 1959, the Dalai Lama seemed to be preparing his people for a possible reconciliation with the PRC.

> Other people feel that the present liberalization policy is a new attempt to fool the Tibetans and that in the end the Tibetan people will not be given rights to equal freedom. The Tibetans should neither suffer such inflated hopes nor ingrained suspicion. They should not be impatient and hold hasty views. . . . It [the resolution] is also an issue which is deeply linked with the changes in the international political scene.[34]

Ten months later he predicted that he would return to Tibet in 1985, although this was not to be.

With the Dalai Lama's return to Tibet, Beijing would gain a powerful ally in the struggle to win the "hearts and minds" of the Tibetan people. The Chinese would also gain a superb goodwill ambassador, who is articulate, intelligent, and well-respected. For the Dalai Lama, return would mean a renewed religious authority over his people, an ability to influence official policy toward ethnic minorities in the PRC and, not least of all, a return to his beloved holy city.

There are many in China and India who would not welcome an agreement of reconciliation. For twenty years Tibetans in exile have put off assimilation and efforts to put down important economic, political, and social roots. If the Dalai Lama makes an agreement with the PRC, those refugees who will not be repatriated will be forced to recognize that these many years have been wasted. They are bound to feel betrayed, and might very well express their anger in some public manner. Nevertheless, it is just such an agreement between Dharamsala and Beijing that holds the best promise for peace and prosperity for the Tibetan people inside *and* outside Tibet.

The overwhelming majority of Tibetans in exile will finally realize they are not returning to their homeland. They will, at last, have an incentive to become totally committed to being productive and influential citizens of their adopted nations. In Tibet itself, the Dalai's presence would help to maintain moderate policies and work to guarantee, as best as can be done, a continuation of the reconciliation between Tibetans and Han. There even appears to be a model of sorts for this type of a relationship in the town of Gonghe in Quinghai Province. There, according to a former Han resident (1968–1973), relations between the two peoples were astonishingly cordial. While Tibetans made up only one-third of the town's population, the security they felt in their ability to continue to maintain their culture (the town was too remote to be seriously affected by the GPCR), along with the Han's stoic acceptance of their lives there, created an atmosphere of harmony. Many Han learned the Tibetan language, Han-Tibetan socializing was common, and animosity appeared to be minimal.[35]

It is appropriate that in a study of Tibet the last word should go to the Dalai Lama himself in setting the only theme by which the problems of the Tibetan people will ever be solved.

> Finally, anger cannot be vanquished by anger, and past history has disappeared into the past. What is more relevant is that in the future there actually be real peace and happiness through developing a friendly, meaningful relationship between China and Tibet. For this to be realized, it is important for both sides to work hard, to have tolerant understanding and be open minded.[36]

12

The Last Decade: 1985–1995

As I completed this book in the mid-1980s, Tibet was in the throes of consequential change. The First Work Forum on Tibet had met in Beijing on 7 April 1980 in a crisis atmosphere where the delegates were warned that "if we do not seize the moment and immediately improve the relationship between the nationalities [Chinese/Tibetan] we will make a serious mistake."[1]

The following month Communist Party chief Hu Yaobang and Vice-Premier Wan Li made an inspection tour of Tibet and were shocked at conditions. They ordered immediate changes while replacing the Tibetan region Communist Party head Ren Rong with Yin Fatang who had twenty years experience in Tibet and was the first high Chinese official who spoke Tibetan. Several urgent measures called for an implementation of real autonomy, a rejection of policies not suited to the TAR, efforts to revive Tibetan culture and religion, and assurances that within a few years two-thirds of all the cadres in the TAR would be Tibetan.

The 1982 Constitution allowed for legal hearings to be held in local languages, and soon after a committee was established in the TAR to make Tibetan the official language there by the year 2000.

In May 1984 a Law on Regional Autonomy for Minority Nationalities was adopted, which encouraged regional autonomy on issues such as education and culture. It allowed regions the right not to implement laws that did not suit their localities.

To encourage economic development, Tibetans were exempted from taxes and industrial development was promoted with the introduction of forty-three major projects worth RMB300 million (about U.S.$36 million). Tourism was also encouraged; foreign visitors increased from 1,500 in 1985 to about 30,000 in 1994. Far more books and magazines in Tibetan were being published, and

Lhasa Television began a second channel in Tibetan.[2] Most important to the Tibetans was their ability to openly practice Buddhism as many, but hardly all, of the restrictions were lifted. Photos of the Dalai Lama became ubiquitous.[3]

In February-March 1984 the Second Work Forum on Tibet was held and devoted exclusively to the economy of the Tibetan region. The Chinese government believed a conspicuous increase in the standard of living and a noticeable decrease in restrictions on Tibetan culture and religion would win more adherents to the idea that Tibet is better off remaining a part of the Chinese state.

Yin Fatang was replaced by Wu Jihnghua (of the Yi minority from Sichuan) in 1985 when, as was described in chapter 11, economic and social conditions for Tibetans had not conspicuously improved. Wu was said to have originally rejected the post, calling for a Tibetan to be named instead, but relented under pressure. Wu began attending religious functions in Tibetan dress, renaming streets in Tibetan, and encouraging policies of Tibetanization. However, by January 1987 Hu Yaobang was ousted in Beijing and reform policies were severely curtailed throughout China.

Because the goals of the first and second work forums on Tibet were not fully achieved (20 percent of all Tibetans are still in poverty; average per capita income is RMB817 [U.S.$98]/year and for farmers and herders it is RMB515 [U.S.$62]), the Third Work Forum on Tibet was convened in Beijing in July 1994 in order to "accelerate development and safeguard stability" in the TAR. These plans outlined sixty-two new projects worth RMB2.4 billion (U.S.$286 million), more tourism, and a more market-oriented economy. These new projects will need, the plans contend, additional skilled Chinese workers who will, undoubtedly, get preferential treatment, be hired more often, and receive monetary incentives. And, as all over China, these new developments will certainly increase the number of karaoke bars, prostitution, gambling, and inflation, all introduced into Tibet since the reforms of the 1980s.[4]

Changes Since 1985

Since the First Work Forum on Tibet, Chinese authorities have managed to transform Tibet in some ways, especially in terms of material goods in the cities. However, they have failed to adequately deal with the underlying issues such as the enmity of Tibetans toward the Han. In almost every sector of Tibetan society there remain serious problems intensified by the persistent racial animosities.

Take, for example, Beijing's difficulties in finding Tibetan officials who are totally loyal to the Chinese state. There is still, after almost half a century, no Tibetan to head the regional branch of the Chinese Communist Party, the most powerful post in the TAR. Until recently older Tibetans who supported China in the 1950s were prominently featured in the media, but these individuals have titles without power.[5]

Membership in the Chinese Communist Party by ethnic minorities is a problem throughout China. In 1957 CCP minority membership stood at 5.5 percent of the total. By 1990 it was only 5.7 percent. Because the minority share of the total population rose from about 5 percent in 1957 to about 9 percent today, the relative representation in the CCP has declined. This is also true for cadres who numbered 5.4 percent in 1981 and 6.6 percent in 1990.[6]

For Tibet, 54.6 percent of the cadres in the TAR were non-Han by 1978, rising to 61.35 percent by 1987[7] but still below the target of two-thirds. Since the late 1980s, more Chinese cadres have been withdrawn than sent in. "Selecting and dispatching cadres to Tibet must be handled strictly and should be carried out on the principle that they should be few in number but high in quality," warned the Ministry of Labor and Personnel. "Cadres transferred to Tibet must be in the most urgent demand in Tibet; those not in need now should be delayed being sent in."[8]

One factor accounting for the lack of Tibetan leadership is certainly the exceptionally high rate of illiteracy/semi-illiteracy among Tibetans, which according to the 1990 census stands at 44.43 percent (28.55 percent higher than the national average) for those over 15 years of age and jumps to 79 percent for women of child-bearing age. Only .57 percent of the Tibetan population receive a college education, only 2.12 percent a high school education, only 3.85 percent go to middle school, and a mere 18.6 percent go to primary school.[9] Chen Kuiyang, the current CCP party secretary in Tibet, admits school attendance is low and dropping and acknowledges the illiteracy rate is the highest for any region in China and any minority group.[10]

In the past two years the government has pumped RMB21.5 million (about U.S.$2.6 million) into education in the region while Tibetans have also privately donated some RMB15 million (about U.S.$1.8 million) in money, labor, and materials through an official program called "Hope Project." The government designated 1993 as the "Tibetan Education Year," and the press has reported that 67 percent of all school-age children are currently enrolled[11] although the official press admits that poor transportation, few schools, and generally poor conditions keep attendance far below expected levels.[12]

Agricultural output is also a problem for Beijing. The First Work Forum decollectivized agriculture and stopped state taxes, which, along with the return of small private entrepreneurship, brought an immediate increase in prosperity due to higher incomes but a decrease in output due to the abandonment of modern techniques such as the use of fertilizer, the sales of which plummeted 74 percent from 1979 to 1986.[13] The Second Work Forum was called largely to deal with this problem.

In the 1990s state taxes were reinstituted in the TAR with rates varying according to region. The beginning of the decade also saw the introduction of new inputs such as better seeds, more machinery, water conservation projects, etc. Unfortunately all of the efforts have proven insufficient and the gap between Tibetans and Chinese continues to increase, so Beijing has pledged an additional

U.S.$1.16 billion to the TAR before the end of the century.[14] According to Gyalsten Norbu, the chairman of the TAR government:

> The financial and taxation situation is not promising; prefectures, cities and units are crying loudly for a supplementary budget; collection of some categories of taxes is not satisfactory, even declining. . . prices for the basic necessities of life and means of production in Tibet are rising rapidly; many residents and people in agricultural and pastoral areas are very resentful because their lives are conspicuously harsh. . . there are many people who have not yet solved the problem of having enough food to eat and clothing to wear . . . all localities are experiencing grain shortages to some extent. Some households have even run out of grain. . . people are strongly complaining about unwarranted price hikes and arbitrary exaction of fees.[15]

Next to the basics of livelihood, the state of religion is most important to Tibetans. After the disasters of the Cultural Revolution, religion was again allowed to be openly practiced, albeit with severe restrictions, in 1978. Hu Yaobang freed religion considerably more in 1980, and there has been a steady expansion in religious endeavors ever since. To be sure, restrictions such as the size of monasteries and number of clergy, curtailment of some religious activities, and the placing of government agents inside monasteries are continuing obstacles, but they vary according to the whims of local officials. Restrictions on religion have also increased of late due to the political activities of some monks and nuns.

There is no accurate count of the clerical community, but Chinese officials put the number of monks and nuns at 40,000 to 45,000 and the number of monasteries at 1,643 for all the Tibetan areas throughout China.[16]

The rapid growth of religious activities and the clerical community along with its participation in political activities against the Chinese state have aroused anger among some Chinese hard-liners who call for a further curtailment of the religious sector.

> The increase of monasteries in Tibet has gone out of control along with the dramatic increase in monks and nuns. . . . It goes without saying that so many people in the prime of their life, neither taking part in production nor studying modern knowledge but subsisting on religious donations, have generated negative impacts on social and economic development as well as on the development of ethnic culture . . . they compete with each other for luxury and grandeur, expending large amounts of manpower and material and financial resources. . . . [Some poor people donate so much to the monasteries that they become welfare recipients, others are kept in perpetual poverty. . . . Moreover,] some monasteries have become the Dalai clique's bastions for carrying out separatist activities and infiltration and some lawless lamas and nuns have become daring vanguards of unrest . . . [We must] intensify the management of religious affairs . . . limit the number of lamas in monasteries and forbid unauthorized construction of monasteries.[17]

The Tibetan Diaspora

There are now about 125,000 Tibetans (120,000 in south Asia and 5,000 elsewhere) living outside of China. I had originally calculated that some 50,000 to 55,000 fled Tibet after the 1959 revolt, and while more have come out since, reliable figures are unavailable. The administration in Dharamsala now says some 85,000 have left since 1959.

There are fifty-four refugee settlements in India, Nepal, and Bhutan where 13 percent of the working adults engage in the handicrafts industry, 29 percent in sweater selling and other trades, and 30 percent in services such as the government, hotels, shops, etc.

The administration in Dharamsala, still unrecognized by any nation and still referred to by the exiles as their government-in-exile, has grown in recent years. There is an Assembly of People's Deputies, which acts as a parliament and which nominally elects a cabinet (*Kashag*) although often the latter consists of the Dalai Lama's nominees. The Assembly is currently made up of forty-six elected members representing the three major regions of Tibet and the five main religious sects.

A Tibetan Supreme Justice Commission was established in 1992 to act as a "judiciary" to deal with civil cases within the Tibetan community. There is a Tibetan Election Commission, a Tibetan Public Service Commission (to oversee the people who work for the administration—350 in 1995), an Office of the Auditor General (to audit accounts), a Department of Religion and Culture, a Department of Home (to handle rehabilitation schemes, welfare offices, etc.), a Department of Education (overseeing eighty-five schools in India, Nepal, and Bhutan for 27,000 children), a Department of Security (which also runs a Research and Analysis Unit to keep track of events in Tibet), a Department of Information and International Relations (to publish and disseminate propaganda and run eleven overseas offices: New York, Geneva, London, Paris, Zurich, Budapest, Moscow, Tokyo, Canberra, Washington, D.C., and Kathmandu, with an additional office in New Delhi), a Department of Health, a Planning Council, and an Office of Reception Centers (to aid new refugees from Tibet).

Greater economic prosperity has not alleviated all the difficulties. Unemployment is 18.5 percent of the adult population. There is little work in the settlements, which compels people to leave; nearly one-third to 80 percent of the adults who live in the settlements migrate each year looking for work. Moreover, some 10 to 15 percent of Tibetan children do not attend school. Health problems persist with 35,000 cases of tuberculosis since 1959 due to poor sanitation and poor hygiene. Land is also an issue with average land-holding down to 2.7 acres for the average household of 5.8 people with only 5 percent of that land irrigated.[18]

There remains little public accountability as to how Dharamsala spends its funds, and some Tibetans question, privately at least, the cost of the Dalai

Lama's extensive travel and the substantial worldwide campaign for Tibetan independence (discussed below) when many of his compatriots in south Asia remain in decidedly poor conditions.

Whatever the problems in exile, Tibetans will probably never return home voluntarily. While the Chinese press may believe that "the figure [of returning exiles] is growing steadily as Tibet opens wider to the outside world" and the TAR government offers monetary incentives such as a RMB1,500–2,000 (about U.S.$180–241) allowance per family in addition to land, pasture, and livestock, only 1,800 have returned permanently although 11,600 have visited Tibet since the border was opened.[19]

Negotiations

Alongside attempts to develop the Tibetan economy and to free Tibetans of excessive restrictions on religion, language, and other cultural activities, Beijing also decided to deal directly with the Dalai Lama who agreed to talks despite a deep lack of trust—on both sides. For China the goal has always been stability and sufficient prosperity in Tibet to minimize difficulties in a sensitive and remote region. For the Dalai Lama there is the hope of returning to Lhasa and influencing the lives of millions of Tibetans rather than the much smaller number of those in exile.

The decision to negotiate was hard for the Dalai Lama who faced problems, as described in chapter 10, over the regional, religious, and political differences among the refugees. In addition, decades of urging his followers to remain stateless in hopes of returning to an independent Tibet and his strident nationalism made any compromise with Beijing difficult to explain to his followers. Further, the Dalai Lama had to be concerned about the possibility that over time Tibetans may become accustomed to being citizens of a Chinese state and that economic advances in Tibet, along with more liberal social policies, could cause Tibetans to be less anxious for his return. A close observer estimated that by 1985–1986 10 percent of the Tibetan inhabitants of Lhasa were pro-Chinese, 10 percent supported independence at any cost, and the majority were in-between, angry at Chinese policies but seeing independence as unrealistic.[20]

In April 1977, Ngabo Ngawang Jigme announced that China, for the first time, would allow Tibetan refugees to visit their families. The following February the Panchen Lama was released from fourteen years of house arrest and prison.

The Dalai Lama reacted favorably, tempering his speeches by speaking less of his hopes for achieving Tibetan independence and more about the economic well-being of his people. "If the six million Tibetans in Tibet are really happy and prosperous as never before," he declared in 1978, "there is no reason for us to argue otherwise."[21] "The core of the Tibetan issue," the Dalai Lama proclaimed in 1980, "is the welfare of the six million Tibetans."[22] He also began to speak publicly about the possibility of reconciling Buddhism with socialism.

In December 1978 Beijing contacted the Dalai Lama's brother, Gyalo Thondup, who was living in Hong Kong at the advice of the CIA who believed (knew?) China would eventually want to negotiate.[23] A new round of Dalai Lama–Beijing contacts immediately began,[24] resulting in an agreement that the Dalai Lama would send an investigative delegation to Tibet in August 1979, the first such visit since the events of 1959.

On 6 January 1979 the TAR established a special committee to receive Tibetans coming back to visit or stay. Pasang, the vice-chairman of the new committee said, "Let bygones be bygones. . . . We welcome all overseas compatriots, including the Dalai Lama. . . ." By March prisoners began to be released starting with 376 who had been held since the abortive 1959 revolt followed by the restoration of civil rights for 6,000 former prisoners.[25]

In 1979 the Dalai Lama visited the Soviet Union, Mongolia, and the United States, all for the first time. The trip to the United States was significant because he had been denied a visa for ten years on the grounds that it was "inconvenient."[26] Although the U.S. State Department insisted that the visa was issued solely for a private religious visit, the Dalai Lama did engage in low profile political activities. Despite Beijing's irritation over these trips, the negotiations were not derailed, and in April 1982 the Dalai Lama sent another delegation (there were to be a total of six) to China and Tibet where it was agreed that he would return to Lhasa in 1985.[27] He even publicly announced his imminent return to Tibet in 1985.

But the optimism was premature. Talks bogged down; the Dalai Lama wanted the freedom to travel, to speak openly, to live in Lhasa and gain a very large measure of autonomy (if not independence) for Tibet. Chinese authorities wanted him to live in Beijing, to regulate his movements, and to accept limited autonomy for Tibet.

At first the Dalai Lama's strategy called for negotiating directly with Beijing. "I tried from 1978 to 1987," he recalled recently, "to resolve the issue by exclusively negotiating with the Chinese government without any international involvement."[28] And he acknowledged as much at the time, writing to Deng Xiaoping in March 1981:

> I have a liking and a belief in the ideology of Communism aiming to improve the lot of human beings and . . . was satisfied with the late Mao tse-t'ung over the ideology and policy on nationalities. Had this ideology, with its related policies, been implemented, it would have brought happiness and contentment to all concerned . . . [In hopes of regaining that momentum I have] throughout been avoiding alignment with any political blocs.[29]

To this point the Tibetan exile's efforts at winning third-party support had been modest. His trips[30] were all dubbed religious in nature although he took every opportunity to meet local officials. Support came from a handful of politicians and a small number of ordinary citizens.[31] Activities on behalf of Tibetan independence were modest, such as designating 1984 as a year to commemorate "25 Years of Struggle and Reconstruction," and the publication of a hagiography of the Dalai Lama and an "official" history by a recent convert to Tibetan Buddhism, John Avedon.[32] The Office of Tibet in New York established a publishing house and store both named Potala.[33] In March 1985, the International Fellowship of Reconciliation and the London-based Scientific Buddhist Association tried to get the United Nations Commission on Human Rights interested in Tibet. Although this UN agency has no powers beyond monitoring and criticism, it provides high visibility and a measure of legitimacy for the causes it addresses.[34]

As long as there was hope of achieving a compromise through negotiations with Beijing, there was no strong need for international support. However, by the mid-1980s talks had broken down, leaving the Dalai Lama nowhere to turn. This development led to the decision to internationalize the Tibet issue with the ultimate hope that outside support for Tibetan independence would force Beijing back to the bargaining table and, in the best case scenario, force China to make concessions. This campaign called for: (1) the Dalai Lama to travel more and make the trips openly political, (2) support groups to be established around the world, especially in the United States, to lobby their governments on the Dalai Lama's behalf, (3) members of parliaments of major nations to be recruited with the eventual goal being open support from the governments of these nations, (4) peaceful civil disobedience inside Tibet to be encouraged, and (5) the Dalai Lama to continue to plead for talks offering flexible terms to Beijing. During late 1986 and early 1987 meetings were held in London, New York, and Washington, D.C., to establish what came to be known, colloquially, as the Tibet Lobby. While not all such efforts were coordinated and some groups only loosely connected to this campaign, together they constituted a major effort on behalf of the Dalai Lama and his goals for Tibet.

While the breakdown of talks was one impetus for this new strategy, an additional catalyst was Michael van Walt van Praag who worked briefly for the powerful Washington, D.C., law firm of Wilmer, Cutler and Pickering, which registered with the U.S. Justice Department as agents for the "Government of Tibet in Exile" on 5 July 1985. van Walt van Praag is a Dutch national and lawyer who has long promoted the Dalai Lama's cause and is now legal adviser to the Dalai Lama and the Office of Tibet in the United States.[35] Wilmer, Cutler and Pickering is a politically powerful lobbying and law firm "known more for its performance in the halls of Congress than inside the courtroom,"[36] and it can be presumed that it played some role in the creation of the public relations campaign in the United States.

In 1986 the Dalai Lama began to travel, diligently visiting several countries in Europe (including the Soviet Union and the Vatican) and building alliances with members of various parliaments. In Austria he demonstrated that even a religious leader can be without scruples in the interests of a political cause when he met with President Kurt Waldheim, a man subject to an international boycott by world leaders due to his Nazi affiliations during World War II.[37]

But it is in the United States that the Tibet Lobby concentrated its efforts. In June 1987 the House of Representatives unanimously passed an amendment to the Foreign Relations Authorization Act denouncing "human rights violations" in Tibet and stating that Tibet is currently forcibly occupied by China. In addition, twenty-six Congress members sent a letter to Chinese Prime Minister Zhao Ziyang denouncing human rights abuses in Tibet.

Beijing responded by having German Chancellor Helmut Kohl and former U.S. President Jimmy Carter visit Tibet separately in June and July for very brief three-day visits. Kohl became the first sitting head of government to ever visit Tibet. Both men made statements to the press implying that things in Tibet were better than the Dalai Lama had portrayed them.[38]

In September 1987 the Dalai Lama visited the United States again despite protests from the Chinese embassy. This time he came with a plan, presented to the Congressional Human Rights Caucus, calling for: (1) Tibet to be a zone of peace, (2) an abandonment of Chinese migration to Tibet, (3) respect for human rights and democratic freedoms, (4) respect for the environment, and (5) negotiations on the future status of Tibet.

Coincidentally,[39] while the Dalai Lama was in the United States, on 24 September the Chinese authorities in Lhasa held a public trial and executed two Tibetans accused of being criminals. Three days later Lhasa saw its first public demonstrations in twenty-eight years. That was followed by another disturbance on 1 October—China's National Day—which led to bloodshed.

These events in Tibet were triggered by deepening hostilities in the Tibetan-Han relationship, anger at the executions, agitation by visitors (both Western and Tibetan), and the knowledge that the Dalai Lama was at that moment in Washington, D.C. In fact, copies of the Congressional resolution along with Dalai Lama's picture superimposed onto the Tibetan flag were widely circulated in Lhasa.

The events in Lhasa helped the Dalai Lama's cause immeasurably because here was a tangible proof of the serious problems in Tibet. On 6 October the U.S. Senate unanimously passed a resolution similar to the earlier House bill while adding provisions that tied the resolving of human rights abuses to future military sales to China.[40] These Congressional acts in the United States were followed by bills in the European Parliament and the German Bundestag supporting the Dalai Lama's Five-Point Plan.

While good for the exiles' morale, these acts did not change official policies. For example, the Deputy Assistant Secretary of State for East Asian and Pacific Affairs, J. Stapelton Roy, testifying in front of two Congressional committees on 14 October 1987, said, "The United States Government considers Tibet to be a part of China and does not in any way recognize the Tibetan government in exile that the Dalai Lama claims to head." Moreover, the United States rejected the

Dalai Lama's Five-Point Plan because it was "a political program advanced by a man who is the head of a government in exile" that no government recognizes.[41] Furthermore, the State Department rejected Tibet Lobby claims of Chinese migration into Tibet, calling them "inaccurate, incomplete and misleading" and arguing that Congressional actions were "insufficient to outweigh the almost certain damage to the U.S.–China bilateral relationship."[42]

Parallel with the efforts to win Congressional approval, efforts were made to win broad popular support. Utopian fantasies of an imaginary Tibet had long held a fascination for Westerners. The Tibetans were successful in endowing Tibet "with all the qualities of a dream, a collective hallucination" and thereby accumulating a significant number of followers supportive of a Shangri-La that never existed. The Dalai Lama announced 1990 as the "Year of Tibet" with a "treasures of Tibet" art exhibit, cultural performances, "debating monks," etc. Also announced was the establishment of an American headquarters in New York City to be dubbed "Tibet House" with actor Richard Gere, another recent convert to Tibetan Buddhism, as head and principal fund-raiser and Elsie Walker (a first cousin of George Bush) as president.[43] Gere swore that "he would put Tibet on the world map, make it a household word in the United States, like Maalox or Lysol" [two commercial products widely known through massive advertising], and sponsor benefit concerts with prominent artists and chic dinners at exclusive restaurants in New York City.[44]

When the Dalai Lama returned to India, he held a news conference, and although questioned repeatedly, he refused to say that he still favored independence, thereby signaling his continued hopes for reconciliation with the authorities in Beijing.[45]

In Tibet things remained quiet until 5 March 1988 when Lhasa saw its biggest demonstration ever. Several thousand Tibetans took part, and the police used tear gas and electric cattle prods to restore order. Many arrests were made, and prisoners, mostly clergy, were routinely tortured. This was, perhaps, more than the Dalai Lama had anticipated for it went beyond civil disobedience and had led to violence, which he has repeatedly repudiated. If the Dalai Lama had hoped that these efforts would prod Beijing toward further compromise, he miscalculated. Unrest in a sensitive border area with a history of rebellion and Western interference at a time when Beijing may have been willing to compromise only strengthened the hand of hard-liners in China. Meanwhile China's harsh crackdown and mistreatment of the Tibetans fueled the flames of nationalism and ethnic hostility. Moreover, the U.S. refusal to acknowledge its covert hand in the contemporary history of Tibet reduced much of the force of its pious pronouncements on human rights abuses in that region. As one senior State Department official put it "at this particular time Congressional support for independence sends the wrong signal to more violent elements and could lead to more bloodshed."[46]

Once the Dalai Lama's plan was launched, however, there was no going back. In March 1988 in Washington, D.C., the International Campaign for Tibet was established. It registered with the Justice Department as a foreign agent for "His Holiness the Dalai Lama" for lobbying purposes and immediately launched publications—*Tibet Press Watch* and *Tibet Forum*, a Chinese language publication written by exiled Tibetan students educated in China. *Tibet Forum* would later be edited by Jigme Ngabo, the son of Ngabo Ngawang Jigme whose recruitment was a major coup for the exiles.[47]

With his newly won support and his organizations in place, the Dalai Lama now decided to make a bold move to get the talks back on track. Speaking in front of the European Parliament in Strasbourg, France, on 15 June 1988, the Dalai Lama publicly said for the first time he would be willing to return to a Tibet that was less than independent. He proposed a "self-governing democratic political entity . . . in association with the People's Republic of China." That is, China would be responsible for foreign affairs and defense while the Tibetans would maintain relations with other nations in "fields of religion, commerce, education, culture, tourism, science, sports and other non-political activities."[48]

Because the Chinese government had repeatedly said it would be willing to meet the Dalai Lama, or his representative, anywhere, anytime, to discuss anything except independence, the Dalai Lama proceeded to name a six-member delegation, with two aides and van Walt van Praag as legal adviser. He said they would be in Geneva in January 1989 waiting for their Chinese counterparts.

The European parliamentarians were less than pleased. "The visit of the Dalai Lama to Strasbourg is in all respects an unofficial one," said Lord Plumb, the British Conservative President of the European Parliament. "It was made very clear to him that the Parliament attaches great importance to the strengthening of good relations with China . . . I do not believe that the Dalai Lama's visit is helpful in the current circumstances of the European Parliament's improving relations with China."[49] Tibetans in exile were also unhappy. Many thought the terms too compromising, and some blamed "foreigners" for influencing the Dalai Lama to abandon full independence.[50]

But the speech was not intended for the Europeans or the Tibetan exiles. The Dalai Lama had used the location as a symbol of his newly won international support. The speech did exactly what it was meant to do—put the Chinese into a difficult position by calling their bluff. The Dalai Lama had publicly agreed to the one condition China had always placed on the talks. "The Dalai Lama's concession landed like a bombshell here and the authorities still do not know how to respond," observed one Chinese source.[51] At first there was even some conciliatory language. Agence France Presse quoted a Chinese official, Mo Zhaoping, as saying that although "partial independence is not acceptable . . . we think there is a change in tone."[52] But in the end Beijing rejected the outstretched hand.

That the Beijing authorities were in difficulty as to how to answer is evidenced by the fact that they did not formally respond to the Dalai Lama's offer until January 1990, nineteen months later. At that time the Chinese embassy in

New Delhi said there would be no talks. The reason, a new one, was the Dalai Lama's refusal to reject the notion that Tibet had at any time been independent.[53]

Meanwhile unrest had continued in Tibet, and while there were differences of opinion among officials there (one observer noted four factions—older Chinese cadres opposed to any compromise with leftist views; older Tibetan cadres supportive of Tibetan integration into a Chinese state; younger, better educated Tibetan cadres supportive of authentic Tibetan autonomy; and younger Chinese cadres who agreed with that)[54]—those who supported less freedoms, more repression and no compromise with the Dalai Lama were becoming more vocal. "We must deal resolute, accurate and rapid blows against the serious crimes of a small number of separatists," read an editorial in *Xizang Ribao* on 13 March 1988. "[They] are the cause of this earthquake and a cancer cell in society."[55] The head of the public security apparatus, Qiao Shi, called for "the government [to] adopt a policy of merciless repression toward all rebels."[56] The hard-liners were winning the political battle in Beijing by pointing to the unrest in Tibet and the interference of foreigners in China's internal affairs, both powerful arguments in a country long worried about such matters.

Nevertheless, the supporters of repression had some formidable opposition. Some officials in Beijing and Lhasa supported compromise with the Dalai Lama and authentic autonomy in Tibet. The Panchen Lama was particularly outspoken. "There are people who think it necessary to strike down the lamas and destroy the monasteries," he said in a speech to the Tibetan delegates at the National People's Congress on 29 March 1988. "We must not fall back to the errors of the past . . . I must seriously warn against people who have the idea of 'dealing merciless blows at the lamas and closing all the temples.'"[57] In January 1989 he spoke to Communist Party members in Shigatse and said, "Although there have been developments in Tibet since its liberation, this development has cost more dearly than its achievements. This mistake must never be repeated."[58] The Panchen Lama's sudden and unexpected death five days later at the age of 50 removed from the scene an important player who had acted as a brake on the hard-liners and who would have contributed greatly to a solution of the Tibet problem.[59]

Prime Minister Zhao Ziyang also opposed repression saying that while the cause of the unrest was due to "splittists in foreign countries" there is the problem of "long-standing leftist policies in Tibet . . . [for example] a serious degree of sectarianism existed among Tibetan leaders. The work of addressing the wrongs were advanced very slowly. The Tibetan people's autonomous rights, the Tibetan language and the customs and habits of this nationality were neglected and such mistakes were not properly and quickly corrected."[60]

Nevertheless, the hard-liners ultimately prevailed when in March 1988 a political rally capping months of marches and protests led Beijing to declare martial law in Lhasa and its environs. It was to last until May 1990. An order, issued in March 1988, to withdraw 10,667 Han cadres from Tibet within a year was now canceled and promises for further Tibetanizaton were forgotten.[61]

Privately, communications continued with private Chinese citizens as go-be-tweens.[62] The Dalai and Panchen Lamas wrote letters to each other and spoke on the telephone several times before the latter's death. Although the calls from Beijing were monitored, the Panchen slipped away from his handlers during a trip to Australia and managed a pre-arranged telephone conversation with the Dalai Lama, then in West Germany.[63]

Meanwhile the internationalization of the Tibet issue was ratcheted up several more notches. The Dalai Lama traveled more frequently,[64] support groups were established in more nations,[65] symposia were held in New Delhi, Copenhagen, and Bonn, "[which] gave Tibet supporters from around the world an opportunity to share thoughts and ideas and work towards more cohesive action in future."[66]

In Washington the Tibet Lobby got the U.S. Senate to pass a resolution condemning human rights abuses in Tibet and to pass resolutions that bestowed on Tibetans a $500,000 grant for refugee relief, thirty college scholarships in the United States for Tibetan students, prohibition on defense goods to China, and an imposition of trade sanctions against China. Only the first two provisions be-came law.

There were significant victories in other fora as well. At the UN Commission on Human Rights, Tibet was discussed for the first time while the General Assembly addressed the Tibet issue twice. In December 1989 the British House of Lords discussed Tibet for the first time.

But it was the rulers of China who were to aid the Dalai Lama's cause the most. While the declaration of martial law in Lhasa was barely noticed, the events in Tiananmen Square in the summer of 1989 were seen live on the world's television sets. The power of those images seriously eroded Beijing's reputation. As Beijing's image tarnished, the Dalai Lama's was proportionally enhanced, especially in the West. While the Tibet Lobby's success can be attrib-uted to the strategies they employed, it was inestimably aided by China's decline in the esteem of Western nations that allowed "Tibet [to] come out of nowhere" as one Western diplomat in Beijing put it.

The most immediate consequence for the Dalai Lama was the awarding of the Nobel Peace Prize. The decision to give it to him had more to do with anti-Chinese sentiment than with anything Tibetan. As the *New York Times* reported, people close to the Norwegian Nobel Committee said their choice of the Dalai Lama "was an attempt both to influence events in China and recognize the efforts of the student leaders of the democracy movement . . ." The Dalai Lama had been nominated in February and the jury had made its decision in September, only weeks after the shooting in Tiananmen Square.[67]

The Nobel prize gave the Dalai Lama a prominence he could never anticipate. Building upon this new awareness, the Tibet Lobby escalated its efforts in 1990, establishing even more parliamentary support committees,[68] having the Dalai

Lama and his advisers travel more fervently to raise money and meet with government officials, and initiating discussion on Tibet at the UN Committee on Human Rights and the Committee for the Elimination of Racial Discrimination. Other Tibetans traveled to make common cause with the now burgeoning group of Chinese dissidents.[69]

But all these ventures were secondary to the hopes that the Dalai Lama had for his efforts in the United States because it was assumed that only Washington could force Beijing back to the bargaining table. In February 1990 President George Bush signed a bill with amendments creating Tibetan language radio broadcasts on the Voice of America (beginning in spring 1991 and currently broadcasting two hours daily in a highly partisan fashion) and setting aside $1 million for thirty U.S. scholarships for Tibetan refugees. In Congress, both houses declared 13 May 1990 National Day in Support for Freedom and Human Rights in China and Tibet.[70]

In Tibet martial law was lifted in May 1990 and tourists once again flocked in. But the conditions in Lhasa did not change markedly; control of the population remained very tight creating even further tensions. Because the situation in Tibet was not changing and because Beijing seemed to be unyielding, the Dalai Lama had little recourse but to continue to pursue his efforts at winning more international recognition and visibility. The Year of Tibet (which actually took place in 1991 and involved 3,000 events in thirty-six countries) proved to be a great success, and the Dalai Lama called for its continuation "to dedicate the year . . . to creating greater awareness and an active international role concerning Tibet's environment and human rights in Tibet."[71] Gere and the fund-raisers were true to their word, raising $525,000 to buy a $825,000 brownstone in New York City that was to be the headquarters of the American operation.[72]

There were also victories at the United Nations, where after repeated efforts the Committee on Human Rights cited "violations of fundamental human rights and freedoms" in Tibet. The resolution used terms such as "national identity" but skirted issues of independence. It was the first time since 1965 that any UN agency had passed a resolution on Tibet.[73]

As always the Dalai Lama continued to travel. He went to Ireland and met President Mary Robinson, to France where he met prominent government officials, to Liechtenstein where he met the prince, and to Austria where he met with Waldheim again. He returned to Mongolia, then visited Lithuania and addressed the Parliament after meeting President Vytauta Landsbergis. In Latvia he met President Anatoligs Gorbunovs; in Bulgaria he was welcomed by President Zhelyu Zhelev. Once again he traveled to the Soviet Union, the United States, Britain, Switzerland, and Germany. He visited Latin America. He made an "official visit" to Sweden, where in 1988 and 1990 he was only permitted private visits and found himself cold-shouldered by the government at the time.[74]

The biggest coup, however, was in the United States where in April 1991 the Dalai Lama met with Congress in the Capitol Rotunda after congressional leaders had refused his request for a speech to a joint session of Congress; the leaders argued that the Rotunda meeting was unusual enough to send a message to China. Afterward he met in the White House with George Bush and National Security Adviser Brent Scowcroft for thirty minutes. (In later years he would return to the White House to meet President Bill Clinton and Vice-President Al Gore.) Government officials insisted the visit was "private," that the Dalai Lama was seen as a spiritual leader. Congressional resolutions concerning Tibet, the White House argued, were only a "sense of Congress" and not binding on the U.S. government nor official U.S. policy.[75]

Be that as it may, twelve years earlier the Dalai Lama was not permitted into the United States and now he was being given the rare honor of a private meeting in the White House with the president of the United States. This dramatic reversal was made possible by the success of the Tibet Lobby, the decline in support for Beijing, and President George Bush's anger at Beijing over their trade policies and refusal to institute political reforms. George Bush went further when on 28 October 1991 he signed a State Department Authorization Act, which included the following paragraph:

> That it is the sense of Congress that Tibet, including those areas incorporated into the Chinese provinces of Sichuan, Yunnan, Gansu, and Qinghai, is an occupied country under established principles of international law whose true representatives are the Dalai Lama and the Tibetan Government in Exile as recognized by the Tibetan people.[76]

In Britain 131 MPs signed a motion seconding the U.S. Congressional amendment that called Tibet an "occupied country."[77]

Talks with China had now stopped altogether with the Chinese blaming the Dalai Lama's intransigence on the independence issue and pointing out that "we have never changed our eagerness to hold negotiations."[78] and the Dalai Lama insisting that he was searching for a middle way. "I am not demanding complete independence from China," he declared at a press conference on 1 August 1990, that demand would be "a little unrealistic."[79]

Whoever was at fault, the Dalai Lama withdrew his Strasbourg plan in September 1991, offering in its stead a somewhat less comprehensive proposition. Speaking at Yale University in October 1991, he asked Beijing to allow him to visit his homeland on a mission of peace under three conditions: (1) the right to travel freely, (2) the freedom to speak to anyone without reprisals against them, and (3) that the world press be allowed to accompany him.[80] The Chinese response this time was swift and clear: the Dalai Lama cannot go home until he unequivocally denounces independence.[81]

The Tibet Lobby also continued its efforts at the UN, joining forces with the newly established dissident China Lobby in getting a resolution through the UN Subcommission on Prevention of Discrimination and Protection of Minorities. This resolution, for the first time in UN history, referred to Tibet as a separate entity.[82] Chinese and Tibetan dissidents have now joined forces to establish the International Coalition for Human Rights in China, which has come close, but as yet has been unsuccessful, to passing a resolution in the UN condemning China's actions.[83]

Chinese leaders' worst nightmare is that the Dalai Lama's efforts will result in a civil war in Tibet and/or in damaging the Chinese economy through the elimination of trade concessions or boycotts. To date all the talk of human rights has had no discernable effect on foreign investment in China or on the Chinese economy.[84] As to their policies in Tibet itself, because China's leaders continue to believe that the difficulties are the work of a "handful" of agitators encouraged by outside forces, their response is a resort to extreme force against peaceful demonstrators while hoping that economic development will make Tibetans less susceptible to the "splittists'" entreaties. This head-in-the-sand attitude ignores the legitimate complaints of many Tibetans and undermines Beijing's own objectives for stability while sharpening the difficulties. As to their internationalization tactics, China has countered with its own campaign but in a staggeringly incompetent fashion when compared to the efforts of the Tibet Lobby.

Outside of China, Beijing's weapon against the constantly growing tide of support for the Dalai Lama's cause has been a plethora of articles in the local, and especially the overseas, press (*Beijing Review, China Today, China Daily News*). The articles emphasize obscure historical points to support the argument that Tibet is a part of China and stress the dismal conditions of the past, arguing that things have improved so much that outsiders are using the wrong measures to judge conditions in Tibet.[85] They have attacked the Dalai Lama for allegedly plotting to restore the old society. "It seems obvious that what he wishes to bring back is the privileges of a few estate holders enslaving the bulk of the Tibetan people."[86] They reject unrest in Tibet as solely the result of agitation by outsiders and a "handful of splittists." Persistent protests are made whenever a foreign leader meets the Dalai Lama. ("The Dalai Lama is not merely a religious leader. He lives in exile and engages in political activities aimed at splitting China and harming national unity. We are opposed to any government leader meeting the Dalai Lama in any form.")[87]

Those who do not read the Chinese press (the vast majority of the populations of the world) have no access to Chinese positions, however poorly presented they may be, because given China's low credibility, the press reports largely from the perspective of the Tibetan exiles. This has been particularly true since the establishment of the Tibet Information Network (TIN) in London, which collects data on Tibet and bombards the world's media with its press statements. While much of what TIN gathers is useful and accurate, the media uses all of their material unquestioningly. A recent study of the media's representation of the Tibet issue in the United States (which found that reporters are woefully ignorant of Tibet and report overwhelmingly in the Dalai Lama's favor) put Beijing's efforts to present its case this way:

The defects of the [Chinese] material on Tibet are the same that blight their articles on other topics; sheer pap ("on the morning of 1 October, when the people of Lhasa were joyfully observing the festive National day in a peaceful and jubilant atmosphere . . .") counterproductive invective ("Oppose Splitting Motherland, Oppose Sabotaging Stability and Unity"), uninterpreted statistics, . . . unlikely sounding quotations from allegedly representative citizens ("scenes of torture perpetuated upon serfs in the old society, such as flaying alive, chopping off hands, and gouging out eyes are still fresh in my mind"). Information packaged this way does not invite serious attention. . . ."[88]

Beijing has also published a large number of books on Tibet for foreign readers and sent Tibetan cultural troupes outside the country.[89]

In March 1993 a Conference on the Work of External Propaganda on the Question of Tibet was convened in which the nature of the problem was clearly delineated and the urgency to counter the Dalai Lama's efforts strongly asserted. With seemingly little concern as to the effect and credibility of this propaganda, the decision was made to do more of the same, and in the two years since there has not been any noticeable change except in quantity.[90]

It's not only journalists whom Beijing handles badly. While the Tibetans took U.S. congressional aides on escorted tours of Tibetan refugee camps and lobbied them continuously in Washington, Beijing refused visas to American Congress members and, apparently, exerted little effort lobbying in Washington on the issue of Tibet.[91] While the Tibetans issue daily press releases and are available for interviews, China refuses journalists permission to visit Tibet. In November 1991, however, Beijing issued a sixty-two-page rebuttal of charges concerning human rights abuses throughout the country and employed several firms including, for a short time, the most notorious and most effective public relations firm in Washington, D.C., Hill & Knowlton, to represent it. In the public relations war, China is monumentally outclassed.[92]

In April 1992, at the request of the Chinese government, the Dalai Lama's brother, Gyalo Thondup, resumed talks in Beijing for the first time since martial law was declared in Lhasa four years earlier. Although the talks produced no concrete developments, according to the Dalai Lama,[93] in September his representative continued the dialogue with the Chinese Ambassador in New Delhi and communication continues sporadically.[94]

China is very angry at the internationalization of the Tibet issue and resents greatly foreign intervention in, what it considers, a domestic matter. It has not bent to that pressure in any meaningful way yet continues to search for, and to need, a solution. The Dalai Lama, for all of his worldwide presence, has yet to get a single country to recognize his government-in-exile or to put significant pressure on Beijing to alter its policies in Tibet where the hard-liners remain ensconced in power. Both sides must understand that a solution can come about, ultimately, only through dialogue, so while they continue to talk in private, in public they continue to play to their respective constituencies.

In September 1995 a Dharamsala official said again that the Dalai Lama "is willing to negotiate with China without insisting on total independence for Tibet."[95] Beijing, for its part, says the Dalai Lama's "so-called concessions are nothing but an adjustment in his tactics. In essence he still sticks to his stand for the independence of Tibet."[96]

"Tibet has been an independent country for a thousand years . . . ," the Dalai Lama counters. "However, it is also a political reality that Tibet is now under Chinese rule . . . I have tried a 'middle-way' approach to the problem . . . over the last fifteen years, six official delegations were sent to China and Tibet, and my personal envoy visited China at least ten times. I also made several proposals to the Chinese government. . . . Unfortunately, the Chinese government's response to these proposals has been one of total rejection."[97]

Pragmatism is possible if both sides are willing. For example, recently China and India, after years of getting nowhere, have agreed to put aside the difficult, and currently unresolvable, matter of where their borders lie in order to improve relations and to move on other issues.[98] So the possibility exists, if both sides are willing, to temporarily put aside the question of Tibetan independence and the issues of a greater Tibet so that other concerns can be meaningfully discussed. Successful negotiations on any other issues may build up the trust needed to go back to the most difficult questions.

Something has to be said about the involvement of the government of Taiwan, which has long tried to influence events as described in previous chapters. In March 1990 the Dalai Lama lifted his ban on contacts with Taiwan and hosted an adviser to the Taiwanese Premier. In May 1993 Gyalo Thondop visited Taiwan, creating the first direct link between the GMD and the Dalai Lama in over three decades. Thondup visited the island again in January 1994 and accepted an invitation for a future visit by the Dalai Lama.[99]

Dharamsala has long accused Taiwan of funding "conflicts and discord in the Tibetan community," and, indeed, in 1990 a Tibetan exile official was forced to resign after it was revealed he had taken money from Taiwan. Taiwanese agents were also caught meddling in Tibetan regional rivalries when they struck a deal with leaders of the Chushi Gangdrug rebel group in March 1994. The rebels apparently agreed to a document that spelled out Tibetan autonomy, which included Kham saying it feared a deal between the Dalai Lama and Beijing that would have left its region out of an autonomous Tibet.[100]

Given all the problems with Beijing in the past, it is not surprising that this current incarnation of the talks has fostered opposition within the Tibetan exile ranks. The most prominent dissident has been the Dalai Lama's oldest brother, Thubten Norbu, who resigned his post as Dharamsala's representative in Tokyo, writing a thirty-seven page letter criticizing any negotiations with the Chinese.[101]

There are dangers in the course the Tibet Lobby has chosen. Elevated expectations among Tibetans, which may not be fulfilled, is but one example just as when during the 1950s and 1960s it was believed CIA aid was all that was needed.[102]

Unfulfilled expectations can lead to additional, and perhaps bloodier, unrest in Tibet where Chinese policies, although improving, continue to fan strife.

It is difficult to predict the future. The Dalai Lama has no option but to continue to escalate this high-risk strategy as long as the talks with Beijing fail to make significant progress.[103] Diplomatic pressure may work, but it is doubtful. He can hope for a collapse of the Beijing government after the death of Deng Xiaoping and a breakup of the country along the lines of the former Soviet Union, although that is doubtful as well.

Beijing holds the trump cards in this high-stakes game. It has the ability to dramatically alter its policies in Tibet in order to ameliorate the serious tensions that currently exist between Chinese and Tibetans. As witnessed in the former Soviet Union, repression only leads to an increase in nationalism.

The key to the solution is at the bargaining table. Any other avenue risks greater tragedy for both sides. "I . . . consider the best way to solve this problem," the Dalai Lama told the Nepali English language newspaper *Independent*, "is that both sides should be reasonable and realistic."[104] On Hungarian radio he said, "I have endeavored to find the middle way, that is to say, not a complete breaking away from China . . . but . . . that Tibet should be a peace zone, an unarmed territory . . . a special relationship would link my homeland to China, on the basis of the one country two systems principle that is often voiced by Beijing."[105]

The Situation at the Moment

As I write this late in 1995, the Chinese government appears to have abandoned any serious efforts to Tibetanize the TAR by encouraging further linguistic, cultural, and religious tolerance. Rather, Beijing has apparently redoubled its efforts to increase economic development, crack down ever harder on the slightest public display of Tibetan nationalism, and slowly assimilate Tibet into the Chinese state by allowing, for the first time, large numbers of Han to migrate into the TAR.

Part of this new policy is to once again crank up the propaganda attacks on the Dalai Lama and continue to argue (one wonders if Chinese officials actually believe this) that *all* the difficulties are caused by outsiders, now dubbed "The Dalai Clique." "Tibet's situation is basically stable," claims the Chinese press, "but . . . the anti-separatist struggle remains very grim."[106]

"The interference of the Dalai clique," Lhasa TV charged, "has made this autonomous region lose many development opportunities and prevented us from concentrating on our undertakings."[107] According to Chen Kuiyuan, the local party secretary, "hostile forces abroad and the Dalai clique have never ceased their heavy interference in Tibet."[108] To Beijing the Dalai Lama is a tool of the West which, wants to Westernize and "disintegrate" China. His organization

> incites religious fanaticism among the Tibetan people. Under a plot hatched by
> ideas men in the West, it has sent home a large number of religious personages

of the upper hierarchy to carry out tactics . . . wildly attempting to use godly strength to poison and bewitch the masses and attain its purpose of making "religion" serve its "political purposes."

Dalai and his clique, while paying lip service to opposing violence, are in fact the creators of unrest who have developed underground organizations and gone all out to infiltrate into rural and pastoral Tibet. They have also tried to infiltrate into Chinese party and government bodies through writing letters and threatening letters to instigate their Tibetan staff to rebel. Some 15,000 such letters were intercepted in Lhasa in 1993 alone. That was seven times greater than the number intercepted in 1992.

[There is a need to] tighten political discipline and purify the ranks of the cadres . . . party members may not hang religious insignias and Dalai's portraits . . . or establish scripture chanting halls or niches for the Buddha's statue . . . they may not send their children to study in schools which the Dalai clique has established outside Tibet.[109]

The Panchen Lama

The tenth Panchen Lama died on 28 January 1989 at age fifty-one. The Dalai Lama offered to send a delegation to, among other things, conduct divination rituals. Meanwhile, China invited the Dalai Lama to take part in the mourning rituals. Both sides declined the respective offers.

In August 1989 the Chinese government announced a plan to search for the new Panchen Lama by using mystical signs, conducting tests on the likely candidates, and using oracles and divinations—in other words, all the traditional rites. However, there was an additional test: the use of the lottery system whereby three finalists have their names inserted into a golden urn that is spun until one name falls out. This procedure was used to select the tenth, eleventh, and twelfth Dalai Lamas after its introduction by the Qing Dynasty in 1792. It was not used in the selection of the recently deceased Panchen. This final step symbolically gives the Chinese government final approval on a crucial Tibetan matter and reasserts its claims to political control over Tibet.

In March 1991 the Dalai Lama informed Beijing that he wanted to be involved in the search by sending his own delegation. China rejected the offer in June. But communication continued quietly, and in July 1993 the head of the search team, Chatral Rinpoche, sent the Dalai Lama a letter describing the progress of the search. For the next two years the Dalai Lama wrote repeatedly to Chatral without a single reply.

By January 1995 the search had narrowed to twenty-eight boys, and the implication could be drawn from Chinese statements that an announcement was imminent. But before Beijing could name a boy, the Dalai Lama, on 14 March, declared his recognition of a six-year-old boy named Dedhun Choekyi Nyima as the eleventh Panchen Lama. There were rumors that Beijing had planned a September announcement of the same boy.

Being preempted did not please Beijing, so a campaign was immediately launched to vilify the Dalai Lama. The Dalai Lama had chosen a boy "through fraud" and "violated the cardinal principles of Buddhism" according to *Xinhua*.[110] Interestingly, China never said that this child was not the official reincarnation; attacks were confined to the Dalai Lama's alleged usurpation of China's authority. Soon, rumors spread outside of China that the search party and the boy were being held incommunicado,[111] that wall posters were appearing in Lhasa critical of Beijing's interference in a religious matter, and that Tashilhunpo Monastery, the home of the Panchen Lamas, was sealed, with monk officials being imprisoned and replaced with pro-Beijing monks.[112]

As I write this, little solid evidence about what transpired is available as new information and rumors appear daily. Two years ago the Chinese government and the Dalai Lama cooperated successfully over the selection of the Karmapa reincarnation and many thought that to be a rehearsal for the Panchen Lama selection. So what happened here? It appears that the Dalai Lama was tipped off to the right boy, which indicates that he was in secret communication with the search party in Tibet. But why did he make his announcement? To exert his authority over religious matters? One rumor has it that the Chinese government learned of the contacts between the search party and the Dalai Lama and was about to punish the monks when the Dalai Lama, hoping to bring world attention to bear, made his announcement.[113] Until we know more about what was happening secretly, the answers to these questions will remain elusive.

Obviously this is not so much an issue of religion (although the Dalai Lama insists this is purely a religious matter) as one of symbolic authority—who has the power to make such momentous decisions. *Xinhua* reported that "what the Dalai Lama really intended to do when he got involved in naming the reincarnation of the Panchen Lama had nothing to do with religious matters. In fact, he attempted to negate China's sovereignty over Tibet and cause disturbances in Tibet by opposing the final decision power of the central government over the reincarnation of the 10th Panchen Lama."[114]

As described in chapter 1, the Panchen Lama position was created by a Dalai Lama in the seventeenth century, and the two major clerical leaders have had close ties, even if somewhat strained at times, ever since. To not have either cleric approve the selection of the other would be a unique circumstance in Tibetan history. The golden urn was only used occasionally when Beijing felt the need to assert its authority. Moreover, it seems very odd for a self-described atheistic and socialist government to be involved in what surely it would term superstitious and feudal practices. All this, of course, has consequences for the future selection of the next Dalai Lama and for rule over Tibet itself.

After the announcement, Beijing had a dilemma: agree that the Dalai Lama's selection was correct and thereby allow him far more authority than he has had since 1959, or reject his selection and pick someone else. This latter option is not without consequence for it could very possibly alienate Tibetans even more, increase ethnic hostilities in Tibet, and perhaps even unite various Tibetan factions against China similar to the late 1950s. Pictures of the boy named by the Dalai Lama immediately began selling briskly in Lhasa's blackmarket. The dangers notwithstanding, it was the latter strategy that was implemented, and from 8–11 November China convened a conference of senior monks and lamas from central Tibet in a hotel in Beijing where the importance of their activities was highlighted by a visit from CCP Party Secretary and President Jiang Zemin. It was reported that attendance was made mandatory as some clerics were pleading illness in attempts to avoid attendance.[115]

On 26 November Beijing announced its own selection, a six-year-old named Gyaincain Norbu selected by lot in a ceremony presided over by Chinese and Tibetan government officials, as well as the requisite clergy. It seems unlikely at this juncture that the boy selected by Beijing will have much credibility among Tibetans. Meanwhile, Beijing and the Dalai Lama have another seemingly insurmountable obstacle to overcome.

Other Problems

The Panchen Lama dispute is an immediate thorn in the sides of the two contenders for power in Tibet, but it is not the greatest problem. The issue with the most dire long-term consequence is the fear that Tibetans have of becoming a minority in their own land.

To understand this situation it is vital to keep in mind that there are two Tibets. When Beijing speaks of Tibet, it is referring to the TAR; when the Dalai Lama speaks of Tibet, he speaks for an area more than three times the size of the TAR in which Tibetans live (Kham and Amdo). The historical reality is that the Dalai Lamas have not ruled these outer areas since the mid-eighteenth century, and during the Simla Conference of 1913, the thirteenth Dalai Lama was even willing to sign away rights to them.[116] As described in earlier chapters, China's policies toward the TAR and other Tibetan-inhabited regions outside the TAR have, since 1950, been significantly different. In 1950 there were few Han Chinese in any of these areas, although there were more in Kham and Amdo. After 1950 Chinese were not permitted to go to the TAR unless assigned there, while there was a slow but steady migration into the other Tibetan areas. Since August 1992 all restrictions on travel for Chinese citizens have been lifted, resulting in a lot of moving around, especially to areas that offer commercial possibilities. Travel was also encouraged when the regulations governing acquisition of business permits were simplified and relaxed in November 1993. By 1994 Beijing was reporting 42,000 registered enterprises in the TAR, the bulk of them run by Han Chinese.[117] "We will implement preferential policies and adopt active measures systematically," Gyalsten Norbu, the TAR chairman, has said, "or freely bring in all kinds of useful qualified personnel, badly needed by our region . . . with the goal of gradually expanding our pool of qualified personnel."[118]

Han officials have been encouraged to volunteer for service in Tibet by a political and media campaign glorifying one Kong Fansen, said to be a selfless cadre who originally worked in Tibet from 1974–1982, returned in 1988, and remained until his death in a car crash in 1994. A native of Shandong Province, he is said to have worked exceedingly hard for the Tibetans with little regard for himself, giving the clothes off his back and change from his pockets to the poor. President Jiang Zemin advised CCP members to "learn from Comrade Kong Fansen."[119]

Registered Chinese residents of Tibet are relatively few, but a considerably larger number of sojourners are not registered with the authorities and therefore not counted in the official population statistics. It is obvious to every visitor to Tibet that there are far more Chinese than the official statistics indicate. The question is how many more?

As I tried to demonstrate in Appendix A, population figures are hard to come by and difficult to believe. The most complete and accurate studies of the population in and around the TAR have been done by the Institute for Sociology at Beijing University because it had access to both officials in the entire region and government documents over a period of several years of continuous research. Outside of China the best effort is, by far, a publication called *New Majority: Chinese Population Transfer into Tibet* by the London-based Tibet Support Group. While every effort is made to be judicious and assertions are carefully worded, these authors had neither access to officials nor documents, so their report is based on "ten weeks of targeted fieldwork ... [and] general observations made in the course of altogether two years of travels in the country from 1985 to 1994." As careful as they were, because the research was based on published materials and "casual observation and conversation," the report's conclusion cannot be taken as definitive.[120]

The 1990 census counted a total of 4,593,330 Tibetans with 2,096,346 in the TAR. It found that registered Hans in the TAR total only 81,217.[121] If we examine the number of officially registered Han over the years, we find their numbers to be relatively small: in 1980 122,356, in 1983 79,650, in 1988 79,781, in 1991 65,101. But we have no reliable numbers for the "floating population," those who are unregistered and uncounted. One official estimate in the late 1980s put that number at 60,000–140,000.[122] Undoubtedly it is far higher today.

The Dalai Lama continues to use the 6 million figure for the population of all Tibetans in the world, a number that has, curiously, remained unchanged for about fifteen years. In recent years he has also claimed that a total of 1.2 million Tibetans have died unnaturally as a result of China's policies since 1950. I am unaware of any Chinese figures as to how many Tibetans have died outside the normal course of events. In Tibet itself there are official monuments to PLA soldiers who have died but none, that I am aware of, to any Tibetans. This figure, like so many of the figures issued from Dharamsala, comes without documentary evidence save for an alleged PLA document from the early 1960s that speaks of 87,000 deaths in the 1959–1960 period. Some scholars have accepted the validity of this document. Undoubtedly, tens of thousands, if not hundreds of thousands of Tibetans died from the revolts of the 1950s, the famine caused by the Great Leap Forward, the turmoil of the Cultural Revolution, the imprisonment of untold numbers of people, and so on. How many we will probably never know. Whatever the figure, it is an unspeakable tragedy.[123]

A decade ago I completed this book with a slim hope for the future and a quote from the Dalai Lama calling for an end to anger and for more tolerance and open-mindedness. While much has happened since then, the difficulties for Tibetans both inside and outside their homeland remain, and the future looks to me, at the moment, bleaker than a decade ago. Nevertheless, the possibility that unforetellable events will bring some solution to bear remains my hope for all the Tibetan people wherever they may live.

Appendix A

The Population of Tibet

In Tibet, as elsewhere, the ethnic boundaries of a people do not always coincide with the political boundaries—the area defined by the former exceeding that defined by the latter in almost every instance. The political boundaries of Tibet are clearly delineated on China's maps and define an area known officially as the Tibet Autonomous Region. Ethnically, however, Tibetans spill over these boundaries on all sides—into Indian Ladakh on the southwest; into Nepal, Sikkim, and Bhutan on the south; and into the Indian-controlled area east of Bhutan, known as the Towang Tract, on the southeast. In China, also, ethnic Tibetans can be found in all the provinces that surround the TAR—Qinghai, Gansu, Sichuan, and Yunnan.

Censuses were held in Tibet from 653 AD onwards, and all were highly inaccurate. The single point of agreement was that the population was declining. The Dalai Lama, himself, has confirmed this trend. The eminent Tibetologist Guiseppe Tucci noted after his eighth visit to Tibet: "there were certainly more [Tibetans] in the past, as may be inferred from surviving traces of intense cultivation and from irrigation works in now almost deserted places."[1] The decline can be attributed to several circumstances: (1) widespread venereal disease, which depressed fertility and increased early mortality; (2) the practice of polyandry, which served to limit the number of children; (3) the climate and topography, which were unable to sustain a large population and precluded large increases; and (4) a large, mostly celibate clergy which did not replace itself.[2] Today the Tibetans in exile and their supporters routinely use the figure of six million for the entire worldwide population of ethnic Tibetans, although this figure does not appear to be supported by any evidence.

Source[3]	Date	Population Estimate (in millions)
a. W.W. Rockhill	1895	3
b. Sarat Chandra Das	1905	2.5 to 3
c. Encyclopaedia Britannica	1910	3
d. David MacDonald	1929	3.9
e. Office of Strategic Services (USA)	1944	4
f. Minister of Interior, GMD	1947	1
g. Tibetan official	1949	15.4
h. A.J. Hopkinson	1950	3
i. O. Edmund Clubb	1956	"well short of 2 million"
j. Heinrich Harrer	1959	4
k. Heinrich Harrer (quoting Zhou Enlai without documentation)	1960	12
l. Hugh Richardson	1961	3
m. Dalai Lama	1962	7 to 8
n. Michel Peissel	1972	7
o. Tibetan exile sources	1976	6 to 7
p. HRH Prince Peter of Greece and Denmark	1979	5

China estimates a total of just under three million in the early 1950s.[4] The GMD is mostly in agreement with these figures,[5] as is at least one noncommunist Western scholar who estimated a total of four million Tibetans if the ethnically related peoples found in Nepal, Sikkim, and Bhutan are included.[6]

The 1982 census reported 1,892,393 residents in the TAR, of whom 1,786,544 (94.41 percent) were ethnic Tibetans. Ethnic Han were said to number 91.592 (4.84 percent), presumably excluding the PLA. The total ethnic Tibetan population of China is placed at 3,870,068.[7]

From a political point of view, there are drawbacks to making estimates—for both sides. As the Dalai Lama continues to raise the population figures, he implicitly admits that a smaller percentage of Tibetans fled their homeland. He thereby diminishes the effects of his argument that the reason for the mass disaffection was China's harsh rule. On the other hand, Beijing's smaller population figure represents an increase in the percentage of Tibetans who fled into exile. If we accept the estimate of, at most, fifty-five thousand Tibetan refugees, then they represented a mere 0.9 percent of the ethnic Tibetans (assuming the population to be six million, as the Dalai Lama does). But, if the population is about three million, as Beijing claims, then almost 2 percent of the population fled their homes.

China's figures are probably closer to the truth than the Dalai Lama's. Beijing has maintained unchallenged control over Tibet for more than thirty years, including control over the marketplace, food production, consumption, and especially the ration coupon system that exists all over China. Control over these aspects of Tibetan life affords the authorities in Lhasa and Beijing opportunities to make population estimates, in spite of their inability to conduct an accurate census. The Tibetans in India not only lack the opportunity to conduct a census, they have not even lived in Tibet for over twenty years.

In 1978 a pamphlet was published in Dharamsala that estimated the pre-1959 clerical population of Tibet at about 200,000 (a figure remarkably similar to Beijing's estimate of 180,000, offered in 1966).[8] If the population of Tibet was indeed six million (the Dalai Lama's figure), then 200,000 would represent 3.3 percent of the total or, roughly 7 percent of the male population (nuns were an insignificant number by all accounts), assuming the male/female population was roughly equal. However, most observers of pre-1950 Tibet agree that the monks equalled approximately 15–20 percent of the male population. If 200,000 clerics represented 20 percent of the male population, there would have been one million Tibetan males—or a total Tibetan population of two million. These figures come closer to the Chinese estimates than to the Tibetan estimates.

When asked about these discrepancies, the Dalai Lama unconvincingly contended that the six million figure was derived from secret Chinese documents he had seen in the late 1950s. Moreover, he added, he believed the three million figure was only for the TAR, in spite of Chinese claims to the contrary. Another three million, he said, were scattered through adjoining regions.[9] If he had indeed seen these alleged secret documents, then why did he cite Tibetan population figures of seven to eight million shortly afterward, in 1962? He could provide no additional substantiation for his claim.

Han in Tibet

It is certainly no easier to determine how many Han live in Tibet and the other pockets of Tibetan habitation than to ascertain Tibetan population figures. These numbers also assume political significance—large numbers of Han migrants indicate that Beijing may be attempting assimilation and ethnic genocide.

Fears of imminent Sinicization were exacerbated by remarks Mao Zedong was alleged to have made to a visiting Tibetan delegation in 1952 that Tibet should eventually have a population of ten million.[10] Zhou Enlai also hinted at impending Han migration in the following statement:

The Hans are greater in number and more developed in economy and culture but in the regions they inhabit there is not much arable land left and underground resources there are not as abundant as in the regions inhabited by fraternal nationalities.[11]

Of course we cannot know for sure whether Mao was talking about Han settlement or an eventual growth in the size of the indigenous Tibetan population at some undetermined future date. In the case of Zhou's statement, it is uncertain how far into the future he meant.

Source[12]	Date	Estimated Number of Han Civilians
a. Hugh Richardson	1960–61	50,000
b. Rev. Ngawang Thubtob	c. 1965	200,000
c. Le Figaro (Paris)	1963	250,000
d. Wallace Liu	1960	300,000 (another 2 million expected)
e. Tingfu F. Tsiang (Taiwan)	1958	300,000
f. Far Eastern Economic Review	1954–56	500,000
g. Taiwanese source	1960	1,000,000
h. O. Edmund Clubb	1959	4,000,000 (another 4 million expected)
i. Taiwanese source	1959	4,500,000
j. Noel Barber	1959	4,500,000
k. Gyalo Thondup	1959	5,000,000 (another 4 million expected)
l. Dalai Lama	1959	5,000,000
m. George Patterson	1965	5,000,000
n. Dalai Lama	1959	5,500,000 (another 4,500,000 expected)
o. Lowell Thomas, Jr.	1959	5,800,000
p. Wadi Rufail (Egypt)	1959	6,000,000
Q. Daily Telegraph (London)	1965	9,000,000
r. Bradford Smith	1961	12,000,000
s. Tibetan Review	1960	"Now almost half the population of Tibet is Chinese"
t. Soviet expert	1974	Half the population, resulting from forced intermarriage
u. Soviet radio	1968	Han a majority in TAR, 80% in Kham
v. Lucien Pye	1976	Han outnumber Tibetans 2 to 1
w. Indian military officer	1966	Han outnumber Tibetans 3 to 1
x. Dorothy Woodman	1960	"a few years time will make the country [Tibet] a Chinese colony"
y. Indian periodical	1964	"several millions"
z. Purshottam Trikamdas	1959	5,000,000 (another 4 million expected)

It is no less confusing to determine the numbers of PLA in the TAR. Here, too, the estimates vary to a remarkable degree.

Source[13]	Date	Estimated Number of PLA
a. Chinese government source	1959	14,000
b. U.S. intelligence	c. 1960	60,000
c. Indian intelligence	c. 1960	150,000
d. George Patterson	1965	250,000
e. The Guardian (Manchester)	1964	300,000
f. Rev. Ngawang Thubtob	c. 1965	300,000
g. Soviet radio	1969	300,000
h. Wallace Liu	1960	300,000
i. Gyalo Thondup	1959	500,000
j. Tibetan Youth Congress (Dharamsala)	1982	500,000
k. Thubten Norbu	1959	600,000
l. Taiwanese source	1959	750,000
m. Noel Barber	1959	750,000

The Chinese themselves have quoted figures on their numbers in the TAR. In 1962 they claimed 40,000 civilians,[14] while in recent years (1976, 1977, 1980) they cite 120,000 civilians.[15] In 1975 Chinese officials admitted a total of 250,000 to 300,000 Han in the TAR, *including* PLA soldiers.[16] For the most part, the Han in the TAR are not there on a permanent basis but are supposed to be rotated every couple of years. This rotation allows officials to deny that there are many settlers; residents are, instead, individuals who are in the capacity of advisers on limited assignment. Since the mid-1980s the situation of the ethnic Han in the TAR has changed dramatically and is discussed in the new chapter added to this edition.

In a study done in 1976, CIA population estimates for the TAR stood at 1,800,000. This figure included the first 1,000 permanent Han settlers who had arrived that very year. As to the entire Han population (permanent settlers, advisers on limited assignments, and PLA) it stood at no more than 234,000, or 13 percent of the total.[17] In 1984, *Beijing Review* reported a total population of 1,930,000 for the TAR, of which only 4.9 percent (94,570) were non-Tibetans. It is presumed the army was not included.[18]

In the past decade some additional information on population has emerged. The Chinese authorities now admit that the 1953 (2.78 million Tibetans throughout the PRC) and 1964 (2.5 million) censuses were estimates while the 1982 (3.87 million) census was based on fieldwork but incomplete. The 1990 census, however, was properly done, Beijing claims, and found a Tibetan population of 4.59 million, about one-half (2.2 million) of whom live within the boundaries of the Tibet autonomous region.[19] These figures do not include Tibetans living outside China. The Tibetans in exile continue to use the 6 million figure as they have for almost two decades, implying no growth in the population whatsoever.

Appendix B

Independence

There are two distinct views of Tibetan "independence." Either Tibet is an independent nation that lost that status to Chinese colonial occupation in 1951, as the Tibetan refugees would have it, or, Tibet has returned to its rightful place under the aegis of the Chinese motherland after a brief period under British influence and, consequently, has once again become "an integral part of China," as China would have it.

The Dalai Lama's Views

1. Tibet has had a continuous central government from, at least, the seventh century.

2. Tibet has its own unique culture and language—a written script derived from Sanskrit, not from Chinese.

3. The relationship between the rulers of Tibet and those of China was known as one of "priest-patron." Tibetans see this as a link between equals—much as Christian world leaders view the Pope. In any case, the "priest-patron" relationship was with the Mongols and Manchus when they ruled China, not with the predominant Han people.

4. The Chinese representatives sent to Lhasa, the ambans, were originally sent as "security guards" to the Dalai Lama and derived all their authority solely through the Lhasan government. Tibetan treaties referred to the Han as "religious disciples."

5. Tibetans did not abide by the Anglo-Chinese treaties of 1890 and 1893 that referred specifically to Tibetan concessions; Tibetans were not consulted in the drafting of these treaties.

6. Lhasan officials signed several foreign treaties: 1856 with Nepal, 1904 with Britain, 1913 with Mongolia, and 1914 with Britain. The 1904 treaty stipulated that "no foreign power" would be permitted to intervene in Tibetan affairs.

7. In 1912 the Lhasa government evicted all Han residents and soldiers from Tibet, while the Dalai Lama simultaneously declared independence.

8. The Chinese government had no control or influence in Lhasa from 1913 to 1950.

9. Tibet was represented as an independent state at the Asian Relations Conference in New Delhi in 1947.

10. The Shakabpa Trade Mission of 1947–1948 traveled to several countries with Tibetan passports as their only travel documents. Various nations affixed their visas to this passport.

11. Tibet has printed and issued its own postage stamps and coins for most of this century.

12. Tibet has its own army and fought, unassisted, against Gurkhas and Kashmiris.

13. Tibet has carried on foreign relations with England, Russia, and the United States (the Tolstoy/Dolan mission).

14. Tibet has hosted foreign diplomatic representatives: the Nepalese from 1856, the British from 1936–1947, and the Indians in 1947–1962.

15. During World War II Tibet remained neutral; in 1943 the Tibet Bureau of Foreign Affairs was established to conduct diplomatic relations.

16. Britain and America forfeited their privileges of extraterritoriality in China on 11 January 1943. Tibet was not included in that agreement, indicating that the United Kingdom and the United States saw Tibet as separate from China. Extraterritoriality did not end in Tibet until 29 April 1954.

17. Tibet has been the subject of three United Nations resolutions condemning Chinese actions.

18. Tibetan representatives were compelled to sign the Seventeen-Point Agreement using forged seals, thereby making the agreement null and void from the very beginning. As a result, all of China's policies since then have been illegal under international law.

The Chinese Government's View

The view of the government of China—whether Mongol, Manchu, or Han, whether imperial, republican, or communist—has remained constant for centuries.

1. Tibet's continuous central government was a local government, not a national one.

2. A distinct language and culture are not necessarily prerequisites for independence. The PRC has over fifty distant ethnic groups and is one of many multinational states in the world.

3. The "priest-patron" relationship was not equal at all but rather one of superior to inferior. The treaty signed in 822 A.D. referred to the two parties as the "Nephew" and the "Uncle"—hardly an equal relationship in traditional family structures. The rulers of China conducted Tibet's foreign affairs.

4. The relationship between China and Tibet began with the imperial marriage of King Songsten Gampo and Tang Dynasty Princess Wen Cheng. This tie was strengthened by similar marriages in later years. Moreover, there were times when the ambans were in almost complete control of the government in Lhasa, such as the period from 1728 to 1911. Tibet was incorporated into China in the mid-thirteenth century when the rulers of China named Phagpa as the ruler of Tibet. The Qing Dynasty "decided on the organization of the local government in Xizang." Since 1712 Manchu power was supreme over China's border areas including Tibet.

5. As for the various treaties signed by Tibet:

—The 1856 treaty was imposed on Lhasa after a defeat at the hands of the Nepalese, while China was in the throes of a major rebellion (the Taiping) and was unable to proffer assistance. The treaty did not mention Tibetan "independence."

—The 1904 treaty was also imposed on Tibet. The reference to a "foreign power" was meant to indicate Russia, not China, as witnessed by the absence of the expulsion of the Han from Tibet at the time, by the Chinese government paying the stipulated indemnity, and by the subsequent 1907 Anglo-Russian pact and the 1908 Angle-Chinese pact that reaffirmed China's suzerainty over Tibet.

—The 1913 Mongolia treaty is most likely a figment of a fertile imagination and even if valid was, in the words of a noted expert in international law, more "a secret intrigue between two parties whose status was doubtful than a clear declaration of independence."[1]

—The 1914 Simla pact was secretly altered after China's delegates pulled out of the conference, and China's refusal to sign the pact raises doubts as to its validity.

6. If the Dalai Lama's declaration of independence in 1912 was valid then why was he willing to sign the original Simla agreement in 1914, which would have recognized Chinese suzerainty in an international agreement? Unilateral declarations of independence are meaningless unless recognized by other nations.

7. The Chinese government, indeed, had no influence over Tibet in the years 1912 to 1951 but neither did it have influence over many areas of China where local warlords ruled as virtual dictators. This condition alone does not represent independence.

8. At the Asian Relations Conference in New Delhi in 1947, the Indian

organizers took down the Tibetan flag after a protest from the Chinese embassy.

9. The Shakabpa Trade Mission was a private business trip. The members traveled on passports that were not recognized by most, if not all, of the nations they visited. Visas were issued as a special expedient, while the Chinese government was repeatedly reassured that Tibet continued to be recognized as part of China.

10. The minting of coins and stamps do not in themselves denote an independent state. The mail service in Tibet was severely restricted, in any case, since the illiteracy rate was over 90 percent of the population. Currency was also seldom used, particularly outside the urban areas. A survey done in Kham in 1940 showed that 29.21 percent of the Tibetan households never used any currency at all, while 35.68 percent never used more than Tibetan $20 a year.[2]

11. Dozens of warlords throughout China during the twentieth century had their own armies, which, in some instances, were in constant conflict. In any event, there were several times when armies were sent by China's rulers to help repel attacks on Tibet.

12. It is true that the government of Lhasa had direct relations with London, St. Petersburg/Moscow, and Washington; but each of these governments has continually and consistently reaffirmed Tibet's status as a part of China. Not a single instance exists when any of these governments recognized Tibet as "independent."

13. The Nepali representatives in Lhasa have always concerned themselves with trade matters, while the British arrived at a time when China was far too weak to adequately protest. The Chinese representatives always saw themselves in a different role from the other two plenipotentiaries. Once again, neither Nepal nor Britain has ever publicly recognized Tibet as an "independent" state.

14. Evicting Han officials at a time when China was ravaged by civil war and could not defend them is more an example of the ability of a regional area to exert its local authority over central government representatives than a display of "independence."

15. Tibet's neutrality during World War II had more to do with its geographic isolation and lack of strategic value than with a conscious effort on the part of the Lhasan authorities. The United States, for one, did not recognize the Tibetan Bureau of Foreign Affairs.

16. Extraterritoriality's continued existence in Tibet was a direct result of the Chinese government's lack of control there and consequent inability to press for an end to this onerous practice in that region. As soon as it was strong enough to do so, it demanded, and received, an end to it. Parenthetically, the existence of extraterritoriality in a region is a demonstration of the weakness of that region and its *lack* of independence rather than the opposite.

17. The UN resolutions were passed at a time when the PRC was not permitted to become a member and of course was not allowed to present its version of events in Tibet.

18. The Seventeen-Point Agreement was valid and the seals were not forged but copied with the assent of the Dalai Lama who also agreed to the provisions of the treaty before the delegation committed its signatures to it. In addition, the Tibetan National Assembly ratified the treaty. The Dalai Lama acquiesced to it for almost a decade without a word of protest, and it was recognized in international treaties with India (1954) and Nepal (1956). There was no international protest at the time of its signing, while the UN refused to discuss it. Complaints were all *ex post facto* and politically motivated.[3]

Third Party Views

No nation has ever publicly accepted Tibet as an independent state, in spite of several instances of government officials appealing to their superiors to do so. Treaties signed by Britain and Russia in the early years of the twentieth century, and others signed by Nepal and India in the 1950s, reaffirmed China's position that Tibet was a part of China.

The Americans presented their views in 1943. On 19 April of that year the British Embassy in Washington presented the State Department an aide-mémoire that stated in part,

> the relationship between China and Tibet is not a matter which can be unilaterally decided by China, but one on which Tibet is entitled to negotiate, and on which she can, if necessary, count on the diplomatic support of the British Government.

On 15 May Washington responded:

> For its part, the Government of the United States has borne in mind the fact that the Chinese constitution lists Tibet among areas constituting the territory of the Republic of China. This Government has at no time raised a question regarding either of these claims.

London replied on 22 July. In a document entitled "Policy of His Majesty's Government Towards Tibetan Relations with China," it asserted that colonial India's interest was to maintain friendly relations with Tibet while at the same time recognizing China's suzerainty. However, "any unconditional admission of Chinese suzerainty should be avoided." London, it continued, would prefer to have Tibet and China negotiate a settlement of their differences, which would recognize both Chinese suzerainty and local Tibetan autonomy. But, if the latter were to be impinged upon the British would not "continue to recognize even a theoretical status of subservience for a people who desire to be free and have, in fact, maintained their freedom for more than thirty years."[4] The irony of this statement, made by the world's largest colonial power, appears to have been lost on policy-makers in Whitehall.

The status quo remained until 1947 when India gained its independence; from then on, London acquiesced with the policy decisions made in New Delhi. The Americans, on the other hand, wavered little from their original policy. This may have resulted from the alliance with the Guomindang, even after the move to Taiwan, for the GMD's attitude toward Tibetan independence was indistinguishable from that of the PRC. The closest the United States came to a policy change was reflected in an official statement made on March 28, 1959, declaring:

> the United States is profoundly sympathetic with the people of Tibet in the face of the barbarous intervention of the Chinese Communist imperialists to deprive a proud and brave people of their cherished religious and political autonomy and to pervert their institutions to Communist ends.[5]

The statement scrupulously avoids mention of Tibetan independence. Aid to Tibetan dissidents to fight communism was one matter, but to champion an independent nation state of Tibet was entirely another.

Not a single state, including India, has extended recognition to the "government-in-exile" of the Dalai Lama in the more than two decades of its existence, despite obvious precedents for such an action. This lack of legal recognition of independence has forced even some strong supporters of the refugees to admit that

> even today international legal experts sympathetic to the Dalai Lama's cause find it difficult to argue that Tibet ever technically established its independence of the Chinese Empire, imperial, or republican.[6]

In spite of these circumstances, there recently has been a concerted effort by lawyers, particularly in the United States, to build a legal case for Tibetan independence, and there is a growing literature on this topic.

Theoretically, the United Nations recognizes four criteria for statehood: (a) a permanent population, (b) a defined territory, (c) a government, and (d) capability of entering into relations with other states.[7] Tibet fulfills those requirements. However, so does the Canadian province of Quebec and, for that matter, any state of the United States. The People's Republic of China met those requirements and was kept out of the UN for over twenty years.

An Historical Look at China's View

Pre-1949

Although China has not always been ruled by ethnic Han dynasties, the occupants of the throne always considered themselves the rulers of all of China. China's conquerors found it more beneficial to adopt Han culture rather than alter it. Consequently, the Chinese world view of Han cultural superiority was reinforced.

While the Han may have believed themselves to be culturally superior, this view, understandably, was not always shared by the non-Han. There are instances in China's past in which non-Han formed alliances that excluded the Han or even openly conspired against them. However, the Han Chinese world view of cultural superiority persisted—at least until Sun Yat-sen's time. Sun appears to have shared this view, hoping for the eventual assimilation of the non-Han peoples into the Han culture through intermarriage. But—perhaps under Soviet influence—he changed his mind. Whether as an expedient or resulting from a fundamental shift in attitude, at the 1924 first National Congress of the Guomindang, Sun asserted that

> the nationalism of the Kuomintang has a two-fold meaning: the self-emancipation of the Chinese nation, and the equality of all national minorities in China.
> The Kuomintang can state with solemnity that it recognizes the right of self-determination of all national minorities in China and it will organize a free and united Chinese republic.[8]

As time went on, there was a GMD-CCP divergence of view on this matter. The Guomindang official view swung back to a more traditional one after Chiang Kaishek's rise to power. Chiang believed that ethnic minorities constituted various "stocks" emanating from a common blood line. The CCP, on the other hand, more closely followed Sun's legacy, viewing China as a multinational state.

The first communist constitution of November 1931, while encouraging citizenship in a Greater China, stated in Article 4 that

> all workers, peasants, Red Army soldiers, and all toilers and their families without distinction of sex, religion, or nationality (Chinese, Manchurian, Mongolians, Moslems, Tibetans . . . living in China) shall be equal before the Soviet Law and shall be citizens of the Soviet Republic.[9]

Not only is there no mention of assimilation, but the constitution even held out the possibility of a loose confederation or even no confederation at all.

> the Soviet Government of China recognizes the right of self-determination of the national minorities of China, their right to complete separation from China and to the formation of an independent state for each national minority. All Mongolians, Tibetans, Miao, Yao, Koreans, and others living in the territory of China shall enjoy the full rights to self-determination, i.e., they may either join the Union of Chinese Soviets or secede from it and form their own state as they may prefer.[10]

While this view prevailed for many years, there was one subtle, yet significant, change. After 1936 there was no further mention of a right to secession. Because the shift remains unacknowledged in China, the reasons are obscured. When CCP leader Mao Zedong spoke to American journalist Edgar Snow in 1936, he made no mention of the possibility of minority secession. "When the people's revolution has been victorious in China," Mao said, "the Outer Mongolian republic will automatically become part of the Chinese federation at their own will. The Mohammedan and Tibetan peoples, likewise, will form autonomous republics attached to the Chinese federation."[11]

Mao reiterated his view that minority-populated areas would attach themselves to central Chinese rule on several occasions. In an interview with journalist Gunther Stein in 1947, Mao stated that "China must first recognize Outer Mongolia as a natural entity and then organize a sort of United States of China to meet Mongol aspirations. The same is true of Tibet."[12]

A year later, writing "On Coalition Government," Mao supported Sun's policy toward the minorities as expressed in the first GMD congress, adding that his own goal was to "give minority nationalities in China better treatment and grant them autonomous rights."[13] Unfortunately, throughout this period the communists never defined their concept of "autonomy." Lack of a definition may stem from the diversity of minority situations. An independent state existed in Outer Mongolia, sponsored by the same Soviet government that was the principal supporter of the CCP. Tibet, at the time, was completely outside the sphere of Chinese rule; and the conditions of minorities in places like Yunnan, Guizhou (Kweichow) and Xinjiang were largely unknown to the CCP—entrenched as they were, in Shaanxi, far from these distant locales.

Post-1949

These pre-1949 policies were, of course, formulated when the communists controlled very few non-Han areas. When they came to national power in 1949 their views appear once again to have undergone a slight transformation, although no official explanation has been given. The first public hint of this change, a seemingly narrower definition of autonomy, can be found only days before the People's Republic of China was officially founded. On 29 September 1949, the Chinese People's Political Consultative Conference called for the implementation of "regional autonomy." While, again, there was no definition of the term, the Chinese were not unequivocal that this new formulation left no room for any notions of separation. On 2 October 1952, the *People's Daily* noted:

> at this juncture any national movement which seeks separation from the Chinese People's Republic for independence will be reactionary, since objectively considered, it would undermine the interests of the various races and particularly the foremost majority of the race considered [the Han], and this would work to the advantage of imperialism.[14]

By 1952, the "General Program of the People's Republic of China for the Implementation of Regional Autonomy for Nationalities"—the basic statement of minority policy at the time—made it quite clear that there would be limitations to this "regional autonomy."

> Each national autonomous region is an integral part of the territory of the People's Republic of China. The autonomous organ of each national autonomous region is a local government led by the people's government of the next

higher level, under the unified leadership of the Central People's Government. (Article 2)

The local government can draw up . . . special regulations for the region . . . but these . . . shall be submitted for approval to the People's Government of the two next higher levels. (Article 23)[15]

These policies were later codified in the PRC's first constitution, in 1954; Article 3 declared China to be a "single multi-national state," of which the "national autonomous areas are inalienable parts."[16]

While a measure of political and social integration had been achieved, however, cultural integration was another matter. In a major speech delivered in 1957, Zhou Enlai pointed out that "assimilation is a reactionary thing if it means one nation destroying another by force. It is a progressive thing if it means a national merger of nations advancing toward prosperity. Assimilation as such has the significance of promoting progress." Yet while Zhou encouraged the "progressive" assimilation and "national merger" of the minority cultures into the numerically superior Han culture, he was at the same time aware of the limits of that assimilation.

So long as religious activity does not hinder political life or economic production, we should not interfere . . . we should not willfully change the minority peoples' customs and habits in the cultural field.

In a national autonomous area, the written language of the major nationality should become the first language.

In all the national autonomous areas minority cadres should hold positions of responsibility.[17]

The PRC's *policy* toward its national minorities remain unchanged in the geopolitical sphere. The three most recent constitutions reaffirmed that policy. The 1975 document referred to China as a "unitary multi-national state" in which the "areas where regional autonomy is exercised are all inalienable" (Article 4). The 1978 document, as well as the one promulgated in 1982, states that "all the national autonomous areas are inalienable parts of the People's Republic of China" (Article 4).[18]

I have already examined how these policies were put into practice. Here we may question why the communist leadership altered its views from the 1930s— when minority secession was deemed possible—to the period after 1949, when the only possibility held out was integration within the Chinese state. There has been much speculation on the reasons for this policy shift; however, although many of the explanations are intriguing, none are borne out by the evidence. Possible explanations include fear of an uprising, such as that in Lhasa in 1959; fear of mass defections, such as those of the Kazaks who fled to the USSR; or even a desire on the part of the communist leadership for retaliation against minorities who mistreated them during the Long March through their areas.

As I have demonstrated, the change in policy came before the Lhasa uprising or the Kazak defections. The Long March argument is interesting but implausible. Although there were some bad experiences, there were as many good ones that led to some local support for the CCP. There was even recruitment to the party of several minority members who later rose to prominent positions, such as Tian Bao and Yang Dongsheng.

June Dreyer has suggested what I believe to be a large part of the answer in that the change in policy was a direct result of a climate of uncertainty on China's borders—by pointing to China's bitterness over having to acknowledge the independence of Outer Mongolia; concern in the early years of the PRC over Soviet designs on Xinjiang (and further worry over Soviet machinations among the minorities); and remembering Japan's earlier successes at winning allies among the Manchus and Mongolians with the advocacy of anti-Han programs.[19]

There were dramatic changes in the world situation immediately following the establishment of the PRC. With the outbreak of the Korean War in June 1950 the PRC was diplomatically and economically isolated from the industrialized nations during a period of urgent economic and technological need. The Soviet Union was alone in its willingness to aid China, although this assistance was not without restrictions. The continued support by the United States for the Guomindang on Taiwan, the establishment of U.S. military bases along China's periphery (in Korea, Japan, and Taiwan), and American support for French colonialism in Indo-China all posed a direct threat to the newly established state. In addition, extensive American-sponsored clandestine activities along the southern rim of China, from Tibet to Laos, is sure to have caused considerable consternation in Beijing. These threats contributed to an upsurge of ardent nationalism, already aroused in the long anti-Japanese resistance and the civil war against the Western-supported Guomidang. As the new Chinese state perceived the dangers of dismemberment by imperialist forces, it sought to reaffirm the unity of the Chinese nation state.

Looking at China's policy shifts in this broader global perspective, they are not so surprising. Nation states, as a whole, are uncomfortable with diverse social and cultural entities within their boundaries, as evidenced by events in Ireland, Belgium, and Canada—to name only a few. Moreover, this discomfort is especially felt following victory in a long and bloody civil war, at a time when newly won power may be threatened from without. In China's case, the CCP's convictions were further heightened by a clear sense of mission for social change.

Conclusion

Tibet has always had a special relationship with China—a relationship that never demonstrated absolute "independence" (as we use the term now); but nor did it demonstrate Tibet to be "an integral part of China." The victory of communist forces in China and the world's political climate brought about a drastic shift in that relationship. I believe that, had the Dalai Lama been able to contain the more aggressive of his officials, the opportunity existed for the Beijing-Lhasa tie to revert to earlier forms. This would only have been possible had the Western nations not isolated China. After 1959 that opportunity, regardless of how slim, was lost. As late as 1978 I would have written "irretrievably lost," but now there is once again slim hope.

China is again speaking of a more realistic interpretation of regional autonomy. The possible return of the Dalai Lama and China's emergence as an accepted and respected member of the world community have set the stage for the forging of a new Beijing-Lhasa link, in which Beijing would continue to control Tibet's security and external relations but the Dalai Lama would lead a truly secular, regional government and once again head the church in Tibet. It remains to be seen just how far along the path to this goal the two parties are willing to travel.[20]

Notes

Introduction

1. For a romanticized view see Rinchen Dolma Taring, *Daughter of Tibet* (London: John Murray, 1970). For an official Chinese view see *Great Changes in Tibet* (Peking: Foreign Languages Press, 1972).

2. A. Tom Grunfeld, "Some Thoughts on the Current State of Sino-Tibetan Historiography," *CQ* 83 (September 1980): 568–576.

3. Luo Fu, "China's Democratic Parties," *BR* 50 (14 December 1979): 24.

4. Howard S. Klein, "History and Historiography in China: Historical Science Society Reestablished—Historical Research Flourishes," *China Exchange News* 8:2 (April 1980): 6–8.

Chapter 1

1. Barbara Nimri Aziz, *Tibetan Frontier Families, Reflections of Three Generations from Ding-ri* (New Delhi: Vikas Publishing House, 1978). The most important recent work is Melvyn C. Goldstein and Cynthia M. Beall, *Nomads of Western Tibet. The Survival of a Way of Life* (Berkeley: University of California Press, 1990). Another example is Ronald D. Schwartz, *Circle of Protest. Political Ritual in the Tibetan Uprising* (New York: Columbia University Press, 1994).

2. Yeh-hu and Ho-shih, "A Preliminary Analysis of the Systems of Feudal Serfdom in Tibet," *MTCY* March 1959 in *ECMM* 171, 8 June 1959. Wang Fen and Wang Fu-jen, "Do Away with Feudal Prerogatives and Exploitation by the Tibetan Lamaseries," *MTYC* August 1959 in *JPRS* 1144-D, 5 February 1960, pp. 17–29. Yen Yu, "How the Feudal Lords Brutally Exploit the Slaves," *MTYC* August 1959 in *JPRS* 1144-D, 5 February 1960, pp. 30–45.

3. Marco Pallis, *Peaks and Lamas* (London: Woburn Books, 1974), pp. 380–390. Marco Pallis, "The Tibetan System of Landed Estates Seen in Perspective," *TR* 12:7 (July 1977): 14–16.

4. Melvyn C. Goldstein, "An Anthropological Study of the Tibetan Political System" (Ph.D., University of Washington, Seattle, 1968), p. 228. Luciano Petech, *Aristoc-*

racy and Government in Tibet, 1728–1959 (Roma: Istituto Italiano per il Medio ed Estremo Orient, 1973).

5. Melvyn C. Goldstein, "The Balance Between Centralization and Decentralization in the Traditional Tibetan Political System," *CAJ* 15:3 (1971): 172 (he cites a former high official on this). Panchen Erdeni, "Democratic Reform for a New Tibet," *PR* 27 (7 July 1959): 6–11 (says 30.9 percent by the government, 39.5 percent by the clergy, 29.6 percent by lay nobility). Ratne Deshapriya Senanayake, *Inside Story of Tibet* (Colombo: Afro-Asian Writer's Bureau, 1967), p. 39 (says 38 percent government, 37 percent clergy, and 25 percent nobility).

6. Taring, pp. 102–103.

7. Ram Rahul, "The Structure of the Government of Tibet, 1644–1911," *IS* 7:3 (January 1962): 289 (says they received a small sum). Amaury de Riencourt, *Roof of the World: Tibet, Key to Asia* (New York and Toronto: Rinehart, 1950), p. 135 (says (U.S.$1,000 a year). Robert W. Ford, *Wind Between the Worlds* (New York: David McKay, 1957), p. 48 (says only foreign employees received salaries).

8. Rahul, "Government of Tibet, 1644–1911," p. 290. David MacDonald, *Twenty Years in Tibet* (Philadelphia: J.B. Lippincott, 1932), p. 141.

9. Robert W. Ford, *Wind Between the Worlds* (New York: David McKay, 1957) pp. 48, 80. Goldstein, "An Anthropological Study," pp. 185–187.

10. This description is drawn from the following sources: Sonam Wangdu, *The Discovery of the 14th Dalai Lama* trans. by Sonam Wangdu, et al. (Bangkok: Klett Thai Publications, 1975). The author was a member of the search party. Heinrich Harrer, *Seven Years in Tibet* (London: Rupert Hart-Davis, 1953), pp. 267–271. B.J. Gould, *Report by Mr. B.J. Gould, C.M.E., C.I.E., Political Officer in Sikkim, On the Discovery, Recognition and Installation of the Fourteenth Dalai Lama* (New Delhi: Government of India Press, 1941), pp. 5–8. Dalai Lama, *The Autobiography of His Holiness the Dalai Lama of Tibet* (London: A Panther Book, 1964), pp. 21–26. For a seventeenth century view see John Pinkerton, *A General Collection of the Best and the Most Intriguing Voyages and Travels in All Parts of the World* (London: Longman, Hurst, Rees, Orme and Brown, Paternoster-Row, and Caldwell and Davis in the Strand, 1811), p. 558. For an account of the discovery of the Thirteenth Dalai Lama see Tada Tōkan, *The Thirteenth Dalai Lama* (Tokyo: The Center for East Asian Cultural Studies, 1965), pp. 2–6. Sir Charles Bell, *Portrait of the Dalai Lama* (London: Collins, 1946), pp. 39–45.

11. Goldstein, "An Anthropological Study," p. 40.

12. Rahul, "Government of Tibet, 1644–1911," p. 296.

13. Melvyn C. Goldstein, "Tibetan Refugees in South India: A New Face to the Indo-Tibetan Interface," *TSB* 9 (1975): 18. United States, Office of Strategic Services (OSS), Research and Analysis Bureau, "Survey of Tibet," No. 757, 1 October 1943, 2d ed., p. 17. National Archives, Diplomatic Branch, Washington, D.C. (Hereafter OSS).

14. Thubten Norbu and Colin M. Turnbull, *Tibet* (New York: Simon and Schuster, 1968), p. 324.

15. Li Shih-Yü Yu, "Tibetan Folk Law," *JRAS* 3 and 4 (1950): 130. Goldstein, "An Anthropological Study," pp. 48–49, 55–56. Melvyn C. Goldstein, "Serfdom and Mobility: An Examination of the Use of 'Human Lease' in Traditional Tibetan Society," *JAS* 30:3 (May 1971): 521–534.

16. *Concerning the Question of Tibet* (Peking: Foreign Languages Press, 1959), pp. 213, 215.

17. Sir Charles Bell, *Tibet Past and Present* (London: Oxford University Press, 1927), pp. 78–79.

18. Tsewang Y. Pemba, "Tibetan Reminiscences," *TR* 12:7 (July 1977): 23.

19. David MacDonald, *Tibet* (London: Humphrey Milford for the Oxford University Press, 1945), p. 12.

20. Hugh Richardson, "Tibet As It Was," *JHKBRAS* 1 (1960–1961): 2.

21. Thubten J. Norbu, "The Social and Economic Structure in Traditional Tibet," in *Tibet: A Handbook*, ed. Helmut Hoffman (Bloomington: Area Studies Research Institute [1976?]), p. 175.

22. Taring, pp. 6–7, 8, 10, 41, 113.

23. Ibid., pp. 10, 43, 52, 78, 90, 109, 126, 145.

24. David MacDonald, "The Tibetan at Home," *Asia* 24:3 (March 1929): 220.

25. Harrer, *Seven Years*, p. 211.

26. Dawa Norbu, *Red Star Over Tibet* (London: William Collins, 1974), p. 244.

27. Jamyang Norbu, *Horseman in the Snow, The Story of Aten, An Old Khampa Warrior* (Dharamsala, India: Information Office, Central Tibetan Secretariat, 1979), p. 52.

28. "Smear Campaign Against Dalai Lama in Lhasa," *N-T* 8:2 (March-June 1973): 1–2.

29. Chen Han-seng, *Frontier Land Systems in Southwestern China* (New York: Institute for Pacific Relations, 1949), p. 136.

30. Sir Charles Bell, *The People of Tibet* (Oxford: At the Clarendon Press, 1928), pp. 95–108. Tsewang Y. Pemba, *Young Days in Tibet* (London: Jonathan Cape, 1957), p. 95. Shên Tsung-lien and Liu Shen-chi, *Tibet and the Tibetans* (New York: E.P. Dutton, 1977), p. 14.

31. Tseten Dolkar, *Girl from Tibet* (Chicago: Loyola University Press, 1971), p. 11. Bell, *Tibet Past and Present*, p. 128. Lowell Thomas and Lowell Thomas, Jr., "Up in the Clouds: Capital of the Lama," *Collier's* 125:8 (25 February 1950): 36.

32. Taring, p. 30. Dolkar, pp. 81–84. OSS, pp. 29–30. Tashi Dorjee, "Education in Tibet," *TJ* 2 (1977): 31–37.

33. Norbu and Turnbull, pp. 329–330.

34. Robert B. Ekvall, *Fields on the Hoof: Nexus of Nomadic Pastoralism in Tibet* (New York: Holt, Reinhart and Winston, 1968), pp. 11–14. Richard P. Palmiere, "The Domestication, Exploitation and Social Functions of the Yak in Tibet and Adjoining Areas," *Proceedings of the American Association of Geographers* 4 (1972): 80–83. Christopher Rand, "A Reporter at Large: The Edge of Outer Darkness," *NY* 26:13 (20 May 1950): 88–104.

35. Taring, p. 105.

36. George Patterson, "The 'Fish' in the 'Sea' of Tibet: Fifteen Years of Guerilla Warfare and Popular Unrest," *CS* 3:23 (15 July 1965): 3. Robert B. Ekvall, *Cultural Relations on the Kansu-Tibet Border* (Chicago: Chicago University Press, 1939), pp. 65–78. Robert B. Ekvall, "Some Differences in Tibetan Land Tenure and Utilization," *Sinologica* 4:1 (1954): 39–48. J.R. Rock, "Konka Risumgongka, Holy Mountain of the Outlaws, *NGM* 60:1 (July 1931):1–65. Robert B. Ekvall, "The Nomadic Pattern of Living Among the Tibetans as Preparation for War," *AA* 63:6 (December 1961): 1250–1263. Cheng Te-k'un and D. Michael Sullivan, *An Introduction to Tibetan Culture* (Chengtu: West China Union University Museum, 1945) Guidebook No. 6. Sven Hedin, "Tibetan Nomads and Valley People," *Asia* 24:1 (January 1924): 37–41, 74–75. "Among the Tibetan Nomads," *North China Herald* 14 March 1944, pp. 766–778.

37. J. Norbu, *Horseman*, p. 63.

38. Harrer, *Seven Years*, p. 137.

39. Dolkar, pp. 45–48. Guiseppe Tucci, *Tibet Land of Snows*, trans. by J.E. Stapleton Driver (London: Elek Books, 1967), p. 154.

40. Harrer, *Seven Years*, p. 176. Dolkar, pp. 45–48. David MacDonald, *The Land of the Lamas* (London: Seeley, Service, 1929), p. 134. R.A. Stein, *Tibetan Civilization*,

trans. by J.E. Stapleton Driver (Stanford: Stanford University Press, 1972), p. 96. PRO FO371/53615 F12114.

41. H.R.H. Prince Peter of Greece and Denmark, "The Tibetan Family System," in *Comparative Family Systems*, ed. M.F. Nimkoff (Boston: Houghton, Mifflin, 1965), p. 203.

42. Ekvall, *Fields on the Hoof*, pp. 27–28. G.A. Combe, *A Tibetan on Tibet. Being the Travels and Observations of Mr. Paul Sherap (Dorje Zoelba) of Tachienlu: With an Introductory Chapter on the Devil Dance* (New York: D. Appleton, 1926), p. 71.

43. Dalai Lama, *Autobiography*, p. 19. George N. Patterson, *Journey with Loshay* (New York: W.W. Norton, 1954), p. 93. Tucci, *Tibet*, p. 154. Marion H. Duncan, *Customs and Superstitions of Tibetans* (London: Mitre Press, 1964), p. 83. For more on Tibetan Women see Barbara Nimri Aziz, "Women in Tibetan Society and Tibetology," in *Tibetan Studies. Proceedings of the 4th Seminar of the International Association for Tibetan Studies*, ed. by Helga Uebach and Jampa L. Panglung (Munchen: Kommission für Zentralasiatische Studien, 1988), pp. 25–34.

44. Li An-che, "Tibetan Family and Its Relations to Religion," *Asian Horizon* 2:1 (Spring 1949): 31.

45. Patterson, *Journey with Loshay*, p. 88.

46. MacDonald, *The Land of the Lamas*, p. 181. Jin Zhou, ed., *Tibet: No Longer Medieval* (Peking: Foreign Languages Press, 1981), p. 195.

47. Robert B. Ekvall, *Religious Observances in Tibet: Patterns and Functions* (Chicago and London: Chicago University Press, 1964), p. 80.

48. Ibid. A.C. McKay, "The Establishment of the British Trade Agencies in Tibet. A Survey," *JRAS* Series 3, 2:3 (1992): 402.

49. Holmes Welch, *Buddhism Under Mao* (Cambridge, MA: Harvard University Press, 1972), p. 32.

50. Albert L. Shelton, *Pioneering in Tibet* (New York, London and Edinburgh: Fleming H. Revell, 1921), p. 67.

51. Dolkar, p. 14.

52. G.E.O. Knight, *Intimate Glimpses of Mysterious Tibet and Neighbouring Countries* (London: Golden Vista Press, 1930), p. 53.

53. Pallis, *Peaks and Lamas*, pp. 384, 386.

54. Norbu and Turnbull, p. 116.

55. Fosco Maraini, *Secret Tibet*, trans. by Eric Mosbacher (New York: Grove Press, 1960), p. 54. Fosco Maraini, "Religion and People in Tibet," *The Geographical Magazine* 24:3 (July 1951): 144. Robert B. Ekvall, "Mis Tong: The Tibetan Custom of Life Indemnity," *Sociologus* 4:2 (1954): 139.

56. Harrer, *Seven Years*, p. 90. Tucci, *Tibet*, p. 133. Dolkar, p. 79. Goldstein, "Centralization," p. 175. Alexandra David-Neel, "Lhasa at Last," *Asia* 26:7 (July 1926): 627.

57. Harrer, *Seven Years*, p. 88. Bell, *People of Tibet*, p. 143. Dolkar, p. 12. Rato Khyongla Nawang Losang, *My Life and Lives. The Story of a Tibetan Incarnation* (New York: E.P. Dutton, 1977), p. 33.

58. Tucci, *Tibet*, p. 206. Maraini, *Secret Tibet*, pp. 124–125. IOLR L/P AND S/12/4202, Ext. 6154.

59. Robert B. Ekvall, "Tibetan Symposium: Law and the Individual Among the Tibetan Nomads," *AA* 66:5 (October 1964): 1110–1148. See, also, Rebecca Redwood French, *The Golden Yoke. The Legal Cosmology of Buddhist Tibet* (Ithaca, NY: Cornell University Press, 1995).

60. Thubten Norbu quoted in James McKenzie Alexander III, "Tibetan National Character" (Ph.D., University of Washington, 1971), pp. 97–98. Goldstein, "An Anthropological Study," pp. 90–94.

61. Swami Pranavanada, *Exploration in Tibet* (Calcutta: University of Calcutta, 1939), pp. 66–67. Duncan, p. 234. MacDonald, *The Land of the Lamas*, pp. 196–197.

62. The original sentence, "amputation of noses and ears," was reduced to "whipping" upon appeal of an American diplomat whose companion's murder had led to these events. Frank Bessac,"This Was the Perilous Trek to Tragedy," *Life* 13 November 1950, pp. 130–36, 138, 141. Ford, p. 37. MacDonald, *The Land of the Lamas*, pp. 196–197.

63. Dolkar, p. 79.

64. Hanna Havnevik, *Tibetan Buddhist Nuns. History, Cultural Norms and Social Reality* (Oslo: Norwegian University Press, 1989?), p. 37.

65. Quoted in Huston Smith, *The Religions of Man* (New York: Harper & Row, 1958), p. 108.

66. Alexandra David-Neel, "Edge of Tibet," *AATA* 44:1 (January 1944): 26–29.

67. Guiseppe Tucci, *The Religions of Tibet*, trans. by Geoffrey Samuel (Berkeley, CA: University of California Press, 1980), p. 187.

68. Tucci, *Tibet*, pp. 73–74.

69. Dalai Lama, *Autobiography*, p. 16. Rosemary Jones Tung, *A Portrait of Lost Tibet* (New York: Holt, Rinehart & Winston, 1980), p. 92. Bell, *People of Tibet*, pp. 217–218.

70. Tucci, *Tibet*, p. 165.

71. Shên and Liu, pp. 141–142.

72. For some photos of "water printing" see Joseph R. Rock, *The Amnye-ma-Chhen Range and Adjacent Regions: A Monographic Study* (Rome: Instituto Italiano Per Il Medio Ed Estreme Oriente, 1956) plates 76, 80.

73. For some photos of oracles in trances see Joseph R. Rock, "Sungmas, The Living Oracles of the Tibetan Church," *NGM* 68:4 (October 1935): 475–486. Dalai Lama quoted in H.R.H. Prince Peter of Greece and Denmark, "Tibetan Oracles," in *Himalayan Anthropology. The Indo-Tibetan Interface* by James F. Fisher (The Hague: Mouton Publishers, 1978), p. 278. Rene de Nebesky-Wojkowitz, *Oracles and Demons of Tibet: The Cult and Iconography of the Tibetan Protective Deities* (S-Gravenhage, Netherlands: Mouton, 1956).

74. de Riencourt, p. 245. Tung, pp. 200–201. Shên and Liu, pp. 87–88.

75. Tucci, *Tibet*, p. 166.

76. The most common translation is W.Y. Evans-Wentz, ed., *The Tibetan Book of the Dead* (London, Oxford, and New York: Oxford University Press, 1960).

77. Bell, *People of Tibet*, pp. 286–296. Shên and Liu, pp. 148–149. Maraini, *Secret Tibet*, p. 58. Dolkar, p. 91. Turrell Wylie, "Ro-Langs: The Tibetan Zombie," *HR* 4:1 (Summer 1964): 68–80. "The Talk of the Town: Our Own Baedeker," *NY* 35:10 (25 April 1959): 34–35.

78. Shên and Liu, pp. 150–151. Dolkar, pp. 58–59. Turrell Wylie, "Mortuary Customs at Sa-skya, Tibet," *Harvard Journal of Asiatic Studies* 25 (1964–1965): 229–242. Michel Peissel, "Mustang, Remote Realm in Nepal," *NGM* 128:4 (October 1964): 594. (Describes a practice of burying bodies within the walls of houses).

79. Bell, *Tibet Past and Present*, p. 165.

80. Barbara Nimri Aziz, "In Real Tibet," interview on radio station WBAI-FM, New York City, 6 July 1978.

81. Berthold Laufer, *Uses of Human Skulls and Bones in Tibet* (Chicago: Field Museum of Natural History, 1928). Andrea Loseries-Leick, "The Use of Human Skulls in Tibetan Rituals," in *Tibetan Studies: Proceedings of the 5th Seminar of the International Association for Tibetan Studies*, ed. by Ihara Shoren and Yamaguchi Zuiho (Narita: Naritasan Shinshoji, 1992), pp. 159–173.

82. *Wrath of the Serfs—A Group of Life-Size Clay Sculptures* (Peking: Foreign Languages Press, 1976).

83. Israel Epstein, "Serfs and Slaves Rule Khaesum Manor," *EH* 16:7 (July 1977): 21.

84. "Visual Denunciation of Serf-Owner's Atrocities," *PR* 29 (19 June 1977): 11.

85. Stein, pp. 132–133, 201. Alexander, p. 69 quotes from unpublished research by H.E. Richardson.

86. Maraini, *Secret Tibet*, pp. 199, 204–205. Pallis, *Peaks and Lamas*, p. 170. Stein, p. 200.

87. H.R.H. Prince Peter of Greece and Denmark, "Zor: A Western Tibetan Ceremonial Goat Sacrifice," *FOLK: Dansk Ethnografisk Tidsskrift* 16–17 (1974–1975): 309–312. H.R.H. Prince Peter of Greece and Denmark, "The Tibetan Ceremony of Breaking the Stone," *FOLK: Dansk Ethnografisk Tidsskrift* 4 (1962): 65–70. Sigebert Hummel, "The Tibetan Ceremony of Breaking the Stone," *HR* 8:2 (November 1968): 139–142.

88. Muriel Percy Brown, "A Welcome Guest in Forbidden Tibet," *Asia* 22:3 (March 1927): 230.

89. Ekvall, *Religious Observances*, pp. 165–166, 169, 172.

90. Bell, *Tibet Past and Present*, p. 80.

91. Khyongla, p. 34.

92. Quoted in Bradford Smith, "Chinese Tyranny in Tibet," *The Atlantic* 207:6 (June 1961): 52.

93. Dorsch Marie de Voe, "The Donden Ling Case: An Essay on Tibetan Refugee Life with Proposals for Change," *TSB* 14 (December 1979): 80. Also in *TR* 15:4 (April 1980): 20.

94. Bell, *Portrait of the Dalai Lama*, pp. 165–166.

95. Combe, p. 22. Goldstein, "An Anthropological Study," p. 165–167.

96. Li An-Che, "A Lamasery in Outline," *Journal of the West China Border Research Society* 14, Series A (1942): 35–68.

97. Hsian Yang, "The Reactionary Nature of the Tibetan Local Government," *MYTC* 4 April 1959 in *JPRS* 862-D, August 1959, p. 29. Goldstein claims that in 1951 there were a total of 22,000 monks (Drepung–10,000, Sera–7,000, Ganden–5,000). Melvyn C. Goldstein, "Religious Conflict in the Traditional Tibetan State," in *Reflections on Tibetan Culture. Essays in Memory of Turrell V. Wylie*, ed. by Lawrence Epstein and Richard B. Sherburne (Lewiston, NY: Edwin Mellin Press, 1990), p. 234.

98. Goldstein, "An Anthropological Study," pp. 216–217.

99. Shên and Liu, pp. 73–76.

100. Khyongla, p. 104. Pedro Carrasco, *Land and Polity in Tibet* (Seattle and London: University of Washington Press, 1959), p. 125. Shên and Liu, pp. 73–76. David MacDonald, "Where a Lama Leads the Way," *Asia* 29:2 (February 1929): 104.

101. Khyongla, pp. 17, 50, 67, 125.

102. Ekvall, *Religious Observances*, p. 193. Shên and Liu, p. 76.

103. Harrer, *Seven Years*, p. 194. Ford, p. 124. Patterson, *Journey with Loshay*, p. 89. Stein, p. 154. H.E. Richardson, "The Rva-sgreng Conspiracy of 1947," in *Tibetan Studies in Honour of H.E. Richardson*, ed. by Michael Aris and Aung San Sui Kyi (Warminster: Aris and Phillips, 1979), p. xvii.

104. Robert B. Ekvall, "Three Categories of Inmates Within Tibetan Monasteries: Status and Function," *CAJ* 5:3 (1960): 210–219. Goldstein, "Religious Conflict in Tibet," p. 234.

105. There are a number of accounts by former and current monks: Khyongla, p. 165 and passim. Chogyam Trungpa, *Born in Tibet* as told to Esmé Cramer Roberts (Baltimore: Penguin Books, 1971) *passim*. Lama Chimpa, "The System of Monastic Education in Tibet," *Indian Studies: Past and Present* 6, 1, 1964, pp. 99–105. (Lama Chimpa spent the years 1943–1949 at the Drepung Monastery.) Alexandra David-Neel, *Magic and Mystery*

in Tibet (Baltimore: Penguin Books, 1971), pp. 94, 110. (Ms. David-Neel was a Frenchwoman who became a Buddhist nun and studied at various Buddhist monasteries in and around Tibet.)

106. Goldstein, "Tibetan Refugees," p. 17, 23.

107. Phuntsog Wangyal, "The Influence of Religion on Tibet's Politics," *TJ* 1:1 (July 1975): 84.

108. The only expert who discusses these issues is Melvyn C. Goldstein. For example, see Goldstein, "Centralization," p. 176. Goldstein, "An Anthropological Study," pp. 137–141.

Chapter 2

1. Zhang Senshui, "Uncovering Prehistoric Tibet," *CR* 30:1 (January 1981): 65–66.

2. There is some confusion as to dates. Tsepon W. Shakabpa, *Tibet: A Political History* (New Haven and London: Yale University Press, 1967), p. 25 says 617–649. Li An-che, "Rñiṅ-ma-pa: The Early Form of Lamaism," *JRAS* 3–4 (1948):143 says 595–650. Ram Rahul, *The Government and Politics of Tibet* (New Delhi: Vikas Publications, 1969), p. 1 says 605–650. Josef Kolmăs, *Tibet and Imperial China: A Survey of Sino-Tibetan Relations up to the End of the Manchu Dynasty in 1912* (Canberra: Australian National University, Center for Oriental Studies, 1976), p. 2.

3. The West's foremost Tibetologist doesn't believe in the story of the Nepali princess. Guiseppe Tucci, "The Wives of Sron btsan sgam po," *Oriens Extremus* 9 (1962): 121–130. Tucci, *Religions of Tibet*, p. 1.

4. Bell, *Tibet Past and Present*, pp. 23–25. Shên and Liu, pp. 22–34. Hoffman, *Tibet: A Handbook*, p. 42. Shakabpa, pp. 26–27. Hugh E. Richardson, *A Short History of Tibet* (New York: E.P. Dutton, 1962), p. 29. Li Tieh-tseng, *Tibet Today and Yesterday* (New York: Bookman Associates, 1960), p. 10. For an account taken from Tang Dynastic sources, see S.W. Bushell, "The Early History of Tibet from Chinese Sources," *JRAS* 12 (1880): 434–541. A.I. Vostrikov, *Tibetan Historical Literature*, trans. by Harish Chandra Gupta (Calcutta: Indian Studies Past and Present, 1970).

5. Tucci, *Religions of Tibet*, p. 2–4, 249. Shakabpa, p. 33. Hoffman, *Tibet: A Handbook*, pp. 42–43. Li An-che "Rñiṅ-ma-pa," p. 143. The best general history of this period is Christopher I. Beckwith, *The Tibetan Empire in Central Asia. A History of the Struggle for Great Power among the Tibetans, Turks, Arabs, and Chinese During the Early Middle Ages* (Princeton: Princeton University Press, 1993).

6. Tucci, *Tibet*, p. 29.

7. Stein, pp. 243–244.

8. Gavin Hambley, ed. *Central Asia* (New York: Delacorte Press, 1969), pp. 81–82.

9. Shakabpa, p. 46.

10. Hoffman, *Tibet: A Handbook*, p. 46.

11. Shakabpa, pp. 50–51. Hambley, p. 80. Tucci, *Tibet*, p. 28, Bell, *Tibet Past and Present*, pp. 27–29. Hoffman, *Tibet: A Handbook*, p. 46.

12. The text of the treaty can be found in Bell, *Tibet Past and Present*, pp. 271–272. See also Jin Zhou, p. 27.

13. Guiseppe Tucci, "The Secret Characters of the Kings of Ancient Tibet," *East and West* 6:3 (October 1955): 197–205. Tucci, *Religions of Tibet*, p. 12.

14. There are at least two versions of Langdarma's death: (1) that a murder weapon, a knife used to cut his throat, was manipulated by the mental processes of a tantric monk and made to look like an accident; de Riencourt, p. 290, and (2) that a Buddhist monk wearing a black robe and black hat, both with white lining, was riding a white horse that had been covered with charcoal. After killing the king, the monk is said to have ridden his

horse through a river—thereby washing off the charcoal—and reversing his robe and hat and making good his getaway; Shakabpa, pp. 52–53. Shên and Liu, p. 27.

15. Li Tieh-tseng, p. 15.

16. Shên and Liu, p. 140. Shakabpa, pp. 65, 71–72.

17. Rahul, *Government and Politics of Tibet*, p. 2. Rahul, "Government of Tibet, 1644–1911," p. 265.

18. Huang Hao, "Tibet's Ties with the Ming Dynasty," *CT* 1:3 (Autumn 1990): 42–43.

19. Li Tieh-tseng, pp. 26–27. Shakabpa, p. 84. Bell, *Tibet Past and Present*, p. 33. Richardson, *Short History*, p. 40.

20. Shakabpa, pp. 84–85. Norbu and Turnbull, pp. 201–15. Tucci, *Tibet*, p. 37. Hoffman, *Tibet: A Handbook*, pp. 55–66.

21. Norbu and Turnbull, p. 216.

22. Richardson, *Short History*, p. 40.

23. Bell, *Tibet Past and Present*, p. 34. Shakabpa, pp. 93–96. Richardson, *Short History*, pp. 40–41.

24. Rahul, *Government and Politics of Tibet*, p. 3. Glen Mullen, "How the Dalai Lamas Established Asia's Foremost Spiritual and Political Institution," *N-T* (May–August 1995): p. 18–22. Ya Hanzhang, *The Biographies of the Dalai Lamas* (Beijing: Foreign Language Press, 1991).

25. Kolmăs, *Tibet and Imperial China*, p. 35. Li Tieh-tseng, pp. 34–38. Rahul, *Government and Politics of Tibet*, p. 15. Shakabpa, pp. 100–124. Tucci, *Tibet*, p. 57. Richardson, *Short History*, pp. 41–46.

26. Lee Wei Kuo, *Tibet in Modern World Politics (1774–1922)* (New York: Columbia University Press, 1931), p. 83. China now claims that the institution of Panchen Lama was created by the Chinese emperor. See archives of the Tibet autonomous region, "Identifying the Reincarnated Bainqen," *BR* 38:37 (11–17 September 1995): 7–10.

27. Shakabpa, pp. 125–126.

28. Ibid., p. 127. Norbu and Turnbull, p. 283. Khyongla, p. 38.

29. Alexandra David-Neel, *Initiations and Initiates in Tibet*, trans. by Fred Rothwell (New York: University Books, 1959), p. 140. Shakabpa, pp. 130–131. Yu Dawchyuan, "Love Songs of the Sixth Dalai Lama," *Academia Sinica Monograph* (Peking) 5, Series A (1930).

30. Luciano Petech, *China and Tibet in the Early 19th Century. History of the Establishment of a Chinese Protectorate in Tibet* (Leiden: E.J. Brill, 1972), p. 17.

31. Li Tieh-tseng, pp. 37–38.

32. Petech, *China and Tibet*, p. 46.

33. Zahiruddin Ahmad, *China and Tibet, 1708–1959. A Resume of Facts* (Oxford: Oxford University Press, 1960), p. 7.

34. Zahiruddin Ahmad, "The Historical Status of China in Tibet," *TJ* 1:1 (July–September 1975): 27.

35. Jedun, "The Establishment of the High Commissionership," *CT* 3:3 (Autumn 1992): pp. 42–44. Josef Kolmăs, "The Ambans and Assistant Ambans of Tibet (1727–1912): Some Statistical Observations," in *Tibetan Studies. Proceedings of the 6th Seminar of the International Association for Tibetan Studies, Afgernes, 1992*, ed. by Per Kvaerne (Oslo: Institute for Comparative Research in Human Culture, 1994), pp. 454–467.

36. For a detailed account see Schuyler Cammann, *Trade Through the Himalayas: The Early British Attempt to Open Tibet* (Princeton, NJ: Princeton University Press, 1951), pp. 102–143.

37. For more on the golden urn, see Joseph Fletcher, "Ch'ing Inner Asia C. 1800," in *The Cambridge History of China. Volume 10. Late Ch'ing, 1800–1911, Part I*, ed. by

John K. Fairbank (Cambridge, UK: Cambridge University Press, 1978), p. 101.
   38. Tucci, *Tibet*, p. 47.
   39. Dalai Lama, *Autobiography*, p. 52.

Chapter 3

   1. The Panchen Lama later wrote to Hastings that he initiated contact with the British in order to see a Buddhist temple built in Calcutta. Calcutta, according to the lama, was the place in which he had been born twice before in previous incarnations. Sudhansu Mohan Banerjee, "A Forgotten Chapter on Indo-Tibetan Contact: A Further Review," *Calcutta Review*, 23:1, April 1952): 32.
   2. Alastair Lamb, "Tibet in Anglo-Chinese Relations: 1767–1842," part I, *JRAS* 3–4 (1957): 163–165.
   3. Li Tieh-tseng, p. 72.
   4. Capt. Samuel Turner, *An Account of an Embassy to the Court of the Teshoo Lama in Tibet; containing a narrative of a journey through Bootan and part of Tibet* (London: W. Bulmer, 1800); see also Lamb, "1767–1842," p. 167.
   5. Taraknath Das, *British Expansion in Tibet* (Calcutta: N.M. Raychowdhury, 1929), p. 5.
   6. Shakabpa, p. 179. Alastair Lamb, "Tibet in Anglo-Chinese Relations: 1767–1842," part II, *JRAS* 1–2, 1958, pp. 40–41.
   7. Sir Olaf Caroe, *Englishmen in Tibet: From Bogle to Gould* (London: A Tibet Society Publication, 1960), p. 3.
   8. C.E.D. Black, "The Trade and Resources of Tibet," *Journal of the East Indian Association*, 41, new series no. 48, (October 1908): 4.
   9. Shakabpa, p. 193. Bell, *Tibet Past and Present*, p. 59. Frederick Spencer Chapman, *Lhasa The Holy City* (New York and London: Harper and Brothers, 1939), pp. 129–130. Sarat Chandras Das, *Indian Pundits in the Land of Snow* (Calcutta: Firma K.L. Mukhopadhyay, 1965). Archibald R. Colquhoun, "In the Heart of the Forbidden Country; or Lhasa Revealed," *The Cornhill Magazine* 14:1 (January 1903): 42. Derek Waller, *The Pundits. British Exploration of Tibet & Central Asia* (Lexington, KY: University Press of Kentucky, 1990).
   10. William Woodville Rockhill, *The Land of the Lamas: Notes of a Journey Through China, Mongolia and Tibet* (New York: Century, 1891). Graham Sandberg, *The Exploration of Tibet: History and Particulars* (New Delhi: Cosmo Publications, 1973). Cornelius Wessels, *Early Jesuit Travellers in Central Asia, 1603–1721* (The Hague: Martinus Nijhoff, 1924). N. Driver, "The Story of the Tibetan Bible," *The International Review of Missions* 40:158 (April 1951): 197–203. George Woodcock, *Into Tibet: The Early British Explorers* (London: Faber and Faber, 1971). Peter Fleming, *Bayonets to Lhasa* (New York: Harper and Brothers, 1961), p. 21.
   11. Shakabpa, p. 199. Li Tieh-tseng, pp. 76–80. Bell, *Tibet Past and Present*, pp. 60, 280–84. Alastair Lamb, *Britain and Chinese Central Asia* (London: Routledge and Kegan Paul, 1960), pp. 176–185.
   12. Bell, *Tibet Past and Present*, pp. 30–31, 104–105.
   13. Dr. Raghuvira, "The British Role in Sino-Tibetan Relations," *TR* 1:2 (November 1968): 16.
   14. Alastair Lamb, "Some Notes on Russian Intrigue in Tibet," *RCAJ* 46:1 (January 1959): 52.
   15. Norman Soong, "See You In Tibet," *Asia* 40:12 (December 1940): 649–654. Lamb, "1767–1842," part I, pp. 161–62. For a fascinating discussion of the "Great Game" see Gerald Morgan, "Myth and Reality in the Great Game," *AAFF* 60:1

(February 1973): 55–65; and Lars-Erik Nynman, "The Great Game: A Comment," *AAFF* 60:3 (October 1973): 299–301; and "Correspondence," *AAFF* 61:1 (February 1974): 119–121.

16. P.L. Mehra, "Tibet and Russian Intrigue," *RCAJ* 45:1 (January 1958): 32.

17. Li Tieh-tseng, p. 120. David J. Dallin. *The Rise of Russia in Asia* (New Haven: Archon Books, 1971), p. 42.

18. Lamb, "Some Notes," p. 60. Parshotam Mehra, "Beginnings of the Lhasa Expedition: Younghusband's Own Words," *Bulletin of Tibetology*, 4:3, (November 1967): 44–45.

19. There was considerable traffic and communication between Tibet and Russia during this period, originally initiated by Tibet's approaches to Russia. John Snelling, *Buddhism in Russia. The Story of Agvan Dorzhiev, Lhasa's Emissary to the Tsar* (Longmean, UK: Element Books, Ltd. 1993), Arasjj Bormanshinov, "A Secret Kalmyk Mission to Tibet in 1904," *CAJ* 36:3–4 (1992):161–187, Nicolai S. Kuleshov, "Agvan Dorjiev—Ambassador of Dalai Lama," *AAFF* 23:1 (1990):13–19. Nicolai S. Kuleshov, "Russia and the Tibetan Crisis at the Beginning of the 20th Century," unpublished manuscript.

20. Sir Charles Bell, "The Dalai Lama, Lhasa 1921," *JRCAS* 11:1 (January 1924): 44–45.

21. Fleming, p. 95.

22. Gordon Enders and Edward Anthony, *Nowhere Else in the World* (New York: Farrer and Rineheart, 1935), p. 74. Powell Millington, *To Lhasa at Last* (London: Smith, Elder, 1905), p. 151.

23. Millington, pp. v-viii.

24. Bell, "The Dalai Lama," p. 44.

25. Fleming, pp. 237–238.

26. A. MacCallum Scott, *The Truth About Tibet* (London: Simpkin, Marshall, Hamilton, Kent, 1905), p. 59.

27. Maj. Gen. P. Neame, "Tibet and the 1936 Lhasa Mission," *JRCAS* 26:2 (1939): 245.

28. Bell, *Tibet Past and Present*, p. 70.

29. MacDonald, *Twenty Years in Tibet*, pp. 17–18, 42–43. "Tibetan Curios for Public Museums," *Times* 5 April 1905, p. 4.

30. Louis T. Siegal, "Ch'ing Tibetan Policy (1906–1910)," in *Papers on China*, vol. 20 (Cambridge, MA: East Asian Research Center, Harvard University, 1966), pp. 181–185.

31. Bell, *Tibet Past and Present*, pp. 93, 210.

32. Eric Teichman, *Travels of a Consular Officer in Eastern Tibet* (Cambridge: Cambridge University Press, 1922), p. 37. Zhao's character ("though ruthless, he was just . . . ") is confirmed by Brig. Gen. M.E. Willoughby, "The Relations of Tibet to China," *JRCAS* 11:111 (1924): 196.

33. Li Tieh-tseng, pp. 66–67. Siegal, p. 189, Lee Wei Kuo, pp. 64–65.

34. Josef Kolmăs, "Ch'ing Shih Kao on Modern History of Tibet," *Archiv Orientalni* (Prague) 32 (1964): 83.

35. Tada, pp. 47–48.

36. Lo Hui-min, ed., *The Correspondence of G.E. Morrison, vol. II, 1919–1920* (Cambridge: Cambridge University Press, 1978), pp. 246–269.

37. Bell, "The Dalai Lama," p. 28–29. Tada, p. 52. Jyotirindra Nath Chowdhury, "British Contributions to the Confusion of Tibet's Status," *Quest* 54 (July-September 1967): 35–36. Kolmăs, *Tibet and Imperial China*, p. 60. Siegal, p. 198. Bell, *Tibet Past and Present*, p. 110. Willoughby, p. 195. Teichman, p. 28. "Tibetan Independence—Fact or Fiction," *BR* 32:7–8 (13–26 February 1989): 26.

38. Nirmal Chandra Sinha, *Tibet: Considerations on Inner Asian History* (Calcutta: Firma K.L. Mukhapadhyay, 1967), p. 5.

39. Bell, *Tibet Past and Present*, p. 113.

40. Alastair Lamb, *The McMahon Line: A Study in the Relations Between India, China and Tibet, 1904–1914* (London: Routledge and Kegan Paul, 1966) vol. 2, part I. Sung Yao-ting, "Chinese Tibetan Relations, 1890–1947," (Ph.D., University of Minnesota, 1949), pp. 81–91. Neville Maxwell, *India's China War* (Garden City, NY: Anchor Books, 1972), pp. 39–46.

41. "The Future of Tibet," *Times* 27 August 1912, p. 5.

42. P.L. Mehra, "Tibet and Outer Mongolia vis-à-vis China, 1911–1936," in *Studies in Asian History: Proceedings of the Asian History Congress, 1961*, ed. by K.S. Lal (New York: Asia Publishing House, 1969), p. 240.

43. "The Mongolian Question: Chinese Rights and Russian Policy," *Times* 3 December 1912, p. 5.

44. H.G.C. Perry-Ayscough and Captain R.B. Otter-Barry, *With the Russians in Mongolia* (London: John Larger, The Bodley Head, 1914), pp. 2–3, 8. Alleged text in Bell, *Tibet Past and Present*, pp. 304–305. China continues to argue that there is no such treaty ("Tibetan Independence—Fact or Fiction," p. 27) while an official publication in Mongolia argues it exists but provides no text (Academy of Sciences, Mongolian People's Republic, ed., *Information Mongolia* [Oxford/New York: Pergamon Press, 1990], p. 119).

45. Sir Charles Bell, "Tibet and Her Neighbours," *PA* 10:4 (December 1937): 435–436. The English text can be found in Michael C. van Walt van Praag, *The Status of Tibet. History, Rights, and Prospects in International Law* (Boulder, CO: Westview Press, 1987), pp. 320–321.

46. Bell, *Tibet Past and Present*, p. 151.

47. Quoted in Teichman, p. 228.

48. Tada, pp. i, 69–70.

49. Alexandra David-Neel, "Tibetan Border Intrigues, *Asia* 41:5 (May 1941): 219.

50. Lamb, *The McMahon Line*, p. 435. Lo Hui-min, p. 75.

51. Quoted in Dorothy Woodman, *Himalayan Frontiers: A Political Review of British, Chinese, Indian and Russian Rivalries* (New York and Washington, DC: Frederick A. Praeger, 1969), pp. 165–166.

52. Quoted in Lamb, *The McMahon Line*, p. 471.

53. *Tibet Under the Dalai Lama* China Chronicle No. 5 (Peiping: The Peiping Chronicle, 1933), p. 17. Tibet's independence was so lacking that during one session of the conference, when the Tibetan delegate was ill, Sir Charles Bell represented Tibet. Ting Tsz Kao, *The Chinese Frontiers* (Aurora, IL: Chinese Scholarly Publishing, 1980), p. 229.

54. W.F. Van Eekelen, "Simla Convention and McMahon Line," *RCAJ* 54:2 (June 1967): 179–181.

55. Sir Charles Bell, "China and Tibet," *JRCAS* 36:1 (January 1949): 54. Bell, "Tibet and Its Neighbours," pp. 437–438.

56. Quoted in Karunakar Gupta, "The McMahon Line 1911–1945—The British Legacy," *CQ* 47 (July–September 1971): 524.

57. Quoted in Maxwell, *India's China War*, p. 49.

58. H.E. Richardson, "Recent Developments in Tibet," *Asian Review* 40:204 (October 1959): 246.

59. Alfred P. Rubin, "Review of The McMahon Line," *The American Journal of International Law* 61 (1967): 827. Parshotam Mehra, "Tibet and its Political Status: An Overview," *Indo-British Review* 18:2 (1990): 140–141. Josef Kolmǎs, "Some Formal Problems of Negotiations and Results of the Simla Conference," *TJ* 16:1 (Spring 1991): 108–114. Josef Kolmǎs, "Was Tibet of 1913–1914 Fully *Sui Iuris* to Enter into Treaty Relations with Another State?" *Archiv Orient' 'aln'i* 60 (1992): 72–78. A recent study

concluded that "the validity of the Simla Convention in International Law is at best questionable, at worst null and void." Premen Addy, "British and Indian Strategic Perceptions of Tibet," in *Resistance and Reform in Tibet*, p. 28.

Chapter 4

1. Shakabpa, pp. 257–58. Goldstein, "An Anthropological Study," p. 213. The most detailed study of this period is Melvyn C. Goldstein, *A History of Modern Tibet, 1913–1951. The Decline of the Lamaist State* (Berkeley: University of California Press, 1989).

2. Tada, p. 65.

3. Willoughby, pp. 201–202.

4. Bell, *Tibet Past and Present*, p. 192. Sir Charles Bell, "A Year in Lhasa," *Geographical Journal* 63 (February 1924): 89–105.

5. Bell, *Portrait of the Dalai Lama*, p. 343.

6. Alfred P. Rubin, "The Position of Tibet in International Law," *CQ* 35 (July-September 1968): 130.

7. C. J. Christie, "Sir Charles Bell: A Memoir," *AAFF* 64:1 (February 1977): 57.

8. A. Doak Barnett, *China on the Eve of Communist Takeover* (New York, London and Washington, DC: Frederick A. Praeger, 1968), pp. 217, 219–220.

9. Ford, pp. 50, 93–94. IOLR L/P&S/12/424.

10. George Patterson, *Peking versus Delhi* (London and New York: Frederick A. Praeger, 1963), pp. 99–100.

11. Heather Stoddard, "The Death of the Thirteenth Dalai Lama," *Lungta* 7 (August 1993): 2–7.

12. Pemba, "Tibetan Reminiscences," pp. 23–24. Richardson, "The Rva-sgreng Conspiracy," p. xvi.

13. Both Hugh Richardson and Tsepon Shakabpa were in Lhasa at the time and were in close contact with all the major officials; but they disagreed on the circumstances of this event. Richardson claims a servant opened the parcel and was wounded when the bomb went off. Shakapba says it was opened by a friend of the Regent and no one was hurt. Richardson, *Short History*, p. 169. Shakabpa, pp. 292–293.

14. Khyongla, pp. 144–46.

15. Grady to Secretary of State, New Delhi, 2 December 1947, 893.00 Tibet/12–247; excerpts from the *Indian Monthly Intelligence Service* 1 October 1947, National Archives, Diplomatic Branch, Washington, DC.

16. Geoffrey T. Bull, *Forbidden Land: A Saga of Tibet* (Chicago: Moody Press, 1967), pp. 108–109.

17. Lincoln C. Brownell, Assistant Military Attache for Air, U.S. Embassy, Chungking, "Recent Political Reports from Sikang Province," 2 May 1944; OSS Report 76122 in National Archives, Diplomatic Branch, Washington, DC.

18. MacDonald, "Where a Lama Leads the Way," pp. 104–105.

19. MacDonald, *Twenty Years in Tibet*, p. 184. Parshotam Mehra, *Tibetan Polity 1904–1937. The Conflict Between the 13th Dalai Lama and the 9th Panchen Lama* (Weisbaden: Otto Harrassowitz, 1976), p. 43. Goldstein, "Centralization," p. 179.

20. Enders and Anthony, pp. 210, 218.

21. Gordon Enders, *Foreign Devil: An American Kim in Modern Asia* (New York: Simon and Schuster, 1942), pp. 278, 290. Li Tieh-tseng, pp. 172–174.

22. F.S. Chapman, "Lhasa in 1937," *The Geographic Journal* 91:6 (June 1938): 304. Chapman, *Lhasa the Holy City*, pp. 10–11. Richardson correspondence, 17 July and 12 August 1981.

23. Bell, *Portrait of the Dalai Lama*, p. 368, C.Y.W. Meng, "Miss Liu's Mission to Tibet," *The China Weekly Review* 6 September 1930, pp. 22–24. Xeirab Nyima, "A Special Envoy of the Nanjing Regime," *CT* Winter 1991, pp. 39–42. Abar Jasbir Singh, "How the Tibetan Problem Influenced China's Foreign Relations, *China Report* 28:3 (July–September 1992): 271–271.

24. Sung Yao-ting, p. 143. Tzu Yuan, "Historical Relations Between the Tibet Region and the Motherland," *MYTC* 4 April 1959 in *JPRS* 862-D, 17 August 1959, p. 10. Li Tieh-tseng, p. 155. Wu Fengpei, "On Relations between the Local Tibetan Government and the Central Government during the Period of the Republic of China," *CT* 3:1 (Spring 1992): 40–44. Meng Xianfan, "A Summary of the Seminar on 'Tibet: Yesterday and Today,'" *Social Sciences in China* 13:1 (Spring 1992): 67–73.

25. Li Tieh-tseng, pp. 168–171, 185–186. Shakabpa, p. 281. IOLR L/PS/12/4177.

26. The Commission of Mongolian and Tibetan Affairs was originally established in Nanjing on 11 February 1928. Sung Yao-ting, pp. 142–143.

27. Taring, p. 121. Margaret D. Williamson, *Memoirs of a Political Officer's Wife in Tibet, Sikkim and Bhutan* (London: Wisdom Publications, 1987).

28. IOLR L/PS/12/4147. Richardson, *Short History*, p. 145. Sir Basil J. Gould, *The Jewel in the Lotus. Recollections of an Indian Political* (London: Chatto and Windus, 1957), p. 208.

29. The question of the Dalai Lama's economic background is an excellent example of the exaggeration so common among those who willingly act as apologists for the Dalai Lama's political positions. It is always emphasized that the lama came from a humble peasant background—"a squalid shack" his aides told an American journalist on a recent U.S. visit. Pete Hamill, "Dalai-ing with the Press: a lama tames the jackals," the *New York Daily News* 5 August 1979, pp. 4, 30.

In fact, however, the family was in the middle to upper peasant economic range (the Dalai Lama's father was the nephew of a high incarnated lama) and became increasingly wealthy after the selection of Thubten Norbu as the incarnation of an abbot; this selection was accompanied by numerous gifts from Kumbum Monastery. By present day U.S. standards the family house may have been "squalid," but it contained many rooms, including servants' quarters. The family employed five full-time workers and as many as forty more during harvesting and sowing season. They also owned sheep, cows, horses, mules, oxen, and hens. Although poor compared to the Tibetan nobility, compared to the general state of the Chinese peasantry during the 1920s and 1930s (the only valid comparison) they were wealthy peasants. British officials considered them " . . . a fairly well-to-do family."

Dalai Lama, *Autobiography*, pp. 19–20. Thubten Jigme Norbu, *Tibet Is My Country: The Autobiography of Thubten Jigme Norbu, Brother of the Dalai Lama* as told to Heinrich Harrer, trans. by Edward Fitzgerald (New York: E.P. Dutton, 1961), pp. 30–31, 33, 41, 47. Norbu and Turnbull, pp. 51–57, 238. IOLR L/P&S/12/4165.

30. There is some dispute regarding how much was paid to Ma. It ranged from several thousand U.S. dollars to $400,000 (Sonam Wangdu, pp. 35–53). Liao Zugui, "Installation of the 14th Dalai Lama," *BR* 38:37 (11–17 September 1995): 10–11. Wu Fengpei, p. 43.

31. U.S. Embassy, London to Secretary of State, Washington, DC., 27 June 1947, 843.00 Tibet/6–2747, National Archives, Diplomatic Branch, Washington, DC.

32. Richardson, *Short History*, p. 173. Li Tieh-tseng, pp. 196–197. de Riencourt, p. 220. de Riencourt was with Richardson in Lhasa at the time, and recounts that almost up to 15 August the diplomat was preparing to leave, unsure what his fate would be.

33. Richardson, *Short History*, p. 174. One scholar claims Nehru didn't want to take over British colonial privileges, "which were a disreputable creation of British imperial-

ism." Amar Jasbir Singh, "How the Tibetan Problem Influenced China's Foreign Relations," *China's Report* 28:3 (July–September 1992): 278.

34. Li Tieh-tseng, p. 199.

35. O.E. Clubb to Secretary of State, Peiping, 12 September 1949, Main Decimal File, Box 7024, National Archives, Diplomatic Branch, Washington, DC.

36. Henderson to Secretary of State, New Delhi, 23 July 1949, 893.00 Tibet/7–2349, National Archives, Diplomatic Branch, Washington, DC.

37. Richardson, *Short History*, p. 177. Richardson correspondence.

38. PRO FO 371/35756 F3268. IOLR L/P&S/12/4155 Reg. No. PZ 7796/39.

39. U.S. Consulate, Calcutta to Secretary of State, 14 December 1949, Main Decimal File, Box 7024, National Archives, Diplomatic Branch, Washington, DC.

40. Shakabpa, p. 259. Ford, p. 96. Dalai Lama, *Autobiography*, p. 55.

41. *Foreign Relations of the United States, 1949, vol. IX, The Far East: China* (Washington, DC: U.S. Government Printing Office, 1974), pp. 1095–1097. (Hereafter *FRUS 1949*.)

42. Donovan to Secretary of State, New Delhi, 22 November 1949, 893.00 Tibet/11–2249, National Archives, Diplomatic Branch, Washington, DC.

43. Ibid.

44. Technology consisted of the following: two unused motorcars, a small hydroelectric plant that did not function when the river froze, one telephone line (Potala to Post Office), one telegraph line (Lhasa-Gyantse-India), one arsenal for small arms, one mint, one photographic studio, one printing office using wooden blocks, two radio transmitters, and a handful of radio receiving sets. OSS, pp. 65–66. de Riencourt, pp. 150–151.

Chapter 5

1. William Woodville Rockhill, *Diary of a Journey Through Mongolia and Tibet in 1891 and 1892* (Washington, DC: Smithsonian Institution, 1894).

2. "So This Is Shangri-la," *Newsweek* 31 January 1944, pp. 24–25. William Boyd Sinclair, *Jump to the Land of God. The Adventures of a United States Air Force Crew in Tibet* (Caldwell, Ohio: Caxton Printers, 1965).

3. *Foreign Relations of the United States,1943. China* (Washington, DC: U.S. Government Printing Office, 1967), p. 631. (Hereafter *FRUS 1943*.)

4. OSS, pp. 1–2.

5. PRO FO 371/93002. IOLR L/P&S/12/4229 Ext. 731/43.

6. R. Harris Smith, OSS. *The Secret History of America's First Central Intelligence Agency* (Berkeley, Los Angeles and London: University of California Press, 1972), pp. 254–255.

7. Ilia Tolstoy, "Across Tibet from India to China," *NGM* 90:2 (August 1946): 169–222. OSS, "Outline of Journey and Observation Made by Ilia Tolstoy, Captain AUS and Brooke Dolan, First Lt. AC," September 1943. In possession of Central Intelligence Agency, Roslyn, VA. IOLR/L/P&S/12/4229.

8. IOLR/L/P&S/12/4229.

9. For the American view see *FRUS 1943*, p. 630; and Charles F. Romanus and Riley Sunderland, *United States Army in World War II. China-Burma-Indian Theater. Stilwell's Mission to China* (Washington, DC: Office of the Chief of Military History, Department of the Army, 1953), p. 287. For the British view see PRO FO 371/35756.

10. PRO FO 371/35690, 35691, 35692.

11. *FRUS 1943*, p. 624.

12. Ibid., p. 626.

13. R.H. Smith, p. 255.
14. Hollis S. Liao, "The United States and Tibet in the 1940s," *Issues and Studies* 26:6 (June 1990): 123.
15. Office of Intelligence Research "Tibet," No. 4731, 19 July 1948, National Archives, Diplomatic Branch, Washington, DC. (Hereafter OIR "Tibet."). George Merrell to Secretary of State, New Delhi, 9 December 1946. Main Decimal File (1945–49) Box 7024, 893.00 Tibet/12–946, National Archives, Diplomatic Branch, Washington, DC.
16. *Foreign Relations of the United States, 1947, vol. VII, The Far East: China* (Washington, DC: U.S. Government Printing Office, 1972), pp. 588–92. (Hereafter *FRUS 1947.*)
17. Ibid., pp. 595–596, 599.
18. Shakabpa, p. 294; Shakabpa claims the decision to send the mission was made in October; but as early as August, American and Indian officials were discussing the proposed trip. *FRUS 1947*, pp. 598–600. Amaury de Riencourt recalled that when he was in Lhasa during the summer of 1947 Shakapba was already planning an overseas trip. de Riencourt, p. 130.
19. Tolstoy, "Outline of Journey," no page numbers, see chapter titled "Economic Report."
20. Shakabpa, p. 295.
21. *FRUS 1947*, pp. 598–600. Shakabpa was not universally liked, see George N. Patterson, *Requiem for Tibet* (London: Aurum Press, 1990), p. 103.
22. *Foreign Relations of the United States, 1948, vol. VII, The Far East: China* (Washington, DC: U.S. Government Printing Office, 1973), pp. 757–58. (Hereafter *FRUS 1948.*) *FRUS 1947*, pp. 603, 604.
23. Shakabpa, p. 296.
24. OIR, "Tibet," p. 37. "Trade Mission to Britain. Dinner in Honour," *Times* 24 November 1948, p. 6. Tsering W. Shakya, "1948 Tibetan Trade Mission to United Kingdom," *TJ* 15:4 (Winter 1990): 97–114.
25. Robert Loup, *Martyr in Tibet: The Heroic Life and Death of Father Maurice Tournay, St. Bernard Missionary to Tibet* (New York: David McKay, 1956), pp. 109–203.
26. *FRUS 1947*, p. 604.
27. *FRUS 1948*, pp. 760–761.
28. Ibid., pp. 1071–1073. Chinese Ambassador Wellington Koo was told without reservation that Washington was fully cognizant of the de jure "sovereignty of China over Tibet." U.S. Department of State, "Policy Review Paper—Tibet," (c. 1949), declassified to author.
29. Shakabpa, p. 323. The Dalai Lama stubbornly clings to the position even today, responding to my findings by arguing that the "passports" were at least "indirectly accepted." Dalai Lama interview, 25 July 1981.
30. *FRUS 1948*, pp. 757–758.
31. *FRUS 1949*, pp. 1064–1078.
32. *FRUS 1949*, pp. 1065–1080.
33. Ibid., pp. 1077–1088.
34. A.T. Steele in the *Chicago Daily News*. A seven-part article in the Pictorial Section; 18, 25 November 2, 9, 16, 23, 30 December 1944. A.T. Steele, "The Boy Ruler of Shangri-La," the *Saturday Evening Post* 13 April 1946, p. 14.
35. Lowell Thomas, Jr., *The Silent War in Tibet* (Garden City, NY: Doubleday, 1959), p. 21.
36. "Lowell Thomas Back from Tibet," *NYT* 17 October 1949, p. 25.
37. *Foreign Relations of the United States, 1950, vol. VI, East Asia and the Pacific*

(Washington, DC: U.S. Government Printing Office, 1976), pp. 272–273, 327–328. (Hereafter *FRUS 1950.*)

38. Memo of conversation, Washington, DC 28 November 1949, 893.00 Tibet/11–2849, National Archives, Diplomatic Branch, Washington, DC.

39. *FRUS 1949*, pp. 1980–1982.

40. Memo of conversation in Kalimpong, June 7, 1951, between one of the Pangdatsang brothers, Rev. G. Tharchin (a converted Christian Tibetan and editor of *Tibet Mirror*, the only Tibetan language newspaper of that time), George Patterson and Fraser Wilkins, First Secretary, U.S. Embassy, New Delhi, #3030, 14 June 1951, declassified to author. *FRUS 1950*, pp. 272–273, 275–276, 330–331. "Department [of State] would not wish Tibetans misinterpret our failure [to] accede [to] their requests as disinterest or lack [of] sympathy [for] their predicaments or difficulties."

41. Ford, pp. 17–19. "Tibet Radio Asks Aid Against Reds," *NYT* 1 February 1950, p. 10.

42. Kenneth W. Condit, *The History of the Joint Chiefs of Staff, vol. II, 1947–1949* (Washington, DC: Historical Division, Joint Secretariat, Joint Chiefs of Staff, undated), pp. 488–489. (This text was a "Top Secret" document until 1976 when it was released to the National Archives, Military Branch, Washington, DC.)

43. Walter H. Waggoner, "Truman Bars Military Help for the Defense of Formosa," *NYT* 6 January 1950, p. 1. Allen S. Whiting, *The Chinese Calculus of Deterrence, India and Indochina* (Ann Arbor: Michigan University Press, 1975), p. 15.

44. Condit, p. 519. Jay Walz, "U.S. May Grant Tibet Recognition in View of Current Asian Situation," *NYT* 25 October 1949, p. 5. "Facts in the Far Eastern Dust," *Economist* 19 November 1949, p. 1130.

45. "Estimate of Effectiveness of Anti-Communist Guerrilla Operations in China," *JCS* Geographic File (1951–1953), REF. OM 519, 28 December 1950. National Archives, Military Branch, Washington, DC.

46. Interview with L. Fletcher Prouty, Washington, DC, 14 August 1979.

47. *Foreign Relations of the United States, 1951, vol. VI, Asia and the Pacific, Part II* (Washington, DC: U.S. Government Printing Office, 1977), pp. 2174–2179. (Hereafter *FRUS 1951.*)

48. *FRUS 1950*, pp. 365–366.

49. Ibid., pp. 361, 364–365.

50. Ibid., pp. 376, 378–618, *passim.*

51. Fraser Wilkins to Secretary of State, New Delhi, 7 June 1961 and 14 June 1951. Declassified to author.

52. It was to be one Lane Lassiter of Darbhanga Airways. U.S. Department of State, 793B.11/11–350.

53. B.N. Mullik, *My Years with Nehru: The Chinese Betrayal* (Bombay: Allied Publishers, 1971), pp. 80–81.

PRO FO 371/84468 FT 1621/2.

PRO FO 371/84450 FT 1015/44.

PRO FO 371/84450 FT 1015/19.

PRO FO 371/92997.

PRO FO 371/92998 FT 10310/79.

Considerable cable traffic between the U.S. Department of State and the U.S. Embassy in New Delhi on this subject. See 793B.00/7–2151. For plans see 7936.00/7–7151. National Archives, Diplomatic Branch, Washington, DC.

54. "Brother of the Dalai Lama Arrives Here to Study," *NYT* 9 July 1951, p. 8. Steve Weissman, "Last Tangle in Tibet," *Pacific Research and World Empire Telegram* 4:5 (July-August 1973): 1–18. Steve Weissman and John Shock, "CIAsia Foundation," *Pa-*

cific Research and World Empire Telegram 3:6 (September-October 1972): 3–4. David W. Conde, *CIA-Core of the Cancer* (New Delhi: Entente Private, 1979), pp. 111–115.

55. *FRUS 1950*, pp. 330–331.

56. Tass, "American Shipment of Arms to Tibet," *Pravda* 13 May 1950 in *SPT* 5:3 (1950): 415. Patterson interview, 27 May 1981.

57. Yu Shah, "The 'Sun of Happiness' is Rising in Tibet," *PC* 11 (1 December 1950): 8–9, 31–32. T. Yershov, "Imperialist Intrigue in Tibet," *NT* 49 (30 November 1949): 8–12. Girlal Jain, *Panscheela and After: A Re-Appraisal of Sino-Indian Relations in the Context of the Tibetan Insurrection* (New York: Asia Publishing House, 1960), pp. 18–19.

58. A.B. Shah, *India's Defense and Foreign Policies* (Bombay: Manaktala, 1966), p. 87.

59. Harry Rositzke, *The CIA's Secret Operations: Espionage, Counterespionage, and Covert Action* (New York: Reader's Digest Press, 1977), p. 173.

60. Weissman, "Last Tangle," p. 5.

61. Quoted in T.D. Allman, "A Half Forgotten Conflict," *FEER* 11 February 1974, p. 27.

62. Letter to author from J.S. Evans, Capt. USN, Chief, Directorate for Print Media, Department of Defense, Washington, DC, 3 July 1979.

63. Rositzke, p. 173.

64. Weissman, "Last Tangle," p. 13.

65. Ibid., p. 3.

66. William O. Douglas, *Beyond the High Himalayas* (Garden City, NY: Doubleday, 1952), p. 202.

67. Robert Trumbull in the *NYT* 22, 23, 24 November 1950, pp. 1, 4, 6. "The Press: All That's News," *Newsweek* 4 December 1960, p. 54.

68. Robert Trumbull correspondence with author, 10 April 1981. The informer was New Zealander Frank Anthony Charlton Thomas; PRO FO 371/84467. CIA National Intelligence Estimate, "Soviet Capabilities and Intentions," 15 November 1950, NIE–3 in *The Declassified Documents Reference System* (Carrollton, VA: Carrollton Press, 1980), p. 226A.

69. *FBIS* Daily Report, Far East-China, 23 November 1949, no. 226.

70. Ibid., January 3, 1950, no. 1.

71. *FRUS 1949, passim.*

72. Christopher Rand, "Chinese Approaches to Tibet Expected to Fall to Reds Soon," *New York Herald Tribune* 6 December 1949, p. 18. K.M. Panikkar, *In Two Chinas: Memories of a Diplomat* (London: George Allen & Unwin, 1955), p. 105.

73. *Xinhua* 10 November 1950 in Ling Nai-min, ed., *Tibet: 1950–1967* (Hong Kong: Union Research Institute, 1968), pp. 8–9.

74. The Soviets referred to Heinrich Harrer as a "Hitlerite" and complained that " . . . Tibet swarms with foreign 'radio specialists . . . ' " and that the United States has " . . . swamped Tibet with spies . . . ." "Tibet Welcomes Its Liberators," *Literaturnaya Gazeta* 9 January 1951 in *SPT* 6:4 (1 March 1951): 102.

75. Robert Trumbull, "Tibet Fears Told By Lowell Thomas, *NYT* 11 October 1949, p. 11. "Lowell Thomas Back from Tibet," p. 25.

76. Michel Peissel, *The Secret War in Tibet* (Boston and Toronto: Little, Brown, 1972), pp. 75–76. Leonard Clark, *The Marching Wind* (New York: Funk & Wagnalls, 1954).

77. Yershov quotes from the *Yorkshire Post* of June 1950. Li Yu-I, "Tibetan People Move Forward," *CR* 1:5 (September-October 1951): 35.

78. Ford, pp. 15, 17–19, 40.

79. T. Norbu, *Tibet*, pp. 246–248.

80. See exchange of notes in Ling, pp. 13–18. Tsering Shakya, "The Genesis of the

Sino-Tibetan Agreement of 1951," in *Tibetan Studies*, ed. by Per Kvaerne, pp. 742–743.

81. Lowell Thomas, Jr., *Out of This World: Across the Himalayas to Forbidden Tibet* (New York: Greystone Press, 1950), p. 32.

82. Patterson interview.

83. Lowell Thomas, Sr., interview with author, New York City, 6 September 1979.

84. It is mentioned for example in "General Conditions in Tibet," *RMRB* 23 November 1950 in Ling, pp. 4–5.

85. George Patterson admits that Beijing had reason to be suspicious of the Americans in 1949–1950. George Patterson, "China and Tibet: Background to Revolt," *CQ* 1 (January–March 1960): 93.

Chapter 6

1. Harrer, *Seven Years*, pp. 239, 259–260.

2. "Chronology of Events in Tibet, 1949–1959," *Hsi-tsang Ta Shih-chi* [Tibet Main Events Record] Peking, May 1959 in *JPRS* 831-D, 28 August 1959.

3. "The Tibetan Autonomous Region in Sikang Province," *RMRB* 14 August 1951 in *CB* 25 September 1951. Tian Bao (Sangye Yeshe) is an ethnic Tibetan born in what is now Sichuan Province around 1917. He joined the communist cause by enlisting in Zhang Guotao's Fourth Front Army around 1935, when the CCP passed through the area in which he lived on its Long March. In 1944 he was in the first graduating class of the Yanan Nationalities Institute and was subsequently wounded in the war against Japan. In 1956 he became the youngest member of the Communist Party Central Committee and has since held a number of high-level positions in nationalities work and in the administration of Sichuan. In 1979 he was appointed the head of the TAR.

4. George N. Patterson, *Tibet in Revolt* (London: Faber & Faber, 1960), pp. 62–63. Fred W. Riggs, "Tibet in Extremis," *Far Eastern Survey* 19:21 (6 December 1950): 224–230.

5. Ford, pp. 135–152. Taring, p. 173.

6. Melvyn C. Goldstein, "Change and Continuity among a Community of Nomadic Pastoralists. A Case Study from Western Tibet, 1950–1990," in *Resistance and Reform in Tibet*, p. 110.

7. "Free Tibet from Foreign Intrigues," *PC* 11 (1 December 1950): 4. Raymond Dennett and Robert K. Turner, eds., *Documents on American Foreign Relations, vol. XII, January 1–December 31, 1950* (Princeton, NJ: Princeton University Press, 1951), pp. 510. United Nations, General Assembly, 5th Session, 1950, *Official Records* (A/1534 and A/1549) annex, vol. 1, pp. 16–18.

8. "Proclamation on Tibet," *PC* 11 (1 December 1950): 9. Qiang Zhai, *The Dragon, the Lion and the Eagle. Chinese/British/American Relations, 1949–1958* (Kent, OH: Kent State University Press, 1994), pp. 46–64.

9. Harrer, *Seven Years*, pp. 281–283. Heinrich Harrer, "The Flight of the Dalai Lama," *Life* 23 April 1951, pp. 130, 140, 142.

10. Harrer, *Seven Years*, pp. 281–286. George Ginsburg and Michael Mathos, *Communist China and Tibet: The First Dozen Years* (The Hague: Martinus Nijhoff, 1964), p. 9. E.H. Rawlings, "The Forbidden Land Today," *Contemporary Review* 182:1043 (November 1952): 302–306. Theodore Burang, "Report from Tibet," *The Canadian Forum* 30:362 (March 1951): 272–273. Patterson, *Requiem for Tibet*, pp. 122–138.

11. Patterson, *Tibet in Revolt*, p. 84. George Patterson, "Kalimpong: The Nest of Spies," *Twentieth Century* 163 (June 1958): 527. Patterson interview. James Cameron, *Point of Departure: An Attempt at Autobiography* (New York: McGraw Hill, 1967), pp. 235–236. Li Weihan, "The Road of Liberation of the Tibetan Nationality—

Commemorating the 30th Anniversary of the Signing of the Agreement on Measures for the Peaceful Liberation of Xizang," *Radio Beijing* 24 May 1981, in *FBIS* 27 May 1981, p. Q7.

12. Memo of conversation between two U.S. Consular officials and Major Bahadur, Calcutta, 14 December 1949.893.00 Tibet/11–949, National Archives, Diplomatic Branch, Washington, DC.

13. Dalai Lama interview. Many authors have claimed that state oracles were consulted on this decision. In an interview the Dalai Lama denied that any oracles were consulted. Tsering Shakya, "The Genesis of the Sino-Tibetan Agreement of 1951," pp. 751–752.

14. Patterson, *Tibet in Revolt*, pp. 79, 81–84. T. Norbu, *Tibet*, p. 244. Patterson, *Requiem for Tibet*, pp. 122–138.

15. Division of Research for the Far East, Office of Intelligence Research, Department of State, '"Peaceful Liberation" of Tibet: Blueprint for Communist Conquest," OIR 60007, 4 June 1951. National Archives, Diplomatic Branch, Washington, DC, Dalai Lama, *Autobiography*, pp. 149–150.

16. Panikkar, p. 105. Mahmudul Huoue, "American and Indian Responses to the Chinese Occupation of Tibet, 1949–1951," *South Asian Studies* 26:1 (January–June 1991): 11–30.

17. Dalai Lama, *Autobiography*, pp. 80–81.

18. "Documents and Speeches on the Peaceful Liberation of Tibet," *PC* 3:12, Supplement to 16 June 1951, p. 12. "The Tibetans Express Full Support of the Central People's Government of China," *Pravda* 21 March 1951 in *SPT* 6:6 (1951): 190–191. The leader of the Tibetan delegation in Beijing says he signed the agreement only *after* the Dalai Lama approved. Ngapoi Ngawang Jigme, "On the 1959 Armed Rebellion," *China Report* 24:3 (1988): 379. Liu Shengqi, "A Review of Some Problems Concerning Foreign Relations in the Peaceful Liberation of Tibet," *Social Sciences in China* 13:3 (September 1992: 174–178. Yuan Shan, "The Dalai Lama and the 17-Article Agreement," *CT* 2:2 (Summer 1991): 2–6. Shokang Soinam Dagyal "Escorting the Representative of the Central Government to Tibet," *CT* 2:1 (Spring 1991): 12–15. Huang Mingxin, "The Tibetan Version of the 17-Article Agreement," *CT* 2:3 (Autumn 1991): 12–14 [Huang was one of the Chinese-Tibetan translators for the agreement].

19. Ling, p. 768. Anna Louise Strong, *When Serfs Stood Up In Tibet* (Peking: New World Press, 1965) 2d ed., pp. 48–49. "On the So-called 'Statement of the Dalai Lama,'"*PR* 2 (21 April 1959): 1–2. "Tibet Affirms Support for People's Government," *PC* 4 (16 November 1951): 13.

20. "On the Politics of Our Work in Tibet—Directive of the Central Committee of the Communist Party of China," *Selected Works of Mao Tse-tung*, vol. V (Peking: Foreign Languages Press, 1977), pp. 74–75.

21. Ginsburg and Mathos, *Communist China*, p. 19. Qiang Zhai, p. 47. Ling, p. 380. Ginsburg and Mathos, *Communist China*, p. 13. They argue that the Chinese ultimatum came only *after* there had been some hard bargaining and the inclusion of changes urged by the Tibetans.

22. Dalai Lama interview. The most comprehensive discussion of these events is in Tsering Shakya, "The Genesis of the Sino-Tibetan Agreement of 1951," pp. 739–754.

23. For text of Seventeen-Point Agreement, see Ling, pp. 19–23.

24. Interview with Chinese participants whose identities must remain anonymous.

25. B. Gurov, "Tibet: Chinese Press Review," *NT* 26 November 1952, pp. 13–15.

26. "Hungarians in Tibet: The Genesis of Revolt," *Eastern Europe* 8:8 (August 1959): 18.

27. PRO FO 371/99661 FT 10310/3.

28. *SWB* 15 February 1980, FE/6346/BII/7–11. The quote is from the wife of Zhang Jingwu. Also, interviews with Chinese officials.

29. Shakabpa, p. 307. Dalai Lama, *Autobiography*, p. 57. Dawa Norbu, "The Democratic Dalai Lama," *TB* 8:2 (August 1976): 4–9. U.S. Department of State, 793B.11/9–1052. National Archives, Diplomatic Branch, Washington, DC.

30. PRO FO 371/99659.

31. Dalai Lama, *Autobiography*, pp. 100–105.

32. Stuart and Roma Gelder, *The Timely Rain: Travels in New Tibet* (New York: Monthly Review Press, 1965), pp. 204–205. Dalai Lama interview.

33. "State Council Resolution on the Establishment of the Preparatory Committee for the Autonomous Region of Tibet," *RMRB* 13 March 1955 in Ling, pp. 141–43. "Degree of People's Republic of China Outline Resolutions Governing Organization of the Preparatory Committee for the Autonomous Region of Tibet," *RMRB* 27 September 1956, in Ling, pp. 171–176.

34. "The Dalai Lama's Report at the Inaugural Meeting of the Preparatory Committee for the Autonomous Region of Tibet," *RMRB* 25 April 1956 and several other reports all in Ling, pp. 144–170.

35. Dalai Lama interview. A CIA memo of 23 April 1959 claims that the Dalai Lama was restricted in his meetings with Gyalo Thondup. However, the Dalai Lama has never acknowledged this. (Memo in author's possession.)

36. Mao Tse-tung, "On the Correct Handling of Contradictions Among the People," in *Selected Works of Mao Tse-tung*, vol. V, p. 406. Mao's "Speaking Notes" of this speech can be found in *The Secret Speeches of Chairman Mao. From the Hundred Flowers to the Great Leap Forward,* ed. by Roderick Macfarquhar, et al. (Cambridge, MA: Harvard University Press, 1989), pp. 131–185.

37. Dalai Lama interview.

38. An American intelligence report estimated that the first two roads cost U.S.$120 million, or roughly U.S.$30 thousand per km. "Background on the Current Situation in Tibet," USIA IRI Intelligence Summary, 8 August 1955, in *Documents on Contemporary China, 1949–1975* #91D.00168, p. 5. National Archives, Diplomatic Branch, Washington, DC.

39. June Treufel Dreyer, *China's Forty Millions* (Cambridge and London: Harvard University Press, 1976), pp. 132–133.

40. *Tibet Under Chinese Communist Rule. A Compilation of Refugee Statements, 1958–1975* (Dharamsala, India: Information and Publicity Office of His Holiness the Dalai Lama, 1976), p. 5.

41. CIA, "Integration of Tibet: China's Progress and Problems," 1976, p. 16 (in author's possession).

42. "Track Laying of Qinghai-Tibet Railway Over Big Salt Lake," *Xinhua Weekly* 30 June 1979, pp. 20–21.

43. *Xinhua* in *AR* 4:14 (1958): 1971. Taring, p. 176.

44. Alan Winnington, *Tibet. Record of a Journey* (New York: International Publishers, 1957), p. 50.

45. PRO FO 371/99659, 16 April 1952.

46. George Ginsburg and Michael Mathos, "Communist China's Impact on Tibet: The First Decade (II)," *FES* 29:8 (August 1960): 123.

47. "Conditions in Tibet and Tibetan Autonomous Areas," *CB* 409 (21 September 1956).

48. Liu Tse-hsi, "Herdsmen on the Tsinghai Pastures Advance Bravely with Flying Red Flags," *MTTC* 6 November 1958 in Ling, pp. 325–329.

49. So-kuan-ying, "After the Democratic Reforms are Carried Out in the Ahpa Tibetan Nationality Autonomous Chou," *RMRB* 28 June 1956 in Ling, pp. 334–339.

50. Dawa Norbu, "The 1959 Rebellion: An Interpretation," *CQ* 77 (March 1979): 79. Robert B. Ekvall, "Nomads of Tibet: A Chinese Dilemma," *CS* 1:3 (23 September 1961): 1–10. Tung Ying and Hsüeh Chien-hua, "Social Reforms in National Minority Areas in China," *RMRB* 15 August 1959 in *SCMP* 2093, 10 September 1959, p. 18.

51. D. Norbu, "The 1959 Rebellion," p. 80.

52. J. Norbu, *Horseman*, p. 95.

53. D. Norbu, "The 1959 Rebellion," p. 81.

54. Li Tsung-hai, "Positively Promote Fixed Abodes and Nomadic Herd Raising," *MTTC* 14 March 1958 in Ling, pp. 294–298.

55. "Outline of Propaganda for CCP Tibet Work Committee Concerning the Policy of Not Implementing Democratic Reforms in Tibet Within Six Years," *XRB* 2 August 1957 in Ling, pp. 206–213.

56. Mao, "On the Policies of Our Work in Tibet," pp. 75–76.

57. Chang Kuo-hua, "Work on the Tibet Region," *RMRB* 21 September 1956 in *CB* 418 (11 October 1956): 18–23.

58. "The Dalai Lama," *CNA* 270 (3 April 1959): 1–7.

59. Dreyer, *China's Forty Millions*, pp. 94–107, 136, 161–162, 165.

60. Bina Roy Burman, *Religion and Politics in Tibet* (New Delhi: Vikas Publishing House, 1979), pp. 110–111, 128.

61. Khyongla, p. 183. J. Norbu, *Horseman*, p. 69. Pemba, *Young Days*, pp. 179–182. Patterson, *Tibet in Revolt*, p. 88. Fei Hsiao-t'ung, "China's Multi-National Family," *CR* 3 (May-June 1952): 23–29. Winnington, *Tibet*, pp. 23–24. Jan Andersson, "Chinese Colonel Who Became a Tibetan Refugee," *TR* 14:10 (October 1979): 21–22.

62. Ford, p. 178.

63. *Policies Towards Nationalities of the People's Republic of China* (Peking: Foreign Languages Press, 1953), pp. 22–25.

64. Chang Chih-i, *The Party and the National Question in China* trans. by George Moseley (Cambridge, MA and London: The MIT Press, 1968), pp. 86–89. Girilal Jain, p. 65.

65. Mao Tse-tung, "Criticize Great Hanism," (10 March 1953) in *Selected Works of Mao Tse-tung,* vol. V, pp. 87–88. A. Tom Grunfeld, "In Search of Equality: Relations between China's Ethnic Minorities and the Majority Han," *BCAS* 17:1 (January–March 1985): 54–67.

66. Quoted in *Tibet Under Chinese Communist Rule,*, p. 38.

67. Dawa Norbu, "The Tibetan Response to Chinese 'Liberation,' " *AAFF* 62:3 (October 1975): 274.

Chapter 7

1. Strong, *When Serfs*, p. 64. Red Guard documents from the mid-1960s claim that in 1952 ". . . the situation was one of touch and go. The atmosphere in Lhasa was extremely tense." Special Group for the Investigation of Teng Hsiao-p'ing, "1018" Revolutionary Rebel Corps, Shanghai Red Metallurgy College, "How the Revolt Broke Out in Tibet. Exposing Teng Hsiao-p'ing, Chief Culprit Responsible for the Tibetan Revolt," *Chih-tien Chang-shan* [Surviving the Rivers and Mountains] 27 October 1967 in *JPRS* 18 December 1967.

2. Mao, "On the Politics of Our Work in Tibet," pp. 75–76.

3. Ngabo quoted in Strong, *When Serfs*, p. 98. "Anti-Red Revolt in Tibet is Growing, Li Says," *FCA* 5:12 (December 1958): 20. P.P. Karan, "The Changing Geography of Tibet," *Asian Profile* 1:1 (August 1973): 43. *The Tibet Revolution and the Free World*

(Taipei: Asian People's Anti-Communism League, 1959), p. 20.

4. Gampo Tashi Andrugstang, *Four Rivers, Six Ranges: Reminiscences of the Resistance Movement in Tibet* (Dharamsala, India: Information and Publicity Office of His Holiness the Dalai Lama, 1973), p. 40.

5. "On the So-called Statement of the Dalai Lama," *PR* 2:16 (21 April 1959): 1–2. Patterson, *Peking versus Delhi*, p. 159. "Man Behind the Tibetan Struggle," *Guardian* 14 November 1963, p. 12. Dalai Lama, *Freedom in Exile. The Autobiography of the Dalai Lama* (New York: Cornelia & Michael Bessie book, HarperCollins, 1990), p.104.

6. Department of State, Division of Research for the Far East, "Unrest in Tibet," no. 7341, 1 November 1956. National Archives, Diplomatic Branch, Washington, DC.

7. Trungpa, pp. 113–142.

8. Andrugstang, pp. 51–53, 58. George N. Patterson, "The Situation in Tibet," *CQ* 6 (April–June 1961): 85. One former rebel said the revolt was "comparable in magnitude to the events in Afghanistan," Jamyang Norbu, "The Tibetan Resistance Movement and the Role of the C.I.A.," in *Resistance and Reform in Tibet*, p. 188.

9. Andrugstang, pp. 51–53.

10. Patterson, "The 'Fish' in the 'Sea,' " p. 67. Patterson, *Peking versus Delhi*, p. 160. Patterson, "The Situation in Tibet," p. 85. Jamyang Norbu, "The Tibetan Resistance Movement . . ." p. 194.

11. Andrugstang, pp. 59–62.

12. Special Group for the Investigation of Teng Hsiao-p'ing. Strong, *When Serfs*, p. 67. Patterson, "The Situation in Tibet," p. 83.

13. Andrugstang, pp. 63, 66. George Patterson, "Tibet," *The Reporter* 32:6 (25 March 1965): 32.

14. "Man Behind the Tibetan Struggle." Patterson, "Tibet," p. 32. Patterson, "The 'Fish' in the 'Sea,' " p. 6. Department of State, "Unrest in Tibet." Lois Lang-Sims, *The Presence of Tibet* (London: Cresset Press, 1963), p. 16. The Dalai Lama believed that Zhou Enlai, at least, was uninformed. John F. Avedon, *In Exile from the Land of Snows. The First Full Account of the Dalai Lama and Tibet since the Chinese Conquest* (New York: Alfred A. Knopf, 1984), p. 46.

15. For a detailed account of events in the early weeks of 1959 see Noel Barber, *From the Land of Lost Content: The Dalai Lama's Fight for Tibet* (Boston: Houghton Mifflin, 1970). A highly condensed version appears in Noel Barber, "Brave and Lost: The Tragic Fall of Tibet," *Reader's Digest* 96:574 (February 1970): 205–248.

Readers should be warned that the reliability of this book is questionable. First, it is based almost exclusively on interviews with former Tibetan officials in exile whom Mr. Barber considers impartial. Second, Mr. Barber's dishonest reporting on Tibet for the *Daily Mirror* as described in this chapter, casts further doubts on the book. Finally, there is Mr. Barber's gratuitous attempt to give his research a scholarly veneer. For example, in his "Acknowledgements" he conveys the impression that he had exclusive access to some important documents. He thanks the British Foreign Office for allowing him to use monitored Chinese radio broadcasts and translations of Chinese newspapers and magazines as well as two personal accounts from Chinese who were in Lhasa in March 1959. What Mr. Barber fails to tell his readers is that the radio broadcasts are readily available at all major research libraries in North America and Europe, and, indeed, are even available by subscription to private individuals. As to the two personal accounts by Chinese, they appeared in *Peking Review*, China's major political publication—accessible to the rest of the world and easy to use since it is fully indexed. Barber's claim that "only by the exercise of great diligence were these documents unearthed" is self-aggrandizing, at best, and dishonest at worst.

16. Dalai Lama, *Autobiography*, p. 156.

17. "Communique on Rebellion in Tibet," *PR* 2 (31 March 1959): 6–8. D. Norbu, "The 1959 Rebellion," p. 91. "How General Tan's First Letter was Brought to the Dalai Lama," *PR* 2 (14 April 1959): 10.

18. The full text of the letters are in Ling, pp. 370–374.

19. Dalai Lama, *Autobiography*, pp. 176, 177.

20. Ibid., p. 188.

21. D. Norbu, "The 1959 Rebellion," p. 88. Dalai Lama interview. Ngapoi, "On the 1959 Armed Rebellion," pp. 378–379. Qiogya, "What Really Happened in Lhasa," *China Report* 24:3 (1988): 383–385.

22. *The Statesman* 25 March 1959 in Raja Hutheesing, ed. *A White Book, Tibet Fights for Freedom: The Story of the March 1959 Uprising as Recorded in Documents, Dispatches, Eyewitness Accounts and World-Wide Reactions* (Bombay, Calcutta, Madras and New Delhi: Orient Longmans, 1960), pp. 64–65.

23. Ou Chaoqui, "Tibet's Potala Palace," *CR* 29:3 (March 1980): 50.

24. Gelder and Gelder, *Timley Rain*, p. 186. Kunsang Paljor, *Tibet: The Undying Flame* (Dharamsala, India: Information and Publicity Office of His Holiness the Dalai Lama, 1977), p. 18.

25. Lorthong Yitsi, "Report on the Anti-Communist Revolution of the Tibetan People by Lorthong Yitsi," *FCA* 6:7 (July 1959): 18.

26. Rodney Gilbert, ed., *Genocide in Tibet: A Study in Communist Aggression* (New York: American-Asian Educational Exchange, [1959?]), pp. 13–14.

27. "Communique on the Revolt," in Ling, p. 350.

28. D. Norbu, "The Tibetan Response," pp. 270–271.

29. Patterson, *Tibet in Revolt*, pp. 181–82. *China Youth Daily* quoted in Reuters, 10 July 1995, Beijing. Mao's comments are in "Summary of a Conversation with the Chairman of the CC CPC Mao Tse-T'ung" from the journal of S.F. Antonov, 21 October 1959, in *Cold War International History Project Bulletin* 3 (Fall 1993): 57.

30. United Nations, General Assembly, *Official Records*, 14th Session, Plenary Meetings (1959), 20–21 October 1959, A/4234, A/4848, pp. 469–530.

31. Quoted in *AR* 6:47 (1959): 3013–3016.

32. "U.S. Affirms Belief in the Principle of Self-Determination for Tibet," *Department of State Bulletin* 42:1082 (21 March 1960): 443–444.

33. "Nehru May Make Statement on Tibet Today," *Statesman* 23 March 1959, pp. 1, 10.

34. "India: The Adventurous Life," *Time* 4 May 1959, pp. 19–20. George Patterson, *Daily Telegraph* and Heinrich Harrer, *Daily Mail* in Hutheesing, p. 98.

35. "Commentary on the So-called Statement of the Dalai Lama."

36. Maxwell, *India's China War* p. 105.

37. *Concerning the Question of Tibet*, p. 141.

38. CIA, "Desire of the Dalai Lama to Continue Struggle for Freedom and Independence of Tibet," 23 April 1959, deposited in Dwight D. Eisenhower Library, Abilene, Kansas.

39. Peissel, *Secret War*, p. 126.

40. *Glimpses of Tibet Today* (Dharamsala, India: Information Office of His Holiness the Dalai Lama, 1978), p. 24.

41. Dalai Lama, "Learn from the Soviet Union and Construct Our Socialist Fatherland," *Hsien-Tai Fo-hsueh* [Contemporary Buddhism] 13 December 1958 in *JPRS* 1461-N, 9 April 1959. Dalai Lama, "Strive for a Glorious Leap Forward in Tibet," *XRB* 1 January 1959 in *JPRS* 951-D, 7 October 1959.

42. Fan Chih-lung, "From Tibet to Peking," *CR* 4:2 (February 1955): 13.

43. Winnington, *Tibet*, p. 135.

44. Dalai Lama, *Autobiography*, p. 13.

45. D. Norbu, "The 1959 Rebellion," p. 86.

46. This argument has changed over the years. From 1959 to December 1964 the Chinese press asserted the Dalai Lama was "kidnapped." [Yang Gongsu, "The Origins and Analysis of the Schemes of the So-called 'Independence of Tibet,'" in *Thesis on Tibetology in China* compiled by Hu Tan (Beijing: China Tibetology Publishing, 1991), p. 370.] When it became evident that he wasn't and that he had no intention of returning, the Chinese press began calling the Dalai Lama a "traitor." ["Dalai Lama Denounced as Traitor," *PR* 5 (25 December 1964): 4–5.] In recent years the official position has reverted to the original claim, undoubtedly because Beijing is engaged in negotiations with the Dalai Lama about his possible return to Tibet. His return would be made easier, Chinese officialdom must believe, if he is not identified as a traitor but, rather, as someone who left Tibet involuntarily.

47. Ibid., pp. 88–89.

48. Our Special Correspondent, "The Pattern of Revolt in Tibet," *The Statesman* 2 March 1959, p. 6. Patterson, *Requiem for Tibet,* pp. 164–175.

49. Dalai Lama, *Freedom in Exile,* p. 126. For a more detailed analysis of these events, see A. Tom Grunfeld, "Some Reflections on the 1959 Revolt in Lhasa," unpublished paper, 1992.

50. "Escape Over the Himalayas: How the Dalai Lama Did It," *USNWR* 20 April 1959, pp. 89–90. "Tibet," *Time* 20 April 1959, pp. 26–36. "Tibet. A God Escapes," *Newsweek* 13 April 1959, pp. 47–48.

51. "Tibet: Lesson from an Escape," *Economist* 11 April 1959, p. 109.

52. Panikkar, p. 113.

53. David S. Connery, "Waiting for the God King," *Atlantic* 205:3 (March 1960): 61–65.

54. *Daily Mail* 6 April 1959, p. 1. Barber began, "Today I flew over the monastery of Towang. . . . " George Patterson said Barber admitted to him that he had filed the story prior to taking the flight. Patterson interview.

55. For a survey of Soviet views up to 1958, see "The Borderlands of Soviet Central Asia—Tibet," *CAR* 6:1 (1958): 57–75.

56. Eremei Parnov, "Tibetan Refugees as Seen by a Russian," *TR* 12:2–3 (February–March 1977): 15–18. Reprinted from *NT* Whiting, pp. 72, 73.

57. Legal Inquiry Committee, *The Question of Tibet and the Rule of Law* (Geneva: International Commission of Jurists, 1959).

58. Legal Inquiry Committee, *Tibet and the Chinese People's Republic* (Geneva: International Commission of Jurists, 1960).

59. Ibid., pp. 3, 5, 13, 139–165.

60. "Brutal 'Modernization' of Tibet," *CSM* 13 August 1960, p. 18.

61. Quoted in *AR* 47 (21–27 November 1959): 3013–3016.

62. *Tibet and Freedom* (London: A Tibet Society Publication, 1969), p. 8.

63. Weissman, "Last Tangle," pp. 9–10. Neil Sheehan, "Aid by CIA Put in the Millions: Group Total Up," *NYT* 19 February 1967, pp. 1, 32. "Units Linked to CIA," *NYT* 19 February 1967, p. 27. Tom Killefer, "Free Lawyers and Cold War. The International Commission of Jurists," *American Bar Association Journal* 41 (May 1955): 417.

64. Niall MacDermott correspondence with author, 3 August 1979.

65. *Afro-Asian Convention on Tibet and Against Colonialism in Asia and Africa* (New Delhi: Afro-Asian Council, 1960), p. 60.

66. See letter in *CSM* 19 January 1961, p. 14. Purshottam Trikamdas, *The Face of Communism* (New Delhi: A Praja Socialist Publication, undated). "China Accused of Killing 65,000 Tibetans," *Times* 6 June 1959, p. 6.

67. George Gale, "Up in Cloud Cuckooland with the Lama," *Daily Express* 16 November 1959, p. 2.
68. Lang-Sims, p. 133.
69. *Tibet and the Chinese People's Republic*, pp. 74, 104.
70. Ibid., pp. 292, 300.
71. Ibid., p. 49.
72. Niall MacDermott correspondence with the author.
73. "Commentary on the So-called Statement of the Dalai Lama."
74. Israel Epstein, "Tsering Pintso—People's Policeman in Lhasa," *EH* 16:9 (September 1977): 23.
75. "Tibet: 'God Said No,'" *Newsweek* 30 March 1959, pp. 50.

Chapter 8

1. *AR* 6:30 (1959): 2785–2786.
2. "The Red Terror in Tibet: Interview with the Dalai Lama," *USNWR* 24 April 1961, p. 79.
3. "Diplomacy and the Dalai Lama," *FEER* 18 March 1974, p. 32.
4. "Interview with the Dalai Lama's Brother—"Holy War" in Tibet—What is it all About?" *USNWR* 13 April 1959, p. 48.
5. *Xinhua* 28 March 1959 quoted in Girilal Jain, p. 84.
6. "China's Hungary," *Economist* 4 April 1959, pp. 16–17.
7. George Patterson, *A Fool at Forty* (Waco, TX and London: Word Books, 1970), pp. 9–10. Harrer, *Seven Years*, p. 123. Dalai Lama interview.
8. Chris Mullin, "The CIA: Tibetan Conspiracy," *FEER* 5 September 1975, p. 31.
9. Patterson, *Tibet in Revolt*, pp. 92–94.
10. Ibid.
11. Ibid., pp. 117–132.
12. Avedon, p. 47. David Allan Mayers, *Cracking the Monolith. U.S. Policy against the Sino-Soviet Alliance, 1949–1955* (Baton Rouge and London: Louisiana State University Press, 1986), pp. 78–87, 95.
13. Mullin, "The CIA," p. 31. L. Fletcher Prouty interview, 14 August 1979.
14. Uncle Sam, "Taiwan and Tibet," *TR* 11:1–2 (January-February 1976): 19.
15. "Chinese Nationalists Report Attacks on Mainland Posts," *NYT* 8 April 1969, p. 8.
16. Khyongla, p. 210.
17. Anna Louise Strong, *Tibetan Interviews* (Peking: New World Press, 1959), p. 115.
18. "Outlook of Anti-Communist Uprising in Tibet," *FCA* 6:4 (April 1959): 9–10.
19. Michel Peissel, *Mustang, the Forbidden Kingdom: Exploring a Lost Himalayan Land* (New York: E.P. Dutton, 1967), p. 38.
20. "Tibet Fights for Freedom," *FCA* 5:9 (September 1958): 29. "Message of President Chiang Kai-shek to Tibetans on March 26, 1959," *FCA* 6:4 (April 1959): 3. *The Tibetan Revolution and the Free World*, p. 37.
21. Igor Oganesoff, "Tibet's Impact: From Indonesia to India, China Loses Good Will It Patiently Built Up," *WSJ* 6 April 1959, p. 19.
22. "Many Rebel Khampas Killed in Nepal," *TR* 9:8 (August 1974): 9–10. Jamyang Norbu says that aid didn't begin to reach the rebels until 1958, "The Tibetan Resistance Movement," p. 195.
23. This extensive account comes largely from the outstanding investigative reporting of British journalist Chris Mullin, who managed to interview many of the actual participants in these events. Mullin, "The CIA." Dalai Lama, *Freedom in Exile*, pp.

126–127. Evan Thomas, *The Very Best Men. Four Who Dared: The Early Years of the CIA* (New York: Simon & Schuster, 1995), p. 276.

24. Poe's real name was Anthony Alexander Poshepny and he recalled his four years with the Khampas as among his fondest memories. "Those Khampas are the best people I ever worked with . . . these guys were *great*." [emphasis in original]. Roger Warner, *Back Fire. The CIA's Secret War in Laos and Its Link to the War in Vietnam* (New York: Simon & Schuster, 1995), pp. 92–93. Michael Morrow, "Super Secret Missions: CIA Spy Teams Inside Red China," *San Francisco Chronicle* 4 September 1970, p. 24. John McBeth, "Letter from Chiang Khong," *FEER* 22 February 1980, p. 66. John Prados, *Presidents' Secret Wars. CIA and Pentagon Covert Operations since World War II* (New York: William Morrow and Company, 1986), pp. 163–164.

25. Mullin, "The CIA," p. 33. George Patterson interview. T.D. Allman, "Cold Wind of Change," *Guardian* 19 December 1973, p. 11.

26. L. Fletcher Prouty, *The Secret Team: The CIA and Its Allies in Control of the United States and the World* (Englewood Cliffs, NJ: Prentice-Hall, 1973), p. 351.

27. David Wise, *The Politics of Lying: Government Deception, Secrecy and Power* (New York: Vintage Books, 1973), p. 252.

28. Dalai Lama, *Autobiography*, p. 186. Dalai Lama interview.

29. "Turmoil in Tibet," *Washington Post* 25 March 1959, p. A12.

30. B.K. Shrivastava, "American Public Opinion on the Tibetan Question," *IS* 10:4 (April 1969): 600.

31. Prouty, *Secret Team*, pp. 345–346.

32. Ibid., pp. 21, 37–82. Evans, p. 277.

33. Ibid., pp. 401–404.

34. Jack Anderson, "A Toll of Dirty Tricks," *Washington Post* 24 April 1977, p. C7.

35. For a full account see Wise, pp. 239–261.

36. L. Fletcher Prouty interview.

37. Maxwell, *India's China War*, p. 488.

38. Panikkar, p. 113. *India, Tibet and China* (Bombay: Democratic Research Service, 1959) passim.

39. Mullik, pp. 182, 183, 194–195.

40. Patterson, *Tibet in Revolt*, pp. 152–153.

41. Mullik, pp. 182, 183, 194–195.

42. Hutheesing, p. 44. George Patterson interview, 27 May 1981. V.H. Coelho, *Sikkim and Bhutan* (New Delhi: Vikas, 1970), p. 71.

43. Roger Hilsman, *To Move a Nation: The Politics of Foreign Policy in the Administration of John F. Kennedy* (Garden City, NY: Doubleday, 1967), pp. 324–327.

44. Avedon, pp. 121–122.

45. Peissel, *Secret War*, p. 191.

46. Mullin, "The CIA," p. 31.

47. Quoted in the *Patriot and the National Herald* in *AR* 28:47 (1972): 11096–11097.

48. A correspondent, "Mustang: Forgotten Corner of Nepal," *FEER* 21 March 1975, pp. 24–25.

49. Koirala interview in the *Statesman* in *AR* 6:39 (1960): 3557.

50. Mahinda Ram Shrestha, "A Challenge from the Khampas," *FEER* 9 August 1974, p. 21.

51. Peissel, *Secret War*, p. 207.

52. Patterson, *A Food at Forty* passim. A. Tom Grunfeld, "Roof of the World," *BCAS* 9:1 (January-March 1977): 60–62.

53. Peissel, *Mustang*, pp. 38, 77.

54. John Hughes, "Tibet—Cloud Shadows Red China," *CSM* 17 February 1966, pp. 1, 4.

55. CIA, National Intelligence Survey, *Communist China. Section 23. Weather and Climate, Part V—Tibetan Highlands,* September 1964 (Carrollton, VA: The Declassified Document Reference Service, Carrollton Press). (77) 161 F.

56. Shrestha. Peissel, *Secret War,* p. 234.

57. M.E. Tackley, Acting Chief, New Branch, Public Information Division, Department of the Army correspondence with the author, 19 June 1979. Prados, pp. 167–169.

58. George Patterson interview.

59. "U.S. Said to Delay Film About Tibet," *NYT* 26 December 1971, p. 21.

60. Peissel, *Secret War,* p. 216.

61. Dawa Norbu, "China Behind Khampa Disarmament," *TR* 10:1 (January 1975): 3–4.

62. One former rebel remembered that the Khampas were ready to fight the Nepalese until the Dalai Lama ordered their surrender. Some of the Tibetan leaders were so angered at the Dalai Lama's order that they committed suicide rather than comply. Michel Acatil Monnier, "Talks with Lhasang Tsering," *Lungta* 7 (August 1993): 32–33. Dalai Lama, *Freedom in Exile,* pp. 192–193.

63. Mullin, "The CIA," p. 31.

64. Evans, p. 278. Gordon H. Chang, *Friends and Enemies. The United States, China and the Soviet Union, 1948–1972* (Stanford: Stanford University Press, 1990), pp. 100–101. John Ranelagh, *The Agency. The Rise and Decline of the CIA* (London: Weidenfeld and Nicolson, 1986), pp. 335–336.

Chapter 9

1. Ginsburg and Mathos, *Communist China,* pp. 132, 136.

2. "Resolutions on the Question of Tibet," *RMRB* 29 April 1959 in Ling, pp. 388–391.

3. P.H.M. Jones, "Respite for Tibet," *FEER* 25 May 1961, pp. 365–366.

4. Li Teh-shen, "A Visit to a Tibetan Farm Co-op," *PR* 25 (23 June 1959): 15–16. Chang Sen, "Democratic Reform: The Road to Happiness," *PR* 24 (16 June 1959): 12–14. Ying Ming, *United and Equal: The Progress of China's Minority Nationalities* (Peking: Foreign Languages Press, 1977), pp. 41–42. Ngabo Ngawang Jigme, "Great Victory of the Democratic Reform in Tibet," *RMRB* 10 April 1960 in Ling, pp. 394–403.

5. Ginsburg and Mathos, *Communist China,* p. 147. "Mutual Aid Teams in Tibet," *PR* 33 (16 August 1960): 5.

6. *Xinhua* 27 September 1962 in Ling, p. 807.

7. Panchen Erdeni, "Report on Work in Tibet in the Past Year," *PR* 2 (13 January 1961): 15, 22.

8. "Regional National Autonomy," *BR* 20 (17 May 1982): 28–29. "Peking Postpones 'Socialist Transformation' in Tibet in Major Policy Shift," *CS* 1:1 (15 May 1961): 1–8.

9. Tsering Lam, "Restoration of Serfdom Must Never Be Allowed," *PR* 6 (7 February 1969: 9–10. *Xinhua* 17 August 1979 in *JPRS* 21 August 1979, p. 14.

10. See Ling, p. 814. Li Weihan, p. Q12.

11. "Dalai Lama Denounced as Traitor," *PR* 52 (25 December 1964): 4–5.

12. Hsieh Fu-chih, "Great Revolutionary Changes in Tibet," *PR* 37 (10 September 1965): 8–10.

13. "Tibet, 1965–1967," *CNA* 657 (1967): 3–4.

14. K. Dhondup, "Panchen Lama, the Enigmatic Tibetan," *TR* 13:2–3 (February–March 1978): 13–17. Avedon, pp. 274–276.

15. Senanayake, p. 151.

16. Ibid.

17. In 1979 the Panchen Lama told an interviewer that in August 1966 the Red Guards had "caught" him, and Zhou Enlai had "protected" him. The clear implication was that this was the first occasion on which he was arrested. This is untrue. Christer Leopold, "An Interview with the Panchen Lama," *TR* 15:11 (November 1980): 14–15.

18. "Panchen Erdeni Interviewed," *PR* 11 (17 March 1978): 41–42.

19. Fox Butterfield, "China's Congress Ending, Appoints 3 Deputy Premiers," *NYT* 11 September 1980, p. 1.

20. *Tibet Under Chinese Communist Rule*, pp. 65–66.

21. Miao P'i-i, "Cadres of the Tibet Nationality Grow Up, Nursed by the Thoughts of Mao Tse-tung," *MTTC* August 1965 in *SCMM* 498, 16 November 1965, p. 18.

22. "The key to national regional autonomy is to have sufficient minority nationality cadres." Ngabo Ngawang Jigme quoted in Jing Wei, "Tibet: An Inside View (I)," *BR* 47 (22 November 1982): 16. (a) *RMRB* 6 January 1964 in "Communist Tibet (Part I)," *CNA* 547 (15 January 1965): 4; (b) *RMRB* 12 November 1964 in Ibid.; (c) "40,000 Non-Han Cadres in Tibet," *Ta Kung Pao* (Hong Kong), 24 August 1978, p. 17. Jing Wei, "Tibet: An Inside View (II)—More Tibetans Assume Leadership," *BR* 48 (29 November 1982): 14; (d) "Tibet Autonomy or Integration?" *China Report* 2:2 (1966): 29; (e) "Flourishing Minority Nationalities Areas," *PR* 9 (3 March 1972): 10–12; (f) "Tibet—From Serfdom to Socialism," *CR* 25:3 (March 1976): 9; (g) "China's Minority Nationalities Today," in *China in Development* (Peking: China Council for the Promotion of International Trade, [1976?]), p. 3; (h) "Local Cadres Form Majority in Tibet," *PR* 34 (25 August 1978): 5; (3) "40,000 Non-Han Cadres in Tibet"; (j) Jing Wei, "Tibet: An Inside View (II)," p. 14; (k) Hu Bangxiu, "Women Cadres in Tibet," *Women in China* (March 1980): 36–38; (l) "Development of Tibet Under the People's Republic of China," *U.S.-China Review* 4:5 (September-October 1980): 16; (m) David Bonavia, "Mistakes on the Roof of the World," *FEER* 8 August 1980, p. 16; (n) Xie Bangmin and Jiang Shunzhang, "Report from Tibet: New Changes on the Plateau," *BR* 21 (25 May 1980): 20; (o) *Radio Peking* 21 May 1981 in *FBIS* 22 May 1981, p. Q4. "Xizang Promotes Minority Cadres in Government," *FBIS* 19 June 1981, p. Q3; (p) Jing Wei, "Tibet: An Inside View (II)," p. 14.

23. "Tibetan Cadres Maturing," *PR* 25 (18 June 1971): 20, 27.

24. Han Suyin, *Lhasa the Open City: A Journey to Tibet* (New York: G.P. Putnam's, 1977), p. 144. "Local Cadres Form Majority in Tibet," p. 5.

25. Paljor, pp. 11–12.

26. Jing Wei, "Tibet: An Inside View (II)," p. 15.

27. "Peking Postpones 'Socialist Transformation' of Tibet," p. 4.

28. Trungpa, p. 126.

29. Huang Lung, "Tibet Makes Up for Lost Centuries," *EW* 16:12 (December 1962): 14–15.

30. "Freedom of Religion in Tibet," *PR* 38 (17 September 1965): 29.

31. Chris Mullin, "Red Roof of the World," *Guardian* 6 June 1975, p. 14.

32. Peter Hazelhurst, "Tibetans Flee Red Guard Terror," *Times* 28 August 1971, p. 2.

33. See Ekvall, "Historical Sites and Cultural Relics," p. 7. John Strong, "Buddhism in Lhasa," *The Atlantic* 231:1 (January 1973): 16, 18–19, 22.

34. Kao Hung, "Commune on the Tibetan Plateau," *PR* 28 (13 May 1973): 14–17.

35. *Hung Ch'i* quoted in "Developments in the Tibetan Autonomous Region," *China Topics* YB 599, September 1976, p. 3. Dawa Norbu, "Changes in Tibetan Economy, 1959–1976," *China Report* 24:3 (1988): 233.

36. CIA, "The Integration of Tibet," pp. 17–18.

37. "Thousands of Chinese Soldiers Killed in Shentse Dzong Uprising," *N-T* 5:1 (1970–1971): 1–2. "Happiness Obstructs Progress," *TB* 13:1 (June 1976): 4–5.

38. (a) "Smear Campaign Against Dalai Lama," pp. 1–2; (b) Dhondup Choedon, pp. 11; (c) J. Norbu, *Horseman*, p. 91; (d) D. Norbu, "The Tibetan Response," p. 274; (e) Choedon, p. 1; (f) "Present Policies in Tibet," *CR* 29:10 (October 1980): 16; (g) Yang Fu-hsing, "The Great Victory of the People's Nationalities in Kanna," *MTTC* October–November 1963, in *SCMM* 20 January 1964, p. 18; (h) Rev. Ngawang Thubtob, *Tibet Today* (New Delhi: Bureau of His Holiness the Dalai Lama, [1965?]), p. 21; (i) "Communist Tibet (Part II)," p. 2; (j) Choedon, p. 7; (k) Senanayake, p. 87; (l) Ibid; (m) Tsering Dorji, "A Guide to Tibet Today," *TR* 9:5 (May 1976): 24–25; (n) T. Ninjee, "Tibet Under Communist Rule: A Brief Survey of Recent Developments," *Journal of African and Asian Studies* 6:1 (Autumn 1967): 24–25; (o) Palijor, pp. 6–7; (p) "Thousands of Chinese Soldiers Killed," pp. 1–2; (q) Rewi Alley, "Among the Tibetans and Chiang," *EH* 12:5 (1973): 23–24; (r) "Smear Campaign Against the Dalai Lama," p. 1; (s) Mullin, "Red Roof"; (t) "People's Communes in Tibet—A Leap in Centuries," *CR* 25:3 (March 1976): 16–19. Tashilhunpo monks were getting 249 kg. in 1975. Israel Epstein, *Tibet Transformed* (Peking: New World Press, 1983), p. 429; (u) D. Norbu, "The Tibetan Response," p. 274; (v) Mullin, "Red Roof"; (w) "Neville Maxwell's Tibet War," *TJ* 8:2 (August 1976): 13; (x) "Recent Military Installations," *TR* 8:1 (January 1976): 3–4; (y) "Economics of Socialism," *TB* 13:5 (May 1978): 5–6; (z) Dalai Lama, "The Dalai Lama Speaks His Mind," *Asian Wall Street Journal* 25 August 1977, p. 23; (aa) "Deceptive Preparations for the Nepalese King," *TB* 9:1 (March-April 1977): 1–4; (bb) "China Increases Investment for Tibetan Agriculture and Animal Husbandry," *Xinhua Weekly* 30 June 1979, p. 20; (cc) Ibid.; (dd) "Big Changes on Estate of Tibetan Lords," *Xinhua Weekly* 30 June 1979, p. 12; (ee) Jing Wei, "Tibet: An Inside View (III): Changes in Gyangze," *BR* 49 (6 December 1982): 23; (ff) "Another Visitor Confirms Poor Conditions in Tibet," *TR* 14:11 (November 1975): 5; (gg) "Increased Farm Production in Tibet," *Xinhua Weekly* 31 March 1979, p. 13; (hh) "What the Second Delegation Saw in Tibet," *TR* 15:9 (September 1980): 7; (ii) "Good Tidings from Tibet," *BR* 7 (16 February 1981): 6. *Xinhua* 1 May 1981 in *FBIS* 1 May 1981, p. 24. "Peasant Income," *Radio Lhasa* 25 April 1981 in *JPRS* 21 May 1981, p. 87; (jj) "County District Production," *Radio Lhasa* in *JPRS* 3 March 1981, p. 111; (kk) Jing Wei, "Tibet: An Inside View (III)," p. 23; (ll) *Radio Lhasa* 24 August 1982 in *SWB* FE/7115/BII/3; (mm) "New Policies Aid Development of Tibet," *Xinhua* 7 June 1982 in *SWB* FE/7948/BII/2.

39. Taring, pp. 102–103.

40. Seymour Topping, "Tibet Struggles for Higher Living Standard," *NYT* 28 October 1979, p. 18.

41. Gordon Bennett, *Huadong: The Story of a Chinese People's Commune* (Boulder, CO and Folkestone, UK: Westview Press, 1978), p. 113.

42. This information was gathered in China and in various cities of the United States from personal interviews with current and past residents of Beijing and Shanghai on the condition their names be withheld. Also, Vaclav Smil, "Who Will Feed China?" *CQ* 143 (September 1995): 810.

43. "State Looks After Old Folk in Tibet," *China Daily* 19 July 1984, p. 3.

44. "Becoming Well-Off Through Collective Strength," *BR* 33 (18 August 1980): 4–5.

45. Chen Muhua, "Controlling Population Growth in a Planned Way," *BR* 46 (16 November 1979): 18.

46. Ibid., p. 3. "Yin Fantang Attends Xizang Party Meeting," *Radio Lhasa* in *FBIS* 1 June 1981, pp. 21–22.

47. The Tibetan government-in-exile disagrees, see *Tibet Under Chinese Communist Rule*, p. 119.

48. Israel Epstein, "Tibet Today," *EH* 5:1 (January 1966): 17–24. "The Far Western

Tip of Tibet," *CR* 21:12 (December 1972): 5. " 'Tent Schools' on the Tibetan Plateau," *PR*, 35 (27 August 1971): 27–28. Yin Hai-shan, "Education and Culture in Tibet," *EW* 16:8 (August 1962): 16.

49. (a) "Rapid Development of Education in Tibet," *Xinhua* 17 August 1966 in Ling, pp. 290–91; (b) "Tibet from Serfdom to Socialism"; (c) Hsi Chan-kao and Kao Yuan-mei, *Tibet Leaps Forward* (Peking: Foreign Languages Press, 1977), pp. 10–11; (d) "Woman in Commune Near Lhasa Tells of Her Life," *NYT* 18 October 1978, p. 18; (e) "Development of Tibet Under the People's Republic of China"; (f) Xie Bangmin and Jiang Shunzhang, p. 20. "Institute Schools Train More Tibetan Cadre Specialists," *Xinhua* 23 February 1981. *Xinhua* 12 September 1978 in *JPRS* November 1978, p. 21; (g) "Tibet: Thirty Years After Liberation," *CR* 30:9 (September 1981): 5. *Xinhua* 25 April 1983 in *SWB* FE/7319/BII/8.

50. "Developments in the Tibet Autonomous Region."

51. Han Suyin, *Lhasa*, p. 147. "Teachers for Tibet," *PR* 13 (16 August 1974): 22.

52. Suzanne Pepper, "Chinese Education After Mao: Two Steps Forward, Two Steps Back and Back Again?," *CQ* 81 (March 1980): 1–65. "Readjustment of Secondary and Primary Education is Essential," *Radio Lhasa* in *FBIS* 30 November 1981, pp. Q1–2.

53. Han Suyin, *Lhasa*, pp. 101–106.

54. Choedon, pp. 24–25. "A Tibetan Barefoot Doctor," *CR* 23:9 (September 1974): 9–11.

55. "Valiant Army Stations on Tangla Range Atop 'Roof of the World,' " *PR* 45 (7 November 1959): 12–14.

56. "New Industrial Center," *CR* 25:3 (March 1976): 22–23.

57. "Report from Tibet. Linchih Today," *CR* 21:6 (June 1976): 16.

58. "The Far Western Tip of Tibet," p. 2.

59. Mullik, pp. 265, 282–283.

60. Wang Lin, "Another Revelation of Indian Expansionism," *PR* 14 (3 April 1964): 30.

61. The Dalai Lama visited Japan in 1967 to attend a conference partially sponsored by the Japanese newspaper *Yomiuri Shimbun*. The government in Beijing retaliated by having the paper's China correspondent expelled. "Liang Ch'eng Chih Office Announces Disqualification of 'Yomiuri Shimbun' Correspondent in Peking," *Xinhua* 12 October 1967 in Ling, pp. 710–712.

62. See the range of documents in Ling, pp. 602–612.

63. Liaison Station of the Rebellion Headquarters in Chengtu, "Cable of September 20 from Chengtu," (Lhasa), 21 September 1967 in *JPRS* 14 March 1968.

64. Dreyer, *China's Forty Millions*, pp. 217–218.

65. "The Inauguration Declaration of the Lhasa Revolutionary Rebel General Headquarters," in Ling, pp. 633–637.

66. Paljor, p. 78. Mullin, "Red Roof."

67. B.C. Nag, "Tibetans Rise in Revolt Again," *Swarajya* 11:26 (24 December 1966): 17–18. "Tibet, 1965–1969, Part I: Rupture Among the Rulers," *CNA* 787, 21 November 1969, p. 3.

68. "All Revolutionaries Unite," *Red Sentry Post* 12 January 1967 in Liang, p. 640.

69. "Struggle for Seizure of Power in Army in Tibet," *Hung t'i-chun Chan-pao* [Red Physical Education Combat News] (Lhasa) no. 5, 8 September 1967 in *JPRS* 7 February 1968.

70. Joint Operational Department of the Children's School of Members of the Department of Communications and the Revolutionary Rebelling Headquarters in Lhasa, "A Question Deserving Our Profound Thought." 13 February 1967 in *JPRS* 14 March 1968. PLA Soldier, "I Also Wish to Make Some Remarks on the 'Public Notice,' "

(Lhasa), 19 August 1967 in *JPRS* 14 March 1968. "Joint Rebelling Army Corps of the Lhasa City Post and Tele-Communications Bureau Under the 'Great Alliance Command, A Solemn Statement,' " (Lhasa), 3 August 1967 in *JPRS* 14 March 1968. Commanding Officer of the Tibet Military Region, "We Won't Permit You to Sabotage the Stability of Border Defense Units," 18 August 1967 in *JPRS* 25 March 1968.

71. Lhasa Revolutionary Rebel Headquarters Meteorological Bureau's United Combat Headquarters, "A Handful of Bad Eggs in the Military Control Committee Will Not Escape from the Crimes of Instigating the Ta-lien-chih's Red Flag Corps to Sabotage Regular Military and Civil Fights and to Set Fire on the Meteorological Bureau (Unsuccessfully)!," 15 September 1967 in *JPRS* 25 March 1968.

72. "Cultural Revolution in Tibet Mainly Inter-Chinese Battle Says London Times,"*TR* 1:12 (December 1968): 7.

73. *Tibet Under Chinese Communist Rule*, pp. 105–106, 160–166.

74. Avedon, p. 270

75. Choedon, p. 64.

76. "Down with Wang Ch'i-wei, the Black Hand of Liu and Teng Stretching into Tibet," *Red Rebel News* 5 July 1967 in Ling, p. 677.

77. Chu Wen-lin, "The Tibet Autonomous Region Revolutionary Committee," *IS* 5:3 (December 1968): 12.

78. Ngapoi Ngawang Jigme, "Xizang's Tremendous Change—In Celebration of the 30th Anniversary of the Signing of the Agreement on Measures for the Peaceful Liberation of Xizang," *Radio Peking* 24 May 1981 in *FBIS* OW261338, 28 May 1981, p. Q5.

79. "Chinese May Be Losing Their Grip on Tibet," *Economist* 6 October 1973, p. 38.

80. Quoted in T.D. Allman, "Cold Wind of Change," *Guardian* 29 December 1973, p. 11.

81. George Patterson, "The Long Journey Home," *FEER* 23 April 1973, p. 29. "Diplomacy and the Dalai Lama," *FEER* 18 March 1974, p. 22.

82. Patterson, "Long Journey Home."

83. Dawa Norbu, "Relations Revisited," *TR* 9:9 (September 1974): 3–4.

84. "Developments in the Tibet Autonomous Region," p. 6.

Chapter 10

1. T.C. Palakshappa, *Tibetans in India: A Case Study of the Mundgod Tibetans* (New Delhi: Sterling, 1978), p. 16.

2. D. Norbu, *Red Star*, p. 246.

3. *Glimpses of Tibet*, p. 25. Dalai Lama, "To China: Open Up Tibet," *NYT* 2 February 1979, pp. 3, 19.

4. Gyatso Tshering, "Tibet's Problems of Spirit and Survival," *TSB* 8 (1974): 25.

5. *Tibetans in Exile, 1959–1969* (Dharamsala, India: Office of His Holiness the Dalai Lama, 1969), p. 179.

6. Gyatso Tshering, "The Continuation of Tibetan Culture," in *Tibetans in Exile*, ed. Germaine Krull (Bombay: Allied, 1968) n.p.

7. "Neville Maxwell's Tibet War," p. 10. Tibetan Youth Congress, "The State of Buddhism Following the Chinese Takeover," *Tibet Society and Tibet Relief Fund of the United Kingdom Newsletter* Summer 1979, pp. 3–4.

8. For the *Canadian* figures see "Tibetan Refugee Study" (Ottawa, Ontario: Research Study Group, Strategic Planning and Research Division, Department of Manpower and Immigration, 1976), p. 5. For *Switzerland* Police Fédérale des Étrangers correspondence with the author, 13 September 1978. "More Tibetans to Settle in Switzerland," *TR* 15:6 (June 1980): 8–9. "New Batch of Refugees for Switzerland," *TR* 1:12 (December

1968): 4–5. For *Taiwan* see Uncle Sam,, p. 18. For *Japan* "Tibetan Students in Japan," *TR* 1:9 (September 1968): 5. For *Europe* "Tibetans in Europe," *TR* 1:4 (April 1968): 5. For *USA* Virginia Lee Warren, "Tibetans Adapt to the U.S., But Miss Their Lofty Homeland," *NYT* 7 April 1976, p. 55. For *Nepal* (7,000 figure), "Tibetan Refugees in Nepal," *TR* 3:1 (January 1970): 5. For 10,000 figure, George Woodcock, "Tibetan Refugees in a Decade of Exile," *PA* 43:3 (Fall 1970): 411. For *India* Woodcock, "Tibetan Refugees," pp. 418–419. Louis J. Holborn, "Refugees: World Problems," in *International Encyclopedia of the Social Services*, ed. David L. Silks (New York: Crowell, Collier and Macmillan, 1968), pp. 361–373. In 1972 the *Statesman* published a story reporting that the Indian government had counted 24,047 Tibetans in India. This was surely an undercount. "Foreign Nationals in India," *TR* 8:4 (April 1973): 5. For *Bhutan* Derek Davis, "Himalayan Honeymoon," *FEER* 24 June 1975, p. 35. A correspondent, "Bhutan: The Go-It-Alone Blueprint," *FEER* 10 January 1975, p. 18. "Tibetans in Bhutan Continue to Be Harassed," *TR* 12:4 (April 1977): 9–10.

9. *Tibet Under Chinese Communist Rule*, pp. 206–207.

10. "Kalon Wangdi Dorji Speaking to the Annual Meeting of the Tibet Society and Relief Fund of the UK, 29 October 1980," *The Tibet Society and Relief Fund of the UK Newsletter* Spring 1981, p. 4.

11. UN High Commissioner for Refugees (UNHCR), *Annual Report, 1969* A/AC.96/396, Section XI-India, p. 26.

12. Ibid., Section XIV—Nepal, p. 50. "10,000 Tibetans Are in Nepal," *NYT* 18 April 1964, p. A25.

13. Gelder and Gelder, *Timely Rain*, p. 223. Han Suyin, *Lhasa*, p. 66. Felix Greene, "Letter from Lhasa," *China Now* 6:6 (November 1976): 6.

14. D. Norbu, *Red Star*, p. 239. For further tales of how little concerned wealthy Tibetans were for their impoverished countrymen, see Lang-Sims, pp. 153–160.

15. Peissel, *Secret War*, p. 212.

16. Martin Jeschke, "Lama in Exile: Prospects for an Expatriot," the *Christian Century* 88:14 (7 April 1971): 446. Patterson, *Requiem for Tibet*, p. 120 says, "The Dalai Lama's Treasure Chest . . . [consisted of a] caravan comprising some 1,500 pack-animals."

17. Henry S. Bradsher, "Tibet Struggles to Survive," *FA* 47:4 (July 1969): 758.

18. "Proceeds of Dalai Lama's Treasure," *Times* 27 February 1969, p. 5. The *Statesman* in *AR* 6:13 (1960): 322. *Tibetans in Exile*, p. xi (this latter book contends that the total was Rs. 7,900,000 [approx. U.S.$900,000]).

19. Paul Grimes, "For Tibetans an End to the Long Exile," *ASIA* 1:6 (March–April 1979): 36.

20. From the *Statesman* in *AR* 6:13 (1960): 3225. Apparently even his mother didn't trust Gyalo Thondup. Patterson, *Requiem for Tibet*, p. 138.

21. *American Emergency Committee for Tibetan Refugees Newsletter* 1 February 1966, p. 3.

22. James O. Mays, "Dilemma of the Dalai Lama," *TSB* 4:1 (1970): 38. Also in *Foreign Service Journal* 46:10 (September 1969): 44–47, 64.

23. Quoted in ibid.

24. "Tibetan Friendship Groups After Mrs. Bedi," *TR* 13:4 (April 1978): 6–7.

25. Stanley D. Bachrack, *The Committee of One Million: "China Lobby" Politics, 1953–1971* (New York: Columbia University Press, 1976), p. 149.

26. Oden Meeker, "Our Far Flung Correspondents: Tibetans Out of the World," *NY* 35:43 (12 December 1959): 174.

27. Bachrack, p. 192. American Emergency Committee for Tibetan Refugees, *Annual Report* 1960.

28. Lowell Thomas interview, 6 September 1979.

29. Ibid.

30. F.N. Beaufort-Palmer, "Moral Indignation and Tibet," *The Tibet Society and Relief Fund of the UK Newsletter* Spring 1981, p. 6.

31. *Tibetans in Exile*, pp. 1–2, 181–182.

32. Peissel, *Secret War*, p. 156.

33. Emil Wiederkehr. *SOS Tibet* (Berne and Lausanne: Comité D'aide Aux Victimes du Communisme, 1960), p. 83.

34. Tsering Wangyal, "Tibetan Settlements in Bylakuppe, South India," *TR* 12:2–3 (February–March 1977): 14.

35. Goldstein, "Tibetan Refugees," p. 16.

36. *Tibetans in Exile*, pp. 48–79. Losang Jinpa, "Maniput: Sluggish Progress," *TR* 13:4 (April 1978): 9–10.

37. T. Wangyal, "Tibetan Settlements in Bylakuppe," pp. 13–14.

38. Palakshappa, p. 43.

39. Goldstein, "Tibetan Refugees," pp. 18–19.

40. Palakshappa, pp. 43, 44, 51–52, 68, 84. de Voe, p. 22.

41. Dawa Norbu, "The State of Tibetan School Education," *TR* 11:4 (April 1976): 3–5. Thubten Samphel, "A Culture in Exile: Tibetan Refugees in India," *China Report* 24:3 (1988): 239.

42. Lang-Sims, pp. 190–191.

43. A correspondent, "Youth Social Work in Dharamsala," *TR* 12:2–3 (February–March 1977): 10.

44. Letter from Jeffrey M. Davis, M.D. to *TR* 14:1 (January 1979): 29.

45. John Billington, "A Visit to Mundgod, South India," *The Tibet Society and Relief Fund of the UK Newsletter* Summer 1981, pp. 13–17. Grania Davis, "Some Problems of Refugee Life—An Inside Look," *TR* 13:1 (January 1978):11–12, 21.

46. Letter from Stephen L. Davis and Grania Davis to *TR* 15:1 (January 1980): 20.

47. Dr. Stephen Howie and Sr. Penny Wagstaff, "Medical Priorities Amongst Tibetan Refugees," *TR* 15:12 (December 1980): 14–15.

48. Avedon, p. 87.

49. Tsering Wangyal, "Son of Kunsang Paljor," *TR* 14:9 (September 1979): 4.

50. *Constitution of Tibet* Promulgated by His Holiness the Dalai Lama, 10 March 1963 (New Delhi: Bureau of His Holiness the Dalai Lama, 1963).

51. Dervla Murphy, *Tibetan Foothold* (Levittown, NY: Transatlantic Arts, 1966), p. 105.

52. Ibid., p. 27. Patterson, *Requiem for Tibet*, pp. 181–182.

53. Ibid., pp. 108–115, 117, 130.

54. "Kalon Wangdi Dorji Speaking," p. 4.

55. Tsering Wangyal, "The Enemy Within," *TR* 16:5 (May 1981): 3–4. "Tibetan Election System Undergoes Drastic Change," *TR* 19:9 (September 1984): 5.

56. Patterson, "Long Journey Home," p. 30.

57. Tsering Wangyal, "Enter the People," *TR* 12:2–3 (February-March 1977): 3–4.

58. "Tibetan Freedom Movement in Delhi," *TR* 12:2–3 (February-March 1977): 7.

59. "Youths Want Election System Changed," *TR* 13:10 (October 1978): 10.

60. Tsering Wangyal, "The Morning After the Night Before," *TR* 12:7 (July 1977): 4.

61. Girja Saklani, "Tibetan Refugees in India. A Sociological Study of an Uprooted Community" (Ph.D., Benares University, 1978), pp. 397–398.

62. Palakshappa, p. 14.

63. R. Vaidyanath, "The Soviet View of the Tibetan System," *IS* 10:4 (April 1969): 602–606.

64. "Freedom Should Be Used Intelligently," *TR* 14:11 (November 1979): 18–19.

65. Henry Kamm, "In India, Aides to Dalai Lama Voice Regrets," *NYT* 19 August 1976, p. 12.

66. United Nations High Commissioner for Refugees, *Annual Report* A/AC.96/277, Section XIII—Nepal, p. 40.

67. Dhondup Namgyal, "Tibetan Refugees in Nepal," the *Tibet Society Newsletter* 4 August 1974, pp. 8–10.

68. Bernard Weintraub, "Bhutan Reports 30 Seized for Plot to Kill King," *NYT* 6 February 1974, p. 24. Derek Davis, "Coups, Kings and Castles in the Sky," *FEER* 10 June 1974, pp. 26–27. "Bhutan King in Tibet Crisis," *TR* 14:2 (February 1979): 7. For the official Tibetan refugee view, see Central Executive Committee, Tibetan Youth Congress, "Tibetan Refugees in Bhutan and Subsequent Developments," *Tibet Society and Tibet Relief Fund of the UK Newsletter* Autumn 1979, pp. 9–12.

69. Barry Shlachter, "Bhutan's King Seeking Balance in Development," *Los Angeles Times* 27 January 1980, pp. 2, 10.

70. Letter from Matthew Nimetz, Acting U.S. Co-ordinator for Refugees Affairs, 10 December 1979 to the *Triple Gem* 33–34, Spring-Summer 1980, pp. 5–6.

71. George Woodcock, "Tibetan Immigration in Switzerland," *Tibetan Refugee Aid Society Newsletter* (Vancouver), 1968.

72. Paul Driben, "On the Possibility of a Resettlement of Tibetan Refugees in Canada," report submitted to the Department of Manpower and Immigration, Prairie Regional Office, Winnipeg, Manitoba, September 1969.

73. Donald A. Messerschmidt, "Innovation to Adoption: Tibetan Immigrants in the United States," *TSB* 10 (1976): 65.

74. David Woodward, *Detour from Tibet* (Chicago: Moody Press, 1976), p. 138.

75. Goldstein, "Tibetan Refugees," pp. 21–22. P. Christiaan Klieger, *Tibetan Nationalism. The Role of Patronage in the Accomplishment of a National Identity* (Meerut, India: Archana Publications, 1992), pp. 67–75.

76. Ernest Weatherall, "A Reluctant Farewell to Tibet," *CSM* 28 May 1969, p. B1.

77. Switzerland's Police Fédérale des Étrangers correspondence with the author, 13 September 1978.

Chapter 11

1. Li Weihan, p. Q2.

2. Ye Jianying, "Comrade Ye Jianying's Speech," *BR* 40 (5 October 1979): 16.

3. Special Commentator, "Is the National Question Essentially a Class Question?" *RMRB* in *BR* 34 (25 August 1980): 17–22.

4. "Cadres in Tibet Carrying Out Party Directives," *Xinhua* 7 June 1980.

5. *Radio Lhasa* 28 May 1980 in *FBIS* OW290547, 29 May 1980, p. Q3.

6. *Radio Lhasa* 21 July 1982 in *SWB* FE/7086/BII/4.

7. An Zhiguo, "Tibet Carries Out New Policies," *BR* 21 (21 May 1984): 4.

8. An Zhiguo, "Tibet. New Policies Bring Changes," *BR* 42 (15 October 1984): 4–5. Shen Yantai, "Lhasa Thrives from Kaleidoscopic Changes," *BR* 48 (26 November 1984): 26–28.

9. Cheng Hsiang, "Changes in Central Policies in Xizang," *Wen Wei Pao* (Hong Kong), 8 October 1983 in *FBIS* HK121221, 14 October 1983, pp. W4-W5.

10. "Dharamsala Refutes New Chinese Claims," *TR* 16:1 (January 1981): 4. "China Calls Tibetan Exiles to 'Return Home,' " *TR* 10:1 (January 1975): 15–16.

11. "Latest Development in Tibet," *BR* 25 (21 June 1982): 20.

12. "Changing Life of Lamas in Tibet," *Xinhua* 24 March 1979, p. 16.

13. Xiao Wen, "Policy on Religion," *BR* 51 (21 December 1979): 14–15.

14. "Constitution of the People's Republic of China," *BR* 52 (27 December 1982): 10–29.

15. "New Monks and Nuns Tonsured," *China Daily* 8 August 1981, p. 1. "Minority Delegates Discuss New 'Law on National Regional Autonomy,' " *CR* 33:8 (August 1984): 12–16. *Xinhua* 23 April 1983 in *SWB* FE/7321/BII/15.

16. Banqen Erdeni Qoigyi Gyancen, "A Great Turning Point for the Development and Prosperity of the Tibetan Nationality," *Radio Peking* 23 May 1981 in *FBIS* OW241912, 28 May 1981, p. Q1.

17. George B. Schaller, "Tibetan Passage," *Animal Kingdom* 83:6 (December-January 1980–1981): 14–19. S. Dillon Ripley, "Tibet: The High and Fragile Land Behind the Range," *Smithsonian* 11:10 (January 1981): 96–105.

18. David Bonavia, "Mistakes on the Roof of the World," p. 16.

19. "Tibet's Han Officials Urged to Learn Tibetan," *Radio Lhasa* in *SWB* FE/7309/BII/17. Yasheng Huang, "China's Cadres Transfer Policy toward Tibet in the 1980s," *Modern China* 21:2 (April 1995): 188–189. Ma Rong, "Residential Patterns and Their Impact on Han-Tibetan Relations in Lhasa City, the Tibet Autonomous Region," in *Urban Anthropology in China* ed. by Greg Guldin and Aidan Southall (Leiden: E.J. Brill, 1993), pp. 268–277.

20. "Dharamsala Delegation Visits Peking and Tibet," *TR* 14:8 (August 1979): 7–8.

21. Harrison E. Salisbury, "Return of the Dalai Lama to Tibet is Expected Soon," *NYT* 31 August 1980, p. 11.

22. "China Outlines Conditions for Dalai Lama's Return," *NYT* 2 May 1977, p. 9.

23. "Any Support Is Welcome," *Asiaweek* 26 August 1977, pp. 22–23.

24. Dalai Lama, "Tibetan Autonomy."

25. An Zhiguo, "Policy Toward the Dalai Lama," *BR* 46 (15 November 1982): 3. Avedon, p. 325.

26. "Second Delegation Returns from Tibet," *TR* 15:8 (August 1980): 4–7. "A Journey Inside Tibet," *Asiaweek* 15 February 1980, pp. 8–10.

27. "Peking Visit Has Dalai Lama's Approval," *TR* 14:9 (September 1979): 5–6.

28. Nancy Nash, "The Dalai Lama Weighs the Chances of Return, *FEER* 3 August 1979, p. 23. Monnier, p. 35 quotes one critic of Dharamsala as saying, "Our government . . . is composed of spineless people who lack the courage to take decisions."

29. "Statement of His Holiness the Dalai Lama on the 23rd Anniversary of the Tibetan National Uprising," *TR* 17:2–3 (February-March 1982): 28.

30. Michael T. Kaufman, "Chinese and Indians Slowly Expanding Ties," *NYT* 15 October 1979, p. A12.

31. "Any Support Is Welcome."

32. V. Ganshin, "Beijing's Proving Ground," *Nedelya* (Moscow), 10–16 November 1980 in *JPRS* 77307, February 1980, pp. 16–19. "Intelligence," *FEER* 16 May 1980, p. 9. *The Statesman* 4 May 1980, in *TR* 15:5 (May 1980): 22. S. Iljin, 'Mao Engineered Tibetan Revolt," *Literaturnay Gazeta* 19 July 1978 in *TR* 13:10 (October 1978): 5.

33. Michael T. Kaufman, "Nepal in Turmoil As Vote to Modernize Nepal Nears," *NYT* 6 October 1979, p. 2.

34. "Statement of His Holiness the Dalai Lama on the 23rd Anniversary of the Tibetan National Uprising," p. 28.

35. Michael B. Frolic, *Mao's People: Sixteen Portraits of Life in Revolutionary China* (Cambridge, MA: Harvard University Press, 1980), pp. 152–155.

36. Dalai Lama, "Statement of His Holiness the Dalai Lama on the 22nd Anniversary of the Tibetan National Uprising Day," *TR* 16:3 (March 1981): 8.

Chapter 12

1. Quoted in Tseten Wangchuck Sharlho, "China's Reforms in Tibet: Issues and Dilemmas," *The Journal of Contemporary China* 1:1 (Fall 1992): 38. For a thorough description of economic and material development in Tibet, see several articles in *CT* 6:4 (1995).

2. "More Than 200,000 Tourists to Tibet since 1980s," *Reuters* 24 December 1994.

3. Melvyn C. Goldstein, "The Dragon and the Snow Lion: The Tibet Question in the 20th Century," in *China Briefing. 1990*, ed. by Anthony Kane (New York: Asia Society, 1990), pp. 140–144. Colin Mackerras, *China's Minorities. Integration and Modernization in the Twentieth Century* (Hong Kong: Oxford University Press, 1994): pp. 153–159. Sharlho, pp. 37–39.

4. There is some dispute about how much money Beijing has provided in subsides to the TAR. One report cites a figure of RMB14.55 billion (about U.S.$1.75 billion) in subsidies for 1952–1990. Rong Ma and Naigu Pan, "The Tibetan Population and Their Geographic Distribution in China," in Kvaerne, *Tibetan Studies*, p. 515. However, in 1988 a Chinese official told me the total was RMB150 billion (about U.S.$18.07 billion) and that most of it had gone for roads, extra salaries, pensions, Chinese-style accommodations, and other perks for the Han officials and not much directly to the Tibetans. "Tibetans Seek Curbs on Powerful Cadres and Bloated Budgets," *Guardian* 8 October 1988, p. 8. Also, a correspondent, "High Stakes," *FEER* 22 (June 1995): 76–80.

5. The only extended field research in Tibet found that life had improved significantly in every single aspect beginning in the early 1980s. Melvyn C. Goldstein, "Change, Conflict and Continuity among a Community of Nomadic Pastoralists. A Case Study from Western Tibet," in *Resistance and Reform in Tibet*, pp. 96–109. Sharlho, pp. 52–54.

6. Mackerras, p. 157.

7. Huang Yasheng, p. 196. The most recent figures cite the population of the TAR as 96 percent Tibetan but Tibetans represent only 72.1 percent of the cadres, 66.4 percent of the top leadership, 64 percent of leading provincial officials, and 60 percent of county representatives. Rod Mickelburgh, "Tibet's Leaders Take Rosy View of the World," *Toronto Globe and Mail* 17 March 1995. Also "Tibet's Raidi on the Dalai Lama: 'The Door Remains Open,'" *Xinhua* 15 March 1995.

8. Huang Yasheng, pp.190–191.

9. An official publication calls these figures, "comparatively horrible." Wang Shaoquan, "Population and Environment in Tibet," *CT* 6:2 (1995): 36. Peng Jianqun, "Economic Development on the Roof of the World," *China Today* 44:8 (August 1995): 14. "China Blames Tibetan Poverty on Numbers," *UPI* 23 November 1995.

10. "Chen Kuiyuan says opposition to 'Dalai clique' is main criterion for Tibetan educators," *XRB* 28 October 1994, in *SWB* 1 November 1994.

11. "On Educational Development in Tibet," *RMRB* 1 November 1994, in *SWB* 21 November 1994. In Qamdo, according to *Qamdo Newspaper* [sic] 15 July 1993, only 34 percent of children attended school, and the illiteracy/semi-illiteracy rate is 78.8 percent. Human Rights Desk, Central Tibetan Administration, Dharamsala, 7 June 1994.

12. "Tibet Government to Put Education at Top of Agenda," *Xinhua* 5 June 1994, in *SWB*.

13. Patrick Peatfeld, "Save Our Tsampa! Modernization, International Aid and the Future of Tibetan Agriculture," *TR* 30:5 (May 1995): 13–19.

14. Ruth Youngblood, "China Pledges Enough Food for Minorities," *UPI* 1 March 1995.

15. "Gyaincain Norbu Tells Meeting: 'Some Households Have Even Run Out of Grain,'" *XRB* 24 May 1994.

16. Jing Wei, *100 Questions About Tibet* (Beijing: Beijing Review Press, 1989), p.

61. United Nations, "Report by the Chinese Delegation to the 44th Session of the Commission on Human Rights," 30 December 1988 (E/CN.4/1989/44), p. 12.

17. "Clearly Understand the True Nature of the Dalai Clique; Oppose Splittism and Safeguard Stability," *XRB* 10 March 1995, in *SWB* 28 March 1995.

18. *Tibetan Refugee Community: Integrated Development Plan—II, 1995–2000* (Dharamsala: Planning Council, May 1994). Excerpts in "Introduction to the Tibetan Refugee Community," *TB* March-April 1995. Also, Vyvyan Cayley, *Children of Tibet: An Oral History of the First Tibetans to Grow Up in Exile* (Balmain, Australia: Pearlfisher Publishers, 1994).

19. Wu Guohua and Qoisang, "Steady Stream of Tibetans Return Home," *CT* 4:1 (Spring 1993): 23–24.

20. Goldstein, "The Dragon and the Snow Lion," pp. 146–150.

21. His Holiness the Dalai Lama, *Collected Statements, Interviews and Articles* (Dharamsala: Information Office of His Holiness the Dalai Lama, 1982), p. 51.

22. Ibid., p. 59.

23. Dawa Norbu, "China's Dialogue with the Dalai Lama 1978–1990: Prenegotiation Stage or Dead End?" *PA* 64:3 (Fall 1991): 369. Tsering Wangyal, "Sino-Tibetan Negotiations Since 1959," in *Resistance and Reform in Tibet*, pp.197–206.

24. Dalai Lama, *Freedom in Exile*, p. 223.

25. Zhang Junyi, "The Story about Delegations from Tibetan Exile Organizations Visiting the Mainland and the Repercussions of Their Visits," in *Collected Essays of Tibetan Studies*, volume 2 (Taipei: Commission for Tibetan Studies, 1989).

26. "Dalai Lama's Tour of Russia and Mongolia," *TR* 14:6 (June 1979): 8–9. Jan Andersson, "Importance of Dalai Lama's U.S. Visit," *TR* 14:12 (December 1979): 14.

27. Zhang Junyi. Dalai Lama, *Freedom in Exile*, pp. 222–223, 240.

28. Dalai Lama, "H.H. The Dalai Lama's Speech to the Chinese Students and Scholars," Boston, 9 September 1995.

29. From His Holiness the Dalai Lama's Private Office, quoted in Singh, p. 285.

30. Japan and Thailand in 1967; Western Europe in 1973; Switzerland in 1974; Japan in 1978; Mongolia, the Soviet Union, Greece, Switzerland and the U.S. in 1979; Italy, Canada, and Japan in 1980; the U.K. and U.S. in 1981; Malaysia, Singapore, Australia, Mongolia, the Soviet Union, Hungary, and Western Europe in 1982; the U.S. in 1983; the U.K., U.S., and Japan in 1984. Rogers Hicks and Ngakpa Chogyam, *Great Ocean. An Authorized Biography of the Buddhist Monk Tenzin Gyatso, His Holiness the Fourteenth Dalai Lama* (Longmead, UK: Element Books, 1984), pp. 198–199.

31. "Plan for Tibetan Commemorative Year in USA," *TR* 18:5 (May 1983): 7.

32. "Year of Tibet," *TR* 19:3 (March 1984): 11.

33. "Interview with Tenzin Namgyal Tethong," *Freedom* 1:1 (October 1991): 16–18.

34. Article 55 of the UN Charter dictates that the UN must promote "universal respect for, and observance of human rights and fundamental freedoms." The UN Commission on Human Rights (fifty-three-member nations that meet for six weeks in February and March of each year in Geneva) and its Subcommission on Prevention of Discrimination and Protection of Minorities (twenty-six experts on the subject selected by their governments) are assigned the task of monitoring compliance of Article 55. China joined these groups in 1970 but did not come under criticism until the mid-1980s and especially after the 1989 events in Tiananmen Square. Philip Baker, "A Long Slow Process," *Human Rights Tribune* 3:3 (Fall 1992): 14–16.

35. "Tibetan Official Meets U.S. Leaders," *TB* 16:3 (August–September 1985): 13. Papers filed with the U.S. Justice Department's Foreign Agents Registration Unit say that Wilmer, Cutler & Pickering will "provide legal advice . . . on a pro-bono basis." Registration No. 3355, 5 July 1985.

36. Jay Rosentstein and Nina Easton, "Charity Call," *American Banker* 4 (November 1985): 38. The major partner, Lloyd Cutler, is a "living legend among Washington's lawyer-lobbyists" as a "corporate Godfather by day and Mother Teresa by night." He built his firm by "providing services to whichever special interests could afford the rates." Cutler has been selected by the *National Law Journal* as one of the 100 most influential lawyers in America and by *Regardies* magazine as one of the most powerful private people in Washington. Michael Binstein et al., "The Power Elite," *Regardies. The Business of Washington* 9:5 (January 1989). Zachary Citron, "Watchdogs that Purr: How Not to Set Up an Ethics Commission," *The New Republic* 6 (March 1989): 10. Michael Binstein, "The Hit List: D.C. Law," the *Washington Post* 14 July 1991, p. W7.

37. On a visit to Chile in June 1992, the Dalai Lama was met at the airport by, among others, the leader of Chile's Nazi party, who told reporters he met the Dalai Lama while he was Chile's Ambassador to India and that the two "are friends." *Reuters,* 16 June 1992. "Dalai Lama in Germany," *TR* 21:6 (June 1986): 6–7. Ngawang Choephill, "Time for Action," *TR* 21:9–10 (September-October 1986): 4–5. "British Parliamentary Committee of Tibet Formed," *TR* 22:4 (April 1987): 7–8. "His Holiness' Europe Visit," *TB* 17:2 (June–July 1986): 2–3.

38. "Jimmy Carter in Tibet," *TB* 18:2 (July–August 1987): 6. Also, "Unprecedented Visit," Ibid.

39. Some people have argued the executions were not coincidental but planned as a demonstration by the Chinese that they indeed control events in Tibet. Although an interesting proposition, there is no evidence apart from hearsay in Tibet.

40. "U.S. Congress Passes Amendments on Tibet," *TR* 22:8 (August 1987): 77–79. "U.S. Senate Adopts Tibet Bill," *TR* 22:11 (November 1987): 11. "Reagan Signs Tibet Bill: China Warns on Tibet," *TR* 23:1 (January 1988): 5.

41. "Human Rights Situation of the Tibetan People," *Department of State Bulletin* 87:2129 (December 1987): 50. Elaine Sciolino, "U.S. Official Defends Stance on Turmoil in Tibet," *NYT* 15 October 1987, p. A18.

42. Elaine Sciolino, "Beijing is Backed by Administration on Unrest in Tibet," *NYT* 7 October 1987, p. A1.

43. Peter Bishop, *The Myth of Shangri-La. Tibet, Travel Writing and the Western Creation of Sacred Landscape* (Berkeley: University of California Press, 1989), p. 7. Douglas C. McGill, "Dalai Lama Promoted an Exhibition," *NYT* 28 September 1987, p. C23. "President Bush's Cousin Visits Dharamsala," *TB* (March–April 1992): 34.

44. "Artists to Take Part in Tibet House Benefit," *NYT* 17 May 1988, p. C16. Amitai Ghosh, "Tibetan Dinner," *Utne Reader* (March–April 1990): 121–122.

45. Sanjoy Hazorika, "Dalai Lama Urges Peaceful Protest," *NYT* 8 October 1987, p. A8.

46. A. Tom Grunfeld, "Letter to the Editor," *NYT* 23 March 1988, p. A26. Sciolino, "Beijing is Backed."

47. "Tibet in Sept./Oct.," *TR* 23:11 (November 1988): 4. *N-T,* 22:4 (September–October 1988): 9.

48. Salamat Ali and Robert Delfs, "One Game, Two Courts," *FEER* 6 October 1988, p. 33.

49. Yojana Sharma, "Tibet: Dalai Lama Proposes New Plan for Self Government," *Interpress* 15 June 1988. Michael C. van Walt van Praag, "Earnest Negotiations. The Only Answer to Growing Unrest in Tibet," *International Relations* 9:5 (May 1989): 377–392.

50. The culprits were alleged to be former British Prime Minister Edward Heath, Lord Ennals, Jimmy Carter, Michael van Walt van Praag, and this author; Norbu, "China's Dialogue with the Dalai Lama," p. 355. Gavin Randall, "Stranger Than Fiction," *TR* 25:7 (July 1990): 15.

51. *AFP* 28 July 1988, in *FBIS* CHI–88–145, 28 July 1988, p. 44.

52. *FBIS* CHI–88–121, 23 June 1988, p. 42.

53. Norbu, "China Dialogue with the Dalai Lama," p. 355.

54. Goldstein, "The Dragon and the Snow Lion," pp. 156–157.

55. *SWB* Part III, Far East, 16 March 1988.

56. Quoted in the *South China Morning Post* 20 July 1988.

57. *FBIS* CHI–88–060, 29 March 1988. *FBIS* CHI–88–066, 6 April 1988.

58. Quoted in *FBIS* 25 January 1989, p. 55.

59. A. Tom Grunfeld, "Enigmatic Buddha Who Works from Within," *Guardian* 8 October 1988, p. 8.

60. Quoted in *Ming Pao* 2 June 1988 in *SWB* FE/0169 - B2/1, 4 June 1988.

61. Huang Yasheng, pp. 196–197.

62. Guy Dinmore, "China in Behind Scenes Attempt to Negotiate with Dalai Lama," *Reuters* 15 December 1989.

63. Dalai Lama, *Freedom in Exile*, p. 260. Norbu, "China's Dialogue with the Dalai Lama," p. 370.

64. "Mexican President Meets Dalai Lama," *TR* 24:8 (August 1989): 6. "His Holiness the Dalai Lama's Scandinavian Visit: Increased Interest in Tibet," *TB* 19:4 (October–November): 2–3. "His Holiness Visits Costa Rica, U.S. and Mexico," *TB* 20:2 (June-July 1989): 3.

65. "British Parliamentary Group for Tibet," *TR* 24:9 (September 1989): 7.

66. "Tibetan Hearing in Germany," *TB* 20:2 (June–July 1989): 1–2, 12. "The Bonn Hearing—A Success," *TR* 24:6 (June 1989): 5. "Danish Government Requested to Support Tibetan Cause," *TR* 24:12 (December 1989): 5.

67. Sheila Rule, "How, And Why, the Dalai Lama Won the Peace Prize," *NYT* 13 October 1989, p. A14. Nicholas D. Kristof, "How Tiananmen Square Helped Support for Tibet," *NYT* 18 August 1991, Section 4, p.4.

68. "Tibet Support Group in Italian Parliament," *TR* 25:3 (March 1990): 6. Tsering Wangyal, "Little Big Nations," *TR* 25:10 (October): 3. "Parliamentary Tibet Committee Formed in Norway," *TR* 26:1 (January 1991): 11.

69. Frank Viviano, "Tibetans Reach Out to Other Dissidents," *San Francisco Chronicle* 3 December 1990, p. A14.

70. *N-T* 24:1 (January–April 1990): 4. "National Day for China and Tibet," *TB* (March–April 1990): 16.

71. Dalai Lama's Statement, 10 March 1992, in *TB* (March–April 1992): 15–16.

72. The groups headquartered in the new building were: the Office of Tibet, Tibet House, the U.S.-Tibet Committee, the Tibetan Woman's Association, The Tibetan Youth Association, Potala Publications, Eco-Tibet, TibetNet, Tibetan Association, Tibet Fund, and the Tibetan–U.S. Resettlement Project. For a discussion of the distorting effects on Tibetan culture that this patronage brings, see Klieger, pp. 84–120.

73. "United Nations Passes Resolutions on Tibet," *TB* (September–October 1991): 1.

74. "Irish President Meets Dalai Lama," *TR* 26:5 (May 1991): 7–8. "Sweden to Receive Dalai Lama Officially," *TR* 26:12 (December 1991): 5. "His Holiness Meets Austrian President, Swiss and French Foreign Ministers," *TB* (September–October 1991): 20. "His Holiness Visits Mongolia, Baltics and Bulgaria," *TB* (November–December 1991): 23. *Snow Lion Newsletter & Catalogue* 6:2 (Summer Supplement 1991): 19.

75. Gwen Ifill, "Lawmakers Cheer Tibetan in Capitol Rotunda," *NYT* 19 April 1991, p. A7. "U.S. President Meets His Holiness," *TB* (May–June 1991): 16. "Dalai Lama's U.K. Visit Most Successful Yet," *TR* 26:5 (May 1991): 6. Interviews with State Department officials on the China Desk, 9 March 1992.

76. "U.S. Congress Declares Tibet an Occupied Country," *TB* (November–December 1991): 22. *N-T* (January–February 1992): 4.

77. "China Sore over a 'Major' Tibetan Victory," *TR* 27:1 (January 1992): 8. "Australia Passes Tibet Resolution," *TB* (January–February 1991): 5. In Australia and New Zealand the Dalai Lama's supporters asked the professional journal *Ad News* to help them find an advertising agency that would be willing to publicize the Dalai Lama's visit and to design an ad campaign for his cause without charge. Six agencies submitted ideas, and Young & Rubican received the account. Michael Magazanik, "Nothing Is Sacred as Admen Try to Sell a Holy Visitation," *Age* (Melbourne) 20 February 1992. Also reprinted in *TR* 27:4 (April 1992): 18–19. These efforts worked. Capacity crowds met the Dalai Lama everywhere he went and he received wide coverage in the press where he spoke on political issues, something he had been forbidden from doing during a previous visit in 1982. Kalinga Seneviratne, "Dalai Lama Ends Two-Week Tour of Australia, *Inter Press Service* 13 May 1992.

78. Fan Cheuk-wan, "Dalai Lama 'Accused' of Blocking Talks," *South China Morning Post* 9 May 1990, p. 6. "Policy on Dalai Lama Remains Unchanged," p. 15.

79. "Dalai Lama to End Institution, Independence Goal," *AFP* 1 August 1990, in *FBIS* CHI–90–148, p. 11. See also, "Dalai Lama Calls for Sino-Tibetan Confederation," *AFP* 13 December 1990, in *FBIS* CHI–90–241, p. 23.

80. Ari L. Goldman, "Dalai Lama Appeals for Help in Going Home," *NYT* 10 October 1991, p. A17. Gerald Renner, "Dalai Lama: Genial Manner, Serious Mission," *The Hartford Courant*, 10 October 1991, p. A15.

81. "China Rejects Dalai Lama's Offer to End Exile," *AFP* 10 October 1991.

82. Ibid. In 1991 the Tibet Lobby in turn supported the China Lobby but to no avail. See also Rene V.L. Wadlow, "Tibet Discussed in UN Commission on Human Rights," *TR* 20:5 (May 1985): 8–10. "Chinese Dissident Organization Supports Tibetans," *TR* 20:7 (July 1985): 7–8.

83. Jean-Michel Stoulling, "Human Rights Commission Decides against Vote on China's Record," *AFP* 5 March 1992. "New World Conscience," *NYT* 13 March 1992, p. A30. "China Thanks Third World for Quashing Tibet Vote," *Reuters* 7 March 1992.

84. Nicholas D. Kristof, "Foreign Investors Pouring Into China," *NYT* 15 June 1992, pp. D1, D6.

85. *Beijing Review*—a weekly—during 1984, for example, ran sixteen articles on Tibet. It ran nineteen in 1990, twenty-seven in 1991, thirty-four in 1992, sixteen in 1993. *China Today*—a monthly—ran six in 1984, four in 1990, twelve in 1991, thirteen in 1992, seven in 1993.

86. Zhang Chunjian and Xeirab Nyima, "Human Rights in Tibet: Past and Present," *BR* 35:8 (February 24–March 1, 1992): 27.

87. Graham Hutchings, "China's Fury at Major's Talk With GodKing." *Daily Telegraph* 6 December 1991, p. 12.

88. Jude Carlson, "Tibet in the News," *BCAS* 24:2 (1992): 40.

89. A list of books can be found on p. 8 of *BR* 35:8 (24 February–1 March 1992) and other issues. "Tibetan Song and Dance Captivate Europeans," *BR* 35:8 (24 February –1 March 1991): 44–45.

90. Several documents are translated in "China's Public Relations Strategy on Tibet." November 1993, International Campaign for Tibet, Washington, D.C.

91. Barbara Crosette, "China Denies Visas to Two Senators," *NYT* 7 April 1992, p. A7. In a discussion with the consul in charge of political affairs at Beijing's New York Consulate, I was informed that there was no program of public relations on the Tibet issue, 27 March 1992.

92. Nicholas D. Kristof, "China Issues Rebuttal to Human Rights Critics," *NYT* 3 November 1991, p. A12. For a $5,000 a month retainer, plus expenses, Hill & Knowlton promised to monitor Congress, provide public relations advice, monitor the media, "build

support to avoid negative effects on China–U.S. relations," "improve China's overall image," "recruit and organize third party allies," and "respond to urgent criticism." U.S. Department of Justice, Foreign Agents Registration Unit, Registration No. 3301, 10 May 1992.

93. "Dalai Lama Calls for Mutual Trust between Tibet and China," *AFP* 24 July 1992.

94. On the Gyalo Thondup visit see Kyodo News Service, 22 July 1992 (an anonymous source confirmed this to me), and on the talks in New Delhi, see press release from "Cabinet of the Tibetan Government in Exile," 24 September 1992.

95. Tsering Wangyal, "Down the Garden Path," *TR* 30:10 (October 1995): 3.

96. "Policy on Dalai Lama Remains Unchanged," p. 15.

97. Dalai Lama, "H.H. The Dalai Lama's Speech to the Chinese Students and Scholars."

98. Jawed Naqvi, "India, China Give Up Quest for Border Settlement," *Reuters* 2 March 1995.

·99. "President Chao Tze-chi's Address at the 39th General Conference of the WLFD ROC Chapter," *WFLD Newsletter* 3:3 (May 1994): 5.

100. "Taiwan Agreement Rejected by Dalai Lama's Government," Tibet Information Network, 3 September 1994.

101. "Tokyo Office Head Resigns," *TR* 27:4 (April 1992): 7. See editorials: Tsering Wangyal, "Yabshi vs. Yabshi," *TR* 27:6 (June 1992): 3, and Tsering Wangyal, "P for Perseverance," *TR* 27:7 (July 1992): 3. For a story on their partial reconciliation, see "Yabshi Controversy Ends," *TR* 27:9 (September 1992): 7.

102. Ibid. "George Bush Joins Buddhist Pantheon in Tibet," *Reuters* 16 December 1991.

103. Melvyn Goldstein, one of the most astute observers of Tibet, has argued (in an unpublished paper presented at Yale University on 24 October 1992) that it is the Dalai Lama who is intransigent. It is he, Goldstein argued, who must accept the reality of a Tibet within a Chinese state and return to preserve cultural and linguistic homogeneity, which is rapidly being lost by the economic integration of Tibet and the free immigration of Han into the areas traditionally inhabited by Tibetans.

104. "Dalai Lama Renews Call to Resolve Tibetan Problem," *Kyodo News Service* 22 July 1992.

105. "Dalai Lama Interviewed in Hungary," *SWB* E/1439/1.

106. "Clearly Understand the True Nature of the Dalai Clique."

107. "Our Important Political Task," Tibet TV, 6 April 1995 in *SWB* 17 April 1995.

108. "Tibet Party Secretary Hails Police and Army Work," *XRB* 24 August 1995, in *SWB* 26 September 1995.

109. "Clearly Understand the True Nature of the Dalai Clique." Teresa Poole, "Tibetan Pupils in India Forced to Return" *The Independent* 28 March 1995 says Dharamsala estimates that since 1985 9,000 children have come to free schools, monasteries, and nunneries outside of Tibet.

110. Patrick Tyler, "China Rejects Choice of Boy as Tibet Lama," *NYT* 13 November 1995, p. 6.

111. Tibet Information Network quotes Chinese officials saying that Chatral Rinpoche was "in the hospital" and that he was "ill." "Signs of Leadership Split over Reincarnation," TIN, 21 September 1995.

112. For a series of attacks on the Dalai Lama and the complete description of Beijing's position, see *CT* supplementary issue (August 1995), which has a photo of the golden urn on its cover. Also, Jasper Becker, "Deputy Abbot Held over Panchen Lama," *South China Morning Post* 30 May 1995. "Tibet CPPCC's statement on 'despicable

means employed by the Dalai clique,' " *Xinhua* 24 May 1995, in *SWB* 27 May 1995. Rone Tempest, "Politics and the Panchen Lama," *Los Angeles Times* 27 May 1995, p. A1, A24-A25. "Statement from H.H. the Dalai Lama," and "Contact with the Chinese Authorities Regarding the Search for the Reincarnation of the Panchen Lama," Dharamsala, 14 May 1995. "Identifying the reincarnated Bainqen," *BR* 38:37 (11–17 September 1995): 7–10. Tsering Shakya, "The Greater Significance of the Panchen Lama Dispute," *TR* 30:8 (August 1995): 14–18.

113. Seth Faison, "Ignoring Dalai Lama's Choice, China Installs Cleric in Tibet," *NYT* 30 November 1995, p. A18.

114. "Panchen Reincarnation System," *Xinhua* 29 November 1995.

115. Geoffrey Crothall, "Secret Meeting on Lama," *South China Morning Post* 7 November 1995. Matt Forney, "Divide and Rule," *FEER* 30 November 1995, p. 26.

116. Goldstein, "Change, Conflict and Continuity," pp. 76–87.

117. Tibet Support Group UK, *New Majority. Chinese Population Transfer into Tibet* (London: Tibet Support Group UK, 1995), pp. 56- 57.

118. *New Majority*, p. 60.

119. Jiang Wandi, "Heroes Admired by Ordinary People," *BR* 38:40 (2–8 October 1995): 9–12.

120. *New Majority*, pp. 101–102.

121. Rong Ma and Naigu Pan, "The Tibetan Population and Their Geographic Distribution in China," in *Tibetan Studies*, ed. by Per Kvaerne, pp. 507–516.

122. *New Majority*, pp. 95, 106.

123. The most vigorous proponent of this 1.2 million number is Paul Ingram, *Tibet. The Facts* (Dharamsala: Tibetan Young Buddhist Association, 1990). My views on this book can be found in a review by A. Tom Grunfeld *CQ* 127 (September 1991): 638–639.

Appendix A

1. Dalai Lama interview. Tucci, *Tibet*, pp. 19–20. For an early census, see Luciano Petech, "The Mongol Census in Tibet," in *Tibetan Studies in Honour of Hugh Richardson*, pp. 233–238.

2. OSS, p. 9.

3. (a) Pradyumna P. Karan, *The Changing Face of Tibet. The Impact of Communist Ideology on the Landscape* (Lexington: University of Kentucky Press, 1976), p. 52; (b) Ibid.; (c) A. Lai, "Sinification and Ethnic Minorities in China, *CS* 8:4 (15 February 1970): 4–5, 19–20; (d) MacDonald, *Land of the Lamas*, p. 115; (e) OSS, Research and Analysis Bureau, "China's Borderlands: Criteria for Claims," no. 2420, 7 August 1944, p. 7. National Archives, Diplomatic Branch, Washington, D.C.; (f) Lal, "Sinification," pp. 4–5, 19–20; (g) William Dunning, "The Mysteries and the Wonder of a Journey Through Tibet," *Holiday* 12:6 (December 1952): 54–57; (h) A.J. Hopkinson, "Tibet Today," *Asiatic Review* 46:168 (October 1959): 141; (i) O.E. Clubb, "Tibet's Strategic Position," *EW* 10:12 (December 1956): 18; (j) Heinrich Harrer, "New Turn of the Wheel," *NYT Magazine* 24 May 1959, p. 21; (k) *Tibet and the Chinese People's Republic*, p. 290; (l) Richardson, "Tibet as It Was," p. 46; (m) Karan, *Changing Face*, p. 52; (n) Peissel, *Secret War* p. 10; (o) "Stop Press," *TR* 11:8 (August 1976): 15; (p) H.R.H. Prince Peter of Greece and Denmark, "The Chinese Colonization of Tibet," *TSB* 13 (1979): 22–31.

4. Theodore Shabad, *China's Changing Map. National and Regional Development, 1949–1971* (New York: Praeger, 1972), pp. 47–48.

5. Tsingfu F. Tsiang, "The Question of Tibet," *FCR* 16:12 (December 1969): 61–64.

6. Albert Kolb, *East Asia: China, Japan, Korea, Vietnam: Geography of a Cultural Region* trans. C.A.M. Sym (London: Methuen, 1971), pp. 365–366.

7. "Xizang Releases Population Census Results," *Radio Lhasa* 20 October 1982 in *JPRS* 9 November 1982, p. 113.

8. *Glimpses of Tibet Today*, p. 50. Senanayake, pp. 39–40.

9. Dalai Lama interview. In the early days of his exile, the Dalai Lama used the figure of 7–8 million as the population of Tibetans, switching to 6 million later on. Zhang Tianlu, "Past and Present Tibetan Population," *China's Tibet* (Winter 1993): 7.

10. "The Tibetan Question," *CNA* 90 (1 July 1955): 5.

11. Zhou Enlai, "Some Questions on Policy Towards Nationalities," *BR* 9 (3 March 1980): 16.

12. (a) Richardson, "Tibet as It Was," p. 46; (b) Thubtob, p. 6; (c) Lal, "Sinification," p. 20; (d) Wallace Liu, "The Meaning of Tibet," *Commonweal* 72:3 (15 April 1960): 57; (e) Tsingfu F. Tsiang, p. 63; (f) P.H.M. Jones, "Tibet and the New Order," *FEER* 3 March 1961, pp. 360–362; (g) "Lhasa. A Hungry City," *FCA* 7:9 (September 1960): 26; (h) O.E. Clubb, "The Old Order Passes in Tibet," *EW* 13:8 (August 1959): 15–16; (i) "Peiping Finally Admits Tibet Revolt," *FCA* 6:4 (April 1959): 22; (j) "Tibet. War Atop of the World," *Newsweek* 12 January, 1959, p. 51; (k) Meeker, "Tibetans Out of This World," pp. 182–183; (l) "Tibet. His Determined Highness," *Time* 29 June 1959, p. 58; (m) Patterson, "The 'Fish' in the 'Sea,' " p. 10; (n) Tillman Durdin, "Tibetans in Peril Dalai Lama Says," *NYT* 21 June 1959, pp. 1, 25; (o) Lal, "Sinification," p. 20; (p) Wadi Rufail, p. 11; (q) Lal, "Sinification," p. 20; (r) B. Smith, p. 50; (s) "Tibetans Becoming a Minority in Tibet," *TR* 4:1 (January 1970): 6–7; (t) Steve Osofosky, "Soviet Criticism of China's National Minorities Policy," *Asian Survey* 14:10 (October 1974): 913; (u) Vaidyanath, p. 603 (quotes a Tashkent International Service Broadcast in the Uygur language); (v) Lucian W. Pye, "China: Ethnic Minorities and national Security," *CS* 14:12 (December 1976): 6–7; (w) Wing Commander Majaraj K. Chopra, "Red China Colonizes Tibet," *Military Review* 46:7 (July 1966): 52–60; (x) Dorothy Woodman, "Tibet: Brain-Washing Buddhism," *New Statesman* 60:1535 (13 August 1960): 202; (y) "Tibet in Ferment," *National Integration* 1964, pp. 13–14; (z) "China Accused of Killing 65,000 Tibetans," *Times* 6 June 1959, p. 6.

13. (a) Strong, *Tibetan Interviews*, p. 117; (B) Lal, "Sinification," p. 20. Patterson "The 'Fish' in the 'Sea,' " p. 10; (c) Ibid; (d) George Patterson, "Tibet," *The Reporter* 32:6 (25 March 1965): 102; (e) "World Press Comments on Tibet Today," *National Integration* 1964, p. 76; (f) Thubtob, p. 6; (g) Vaidyanath, p. 603; (h) Wallace Liu, p. 57; (i) "Peiping Turning Tibet Into Military Base," *FCA* 6:11 (November 1959): 25; (j) "Half-Million PLA troops in TAR Alone" *TR* 17:2–3 (February-March 1982): 4; (k) "Interview with Dalai Lama's Brother"; (l) "Peiping Finally Admits Tibet Revolt"; (m) "Tibet: War Atop of the World."

14. Gelder and Gelder, *Timely Rain*, p. 108.

15. Robert L. Bartley, "Tibet: Roof of the World," *WSJ* 22 September 1976, p. 20.

16. Han Suyin, *Lhasa*, p. 146.

17. CIA, "The Integration of Tibet," p. 13.

18. "Tibetans Healthier, Better Educated," *BR* 42 (15 October 1984): 11.

19. Zhang Tianlu, pp. 7–8.

Appendix B

1. Rubin, "The Position of Tibet," p. 123.

2. Chen Han-seng, p. 142.

3. The most complete summary of the Tibetan exile position can be found in van

Walt van Praag and also in Hilary K. Jacobs et al., "Independence for Tibet: An International Legal Analysis," *China Law Reporter* 8:1–2 (1994): 22–72. While there is nothing as comprehensive for the Chinese side, good sources are *Tibet—Its Ownership and Human Rights Situation* (Beijing: Information Office of the State Council of the People's Republic of China, 1992); *100 Questions about Tibet* (Beijing: Beijing Review Press, 1989).

4. For the entire text of this exchange, see *FRUS 1943*, pp. 626–628, 630, 634–636.

5. *Department of State Bulletin* 40 (1959): 515.

6. Bradsher, p. 753.

7. Rosalyn Higgens, *The Development of International Law Through the Political Organs of the United Nations* (London: Oxford University Press, 1963), pp. 11–57.

8. Quoted in John deFrancis, "National and Minority Policies, *The Annals of the American Academy of Political and Social Sciences: Report on China* 277, 1951, pp. 148–149.

9. Conrad Brandt, Benjamin Schwartz and John K. Fairbank, eds., *A Documentary History of Chinese Communism* (New York: Athenaeum, 1960), pp. 64, 124.

10. Ibid., pp. 223–224.

11. Edgar Snow, "Interviews with Mao Tse-tung, Communist Leader," in *China: The March Towards Unity* (New York: Workers Library Publishers, 1937), pp. 40–41.

12. Quoted in *Foreign Relations of the United States, 1944, vol. VI China* (Washington, DC: U.S. Government Printing Office, 1967), p. 537.

13. Mao Tse-tung, "On Coalition Government," in *Selected Works of Mao Tse-tung* vol. III (Peking: Foreign Languages Press, 1965), pp. 255–320.

14. Cited in Harold Hinton, "The Status of National Minorities in Communist China," USIA, IRI, Intelligence Survey (IS–63–55), July 1955, pp. 7, 9, National Archives, Diplomatic Branch, Washington, DC.

15. Ibid.

16. *The Constitution of the People's Republic of China* (Peking: Foreign Languages Press, 1954).

17. Zhou Enlai, "Some Questions on Policy Towards Nationalities," Part 1, pp. 14–23.

18. *The Constitution of the People's Republic of China* (Peking: Foreign Languages Press, 1975). *The Constitution of the People's Republic of China* (Peking: Foreign Languages Press, 1978). "Constitution of the People's Republic of China," *BR* 52 (17 December 1982): 12.

19. Dreyer, *China's Forty Millions*, p. 70.

20. For a more detailed discussion of these issues, see A. Tom Grunfeld, "In Search of Equality: Relations Between China's Ethnic Minorities and the Majority Han," *BCAS* 17:1 (January–March 1985): 54–67.

Bibliography

Unpublished Materials

Alexander III, James McKenzie, "Tibetan National Character" (Ph.D., University of Washington, 1971).

Aziz, Barbara Nimri, "In Real Tibet," interview on radio station WBAI-FM, New York City, 6 July 1978.

Goldstein, Melvyn C.,"An Anthropological Study of the Tibetan Political System" (Ph.D., University of Washington, Seattle, 1968).

Grunfeld, A. Tom, "Some Reflections on the 1959 Revolt In Lhasa," unpublished paper, 1992.

Kuleshov, Nicolai S., "Russia and the Tibetan Crisis at the Beginning of the 20th Century," unpublished manuscript.

Saklani, Sakni, "Tibetan Refugees in India. A Sociological Study of an Uprooted Community" (Ph.D., Benares University, 1978).

Sung Yao-ting, "Chinese Tibetan Relations, 1890–1947," (Ph.D., University of Minnesota, 1949).

"Tibetan Refugee Study" (Ottawa, Ontario: Research Study Group, Strategic Planning and Research Division, Department of Manpower and Immigration, 1976).

Correspondence/Interviews

Dalai Lama interview, 25 July 1981.

J.S. Evans, Capt. USN, Chief, Directorate for Print Media, Department of Defense, correspondence, Washington, DC, 3 July 1979.

Niall MacDermott correspondence, 3 August 1979.

Police Fédérale des Étrangers correspondence, 13 September 1978.

L. Fletcher Prouty interview, Washington, DC, 14 August 1979.

Hugh Richardson correspondence, 17 June, 17 July, 12 August 1981.

M.E. Tackley, Acting Chief, New Branch, Public Information Division, Department of the Army correspondence, 19 June 1979.

Lowell Thomas, Sr., interview, New York City, 6 September 1979.

Robert Trumbull correspondence, 10 April 1981
State Department officials on the China Desk, interviews, 9 March 1992.

Government Documents

"Background on the Current Situation in Tibet," USIA IRI Intelligence Summary, 8 August 1955, in *Documents on Contemporary China, 1949–1975,* #91D.00168, p. 5. National Archives, Diplomatic Branch, Washington, DC.

British Broadcasting Company, Summary of World Broadcasts (SWB), The Far East.

CIA, "Desire of the Dalai Lama to Continue Struggle for Freedom and Independence of Tibet," 23 April 1959, deposited in Dwight D. Eisenhower Library, Abilene, Kansas.

CIA, "Integration of Tibet: China's Progress and Problems," 1976. (In author's possession).

CIA National Intelligence Estimate, "Soviet Capabilities and Intentions," 15 November 1950, NIE–3 in *The Declassified Documents Reference System* (Carrollton, VA: Carrollton Press, 1980) p. 226A.

CIA, National Intelligence Survey, "Communist China. Section 23. Weather and Climate, Part V—Tibetan Highlands," September 1964 in *The Declassified Document Reference Service* (Carrollton, VA: Carrollton Press). (77) 161 F.

O.E. Clubb to Secretary of State, Peiping, 12 September 1949, Main Decimal File, Box 7024, National Archives, Diplomatic Branch, Washington, DC.

Condir, Kenneth, *The History of the Joint Chiefs of Staff, vol. II, 1947–1949* (Washington, DC: Historical Division, Joint Secretariat, Joint Chiefs of Staff, undated) National Archives, Military Branch, Washington, DC.

Division of Research for the Far East, Office of Intelligence Research, Department of State, "'Peaceful Liberation' of Tibet: Blueprint for Communist Conquest," OIR 60007, 4 June 1951. National Archives, Diplomatic Branch, Washington, DC,

Donovan to Secretary of State, New Delhi, 22 November 1949, 893.00 Tibet/11–2249, National Archives, Diplomatic Branch, Washington, DC.

Driben, Paul, "On the Possibility of a Resettlement of Tibetan Refugees in Canada," report submitted to the Department of Manpower and Immigration, Prairie Regional Office, Winnipeg, Manitoba, September 1969.

"Estimate of Effectiveness of Anti-Communist Guerrilla Operations in China," *Joint Chiefs of Staff Geographic File (1951–1953),* REF. OM 519, 28 December 1950. National Archives, Military Branch, Washington, DC.

Foreign Broadcast Information Service (FBIS), U.S.A.

Henderson to Secretary of State, New Delhi, 23 July 1949, 893.00 Tibet/7–2349, National Archives, Diplomatic Branch, Washington, DC.

Hinton, Harold, "The Status of National Minorities in Communist China," USIA, IRI, Intelligence Survey (IS–63–55), July 1955, National Archives, Diplomatic Branch, Washington, DC.

India Office Library and Records (IORL), London, England.

Memo of conversation between two U.S. Consular officials and Major Bahadur, Calcutta, 14 December 1949, 893.00 Tibet/11–949, National Archives, Diplomatic Branch, Washington, DC.

Memo of conversation, Washington, DC, 28 November 1949, 893.00 Tibet/11–2849, National Archives, Diplomatic Branch, Washington, DC.

George Merrell to Secretary of State, New Delhi, 9 December 1946. Main Decimal File (1945–49) Box 7024, 893.00 Tibet/12–946, National Archives, Diplomatic Branch, Washington, DC.

Office of Intelligence Research "Tibet," No. 4731, 19 July 1948, National Archives, Diplomatic Branch, Washington, DC.

OSS, Lincoln C. Brownell, Assistant Military Attache for Air, U.S. Embassy, Chungking, "Recent Political Reports from Sikang Province," 2 May 1944; Report 76122 in National Archives, Diplomatic Branch, Washington, DC.

OSS, "Outline of Journey and Observation Made by Ilia Tolstoy, Captain AUS and Brooke Dolan, First Lt. AC," September 1943. In possession of Central Intelligence Agency, Roslyn, VA.

OSS, Research and Analysis Bureau, "China's Borderlands: Criteria for Claims," no. 2420, 7 August 1944, p. 7. National Archives, Diplomatic Branch, Washington, D.C.

OSS, Research and Analysis Bureau, "Survey of Tibet," No. 757, 1 October 1943, 2d ed. National Archives, Diplomatic Branch, Washington, D.C.

U.S. Consulate, Calcutta to Secretary of State, 14 December 1949, Main Decimal File, Box 7024, National Archives, Diplomatic Branch, Washington, DC.

U. S. Department of Justice, Foreign Agents Registration Unit, Registration No. 3301, 10 May 1992.

U.S. Department of State, "Policy Review Paper—Tibet," (c. 1949). (Declassified to author.)

U.S. Department of State and the U.S. Embassy in New Delhi, 793B.00/7–2151; 793B.11/9–1052, 793B.11/11–350, 7936.00/7–7151. National Archives, Diplomatic Branch, Washington, DC.

U.S. Department of State, Division of Research for the Far East, "Unrest in Tibet," no. 7341, 1 November 1956. National Archives, Diplomatic Branch, Washington, DC.

U.S. Embassy, London to Secretary of State, Washington, DC., 27 June 1947, 843.00 Tibet/6–2747, National Archives, Diplomatic Branch, Washington, DC.

Grady to Secretary of State, New Delhi, 2 December 1947, 893.00 Tibet/12–247; excerpts from the *Indian Monthly Intelligence Service,* 1 October 1947, National Archives, Diplomatic Branch, Washington, DC.

U.K. Foreign Office records in Public Records Office (PRO), Kew Gardens (London) England.

United Nations, General Assembly, 5th Session, 1950, *Official Records* (A/1534 and A/1549) annex, vol. 1, pp. 16–18.

United Nations, General Assembly, *Official Records,* 14th Session, Plenary Meetings (1959), 20–21 October 1959, A/4234, A/4848, pp. 469–530.

UN High Commissioner for Refugees (UNHCR), *Annual Report, 1969,* A/AC.96/396, Section XI-India, Section XIV—Nepal.

United Nations High Commissioner for Refugees, *Annual Report, 1970* A/AC.96/277, Section XIII—Nepal.

Fraser Wilkins to Secretary of State, New Delhi, 7 June 1951 and 14 June 1951. (Declassified to author.)

Books

Academy of Sciences, Mongolian People's Republic, ed., *Information Mongolia* (Oxford/New York: Pergamon Press, 1990).

Afro-Asian Convention on Tibet and Against Colonialism in Asia and Africa (New Delhi: Afro-Asian Council, 1960).

Ahmad, Zahiruddin, *China and Tibet, 1708–1959. A Resume of Facts* (Oxford: Oxford University Press, 1960).

Andrugstang, Gampo Tashi, *Four Rivers, Six Ranges: Reminiscences of the Resistance Movement in Tibet* (Dharamsala, India: Information and Publicity Office of His Holiness the Dalai Lama, 1973).

Aris, Michael and Aung San Sui Kyi, *Tibetan Studies in Honour of H.E. Richardson* (Warminster: Aris and Phillips, 1979).

Avedon, John F., *In Exile From The Land of Snows. The First Full Account of The Dalai Lama and Tibet Since The Chinese Conquest* (New York: Alfred A. Knopf, 1984).

Aziz, Barbara Nimri, *Tibetan Frontier Families, Reflections of Three Generations from Ding-ri* (New Delhi: Vikas Publishing House, 1978).

Bachrack, Stanley D. *The Committee of One Million: "China Lobby" Politics, 1953–1971* (New York: Columbia University Press, 1976).

Barber, Noel, *From the Land of Lost Content: The Dalai Lama's Fight for Tibet* (Boston: Houghton Mifflin, 1970).

Barnett, A. Doak, *China in the Eve of Communist Takeover* (New York, London and Washington, DC: Frederick A. Praeger, 1968).

Barnett, Robert and Shirin Akiner, eds., *Resistance and Reform in Tibet* (Bloomington: Indiana University Press, 1994)

Beckwith, Christopher I., *The Tibetan Empire in Central Asia. A History of the Struggle for Great Power Among the Tibetans, Turks, Arabs, and Chinese During The Early Middle Ages* (Princeton: Princeton University Press, 1993).

Bell, Sir Charles, *Portrait of the Dalai Lama* (London: Collins, 1946).

————. *The People of Tibet* (Oxford: At the Clarendon Press, 1928).

————. *Tibet Past and Present* (London: Oxford University Press, 1927).

Bennett, Gordon, *Huadong: The Story of a Chinese People's Commune* (Boulder, CO and Folkestone, UK: Westview Press, 1978).

Bishop, Peter, *The Myth of Shangri-La. Tibet, Travel Writing and the Western Creation of Sacred Landscape* (Berkeley: University of California Press, 1989).

Brandt, Conrad, Benjamin Schwartz and John K. Fairbank, eds., *A Documentary History of Chinese Communism* (New York: Athenaeum, 1960)

Bull, Geoffrey T. *Forbidden Land: A Saga of Tibet* (Chicago: Moody Press, 1967).

Burman, Bina Roy, *Religion and Politics in Tibet* (New Delhi: Vikas Publishing House, 1979).

Cameron, James, *Point of Departure: An Attempt at Autobiography* (New York: McGraw Hill, 1967).

Cammann, Schuyler, *Trade Through the Himalayas: The Early British Attempt to Open Tibet* (Princeton, NJ: Princeton University Press, 1951).

Caroe, Sir Olaf, *Englishmen in Tibet: From Bogle to Gould* (London: A Tibet Society Publication, 1960).

Carrasco, Pedro, *Land and Polity in Tibet* (Seattle and London: University of Washington Press, 1959).

Cayley, Vyvyan, *Children of Tibet: An Oral History of the First Tibetans to Grow Up in Exile* (Balmain, Australia: Pearlfisher Publishers, 1994).

Chang Chih-i, *The Party and the National Question in China* trans. by George Moseley (Cambridge, MA and London: The MIT Press, 1968).

Chang, Gordon H., *Friends and Enemies. The United States, China and the Soviet Union, 1948–1972* (Stanford: Stanford University Press, 1990).

Chapman, Frederick Spencer, *Lhasa The Holy City* (New York and London: Harper and Brothers, 1939).

Chen Han-seng, *Frontier Land Systems in Southwestern China* (New York: Institute for Pacific Relations, 1949).

Cheng Te-k'un and D. Michael Sullivan, *An Introduction to Tibetan Culture* (Chengtu: West China Union University Museum, 1945), Guidebook No. 6.

China in Development (Peking: China Council for the Promotion of International Trade, [1976?]).

China: The March Towards Unity (New York: Workers Library Publishers, 1937).

Choedon, Dhondup, *Life in the Red Flag Commune* (Dharamsala, India: The Information Office of His Holiness the Dalai Lama, 1978).

Clark, Leonard, *The Marching Wind* (New York: Funk & Wagnalls, 1954).

Coelho, V.H., *Sikkim and Bhutan* (New Delhi: Vikas, 1970).

Combe, G.A., *A Tibetan on Tibet. Being the Travels and Observations of Mr. Paul Sherap (Dorje Zoelba) of Tachienlu: With an Introductory Chapter on the Devil Dance* (New York: D. Appleton, 1926).

Concerning the Question of Tibet (Peking: Foreign Languages Press, 1959).

Conde, David W. *CIA-Core of the Cancer* (New Delhi: Entente Private, 1979).

Constitution of Tibet, Promulgated by His Holiness the Dalai Lama, 10 March 1963 (New Delhi: Bureau of His Holiness the Dalai Lama, 1963).

Dalai Lama, His Holiness The, *Collected Statements, Interviews and Articles* (Dharamsala: The Information Office of His Holiness the Dalai Lama, 1982).

Dalai Lama, *Freedom in Exile. The Autobiography of the Dalai Lama* (New York: A Cornelia & Michael Bessie Book, HarperCollins, 1990).

———. *The Autobiography of His Holiness the Dalai Lama of Tibet* (London: A Panther Book, 1964).

Dallin, David J., *The Rise of Russia in Asia* (New Haven: Archon Books, 1971).

Das, Sarat Chandras, *Indian Pundits in the Land of Snow* (Calcutta: Firma K.L. Mukhopadhyay, 1965).

Das, Taraknath, *British Expansion in Tibet* (Calcutta: N.M. Raychowdhury, 1929).

David-Neel, Alexandra, *Initiations and Initiates in Tibet,* trans. by Fred Rothwell (New York: University Books, 1959).

———. *Magic and Mystery in Tibet* (Baltimore: Penguin Books, 1971).

De Nebesky-Wojkowitz, Rene, *Oracles and Demons of Tibet: The Cult and Iconography of the Tibetan Protective Deities* (S-Gravenhage, Netherlands: Mouton, 1956).

Dennett, Raymond and Robert K. Turner, eds. *Documents on American Foreign Relations, vol. XII, January 1–December 31, 1950* (Princeton, NJ: Princeton University Press, 1951).

de Riencourt, Amaury, *Roof of the World: Tibet, Key to Asia* (New York: Rinehart, 1950).

Dolkar, Tseten, *Girl from Tibet* (Chicago: Loyola University Press, 1971).

Douglas, William O., *Beyond the High Himalayas* (Garden City, NY: Doubleday, 1952).

Dreyer, June Treufel, *China's Forty Millions* (Cambridge and London: Harvard University Press, 1976).

Duncan, Marion H., *Customs and Superstitions of Tibetans* (London: Mitre Press, 1964).

Ekvall, Robert B., *Cultural Relations on the Kansu-Tibet Border* (Chicago: Chicago University Press, 1939).

———. *Fields on the Hoof: Nexus of Nomadic Pastoralism in Tibet* (New York: Holt, Reinhart and Winston, 1968).

———. *Religious Observances in Tibet: Patterns and Functions* (Chicago and London: Chicago University Press, 1964).

Enders, Gordon, *Foreign Devil: An American Kim in Modern Asia* (New York: Simon and Schuster, 1942).

Enders, Gordon and Edward Anthony, *Nowhere Else in the World* (New York: Farrer and Rineheart, 1935).

Epstein, Israel, *Tibet Transformed* (Peking: New World Press, 1983).

Epstein, Lawrence and Richard D. Sherburne, eds., *Reflections in Tibetan Culture. Essays in Memory of Turrell V. Wylie* (Lewiston, NY: The Edwin Mellin Press, 1990).

Evans-Wentz, W.Y. ed., *The Tibetan Book of the Dead* (London, Oxford, and New York: Oxford University Press, 1960).

Fairbank, John D., ed., *The Cambridge History of China. Volume 10. Late Ch'ing, 1800–1911, Part I* (Cambridge: Cambridge University Press 1978).

Fisher, James F., *Himalayan Anthropology. The Indo-Tibetan Interface* (The Hague: Mouton Publishers, 1978).

Fleming, Peter, *Bayonets to Lhasa* (New York: Harper and Brothers, 1961).

Ford, Robert W., *Wind Between the Worlds* (New York: David McKay, 1957).

Foreign Relations of the United States, 1943, China (Washington, DC: U.S. Government Printing Office, 1967).

Foreign Relations of the United States, 1944, vol. VI. China (Washington, DC: U.S. Government Printing Office, 1967).

Foreign Relations of the United States, 1947, vol. VII, The Far East: China (Washington, DC: U.S. Government Printing Office, 1972).

Foreign Relations of the United States, 1948, vol. VII, The Far East: China (Washington, DC: U.S. Government Printing Office, 1973).

Foreign Relations of the United States, 1949, vol. IX, The Far East: China (Washington, DC: U.S. Government Printing Office, 1974).

Foreign Relations of the United States, 1950, vol. VI, East Asia and the Pacific (Washington, DC: U.S. Government Printing Office, 1976).

Foreign Relations of the United States, 1951, vol. VI, Asia and the Pacific, Part II (Washington, DC: U.S. Government Printing Office, 1977).

French, Rebecca Redwood, *The Golden Yoke. The Legal Cosmology of Buddhist Tibet* (Ithaca, NY: Cornell University Press, 1995).

Frolic, Michael B., *Mao's People: Sixteen Portraits of Life in Revolutionary China* (Cambridge, MA: Harvard University Press, 1980).

Gelder, Stuart and Roma, *The Timely Rain: Travels in New Tibet* (New York: Monthly Review Press, 1965).

Gilbert, Rodney, ed., *Genocide in Tibet: A Study in Communist Aggression* (New York: American-Asian Educational Exchange [1959?]).

Ginsburg, George and Michael Mathos *Communist China and Tibet: The First Dozen Years* (The Hague: Martinus Nijhoff, 1964).

Glimpses of Tibet Today (Dharamsala, India: Information Office of His Holiness the Dalai Lama, 1978).

Goldstein, Melvyn C., *A History of Modern Tibet, 1913–1951. The Decline of the Lamaist State* (Berkeley, University of California Press, 1989).

Goldstein, Melvyn C. and Cynthia M. Beall, *Nomads of Western Tibet. The Survival of a Way of Life* (Berkeley: University of California Press, 1990).

Gould, Sir Basil J., *The Jewel in the Lotus. Recollections of an Indian Political* (London: Chatto and Windus, 1957).

———. *Report by Mr. B.J. Gould, C.M.E., C.I.E., Political Officer in Sikkim, On the Discovery, Recognition and Installation of the Fourteenth Dalai Lama* (New Delhi: Government of India Press, 1941).

Great Changes in Tibet (Peking: Foreign Languages Press, 1972).

Guldin, Geg and Aidan Southall, eds., *Urban Anthropology in China* (Leiden: E.J.Brill, 1993).

Hambley, Gavin, ed., *Central Asia* (New York: Delacorte Press, 1969).

Han Suyin, *Lhasa the Open City: A Journey to Tibet* (New York: G.P. Putnam's, 1977).

Harrer, Heinrich, *Seven Years in Tibet* (London: Rupert Hart-Davis, 1953).

Havnevik, Hanna, *Tibetan Buddhist Nuns. History, Cultural Norms and Social Reality* (Oslo: Norwegian University Press, 1989?).

Hicks, Rogers and Ngakpa Chogyam, *Great Ocean. An Authorized Biography of the Buddhist Monk Tenzin Gyatso, His Holiness the Fourteenth Dalai Lama* (Longmead, UK: Element Books, 1984).

Higgens, Rosalyn, *The Development of International Law Through the Political Organs of the United Nations* (London: Oxford University Press, 1963).

Hilsman, Roger, *To Move a Nation: The Politics of Foreign Policy in the Administration of John F. Kennedy* (Garden City, NY: Doubleday, 1967).

Hoffman, Helmut, ed., *Tibet: A Handbook* (Bloomington: Area Studies Research Institute, 1976?).

Hsi Chan-kao and Kao Yuan-mei, *Tibet Leaps Forward* (Peking: Foreign Languages Press, 1977).

Hu Tan, ed., *Thesis on Tibetology in China* (Beijing: China Tibetology Publishing House, 1991).

Hutheesing, Raja, ed., *A White Book, Tibet Fights for Freedom: The Story of the March 1959 Uprising as Recorded in Documents, Dispatches, Eyewitness Accounts and World-Wide Reactions* (Bombay, Calcutta, Madras and New Delhi: Orient Longmans, 1960).

Ihara Shoren and Yamaguchi Zuiho, eds., *Tibetan Studies: Proceedings of the 5th Seminar of the International Association For Tibetan Studies* (Narita: Naritasan Shinshoji, 1992).

India, Tibet and China (Bombay: Democratic Research Service, 1959).

Ingram, Paul, *Tibet. The Facts* (Dharamsala: Tibetan Young Buddhist Association, 1990).

Jain, Girlal, *Panscheela and After: A Re-Appraisal of Sino-Indian Relations in the Context of the Tibetan Insurrection* (New York: Asia Publishing House, 1960).

Jin Zhou, ed., *Tibet: No Longer Medieval* (Peking: Foreign Languages Press, 1981).

Jing Wei, *100 Questions About Tibet* (Beijing: Beijing Review Press, 1989).

Kane, Anthony, ed., *China Briefing. 1990* (New York: The Asia Society, 1990).

Kao, Ting Tsz, *The Chinese Frontiers* (Aurora, IL: Chinese Scholarly Publishing, 1980).

Karan, Pradyumna P., *The Changing Face of Tibet. The Impact of Communist Ideology on the Landscape* (Lexington: University of Kentucky Press, 1976).

Khyongla Nawang Losang, Rato, *My Life and Lives. The Story of a Tibetan Incarnation* (New York: E. P. Dutton, 1977).

Klieger, P. Christiaan, *Tibetan Nationalism. The Role of Patronage in the Accomplishment of a National Identity* (Meerut, India: Archana Publications, 1992).

Knight, G.E.O., *Intimate Glimpses of Mysterious Tibet and Neighbouring Countries* (London: Golden Vista Press, 1930).

Kolb, Albert, *East Asia: China, Japan, Korea, Vietnam: Geography of a Cultural Region*, trans. C.A.M. Sym (London: Methuen, 1971).

Kolmăs, Josef, *Tibet and Imperial China: A Survey of Sino-Tibetan Relations up to the End of the Manchu Dynasty in 1912* (Canberra: Australian National University, Center for Oriental Studies, 1976).

Krull, Germaine, ed., *Tibetans in Exile* (Bombay: Allied, 1968).

Kvaerne, Per, *Tibetan Studies. proceedings of the 6th Seminar of the International Association for Tibetan Studies, Fagernes, 1992* (Oslo: The Institute for Comparative Research in Human Culture, 1994), 2 volumes.

Lal, K.S., ed., *Studies in Asian History: Proceedings of the Asian History Congress, 1961* (New York: Asia Publishing House, 1969).

Lamb, Alastair, *Britain and Chinese Central Asia* (London: Routledge and Kegan Paul, 1960).

———. *The McMahon Line: A Study in the Relations Between India, China and Tibet, 1904–1914* (London: Routledge and Kegan Paul, 1966), 2 vols.

Lang-Sims, Lois, *The Presence of Tibet* (London: Cresset Press, 1963).

Laufer, Berthold, *Uses of Human Skulls and Bones in Tibet* (Chicago: Field Museum of Natural History, 1928).

Lee Wei Kuo, *Tibet in Modern World Politics (1774–1922)* (New York: Columbia University Press, 1931).

Legal Inquiry Committee, *The Question of Tibet and the Rule of Law* (Geneva: International Commission of Jurists, 1959).

———. *Tibet and the Chinese People's Republic* (Geneva: International Commission of Jurists, 1960).

316 • BIBLIOGRAPHY

Li Tieh-tseng, *Tibet Today and Yesterday* (New York: Bookman Associates, 1960).

Ling Nai-min, ed., *Tibet: 1950–1967* (Hong Kong: Union Research Institute, 1968).

Lo Hui-min, ed., *The Correspondence of G.E. Morrison, vol. II, 1919–1920* (Cambridge: Cambridge University Press, 1978).

Loup, Robert, *Martyr in Tibet: The Heroic Life and Death of Father Maurice Tournay, St. Bernard Missionary to Tibet* (New York: David McKay, 1956).

MacDonald, David, *The Land of the Lamas* (London: Seeley, Service, 1929).

———. *Tibet* (London: Humphrey Milford for the Oxford University Press, 1945).

———. *Twenty Years in Tibet* (Philadelphia: J.B. Lippincott, 1932).

Mackerras, Colin, *China's Minorities. Integration and Modernization in the Twentieth Century* (Hong Kong: Oxford University Press, 1994).

Mao Tse-t'ung, *Selected Works of Mao Tse-tung*, vol. III (Peking: Foreign Languages Press, 1965).

———. *Selected Works of Mao Tse-tung*, vol. V (Peking: Foreign Languages Press, 1977).

———. *The Secret Speeches of Chairman Mao. From the Hundred Flowers to the Great Leap Forward*, Edited by Roderick MacFarquhar et. al. (Cambridge, MA: Harvard University Press, 1989).

Maraini, Fosco, *Secret Tibet*, trans. by Eric Mosbacher (New York: Grove Press, 1960).

Mayers, David Allan, *Cracking the Monolith. U. S. Policy Against the Sino-Soviet Alliance, 1949–1955* (Baton Rouge and London: Louisiana State University Press, 1986).

Maxwell, Neville, *India's China War* (Garden City, NY: Anchor Books, 1972).

Mehra, Parshotam, *Tibetan Polity 1904–1937. The Conflict Between the 13th Dalai Lama and the 9th Panchen Lama* (Weisbaden: Otto Harrassowitz, 1976).

Millington, Powell, *To Lhasa at Last* (London: Smith, Elder, 1905).

Mullik, B.N., *My Years with Nehru: The Chinese Betrayal* (Bombay: Allied Publishers, 1971).

Murphy, Dervla, *Tibetan Foothold* (Levittown, NY: Transatlantic Arts, 1966).

Nimkoff, M.F., ed.,*Comparative Family Systems* (Boston: Houghton, Mifflin, 1965).

Norbu, Dawa, *Red Star Over Tibet* (London: William Collins, 1974).

Norbu, Jamyang, *Horseman in the Snow, The Story of Aten, An Old Khampa Warrior* (Dharamsala, India: Information Office, Central Tibetan Secretariat, 1979).

Norbu, Thubten Jigme, *Tibet is My Country: The Autobiography of Thubten Jigme Norbu, Brother of the Dalai Lama* as told to Heinrich Harrer, trans. by Edward Fitzgerald (New York: E.P. Dutton, 1961).

Norbu, Thubten and Colin M. Turnbull, *Tibet* (New York: Simon and Schuster, 1968).

Palakshappa, T.C., *Tibetans in India: A Case Study of the Mundgod Tibetans* (New Delhi: Sterling, 1978).

Paljor, Kunsang, *Tibet: The Undying Flame* (Dharamsala, India: Information and Publicity Office of His Holiness the Dalai Lama, 1977).

Pallis, Marco, *Peaks and Lamas* (London: Woburn Books, 1974).

Panikkar, K.M., *In Two Chinas: Memories of a Diplomat* (London: George Allen & Unwin, 1955).

Patterson, George N., *A Fool at Forty* (Waco, TX and London: Word Books, 1970).

———. *Journey with Loshay* (New York: W.W. Norton, 1954).

———. *Peking versus Delhi* (London and New York: Frederick A. Praeger, 1963).

———. *Requiem for Tibet* (London: Aurum Press, 1990).

———. *Tibet in Revolt* (London: Faber & Faber, 1960).

Peissel, Michel, *Mustang, the Forbidden Kingdom: Exploring a Lost Himalayan Land* (New York: E.P. Dutton, 1967).

Peissel, Michel, *The Secret War in Tibet* (Boston and Toronto: Little, Brown, 1972).

Pemba, Tsewang Y., *Young Days in Tibet* (London: Jonathan Cape, 1957).

Perry-Ayscough H.G.C. and Captain R.B. Otter-Barry, *With the Russians in Mongolia* (London: John Larger, The Bodley Head, 1914).

Petech, Luciano, *Aristocracy and Government in Tibet, 1728–1959* (Roma: Istituto Italiano Per Il Medio Ed Estremo Orient, 1973).

———. *China and Tibet in the Early 19th Century. History of the Establishment of a Chinese Protectorate in Tibet* (Leiden: E.J. Brill, 1972).

Pinkerton, John, *A General Collection of the Best and the Most Intriguing Voyages and Travels in All Parts of the World* (London: Longman, Hurst, Rees, Orme and Brown, Paternoster-Row, and Caldwell and Davis in the Strand, 1811).

Policies Towards Nationalities of the People's Republic of China (Peking: Foreign Languages Press, 1953).

Prados, John, *Presidents' Secret Wars. CIA and Pentagon Covert Operations Since World War II* (New York: William Morrow and Compnay, Inc., 1986).

Pranavanada, Swami, *Exploration in Tibet* (Calcutta: University of Calcutta, 1939).

Prouty, L. Fletcher, *The Secret Team: The CIA and Its Allies in Control of the United States and the World* (Englewood Cliffs, NJ: Prentice-Hall, 1973).

Rahul, Ram, *The Government and Politics of Tibet* (New Delhi: Vikas Publications, 1969).

Ranelagh, John, *The Agency. The Rise and Decline of the CIA* (London: Weidenfeld and Nicolson, 1986).

Richardson, Hugh H., *A Short History of Tibet* (New York: E.P. Dutton, 1962).

Rock, Joseph R., *The Amnye-ma-Chhen Range and Adjacent Regions: A Monographic Study* (Rome: Instituto Italiano Per Il Medio Ed Estreme Oriente, 1956).

Rockhill, William Woodville, *Diary of a Journey Through Mongolia and Tibet in 1891 and 1892* (Washington, DC: Smithsonian Institution, 1894).

———. *The Land of the Lamas: Notes of a Journey Through China, Mongolia and Tibet* (New York: Century, 1891).

Romanus,Charles F. and Riley Sunderland, *United States Army in World War II. China-Burma-Indian Theatre. Stilwell's Mission to China* (Washington, DC: Office of the Chief of Military History, Department of the Army, 1953).

Rositzke, Harry, *The CIA's Secret Operations: Espionage, Counterespionage, and Covert Action* (New York: Reader's Digest Press, 1977).

Sandberg, Graham, *The Exploration of Tibet: History and Particulars* (New Delhi: Cosmo Publications, 1973).

Schwartz, Ronald D., *Circle of Protest. Political Ritual in the Tibetan Uprising* (New York: Columbia University Press, 1994).

Scott, A. MacCallum, *The Truth About Tibet* (London: Simpkin, Marshall, Hamilton, Kent, 1905).

Senanayake, Ratne Deshapriya, *Inside Story of Tibet* (Colombo: Afro-Asian Writer's Bureau, 1967).

Shabad, Theodore, *China's Changing Map. National and Regional Development, 1949–1971* (New York: Praeger, 1972).

Shah, A.B., *India's Defense and Foreign Policies* (Bombay: Manaktala, 1966).

Shakabpa, Tsepon W., *Tibet: A Political History* (New Haven and London: Yale University Press, 1967).

Shelton, Albert L., *Pioneering in Tibet* (New York, London and Edinburgh: Fleming H. Revell, 1921).

Shên Tsung-lien and Liu Shen-chi, *Tibet and the Tibetans* (New York: E.P. Dutton, 1977).

Siks, David Ll, ed., *International Encyclopedia of the Social Services* (New York: Crowell, Collier and Macmillan, 1968).

Sinclair, William Boyd, *Jump to the Land of God. The Adventures of a United States Air Force Crew in Tibet* (Caldwell, Ohio: Caxton Printers, 1965).

Sinha, Nirmal Chandra, *Tibet: Considerations on Inner Asian History* (Calcutta: Firma K.L. Mukhapadhyay, 1967).

Smith, Huston, *The Religions of Man* (New York: Harper & Row, 1958).

Smith, R. Harris, *OSS. The Secret History of America's First Central Intelligence Agency* (Berkeley, Los Angeles and London: University of California Press, 1972).

Snelling, John, *Buddhism in Russia. The Story of Agvan Dorzhiev, Lhasa's Emissary to the Tsar* (Longmean, UK: Element Books, Ltd. 1993).

Stein, R.A., *Tibetan Civilization,* trans. by J.E. Stapleton Driver (Stanford: Stanford University Press, 1972).

Strong, Anna Louise, *Tibetan Interviews* (Peking: New World Press, 1959).

————. *When Serfs Stood Up In Tibet* (Peking: New World Press, 1965) 2d ed.

Tada Tōkan, *The Thirteenth Dalai Lama* (Tokyo: The Center for East Asian Cultural Studies, 1965).

Taring, Rinchen Dolma, *Daughter of Tibet* (London: John Murray, 1970).

Teichman, Eric, *Travels of a Consular Officer in Eastern Tibet* (Cambridge: Cambridge University Press, 1922).

The Constitution of the People's Republic of China (Peking: Foreign Languages Press, 1954).

The Constitution of the People's Republic of China (Peking: Foreign Languages Press, 1975).

The Constitution of the People's Republic of China (Peking: Foreign Languages Press, 1978).

The Tibet Revolution and the Free World (Taipei: Asian People's Anti-Communism League, 1959).

Thomas, Evan, *The Very Best Men. Four Who Dared: The Early Years of the CIA* (New York: Simon & Schuster, 1995).

Thomas, Lowell Jr., *Out of This World: Across the Himalayas to Forbidden Tibet* (New York: Greystone Press, 1950).

————. *The Silent War in Tibet* (Garden City, NY: Doubleday, 1959).

Thubtob, Rev. Ngawang, *Tibet Today* (New Delhi: Bureau of His Holiness the Dalai Lama 1965?).

Tibet and Freedom (London: A Tibet Society Publication, 1969).

Tibet-Its Ownership and Human Rights Situation (Beijing: Information Office of the State Council of the People's Republic of China, 1992).

Tibet Support Group UK, *New Majority. Chinese Population Transfer into Tibet* (London: Tibet Support Group UK, 1995).

Tibet Under Chinese Communist Rule. A Compilation of Refugee Statements, 1958–1975 (Dharamsala, India: Information and Publicity Office of His Holiness the Dalai Lama, 1976).

Tibet Under the Dalai Lama, China Chronicle No. 5 (Peiping: The Peiping Chronicle, 1933).

Tibetan Refugee Community:Integrated Development Plan—II, 1995–2000 (Dharamsala: The Planning Council, May 1994).

Tibetans in Exile, 1959–1969 (Dharamsala, India: Office of His Holiness the Dalai Lama, 1969).

Trikamdas, Purshottam, *The Face of Communism* (New Delhi: A Praja Socialist Publication, undated).

Trungpa, Chogyam, *Born in Tibet* as told to Esmé Cramer Roberts (Baltimore: Penguin Books, 1971).

Tucci, Guiseppe, *The Religions of Tibet,* trans. by Geoffrey Samuel (Berkeley, CA: University of California Press, 1980).
————. *Tibet Land of Snows,* trans. by J.E. Stapleton Driver (London: Elek Books, 1967.)
Tung, Rosemary Jones, *A Portrait of Lost Tibet* (New York: Holt, Rinehart & Winston, 1980).
Turner, Capt. Samuel, *An Account of an Embassy to the Court of the Teshoo Lama in Tibet; containing a narrative of a journey through Bootan and part of Tibet* (London: W. Bulmer, 1800).
Uebach, Helga and Jampa L. Panglung, eds., *Tibetan Studies. Proceedings of the 4th Seminar of the International Association For Tibetan Studies* (Munchen: Kommission Für Zentralasiatische Studien, 1988).
Van Walt Van Praag, Michael, *The Status of Tibet. History, Rights, and Prospects in International Law* (Boulder: Westview Press, 1987).
Vostrikov, A.I., *Tibetan Historical Literature* translated by Harish Chandra Gupta (Calcutta: Indian Studies Past and Present, 1970).
Waller, Derek, *The Pundits. British Exploration of Tibet & Central Asia* (Lexington, KY: The University Press of Kentucky, 1990).
Wangdu, Sonam, *The Discovery of the XIVth Dalai Lama,* translated by Sonam Wangdu, et. al. (Bangkok: Klett Thai Publications, 1975).
Warner, Roger, *Back Fire. The CIA's Secret War in Laos and its Link to the War in Vietnam* (New York: Simon & Schuster, 1995).
Welch, Holmes, *Buddhism Under Mao* (Cambridge, MA: Harvard University Press, 1972).
Wiederkehr, Emil, *SOS Tibet* (Berne and Lausanne: Comité D'aide Aux Victimes du Communisme, 1960).
Wessels, Cornelius, *Early Jesuit Travellers in Central Asia, 1603–1721* (The Hague: Martinus Nijhoff, 1924).
Whiting, Allen S., *The Chinese Calculus of Deterrence, India and Indochina* (Ann Arbor: Michigan University Press, 1975).
Williamson, Margaret D., *Memoirs of a Political Officer's Wife in Tibet, Sikkim and Bhutan* (London: Wisdom Publications, 1987).
Winnington, Alan, *Tibet. Record of a Journey* (New York: International Publishers, 1957).
Wise, David, *The Politics of Lying: Government Deception, Secrecy and Power* (New York: Vintage Books, 1973).
Woodcock, George, *Into Tibet: The Early British Explorers* (London: Faber and Faber, 1971).
Woodman, Dorothy, *Himalayan Frontiers: A Political Review of British, Chinese, Indian and Russian Rivalries* (New York and Washington, DC: Frederick A. Praeger, 1969).
Woodward, David, *Detour from Tibet* (Chicago: Moody Press, 1976).
Wrath of the Serfs—A Group of Life-Size Clay Sculptures (Peking: Foreign Languages Press, 1976).
Ya Hanzhang, *The Biographies of the Dalai Lamas* (Beijing: Foreign Language Press, 1991).
Ying Ming, *United and Equal: The Progress of China's Minority Nationalities* (Peking: Foreign Languages Press, 1977).
Zhai, Qiang, *The Dragon, The Lion and the Eagle. Chinese/British/American Relations, 1949–1958* (Kent, OH: The Kent State University Press, 1994).

Articles

"10,000 Tibetans Are in Nepal," *New York Times* 18 April 1964, p. A25.
A correspondent, "Bhutan: The Go-It-Alone Blueprint," *Far Eastern Economic Review* 10 January 1975, p. 18.

A correspondent, "High Stakes," *Far Eastern Economic Review* 22 June 1995, pp. 76–80.

A correspondent, "Mustang: Forgotten Corner of Nepal," *Far Eastern Economic Review* 21 March 1975, pp. 24–25.

"A Journey Inside Tibet," *Asiaweek* 15 February 1980, pp. 8–10.

"A Tibetan Barefoot Doctor," *China Reconstructs* 23:9 (September 1974): 9–11.

Ahmad, Zahiruddin, "The Historical Status of China in Tibet," *Tibet Journal* 1:1 (July-September 1975): 24–35.

Ali, Salamat and Robert Delfs, "One Game, Two Courts," *Far Eastern Economic Review* 6 October 1988, p. 33.

Alley, Rewi, "Among the Tibetans and Chiang," *Eastern Horizons* 12:5 (1973): 17–42.

Allman, T.D., "A Half Forgotten Conflict," *Far Eastern Economic Review* 11 February 1974, p. 27.

Allman, T.D.,"Cold Wind of Change," *Guardian* 19 December 1973, p. 11.

American Emergency Committee for Tibetan Refugees Newsletter 1 February 1966,

"Among the Tibetan Nomads," *North China Herald* 14 March 1944, pp. 766–767.

An Zhiguo, "Policy Toward the Dalai Lama," *Beijing Review* 25 (15 November 1982): 3–4.

———. "Tibet Carries Out New Policies," *Beijing Review* 27 (21 May 1984): 4–5.

———. "Tibet. New Policies Bring Changes," *Beijing Review* 27 (15 October 1984): 4–5.

Anderson, Jack, "A Toll of Dirty Tricks," *Washington Post* 24 April 1977, p. C7.

Andersson, Jan, "Chinese Colonel Who Became a Tibetan Refugee," *Tibetan Review* 14:10 (October 1979): 21–22.

———. "Importance of Dalai Lama's U.S. Visit," *Tibetan Review* 14:12 (December 1979): 14–16.

"Another Visitor Confirms Poor Conditions in Tibet," *Tibetan Review* 14:11 (November 1975): 5.

"Anti-Red Revolt in Tibet is Growing, Li Says," *Free China And Asia* 5:12 (December 1958): 20.

"Any Support Is Welcome," *Asiaweek* 26 August 1977, pp. 22–23.

Archives of the Tibet Autonomous Region, "Identifying the·Reincarnated Bainqen," *Beijing Review* 38 (11–17 September 1995): 7–10.

"Artists to Take Part in Tibet House Benefit," *New York Times* 17 May 1988, p. C16.

"Australia Passes Tibet Resolution," *Tibetan Bulletin* (January-February 1991): 5.

Baker, Philip, "A Long Slow Process," *Human Rights Tribune* 3:3 (Fall 1992): 14–16.

Banerjee, Sudhansu Mohan, "A Forgotten Chapter on Indo-Tibetan Contact: A Further Review," *Calcutta Review* 123:1 (April 1952): 29–36.

Banqen Erdeni Qoigyi Gyancen, "A Great Turning Point for the Development and Prosperity of the Tibetan Nationality," *Radio Peking* 23 May 1981 in *FBIS* OW241912, 28 May 1981, p. Q1.

Barber, Noel, "Brave and Lost: The Tragic Fall of Tibet," *Reader's Digest* 96:574 (February 1970): 205–248.

———. "Noel Barber Moves up to the 'end of the line' as Dalai Lama prepares for the next lap of freedom," *Daily Mail* 6 April 1959, p. 1.

Bartley, Robert L., "Tibet: Roof of the World," *Wall Street Journal* 22 September 1976, p. 20.

Beaufort-Palmer, F.N., "Moral Indignation and Tibet," *The Tibet Society and Relief Fund of the UK Newsletter* Spring 1981, p. 6.

Becker, Jasper, "Deputy abbot held over Panchen Lama," *South China Morning Post* 30 May 1995.

"Becoming Well-Off Through Collective Strength," *Beijing Review* 23 (18 August 1980): 4–5.

Bell, Sir Charles, "A Year in Lhasa," *Geographical Journal* 63 (February 1924): 89–105.

————. "China and Tibet," *Journal of the Royal Central Asian Society* 36:1 (January 1949): 54–57.

————. "The Dalai Lama, Lhasa 1921," *Journal of the Royal Central Asiatic Society* 11:1 (January 1924): 36–52.

————. "Tibet and Her Neighbours," *Pacific Affairs* 10:4 (December 1937): 428–440.

Bessac, Frank, "This Was the Perilous Trek to Tragedy," *Life* 13 November 1950, pp. 130–136, 138, 141.

"Bhutan King in Tibet Crisis," *Tibetan Review* 14:2 (February 1979): 7.

"Big Changes on Estate of Tibetan Lords," *Xinhua Weekly* 30 June 1979, p. 12.

Billington, John, "A Visit to Mundgod, South India," *The Tibet Society and Relief Fund of the UK Newsletter* Summer 1981, pp. 13–17.

Binstein, Michael, "The Hit List: D.C. Law," *The Washington Post*, 14 July 1991, p. W7.

Binstein, Michael et. al. "The Power Elite," *Regardies. The Business of Washington* 9:5 (January 1989).

Black, C.E.D., "The Trade and Resources of Tibet," *Journal of the East Indian Association* 41, new series no. 48 (October 1908): 1–19.

Bonavia, David, "Mistakes on the Roof of the World," *Far Eastern Economic Review* 8 August 1980, p. 16.

Bormanshinov, Arasjj, "A Secret Kalmyk Mission to Tibet in 1904," *Central Asian Journal* 36:3–4 (1992): 161–187.

Bradsher, Henry S., "Tibet Struggles to Survive," *Foreign Affairs* 47:4 (July 1969): 750–762.

"British Parliamentary Committee of Tibet Formed," *Tibetan Review* 22:4 (April 1987): 7–8.

"British Parliamentary Group for Tibet," *Tibetan Review* 4:9 (September 1989): 7.

"Brother of the Dalai Lama Arrives Here to Study," *New York Times* 9 July 1951, p. 8.

Brown, Muriel Percy, "A Welcome Guest in Forbidden Tibet," *Asia* 22:3 (March 1927): 179–185.

"Brutal 'Modernization' of Tibet," *Christian Science Monitor* 13 August 1960, p. 18.

Burang, Theodore, "Report from Tibet," *The Canadian Forum* 30: 362 (March 1951): 272–273.

Bushell, S.W., "The Early History of Tibet from Chinese Sources," *Journal of the Royal Asiatic Society* 12 (1880): 434–541.

Butterfield, Fox, "China's Congress Ending, Appoints Three Deputy Premiers," *New York Times* 11 September 1980, p. 1.

Carlson, Jude, "Tibet in the News," *Bulletin of Concerned Asian Studies* 24:2 (1992): 25–42.

Central Executive Committee, Tibetan Youth Congress, "Tibetan Refugees in Bhutan and Subsequent Developments," *Tibet Society and Tibet Relief Fund of the UK Newsletter* Autumn 1979, pp. 9–12.

Chang Kuo-hua, "Work on the Tibet Region," *Renmin Ribao* 21 September 1956 in *Current Background* 418 (11 October 1956): 18–23.

Chang Sen, "Democratic Reform: The Road to Happiness," *Peking Review* 24 (16 June 1959): 12–14.

"Changing Life of Lamas in Tibet," *Xinhua* 24 March 1979, p. 16.

Chapman, F.S., "Lhasa in 1937," *The Geographic Journal* 91:6 (June 1938): 497–507.

Chen Muhua, "Controlling Population Growth in a Planned Way," *Beijing Review* 46 (16 November 1979):17–20.

Cheng Hsiang, "Changes in Central Policies in Xizang," *Wen Wei Pao* (Hong Kong), 8 October 1983 in *FBIS* HK121221, 14 October 1983, pp. W4-W5.

"China Accused of Killing 65,000 Tibetans," *Times* 6 June 1959, p. 6.

"China Blames Tibetan Poverty on Numbers," *United Press International* 23 November 1995.

"China Calls Tibetan Exiles to 'Return Home,' " *Tibetan Review* 10:1 (January 1975): 15–16.

"China Increases Investment for Tibetan Agriculture and Animal Husbandry," *Xinhua Weekly* 30 June 1979, p. 20

"China Outlines Conditions for Dalai Lama's Return," *New York Times* 2 May 1977, p. 9.

"China Sore Over a 'Major' Tibetan Victory," *Tibetan Review* 27:1 (January 1992): 8.

"China's Hungary,"*Economist* 4 April 1959, pp. 16–17.

"Chinese Dissident Organization Supports Tibetans," *Tibetan Review* 20:7 (July 1985): 7–8.

"Chinese May Be Losing Their Grip on Tibet," *Economist* 6 October 1973, pp. 37–38.

"Chinese Nationalists Report Attacks on Mainland Posts," *New York Times* 8 April 1969, p. 8.

Choephill, Ngawang, "Time for Action," *Tibetan Review* 21:9–10 (September-October 1986): 4–5.

Chopra, Wing Commander Majaraj K., "Red China Colonizes Tibet," *Military Review* 46:7 (July 1966): 52–60.

Chowdhury, Jyotirindra Nath, "British Contributions to the Confusion of Tibet's Status," *Quest* 54 (July-September 1967): 32–38.

Christie, C. J., "Sir Charles Bell: A Memoir," *Asian Affairs* 64:1 (February 1977): 48–62.

'Chronology of Events in Tibet, 1949–1959," *Hsi-tsang Ta Shih-chi* [Tibet Main Events Record] Peking, May 1959 in *JPRS* 831-D, 28 August 1959.

Chu Wen-lin, "The Tibet Autonomous Region Revolutionary Committee," *Issues and Studies* 5:3 (December 1968): 12–21.

Citron, Zachary, "Watchdogs That Purr: How not to set up an ethics commission," *The New Republic* 6 March 1989, p. 10.

Clubb, O.E., "The Old Order Passes in Tibet," *Eastern World* 13:8 (August 1959): 15–16.

———. "Tibet's Strategic Position," *Eastern World* 10:12 (December 1956): 18–19.

Colquhoun, Archibald R., "In the Heart of the Forbidden Country; or Lhasa Revealed," *The Cornhill Magazine* 14:1 (January 1903): 39–52.

Commanding Officer of the Tibet Military Region, "We Won't Permit You to Sabotage the Stability of Border Defense Units," 18 August 1967 in *JPRS* 44802, 25 March 1968.

"Communique on Rebellion in Tibet," *Peking Review* 2 (31 March 1959): 6–8.

"Conditions in Tibet and Tibetan Autonomous Areas," *Current Background* 409 (21 September 1956).

Connery, David S. "Waiting for the God King," *Atlantic* 205:3 (March 1960): 61–65.

"Constitution of the People's Republic of China," *Beijing Review* 52 (27 December 1982): 10–29.

Crosette, Barbara, "China Denies Visas to Two Senators," *New York Times* 7 April 1992, p. A7.

Crothall, Geoffrey, "Secret Meeting on Lama," *South China Morning Post* 7 November 1995.

"Cultural Revolution in Tibet Mainly Inter-Chinese Battle Says London Times,"*Tibetan Review* 1:12 (December 1968): 7.

"Dalai Lama Denounced as Traitor," *Peking Review* 52 (25 December 1964): 4–5.

"Dalai Lama in Germany," *Tibetan Review* 21:6 (June 1986): 6–7.

"Dalai Lama's Tour of Russia and Mongolia," *Tibetan Review* 14:6 (June 1979): 8–9.

"Dalai Lama's U.K. Visit Most Successful Yet," *Tibetan Review* 26:5 (May 1991): 6.

Dalai Lama, "H. H. The Dalai Lama's Speech to the Chinese Students and Scholars," Boston, 9 September 1995.

———. "Learn from the Soviet Union and Construct Our Socialist Fatherland," *Hsien-Tai Fo-hsueh* [Contemporary Buddhism] 13 December 1958 in *JPRS* 1461-N, 9 April 1959.

———. "Statement of His Holiness the Dalai Lama on the 22nd Anniversary of the Tibetan National Uprising Day," *Tibetan Review,* 16:3 (March 1981): 8.

———. "Strive for a Glorious Leap Forward in Tibet," *Xizang Ribao* 1 January 1959 in *JPRS* 951-D, 7 October 1959.

———. "The Dalai Lama Speaks His Mind," *Asian Wall Street Journal* 25 August 1977, p. 23.

"Danish Government Requested to Support Tibetan Cause," *Tibetan Review* 24:12 (December 1989): 5.

David-Neel, Alexandra, "Edge of Tibet," *Asia and the Americas* 44:1 (January 1944): 26–29.

David-Neel, Alexandra, "Lhasa at Last," *Asia* 26:7 (July 1926): 624–633, 644–646.

David-Neel, Alexandra, "Tibetan Border Intrigues, *Asia* 41:5 (May 1941): 219–222.

Davis, Derek, "Coups, Kings and Castles in the Sky," *Far Eastern Economic Review* 10 June 1974, pp. 26–27.

Davis, Derek, "Himalayan Honeymoon," *Far Eastern Economic Review* 24 June 1974, p. 35.

Davis, Grania, "Some Problems of Refugee Life—An Inside Look," *Tibetan Review* 13:1 (January 1978): 11–12, 21.

"Deceptive Preparations for the Nepalese King," *Tibetan Bulletin* 9:1 (March-April 1977): 1–4.

deFrancis, John, "National and Minority Policies, *The Annals of the American Academy of Political and Social Sciences: Report on China* 277 (September 1951): 146–155.

"Development of Tibet Under the People's Republic of China," *U.S.-China Review* 4:5 (September-October 1980): 16.

"Developments in the Tibetan Autonomous Region," *China Topics* YB 599, September 1976, p. 3.

de Voe, Dorsch Marie, "The Donden Ling Case: An Essay on Tibetan Refugee Life with Proposals for Change," *Tibet Society Bulletin* 14 (December 1979): 61–91. Also in *Tibetan Review* 15:4 (April 1980): 13–22.

"Dharamsala Delegation Visits Peking and Tibet," *Tibetan Review* 14:8 (August 1979): 7–8.

"Dharamsala Refutes New Chinese Claims," *Tibetan Review* 16:1 (January 1981): 4.

Dhondup, K., "Panchen Lama, the Enigmatic Tibetan," *Tibetan Review* 13:2–3 (February-March 1978): 13–17.

"Diplomacy and the Dalai Lama," *Far Eastern Economic Review* 18 March 1974, p. 32.

"Documents and Speeches on the Peaceful Liberation of Tibet," *People's China* 3:12, Supplement to 16 June 1951.

Dorjee, Tashi, "Education in Tibet," *Tibet Journal* 2 (1977): 31–37.

Dorji, Tsering, "A Guide to Tibet Today," *Tibetan Review* 11:5 (May 1976): 24–25.

Driver, N. "The Story of the Tibetan Bible," *The International Review of Missions* 40:158 (April 1951): 197–203.

Dunning, William, "The Mysteries and the Wonder of a Journey Through Tibet," *Holiday* 12:6 (December 1952): 54–57.

Durdin, Tillman, "Tibetans in Peril Dalai Lama Says," *New York Times* 21 June 1959, pp. 1, 25.

"Economics of Socialism," *Tibetan Bulletin* 13:5 (May 1978): 5–6.

Ekvall, Robert B. "Mis Tong: The Tibetan Custom of Life Indemnity," *Sociologus* 4:2 (1954): 136–145.

———. "Nomads of Tibet: A Chinese Dilemma," *Current Scene* 1:3 (23 September 1961): 1–10.

————. "Some Differences in Tibetan Land Tenure and Utilization," *Sinologica* 4:1 (1954): 39–48.

————. "The Nomadic Pattern of Living Among the Tibetans as Preparation for War," *American Anthropologist* 63:6 (December 1961): 1250–1263.

————. "Three Categories of Inmates Within Tibetan Monasteries: Status and Function," *Central Asiatic Journal* 5:3 (1960): 206–220.

————. "Tibetan Symposium: Law and the Individual Among the Tibetan Nomads," *American Anthropologist* 66:5 (October 1964): 1110–1115.

Epstein, Israel, "Serfs and Slaves Rule Khaesum Manor," *Eastern Horizon* 16:7 (July 1977): 21–35.

————. "Tibet Today," *Eastern Horizon* 5:1 (January 1966): 17–24.

————. "Tsering Pintso—People's Policeman in Lhasa," *Eastern Horizon* 16:9 (September 1977): 20–24, 29.

"Escape Over the Himalayas: How the Dalai Lama Did It," *US News & World Report* 20 April 1959, pp. 89–90.

"Facts in the Far Eastern Dust," *Economist* 19 November 1949, p. 1130.

Faison, Seth, "Ignoring Dalai Lama's Choice, China Installs Cleric in Tibet,"*New York Times* 30 November 1995, p. A18.

Fan Cheuk-wan, "Dalai Lama 'Accused' of Blocking Talks," *South China Morning Post* 9 May 1990, p. 6.

Fan Chih-lung, "From Tibet to Peking," *China Reconstructs* 4:2 (February 1955): 12–13.

Fei Hsiao-t'ung, "China's Multi-National Family," *China Reconstructs* 2:5–6 (May-June 1952): 23–29.

"Flourishing Minority Nationalities Areas," *Peking Review* 9 (3 March 1972): 10–12.

"Foreign Nationals in India," *Tibetan Review* 8:4 (April 1973): 15.

Forney, Matt, "Divide and Rule," *Far Eastern Economic Review* 30 November 1995, p. 26.

"Free Lawyers and Cold War. The International Commission of Jurists," *American Bar Association Journal* 41 , 1955, p. 417.

"Freedom of Religion in Tibet," *Peking Review* 38 (17 September 1965): 29.

"Freedom Should Be Used Intelligently," *Tibetan Review* 14:11 (November 1979): 18–19.

Gale, George, "Up in Cloud Cuckooland with the Lama," *Daily Express* 16 November 1959, p. 2.

Ganshin, V.,"Beijing's Proving Ground," *Nedelya* (Moscow), 10–16 November 1980 in *JPRS* 77307, February 1980, pp. 16–19.

Ghosh, Amitai, "Tibetan Dinner," *Utne Reader* (March-April 1990): 121–122.

Ginsburg, George and Michael Mathos, "Communist China's Impact on Tibet: The First Decade (II)," *Far Eastern Survey* 29:8 (August 1960): 120–124.

Goldman, Ari L., "Dalai Lama Appeals for Help in Going Home," *New York Times* 10 October 1991, p. A17.

Goldstein, Melvyn C., "Serfdom and Mobility: An Examination of the Use of 'Human Lease' in Traditional Tibetan Society," *Journal of Asian Studies* 30:3 (May 1971): 521–534.

————. "The Balance Between Centralization and Decentralization in the Traditional Tibetan Political System," *Central Asiatic Journal,* 15:3, (1971): 170–182.

————. "Tibetan Refugees in South India: A New Face to the Indo-Tibetan Interface," *Tibet Society Bulletin* 9 (1975): 12–29.

"Good Tidings from Tibet," *Beijing Review* 7 (16 February 1981): 6.

Felix Greene, "Letter from Lhasa," *China Now* 6:6 (November 1976): 3–7.

Paul Grimes, "For Tibetans an End to the Long Exile," *ASIA* 1:6 (March-April 1979): 36.

Grunfeld, A. Tom, "Enigmatic Buddha Who Works From Within," *Guardian* 8 October 1988, p. 8.
———. "In Search of Equality: Relations Between China's Ethnic Minorities and the Majority Han, " *Bulletin of Concerned Asian Scholars* 17:1 (January-March 1985): 54–67.
———. "Letter to the Editor," *New York Times* 23 March 1988, p. A26.
———. "Roof of the World,"*Bulletin of Concerned Asian Scholars* 9:1 (January-March 1977): 60–62.
———. "Review," *China Quarterly* 127 (September 1991): 638–639.
———. "Some Thoughts on the Current State of Sino-Tibetan Historiography," *China Quarterly* 83 (September 1980): 568–576.
———. "Tibetans Seek Curbs on Powerful Cadres and Bloated Budgets," *Guardian* 8 October, 1988, p. 8.
Gupta, Karunakar,"The McMahon Line 1911–1945—The British Legacy," *China Quarterly* 47 (July-September 1971): 521–545.
Gurov, B. "Tibet: Chinese Press Review," *New Times* 26 November 1952, pp. 12–15.
"Gyaincain Norbu tells meeting: 'some households have even run out of grain' " *Xizang Ribao* 24 May 1994.
Hamill, Pete, "Dalai-ing with the Press: a lama tames the jackals," *New York Daily News* 5 August 1979, pp. 4, 30.
"Happiness Obstructs Progress," *Tibetan Bulletin* 13:1 (June 1976): 4–5.
Harrer, Heinrich, "New Turn of the Wheel," *New York Times Magazine* 24 May 1959, p. 21.
Hazelhurst, Peter, "Tibetans Flee Red Guard Terror," *Times* 28 August 1971, p. 2.
Hedin, Sven, "Tibetan Nomads and Valley People," *Asia* 24:1 (January 1924): 37–41, 74–75.
"His Holiness' Europe Visit," *Tibetan Bulletin* 17:2 (June-July 1986): 2–3.
"His Holiness the Dalai Lama's Scandinavian Visit: Increased Interest in Tibet," *Tibetan Bulletin* 19:4 (October-November 1988): 2–3.
"His Holiness Visits Costa Rica, U.S. and Mexico," *Tibetan Bulletin* 20:2 (June-July 1989): 3.
Hopkinson, A.J., "Tibet Today," *Asiatic Review* 46:168 (October 1950): 1139–1151.
"How General Tan's First Letter was Brought to the Dalai Lama," *Peking Review* 2 (14 April 1959): 10.
Howie, Dr. Stephen and Sr. Penny Wagstaff, "Medical Priorities Amongst Tibetan Refugees," *Tibetan Review* 15:12 (December 1980): 14–15.
Hazorika, Sanjoy, "Dalai Lama Urges Peaceful Protest," *New York Times* 8 October 1987, p. A8.
"His Holiness Meets Austrian President, Swiss and French Foreign Ministers," *Tibetan Bulletin* (September-October 1991): 20.
"His Holiness Visits Mongolia, Baltics and Bulgaria," *Tibetan Bulletin* (November-December 1991): 23.
Hsian Yang, "The Reactionary Nature of the Tibetan Local Government," *MYTC* 4 April 1959 in *JPRS* 862-D, August 1959, p. 29.
Hsieh Fu-chih, "Great Revolutionary Changes in Tibet," *Peking Review* 37 (10 September 1965): 8–10.
Hu Bangxiu, "Women Cadres in Tibet," *Women in China* (March 1980): 36–38.
Huang Hao, "Tibet's Ties With The Ming Dynasty," *China's Tibet* 1:3 (Autumn 1990): 42–43.
Huang Lung, "Tibet Makes Up for Lost Centuries," *Eastern World* 16:12 (December 1962): 14–15.
Huang Mingxin, "The Tibetan Version of the 17-Article Agreement, " *China's Tibet* 2:3 (Autumn 1991): 12–14.

Huang, Yasheng, "China's Cadre Transfer Policy Toward Tibet in the 1980s," *Modern China* 21:2 (April 1995): 184–204.

Hughes, John, "Tibet—Cloud Shadows Red China," *Christian Science Monitor* 17 February 1966, pp. 1, 4.

"Human Rights Situation of the Tibetan People," *Department of State Bulletin* 87:2129 (December 1987): 50.

Hummel, Sigebert, "The Tibetan Ceremony of Breaking the Stone," *History of Religions* 8:2 (November 1968): 139–142.

"Hungarians in Tibet: The Genesis of Revolt," *East Europe* 8:8 (August 1959): 12–19.

Huoue, Mahmudul, "American and Indian Responses to the Chinese Occupation of Tibet, 1949–1951," *South Asian Studies* 26:1 (January-June 1991): 11–30.

Hutchings, Graham, "China's Fury at Major's Talk With God-King." *The Daily Telegraph* 6 December 1991, p. 12.

Ifill, Gwen, "Lawmakers Cheer Tibetan in Capitol Rotunda," *New York Times* 19 April 1991, p. A7.

Iljin, S. "Mao Engineered Tibetan Revolt," *Literaturnay Gazeta* 19 July 1978 in *Tibetan Review* 13:10 (October 1978): 5.

"Increased Farm Production in Tibet," *Xinhua Weekly* 31 March 1979, p. 13.

"India: The Adventurous Life," *Time* 4 May 1959, pp. 19–20.

"Institute Schools Train More Tibetan Cadre Specialists," *Xinhua* 23 February 1981. *Xinhua* 12 September 1978 in *JPRS* 72017, November 1978, p. 21.

"Intelligence," *Far Eastern Economic Review* 16 May 1980, p. 9.

"Interview with Tenzin Namgyal Tethong," *Freedom* 1:1 (October 1991): 16–18.

"Interview with the Dalai Lama's Brother—"Holy War" in Tibet—What is it all About?" *US News & World Report* 13 April 1959, pp. 46–48.

"Irish President Meets Dalai Lama," *Tibetan Review* 26:5 (May 1991): 7–8.

Jacobs, Hilary K., et al., "Independence For Tibet: An International Legal Analysis," *China Law Reporter* 8:1–2 (1994): 22–72.

Jedun, "The Establishment of the High Commissionership," *China's Tibet* 3:3 (Autumn 1992): 42–44.

Jeschke, Martin, "Lama in Exile: Prospects for an Expatriot," *The Christian Century* 88:14 (7 April 1971):443–446.

Jiang Wandi, "Heroes Admired by Ordinary People," *Beijing Review* 38:40 (2–8 October 1995): 9–12.

"Jimmy Carter in Tibet," *Tibetan Bulletin* 18:2 (July-August 1987): 6.

Jing Wei, "Tibet: An Inside View (I)," *Beijing Review* 47 (22 November 1982): 14–18.

———. "Tibet: An Inside View (II)—More Tibetans Assume Leadership," *Beijing Review* 48 (29 November 1982): 14–17.

———. "Tibet: An Inside View (III): Changes in Gyangze," *Beijing Review* 49 (6 December 1982): 21–24.

Jinpa, Losang, "Maniput: Sluggish Progress," *Tibetan Review* 13:4 (April 1978): 9–10.

Joint Operational Department of the Children's School of Members of the Department of Communications and the Revolutionary Rebelling Headquarters in Lhasa, "A Question Deserving Our Profound Thought." 13 February 1967 in *JPRS* 44680, 14 March 1968.

"Joint Rebelling Army Corps of the Lhasa City Post and Tele-Communications Bureau Under the 'Great Alliance Command, A Solemn Statement,' " (Lhasa), 3 August 1967 in *JPRS* 44680, 14 March 1968.

Jones, P.H.M., "Respite for Tibet," *Far Eastern Economic Review* 25 May 1961, pp. 365–366.

Jones, P.H.M., "Tibet and the New Order," *Far Eastern Economic Review* 3 March 1961, pp. 360–362.

"Kalon Wangdi Dorji Speaking to the Annual Meeting of the Tibet Society and Relief Fund of the UK, 29 October 1980," *The Tibet Society and Relief Fund of the UK Newsletter*, Spring 1981, p. 4.

Kamm, Henry, "In India, Aides to Dalai Lama Voice Regrets," *New York Times* 19 August 1976, p. 12.

Kao Hung, "Commune on the Tibetan Plateau," *Peking Review* 28, (13 May 1973): 14–17.

Karan, P.P., "The Changing Geography of Tibet," *Asian Profile* 1:1 (August 1973): 39–62.

Kaufman, Michael T., "Chinese and Indians Slowly Expanding Ties," *New York Times* 15 October 1979, p. A12.

Kaufman, Michael T., "Nepal in Turmoil As Vote to Modernize Nepal Nears," *New York Times* 6 October 1979, p. 2.

Killefer, Tom, "Free Lawyers and Cold War. The International Commission of Jurists," *American Bar Association Journal* 41 (May 1955): 417–420.

Klein, Howard S., "History and Historiography in China: Historical Science Society Reestablished—Historical Research Flourishes," *China Exchange News* 8:2 (April 1980): 6–8.

Kolmǎs, Josef, "Ch'ing Shih Kao on Modern History of Tibet," *Archiv Orient'aln'i* 32 (1964): 77–99.

———. "Some Formal Problems of Negotiations and Results of the Simla Conference," *Tibet Journal* 16:1 (Spring 1991): 108–114.

———. "Was Tibet of 1913–1914 Fully *sui iuris* to Enter Into Treaty Relations With Another State?" *Archiv Orient'aln'i* 60 (1992): 72–78.

Nicholas D. Kristof, "China Issues Rebuttal To Human Rights Critics," *New York Times* 3 November 1991, p. A12.

———. "Foreign Investors Pouring Into China," *New York Times* 15 June 1992, pp. D1, D6.

———. "How Tiananmen Square Helped Support for Tibet," *New York Times* 18 August 1991, Section 4, p.4.

Kuleshov, Nicolai S., "Agvan Dorjiev - Ambassador of Dalai Lama," *Asian Affairs* 23:1 (1990): 13–19.

Lai, A., "Sinification and Ethnic Minorities in China, *Current Scene* 8:4 (15 February 1970): 4–5, 19–20.

Lama Chimpa, "The System of Monastic Education in Tibet," *Indian Studies: Past and Present* 6:1 (October-December 1964): 99–105.

Lamb, Alastair, "Some Notes on Russian Intrigue in Tibet," *Royal Central Asian Journal* 46:1 (January 1959): 52.

———. "Tibet in Anglo-Chinese Relations: 1767–1842," part I, *Journal of the Royal Asiatic Society* 3–4 (1957): 161–176.

———. "Tibet in Anglo-Chinese Relations: 1767–1842," part II, *Journal of the Royal Asiatic Society* 1–2 (1958): 26–43.

"Latest Development in Tibet," *Beijing Review* 25 (21 June 1982): 18–22.

Leopold, Christian, "An Interview with the Panchen Lama," *Tibetan Review* 15:11 (November 1980): 14–15.

"Lhasa. A Hungry City," *Free China and Asia* 7:9 (September 1960): 26.

Lhasa Revolutionary Rebel Headquarters Meteorological Bureau's United Combat Headquarters, "A Handful of Bad Eggs in the Military Control Committee Will Not Escape from the Crimes of Instigating the Ta-lien-chih's Red Flag Corps to Sabotage Regular Military and Civil Fights and to Set Fire on the Meteorological Bureau (Unsuccessfully)!," 15 September 1967 in *JPRS* 44802, 25 March 1968.

Li An-Che, "A Lamasery in Outline," *Journal of the West China Border Research Society* 14: Series A (1942): 35–68.

———. "Rñiñ-ma-pa: The Early Form of Lamaism," *Journal of the Royal Asiatic Society* 3–4 (1948): 142–163.

———. "Tibetan Family and Its Relations to Religion," *Asian Horizon* 2:1 (Spring 1949) 25–36.

Li Shih-Yü Yu, "Tibetan Folk Law," *Journal of the Royal Asiatic Society* 3–4 (1950): 127–148.

Li Teh-shen, "A Visit to a Tibetan Farm Co-op," *Peking Review* 25 (23 June 1959): 15–16.

Li Weihan, "The Road of Liberation of the Tibetan Nationality—Commemorating the 30th Anniversary of the Signing of the Agreement on Measures for the Peaceful Liberation of Xizang," *Radio Beijing* 24 May 1981 in *FBIS* OW241709, 27 May 1981, p. Q7.

Li Yu-I, "Tibetan People Move Forward," *China Reconstructs* 1:5 (September-October 1951): 35–39.

Liaison Station of the Rebellion Headquarters in Chengtu, "Cable of September 20 from Chengtu," (Lhasa), 21 September 1967 in *JPRS* 44680, 14 March 1968.

Liao, Hollis S., "The United States and Tibet in the 1940s," *Issues and Studies* 26:6 (June 1990): 123.

Liao Zugui, "Installation of the 14th Dalai Lama," *Beijing Review* 38:37 (11–17 September 1995): 10–13.

Liu Shengqi, "A Review of Some Problems Concerning Foreign Relations in the Peaceful Liberation of Tibet," *Social Sciences in China* 13:3 (September 1992): 174–178.

Liu,Wallace, "The Meaning of Tibet," *Commonweal* 72:3 (15 April 1960): 55–57.

"Local Cadres Form Majority in Tibet," *Peking Review* 34 (25 August 1978): 5.

"Lowell Thomas Back from Tibet," *New York Times* 17 October 1949, p. 25.

Luo Fu, "China's Democratic Parties," *Beijing Review* 50 (14 December 1979): 19–27, 30.

MacDonald, David, "The Tibetan at Home," *Asia* 24:3 (March 1929): 214–221, 246–249.

———. "Where a Lama Leads the Way," *Asia* 29:2 (February 1929): 98–105, 147–152.

Mays, James O., "Dilemma of the Dalai Lama," *Tibet Society Bulletin* 4:1 (1970): 35–45. Also in *Foreign Service Journal* 46:10 (September 1969): 44–47, 64.

"Man Behind the Tibetan Struggle," *Guardian* 14 November 1963, p. 12.

"Many Rebel Khampas Killed in Nepal," *Tibetan Review* 9:8 (September 1974): pp. 9–10.

Maraini, Fosco, "Religion and People in Tibet," *The Geographical Magazine* 24:3 (July 1951): 141–144.

McBeth, John, "Letter from Chiang Khong," *Far Eastern Economic Review* 22 February 1980, p. 66.

McGill, Douglas C., "Dalai Lama Promoted an Exhibition," *New York Times* 28 September 1987, p. C23.

McKay, A. C. "The Establishment of the British Trade Agencies in Tibet. A Survey," *Journal of the Royal Asiatic Society* Series 3, 2:3 (1992): 399–421.

Meeker, Oden, "Our Far Flung Correspondents: Tibetans Out of the World," *New Yorker* 35:43 (12 December 1959): 35–43, 160, 162–188.

Mehra, Parshotam, "Beginnings of the Lhasa Expedition: Younghusband's Own Words," *Bulletin of Tibetology* 4:3 (November 1967): 9–18.

———. "Tibet and its Political Status: An Overview," *Indo-British Review* 18:2 (1990): 140–141.

Mehra, P.L., "Tibet and Russian Intrigue," *Royal Central Asian Journal* 45:1 (January 1958): 32.

Meng, C.Y.W., "Miss Liu's Mission to Tibet," *The China Weekly Review* 6 September 1930, pp. 22–24.

Meng Xianfan, "A Summary of the Seminar on 'Tibet: Yesterday and Today'," *Social Sciences in China* 13:1 (Spring 1992): 67–73.

"Message of President Chiang Kai-shek to Tibetans on March 26, 1959," *Free China and Asia* 6:4 (April 1959): 3.

Messerschmidt, Donald A., "Innovation to Adoption: Tibetan Immigrants in the United States," *Tibet Society Bulletin* 10 (1976): 48–70.

"Mexican President Meets Dalai Lama," *Tibetan Review* 24:8 (August 1989): 6.

Miao P'i-i, "Cadres of the Tibet Nationality Grow Up, Nursed by the Thoughts of Mao Tse-tung," *MTTC* August 1965 in *SCMM* 498, 16 November 1965, p. 18.

Mickelburgh, Rod "Tibet's Leaders Take Rosy View of the World," *Toronto Globe and Mail* 17 March 1995.

"Minority Delegates Discuss New 'Law on National Regional Autonomy,' " *China Reconstructs* 33:8 (August 1984): 12–16.

Monnier, Michel Acatil, "Talks With Lhasang Tsering," *Lungta* 7 (August 1993): 32–33.

"More Than 200,000 Tourists to Tibet Since 1980s," *Reuters* 24 December 1994.

"More Tibetans to Settle in Switzerland," *Tibetan Review* 15:6 (June 1980): 8–9.

Morgan, Gerald, "Myth and Reality in the Great Game," *Asian Affairs* 60:1 (February 1973): 55–65.

Morrow, Michael, "Super Secret Missions: CIA Spy Teams Inside Red China," *San Francisco Chronicle* 4 September 1970, p. 24.

Mullen, Glen, "How the Dalai Lamas Established Asia's Foremost Spiritual and Political Institution," *News-Tibet* (May-August 1995): 18–22.

Mullin, Chris, "Red Roof of the World," *Guardian* 6 June 1975, p. 14.

———. "The CIA: Tibetan Conspiracy," *Far Eastern Economic Review* 5 September 1989, pp. 30–34.

"Mutual Aid Teams in Tibet," *Peking Review* 33 (16 August 1960): 5.

Nag, B.C.,"Tibetans Rise in Revolt Again," *Swarajya* 11:26 (24 December 1966): 17–18.

Namgyal, Dhondup, "Tibetan Refugees in Nepal," *Tibet Society Newsletter* 4 August 1974, pp. 8–10.

Nash, Nancy, "The Dalai Lama Weighs the Chances of Return, *Far Eastern Economic Review* 3 August 1979, pp. 22–23.

"National Day for China and Tibet," *Tibetan Bulletin* (March-April 1990): 16.

Neame, Maj. Gen. P., "Tibet and the 1936 Lhasa Mission," *Journal of the Royal Central Asiatic Society* 26:2 (1939): 234–246.

"Nehru May Make Statement on Tibet Today," *Statesman* 23 March 1959, pp. 1, 10.

"Neville Maxwell's Tibet War," *Tibet Journal* 8:2 (August 1976): 9–15.

"New Batch of Refugees for Switzerland," *Tibetan Review* 7:12 (December 1968): 4–5.

"New Industrial Center," *China Reconstructs* 25:3 (March 1976): 22–23.

"New Monks and Nuns Tonsured," *China Daily* 8 August 1981, p. 1.

"New Policies Aid Development of Tibet," *Xinhua* 7 June 1982 in *SWB* FE/7948/BII/2.

Nimetz, Matthew, Acting U.S. Co-ordinator for Refugees Affairs, letter, 10 December 1979 to the *Triple Gem* 33–34 (Spring-Summer 1980): 5–6.

Ninjee, T, "Tibet Under Communist Rule: A Brief Survey of Recent Developments," *Journal of African and Asian Studies* 6:1 (Autumn 1967): 17–38.

Ngapoi Ngawang Jigme, "On the 1959 Armed Rebellion," *China Report* 24:3 (1988): 379.

———. "Xizang's Tremendous Change—In Celebration of the 30th Anniversary of the Signing of the Agreement on Measures for the Peaceful Liberation of Xizang," *Radio Peking* 24 May 1981 in *FBIS* OW261338, 28 May 1981, p. Q5.

Norbu Dawa, "Changes in Tibetan Economy, 1959–1976," *China Report* 24:3 (1988): 221–235.

———. "China Behind Khampa Disarmament," *Tibetan Review* 10:1 (January 1975): 3–4.

———. "China's Dialogue with the Dalai Lama 1978–1990: Prenegotiation Stage or Dead End?" *Pacific Affairs* 64:3 (Fall 1991): 351–372.

———. "Relaxation Revisited," *Tibetan Review* 9:9 (September 1974): pp. 3–4.

———. "The 1959 Rebellion: An Interpretation," *China Quarterly* 77 (March 1979): 74–93.

———. "The Democratic Dalai Lama," *Tibetan Bulletin* 8:2 (August 1976): 4–9.

———. "The State of Tibetan School Education," *Tibetan Review* 11:4 (April 1976): 3–5.

———. "The Tibetan Response to Chinese 'Liberation,' " *Asian Affairs* 62:3, (October 1975): 264–274.

Nynman, Lars-Erik, "The Great Game: A Comment," *Asian Affairs* 60:3 (October 1973): 299–301.

Oganesoff, Igor, "Tibet's Impact: From Indonesia to India, China Loses Good Will It Patiently Built Up," *Wall Street Journal* 6 April 1959, p. 19.

"On the So-called 'Statement of the Dalai Lama,' " *Peking Review* 2:16 (21 April 1959): 1–2.

Osofosky, Steve, "Soviet Criticism of China's National Minorities Policy," *Asian Survey* 14:10 (October 1974): 907–917.

Ou Chaoqui, "Tibet's Potala Palace," *China Reconstructs* 29:3 (March 1980): 44–50, 69.

Our Special Correspondent, "The Pattern of Revolt in Tibet," *The Statesman* 2 March 1959, p. 6.

"Outlook of Anti-Communist Uprising in Tibet," *Free China and Asia* 6:4 (April 1959): 8–11.

Palmiere, Richard P.,"The Domestication, Exploitation and Social Functions of the Yak in Tibet and Adjoining Areas," *Proceedings of the American Association of Geographers* 4 (1972): 80–83.

Pallis, Marco, "The Tibetan System of Landed Estates Seen in Perspective," *Tibetan Review* 12:7 (July 1977): 14–16.

"Panchen Erdeni Interviewed," *Peking Review* 11 (17 March 1978): 41–42.

———. "Democratic Reform for a New Tibet," *Peking Review* 27 (7 July 1959): 6–11.

———. "Report on Work in Tibet in the Past Year," *Peking Review* 2 (13 January 1961): 15–22.

"Parliamentary Tibet Committee Formed in Norway," *Tibetan Review* 26:1 (January 1991): 11.

Parnov, Eremei, "Tibetan Refugees as Seen by a Russian," *Tibetan Review* 12: 2 and 3 (February-March 1977): 15–18.

Patterson, George, "China and Tibet: Background to Revolt," *China Quarterly* 1 (January-March 1960): 87–102.

———. "Kalimpong: The Nest of Spies," *Twentieth Century* 163 (June 1958): 523–531.

———. "The 'Fish' in the 'Sea' of Tibet: Fifteen Years of Guerilla Warfare and Popular Unrest," *Current Scene* 3:23 (15 July 1965): 1–10.

———. "The Long Journey Home," *Far Eastern Economic Review* 23 April 1973, pp. 29–30.

———. "The Situation in Tibet," *China Quarterly* 6 (April-June 1961): 81–86..

———. "Tibet," *The Reporter*, 32:6 (25 March 1965): 31–33.

"Peiping Finally Admits Tibet Revolt," *Free China and Asia* 6:4 (April 1959): 20–24.

Peissel, Michel, "Mustang, Remote Realm in Nepal," *National Geographic Magazine* 128:4 (October 1965): 578–604.

"Peking Postpones 'Socialist Transformation' in Tibet in Major Policy Shift," *Current Scene* 1:1 (15 May 1961): 1–8.

"Peking Visit Has Dalai Lama's Approval," *Tibetan Review* 14:9 (September 1979): 5–6.

Pemba, Tsewang Y., "Tibetan Reminiscences," *Tibetan Review* 12:7 (July 1977): 22–25.

Peng Jianqun, "Economic Development on the Roof of the World," *China Today* 44:8 (August 1995): 10–14.

"People's Communes in Tibet—A Leap in Centuries," *China Reconstructs* 25:3 (March 1976): 16–19.

Pepper, Suzanne, "Chinese Education After Mao: Two Steps Forward, Two Steps Back and Back Again?," *China Quarterly* 81 (March 1980): 1–65.

PLA Soldier, "I Also Wish to Make Some Remarks on the 'Public Notice,' " (Lhasa), 19 August 1967 in *JPRS* 44680, 14 March 1968.

"Plan for Tibetan Commemorative Year in USA," *Tibetan Review* 18:5 (May 1983): 7.

"Policy on Dalai Lama Remains Unchanged," *Beijing Review* 37: (16–22 May 1994): 13–16.

Poole, Teresa, "Tibetan Pupils in India Forced to Return' " *The Independent* 28 March 1995.

"Present Policies in Tibet," *China Reconstructs* 29:10 (October 1980): 16–20.

"President Bush's Cousin Visits Dharamsala," *Tibetan Bulletin* (March-April 1992): 34.

"President Chao Tze-chi's Address at the 39th General Conference of the WLFD ROC Chapter," *WFLD Newsletter* 3:3 (May 1994): 3–5.

H.R.H. Prince Peter of Greece and Denmark, "The Chinese Colonization of Tibet," *Tibet Society Bulletin* 13 (1979): 22–31.

———. "The Tibetan Ceremony of Breaking the Stone," *FOLK: Dansk Ethnografisk Tidsskrift* 4 (1962): 65–70.

———. "Zor: A Western Tibetan Ceremonial Goat Sacrifice," *FOLK: Dansk Ethnografisk Tidsskrift* 16–17 (1974–1975): 309–312.

"Proceeds of Dalai Lama's Treasure," *Times* 27 February 1969, p. 5.

"Proclamation on Tibet," *People's China* 11 (1 December 1950): 9.

Pye, Lucian W., "China: Ethnic Minorities and National Security," *Current Scene* 14:12 (December 1976): 1–17.

Qiogya, "What Really Happened in Lhasa," *China Report* 24:3 (1988): 383–385.

Raghuvira, Dr., "The British Role in Sino-Tibetan Relations," *Tibetan Review* 1:2 (November 1968): 16.

Rahul, Ram, "The Structure of the Government of Tibet, 1644–1911," *International Studies* 7:3 (January 1962): 263–298,

Rand, Christopher, "A Reporter at Large: The Edge of Outer Darkness," *New Yorker* 26:13 (20 May 1950): 88–104.

———. "Chinese Approaches to Tibet Expected to Fall to Reds Soon," *New York Herald Tribune* 6 December 1949, p. 18.

Randall, Gavin, "Stranger Than Fiction," *Tibetan Review* 25:7 (July 1990): 15.

Rawlings, E.H.,"The Forbidden Land Today," *Contemporary Review* 25:7 (July 1990): 15. 182:1043 (November 1952): 302–306.

"Readjustment of Secondary and Primary Education is Essential," *Radio Lhasa* in *FBIS* HK280347, 30 November 1981, pp. Q1–2.

"Reagan Signs Tibet Bill: China Warns on Tibet," *Tibetan Review* 23:1 (January 1988): 5.

"Recent Military Installations," *Tibetan Review* 8:1 (June 1976): 3–4.

"Regional National Autonomy," *Beijing Review* 20 (17 May 1982): 28–29.

Renner, Gerald, "Dalai Lama: genial manner, serious mission," *The Hartford Courant* 10 October 1991, p. A15.

"Report from Tibet. Linchih Today," *China Reconstructs* 21:6 (June 1972): 16.

Richardson, H.E., "Recent Developments in Tibet," *Asian Review* 40:204 (October 1959): 243–257.

————. "Tibet As It Was," *Journal of the Hong Kong Branch of the Royal Asiatic Society* 1 (1960–1961): 42–49.

Riggs, Fred W., "Tibet in Extremis," *Far Eastern Survey* 19:21 (6 December 1950): 4224–4230.

Ripley, S. Dillon, "Tibet: The High and Fragile Land Behind the Range," *Smithsonian* 11:10 (January 1981): 96–105.

Rock, Joseph R., "Konka Risumgongka, Holy Mountain of the Outlaws, *National Geographic Magazine* 60:1 (July 1931): 1–65.

————. "Sungmas, The Living Oracles of the Tibetan Church,"*National Geographic Magazine* 68:4 (October 1935): 475–486.

Rosentstein, Jay and Nina Easton, "Charity Call," *American Banker* 4 November 1985, p. 38.

Rubin, Alfred P., "Review of The McMahon Line," *The American Journal of International Law* 61 (1967): 827–829.

————. "The Position of Tibet in International Law," *China Quarterly* 35 (July-September 1968): 110–154.

Rule, Sheila, "How, And Why, the Dalai Lama Won the Peace Prize," *New York Times* 13 October 1989, p. A14.

Salisbury, Harrison E., "Return of the Dalai Lama to Tibet is Expected Soon," *New York Times* 31 August 1980, p. 11.

Samphel, Thubten, "A Culture in Exile: Tibetan Refugees in India," *China Report* 24:3 (1988): 237–242.

Schaller, George B., "Tibetan Passage," *Animal Kingdom* 83:6 (December-January 1980–1981): 14–19.

Sciolino, Elaine, "Beijing is Backed By Administration on Unrest in Tibet," *New York Times* 7 October 1987, p. A1.

————. "U.S. Official Defends Stance on Turmoil in Tibet," *New York Times* 15 October 1987, p. A18.

"Second Delegation Returns from Tibet," *Tibetan Review* 15:8 (August 1980): 4–7.

Shakya, Tsering W., "1948 Tibetan Trade Mission to United Kingdom," *Tibet Journal* 15:4 (Winter 1990): 97–114.

Sharlho, Tseten Wangchuck, "China's Reforms in Tibet: Issues and Dilemmas," *The Journal of Contemporary China* 1:1 (Fall 1992): 34–60.

Sharma, Yojana, "Tibet: Dalai Lama Proposes New Plan for Self Government," *Interpress* 15 June 1988.

Sheehan, Neil, "Aid by CIA Put in the Millions: Group Total Up," *New York Times* 19 February 1967, pp. 1, 32.

Shen Yantai, "Lhasa Thrives from Kaleidoscopic Changes," *Beijing Review* 48 (26 November 1984): 26–28.

Shlachter, Barry, "Bhutan's King Seeking Balance in Development," *Los Angeles Times* 27 January 1980, pp. 2, 10.

Shokang Soinam Dagyal "Escorting the Representative of the Central Government to Tibet," *China's Tibet* 2:1 (Spring 1991): 12–15.

Shrestha, Mahinda Ram, "A Challenge from the Khampas," *Far Eastern Economic Review* 9 August 1974, p. 21.

Shrivastava, B.K., "American Public Opinion on the Tibetan Question," *International Studies* 10:4 (April 1969): 584–601.

Siegal, Louis T., "Ch'ing Tibetan Policy (1906–1910)," in *Papers on China* vol. 20, 1966.

Singh, Abar Jasbir, "How the Tibetan Problem Influenced China's Foreign Relations, *China Report* 28:3 (July-September 1992): 271–277.

"Smear Campaign Against Dalai Lama in Lhasa," *News-Tibet* 8:2 (March-June 1973): pp. 1–2.

Smil, Vaclav, "Who Will Feed China?" *China Quarterly* 143 (September 1995): 801–813.

Smith, Bradford, "Chinese Tyranny in Tibet," *The Atlantic* 207:6 (June 1961): 49–52.

"So This is Shangri-la," *Newsweek* 31 January 1944, pp. 24–25.

Soong, Norman, "See You In Tibet," *Asia* 40:12 (December 1940): 649–54.

Special Commentator, "Is the National Question Essentially a Class Question?" *Renmin Ribao in Beijing Review* 34 (25 August 1980): 17–22.

Special Group for the Investigation of Teng Hsiao-p'ing, "1018" Revolutionary Rebel Corps, Shanghai Red Metallurgy College, "How the Revolt Broke Out in Tibet. Exposing Teng Hsiao-p'ing, Chief Culprit Responsible for the Tibetan Revolt," *Chih-tien Chang-shan* [Surviving the Rivers and Mountains] 27 October 1967 in *JPRS* 4086, 18 December 1967.

"State Looks After Old Folk in Tibet," *China Daily* 19 July 1984, p. 3.

"Statement of His Holiness the Dalai Lama on the 23rd Anniversary of the Tibetan National Uprising," *Tibetan Review* 17:2–3 (February-March 1982): 24, 28.

Steele, A.T. in the *Chicago Daily News*. A seven-part article in the Pictorial Section; 18 (pp. 4–5), 25 (pp. 4–5) November; 2 (pp.4–5), 9 (pp.8–9), 16 (pp.4–5), 23 (pp. 4–5), 30 (pp. 8–9) December 1944.

———. "The Boy Ruler of Shangri-La," *Saturday Evening Post*, 13 April 1946, p. 14.

Stoddard, Heather, "The Death of the Thirteenth Dalai Lama," *Lungta* 7 (August 1993): 2–7.

Strong, John, "Buddhism in Lhasa," *Atlantic* 231:1 (January 1973): 16, 18–19, 22.

"Struggle for Seizure of Power in Army in Tibet," *Hung t'i-chun Chan-pao* [Red Physical Education Combat News] (Lhasa) no. 5, 8 September 1967 in *JPRS* 44278, 7 February 1968.

"Summary of a Conversation with the Chairman of the CC CPC Mao Tse-T'ung" From the Journal of S.F. Antonov, 21 October 1959 in *Cold War International History Project Bulletin* 3 (Fall 1993): 56–58.

"Sweden to Receive Dalai Lama Officially," *Tibetan Review* 26:12 (December 1991): 5.

Tass, "American Shipment of Arms to Tibet," *Pravda* 13 May 1950 in *Soviet Press Translations* 5:3 (1950): 415.

"Teachers for Tibet," *Peking Review* 13 (16 August 1974): 22.

Tempest, Rone, "Politics and the Panchen Lama," *Los Angeles Times* 27 May 1995, p. A1, A24-A25.

" 'Tent Schools' on the Tibetan Plateau," *Peking Review* 35 (27 August 1971): 27–28.

"The Bonn Hearing-A Success," *Tibetan Review* 24:6 (June 1989): 5.

"The Borderlands of Soviet Central Asia—Tibet," *Central Asian Review* 6:1 (1958): 57–75.

"The Dalai Lama," *China News Analysis* 270 (3 April 1959): 1–7.

"The Far Western Tip of Tibet," *China Reconstructs* 21:12 (December 1972): 2–5.

"The Flight of the Dalai Lama," *Life* 23 April 1951, pp. 130, 140, 142.

"The Future of Tibet," *Times* 27 August 1912, p. 5.

"The Mongolian Question: Chinese Rights and Russian Policy," *Times* 3 December 1912, p. 5.

"The Press: All That's News," *Newsweek* 4 December 1960, p. 54.

"The Red Terror in Tibet: Interview with the Dalai Lama," *US News & World Report* 24 April 1961, p. 79.

"The Talk of the Town: Our Own Baedeker," *New Yorker* 35:10 (25 April 1959): 34–35.

"The Tibetan Autonomous Region in Sikang Province," *Renmin Mibao* 14 August 1951 in *Current Background* 118 (25 September 1951).

"The Tibetan Question," *China News Analysis* 90 (1 July 1955): 1–7.

"The Tibetans Express Full Support of the Central People's Government of China," *Pravda* March 21, 1951 in *Soviet Press Translations* 6:6 (1951): 190–191.

Thomas, Lowell and Lowell Thomas, Jr., "Up in the Clouds: Capital of the Lama," *Collier's* 125:8 (25 February 1950): 36.

"1000 Visas to the U.S.A.," *Tibetan Bulletin* (July-August 1991): 17.

"Thousands of Chinese Soldiers Killed in Shentse Dzong Uprising," *News-Tibet* 5:1 (December-January 1970–1971): 1–2.

"Tibet," *Time* 20 April 1959, pp. 26–36.

"Tibet, 1965–1967," *China News Analysis* 657 (28 April 1967): 1–7.

"Tibet, 1965–1969, Part I: Rupture Among the Rulers," *China News Analysis* 787 (21 November 1969): 1–7.

"Tibet. A God Escapes," *Newsweek* 13 April 1959, p. 47–48.

"Tibet Affirms Support for People's Government," *People's China* 4 (16 November 1951): 13.

"Tibet Fighting for Freedom," *Free China and Asia* 5:9 (September 1958): 29.

"Tibet—From Serfdom to Socialism," *China Reconstructs* 25:3 (March 1976): 6–10.

"Tibet: 'God Said No,' " *Newsweek* 30 March 1959, p. 50.

"Tibet. His Determined Highness," *Time* 29 June 1959, p. 28.

"Tibet in Ferment," *National Integration* (1964): 13–14.

"Tibet in Sept./Oct.," *Tibetan Review* 23:11 (November 1988): 4.

"Tibet: Lesson from an Escape," *Economist* 11 April 1959, p. 109.

"Tibet Radio Asks Aid Against Reds," *New York Times* 1 February 1950, p. 10.

"Tibet Support Group in Italian Parliament," *Tibetan Review* 25:3 (March 1990): 6.

"Tibet: Thirty Years After Liberation," *China Reconstructs* 30:9 (September 1981): 4–5.

"Tibet. War Atop of the World," *Newsweek* 12 January 1959, p. 51.

"Tibet Welcomes Its Liberators," *Literaturnaya Gazeta* 9 January 1951 in *Soviet Press Translations* 6:4 (1 March 1951): 102–104.

"Tibet's Raidi on the Dalai Lama: 'the door remains open'" *Xinhua*, 15 March 1995.

"Tibetan Cadres Maturing," *Peking Review* 25 (18 June 1971): 20, 27.

"Tibetan Curios for Public Museums," *Times* 5 April 1905, p. 4.

"Tibetan Election System Undergoes Drastic Change," *Tibetan Review* 19:9 (September 1984): 5.

"Tibetan Friendship Groups After Mrs. Bedi," *Tibetan Review* 13: 4 (April 1978): 6–7.

"Tibetan Hearing in Germany," *Tibetan Bulletin* 20:2 (June-July 1989): 1–2, 12.

"Tibetan Independence - Fact or Fiction," *Beijing Review* 32 (13–26 February 1989): 25–30.

"Tibetan Official Meets U.S. Leaders," *Tibetan Bulletin* 16:3 (August-September 1985): 13.

"Tibetan Refugees in Nepal," *Tibetan Review* 5:3 (March 1970): 5.

"Tibetan Students in Japan," *Tibetan Review* 1:9 (September 1968): 5.

Tibetan Youth Congress, "The State of Buddhism Following the Chinese Takeover," *Tibet Society and Tibet Relief Fund of the United Kingdom Newsletter* (Summer 1979): 3–4.

"Tibetans Becoming a Minority in Tibet," *Tibetan Review* 4:1 (1 July 1970): 6–7.

"Tibetans Healthier, Better Educated," *Beijing Review* 42 (15 October 1984): 11.

"Tibetans in Bhutan Continue to Be Harassed," *Tibetan Review* 12:4 (April 1977): 9–10.

"Tibetans in Europe," *Tibetan Review* 1:4 (April 1968): 5.

"To China: Open Up Tibet," *New York Times* 2 February 1979, pp. 3, 19.

"Tokyo Office Head Resigns," *Tibetan Review* 27:4 (April 1992): 7.

Tolstoy, Ilia, "Across Tibet from India to China," *National Geographic Magazine* 90:2 (August 1946): 169–222.

Topping, Seymour, "Tibet Struggles for Higher Living Standard," *New York Times* 28 October 1979, p. 18.

"Tracklaying of Qinghai-Tibet Railway Over Big Salt Lake," *Xinhua Weekly* 30 June 1979, pp. 20–21.

"Trade Mission to Britain. Dinner in Honour," *Times* 24 November 1948, p. 6.

Trumbull, Robert, "Soviet Maps Tibet Air Bases in Potential Threat to India," *New York Times* 22 November 1950, pp. 1, 4.

———. "Acheson Credits Dispatch," *New York Times* 23 November 1950 p. 6.

———. "Red Strategy Aims at Kashmir, Nepal," *New York Times* 24 November 1950, p. 6.

———. "Tibet Fears Told By Lowell Thomas, *New York Times* 11 October 1949, p. 11.

Tsering, Lam, "Restoration of Serfdom Must Never Be Allowed," *Peking Review* 6 (7 February 1969): 9–10.

Tshering, Gyatso, "Tibet's Problems of Spirit and Survival," *Tibet Society Bulletin* 8 (1974): 8–26.

Tsingfu F. Tsiang, "The Question of Tibet," *Free China and Asia* 16:12 (December 1969): 61–64.

Tucci, Guiseppe, "The Secret Characters of the Kings of Ancient Tibet," *East and West* 6:3 (October 1955): 197–205.

———. "The Wives of Sron btsan sgam po," *Oriens Extremus* 9 (1962): 121–130.

Tung Ying and Hsüeh Chien-hua, "Social Reforms in National Minority Areas in China," *Renmin Ribao* 15 August 1959 in *SCMP* 2093, 10 September 1959, p. 18.

"Turmoil in Tibet," *Washington Post* 25 March 1959, p. A12.

Tyler, Patrick, "China Rejects Choice of Boy as Tibet Lama," *New York Times* 13 November 1995, p. 6.

Tzu Yuan, "Historical Relations Between the Tibet Region and the Motherland," *MYTC* 4 April 1959 in *JPRS* 862-D, 17 August 1959, p. 10.

Uncle Sam, "Taiwan and Tibet," *Tibetan Review* 11:1–2 (January-February 1976): 18–19, 25.

"United Nations Passes Resolutions on Tibet," *Tibetan Bulletin* (September-October 1991): 1.

"U.S. Affirms Belief in the Principle of Self-Determination for Tibet," *Department of State Bulletin* 42:1082 (21 March 1960): 443–444.

"U.S. Congress Declares Tibet an Occupied Country," *Tibetan Bulletin* (November-December 1991): 22.

"U.S. Congress Passes Amendments on Tibet," *Tibetan Review* 22:8 (August 1987): 77–79.

"U.S. President Meets His Holiness," *Tibetan Bulletin* (May-June 1991): 16.

"U.S. Said to Delay Film About Tibet," *New York Times* 26 December 1971, p. 21.

"U.S. Senate Adopts Tibet Bill," *Tibetan Review* 22:11 (November 1987): 11.

"Units Linked to CIA," *New York Times* 19 February 1967, p. 27.

"Unprecedented Visit," *Tibetan Bulletin* 18:2 (July-August 1987): 6.

Vaidyanath, R., "The Soviet View of the Tibetan System," *International Studies* 10:4 (April 1969): 602–606.

"Valiant Army Stations on Tangla Range Atop 'Roof of the World,' " *Peking Review* 45 (7 November 1959): 12–14.

Van Eekelen, W.F., "Simla Convention and McMahon Line," *Royal Central Asiatic Journal* 54:2 (June 1967): 179–184.

van Walt van Praag, Michael C., "Earnest Negotiations. The Only Answer to Growing Unrest in Tibet," *International Relations* 9:5 (May 1989): 377–392.

"Visual Denunciation of Serf-Owner's Atrocities," *Peking Review* 29 (19 June 1977): 11.

Viviano, Frank, "Tibetans Reach Out to Other Dissidents," *San Francisco Chronicle* 3 December 1990, p. A14.

Wadlow, Rene V.L., "Tibet Discussed in UN Commission on Human Rights," *Tibetan Review* 20:5 (May 1985): 8–10.

Waggoner, Walter H., "Truman Bars Military Help for the Defense of Formosa," *New York Times* 6 January 1950, p. 6.

Walz, Jay, "U.S. May Grant Tibet Recognition in View of Current Asian Situation," *New York Times* 25 October 1949, p. 5.

Wang Fen and Wang Fu-jen, "Do Away with Feudal Prerogatives and Exploitation by the Tibetan Lamaseries," *MTYC* August 1959 in *JPRS* 1144-D, 5 February 1960, pp. 17–29.

Wang Lin, "Another Revelation of Indian Expansionism," *Peking Review* 14 (3 April 1964): 30.

Wang Shaoquan, "Population and Environment in Tibet," *China's Tibet* 6:2 (1995): 34–36.

Wangyal, Phuntsog, "The Influence of Religion on Tibet's Politics," *Tibet Journal* 1:1 (July-September 1975): 78–86.

Wangyal, Tsering, "Down the Garden Path," *Tibetan Review* 30:10 (October 1995): 3.

———. "Enter the People," *Tibetan Review* 12:2–3 (February-March 1977): 3–4.

———. "Little Big Nations," *Tibetan Review* 25:10 (October): 3.

———. "P for Perseverance," *Tibetan Review* 27:7 (July 1992): 3.

———. "Son of Kunsang Paljor"," *Tibetan Review* 14:9 (September 1979): 4.

———. "The Enemy Within," *Tibetan Review* 16:5 (May 1981): 3–4.

———. "The Morning After the Night Before," *Tibetan Review* 12:7 (July 1977): 4.

———. "Tibetan Settlements in Bylakuppe, South India," *Tibetan Review* 12:2–3 (February-March 1977): 12–14.

———. "Yabshi vs. Yabshi," *Tibetan Review* 27:6 (June 1992): 3.

Warren, Virginia Lee, "Tibetans Adapt to the U.S., But Miss Their Lofty Homeland," *New York Times* 7 April 1976, p. 55.

Weatherall, Ernest, "A Reluctant Farewell to Tibet," *Christian Science Monitor* 28 May 1969, p. B1.

Weintraub, Bernard, "Bhutan Reports 30 Seized for Plot to Kill King," *New York Times* 6 February 1974, p. 24.

Weissman, Steve, "Last Tangle in Tibet," *Pacific Research and World Empire Telegram* 4:5 (July-August 1973): 1–18.

Weissman, Steve and John Shock, "CIAsia Foundation," *Pacific Research and World Empire Telegram* 3:6 (September-October 1972): 3–4.

"What the Second Delegation Saw in Tibet," *Tibetan Review* 15:9 (September-October 1980): 7.

Willoughby, Brig. Gen. M.E., "The Relations of Tibet to China," *Journal of the Royal Central Asiatic Society* 11:111 (1924): 187–203.

"Woman in Commune Near Lhasa Tells of Her Life," *New York Times* 18 October 1978, p. 18.

Woodcock, George, "Tibetan Immigrants in Switzerland," *Tibetan Refugee Aid Society Newsletter* (Vancouver), 1968.

———. "Tibetan Refugees in a Decade of Exile," *Pacific Affairs* 43:3 (Fall 1970): 410–420.

Woodman, Dorothy, "Tibet: Brain-Washing Buddhism," *New Statesman* 60:1535 (13 August 1960): 202.

"World Press Comments on Tibet Today," *National Integration* (1964): 73–76.

Wu Fengpei, "On Relations Between the Local Tibetan Government and the Central Government During the Period of the Republic of China," *China's Tibet* 3:1 (Spring 1992): 40–44.

Wu Guohua and Qoisang, "Steady Stream of Tibetans Return Home," *China's Tibet* 4:1 (Spring 1993): 23–24.

Wylie, Turrell, "Mortuary Customs at Sa-skya, Tibet," *Harvard Journal of Asiatic Studies* 25 (1964–65): 229–42.

————. "Ro-Langs: The Tibetan Zombie," *History of Religions* 4:1 (Summmer 1964): 68–80.

Xie Bangmin and Jiang Shunzhang, "Report from Tibet: New Changes on the Plateau," *Beijing Review* 21 (25 May 1980): 19–25.

Xeirab Nyima, "A Special Envoy of the Nanjing Regime," *China's Tibet* (Winter 1991): 39–42.

Xiao Wen, "Policy on Religion," *Beijing Review* 51 (21 December 1979): 14–16, 22.

"Xizang Promotes Minority Cadres in Government," *FBIS* OW121308, June 19, 1981, p. Q3.

"Xizang Releases Population Census Results," *Radio Lhasa* 20 October 1982 in *JPRS* 82204, 9 November 1982, p. 113.

"Yabshi Controversy Ends," *Tibetan Review* 27:9 (September 1992): 7.

Yang Fu-hsing, "The Great Victory of the People's Nationalities in Kanna," *MTTC* October–November 1963, in *SCMM* 400, 20 January 1964, p. 18.

Ye Jianying, "Comrade Ye Jianying's Speech," *Beijing Review* 40 (5 October 1979): 7–32.

"Year of Tibet," *Tibetan Review* 19:3 (March 1984): 11.

Yeh-hu and Ho-shih, "A Preliminary Analysis of the Systems of Feudal Serfdom in Tibet," *MTCY* March 1959 in *ECMM* 171, 8 June 1959.

Yen Yu, "How the Feudal Lords Brutally Exploit the Slaves," *MTYC* August 1959 in *JPRS* 1144-D, 5 February 1960, pp. 30–45.

Yershov, T., "Imperialist Intrigue in Tibet," *New Times* 49 (30 November 1949): 8–12.

Yin Hai-shan, "Education and Culture in Tibet," *Eastern World* 16:8 (August 1962): 16.

"Yin Fantang Attends Xizang Party Meeting," *Radio Lhasa* in *FBIS* 1 June 1981, pp. 21–22.

Yitsi, Lorthong, "Report on the Anti-Communist Revolution of the Tibetan People by Lorthong Yitsi," *Free China and Asia* 6:7 (July 1959): 17–20.

Youngblood, Ruth "China pledges enough food for minorities," *United Press International* 1 March 1995.

"Youth Social Work in Dharamsala," *Tibetan Review* 12:2–3 (February-March 1977): 10.

"Youths Want Election System Changed," *Tibetan Review* 13:4 (April 1978): 10, 14..

Yu Dawchyuan, "Love Songs of the Sixth Dalai Lama," *Academia Sinica Monograph* (Peking) Series A, No. 5, 1930.

Yu Shah, "The 'Sun of Happiness' is Rising in Tibet," *People's China* 11 (1 December 1950): 8–9, 31–32.

Yuan Shan, "The Dalai Lama and the 17-article Agreement, " *China's Tibet* 2:2 (Summer 1991): 2–6.

Zhang Chunjian and Xeirab Nyima, "Human Rights in Tibet: Past and Present," *Beijing Review* 35 (24 February –1 March 1992): 24–27.

Zhang Junyi, ed. *Collected Essays of Tibetan Studies* (Taipei: Commission for Tibetan Studies, 1989), 2 volumes.

Zhang Senshui, "Uncovering Prehistoric Tibet," *China Reconstructs* 30:1 (January 1981): 65–66.

Zhang Tianlu, "Past and Present Tibetan Population," *China's Tibet* (Winter 1993): 7–10.

Zhou Enlai, "Some Questions on Policy Towards Nationalities," *Beijing Review* 9 (3 March 1980): 14–23; 10 (10 March 1980): 18–23.

Index

A. Tom Grunfeld is a Canadian Sinologist who was educated at the School of Oriental and African Studies in London and New York University. Currently he is professor of history at SUNY—Empire State College. He has authored, edited, and contributed to several books on East Asian history as well as several dozen articles in journals such as *The China Quarterly, Tibetan Review, Trends in History, Far Eastern Economic Review,* and *China Tibetology.*